Women's Words, Women's Stories

AN AMERICAN DAYBOOK

For Mie Abe
to celebrate her courage,
patience, and loving kindness

Women's Words, Women's Stories

AN AMERICAN DAYBOOK

Edited and Compiled by
Lois Stiles Edgerly

Tilbury House, Publishers
GARDINER, MAINE

Tilbury House, Publishers
132 Water Street
Gardiner, Maine 04345

Library of Congress Cataloging-in-Publication Data

Women's Words, Women's Stories: An American Daybook /
edited and compiled by Lois Stiles Edgerly.
     p.   cm.
  Includes bibliographical references.
  ISBN 0-88448-143-3 (hardcover) $24.95
  1. Women--United States--Biography. I. Edgerly, Lois Stiles, 1929-   .
HQ1410.G583   1994
305.4'0973'09034--dc20   94-15754
                                                    CIP

Grateful acknowledgment is made to the following publishers and journals for permission to reprint this material:

The Adolescent Diaries of Karen Horney, Copyright 1980. Reprinted with permission of Basic Books, Inc.

An Autobiography of a West Texas Pioneer — Ella Elgar Bird Dumont, edited by Tommy J. Boley. Copyright 1988. Reprinted with permission of the University of Texas Press.

Black Women in Bands and Orchestras, D. Antoinette Handy. Copyright 1981. Reprinted with permission of The Scarecrow Press.

The Civil War Diary of Sarah Morgan, edited by Charles East. Copyright 1991. Reprinted with permission of the University of Georgia Press.

Covered Wagon Women, Diaries and Letters from the Western Trails, 1840-1890, edited and compiled by Kenneth L. Holmes. Copyright 1990. Reprinted with permission of the Arthur H. Clark Company.

Covered Wagon Women — Volume II, edited and compiled by Kenneth L. Holmes. Copyright 1983. Reprinted with permission of the Arthur H. Clark Company.

Covered Wagon Women — Volume IV, edited and compiled by Kenneth L. Holmes. Copyright 1985. Reprinted with permission of the Arthur H. Clark Company.

The Diary of Caroline Seabury, edited by Suzanne L. Bunkers. Copyright 1991. Reprinted with permission of the University of Wisconsin Press.

Dorothy Thompson and Rose Wilder Lane: Forty Years of Friendship Letters, 1921 - 1960, edited by William Holtz. Copyright 1991. Reprinted with permission of the University of Missouri Press.

Little House in the Ozarks, edited by Stephen W. Hines. Copyright 1991. Reprinted with permission of Guideposts.

Lizzie, The Letters of Elizabeth Chester Fisk 1864-1893, edited by Rex C. Myers. Copyright 1989. Reprinted with permission of the Mountain Press Publishing Company.

More Than Common Powers of Perception — The Diary of Elizabeth Rogers Mason Cabot, edited by P.A.M. Taylor. Copyright 1991. Reprinted with permission of Beacon Press.

Sara Jane Foster, Teacher of the Freedmen, edited by Wayne E. Reilly. Copyright 1990. Reprinted with permission of the University Press of Virginia.

The Shattered Dream, edited by Harold Woodell. Copyright 1991. Reprinted with permission of the University of South Carolina Press.

Wartime Washington, The Civil War Letters of Elizabeth Blair Lee, edited by Virginia Jeans Laas. Copyright 1991. Reprinted with permission of the University of Illinois Press.

Willa Cather in Person; Interviews, Speeches and Letters, selected and edited by L. Brent Bohlke. Copyright 1986. Reprinted with permission of the University of Nebraska Press.

Jacket and text designed by Edith Allard
Keyboarding by Cheryl Moloney, Perfection Typing, Weymouth, Massachusetts
Editing and production: Mark Melnicove, Lisa Reece, Devon Phillips, Dianne Smith, Jennifer Littlefield, Annette Watson, and Jennifer Elliott
Printing (jackets): John P. Pow Co., Boston, Massachusetts
Printing (text) and binding: Maple-Vail, Binghamton, New York

Contents

Acknowledgments

I am grateful to the researchers, librarians, archivists, relatives, and friends who helped me to find and assemble the writings and stories of the women that this book celebrates.

I extend my special appreciation and gratitude to
Lynne Spiegel and Jennifer Pulver

and to

Karen Hammerness • Julie Rikleman • Stephanie Yuhl
Sarah Stiles Edgerly • Cheryl Moloney • Margaret Dines
Sheila Hanlon • Mary Poynter Martin • G. Lloyd Martin
Patricia Emerson Watson • Mary Emerson Stevens
Eugene Emerson • Richard Boyle O'Reilly Hocking
June Lloyd • Ann Sims Morison • Stephanie E. Adcock
Len Edgerly • Doris Clements • Rebecca Fairbank
Mary Louise Taft • Betsy H. Woodman • Delia H. Cantor
Joanne Martell • Caroline Creal • Lacine Edwards
Joan Hocking Kracke • Joanne Kronauer • Janet Howell
Barbara Groves Clark • Noel Peattie • Joan Falcone
Barrie B. Greenbie • Linda Lipsett • Molly Ackerman
Mark Melnicove, my creative publisher, and
Will, my dear partner in all things.

Lois Stiles Edgerly

Foreword

After collecting the words and stories of seven hundred thirty-two nineteenth-century American women in *Women's Words, Women's Stories* and *Give Her This Day* (published in 1990), I find myself with a new perspective with regard to my work. When I began collecting women's writings in 1978, I was not searching for evidence to support some preconceived theory or expecting any particular conclusions to emerge. I was interested in women's lives and drawn to books from the Victorian era. My search for writings by women that revealed their personalities and provided a glimpse into their lives was like a treasure hunt. When organizing my books, I decided to celebrate each woman by presenting her words and story on her birthdate. My effort has been to have each one tell her own story, speak to us through her own words.

I found women carrying on careers to the age of eighty and beyond, others making their way in life after the early loss of parents; born sculptors and painters succeeding in spite of barriers placed in their ways; and black women refusing to accept the limitations of race. Women rose to the challenges of war and brought heroism to the westward trek of the pioneers. Many were discovering that they had the ability to write or to captivate an audience. Revealing patterns emerged from this patchwork of unforgettable stories and gave me new insight into my own life.

The women in my books were some of the first participants in the movement for women's enfranchisement in this country. The barriers and challenges they faced started to give way to their indomitable desire to participate. They began speaking, influencing public opinion, publishing under their own names, and establishing professional careers. These remarkable women and their memorable stories were part of the evolution of consciousness that flowered in the nineteenth century and continues today.

Lois Stiles Edgerly
Cambridge, Massachusetts
August 1994

JANUARY

Carrie Adell Strahorn

1911

I do not know whether there ever was a worse terminal town than Shoshone (Idaho). It seemed to call the roughest and toughest elements that it had been my lot to see. There was a fight on the streets almost every hour of the day and night.

It was my misfortune to arrive alone in Shoshone one day soon after the line was opened. The telegram telling Pard of my coming had miscarried, and he was at Hailey. It was a matter of most serious moment what I should do for a night's shelter, and there could not have been a gloomier prospect. . . . Shots were singing through the air, drunken brawlers were yelling and swearing. . . .

There was no respectable hotel in the place, and what rude shacks there were about the town were given up to saloons and dance halls. Hardened, weather-beaten, dissipated countenances glowered from under every hat brim in sight. I sat down on a rude bench in the depot to think over my situation and get up courage to ask if I might spend the night in the passenger car there by the station. . . .

Then the ticket man slammed his window, and a feeling of desolation and abhorrence was creeping over me, when a man came in and pounded on the ticket window, which was quickly thrown open again, and I heard him ask if Mrs. Strahorn had arrived on that train. Well, he just looked like an angel from heaven to me when he made known his errand and said Pard had told him to look out for me on every train. . . .

Carrie Adell Green Strahorn was born January 1, 1854, in Marengo, Illinois. Her father was a physician. She graduated from the University of Michigan and studied music in America and Europe.

Adell's best friend had settled in Denver, where she became engaged to Robert "Pard" Strahorn. When she came down with a grave illness, he brought her home to Marengo. He and Adell stayed by her bedside, nursing her until her death.

A tough place

Adell's writing is from Volume II of Fifteen Thousand Miles by Stage, *published by Knickerbocker Press in 1911.*

Pard returned to the West, taking a job as a newspaper reporter. He wrote a guide book extolling the virtues of the Wyoming and Dakota territories, which ultimately led to the establishment of a "literary bureau" to issue similar guide books for prospective settlers.

Adell and Pard were married in 1877; he was hired by the "bureau" the following week. The job required much travel under primitive conditions, and railroad officials did not think it suitable for a woman to go along. Pard refused to leave his bride and declined the position unless Adell could accompany him. The officials ultimately gave in, and the Strahorns travelled together 6,000 miles in the first three years. Adell assisted Pard in writing his informative travel books.

After years spent exploring the West, the couple began the second phase of their career, settling the West. They founded Ontario, Oregon, and six towns in Idaho along the Union Pacific route — "our children of which we are justly proud," Adell called them.

After inching their way West, the Strahorns settled permanently in Spokane, Washington, in 1898. Pard continued to work for the railroad, and Adell began writing her memoirs, *Fifteen Thousand Miles by Stage.*

She died March 15, 1925, at the age of seventy-one.

Florence Lawrence

*O*ut of action

1916
Yes, I've come back to you, dear old public. You've always been so kind to me. You've laughed when I laughed, and cried when I cried — we've been good friends, you and I.

It's much more than a year now since I went away and left you. But I was tired — oh, so tired! You didn't know where I went to, and I didn't quite want you to, because I needed to be very quiet for a long, long time, it seemed to me just then. I used to sit in my little dressing-room at the Victor studio, and wonder just how much longer I could keep on "making believe."

I did keep on "making believe," too, for a long time after I thought I couldn't. And then one day I packed my things and said I was going home, and I went. Where was my home? At Westwood, New Jersey — fifty acres mostly planted out with fruit trees. . . . I

Florence's writing, describing her return to the movies after suffering an injury during filming, is from "Why I Came Back," Motion Picture Magazine, March 1916.

Women's Words, Women's Stories

have some cows and horses and pigs, and some chickens too. Then in the house I have the dearest cat named "Buggs" — just an ordinary, everyday cat who once was a homeless kitten. But Buggs has had good bringing-up and does his bit toward the entertainment of favored guests. In fact, he enjoys the distinction of being inquired after along with more important members of the family.

Florence Annie Bridgewood (Florence Lawrence) was born January 2, 1886, in Ontario, Canada. She made her stage debut at age three with her parents' travelling tent show.

Mrs. Bridgewood and Florence changed their last name to Lawrence and began looking for work in the fledgling film industry. Florence was quickly cast in the Edison Company films *Daniel Boone* and *The Shaughraun* and she decided to establish a career in the movies. In 1908 D. W. Griffith sent several agents, including Harry Solter, to search for a star for his Biograph Company. Solter discovered Florence, married her within the month, and she became "The Biograph Girl."

After two years Florence and Harry left Biograph for Carl Laemmle's Independent Motion Picture Company. Laemmle recognized the public's fascination with screen stars and began a publicity campaign around Florence. He started a rumor that she had been killed in an accident, then presented her at elaborately staged public appearances to prove she was indeed alive.

In 1915 Florence was injured filming a scene in a burning building. She was totally paralyzed for four months and remained partially paralyzed for several years. Her husband died in 1920, and she spent the next two years as a bit player for MGM. She remarried and divorced twice and operated a small cosmetics store in Hollywood, but she became increasingly depressed. In 1938 she drank a fatal mixture of ant poison (arsenic) and cough syrup and was buried in an unmarked grave in Hollywood Memorial Cemetery.

Emily Huntington

1901

Happier housekeeping

I spent hours of thought by day and night, when I came to really live among the poor of New York City. How prematurely old the little faces that gathered around me looked, how puzzled and anxious over every task, and yet how bravely those tasks were performed when explained and understood! How uncomplainingly they toiled, and yet how evident was their disgust at the toil, and how it was hurried through to be ready for the play-time. Poor little children! Must they always do what they hate? My little lessons to little housekeepers, published by A. D. F. Randolph & Co. in 1876, was the first step; through that I was introduced to Miss Haines, so well known as a teacher in New York, and by her was invited to visit her "Kindergarten." How shall I describe my joy! My mystery was all solved. There in a pretty, sunny room, among birds and flowers, sat children of the wealthy, building with blocks and gradually learning the rudiments of geometry. In a moment my fancy painted my poor children in the same pretty framing, setting little tables, washing little dishes, all the time listening to corrections and suggestions from kind teachers. What happy little faces! Work had become play, and the instruments of toil were playthings.

Emily Huntington, welfare worker and founder of the "kitchen garden" movement, was born January 3, 1841, in Lebanon, Connecticut. Little is known of her early years. She attended Wheaton Seminary for awhile and then worked in a mission school for poor children in Norton, Connecticut.

In 1875 Emily moved to New York City, where she took a position as matron of the Wilson Industrial School for Girls in the East Side tenement district. She was dismayed by the poverty and degradation of the immigrant children who attended the school. The little girls could not perform even the simplest and most fundamental household tasks.

Emily changed how the "housework" classes were taught, making them fun and instructive instead of dreary and lifeless. She published her new teaching ideas in *Little Lessons for Little Housekeepers* in 1876. She had the idea of adapting Friedrich Froebel's kindergarten teaching concept to the teaching of elementary housekeeping arts. For the cubes and spheres and geometric forms, she substituted pots, pans, brooms, and other household tools. Her system of instruction included songs to be sung while doing different tasks. Her instruction book for teachers included such songs as "Washing Dishes, Washing Dishes," "Waste Not," "Beating Eggs," "Bedmaking," and "Boiling Potatoes." She taught her pupils how to cheerfully create clean, well-run homes preparatory to becoming household servants.

Emily strongly believed that all young girls, rich or poor, should be taught domestic science. She chose the name

Emily's writing is from the introduction to her book, How to Teach Kitchen Garden or Object Lessons in Household Work including Songs, Plays, Exercises and Games Illustrating Household Occupations, *published in 1901 by Doubleday.*

"kitchen garden" for her system of teaching, thereby recognizing her debt to the kindergarten idea and acknowledging that her program focused on elementary domestic training. She later admitted that she could have chosen a more descriptive name and that "domestic kindergarten" might have been better.

Emily trained teachers in her methods, and by 1879 kitchen garden classes were under way in fourteen industrial schools and missions in New York City. Her Kitchen Garden Organization spread to other parts of the country and later became the Industrial Education Association.

In 1892 Emily left the Wilson Industrial School and became the superintendent of the New York Cooking School. She never married and died of heart trouble in 1909.

Addie Melvina Billings

circa 1917

Against prohibition

Mr. Billings is not well. . . . Our children are still going to school. Our 40 acres in wine grapes make us a good living, even though we have to have all the work done by hired help which is difficult to secure now that so many of our grape growers' sons have gone to war. If prohibition makes our grapes worthless, we won't have anything left. We're old. We have not the strength to make a new start. I don't know what will become of us.

Addie Melvina Billings was born January 4, 1858, in Pecotonica, Illinois. She began teaching school at sixteen while taking classes herself at the Iowa State Normal School. In 1880 she married Elmore M. Billings, a lawyer, and settled in Geneva, Nebraska.

After her marriage, Addie became her husband's secretary. She liked working in his firm and became familiar with the law. She was also a correspondent for the Omaha newspapers, which enabled her to get free publicity for her husband. When he would win a case, she would include it in her column; but when he lost a case, she would, of course, forget to mention it.

In 1887 Addie was admitted to the Nebraska bar and became Elmore's law partner. They moved to Benicia, California, four years later, seeking a milder climate for Elmore's health. When his health failed to improve and he

Addie's writing is from "How the Bone-Dry National Amendment Would Affect Me and My Neighbors," an address she delivered to the California Grape Protective Association.

retired, she continued to practice law, joining the Wallace Rutherford firm in Napa.

In 1908 the Billings invested in a wine vineyard near Calistoga. For many years Addie served as executive secretary of the California Grape Growers' Association. When the Woman's Christian Temperance Union, of which she was also a member, discovered her affiliation with grape growers, she was "read out" of the organization.

Addie was a member of the Order of the Eastern Star for more than fifty years. She served for two years as Grand Matron of Nebraska before her move to California. After Elmore's death in 1920, she relocated to Berkeley so that her two adopted daughters could attend the University of California there. In her later years, Addie took up the hobby of rug hooking and made more than fifty beautiful rugs. She died at home in Berkeley in 1948 at the age of ninety.

JANUARY 5

Olympia Brown

Leading the way

1926
In the course of my second year (1861 — St. Lawrence University Theological School in Canton, NY), I learned that the Northern Universalist Association would hold its annual meeting at Malone, New York. I resolved to go there and formally ask for ordination. I felt more uncertain of securing ordination later, and therefore determined to get it there if possible, since I thought that this ordaining council, knowing something of my work and character, might be more favorable than some other body elsewhere. . . . The week before, I had preached at Huvelton, and the people there had invited me to be their pastor. A delegate from Huvelton was a member of the ordaining council, so I went into the presence of that body feeling quite confident, and although there was much discussion and opposition, I spoke for myself, and when the vote was taken it was in my favor. The ceremony took place. Mr. Fisher had so far overcome his feelings that he took part in the exercises. This was the first time that the Universalists, or indeed any denomination had formally ordained any women as a preacher. They took that stand, a remarkable one for the day, which shows the courage of those men.

Olympia's writing is from her unpublished autobiography, which is part of the Olympia Brown Papers, Schlesinger Library, Radcliffe College, Cambridge, Massachusetts.

Olympia Brown was born January 5, 1835, in Prairie Ronde, Michigan. After one unhappy year at Mt. Holyoke College she graduated from Antioch College in 1860. While at Antioch she arranged for Congregational minister Antoinette Brown Blackwell to preach at the school. It was the first time she had heard a woman preach, and despite widespread opposition to female ministers, she decided to become one.

Olympia entered the St. Lawrence University Theological School in Canton, New York, where she endured prejudice and harassment from her classmates and professors. Following graduation she was immediately ordained at the Northern Universalist Association meeting and assumed a vacant position at a small parish in Vermont.

In 1873 after being installed in Weymouth, Massachusetts, Olympia married John Henry Willis, a local merchant on the board of trustees of her church. With his agreement she kept her maiden name. Five years later they moved to Racine, Wisconsin, where Olympia became active in the women's suffrage movement.

Olympia resigned from her Racine pastorate in 1887 to concentrate on suffrage work. She travelled tirelessly throughout the state, speaking on behalf of the movement and organizing suffrage clubs.

Olympia moved in with her daughter in 1914 after her husband's death, but she continued to work for her causes. At the age of ninety-one she took her first trip to Europe and suffered a fatal heart attack a few months after her return.

Jean Kenyon Mackenzie

September 15, 1904

Really in Africa

To-night I was reading about Stanley's search for Livingstone, when suddenly I asked myself, "Am I really in the country of which he writes?" I went to the window to look out, to see, my dears, if I were. It was raining heavily, but for all that the moonlight penetrated the clouds and fell with a most impartial ray and no glamour. There were the worn paths leading from little gray huts to little gray huts; there were the innumerable banners of the plantain trees, and the slim, up-standing pawpaws, and beyond these the great columns of the trees of the forest, all patient under the vehement rain. And I know perfectly, and for the first time, that I am in Africa.

Nowadays during half of the school hours I teach

Jean's writing is from Black Sheep, Adventures in West Africa, *published in 1916 by Houghton, Mifflin and Company.*

several classes in the primer. Zambe has graduated to the primer and reads, with inexplicable pauses and with strange agitation of his arms and legs, sentences of three words each. Always his eyes plead with me not to desert him in this adventurous country of learning. Do you know, I am happy in this: that all these people are real and individual. One is clever, another is stupid; another's lips, when he recites, tremble with trepidation; another, bless her little heart, has a little frightened pulse that throbs in her neck when she grapples with the chart. Who could resist such allurements, such weaknesses, such eagerness?

Jean Kenyon Mackenzie was born January 6, 1874, in Elgin, Illinois, the eldest of six children of a Presbyterian minister. After graduating from the Van Ness Seminary in San Francisco, she spent two years at the Sorbonne in Paris and two years at the University of California. In 1902, determined to do something useful beyond studying, she applied to the Presbyterian Board of Foreign Missions to become a missionary in Africa.

In 1904 Jean was sent to the German colony of Kamerun where she remained for ten years. She worked at several remote bush villages that were accessible only on foot. An accident in 1914 forced her to return to America, where she began writing about her African experiences.

Jean published the first of many articles for *Atlantic Monthly* in 1914. Two years later she published her first book and returned to Africa for two more years of special duty during World War I. Upon her second homecoming she resumed her writing career until 1930. Critics praised her work, proclaiming it a "valuable contribution to the literature of missions" that presented a clear "picture of the hearts of black men and women."

The Presbyterian Board of Foreign Missions elected Jean a member in 1923. She was sent as the board's special representative to the 1926 international and interdenominational conference in Belgium, where she spoke on the future of African missions.

Jean died of lung cancer in 1936 at the age of sixty-two.

Emma Schoenmacher Mott

1909

Dr. Sutton came, and while they sat talking, Dr. beside the bed, the Death Angel came also. I had been leaning on the foot of the bed, after giving him two tiny pills by order of Dr. who had also given him a hypo injection at 9:15 PM. I sat down in the front room with the stove obstructing sight of them. Almost immediately Dr. went without stopping to say "Good Night." The door hardly closed when a gasp reached my ear. One step and I was in sight of my loved one, but too late. He had entered in. I started to rub his hands but I knew that were futile, then I ran to the door and called "Dr.! Dr.! Come right back." He had gotten only in front of the next neighbor's door — it all happened so quickly — and instantly returned. I plead, "Do something for him, you must." He said, "No use Mrs. Mott." I, with a single stroke composed his face and it took on a look which I shall ever remember, an expression so familiar to me when he had been thinking on some life problems, a sort of quizzical smile that expected me to ask of him "What is it Harry?" And I asked it of him over and over but no response ever came. And I still am asking "What would you say Harry if you could speak."

A look to remember

Emma Schoenmacher Mott was born January 7, 1849, in Branchville, New Jersey. She began teaching in Pennsylvania at the age of fifteen because she was too young to be certified in New Jersey. She used her earnings to pay for college courses to improve herself, concentrating on speech and music.

Emma married Henry Harrison Mott, the well-known suffragist and Lucretia Mott's first cousin, in her early thirties. They relocated to Grafton, North Dakota, where Emma started the first school in 1882. The tiny fifty-by-thirty-foot building had desks but no blackboard, and she supplied the textbooks for her seventy pupils. Henry set up a law practice but soon found his services were not in much demand in Grafton. He changed careers to become a surveyor; his son and grandson continued in the same profession.

In 1884 the University of North Dakota opened in a four-

Emma's writing is from a letter to Mrs. E. A. Thorpe. The penciled first draft is among the Henry Mott family papers in the Orin G. Libby Manuscript Collection at the University of North Dakota in Grand Forks.

story brick building in Grand Forks. Emma joined the faculty and boarded on campus, as Grafton was forty miles away. The first year conditions were primitive, and tempers clashed over the ideal of establishing another Harvard on the prairie and the reality of poor heating and plumbing and ill-prepared students. Following the inaugural year the president, the janitor, and Emma were not asked back, and she returned to Grafton disillusioned.

Emma joined the Woman's Christian Temperance Union and began writing a column, "Letter from the Grafton Union," for its North Dakota magazine, *Western Womanhood*. With her husband's help, she took an ax and broke up all twenty-seven saloons in Grafton. Thereafter she wore twenty-seven keys attached to her belt as a statement of her accomplishment.

Henry died in 1909 at fifty-six, leaving Emma bereft. When her house burned to the ground several years later, all that she could salvage were her husband's four diaries, written from 1899 to 1908. She moved in with her son and lived there until her death in 1941.

JANUARY   8

Mary Kenney O'Sullivan

Her first strike

Mary's writing is taken from her unfinished and unpublished autobiography given to Schlesinger Library, Radcliffe College, by Professor Oscar Handlin. He was given the autobiography by Mary's long-time neighbor, Mrs. I. B. Cohen.

1936

There was a public school in Hannibal where the children were taught the three R's. There was also a parochial school and a convent school. The parochial school cost fifty cents a month, the convent, $2.00 a month. When I was nine years old, my parents sent me to the convent. They were determined that their baby should have the best.

I learned easily, and I was ambitious to get ahead. Mother Gabriel chose me to help her in teaching the younger children elementary spelling and reading. One day, three classmates danced in, collected their books, and told me with happy faces they were going to the higher room. There were no examinations for promotions. The Mother Superior made the decisions. I went right to her and asked if I might not be sent to the higher class, too. She answered, "Not this time. But when the next vacancy occurs, you shall be sent up." Some weeks afterward, when I arrived at school one morning, two children of my class ran up to me, their faces all smiles, and said, "We are going up to the higher room!"

I went to the Mother and asked if I was going up to the higher room, too. She answered as before, "Not this time. But at the very next vacancy you shall."

I knew I had been wronged. I rushed to my desk, took my books and my slate and marched out of the room. On the way out, I met some girls coming in late, and I shocked them by telling them I was leaving. "I shall never come back to this school again," I said.

When I reached home Mother was sewing. I told her about the Mother Superior, the broken word, and my telling the girls I had left school and would never return. She was distressed, I could see, but she said nothing. At noon there came a knock at the door. The Mother Superior and the head teacher had come. They said to my mother that I had set a bad example and had disgraced the school. The two insisted that I must go back to atone for the wrong I had done. My mother, a pious Catholic, was overwhelmed to think that her youngest child had disgraced the school. So she joined her pleadings to those of the Mother and Sister. But I would not yield.

I didn't go back. I won my first strike.

Now I think perhaps my parents were secretly proud of me. At any rate, there were no reproaches. The next week I entered the public school. I was happy there. I liked everybody and everybody liked me!

Mary Kenney O'Sullivan was born January 8, 1864, in Hannibal, Missouri. She started school when she was nine, first attending the local convent school and later transferring to the public school. In her early teens she left school to work as an apprentice dressmaker.

Mary turned to factory work at a book binding company when the death of her father left her with an invalid mother to support. She learned every job open to women and became a forewoman. Her experiences at several Chicago binderies propelled her to organize her co-workers to form a union to fight for better hours and conditions.

Mary was appointed the first woman general organizer of the American Federation of Labor in 1891. She travelled throughout New York, Massachusetts, and Illinois, organizing women's unions.

Mary married John F. O'Sullivan, labor editor of the

Boston Globe, in 1894. They had four children, but Mary continued her labor work, organizing local rubber makers and laundry workers and speaking frequently at union meetings.

In 1902 John O'Sullivan was run over by a train. Mary had to support herself and her children, yet she remained in the forefront of the labor movement. When she was fifty she became a factory inspector for the Massachusetts Department of Labor and Industries. She held the position through her seventieth year. Mary died in 1943 when she was seventy-nine.

Elizabeth Knight Britton

*A*merican mosses

Elizabeth's writing is from a letter to Mr. Kennedy, a fellow botanist. It is part of a collection of manuscript letters in the archives of the Gray Herbarium, Harvard University.

1898
I shall be very glad to see a good, patient, clever worker at Harvard, and hope the appointment will be made soon, as I know we shall all ask for questions to be answered there and send material there as soon as there is someone to use those valuable collections which are now idle. Unity of work and purpose is what we need in American Bryology and then we shall stop and put an end to this sending of American mosses abroad to be named and also such abominable results as Kindberg's garbling of Macoun's mosses. I think we are all agreed that no matter what we call our plants, they can be better known and studied by those who see them growing, than by those who do not even know whether Boston is a suburb of New York, nor the differences and varieties of our geography and topography. Those of us who have been abroad and realized how little they know about us, feel very keenly about this, and are doing our best to stop it. And this is true not only of mosses but of insects, etc. etc. We are trying to keep the types here, and by creating new types and monographs we are succeeding in doing this much better than we did half a century ago.

Elizabeth Gertrude Knight Britton was born January 9, 1858, in New York City. She spent a large part of her childhood in Cuba, where her father and grandfather operated a variety of businesses. It was there that she first developed her interest in botany.

Upon graduation from Normal College (later Hunter

College) in New York, she was asked to teach there, although she was only seventeen years old. In 1883 she presented her first scientific paper on albinism in plants. Several months later she presented a paper on mosses, the first in a long line that would establish her as a leader in the study of mosses (bryology).

Elizabeth married Nathaniel Lord Britton, a botany professor at Columbia University in 1885. They made a good team; she accompanied him on all his field expeditions to assist him, as well as to further her own bryological studies. She assumed charge of Columbia's small moss collection and worked to increase its size.

Elizabeth and her husband were the principal force behind the establishment of the New York Botanical Gardens on 250 acres in the Bronx. Professor Britton served as its director-in-chief for more than thirty-three years, and in 1912 his wife was appointed honorary curator of mosses.

Elizabeth was also interested in the study and conservation of wildflowers. In 1902 she helped found the Wild Flower Preservation Society of America. As secretary and treasurer she helped pass legislation in several states to protect vanishing native plants. She staged a successful national boycott against the use of wild holly at Christmas. Wild holly was replaced by holly that was cultivated for that purpose.

Elizabeth died at home in 1934. The following year a double peak in Puerto Rico was named Mt. Britton in honor of Elizabeth and her husband. Fifteen plant species and one moss genus bear her name as well.

Sarah Lee Brown Fleming

1918
John Vance's name was held in reverence by every Negro in and around Santa Maria. How many Black men and women in slavery had heard of this good man and prayed that some day they might become his property! Often, on moonlight nights, he would listen to the singing of his slaves, as they sat in their cabin doors, voicing the familiar plantation melodies — the effect of which was marvelous — as it passed from door to door on the balmy breezes. . . .

John Vance was in the habit of visiting his slaves in their cabins, he would talk with them, and thus he became a part of their lives. He never had occasion to whip a slave, never kept an overseer, neither did he ever

A benevolent master

Sarah's writing is from Hope's Highway, *published in 1918 by Neale Publishing Company, New York.*

have a runaway. When a slave became in any way obstinate or unruly, the master would only have to suggest in a kindly way, that perhaps the bondman would like another master; and, almost invariably, he would get the result he desired.

Sarah Lee Brown Fleming was born January 10, 1875, in Charleston, South Carolina. The family resettled in Brooklyn, New York when she was two. From the time she began attending school she knew she wanted to be a teacher. Sadly, she received no encouragement from her parents, who recognized that there were no black teachers in Brooklyn at the time. Sarah, undaunted, remained in school, declaring she would rather die than forego education.

Sarah became the first black schoolteacher in Brooklyn and taught for several years until her marriage in 1906 to Dr. Richard Stedman Fleming. They moved to New Haven, Connecticut where he was the first black dentist in the state.

Sarah took up writing while she raised their two children. In her novel *Hope's Highway*, a kind white man, John Vance, establishes Vance Institute to educate former slaves. An evil white politician closes the institute in an attempt to prevent blacks from advancing. In the end, after many trials and setbacks, a young black man is able to reopen the institute so that people of color can turn "the rough road of ignorance into the happy highway of hope."

In addition to her writing, Sarah was deeply involved in community charities. She was most concerned with the needs of young, single, black women moving to cities, and in 1936 she opened the Phillis Wheatley Home for Girls. In appreciation for her efforts in the community, she was proclaimed Connecticut's Mother of the Year in 1952, the first black to receive the award. Sarah died in 1962 at home in New Haven, a few days short of her eighty-seventh birthday.

Harriet Maxwell Converse

*A*n ancient order

1908

"How swift he flies bearing the sun to the morning,
See how he sits down in the trails of the east sky!
Whip-poor-will, Whip-poor-will, no more I follow thee!
When the night comes again, wilt thou say 'Follow me'?"

The singing ends and the matrons bring in the kettles of soup and distribute it to all.

A few words in which I thank my Indian friends for consenting that I may hereafter "sit" with them and their friendly replies fill the moments that are swiftly bringing the day. It is the law that the sun shall not see us separate.

As I stand in the farmhouse door and hear the rumble of wheels grow faint and fainter, the sun casts a foreglow of its coming in the east sky, and the night seems a dream and it is difficult to realize that it has made me a member of the most ancient order of North American Indians.

Harriet Maxwell Converse was born January 11, 1836, in Elmira, New York, the youngest of seven children. Harriet's mother died when she was nine, after which she was sent to live with relatives in Ohio.

As a teenager, Harriet married George Clarke, but he died within a few years. Her inheritance from her husband, as well as from her father two years later left her a very wealthy young woman. She returned to New York in 1861 to marry a childhood friend, Franklin Buchanan Converse.

The Converses spent the first five years of their marriage travelling throughout the United States, Europe, Asia, and Africa, documenting native musical instruments. Upon their return, they settled in New York City, where Harriet occupied herself writing poetry and essays for several magazines. She published one book of her collected poems, *Sheaves* (1882), which was well received.

Harriet's life changed completely in the early 1880s after a chance meeting with a fellow New Yorker, General Ely S. Parker. General Parker was a Seneca Indian chief who had become an engineer and served as commissioner of Indian affairs under President Ulysses Grant. Although residing in New York City, he continued to preserve the history of the Iroquois Confederacy, and delighted in telling Harriet about his culture. Harriet became a champion of Indian rights and lobbied in New York and Washington on behalf of native Americans. The Indians showed their appreciation by adopting her, naming her "Ya-ie-wa-noh," and eventually making her an honorary chief of the Six Nations.

General Parker described Harriet as "the best informed woman in Indian lore in America." Committed to preserving the Iroquois culture, she began purchasing Indian relics which she donated to the New York State Museum. She also donated extensively to the American Museum of Natural

Harriet's description of her induction into the secret Little Water Medicine Society is from Myths and Legends of the New York State Iroquois, *published in 1908 by the University of New York.*

History, the Museum of the American Indian, and Harvard's Peabody Museum.

Harriet died in 1903, two months after her husband. Many members of the Six Nations attended her funeral, which combined Iroquois and Episcopal rituals.

Theresa Helburn

*T*wo diverse people

Theresa's writing is from her autobiography, A Wayward Quest, *published in 1960 by Little, Brown and Company, Boston.*

1960

It's hard to imagine two people more completely different. I was an extrovert, Oliver an introvert; I lived with a crowded calendar of lunches, teas (there weren't cocktail parties then), dinners, always the theater or music in the evenings, and people-people-people all day and every day. To Oliver the thought of more than three people in a room at one time was horror. . . .

I was conventional, snobbish, priggish and reserved. Oliver wanted people to be themselves, to be honest and real and courageous. He came into my life like a high wind that blew away everything that was artificial.

No wonder I was afraid. We were so different that I could not imagine being able to build a marriage while two diverse people tugged in different ways. Anyhow, I felt about marriage as I felt about the theater. No one should enter it unless he can't help it.

Theresa Helburn was born January 12, 1887, in New York City. When Theresa was a child, her mother frequently took her to the theater, which enthralled her. She later wrote: "I entered a world that was unlike anything I have ever imagined, but that I recognized at once as my own. The theatre was not a dream, or a goal — it was home."

Theresa graduated from Bryn Mawr College in 1908, after which she had a nervous breakdown. Her mother bought her a farm at Cape May, New Jersey, where she rested and recuperated. She took up writing and produced a few plays, none of them successful. In 1914 she co-founded the Washington Street Players in New York City, later called the Theatre Guild, which presented European plays.

The guild enjoyed a successful first season and established its reputation as America's foremost art theater. Theresa served as executive director and took part in all aspects of production from choosing plays to casting. She used her writing talents to rewrite dialogue — sometimes with the playwright's approval, sometimes not — and she became known as a "play doctor."

Theresa married John Baker Opdycke ("Oliver") in 1919. He was her constant companion until his death in 1956.

Despite some success, the guild was bankrupt by 1943. Theresa came up with the idea of turning the play *Green Grow the Lilacs* into a musical and hired Richard Rodgers and Oscar Hammerstein to write it. The resulting musical *Oklahoma!* became a phenomenal success and revolutionized the American musical theater. The Kiowa Indian tribe of Oklahoma made Theresa a chief and named her "Little Lady Who Sees Far."

Two years later Theresa again hired Rodgers and Hammerstein to turn the play *Liliom* into a musical, and the resulting *Carousel* was another tremendous hit. She continued to bring serious plays to the American public as well, establishing close working relationships with Eugene O'Neill and George Bernard Shaw. Theresa retired from the guild in 1953 and died at her Connecticut home in 1959.

Lilla Cabot Perry

1927

*H*er own impression

Monet was a man of his own opinions though he always let you have yours and liked you all the better for being outspoken about them. He used to tell me that my forté was "plein air," figures out-of-doors, and once in urging me to paint more boldly he said to me: "Remember that every leaf on the tree is as important as the features of your model. I should like just for once to see you put her mouth under one eye instead of under her nose!"

"If I did that, no one would ever look at anything else in the picture!"

He laughed heartily and said:

"Vous avez peut-être raison, Madame!"

In spite of his intense nature and at times rather severe aspect, he was inexpressibly kind to many a struggling young painter. I remember him once saying to me:

"When you go out to paint, try to forget what objects you have before you, a tree, a house, a field or whatever. Merely think here is a little square of blue,

Lilla's writing is from "Reminiscences of Monet, 1889 to 1909," American Magazine of Art, *March 1927.*

here an oblong of pink, here a streak of yellow, and paint it just as it looks to you, the exact color and shape, until it gives your own naive impression of the scene before you."

Lilla Cabot Perry was born January 13, 1848, in Boston, Massachusetts, the eldest of eight children of a prominent surgeon. She grew up in the company of Boston's intelligentsia: Louisa May Alcott, Ralph Waldo Emerson, and James Russell Lowell were her parents' frequent guests.

When she was twenty-one Lilla met Thomas Sargent Perry. They were married after a five-year courtship and had three daughters. Although Lilla had been interested in art since childhood, she didn't start to paint until she was thirty.

The Perry family moved to Paris for two years in 1887, and Lilla immersed herself in art classes. In May 1887 she attended an exhibit of Claude Monet's impressionist paintings and experienced the "revelation" of her career. She decided to move to Giverny and rented a house next door to Monet.

Monet never took pupils, but he did critique Lilla's work, praising her and recommending that she concentrate on her specialties: plein-air and landscapes. However, her husband did not earn much money, so Lilla was forced to paint portraits to support the family.

In 1905 Lilla suffered a nervous breakdown which her husband attributed to "thirty years of insomnia." In 1909 they spent their final season in Giverny and returned to the United States. She brought with her hollyhock seeds from Monet's garden, which bloomed at her New Hampshire home for many summers.

After years of trying to promote American interest in Impressionism, which she called the "new truth" in painting, Lilla finally began to realize some success in her own country. In 1915 she received the bronze medal at the Panama-Pacific International Exposition in San Francisco.

Lilla's late impressions, painted in her early eighties, were some of her best works. She was still painting on the day she died in 1934 at the age of eighty-six.

Katharine Prescott Wormeley

Headquarters U.S. Sanitary Commission
Steamer "Wilson Small"
May 13, 1862

On a hospital ship

Dear Mother,

. . . I took my first actual watch last night. . . . We begin the day by getting them all washed, and freshened up, and breakfasted. Then the surgeons and dressers make their rounds, open the wounds, apply the remedies, and replace the bandages. This is an awful hour; I sat with my fingers in my ears this morning. When it is over, we go back to the men and put the ward in order once more; remaking several beds, and giving clean handkerchiefs with a little cologne or bay-water on them, — so prized in the sickening atmosphere of wounds. We sponge the bandages over the wounds constantly, which alone carries us round from cot to cot almost without stopping, except to talk to some, read to others, or write letters for them; occasionally giving medicine or brandy, etc., according to order. Then comes dinner. After that we go off duty, and get first washed and then fed ourselves; our dinner-table being the top of an old stove, with slices of bread for plates, fingers for knives and forks, and carpet-bags for chairs. . . . After dinner other ladies keep the same sort of watch through the afternoon and evening.

Katharine Prescott Wormeley was born January 14, 1830, in Ipswich, Suffolk, England. Her family sailed to America in 1848 for an extended visit, which became permanent following her father's death in 1852.

The Wormeleys settled in Newport, Rhode Island. At the beginning of the Civil War Katharine was one of the first to join the local relief effort. She organized a Women's Union Aid Society to assist the families of the soldiers. She obtained a government clothing contract, and her seamstresses produced more than 50,000 shirts in one year.

In 1862 Katharine joined the United States Sanitary Commission, a private volunteer organization. She served as a matron on a hospital ship that searched for sick and wounded soldiers along the rivers of the Virginia peninsula. After several months the program was taken over by the army, and she moved on to become "lady superintendent" of

Katharine's writing is from The Other Side of War, *published in 1889 by Ticknor Field and Company.*

Lowell General Hospital near Newport. Her health soon failed, however, and she was forced to resign. While recovering, bedridden at home, she wrote a book about the purpose of the Sanitary Commission that raised hundreds of dollars for commission efforts.

After the war Katharine founded the Newport Charity Organization Society, as well as an industrial school that offered classes in cooking, sewing, and domestic work for poor women.

Katharine spent the last fifteen years of her life at her farm in Jackson, New Hampshire, where she died of pneumonia in 1908.

Elia Wilkinson Peattie

Glorious freedom

1914

"I often have dreamed of bringing you up on this trail," said Wander whimsically, "but never for the purpose of hearing you make your declaration of independence."

"Why not?" demanded Kate. "In what better place could I make it?"

Beside the clamorous waterfall was a huge boulder squared almost as if the hand of a mason had shaped it. Kate stepped on it, before Wander could prevent her, and stood laughing, the wind blowing her garments about her and lifting strands of her loosened hair.

"I declare my freedom!" she cried with grandiose mockery. "Freedom to think my own thoughts, preach my own creeds, do my own work, and make the sacrifices of my own choosing. . . ."

Elia Wilkinson Peattie was born January 15, 1862, in Kalamazoo, Michigan. Her family relocated to the outskirts of Chicago after the 1871 fire there, and her father built their new house by hand. Elia returned to the house as an adult and raised her three sons there.

In 1883 Elia married Robert Burns Peattie and began work as the first "girl reporter" at the *Chicago Tribune*. When her husband was offered a job at the *World-Herald* in Omaha, he required that there be a job for his wife as well. They remained in Nebraska for ten years.

From 1901 to 1917 Elia was the literary critic at the *Chicago Tribune*. She complained that it was tedious work, taking time away from her other writing, but it was also

Elia's writing is from The Precipice, *which she wrote to help women gain the right to vote. It was published in 1914 by the University of Illinois Press.*

lucrative. Elia was determined to earn money to improve her family's lot and pay for her children's education. Once she wrote 100 short stories in 100 days to pay for renovations in her home. During her lifetime she published thirty-two books.

Elia also belonged to numerous women's clubs and gave lectures at Jane Addams' Hull House. When women authors were refused membership at the all-male Cliff Dwellers Club, she founded the Cordon Club. Her well-known Sunday brunches were one of the central gathering places for Chicago's literary set.

The Peatties retired to North Carolina in 1920. Elia died in 1935 during a July vacation in Vermont.

Ellen Russell Emerson

1884

*I*ndian beliefs

The Indian believes that the spirit of the animal slain walks about his cabin, watchful of the disposition of his bones.

. . . if the hunter neglects to take care of the bones, the offended spirit communicates the fact to his former companions, who then conspire to keep concealed from the hunter, that he may famish for want of food. This belief is an illustration of the ancient teaching, that the Great Spirit bade the animals allow themselves to be killed by the Indian for his sustenance. . . .

It was the occasion of remark among the Jesuits that the Indian questioned, "What animal do you pray for; is it a bear, or a deer?" And the zealous Fathers asseverated: "These savages are utterly brutish. They think only of eating." Yet the Jesuit taught the Indian convert the words of our Lord's Prayer that bear the burden of a similar appeal — "Give us this day our daily bread."

Ellen Russell Emerson was born January 16, 1837, in New Sharon, Maine. Her father, a physician, sent her away to school at the Mount Vernon Seminary in Boston, where the president, Dr. Robert Cushman, took a special interest in her. In 1862 at the age of twenty-five, she married Edwin Ruthven Emerson.

Ellen became interested in the ethnology of American

Ellen's writing is from Indian Myths; or Legends, Traditions, and Symbols of the Aborigines of America Compared with Those of Other Countries, including Hindostan, Egypt, Persia, Assyria and China, *published in 1884 by J. R. Osgood and Company.*

Indians and began extensive research. She published her first book, *Indian Myths; or Legends, Traditions, and Symbols of the Aborigines of America Compared with Those of Other Countries, including Hindostan, Egypt, Persia, Assyria and China*, in 1884. In 1886 she departed for Europe for four years of study, spending most of her time on Egyptology in Paris, where she was made an honorary member of the Société Américaine. Upon her return to America she published her second book, *Masks, Heads, and Faces with Some Considerations Respecting the Rise and Development of Art.*

Ellen returned to Europe in 1892 to assist with the exposition being held in Madrid to celebrate the 400th anniversary of the discovery of America. For her efforts she received a medal from the Junta Directiva of the Columbian Historical Exposition.

Ellen died at home in Cambridge, Massachusetts in 1907 at the age of seventy. She was survived by her husband and daughter.

Evelyn Dunn Scott

Unended quest

1937

Once, while we were living in Russellville, my mother, who had been out afternoon-calling, entered our yard (she was looking so pretty in her grey broadcloth gown with her ostrich-plumed hat and her furs and violets, that I remember it still), and discovered me squatting in the grass, digging violently and laboriously with a large tin spoon. Questioned on my preoccupation, I explained to her that I did not like Russellville and was digging to reach China, which I understood to be at the other side of the world. I think this began an adventure, which has always had a somewhat desperate character, and is not yet done. I was like a trapped rat, forging a way through obstacles with a new burrow! Like a convict frenziedly employing a pocketknife as he seeks for freedom through ten yards of solid masonry with a guarded continent beyond! I wanted to get out, and be able to arrive somewhere else — on the other side of the strange taboos and inscrutable injunctions which hedged and hemmed me in.

Evelyn's writing is taken from Background in Tennessee, *published in 1937 by R. M. McBride.*

Elsie Dunn (Evelyn Scott) was born January 17, 1893, to a

prominent Southern family in Clarksville, Tennessee. Just shy of her twenty-first birthday she ran away to Brazil with Frederick Creighton Wellman, the director of tropical medicine at Tulane University, who was still married to his second wife. They took with them a few clothes, some money, and two books: Tolstoy's *War and Peace* and a volume of Keats's poetry.

Frederick and Elsie changed their names to Cyril Kay and Evelyn Scott upon arrival in Brazil. They remained in South America for six years, despite their poverty and various illnesses. Evelyn's mother came for a visit and was forced to remain with them when her husband failed to send money for her return trip. They all returned to the United States in 1920, and Evelyn published her first novel the following year. Evelyn became a literary sensation, producing a tremendous amount of work in a short time. She published thirteen novels, a biography, a play, a mystery, three children's books, and two volumes of poetry. She was named honorary vice-president of the Author's League of America and widely hailed as one of the outstanding literary figures of the time.

Evelyn married British novelist John Metcalfe in 1928. During World War II he served in the Royal Air Force, leaving Evelyn stranded in England. She suffered a breakdown, possibly a stroke, which left her unstable, tormented by voices in her head. Her literary career was finished, and she was unable to save enough money to return to the United States until 1954. Evelyn spent the last years of her life with her husband in a small room in a New York City hotel. She died in 1963.

Ann Browder Pruett

1867
Thursday, July 4th
Today, the one that was once celebrated so heartily and joyously, has passed very quietly — no demonstrations whatever with the white people, pro or con. The freedmen had a dinner. I heard the drum and I suppose the "Stars and Stripes" were floating in the breeze. We have no national day — no day that is an anniversary of any event that brings joy to us. The days when our great battles were fought roll around, but we only sigh or drop a tear for some loved one who fell! We think not of them now as victories, since the end was not a victory. God, in His great wisdom, has caused us

*O*ur defeat

Ann's writing, from her diary written during the Reconstruction period following the Civil War, was privately published by Dorothy Sturgis Pruett in 1984.

almost to forget the war — it is so strange, but it is very seldom spoken of, and each one seems to think of one in defeat as the will of God — and each one seemed to yield and say: "Thy will be done." It's best for us that we do not think of it. We have adopted a very beautiful custom that I hope will be kept up by Southern women as long as there's one of us left that is of decorating our soldiers' graves the twenty-sixth of April. I assisted this year. It was a sad pleasure.

Ann Browder Pruett was born January 18, 1843, in Barbour County, Alabama. She was descended from two long-established, prominent Southern families. When the slaves were freed, Ann's father lost a great deal and the family's wealth was greatly reduced. However, they retained a staff of servants and had means to ensure a good education and travel opportunities for Ann and her brother.

Ann became engaged to Maj. William Pruett in October 1867. They planned to be married on December 3, but at the last moment Ann postponed it a week because she "wanted to remain one more week in single blessedness." She confided in her diary her fears for her future: "Will his family love me? Will he love me then as now? Will I suit him? Will I be a good companion?"

Ann's fears were unfounded, and she and William enjoyed a happy union. They remained in Barbour County, where he was elected probate judge. Ann had three children, two sons and a daughter. Her health had always been fragile, and she passed away prematurely in 1880 at the age of thirty-seven. She was buried in the Pruett family plot; her husband was placed by her side thirty years later.

JANUARY 19

Effie Lee Newsome

Imagination

1927
SKY PICTURES
Sometimes a right white mountain
Or great soft polar bear,
Or lazy little flocks of sheep
Move on in the blue air.
The mountains tear themselves like floss,
The bears all melt away.
The little sheep will drift apart
In such a sudden way.

And then new sheep and mountains come.
New polar bears appear
And roll and tumble on again
Up in the skies so clear.
The polar bears would like to get
Where polar bears belong.
The mountains try so hard to stand
In one place firm and strong.
The little sheep all want to stop
And pasture in the sky,
But never can these things be done,
Although they try and try!

Mary Effie Lee Newsome was born January 19, 1885, in Philadelphia, where her father was editor of the African Methodist Episcopal Church's paper, *The Christian Record*. Reading was favored by the Lee family, and Effie spent many hours of her childhood reading the Bible, poetry, fables, and nature books. She began writing herself at five years of age.

In 1896 the family relocated to Wilberforce, Ohio. Effie attended her father's alma mater, Wilberforce University, graduating in 1904. She continued to pursue her studies until 1914, attending Oberlin College, the Academy of Fine Arts, and the University of Pennsylvania.

Effie married the Reverend Henry Newsome in 1920. They continued to reside in Wilberforce, where Effie became a librarian. She began her career at Central State College and later transferred to Wilberforce University, where she remained until 1963.

In addition to her duties at the library, Effie wrote poetry and prose, primarily for children. She was a frequent contributor to W. E. B. Dubois's magazine for black children, *The Brownies' Book*, and to another of his publications, *The Crisis*. Her book of children's poems, *Gladiola Garden: Poems of Outdoors and Indoors for Second Grade Readers*, was published in 1944. The pervasive theme of her work was optimism. She tried to instill in her readers an appreciation of the world around them and a sense of racial pride.

She died in 1979 at the age of ninety-four.

Effie's "Sky Pictures" is from Caroling Dusk: An Anthology of Verse by Negro Poets, edited by Countee Cullen, published in 1927 by Harper & Row.

Ellis Reynolds Shipp

*W*anting more

1872

I do not wish to make too many resolutions lest I shall not be enabled to execute them, but I believe it is better to make them and break them than do nothing. I know that I am tired of this life of uselessness and unaccomplished desires, only as far as cooking, washing dishes and doing general housework goes. I believe that woman's life should not consist wholly and solely of these routine duties. I think she should have ample time and opportunity to study and improve her mind, to add polish and grace to her manners, to cultivate those finer tastes and refined and delicate feelings that are so beautiful in women and that are so truly requisite in a mother.

Ellis Reynolds Shipp was born January 20, 1847, in Davis County, Iowa. At the age of five she travelled with her family by covered wagon to the new Mormon settlement in the Valley of the Great Salt Lake, Utah. Mormon leader Brigham Young met her at a church conference in 1864 and was so impressed that he invited her to move in with his large family and attend their school.

Ellis resided with the Youngs until her marriage in 1866 to Milford Bard Shipp. Brigham Young disapproved of Shipp because he was eleven years older and twice divorced, but Ellis ignored the advice of family and friends. In keeping with the Mormon tradition of polygamy, Milford gradually took on three more wives.

In 1873 Brigham Young declared in a sermon that "the time has come for women to come forth as doctors in these Valleys." Within two years Ellis's sister-wife Maggie was sent off to Woman's Medical College in Philadelphia. However, she suffered terribly from homesickness and returned to the family after one month. Since the tuition was prepaid, Ellis was sent in her place.

Ellis worked hard to catch up, and graduated with honors despite the fact that she was pregnant during her final year. She returned to Salt Lake and opened her private practice, advertising in the newspapers as a "Physician and Surgeon; Special attention given to Obstetrics, diseases of women and minor surgery." She also opened her own School of Obstetrics and Nursing, training other women for service in the western Mormon communities.

Ellis's writing is from her diary entry written November 13, 1872. The diary is included in The Early Autobiography and Diary of Ellis Reynolds Shipp, M.D., *published by Desert News Press, Salt Lake City, 1962.*

Ellis continued teaching and practicing medicine well into her eighties, earning the title of "Grand Old Lady of Utah." She delivered more than 5,000 babies during her fifty-year career in addition to having ten of her own, and did much to educate local women in first aid, sanitation, and disease prevention. Upon her death at ninety-two, a renowned doctor wrote that she was the "outstanding woman of the last one hundred years, and I believe it will be another one hundred years before Utah produces another woman whose service to mankind exceeds that which she had rendered."

Anna White

1903

The Shaker Eldress is a bishop . . . a pastor; but no pastor of any outside church holds such a cure of souls. To her come the members of her flock, soul by soul, with the burden of sin, the frailty of nature, the weakness of character. . . . Here must be the power to arise with zeal and fervor to their true mission — to be a centre of pure spiritual life. . . .

She is the family mother. Her door is ever open. Her smile is the sunshine of the home. From aged sister to youngest child her eye is ever on the watch for need of body or ache of heart. The dying look to her for love to bear them thru the cold river of death, and her bosom is the resting place of every weary head.

Anna White was born January 21, 1831, in Brooklyn, New York. She was raised as a Quaker, and one of her earliest memories was of hearing Lucretia Mott deliver an antislavery message at a meeting. After graduating from a Quaker boarding school in Poughkeepsie, Anna returned to her family in New York City.

Anna helped her father with his hardware store and took in tailoring. One of her father's clients was the Shaker Community in Hancock, Massachusetts. Anna often accompanied him on his visits there and was impressed by the Shakers' ideal of Christian perfection. She loved their meetings, their songs, the beauty of their settlement, and in 1849, despite the warnings of her relatives, she joined the sect.

Anna spent the rest of her life at the Shaker Community in New Lebanon, New York, where she was a member of the "North Family." She became an associate eldress in 1865, in

Soul by soul

Anna's writing is from her essay "Woman's Mission," written for the January 1891 issue of the official Shaker periodical, Manifesto.

charge of the young female members. Following the death of Eldress Antoinette Doolittle in 1887, she became First Eldress of North Family.

In addition to her work at New Lebanon, Anna endeavored to improve the secular world as well. She served as vice-president of the Alliance of Women for Peace, which supported the cause of international disarmament. She was also a member of the National American Woman Suffrage Association and the National Council of Women of the United States. She was fascinated by Shaker history and music and compiled two volumes of Shaker songs. Her greatest contribution to the Shakers was her book *Shakerism: Its Meaning and Message*, co-authored with Eldress Leila Taylor. It was the only history published by the Shakers themselves. At a time when the movement was in decline, she hoped to attract new members by presenting the case for Shakerism to the world.

Anna died in 1910 and was buried in the North Family plot in the New Lebanon Cemetery.

Jennie Fowler Willing

*W*ith ghosts

1873

I once knew a girl who had a cold, selfish enjoyment of her power over young men, and practiced upon them accordingly. One of her victims was found stone dead with a laudanum-vial and a note to her, on the stand beside his bed. Another to whom she was pleased to call herself "engaged" for a while, went off to the Western plains, and none of his friends ever knew his fate. A third "threw himself away" upon a poor, ignorant servant girl, who had the merit of being, at least, honest. Do you think that young woman could enjoy the home, the husband, and children of her later years, with ghosts like those peeping in at her windows?

Jennie Fowler Willing was born January 22, 1834, in Burford, Canada West (later Ontario). The family relocated when she was eight to a farm in Newark, Illinois. Jennie's poor health precluded her attendance at local schools; however, she was so thorough in self-education that she was permitted to begin teaching at fifteen.

In 1853 Jennie married William C. Willing, a lawyer who had recently abandoned the law to become a Methodist

Jennie's writing is from "Our Mother," published in the September 1873 issue of the Methodist magazine for women, Ladies' Repository.

minister. For several years she followed him around rural New York and Illinois as he transferred from pastorate to pastorate. He encouraged her to become a minister as well, arranging for a local preacher's license and giving her one of his congregations for her own.

The Willings heard a lecture in 1868 by returning missionaries from India, and the following year the Woman's Foreign Missionary Society of the Methodist Episcopal Church was established in Boston. Jennie formed an auxiliary branch in her hometown of Rockford, Illinois, as well as the northwestern branch in Chicago and the western branch in St. Louis.

In 1874 Jennie and two other women organized the national women's temperance meeting in Cleveland. Delegates from seventeen states attended, and they officially established the Woman's Christian Temperance Union. Jennie served as first president of the Illinois WCTU and as editor of the group's monthly paper, *Our Union*.

In 1889 the Willings moved to New York City, where William accepted a new pastorate. Although he died five years later, Jennie remained in New York to continue her work with poor immigrant girls. In 1895 she founded the New York Evangelistic Training School. She died in 1916 at the age of eighty-two, dividing her estate between the WCTU and the school.

Mary Blanche Norton

1920

Finally Platona is reached after what would be to most Americans a dangerous ride along the steep mountain road overlooking the sea. The clinic is held in what on other days is the "Mayor's office." It has no medical conveniences or apparatus and but little furniture, so I commandeer a soap box to stand or sit upon and the Mayor's rickety desk for my medicine table.

The crowd has been gathering for several hours, a ragged, dirty, clamorous throng, regardless of the rain. They have gone through so much suffering and misery that a little rain means nothing.

Every one is anxious to see the American doctor. Many of the women never had had a doctor examine them for anything. It is a steady stream of woes, of indescribable diseases.

A stream of woes

Mary's writing is from a letter written to friends from Turkey. It appeared in the June 12, 1920, edition of the New York Sun.

More than 100 people have been attended at Platona. Hundreds more need treatment, and it will be another week before medical help or medicines reach the village again. But we have so few workers, and so little medicine. If Americans could only realize the conditions and the needs!

Mary Blanche Norton was born January 23, 1875, in Perryville, Pennsylvania. Her father worked for the railroad, which relocated the family to Eldon, Iowa, soon after Mary's birth. She attended local schools and graduated from Parsons College.

Following graduation, Mary taught school for several years and worked her way up to principal of the Eldon High School. She also did a great deal of social work with the poor, and her experiences with the sick and hungry led her toward a career in medicine.

In 1911 at the age of thirty-six, Mary enrolled in the Cornell University Medical School. She opened a private practice, first in Maine and later in New York City. She affiliated herself with several women's clinics, and often worked free of charge.

At the close of World War I Mary wanted to help the needy abroad. She joined the medical unit of the Near East Relief stationed in Turkey.

Mary worked with refugees at the clinics and with hundreds of abandoned orphans. Local women would not let male doctors see more than their tongues and wrists, so she proved invaluable to the female population. During an epidemic of Egyptian trachoma, Mary was stricken with the disease and spent months alone in an attic recuperating. She recovered but lost her sight in one eye.

In 1920 King Alexander of Greece bestowed upon her the Military Order of King George I, which carried the title of Chevalier. She was the first and only woman to receive this honor.

Mary retired from medicine in 1929 and began teaching science at the Holmquist School for Girls in New Hope, Pennsylvania. She died in 1971 at the age of ninety-six.

Katherine Mayo

1920

That was a happy Christmas at Mailly; these trench-
mortar boys and the Y girls with them doing their best
to make it so. On the day before Christmas they did an
enormous baking of pies, so that every lad should have
all he liked for once. . . . Then there had been the
usual day's work to do. And at the end the boys had
lingered, reluctant, on that night of nights, to quit their
closest link with home.

But at last the coast cleared. Then, hastily darkening the windows, the girls dragged in the trees that they
had managed to smuggle into camp. Alone they set
them up — for Y girls developed muscle, over there —
planted tables on tables in lieu of stepladders, proceeded to dress the boughs and to hang them with tomorrow's long-planned presents.

Toward midnight they finished. . . . And so it happened that one girl whispered to another, as they
tramped along toward bed:

"It's all so beautiful — someway, I'd like to be in a
real church while Christmas Day comes in. There's the
ruin, of course. — Would you come?"

So the two stole off at a tangent, in the quiet, across
the snow. No one, they knew, would pass that way.
For the church was an utter wreck, its roof demolished
by bombs, its walls rent or pierced with yawning holes
where shot had gone crashing through.

"But people have said prayers in it, these hundreds
of years," said one to the other. "You can feel it still.
We can just kneel there till the time comes, and then
creep home again. No one will know."

Silent again they plodded on — and came at last to
where the roofless walls loomed black and jagged
against a star-hung sky.

At last they crossed the threshold, and stood at the
foot of the nave. And they looked. And they saw a
wonderful thing.

That church was not empty, but full — full of their

Holy night

Katherine's writing is from
That Damn Y — A Record
of Overseas Service, *published
in 1920 by Houghton, Mifflin
and Company.*

own American boys, kneeling among the ruins, under the stars, waiting there in stillness for the coming of The Hour.

Katherine Mayo was born January 24, 1867, in Ridgway, Pennsylvania. Her father, a miner, continually relocated the family in search of a big strike, so Katherine travelled extensively throughout the United States and abroad.

At the age of twenty-five Katherine sold her first article to *Life* magazine for five dollars. Thereafter she contributed frequently to popular magazines and newspapers. A true freelance writer, her topics ranged from "Odd New Jersey Epitaphs" to "Cat Breeding for Profit."

Upon her return to the United States from a trip to Europe, she met and befriended Moyca Newell, a wealthy woman in her early twenties. They built a house together in 1911 in Bedford Hills, New York, called "Maaikenshof," Dutch for Moyca's estate. Thereafter the two friends travelled together throughout the world, gathering material for Katherine's books.

Katherine perceived herself as "a volunteer spokesman for the voiceless underdog." During World War I she received a cable from the Overseas YMCA asking her to go abroad to "let the American public know in print how the Overseas Y was using American trust money." Her observations resulted in a book, *That Damn Y — A Record of Overseas Service*. In 1940 Katherine died of cancer at home in Bedford Hills at the age of seventy-three.

Maud Wood Park

*A*t the circus

Maud's writing is from "Campaigning State by State," an article she contributed to the National American Woman Suffrage Association anthology, Victory, How Women Won It: A Centennial Symposium 1840-1940, *published in 1940 by the H. W. Wilson Company.*

1940
Sometimes we stumbled on unexpected friends. We came across one in Ohio when we were helping local workers in a northern county during a referendum campaign. There we found that a circus was to have a tight-rope performance, preceded by a band concert, in the square late that afternoon. . . . We asked the manager for permission to speak to the crowd between the concert and the acrobatic feat. He proved to be an Australian, enthusiastic about woman suffrage in his own country, and volunteered to introduce me. When the time came, he did so with as much gusto as if I had been a lady with two heads. Afterwards he invited us to

join the circus procession back to the big tent and offered to let me speak from one of the rings during the regular performance. So our car fell in behind the elephants. Again I was introduced with flourishes. Unfortunately, a troupe of trained dogs, waiting for their turn, took offense at my voice and their yapping, combined with the noise of an engine on a nearby railway track, drowned my words. "Never mind," said the sympathetic manager, "if you'll let me get the pile of leaflets I saw in your car, I'll have them distributed," and in a few minutes the two clowns were giving our suffrage leaflets to the audience.

Maud May Wood Park was born January 25, 1871, in Boston. She taught in local high schools until she saved enough money to enroll in Radcliffe at the age of twenty-four. It was in college that she first became involved in the women's suffrage movement. After graduating summa cum laude, Maud and her new husband, fellow student Charles Edward Park, moved into a Boston housing project, and she began her long career as a social reformer and suffragist.

Maud organized the first Boston Parent-Teacher Association and established several social clubs for immigrant women. She concentrated her suffrage work on college educated women and founded the College Equal Suffrage League.

Shortly after Charles's death in 1904, Maud spent a year and a half touring remote areas of the world, studying women in other cultures. She lectured extensively on her findings upon her return to America.

In 1909 Maud married New York theatrical agent Robert Hunter, although their work prevented them from living together. They met in hotels during Maud's lecture tours and spent vacations at her summer home in Maine. In 1919 Maud accepted the presidency of the newly formed League of Women Voters.

Maud worked tirelessly for the League of Women Voters until illness finally forced her to resign. She died in 1955 at her home in Massachusetts.

Elisabet Ney

To a friend

Elisabet's writing is from a letter to Arthur Schopenhauer and is included in Elisabet Ney by Jan Fortune and Jean Burton. She did a highly acclaimed bust of Schopenhauer a few months before he died. He described her in a letter to a friend as "twenty-four years old, very pretty and indescribably charming."

Berlin
March 2, 1860
Most Honoured Friend:

. . . The very sight of your handwriting made the day gloriously happy, just as it always does. You are always enthroned high in the altar of my heart, and letters from you bring back to me those wonderful days — only there were not enough of them — which we spent together last autumn in Frankfurt. Those dearest hours! They constitute one of the loveliest periods of my life.

. . . Soon after your letter arrived I had a visitor, Stockhausen, the great classical singer from Paris, from whose artistry I have learned many truths. He, too, has read a great deal of your work and was burning to know more about you. We talked of you for hours. I was overjoyed to be able to tell about all the wonderful things that happened at Frankfurt, and he took it all in eagerly. As I found him such an understanding person, and so keenly interested in you, I showed him your bust.

And is your bust still here? How can you ask? It has never left my side. I simply could not bring myself to part with it, which is why it has not yet been cast. I dared not trust such an important task to anyone save myself.

Elisabet Ney was born January 26, 1833, in Münster, Westphalia, Prussia. Her father was a professional stonecutter, and although he mostly made tombstones, he fancied himself an artist. Elisabet spent a great deal of time in her father's studio and declared at the age of eight that she too would be a sculptor.

Elisabet enrolled in the Royal Bavarian Academy of the Fine Arts in Munich when she was twenty. Soon after graduation, she began sculpting busts of Europe's elite: composer and pianist Franz Liszt, Prince Otto von Bismarck, philosopher Arthur Schopenhauer, King George V of Hanover, King Wilhelm I of Prussia. Her fame grew; in 1867 she received a royal command from King Ludwig III to become court sculptor in Munich.

Elisabet had married a physician, Edmund Duncan Montgomery, four years prior to her arrival in Munich as court sculptor. However, she never assumed his name and denied the marriage, preferring that people believe she was living in sin with her "best friend." Her feminism and eccentric lifestyle were not tolerated in Ludwig's court; she and her "best friend" were forced to flee Munich in 1870, leaving Ludwig II's unfinished statue behind.

Dr. Montgomery and Elisabet emigrated to the United States the following year and settled in Liendo Plantation near Houston, Texas. Elisabet's eccentricities were accepted in America. She finished her masterpiece — a statue of Lady Macbeth, her favorite literary heroine — when she was seventy-two. She died two years later in 1907 and was buried under a stand of live oaks at Liendo.

Catharine Marvin Dimmick

April 1, 1821

A need for grace

A paragraph in the Boston Recorder recently struck me with great force. Speaking of ministers' wives, it said, "They will not have a common place either in heaven or hell!" I tremble to be in a station of such responsibility. I need more grace — more grace that I may act my part aright. Especially in visiting the sick do I often feel this need.

Catharine Mather Marvin Dimmick was born January 27, 1793, in Norwich, Connecticut. Due to frail health, most of her education occurred at home. Her father, a physician, passed away when Catharine was five, and she became an orphan at fifteen upon the death of her mother.

Following Mrs. Marvin's death the six children were separated and placed with relatives. Catharine went to live with her uncle, Benjamin Snow. She opened a small girls' school in the autumn of 1809 when she was sixteen.

Catharine was religious and extremely studious, rising at 4:00 a.m. each day to pray and prepare her lessons. She was never idle; while reading, her hands would be active knitting or sewing. She referred to her pupils as her "little friends" and remained in contact with many throughout their lives.

When Catharine was twenty-seven she married Luther F. Dimmick, minister of North Church in Newburyport, Massachusetts. She closed her school to assume the role of minister's wife until her death in 1844.

Catharine's writing is from her journal which is partially reprinted in her husband's Memoir, *published by her brother T. R. Marvin in 1846.*

Grace Gallatin Seton

Success in the West

1900
"This thing has been done before, and done well. Good; then I can do it, and enjoy it too."

I particularly insisted upon the latter clause — in the East. This formula is applicable in any situation. I never should have gotten through my Western experiences without it, and I advise you, my dear Woman-who-goes-hunting-with-her-husband, to take a large stock of it made up and ready for use. There is one other rule for your conduct, if you want to be a success: think what you like, but unless it is pleasant, don't say it.

I had a man's saddle, with a narrow tree and high pommel cantle, such as is used out West, and as I had not ridden a horse since the hazy days of my infancy, I got on the huge creature's back with everything to learn. Fear enveloped me as in a cloud during my first ride, and the possibilities of the little cow pony they put me on seemed more awe-inspiring than those of a locomotive. But I had been reading Professor William James and acquired from him the idea (I hope I do not malign him) that the accomplishment of a thing depends largely upon one's mental attitude. . . .

Grace Gallatin Thompson Seton was born January 28, 1872, in Sacramento, California. When she was nine her parents divorced, and her mother took her to New York to live, leaving two older siblings with their father. After graduating from Packer Collegiate Institute in Brooklyn, Grace studied hand bookmaking and printing.

Grace met her future husband, Ernest Thompson Seton, a naturalist and author, while travelling abroad. They were married in 1896, and Grace began helping him design and edit his books. She accompanied him on his camping trips and learned to shoot and ride. Grace, who had grown up in a city, wrote about these new experiences in her first two books. Her newfound love of the outdoors led her to co-found the Camp Fire Girls in 1912.

From the age of seventeen Grace was active in the women's suffrage movement, serving as president of the Connecticut Woman's Suffrage Association from 1910 to 1920. She spent World War I in France, directing a women's unit that delivered food and assistance to soldiers behind the

Grace's writing is from her first book, A Woman Tenderfoot, *about a trip on horseback through the Rockies, published in 1900 by Doubleday.*

trenches, and she later received a medal from the French government for her efforts. Upon her return to America, she established the Biblioteca Femina, a collection of women's writings from thirty-seven countries, and presented it to Northwestern University.

In the 1920s Grace began travelling extensively to study the status of women in other cultures; each journey resulted in one or more books on the subject. She went to Egypt in 1921, then to China, India, South America, Vietnam, and Cambodia. Never one to stick to the beaten path, Grace caravanned by camel through the Egyptian desert, hunted tigers in the Himalayas, and shot a jaguar in the Peruvian jungle. Fascinated by the condition of women's lives, she hired a guide to lead her to the remote Moi tribe in Vietnam, which used poison arrows, ate raw flesh, and had a matriarchal society. Her last book, *Poison Arrows*, about the Mois was published in 1938.

In 1930 she moved in with her daughter Anya, who was also a well-known author, and studied mysticism and Eastern religions until her death in 1959.

Jeannette Meyers Thurber

1919

Symphonic masterpiece

In looking back over my thirty-five years of activity as President of the National Conservatory of Music of America there is nothing I am so proud of as having been able to bring Dr. Dvořák to America, thus being privileged to open the way for one of the world's symphonic masterpieces, as well as some chamber works which are admittedly even better than the chamber music he wrote in Europe. Well do I remember how the Kneisel Quartet came to the Conservatory to try over this music in the composer's presence! A gala day in New York's concert life was the first performance of the New World Symphony by the Philharmonic Orchestra under Anton Seidl. It was the most important event in the long history of the Philharmonic.

On the whole, Dvořák seemed to be happy in his new surroundings, although he suffered much from homesickness, being intensely patriotic. He passed two of his summers in Iowa, at Spilville, because of the number of Bohemians living there. Anton Seidl was

Jeannette's writing is taken from "Personal Recollections of a Great Master, A Thumbnail Biography of Antonín Dvořák" in the November 1919 issue of Etude.

probably right in declaring that the intense pathos of the slow movement of the New World Symphony was inspired by nostalgia — by longing for home.

Jeannette Meyers Thurber was born January 29, 1850, in New York City. From the time she was a child her parents encouraged her to study music. She attended private schools in New York and Paris, where she became fluent in French and German.

Jeannette married Francis Beattie Thurber when she was nineteen. Shortly after the wedding, she began working at her lifelong dream to improve the teaching facilities for music in America. She planned to build a national conservatory where instruction would follow European guidelines.

Jeannette obtained a charter from the state of New York for a National Conservatory of Music. In 1885 she opened its first department, the American School of Opera. Unfortunately, since she failed to show a profit in the first year, the incorporators withdrew, and the school was closed in June of 1887.

Undaunted, Jeannette continued to work to establish a national conservatory. In March 1891 Congress passed an act investing the conservatory with power to grant diplomas and confer honorary degrees. All students were admitted, regardless of race or religion, with only nominal tuition and none at all for extremely talented students. Well-known musicians joined the faculty, and Czech composer Antonín Dvorák became its director. Jeannette died in 1945, having contributed more than any other non-professional to American music.

Louise Beebe Wilder

Creative gardening

1918

In his garden every man may be his own artist without apology or explanation. Here is one spot where each may experience the "romance of possibility," may give free rein to his fancy, and gather his living materials into compositions as gay, as splendid, or as wan as his individual enjoyment of colour dictates. . . . No phase of gardening is to me so fascinating as this scheming with flower colours, the more so perhaps that no arbitrary laws may be laid down for our following. Each within his green inclosure is a creator, and no two shall

Louise's writing is from her foreword to Color in My Garden, *published in 1918 by Doubleday.*

reach the same conclusion; nor shall we, any more than other creative workers, be ever wholly satisfied with our accomplishment.

Louise Morris Beebe Wilder was born January 30, 1878, in Baltimore, Maryland. Her love of gardening began when she was a child playing in her parents' garden and at her grandparents' home, Beebe Farm, in Wakefield, Massachusetts, where she spent most of her summers. She started her first garden at the age of six.

In November 1902 Louise married New York architect Walter Robb Wilder and had two children. They divided their time between a home in Bronxville, New York, and their 200-acre country estate "Balderbrae" in Pomona, New York. It was at Balderbrae that Louise created her beautiful enclosed garden, sheltered behind high stone walls, that was the basis for her first two gardening books. Outside the walled garden Louise had her nursery beds, greenhouse, and herb garden. Inside, Louise's plantings were specifically arranged for height and color to bloom in a continuous spectacular array.

Louise collected plants, concentrating especially on alpine specimens from around the world. From 1925 to 1938 she wrote monthly columns for *House and Garden* magazine. She turned her years of experience working on her knees in her garden into ten highly successful books on gardening. T. H. Everett, author of the ten-volume *Encyclopedia of Horticulture*, referred to Louise as "one of the finest horticulturists of her time and one of the best writers of horticulture books."

Louise died in New York City in April 1938 at the age of sixty and was buried in Wakefield, Massachusetts.

Alice Bennett

1883

I do not believe the patient can be found so demented as to be insensible to the voice of kindness, and the influence of affection upon some of them is really wonderful.

. . . An immensely powerful, muscular German woman, one of the first admissions to the hospital, brought with her a reputation for ferocity calculated to strike terror to the soul of the uninitiated. For months she had been chained in a dungeon, the limited space of which scarcely permitted her to lie at full length on her

A transformation

Alice's writing is from her paper "Mechanical Restraint in the Treatment of the Insane," which she read before the Medico-Legal Society of New York on June 6, 1883.

heap of straw. Through the grating of the heavy door was thrust the food, which she must eat as best she could, with hands confined. Here also the curious were privileged to gaze upon this monster in human form, who, with her hair long ago torn out by her own hands and her expression of savage distrust and defiance, might well seem something less than human. A year ago I introduced a gentleman interested in public charities to this same woman, standing in the door of her neat little room, which she invited us to enter and inspect. Her thick gray curls surrounded a face strongly-marked and resolute, yet not unpleasant to look upon, and her general appearance was such as to attract a stranger at once.

She was led to speak of her former experience: "And why were you locked up in a dungeon?" asked my friend. "Because" — but I can not repeat her language. At the mere recollection, a tithe of her old fury was aroused and her mien hinted at the total annihilation of anybody in her path.

"But *why* did you have those feelings there and not here?" persisted the visitor.

"Because they locked me up. Would you like to be locked up like a beast?" came the answer, with an emphasis which was a whole sermon in itself. This patient also belongs to the chronic class, and is probably a "life-member" of our little community, but she is a busy worker, she has a quick, ready intelligence and warm affections, and her life is not altogether an unhappy one.

Alice Bennett was born January 31, 1851, in Wrentham, Massachusetts. At twenty-five she graduated with an M.D. degree from the Woman's Medical College of Pennsylvania. She began teaching anatomy at the college and opened a private practice.

Dr. Bennett continued her studies and in 1880 became the first female recipient of a Ph.D. degree from the University of Pennsylvania; her dissertation was on the anatomy of the forelimb of the marmoset.

Following graduation, Alice was appointed superintendent of the women's division of the State Hospital for the Insane at Norristown, Pennsylvania, another first for a woman. She immediately abolished all forms of patient restraint — chains, strait jackets, and cells — citing a need for "moral treatment with a bond of respect between patient and attendant." She also initiated occupational therapy with music, art, and handicrafts.

Dr. Bennett resigned from the Hospital for the Insane after sixteen years and resumed private practice in her hometown of Wrentham. In 1910 she moved to New York City, where she worked without pay for the last fifteen years of her life at the New York Infirmary for Women and Children.

FEBRUARY

Cordelia Howard

1928

Eva was not my first part. There was a scene in *Oliver Twist* usually cut out, as it is not important to the plot, where Oliver is running away from the workhouse and stops to say goodbye to his friend Little Dick, a consumptive child who is digging in the garden. My mother, who was playing Oliver, taught me this part, as I had shown some dramatic instinct. Of course it is taken from the novel and is quite pathetic as the child says he heard the doctor tell them he was dying, and throwing his arms about Oliver's neck, he says, "Goodbye, God bless you."

Fanny Wallack who was starring as Nancy Sykes, stood in the wings with the tears rolling down her face and pronounced me a wonderful child. It seems incredible that such a baby could have had any idea of the pathos of the situation. I must have been an exceptional child. The worst thing about these prodigies is that they generally prove nonentities in their later years, and I am no exception to the rule!

Cordelia Howard was born February 1, 1848, in Boston. Her grandfather was resident custodian at the local Federal Street Theatre, and his three sons and one daughter all acted as children. His daughter, Caroline, married George Howard, also an actor, at fifteen. They settled in Providence, Rhode Island, where Cordelia was born, the second of eight children.

Cordelia made her stage debut at the age of two and a half as a fairy sprite in a dramatic ballet. At four she played Little Dick in *Oliver Twist;* her performance was so moving it consistently brought tears to both the audience and her fellow thespians. Her success at melodrama inspired her father to cast her as little Eva in *Uncle Tom's Cabin.*

Mrs. Howard's cousin wrote a dramatization of Harriet Beecher Stowe's book, and the play opened in Troy, New York, in September 1852. Cordelia was a huge success as Eva; the Howard family was supported by *Uncle Tom's Cabin* for many years. Cordelia was billed as "The Youthful Wonder." She gave her final performance as Eva in Boston in 1861 when she was thirteen. Two months later she retired from the theater.

Pathos

Cordelia's writing is from "Memoirs of the Original Little Eva," which she wrote in 1928 at the age of eighty. It was published for the first time in the December 1956 issue of Educational Theatre Journal.

Cordelia married Edmund Macdonald, a book binder, in 1871. They lived in Cambridge, Massachusetts, until her death in 1941 when she was ninety-three.

Anne Bauchens

How to cut film

1937

Many people ask me what film editing is. I would say it is very much like a jigsaw puzzle, except that in a jigsaw puzzle the little pieces are all cut out in the various forms and you try to fit them together to make a picture, while in cutting films you have to cut your pieces first and then put them together. . . .

I have often been asked what methods are used in cutting different types of scenes, such as dramatic and comedy scenes. I cannot say there is any particular method or rule for cutting. Sometimes the length of the scene, sometimes its action, creates the tempo. My opinion is that we handle the feel and tempo of the picture entirely by instinct and feeling, and not by any set rule.

Anne Bauchens was born February 2, 1881, in St. Louis, Missouri. She studied acting, dancing, and gymnastics in hopes of becoming an actress. When she felt ready, she moved to New York to audition on Broadway. She was unsuccessful and took a position as secretary to William DeMille, the director and playwright. When his brother, Cecil B. DeMille, invited him to Hollywood to work with him, Anne went along. She invented the job title of script clerk, and became Cecil's indispensable production secretary.

William DeMille recommended Anne to edit a film in 1917, thus beginning her long career in the editing room. The following year she assisted Cecil B. DeMille with the editing of his film *We Can't Have Everything*. He had been unhappy with the editing of his first two films, so he had taken to doing it himself. After working with Anne he trusted her completely, and thereafter she had sole responsibility for editing all his movies. He called her "the best film editor I know" and would not sign a contract unless it specified Anne as the editor.

Anne collaborated with Cecil B. DeMille from 1918 until his death in 1959, producing thirty-nine films. Her nickname was "Trojan Annie" because she worked so hard, often

Anne's writing is from "Cutting the Film," which was included in We Make the Movies, *edited by Nancy Naumburg and published by W. W. Norton and Company, Inc., in 1937.*

putting in sixteen- to eighteen-hour days. In 1940 she became the first woman to win an Academy Award for film editing, and in 1952 she was the first recipient of the ACE, the Achievement Award of the American Cinema Editors. She received three more Academy Award nominations, the last for *The Ten Commandments* in 1956 when she was seventy-five years old. DeMille admitted that editing that epic film was "the most difficult operation of film editing in motion picture history." He had used sixteen cameras, and Anne had to edit 100,000 feet of film down to 12,000 feet without losing the continuity of the plot.

Anne retired from film editing after Cecil B. DeMille's death. She wrote a tribute to him which was published in France a year after her death. She died in 1967 at the Motion Picture Country House and Hospital in Woodland Hills, California.

Elizabeth Blackwell, M.D.

1852

The feeble cry

How eagerly we await that first inspiration! The mother, forgetful of weariness and suffering, lifts her pale face from the pillow, and listens with her whole soul. The physician, profoundly penetrated with the mystery of birth, bends in suspense over the little being hovering on the threshold of a new existence — for one moment they await the issue — life or death! — the feeble cry is the token of victory — the mother's face lights up with ineffable joy, as she sinks back exhausted, and the sentiment of sympathy, of reverence, thrills through the physician's heart.

Elizabeth Blackwell was born February 3, 1821, in Counterslip, England. After her father's sugar refinery was destroyed by fire in 1832, the family moved to America. Elizabeth and her eight siblings were educated at home by their parents, private tutors, and four maiden aunts who shared their house. They were raised in a stimulating, liberal environment, and all the Blackwell children grew up to be successful, independent thinkers. Elizabeth became the first female doctor of medicine in the United States and was joined in the profession by her younger sister Emily (October 8). Two of her brothers became well-known social reformers; Samuel married Antoinette Brown (May 20), and Henry married Lucy Stone.

Elizabeth's writing is from The Laws of Life, with Special Reference to the Physical Education of Girls, *published in 1852 by the George P. Putnam Company.*

In her twenties, Elizabeth's desire for a medical degree, considered inappropriate for women of that day, became her greatest challenge. She was denied admission to every medical school in Philadelphia and New York, as well as Harvard, Yale, and Bowdoin. She was finally accepted at Geneva College in west-central New York, although she later found out she had been accidentally admitted by a panel of students who thought her application was a joke being played on them by a rival school.

Initially, Elizabeth was met with hostility from local townspeople and angry male students, but she persevered and was awarded her medical degree in January 1849. Her thesis, which was later published in the *Buffalo Medical Journal and Monthly Review*, stressed the importance of sanitation and personal hygiene in fighting disease, which became the mainstay of her medical philosophy.

After graduation Elizabeth studied abroad for two years. While in France she contracted purulent ophthalmia from one of her patients. As a result, she lost sight in one eye which ended her dreams of becoming a surgeon. Upon her return to New York in 1851, she was barred from practice in city hospitals and dispensaries, ignored by her peers, and attacked in a series of anonymous letters. She bought a house and opened a private practice. While waiting for patients, she gave lectures on hygiene which she published in book form in 1852. She was so lonely and discouraged that she adopted a seven-year-old orphan, Kitty Barry in 1854, who acted as daughter, companion, nurse, and secretary for the rest of her life.

In 1853 Elizabeth opened a one-room dispensary for women in New York's tenement district. After four years of active fundraising, she was able to open the New York Infirmary for Women and Children where she was ably assisted by her sister Emily. During the Civil War Elizabeth devoted her time to the Woman's Central Association of Relief, and both Blackwell sisters selected and trained nurses.

In 1868 Elizabeth established the Woman's Medical College of the New York Infirmary where women could receive an excellent education in addition to receiving clinical experience at the adjacent infirmary. After seeing her lifelong dream for a women's medical college firmly established, she left it in Emily's capable hands. Although Elizabeth had become a naturalized American citizen in 1849, she returned to England in 1869 where she resided until her death in 1910. In 1871 she created the National Health Society in London to further her beliefs on the importance of good hygiene. The Society's motto was "Prevention is better than cure." However, she suffered from biliary colic and was forced to retire in 1875. Thereafter, she lived with Kitty in a house by the sea in Hastings, publishing articles on hygiene and sanitation.

Elizabeth made her last visit to America in 1906 at the age of eighty-six. The following year she fell down the stairs at home and never fully recovered. She died three years later and was buried beneath a large Celtic cross in the Scotland Highlands.

Ella Sheppard Moore

circa 1909

*A*gony of slavery

My earliest recollections was of my mother's tears over the cruelties of slavery, as she realized that its degradation fell heaviest upon the young Negro girl. Mother's fears and sufferings were intensified one day by the discovery that the mistress had already begun to train me as a spy upon her, as a nurse. I had made my first report, which the mistress had magnified, and threatened mother. Stung by this revelation and realizing that it would lead eventually to the alienation of our affection and teach me to lie and deceive, in agony of soul and despair, she caught me in her arms, and while rushing to the river to end it all, was overtaken by Mammy Viney, who cried out, "Don't you do it, Honey, don't take that that you cannot give back." She raised her eyes to Heaven and said, "Look, Honey, don't you see the clouds of the Lord as they pass by? The Lord has got need of this child." My mother took courage, and hugging her helpless baby to her breast, walked back into slavery to await God's own time.

Ella Sheppard Moore was born February 4, 1851, to a slave couple in Nashville, Tennessee. Her father bought his freedom for $1,800 but his master reneged on his promise to sell her mother Sarah to the same purchaser. Sarah threatened to drown herself and her child, and, fearing the financial loss, the master sold Ella to her father but kept Ella's mother and relocated her to Mississippi.

Ella's father realized he would never see Sarah again. He married another slave woman, bought her freedom for $1,300, and moved the family to Cincinnati. Ella thrived in Ohio, attending school and taking piano lessons. As she was the only black pupil of a white piano teacher, she had to enter the school at night through the back door.

Ella's writing is from "Before Emancipation," which she wrote circa 1909 published by the American Missionary Association, New York, no date.

In 1868 Ella returned to Tennessee to teach at a black school near Nashville. She gave piano lessons and waited on tables to earn enough money to attend Fisk University. After two years at Fisk she was hired as a music teacher, the university's first black staff member.

Ella was selected as one of nine black singers to raise funds for Fisk. In October 1871 the Jubilee Singers left on their first tour. They earned $20,000, which was used to erect Jubilee Hall, a women's dormitory at Fisk. Initially, they sang "white man's music," feeling that the sorrowful songs associated with slavery were too private and sacred. Ella encouraged the singers to incorporate slave songs into their repertoire, and she is now credited with preserving the spiritual and presenting it to the world.

The Jubilee Singers enjoyed tremendous national and international success. The group disbanded after seven years and two lengthy European tours, having earned more than $150,000 for Fisk.

Ella returned to Fisk and invested her savings in a home on campus. She went to Mississippi in 1881, found her mother, and brought her and a younger sister back to live with her and her stepmother. The following year she married George W. Moore, a pastor active in the American Missionary Association. On June 9, 1914, she was stricken with appendicitis and received medical help too late to save her.

FEBRUARY 5

Mary Sewall Gardner

Nurses at sea

At sea
Monday, Sept. 22, 1918
Dear Milly

I do *not* like the sea. We have been out a week and so far I have gotten along much better than usual, but I always feel more or less miserable. I am rooming with three other nurses and the last unbearable touch is that all our clothes are exactly alike, even our underclothes. But how absurd even to mention these trifling uncomfortablenesses when we are safe so far and perfectly all right. Also I am really proving myself a better sailor than ever before.

The general situation causes the authorities to allow us to sleep on deck which I have done every night since that first awful one in our crowded and wholly airless

Mary's letter to her friend Milly is in the Mary Sewall Gardner Papers at Schlesinger Library, Radcliffe College, Cambridge, Massachusetts.

Women's Words, Women's Stories

stateroom. A good many others do the same, some forty or fifty men and women perhaps. After struggling unsuccessfully with steamer chairs, most of us have given them up and just crawl into our sleeping bags and lie flat on the deck. It is astonishing how well one can sleep on anything so hard, but alas we have to get up at five in the morning when they wash the decks.

My dear, the voyage is full of interest. Most of these details I cannot tell you on account of the censor. For one thing there have been no gulls following the ship, for it is against the rules to throw anything even the smallest crumb overboard. As people come up on deck at night to go to bed they all appear fully dressed and each one carries a life preserver which is placed by their side as they lie down.

Mary Sewall Gardner was born February 5, 1871, in Newton, Massachusetts. After her mother's death when she was four, her father married a physician.

Mary received her early education in local private schools and later attended Miss Porter's School in Farmington, Connecticut. In 1890 she returned home and spent the next years nursing her invalid stepmother and doing community work. In 1901 at the age of thirty Mary enrolled in the Newport Rhode Island Hospital Training School, realizing at last her long ambition that had been inspired by her step-mother, to become a physician. Upon completion of the four-year program, she became superintendent of nurses of the Providence District Nursing Association. Under her leadership, the organization became a model for other district nursing associations. She organized regular meetings, established an efficient record-keeping system, and introduced uniforms.

Mary and another nurse founded the National Organization of Public Health Nursing in 1912, and she served as president. She was instrumental in creating the organization's monthly periodical *Public Health Nursing*, contributing numerous articles and editorials.

With the advent of World War I, Mary took a leave of absence and went to Italy as chief nurse of the American Red Cross Tuberculosis Commission. She established training programs for Italian women who wanted to become nurses.

Mary published *Public Health Nursing* in 1916, her greatest contribution to her profession. The book was revised twice and translated into several languages, and was long hailed as a classic. She died at home in Providence, Rhode Island, at the age of ninety.

Anne Spencer

Face and hands

circa
1924

Lady, Lady, I saw your face,
Dark as night withholding a star . . .
The chisel fell, or it might have been
You had borne so long the yoke of men.

Lady, Lady, I saw your hands,
Twisted, awry, like crumpled roots,
Bleached poor white in a sudsy tub,
Wrinkled and drawn from your rub-a-dub.

Anne Bethel Bannister Spencer was born February 6, 1882, in Henry County, Virginia. After her parents' divorce when she was a child, her mother placed her with the Dixies of Bramwell, West Virginia, a respected family in the black community. Her mother lived and worked nearby and took part in supervising Anne's education. She refused to let her daughter attend black "free schools" and enrolled her instead in the Virginia Seminary in 1893. Anne thrived at the seminary and was asked to give the valedictory at her graduation in 1899.

Anne married Edward Spencer, a classmate from the Virginia Seminary, in May 1901, and established a lifelong residence in Lynchburg, Virginia. Their home soon became a gathering place for local black intellectuals and visitors travelling to the South.

From 1923 to 1945 Anne was the librarian at the local Dunbar High School in Lynchburg, where she exposed black students to a world of literature otherwise unavailable to them. She began writing poetry, and several of her poems appeared in anthologies of black poetry. Although several editors sought her work, she preferred to remain out of the limelight, and therefore less than thirty of her poems were published during her lifetime. Most of her work did not address issues of race because, as she explained in an interview: "I react to life more as a human being than as a Negro being. The Tom-Tom FORCED into poetry seems a sad state to me." Unfortunately, many of her writings were lost due to her habit of writing on odd pieces of paper such as old envelopes, paper bags, or even the backs of telephone bills.

Anne became a recluse after her husband's death in 1964. Her health gradually declined, and she spent the last two

Anne's writing is from her poem "Lady, Lady" and is included in The Poetry of Black America, *edited by Arnold Adoff and published in 1973 by Harper Collins.*

Women's Words, Women's Stories

years of her life in and out of the hospital. She died in July 1975 at the age of ninety-three.

Laura Ingalls Wilder

1916

As Thanksgiving day draws near again, I am reminded of an occurrence of my childhood.

We were living on the frontier in South Dakota then. There's no more frontier within the boundaries of the United States, more's the pity, but then we were ahead of the railroad in a new unsettled country.

Father had laid in a supply of provisions for the winter, and among them were salt meats; but for fresh meats we depended on Father's gun and the antelope which fed in herds across the prairie. So we were quite excited, one day near Thanksgiving, when Father hurried into the house for his gun and then away again to try for a shot at a belated flock of wild geese hurrying south.

We would have roast goose for Thanksgiving dinner! "Roast goose and dressing seasoned with sage," said sister Mary. "No, not sage! I don't like sage, and we won't have it in the dressing," I exclaimed. Then we quarreled, sister Mary and I, until Father returned — without the goose!

I remember saying in a meek voice to sister Mary, "I wish I had let you have the sage," and to this day when I think of it, I feel again just as I felt then and realize how thankful I would have been for roast goose and dressing with sage seasoning.

A futile argument

Laura Ingalls Wilder was born February 7, 1867, near Pepin, Wisconsin. Millions of people are familiar with Laura's childhood through her Little House series of books, and later from the long-running television show "Little House on the Prairie."

The Ingalls family settled in De Smet, South Dakota in 1876. Their first winter there is still in the record books as one of the worst ever. It was during this blizzard season when she was nine that Laura met her future husband, Almanzo Wilder.

Laura's writing is from Little House in the Ozarks, *edited by Stephen W. Hines and published in 1991 by Guideposts, Carmel, New York.*

Laura received her teaching certificate at fifteen. She immediately took a teaching job in a small town 12 miles from her home. She boarded with a family during the week and on weekends Almanzo would fetch her in his buggy and return her to her family. She and Almanzo were married in August 1885, and their only child, Rose, was born the following year. During the wedding ceremony Laura refused to say the word "obey" because she did not want to make a promise she could not keep.

The Wilders settled in Mansfield, Missouri. He planted apple orchards while Laura raised chickens. Her chickens led indirectly to her writing career when in 1911 she wrote a speech on poultry raising for a local farm organization meeting. The editor of the *Missouri Realist*, a magazine about country life, was impressed and asked Laura to write for his publication. For the next twelve years, Laura had her own column and edited the home section.

Rose Wilder encouraged her mother to write her life story and assisted her with editing. She took her mother's finished manuscript *Little House in the Big Woods* and sold it to Harper and Brothers.

Before it was even published in 1932, *Harper's* was touting it as the "miracle book that no depression could stop." Thus the Little House series began, followed by seven more books between 1933 and 1943.

Laura and her books enjoyed tremendous success; she received numerous awards, and several libraries were named in her honor. Almanzo passed away in 1949, after which her health began to fail, and she died eight years later. Almanzo, Laura, and Rose are all buried in the cemetery at Mansfield, Missouri.

FEBRUARY 8

Harriet Hanson Robinson

*M*ill girl

1898

I was about ten years of age, when my mother, feeling obliged to have help in her work besides what I could give, and also needing the money which I could earn, allowed me, at my urgent request (for I wanted to earn *money* like the other little girls), to go to work in the mill. I worked first in the spinning-room as a "doffer." The doffers were the very youngest girls, whose work was to doff, or take off, the full bobbins, and replace them with the empty ones.

I can see myself now, racing down the alley, between

Harriet's writing is from Loom and Spindle or Life Among the Early Mill Girls, *published in 1898 by T. Y. Crowell and Company.*

Women's Words, Women's Stories

the spinning-frames, carrying in front of me a bobbin-box bigger than I was. These mites had to be very swift in their movements, so as not to keep the spinning-frames stopped long, and they worked only about fifteen minutes in every hour. The rest of the time was their own, and when the overseer was kind they were allowed to read, knit, or even to go outside the mill-yard to play. . . .

Harriet Jane Hanson Robinson was born February 8, 1825, in Boston. Her father's death in 1831 plunged the family into poverty. They moved to Lowell, Massachusetts, where her mother took in boarders, and the four children went to work in the local mills.

Harriet started working at the age of ten. A year later the older girls went out on strike over a cut in wages. She led the younger workers out with them until the situation was resolved. In later years she commented: "I was more proud than I have ever been since of any success I may have achieved."

Despite her fourteen-hour days, Harriet managed to attend school until she was fifteen. After her schooling ended she continued working at the mill. From 1839 to 1845 the mill girls published the *Lowell Offering*, a monthly magazine of short stories, essays, and poetry. One of Harriet's poems caught the attention of William Stevens Robinson, an editor at the *Lowell Courier* newspaper. They were married in 1848 and had four children.

Harriet's husband wrote militant anti-slavery articles under the pen name "Warrington." She embraced the cause, assisting him in whatever way she could. Following the Civil War, they became involved in the new cause of women's suffrage. Harriet found Lucy Stone to be too moderate, so she aligned herself with the more radical Susan B. Anthony (February 15). Harriet and her eldest daughter organized the National Woman Suffrage Association of Massachusetts. She continued to speak and write on behalf of suffrage until her death in 1912.

Amy Lowell

A poet's wish

1917

The April *North American Review* came safely, and a day or two later came my twelve copies. I think "Sea-Blue and Blood-Red" looks exceedingly well, and the faithfulness with which the printing has been done fills me with gratitude. I wonder whether people will like the poem, or whether they will not be able to make head nor tail of it. This is hardly a moment, I suppose, when poetry is likely to have very much attention paid to it, which is sad, because I think it is the only way I can serve my country, my wretched health making me quite useless for anything else. Perhaps the country needs poets, I hope she does, and perhaps *Le Bon Dieu* will give me a chance to say something that counts, so that I can feel that I am doing my bit.

Amy Lowell was born February 9, 1874, in Brookline, Massachusetts, into a prominent New England family that traced its roots back to Percival Lowle, who settled on the North Shore in 1639. Her closest sibling was twelve years older. Left alone a great deal as a child, she turned to reading. As a teenager she confided in her diary: "I should like best of anything to be literary."

Although Amy always longed to write and was inspired by her cousin, the poet James Russell Lowell, she did not begin writing poetry until her early thirties. Her first sonnet was published in the *Atlantic Monthly* in 1910. From then on she became prolific, publishing four volumes of poetry between 1916 and 1921. She also edited three anthologies of imagist poetry and wrote two volumes of critical analysis.

Amy became a literary celebrity. She was very overweight, smoked cigars, and spoke in a loud, flamboyant manner. She was the center of attention wherever she went and was in great demand as a lecturer.

Amy's writing is from a letter to Elizabeth Cutting, her editor at the North American Review. *It is among her papers at the Houghton Library, Harvard University, Cambridge, Massachusetts.*

In 1918 her health began to fail. She had the first of several operations for an umbilical hernia. She was able to complete her last work, a biography of Keats, which was published in early 1925. She died that spring of a cerebral hemorrhage at the age of fifty-one and was buried in Cambridge's Mount Auburn Cemetery.

Marguerite Milton Wells

1941

*T*ell the people

We are familiar with the old couplet: "Of all sad words of tongue and pen, the saddest are these 'it might have been!'" How poignant those sad words became when too late people realized that it was not for lack of warnings that fate overtook them but because they would not listen. There have been everywhere voices crying in the wilderness; Winston Churchill warned the French novelist, André Maurois — do not write any more novels, nor any more biographies, write one thing always with the same idea, one thing every day and let that one thing be: the French air force, once the greatest, is slipping back to fourth or fifth while Germany's becomes the best in the world. This was six years ago, three years before Munich, five years before Dunkirk....

I recall these incidents to illustrate what havoc a lag in public understanding may work. It is for you and me to discover what lags exist among people in this country and to consider how we can help take up those lags.

Marguerite Milton Wells was born February 10, 1872, in Milwaukee, Wisconsin. When she was a child, her family moved to the remotest corner of the Dakota Territories where she witnessed firsthand the creation of new towns and eventually a new state. Seeing many strangers come together to create laws that worked for their community left a lasting impression on her and formed the basis for her fervent belief in democracy.

After graduating from Smith College in 1895, Marguerite occupied herself with teaching and volunteer work in Minneapolis, serving on the boards of many charities and civic organizations. One day in 1917 for no explicable reason, she resigned from every office she held and presented herself at the Minnesota Woman Suffrage Association to serve wherever needed.

Marguerite participated in the final suffrage battle until Minnesota ratified the Nineteenth Amendment. In 1919, while attending the National American Woman Suffrage Association Convention in St. Louis, she heard president Carrie Chapman Catt call for a league to be formed to educate new voters. The result was the creation of the National League of Woman Voters in 1920, to which Marguerite devoted the next twenty-five years of her life.

Marguerite's writing is from a letter she wrote to members of the League of Women Voters. It appeared in the August 1941 issue of the League's newsletter, Citizens All.

Marguerite served as president of the Minnesota League of Women Voters for ten years and was the third president of the national league from 1934 to 1944. She believed that an informed majority would make wise decisions within a democratic system. Her philosophy became the league's philosophy, and education became its primary goal.

Marguerite died at her sister's home in Minneapolis in 1959 at the age of eighty-seven.

Agnes Christina Laut

Use the ballot

Agnes's writing is from "Am I My Brother's Keeper?," an article in Saturday Night, *a magazine published in Toronto in 1913.*

1913

"I know," he said, "we are not striking for what you would call anything special — any special grievance. We are striking to paralyze every wheel of commerce, to tie up industry, to stop the mills, the railroads, the mines, the factories, by passive force to compel the expropriation of industry and to overturn the capitalistic system —"

"Hold on," I said, "it has taken civilization millions of years to come up from the status of the wild beast; and I admit there are still ravening wild beasts masquerading in civilized garb, that would make the creatures of the jungle look innocent. I see the evils! We all do; but instead of overturning, why don't you fight to remedy the ills and purge the evils? You have the ballot. It takes you only three years to get the vote in Canada. Why don't you use the ballot and vote things right, instead of smashing everything upside down over the edge of a precipice to build up a new system from the ruins?"

Agnes Christina Laut was born February 11, 1871, in Ontario, Canada. She spent her childhood in Winnipeg, then a remote frontier town where trappers came to sell their furs to the Hudson's Bay store. Agnes listened to trappers' and Indians' tales of adventure and preserved them in her memory for later use.

Agnes published her first book in 1900, her second two years later. Both concerned the first explorers of the Canadian wilderness and the lucrative fur trade. A prolific writer, she wrote eighteen books over the next twenty-one years, all of which were about the exploration and settlement of the vast North American continent. She believed that civilization followed a predictable course: first the explorers, then the traders, then the settlers. She was most fascinated with the explorers and traders, and her best books drew on recollections of these men.

In her later years, Agnes wrote several travel books on Canada and the American Southwest. She died at her home in Passaic, New Jersey, in 1936.

Fannie Barrier Williams

1904

I went to a New England city, but even here, in the very cradle of liberty, white Southerners were there before me, and to save their feelings I was told by the principal of the school, a man who was descended from a long line of abolition ancestors, that it would imperil the interests of the school if I remained, as all of his Southern pupils would leave, and again I had to submit to the tyranny of a dark complexion. But it is scarcely possible to enumerate the many ways in which an ambitious colored young woman is prevented from being all that she might be in the higher directions of life in this country. Plainly I would have been far happier as a woman if my life up to the age of eighteen years had not been so free, spontaneous and unhampered by race prejudice. I have still many white friends and the old home and school associations are still sweet and delightful and always renewed with pleasure, yet I have never quite recovered from the shock and pain of my first bitter realization that to be a colored woman is to be discredited, mistrusted and often meanly hated.

A bitter realization

Fannie Barrier Williams was born February 12, 1855, to the only black family in Brockport, New York. After graduating from the State Normal School she began teaching in Washington, D.C., and farther south, where she encountered overt prejudice for the first time.

Following her marriage to S. Laing Williams, a lawyer, in 1887, they settled in Chicago. She was instantly thrown into the public eye in 1893 with her speech, "The Intellectual Progress of the Colored Women in the United States since the Emancipation," delivered before the World's Congress of

Fannie's writing is from "A Northern Negro's Autobiography," published in the July 14, 1904, issue of The Independent.

Representative Women. Her words were highly acclaimed, and she was sought as a speaker by church groups and clubs throughout the country.

As a result of Fannie's newfound notoriety, she was nominated for membership in the Chicago Woman's Club. After a year of controversy both within the club and in the press, she was accepted as the only black member, a distinction she held for the next thirty years.

Fannie realized that legislation alone could not improve conditions for the black race. She endorsed the creation of clubs for black women, believing that such an organized movement would be "a new intelligence against an old ignorance." She helped to found the National League of Colored Women, the National Association of Colored Women, and the Illinois Woman's Alliance. These clubs sponsored many welfare organizations in addition to providing daycare, employment bureaus, classes, and other forms of self-help.

Following her husband's death in 1921, Fannie curtailed her public activities. After completing her term as the first woman and first black on the Chicago Library Board, she retired and returned to Brockport to live with her sister. Fannie died in 1944 at the age of eighty-nine. She is remembered as a pioneer in the social and political development of black women in America.

FEBRUARY 13

Susan McGroarty (Sister Julia)

A Sister from America

Namur
November 22, 1868
I am sure that our dear Sisters are anxious to hear all that I can tell them, and I shall give them a full account of all that has transpired up to this time; not of my feelings, however, nor of the emotions which almost overpowered me as I stood for the first time in the presence of that venerable and venerated Mother whom I had so long desired to see! There I was, at last! But, oh, I regretted that I was alone where so many wished to be. O my dear Sisters, if you could only see her more than maternal kindness! But you know it without ever having seen her, and you must know that you all had a part in the reception she gave to her American child. . . .

While we were at breakfast, Sister Beatrice, an old Sister who had lived with Mother Julia, came in; when she heard that I was the Sister from America, she

Susan's letter to her sister nuns in Philadelphia was written on her first trip to Namur, Belgium, the headquarters of the Order of Notre Dame de Namur. It is included in Sister Julia, *by Sister Helen Louise, published in 1928 by Benziger Brothers.*

literally lifted up her voice and wept, and exclaimed: "Welcome! May God bless you," etc., a blessing of the patriarchs; which blessing she repeated when she learned that I was called "Julia."

Was it not delightful to tread for the first time the soil of Belgium?

Susan McGroarty (Sister Julia) was born February 13, 1827, at the McGroarty farm near Donegal, Ireland. Four years later the family emigrated to Ohio. Shortly after her father's death, Susan entered the Convent School of the Sisters of Notre Dame de Namur, a Belgian Catholic order that had recently opened its first American home in Cincinnati.

At nineteen Susan took the name Sister Julia after the founder of the order; she took her vows within two years and was placed in charge of the convent day school.

Sister Julia's main concern was to improve the education system of her order. She was made superior of the Philadelphia Academy in 1860 — the first American superior within the order — and later, provincial superior. During her administration she standardized the curriculum, established a system of general exams, and founded fourteen new schools.

Sister Julia is best known as the founder of Trinity College in Washington, D.C. The Catholic University of America had been operating in Washington since 1889, but it was exclusively male. Sister Julia and another nun modeled Trinity after an English teaching college and Vassar and Wellesley colleges.

Although Sister Julia died in 1901, one year after the college opened, she left a plan for its direction that continued to influence its development for years. She was buried in the chapel of The Summit, one of the schools she had founded in Cincinnati.

Frances Anne Boyd

1894

On leaving the breakfast-table at Virginia City, we were greatly surprised to find our coach almost full of passengers; but we climbed in, and for five days and nights were carried onward without the slightest change of any sort. There was a front and back seat, and between the two a middle one, which faced the back that we occupied. Whenever in the course of the

A weary ride

succeeding five days and nights it was needful to move even our feet, we could only do so by asking our *vis-à-vis* to move his at the same time, as there was not one inch of space unoccupied.

The rough frontiersmen who were our fellow-passengers tried in every way to make our situation more endurable. After we had sat bolt upright for two days and nights, vainly trying to snatch a few moments' sleep, which the constant lurching of the stage rendered impossible, the two men directly facing us proposed, with many apologies, that we should allow them to lay folded blankets on their laps, when, by leaning forward and laying our heads on the rests thus provided, our weary brains might find some relief. We gratefully assented, only to find, however, that the unnatural position rendered sleep impossible, so decided to bear our hardships as best we could until released by time.

Frances Anne Mullen Boyd was born February 14, 1848, in New York City. She married Orsemus B. Boyd, a lieutenant in the army when she was nineteen. Soon after their wedding, Orsemus was ordered to Camp Halleck, Nevada, to protect the crews of the Central Pacific Railroad from the Indians. Three months later, Frances began the long journey to join her husband.

Growing up sheltered in New York, Frances embraced the trip as an exciting adventure. She took a steamer to Panama, which she then crossed by train to another steamer to San Francisco. There she took a train to the terminus of the Pacific Railroad, crossed the Sierras by sled and stagecoach, and finally completed the trip to Camp Halleck in an army ambulance.

Upon arrival she discovered that her new home was a two-room tent with a barley sack carpet. Food was scarce, there was no female companionship, and temperatures rose to 100 degrees in the summer and plummeted to minus thirty-three degrees in the winter.

Despite the hardships Frances adjusted to army life with courage and a sense of humor. She followed her husband from fort to fort, from New Mexico to Texas, and grew to love the wild beauty of the West.

Her husband died after a short illness in 1885 while on campaign against Geronimo, abruptly putting an end to Frances's army life. With her three children she moved to New Jersey, where she remained until her death in 1926.

Frances's reminiscences about the stagecoach trip she and another army wife took from Virginia City, Nevada, to meet their husbands in Austin, Texas, is included in Cavalry Life in Tent and Field, *published in 1894 by J. Selwin Tait and Sons, New York.*

Women's Words, Women's Stories

Susan B. Anthony

Rochester, NY
August 24, 1881

. . . Dear Aunt on looking over your beautiful letter — that carries me back so to my dear Mother's letters — wakes up all the old and precious memories — I am afraid I haven't done myself justice — that is, my feeling of thankfulness that you, my dear Aunt, appreciate my work — my efforts — so much as to make you feel to send me this beautiful and generous present. [She had sent her five dollars.] It comforts & cheers me a great deal more than the bare money will pay or purchase — it is what it *represents* that gives me so much pleasure — that is — it is the *fact* of your *sympathy* & sort of *sanction* of the aim and purpose of my life work —

If my dear father & mother can and do look back here — *it rejoices their hearts* to see *you* thus holding up their Susan's hands, in her work — which they highly approved when in the body.

Susan Brownell Anthony was born February 15, 1820, on a farm near Adams, Massachusetts. Raised in the Quaker faith, her liberal ideas were inspired by her religion.

Susan became a schoolteacher when she was nineteen. She enjoyed her students and her work but left teaching when she was twenty-nine, disturbed by the disparity in pay between male and female teachers. She became convinced after she met Amelia Bloomer and Elizabeth Cady Stanton that the way to improve women's rights was through the ballot, and she devoted the next fifty-six years to securing the vote for women.

In 1868 Susan co-founded a weekly newspaper, *Revolution*. The following year she called together a women's suffrage convention in Washington, D.C., and organized the National Woman Suffrage Association. She began a thirty-year period of travel throughout America, primarily in the Middle and Far West.

In 1872 Susan voted in the presidential election and was immediately arrested, found guilty of voting illegally, and fined $100. She refused to pay the fine, hoping to carry the case to the Supreme Court, but she was foiled when no action was taken to enforce her sentence. She decided that incidents

Susan's writing is from a letter to her Aunt Eliza Wadsworth Anthony in Colet, Illinois. It is part of the Sophia Smith Collection, Smith College, Northampton, Massachusetts.

like these should not be lost to history, so she began writing the *History of Woman Suffrage* with Stanton and Matilda Gage. It was published in 1886 by Fowler and Wills.

Susan spent most of her life travelling to promote her cause. Hotels were her home until 1890 when, at the age of seventy, she decided to live with her sister in Rochester, New York. Retirement was unimaginable for her, and, as the aged symbol of the women's movement, she continued her busy schedule. At her last suffrage convention when she was eighty-six, she imparted her final message for the future: "Failure is impossible." One month later, in March 1906, she died at her home in Rochester.

Sarah Anne Dorsey

Loving scrutiny

1866
It is enough for me to know that my friend considered it wise to intrust the rendering of his life's history to my feeble hand, although I feel it to be a task better fitted to fingers used rather to handle the sword than the distaff.

It is an ambitious venture for a woman, with her feminine mind, which, though often acute, subtle, penetrating, and analytic, is too entirely *subjective*, to attempt in any way the writing of *history*. . . . It needs the broad, objective grasp of the masculine soul . . . but women may perhaps write Biographies, just as they paint best, flowers, animals, subjects of still life, that require close, refined, loving scrutiny, in which affection and patience may be useful in giving accuracy and penetration to the eye, and which require fine, dainty touches of the pencil, and minute, careful elaboration.

Sarah Anne Ellis Dorsey was born February 16, 1829, on her father's plantation near Natchez, Mississippi. Although her beloved father died when she was nine, her large inheritance enabled her mother to give her the best private education available.

In 1853 Sarah married Samuel Worthington Dorsey, the overseer of her mother's family's plantations in Louisiana. They settled on a plantation at Lake St. Joseph in northeast Louisiana where she immediately set out to improve the conditions of their slaves. Sarah taught them to read and write and opened a Sunday School for their education and worship.

Sarah's writing is from the preface of her biography of her good friend, the Brigadier General of the Confederate Army and Confederate Governor of Louisiana, Henry Watkins Allen. Recollections of Henry Watkins Allen *was published in 1866 by M. Doolady.*

During the Civil War their home was burned by the Union Army, and the Dorseys fled with their slaves to Crockett, Texas for the duration of the war. Sarah worked as a nurse in a Confederate hospital until their return to Louisiana.

With the encouragement of an aunt who had published several novels, Sarah began to write. Her first work, *Agnes Graham*, was serialized in the *Southern Literary Messenger* in 1863 and published in book form six years later. She published four other novels and several biographies of Confederate heroes.

Sarah moved permanently to "Beauvoir," the family's summer home on the Gulf Coast near Biloxi, Mississippi, after her husband's death in 1875. The following year, learning that Jefferson Davis, the president of the Confederacy, was looking for a secluded spot to write his memoirs, she invited him to Beauvoir. As a childhood friend of his wife Varina Howell Davis, Sarah had kept in touch with Varina and greatly admired her husband. Jefferson Davis wrote of Sarah, "Some of her own sex resent her because she prefers the more serious conversation of men." He could well have been writing about his own wife who was jealous of Sarah and refused to join her husband at Beauvoir for over a year. During that time Sarah assisted him in the writing of his autobiography by taking dictation for several hours each day and by entertaining former Confederates who visited Davis.

Jefferson Davis was so enamoured of "Beauvoir" that Sarah made arrangements to sell it to him in February 1879. Meanwhile, suspecting that she was terminally ill, she secretly willed all of her property, including two Louisiana plantations, to Davis. Soon after, she was diagnosed with cancer and died in July 1879 at the age of fifty. Beauvoir is now the Jefferson Davis Shrine and several of Sarah's books, correspondence, and other personal effects are displayed there.

Dorothy Canfield Fisher

1922

*W*hat is important

The Author's Club of New York is giving a dinner for me on the twenty-third . . . I accepted this invitation only because Father belonged to that club for a long time and was always very unhappy (you know that he was very much of a "feminist") that they did not recognize women writers. This is the very first time they have offered a dinner for a woman writer and they are going to continue to do so from now on, so they say.

How many doors are opening up everywhere for women! But it is all the same to me whether the door is opened or remains closed! What is the use of all those dinners "in honor of someone!" All that is important is to do one's work well, and dinners don't help you in that — on the contrary!

Dorothy Frances Canfield Fisher was born February 17, 1879, in Lawrence, Kansas, where her father was a professor at the University of Kansas. Her mother took her to France for a year's schooling when she was eleven. Upon their return, they settled in Nebraska, where Mr. Canfield had become chancellor of the University of Nebraska. There she began a lifelong friendship with her brother's classmate, Willa Cather (December 7). In 1895 her father became president of Ohio State University, from which she graduated with a degree in French in 1899. She continued following her father from job to job, earning a doctorate from Columbia University when he transferred there.

Dorothy began writing upon completing her doctorate. After publishing numerous short stories, her first novel appeared in 1907, the same year she married John Bedwood Fisher. They moved to one of the Canfield family properties in Arlington, Vermont, so that they could both concentrate on their writing careers. Dorothy became a prolific writer, publishing fiction and non-fiction, essays, and short stories. Her stories were rich with details and beautifully written.

While travelling abroad in 1911, Dorothy discovered Maria Montessori's innovative school. She helped popularize the Italian educator's ideas in America through four articles and two novels.

In 1926 Dorothy was chosen to be the only woman on the board of selection of the Book-of-the-Month Club, a position she held for the next twenty-five years. She died of a stroke at her home in Vermont in 1958.

Dorothy's writing is from a March 5, 1922, letter to her friend Célene Sibut. It is in the Wilbur Collection of the University of Vermont, Burlington.

Elizabeth Chester Fisk

Journey to Montana

1871

In the valley before us, "Beaverhead," we saw a fearful storm arising and soon the wind and dust swept toward us. The driver handed me the lines while he put on his coat and allowed me to retain them while he used the whip. Our team of four horses was one of the best on the road, and we flew along through wind and dust

Women's Words, Women's Stories

with ribbons fluttering and shawls breaking loose from pins, even with difficulty retaining our seats on the coach. My bonnet flew off and rested on the back of my neck, my veil went up a thousand feet, and tears ran down my cheeks but amid it all I held fast the lines with the horses galloping furiously. All my fatigue seemed to blow away and the deep draughts of mountain air invigorated me for the rest of the journey.

Your daughter, L. C. Fisk

Elizabeth (Lizzie) Chester Fisk was born February 18, 1846, in East Haddam, Connecticut. She completed her schooling when she was seventeen.

In 1864 members of the Vernon, Connecticut, Patriotic Society made quilts which they sent to the U.S. Sanitary Commission for the Union soldiers. Lizzie's younger sister Fannie hid a note in her quilt, which was received by Capt. Robert Emmett Fisk. He replied to the note, but Fannie was too young and too shy to answer so she asked her sister for assistance. Lizzie began a correspondence that lasted until the war ended.

Immediately upon being discharged from the army Robert went to Connecticut to meet Lizzie. They became engaged within weeks. He left soon afterward to join his brother in the gold fields of Montana in search of a home and income to offer Lizzie.

Lizzie and Robert were married two years later in March 1867. They left the following month on the long journey to Montana. They settled in Helena, where Robert had started a newspaper, the *Helena Herald*. Lizzie tutored a small group of children at home for $1 per week.

Over the years Helena grew from a rowdy mining camp to a prosperous city. Lizzie wrote long, detailed letters home describing life in Montana. She thought of writing a book about her state, but raising six children preoccupied her. The letters were handed down from generation to generation, and in 1989 they were published, finally fulfilling her dream.

In 1902 Robert sold his newspaper business and retired to Berkeley, California. He died six years later. Lizzie survived him by nineteen years and died in 1927 when she was eighty-one.

Lizzie's writing is from a letter to her mother in Connecticut. Her letters are in the Montana Historical Society at Helena and have been published in Lizzie, The Letters of Elizabeth Chester Fisk 1864-1893, *edited by Rex C. Myers, Mountain Press Publishing Company, 1989.*

Lugenia Burns Hope

Control your men

1920

We have become a little discouraged. We have begun to feel that you are not after all, interested in us. . . . The Negro women of the South lay everything that happens to the members of [their] race at the door of the Southern white women. . . . We all feel that you can control your men. We feel as far as lynching is concerned that, if the white woman would take hold of the situation, that lynching would be stopped. . . . I want to say to you, when you read in the paper where a colored man has insulted a white woman, just multiply that by one thousand and you have some idea of the number of colored women insulted by white men.

I want to ask . . . won't you help us, friends, to bring to justice the criminal of your race who is just as much [a] criminal when [he] tramps on the womanhood of my race.

Lugenia Burns Hope was born February 19, 1871, in St. Louis, Missouri. She attended the Chicago Art Institute and the Chicago Business College. In December 1897 she married John Hope, a professor at Roger Williams University in Nashville. Always concerned with the need for recreational activities for young blacks, she organized classes in physical education and arts and crafts at the university.

The Hopes moved in 1899 to Atlanta, where John took a position as classics professor at Atlanta Baptist College (subsequently Morehouse College). In 1906 he became Morehouse's first black president. Lugenia founded the Neighborhood Union, an all-female social welfare agency for blacks. She served as its president for more than twenty-five years.

Through the Neighborhood Union, Lugenia became affiliated with the YWCA's Atlanta War Work Council for black soldiers during World War I. She was the national supervisor of the YWCA's black hostess-house program, which established recreation centers for soldiers and their families. She worked closely with the all-white Association of Southern Women for the Prevention of Lynching, and in 1916 became a founding member of the National Association of Colored Women's Clubs. In 1932 she was elected first vice-president of the Atlanta Chapter of the National Association for the Advancement of Colored People (NAACP).

Lugenia's writing is from a talk she gave to a Commission of Interracial Cooperation meeting in Memphis, July 1920.

Women's Words, Women's Stories

Lugenia constantly used her influence to strive for racial equality. She was a popular, charismatic speaker, addressing both black and white audiences about the need for better black schools and better recreational facilities for city children. She died of a heart attack in August 1947, and her ashes were scattered around the Morehouse campus.

Margaret Bayard Smith

1837

In December, 1800, a few days after Congress had for the first time met in our new Metropolis, I was one morning sitting alone in the parlour, when the servant opened the door and showed in a gentlemen who wished to see my husband. . . . after taking the chair I offered him in a free and easy manner, and carelessly throwing his arm on the table near which he sat, he turned towards me a countenance beaming with an expression of benevolence and with a manner and voice almost femininely soft and gentle, entered into conversation on the commonplace topics of the day, from which, before I was conscious of it, he had drawn me into observations of a more personal and interesting nature. I know not how it was, but there was something in his manner, his countenance and voice that at once unlocked my heart, and in answer to his casual enquiries concerning our situation in our *new home*, as he called it, I found myself frankly telling him what I liked or disliked in our present circumstances and abode. I knew not who he was, but the interest with which he listened to my artless details, induced the idea he was some intimate acquaintance or friend of Mr. Smith's and put me perfectly at ease; in truth so kind and conciliating were his looks and manners that I forgot he was not a friend of my own, until on the opening of the door, Mr. Smith entered and introduced the stranger to me as *Mr. Jefferson.*

I felt my cheeks burn and my heart throb, and not a word more could I speak while he remained.

Margaret Bayard Smith was born February 20, 1778, on her family's farm in Pennsylvania.

A gracious stranger

Margaret's writing is from The First Forty Years of Washington Society, *a collection of reminiscences, edited by Gaillard Hunt and published in 1906 by Charles Scribner and Sons.*

As a young woman Margaret had many suitors, but her heart belonged to her second cousin, Samuel Harrison Smith. Although he was an agnostic and a Republican while she was a Presbyterian and a Federalist, they overcame their differences and became engaged in 1797. After three years of family disapproval, financial setbacks, and illness, they finally were able to marry.

Shortly after their wedding the Smiths moved to Washington at the request of Samuel's mentor, Thomas Jefferson. He started the Jeffersonian newspaper, the *National Intelligencer*, and later became the president of the Washington branch of the Bank of the United States. Thus, the Smiths enjoyed a position of prominence in Washington society.

Margaret had four children and devoted the first twenty years of her marriage to raising her family and entertaining her husband's friends and business associates. As her children grew, she began writing for publication. She wrote several novels; biographies of her friends, including Dolly Madison; and essays and short stories for magazines. Most of her work was published anonymously, although it was generally known that she was the author.

Margaret died in 1844. Her most important work was published posthumously in 1906 as *The First Forty Years of Washington Society*. It is a compilation of her letters and diaries written between 1800 and 1841 and is a major resource for the social and political history of the United States.

Elizabeth Pennell

Knowing how to ride

1898

I am told I have made a record. I think I have, and one to be proud of. I went over nine passes — six in less than a week. I worked at times as hard as a dock labourer. . . . I wanted to see if I could cross the Alps on a bicycle. I did, and any woman who rides — and knows how to ride — a good strong machine fitted with a good strong brake on each wheel, who will be wise enough not to let it get away with her on the down grade, nor to play herself out by riding it on a long steep ascent, and who is not afraid of work, may learn what pleasure there is in the exploit. But all these conditions must be fulfilled, otherwise I can answer neither for her wheel nor her life.

Elizabeth's writing is from Over the Alps on a Bicycle, *published in 1898 by T. Fisher Unwin.*

Elizabeth Robins Pennell was born February 21, 1855, in Philadelphia. After graduating from convent school, she was encouraged by her uncle, writer Charles Leland, to become a writer herself. He gave her her first job, as his assistant in organizing arts and crafts classes in the local public school system. In 1881 he helped her get her first article published in the *Atlantic Monthly*.

In 1882 *Scribner's Magazine* hired Uncle Charles to write the text to accompany the etchings of a young Philadelphia artist, Joseph Pennell. Too busy himself he turned the job over to Elizabeth, thus beginning a forty-four year working relationship between the two.

Elizabeth and Joseph were married in 1884. They immediately set sail for England, where they spent the summer bicycling through the British countryside. That trip inspired their first joint book, which led to other commissions that enabled them to remain in Europe. Every summer they bicycled through a different country and then wrote articles and books about their journeys.

Joseph became the art critic for the London *Star* in 1888 but often was too busy to complete the work, so Elizabeth did it for him. She also turned one of her hobbies, cooking, into a series of books of culinary essays.

With the outbreak of World War I, after decades of residing abroad, the Pennells returned to the United States. After Joseph's death in 1926, Elizabeth devoted herself to cataloging his illustrations and wrote one of her best works, a two-volume book entitled *The Life and Letters of Joseph Pennell*. She died in 1935, just two weeks shy of her eighty-first birthday.

Margaret Munson Sangster

1909

A need for friends

A group of women, who sold newspapers at a ferry terminal and wore three-cornered shawls pinned over their shoulders, were friends with whom I exchanged greetings morning and afternoon for nearly a decade. They told me in our brief communications about their home and their lives, and I knew their trials and triumphs. I was stronger in that I knew their affectionate prayers were offered for me day-by-day. Unless one makes friends of all sorts, and never ceases to add to their number, a time will inevitably come when life will be shorn of that spice of interest which redeems it from dullness.

Margaret's writing is from her autobiography, From My Youth Up, *published in 1909 by the Fleming H. Revell Company.*

Margaret Elizabeth Munson Sangster was born February 22, 1838, in New Rochelle, New York. Her mother took charge of her education at an early age. She could read fluently when she was four, and at eight she entered the Passaic Seminary, a Baptist school.

When she was seventeen Margaret submitted her first story for publication and it was accepted immediately. However, her budding career was sidetracked when she married George Sangster, a widower with two young children, in 1858. They had one son together.

George died in 1871 leaving Margaret with three children to support, so she resumed her writing in earnest. She contributed articles to all the major magazines of the day and soon became an assistant editor of *Hearth and Home*. Thereafter, she was the editor of *Harper's Bazaar* for ten years. She perceived herself as a Christian leader of women, answering letters and writing essays with advice to America's women.

Margaret had always been opposed to women's suffrage and expressed this view in her writings. She believed it was a threat to the welfare of the family. However, she had a complete change of heart in her early seventies, having decided that woman was helpless without the vote to protect her. Although blind for the last few years of her life, Margaret continued to write with the help of secretaries until her death in 1909 when she was seventy-four.

Katherine Pettit

College material.

Katherine's writing is from a May 12, 1933, letter to Howard E. Taylor, the business manager of Berea College. It is in the Pine Mountain Settlement School Collection, Southern Appalachian Archives, at Berea College, Berea, Kentucky.

1933
My dear Mr. Taylor,

Here is a letter from Eva Lewis, whom I've told never to stop writing to you until she gets into Berea. I just wish you could see the house that she comes from. Such disorder and filth. She has never lived in our school and her mother has never given her the chance to learn about "clean living and pretty fixin's." If you only had one scholarship please give it to her. She is college material. She had wonderful old fashioned grandparents on both sides.

. . . If you do not want to keep Eva's letter will you let me have it. However, if you do just keep it, It may help you get the scholarship.

Katherine Pettit was born February 23, 1868, near Lexington, Kentucky. She received her early schooling in the local schools of Lexington and Louisville.

When Katherine was in her twenties her membership in the rural library service of the State Federation of Women's Clubs and in the Woman's Christian Temperance Union, both of which were doing work in the Appalachian Mountains, brought her into that region for the first time. Seeing the grim poverty, the lack of educational opportunities for the children, and the hard lives of the women made her resolve to do whatever she could to help them. During several summers, she went back to the area to run WCTU "homemakers' summer camp meetings," in which she helped mountain women with home problems. She and her friend, May Stone from Louisville, showed the women how to sew, make cottage cheese, and raise bread. They read to the children, taught them games and songs, and gave daily temperance and Bible readings.

In 1902 Katherine and May raised money and started the Hindman Settlement School in Knott County. Using Jane Addams's urban school at Hull House in Chicago as a model, they created a program especially designed for mountain children, with an emphasis on manual skills and crafts as well as the three R's. Some children travelled long distances through the mountains to attend. Encouraged by the success of the Hindman Settlement School, Katherine established another school at Pine Mountain, Kentucky, in 1913, which became equally successful. She was a good manager and creative planner as well as a kind and patient director. The children and women who attended the school loved her dearly. Katherine made a great difference in their lives by teaching them skills and giving them hope.

In 1930 she retired from Pine Mountain to work in the Harlan County area doing what she termed "free lance" work, helping the small farmers who, hard hit by the Depression, had sold their land. She encouraged them to leave the welfare rolls and return to farming. She taught the men better farming techniques and organized a partnership between them and gift shops that sold their handcrafts.

In 1932 Katherine was awarded a medal by the University of Kentucky for her many contributions to the state. She died in 1936 of cancer and is buried in Lexington. She had never married. Not long before she died, Katherine wrote to an old friend, "This has been a glorious world to work in and am eager to see what the next will be."

Anna Morgan

An important event

1917

My next appearance was at Austin, Illinois, where I received my first five dollars. The town was deluged with posters announcing that Miss Anna Morgan, Chicago's Favorite Reader, would appear in the town hall on Tuesday evening November 16th. Admission twenty five cents.

I now considered myself a professional. Soon after that on a never-to-be-forgotten evening about seven o'clock the doorbell rang, and I opened the door. A very dignified man said:

"I am looking for Miss Anna Morgan, the dramatic reader."

I was greatly annoyed to have been deprived of the privilege then in vogue, and thought an essential point in business, of keeping him waiting and then sailing into the "parlor" with an air of great importance, calculated to impress the caller. In this case I had to admit that I was Anna Morgan, and ask him to be seated. He told me he had been sent by the Bryant Literary Society to engage me to read on a program to be given the following week. He said he wanted two numbers and would send a carriage and pay me ten dollars. I remember I straightened up, assumed much dignity, knit my brows, and tried to figure out whether my engagements would permit my accepting this date. I finally said I could, and the man left with what seemed to me much satisfaction at having secured my services. I don't remember who composed the Bryant Literary Society, nor where it was situated, nor whether I ever had been on the north side before. I remember I recited "The Maiden Martyr" and "Asleep at the Switch," and some humorous encores, and regarded it as the most important event in my life up to then.

Anna's writing about her early career is from her book My Chicago, *published in 1918 by R. F. Seymour.*

Anna Morgan was born February 24, 1851, in Fleming, New York. She moved with her mother and four siblings to Chicago when she was twenty-five following the death of her father. There she commenced her study of elocution at the Hershey School of Music.

Anna quickly gained a reputation as a dramatic reader, appreciated for her natural style as well as her interesting mixture of reading material. She toured the United States from 1880 to 1883 and then took the position of drama teacher at the Chicago Opera House Conservatory. Thereafter she performed only occasionally, devoting herself instead to teaching drama.

In 1898 Anna left the conservatory staff to open her own school, the Anna Morgan Studios, where she presided until her retirement in 1925. She was a pioneer in set design, in addition to premiering the works of numerous European playwrights such as Henrik Ibsen, George Bernard Shaw, and Maurice Maeterlinck. Choosing to remain in Chicago, Anna declined offers to teach in New York, Paris, London, and Florence. She wrote three books on speech and theater, and she remained active in the Chicago dramatic scene until her death in 1936.

Jane Goodwin Austin

1881

Anxious love

. . . the baron François was as nearly handsome as a manly man should be, and had inherited from his Norman mother all the high and haughty characteristics of her race, — the cold, clear eyes, blue as steel, and betimes as trenchant and as cruel, the fair complexion, proud, thin-lipped mouth, and tawny golden hair . . . .

But just now the steely eyes were dim with tender fears, and the severe mouth was tremulous with loving words; and the hand fit to wield a battle-axe was clasped in timid constraint over the tiny fingers of the Provençal girl, as he slowly answered: —

"Because, if you do not love me, and love me always, you will be the misfortune of my life."

Jane Goodwin Austin was born February 25, 1831, in Worcester, Massachusetts. Her family took great pride in being Mayflower descendants on both sides, and most of her relatives continued to live in Plymouth. Her father was a lawyer and antiquarian who was an authority on the Pilgrims, and her mother wrote poetry.

Jane's father died when she was a child. She was educated at private schools in Boston and began writing short stories as

Jane's writing is from A Nameless Nobleman, *the third of her Pilgrim Books, published in 1881 by J. R. Osgood and Company.*

a teenager. At nineteen she married Loring Henry Austin.
They had three children, and she put aside her writing for
many years while she raised her family. When she resumed
writing she contributed numerous stories, always about early
New England life, to the *Atlantic Monthly*, *Harper's Bazaar*,
Putnam's, and other current periodicals. Buoyed by her success, she published her first book, *Fairy Dreams*, in 1859.

Jane was respected in her field and socialized with Ralph
Waldo Emerson, Nathaniel Hawthorne, Louisa May Alcott,
and other well-known Boston authors. In 1881 she published
the first in her series of "Pilgrim Books." She spent summers
in Plymouth conducting research so as to be certain her
books were factual, and the result was an accurate portrayal of
the customs and daily existence of the early New England settlers.

Jane's Pilgrim Books included four volumes, which covered the period from the Pilgrims' landing at Plymouth Rock
to 1775. She had planned a fifth book but did not live to
achieve it. During her long career Jane published twenty
novels, the last in 1892. She died two years later at the age of
sixty-three.

FEBRUARY 26   # Louise deKoven Bowen

*T*opsy-turvy world

1944
Capt. Wm. McCormick Blair, Jr.
Somewhere in Burma.
Dear Bill:

I have been thinking a great deal about you in India
lately, and you seem very far away. I wonder about
your work, what you are doing, what you read; if you
know what is going on in this country, and if you realize the love and pride we all feel for the men in the
Service, for their courage, unselfishness and heroism,
which will be told and retold in the centuries to
come. . . .

As you know, I am eighty-five years old — on what
I call the sunny side of ninety — and my mind goes
back to things which happened many years ago. I think
especially about Baymeath at Bar Harbor, Maine,
where all you grandchildren came to visit every summer, and then later, the great-grandchildren. I cannot
help but think how the world has changed since that
time. The whole world seems to have been turned so

*Louise's writing is from a letter
to her grandson, which she
wrote as a preface-dedication
for* Baymeath, *privately
printed in 1944.*

topsy-turvy that one does not know what to do or to think. Even women's dress has changed tremendously. Many women do not even wear hats in the cities. It makes one feel as if the whole population had rushed out to a fire and had forgotten to don their head-gear. . . . I remember that you are the one in the family who has always seemed most interested in that old memory book of mine. You have asked me many times how we lived in the early days, so I am going to try to write you a description of those days. . . . It makes me feel rather sad to do it, because I think those were the happiest years of my life, but at the same time it gives me something to do. . . .

Louise deKoven Bowen was born to a wealthy family on February 26, 1859, in Chicago.

Following graduation at sixteen from the Dearborn Seminary, she asked her minister to assist her in finding social service work. He entrusted her with a Sunday school class of mischievous boys that other church members had turned down. She taught the class successfully for eleven years, increased its membership, and built the Huron Street Club for the boys.

Louise married a Chicago businessman, Joseph Tilton Bowen, in June 1886. She temporarily left her career as a social worker to raise her four children, until Jane Addams offered her a position at Hull House.

Louise became a trustee and later a treasurer of Hull House, and most of her social service work revolved around that organization. She helped found the Juvenile Protection Association and published *Safeguards for City Youth at Work and at Play*.

Jane Addams died in 1935, and Louise succeeded her as president of Hull House for the next nine years. She often contributed her own money to Hull House in addition to her tireless fund raising. Louise retired from social work when she turned eighty-five. She died at her Chicago home in 1953 at the age of ninety-four.

Emma Marwedel

Budding souls

1887

Having found the cradle to be the right spot wherein to begin education, a knowledge of the nature of the inhabitant of the cradle was found to be necessary to that beginning. This presupposed a knowledge of the mother and of motherhood, which make the first and second parts of my work. Thus the book in all its parts leads, like a circle, back to its starting-point — from the commencement of life in the child to the creation of life in the mother.

It reflects the many sacred hours spent in watching and directing the unfolding of their budding souls, and in loving study of their educational needs. It reflects also a thousand divine sparks of childhood's purity, poetry, righteousness, and reason; its devotion to duty, and its hitherto so much unappreciated altruism. My inspiration in writing this book has been, *sympathy* with the mother in her immeasurable responsibility; *the condition of childhood's rights to justice and happiness;* and finally, an abiding faith in the mental and physical evolution of the race. So let me hope that it will lead the mother and the educator, as it did me, inward to the depths of the nature of the child, and onward *with* the child.

Emma Jacobina Christiana Marwedel was born February 27, 1818, in Münden, Germany. Her father was a district judge, which gave the family a prominent social position. However, both parents died when Emma was a young girl, forcing her to abandon high society and go to work. This early experience began her lifelong commitment to the plight of working women.

Emma studied extensively on her own and with Friedrich Froebel, the founder of the kindergarten movement.

Froebel's belief that the public school system in America was ideally suited to his method influenced Emma to emigrate to New York to establish a training school for kindergarten teachers. After her first efforts in New York failed, she tried again in Washington, D.C., and California. In 1876 she opened the California Model Kindergarten and the Pacific Model Training School for Kindergartners, but lack of enrollment forced her to close within one year.

Emma's writing is from her preface to Conscious Motherhood; or the Earliest Unfolding of the Child in the Cradle, Nursery, and Kindergarten, *published by D. C. Heath & Company, 1889.*

Emma retired from teaching in 1885 but continued to crusade on behalf of the kindergarten concept; at sixty-nine she published her major work on the subject, *Conscious Motherhood; or the Earliest Unfolding of the Child in the Cradle, Nursery, and Kindergarten.* Although practically penniless, she spent what little money she had to manufacture the colored blocks and charts she had invented as kindergarten teaching tools.

Upon her death in 1893, California kindergartners built at her gravesite a monument exactly like Froebel's, consisting of the cube, cylinder, and sphere used in the training of a child's senses.

Sarah Morgan Dawson

July 24, 1862

All dressed, we went to the north west corner, as far as possible from the rest of the household, and sat in a splendid breeze for hours. . . .

We discussed our favorite books, characters, authors, repeated scraps here and there of the mock sentimental, talked of how we would one day like to travel, and where we would go; discussed love and marriage, and came to the conclusion neither was the jest it was thought to be. (O wise young women!)

Dena says marriage is awful, but to be an old maid more awful still. I won't agree. I mean to be an old maid myself, and show the world what such a life can be. It shocks me to hear a woman say she would hate to die unmarried. I have heard girls say they would rather be wretched, married, than happy as old maids. Is it not revolting? If I had my choice of wretchedness on either hand, I would take it alone; for then I only would be to blame, while married, *he* would be the iron that would pierce my very soul.

Sarah Ida Fowler Morgan Dawson was born February 28, 1842, in New Orleans, Louisiana, during the period her father was collector of customs for the Port of New Orleans. The family returned to their home in Baton Rouge when she was eight.

From 1862 to 1865 Sarah compiled five volumes of diaries that chronicled the Civil War. She wrote long entries —

Show the world

Sarah's writing is from her October 2, 1862, diary entry. The original diary is in the University of Georgia archives and has been published as The Civil War Diary of Sarah Morgan, *edited by Charles East, University of Georgia Press, Athens, 1991.*

often ten pages for one day — and as a result, left behind a priceless personal history of the war.

Initially Sarah and her family were against the war, despite the fact that they owned eight slaves, and they were optimistic that it would be a short war with a Confederate victory. After New Orleans fell to Union soldiers, who were approaching Baton Rouge, Sarah's tone changed. The Yankees became the enemy and she remarked that her heart had turned bitter. As she and her younger brother and sister prepared to flee the city, her brother-in-law burned their cotton to keep it from the Yankees.

The Morgans hid in various places throughout the countryside, eventually arriving in New Orleans, where they remained until the war's end. The war years took a grievous toll on Sarah's family; her father died of natural causes, one brother died in a duel, and two others were killed fighting for the Confederacy. Sarah never returned to Baton Rouge. She left New Orleans soon after the war ended to begin a new life in South Carolina. She wrapped her diaries in linen and did not look at them again until 1896, when she wrote in the margin at the end: "I have so cried my heart out today for my dead brothers. Thirty-two years and a half have passed, and still I can recall the agony. . . ."

Sarah married Frank Dawson in 1874 (her previous sentiments about marriage notwithstanding) and had a brief newspaper career as a feminist essayist until she retired to raise her two children. Frank was murdered in 1889. The acquittal of his murderer plus financial disputes with his business partner left Sarah a broken woman. She moved to Paris to live with her son Warrington. He described her during her final years as "dreaming of a tragic distant past." Following her death in 1909 her body was returned to Charleston, South Carolina, to be buried beside her husband.

Augusta Christine Fells Savage

A born sculptor

Augusta's writing is from "Augusta Savage, an Autobiography," The Crisis magazine, August 1929.

1929

I was born in Florida of poor parents. I am the seventh child in a family of fourteen. Nine of us reached maturity. My father, who died in January this year, was a minister and very fond of good books. I had very little schooling and most of my school hours were spent in playing hookey in order to go to the clay pit — we had a brick yard in our town — and there made ducks out of clay.

Our family moved to West Palm Beach in 1915, and as there was no clay soil down there, so my clay modelling came to an end until I chanced to pass a pottery on the outskirts of the town and having begged a bit of clay from the potter, I resumed my modelling. The objects created from this clay were brought to the attention of the superintendent of the county fair which was due to open within three weeks. This man, the late Mr. George Graham Currie, persuaded me to enter my models in the fair, which I did. Being the only work of its kind on exhibit, it created a small sensation. A special prize of $25 was awarded me, and this together with public contributions donated by the tourists with the admonition to go to New York and study art, netted me $175.

Augusta Christine Fells Savage was born February 29, 1892, in Green Cove Springs, Florida. As a young child, she began sculpting the local red clay despite her father's objections that she was making "graven images" prohibited in the Bible.

At fifteen Augusta married John T. Moore. They had a daughter, Irene. John died in 1915 and she returned to her family, by then living in West Palm Beach. She soon married a carpenter named James Savage, but they were divorced in the early 1920s after she left for New York City to study sculpture.

Augusta attended Cooper Union's four-year tuition-free art program and received a scholarship for her room and board. After being denied admission to a summer school in France because she was not white, she was asked to study with the well-known American sculptor Hermon MacNeil instead.

In October 1923 Augusta married again, this time to Robert L. Poston, but he died the following year. She was fast becoming a semi-successful portrait sculptor. In 1929 she went to Paris to study and exhibited her work in several galleries, where she won citations and a medallion at the Colonial Exposition.

Augusta founded the Savage Studio of Arts and Crafts in 1932 in New York City, and in 1937 she became the first director of the Harlem Community Art Center. She loved teaching and helping young black artists develop their talents.

Augusta was the first black to be elected a member of the National Association of Women Painters and Sculptors and the only black woman to receive a commission for a sculpture for the 1939 New York World's Fair. In 1945 she moved to Saugerties, New York. She lived there until her death from cancer in 1962 at the age of seventy.

MARCH

Lillian M. N. Stevens

1899

I cannot too strongly emphasize the desire I feel that in all our large cities the nation over there should be held a daily Gospel Temperance meeting at the noon hour under the leadership of our local unions, a service of prayer, testimony and sacred song, designed especially to reach the drinking classes, and where the total abstinence pledge is always offered. Let there be a "Lookout Committee" appointed to invite those who are away from their homes, and in the midst of the counter currents of city life, to attend this meeting, where they will find warm sympathy and help from our mother-hearted white-ribboners. Many of our unions already support such a meeting, but let me lovingly urge its vital importance upon all. In these meetings held weekly if not daily, the music ought to be an important feature. I cannot sing a note myself, but I love to hear you "Sing them over again to me," those "wonderful words of life," and everywhere there are hungry souls to whom some sweet refrain of a Gospel hymn will be the very bread of life.

A strong desire

Lillian Marion Norton Ames Stevens was born March 1, 1844, in Dover, Maine. The death of her only brother in childhood profoundly affected her, prompting her to become very religious.

Following an education at local private academies, Lillian taught for several years until her marriage at twenty-one to Michael Stevens, a grain and salt wholesaler. As a young bride with one child, she became involved in the local crusades against alcohol and saloons. In 1875 she co-founded and became treasurer of the Maine Woman's Christian Temperance Union.

Lillian became president of the Maine WCTU in 1878. She spent much time away from home lobbying the Maine legislature for temperance laws. Eventually, with her husband's approval she hired a nanny to help raise her daughter.

Lillian befriended Frances Willard, the president of the National WCTU, and succeeded her as president following her death in 1898. As president she travelled to many conventions in the United States and abroad and lectured all over the world. Membership expanded from 168,000 to 248,000,

Lillian's writing is from an address she delivered before the annual WCTU convention in October 1899 in Seattle, Washington. It is included in What Lillian M. N. Stevens Said, *compiled by Anna A. Gordon and published by the Regional Woman's Christian Temperance Union in 1914.*

the sale of alcohol was banned on military bases, and six new states passed prohibition laws.

In 1911 Lillian proclaimed a goal of national prohibition within the decade, and she devoted most of her time to demonstrating and petitioning in Washington, D.C. She died in 1914, leaving an assistant, Anna Gordon, to lead the WCTU in achieving her goal.

MARCH 2

Inez Haynes Irwin

Should women propose?

1912

It would be impossible to collect exact statistics on this matter; for it concerns itself with the most delicate and elusive, the most subtle and sacred of human conditions — the period when, either by gentle and imperceptible degrees or by violent cataclysmic outburst, friendship between a man and a woman bursts into the flame of love. It would be as easy to make an exact study of the song of the uncaged skylark, the perfume of a climbing rose, the color-values of an opal. In brief, it is one thing to say, "Do you believe women should propose?" and quite another, "But what happened in your case?" And, "Have you ever proposed to a man?" or "Would you?"

Nevertheless, ever since this conundrum was put to me, I have been submitting it to everybody I met. There has been extraordinary diversity in the answers. They have run from a shocked, *"No! No! No!!"* through a hesitating, "Well, I don't see why — and yet I could never do it myself," to a decided, "Yes, certainly!" . . .

Inez Haynes Irwin was born March 2, 1873, in Rio de Janeiro, Brazil, where her parents had relocated from New England in hopes of becoming financially successful in the coffee business. Their efforts failed when Inez was a child, and the family moved back to Boston.

Inez was the ninth of twelve children. From observing her mother's life of tedious housework and constant childbearing, she developed "a profound horror of the woman's life" that formed the basis of her feminist views. At fourteen, while researching the topic "Should Women Vote?" for a school paper, she became a confirmed suffragist.

Inez's writing is from "Should Women Propose?," Harper's Bazaar, July 1912.

In August 1897 Inez married Rufus Hamilton Gillmore, a newspaper reporter. The next month, with his support, she entered Radcliffe College. With a classmate she founded the College Equal Suffrage League to organize undergraduates and alumnae and bring feminist speakers such as Alice Stone Blackwell to the college.

The Gillmores moved to New York City after Inez's graduation and became leaders in the avant-garde Greenwich Village community. Inez published magazine articles, short stories, and in 1908 her first novel, *June Jeopardy*. During this time, she met William Henry Irwin, a Californian who had come to New York as managing editor of *McClure's Magazine*. She left her first husband in 1913, obtained a divorce, and married Irwin in February 1916.

Inez now turned to writing full time. She accompanied her husband to Europe during World War I and reported on the progress of the war in Italy and France for American magazines. In 1921 she published an inspiring history of the suffrage campaign, *The Story of the Woman's Party*. She produced twelve novels, and in 1924 won the O. Henry Memorial Prize for her short story "The Spring Flight." Her biggest success, however, was her Maida series of children's books, which began with *Maida's Little Shop* in 1910 and ended with an eleventh volume in 1951.

Following her husband's death in 1948, Inez retired to their Scituate, Massachusetts, summer home. She died in 1970 at the age of ninety-seven.

Nellie Mason Auten

1901

The sweat-shop

There are various ideas as to what constitutes a sweat-shop. The term was first used by the employees of the contractor who made a shop of his living rooms and worked his toilers to the utmost limit of their strength. The rooms were sometimes used for bedrooms at night, and kitchen, dining-room, and workshop in the daytime. The people were crowded together, and real home life was undermined, if not destroyed.

Nellie Mason Auten was born March 3, 1875, in Princeville, Illinois. After graduating from Princeville Academy, she enrolled in Wellesley College, receiving her A.B. degree in 1898. She was awarded a master's degree in 1900 from the University of Chicago. Her thesis, "Some Phases of the

Nellie's writing is from "Some Phases of the Sweating System in the Garment Trades of Chicago," which was published in the March 1901 issue of the American Journal of Sociology.

Sweating System in the Garment Trades of Chicago," was published in the *American Journal of Sociology*.

Miss Auten began her career as a teacher in the local grade school in Princeville. In 1902 she opened a private school for boys with her brother, but they closed it the following year. She transferred to the public high school as a teacher of Latin, and there she remained for many years.

In the 1933 *Wellesley College Record Book*, Nellie wrote that she was unable to attend her reunion because "I am still at home, happy in the privilege of helping care for father and mother, who are now ninety-four and ninety." Her mother died later that year, but she continued to nurse her bedridden father until he died. She never married. Her brother Edward, a botanist who developed several new strains of peonies, lived nearby, and she often assisted him in his gardens.

Through her church Nellie gathered books and clothing, which she then dispersed to missions in India, China, and Africa. She was a member of the American Bible Society, the American Mission to Lepers, the Woman's Christian Temperance Union, and the Red Cross. She also helped subsidize two schools for black children in the South and a rural school in the Kentucky mountains, to which she sent books and writing supplies.

Nellie died at home in September 1948 at the age of seventy-three.

MARCH 4

Rebecca Gratz

Losing a daughter

Rebecca's letters are from a large collection written to her brother Benjamin and his two wives (Maria, 1819-1841, and Ann, 1843-1866), composed during the period 1808 to 1866. These letters were compiled into a book, Letters of Rebecca Gratz, *edited by Rabbi David Philipson and published by the Jewish Publication Society of America in 1929.*

January 2, 1848
My dear Sara — the child of my tenderest affection has just engaged herself and I shall lose her society — the gentleman Mr. Joseph of Canada, is I believe better known (personally) to Mary Boswell than myself — for the intimacy was commenced when they were at Cape May last summer — Tho I can make no reasonable objection if her happiness is concerned, it is a very severe trial to me — no one can look into the uncertain future — and the child you have reared and cherished and treasured so dearly can hardly be transferred to other protectors without reluctance & misgivings — Sara is one of the most lovely & gifted characters I know so it would be difficult to find a person we think should be good enough to match her to — . . .

Thank God all our family circle are well — and I ought to be happy & grateful — but My dear Ben when your darling daughter is going to be married you will be able to understand a feeling not easily defined — but certainly too full of anxious care to be called happiness — believe me with sincerest affection My dear Brother devotedly Yours R. Gratz

Rebecca Gratz, charity worker and Sabbath School founder, was born March 4, 1781, in Philadelphia. The Gratz family was a large one: seven sons (two of whom died in childhood) and five daughters. They comprised the foremost Jewish family of their day in the United States, and their home was constantly filled with writers, politicians, and other distinguished Philadelphians.

When she was twenty, Rebecca helped organize the Female Association for the Relief of Women and Children in Reduced Circumstances. Her most significant accomplishment was the founding in 1838 of the Hebrew Sunday School Society to provide religious education for Jewish children. She served as its president until 1864, and it was the model for all similar institutions in the United States.

Rebecca was devoted to her family and served as homemaker for her unmarried brothers. She never married. When her younger sister Rachel died leaving nine children, Rebecca took them in and raised them as her own. She was especially close to her brother Benjamin, who lived in Kentucky. Her many letters to him reveal her intelligence, compassion and deep religious spirit. She died in Philadelphia in 1869 and was buried in the old Jewish Cemetery on Spruce Street.

Walter Scott used Rebecca as his model for the beautiful and noble Jewess Rebecca in his novel *Ivanhoe*. Scott became aware of Rebecca through Washington Irving, a longtime family friend.

Constance Fenimore Woolson M A R C H   5

1880

Boston people — I mean those that belong to the old families there — are like nobody but themselves. I have had to learn their ways slowly, inch by inch, just as I have the ways of the English. They are quite as unlike other Americans as the English are unlike all

*B*oston people

Americans. I have been surrounded by Boston people ever since I came to Italy, and after burning my fingers a good many times, I have at last succeeded, I think, in comprehending them. They are cold, cold, cold, but only in manner, and on the outside. They are stiff. They never gush, and hate gush. They have an inborn belief that Boston "ways" are by far the best in the world, and *secretly* they think all other ways vulgar. Having accustomed myself to their immense serenity about themselves and their views, I now know how to take them. And I can see, too, their really good points which are many. . . .

Constance Fenimore Woolson was born March 5, 1840, in Claremont, New Hampshire. Her great-uncle was the author James Fenimore Cooper, who helped to influence her to pursue her interest in writing. The Woolsons relocated to Cleveland when Constance was a young child. She attended local private schools in Ohio and graduated in 1858 at the head of her class from a finishing school in New York.

Constance served as a nurse during the Civil War and fell in love with an injured colonel. She never married after he spurned her romantic advances. Following her father's death in 1869 she travelled up and down the Eastern Seaboard with her mother. Her first short stories, descriptive tales of her journeys, appeared in *Harper's Bazaar* and *Putnam's* magazines in 1870. Her first book, a collection of short stories, appeared in 1875.

Constance's first and most popular novel, *Anne*, was completed in 1879 and published in book form three years later after being serialized in *Harper's*. It sold more than 57,000 copies and enabled her to move to Europe, where she remained for the last fourteen years of her life. She travelled extensively and maintained residences in England and Italy. She met the author Henry James in Florence, and they became close friends. He would often sublet a room from her for lengthy periods at her villa at Bellosquardo in the hills above Florence.

Constance produced four novels during her years abroad. She suffered from bouts of depression, which she considered to be normal for a creative temperament. She became very ill with influenza in the summer of 1893 and moved into an apartment in Venice to complete her last book, *Horace Chase*. Another bout with influenza the following year turned into typhoid fever. On January 24, 1894, she either threw herself out the window, or fell, while her nurse had momentarily left the room. Although no one witnessed the accident, Henry James was convinced she had killed herself due to depression

Constance's writing is from a letter to her friend Katherine Livingston Mather and is included in Constance Fenimore Woolson, *edited by her niece Clare Benedict and published by Ellis, London, 1930.*

Women's Words, Women's Stories

over her illness. She was buried in Rome's Protestant Cemetery.

Anna Claypoole Peale

1825

Dearest Father,

 I would have written yesterday as I promised but there was no letter paper in the house and everyone in the house was as you suppose very busy, all of the paper had been used the night before for the dreaming cake . . . . I have one for you which I will send on by the first opportunity. Sally desired me to give you a description of the wedding, but that is a task I shall leave to her. . . . She never looked so well, she almost frightened the Baltimoreans by her modish appearance, her dress stuck out so prodigiously that she was obliged to enter in sideways and her headdress so high that Mr. Erskine had to get upon a chair to get her calosh on and even then it was no easy matter. It was a very merry wedding, everybody was in a rose coloured humor. . . . I could not conceive when it was eleven o'clock how the evening had flown so quickly. Yesterday we dined with the Bride the gentlemen had a brunch drinking. . . .

 Yours and grateful, Daughter Anna

A merry wedding

Anna Claypoole Peale was born March 6, 1791, in Philadelphia. Her father, James Peale, was a portrait painter and brother of the better-known artist Charles W. Peale. James worked in his brother's studio, assisting him with the detailed background work of his portraits. As Charles' eyesight began to fail, James took over the meticulous work required for his miniatures.

 Anna and her two older sisters, Margaretta and Sarah, joined the family's art studio as teenagers. Anna exhibited her first painting, "Fruit Piece (first attempt)," at the 1811 exhibition of the Pennsylvania Academy of Fine Arts. Her Uncle Charles found her work in miniature to be "excellent" and brought her to his Washington studio in 1818 to paint miniatures on ivory. In a letter to a cousin he remarked, "Her merit in miniature painting brings her into high estimation, and so many Ladies and Gentlemen desire to sit for her that

Anna's October 6, 1825, letter to her father describing the wedding of a family friend is in the American Philosophical Society Library, Philadelphia.

she frequently is obliged to raise her prices." Some of her famous subjects included President James Monroe, Andrew Jackson, and Henry Clay.

In 1824 Anna was elected an academician of the Pennsylvania Academy of Fine Arts, where she exhibited each year through 1842. In August 1829 she married the Reverend William Staughton, but he died within four months. In June 1841 she married General William Duncan and retired from professional portraiture. She was widowed again in 1864, and several years later her sister Sarah retired from her successful career as a portrait painter in St. Louis to return to Pennsylvania to share Anna's home. Anna died in 1878 and was buried with her sisters in the James Peale vault in Philadelphia's Ronaldson Cemetery.

Edna Adelaide Brown

Born to write

Edna's writing is from The Junior Book of Authors, *edited by Stanley J. Kunitz and Harold Haycraft and published by the H. W. Wilson Company in 1934.*

1934

Because I had few child playmates, I created imaginary ones, and entertained myself making stories. When I did go to school, which was not until I was ten, I perfectly adored writing compositions. Indeed, all through my school days, English lessons and written exercises held no terrors, but I never have been able to add a column of figures twice and attain the same result.

Edna Adelaide Brown was born March 7, 1875, in Providence, Rhode Island. Because of frail health she received her early education at home and did not go to school until she was ten.

Edna graduated from the Girls High School, Brown University, and the New York State Library School. In later years, she reflected that her choice of a library career due to her love of books was amusing in that as a child she had never been permitted to use the public library for fear of germs.

Upon graduation from library school she travelled in Europe for two years, gathering ideas for her books. Edna returned to a job at the Providence Public Library and later joined the staff of the Rosenberg Library in Galveston, Texas. She found working in a large library difficult and was happy to return to New England in 1906 as the chief librarian of Andover Hall Memorial Library, Andover, Massachusetts, a position she held for thirty years.

Edna wrote more than twenty children's books and plays; most of her stories were about animals. All of them were recommended by the American Library Association Booklist. She retired from the Andover Library in 1939 to devote her time to writing and working in her garden. Edna never married. She published her last book, *How Many Miles to Babylon?*, in 1941. She died three years later and is buried in Andover.

Mary Wright Plummer

1909

A rare surprise

A few years ago a strange figure appeared in my office, a little man, a foreigner, of Hebrew race, I judged, who offered for sale very simply a volume of philosophy of his own writing, printed by some third-rate printer, cheaply bound and in no way attractive. The author told me he was a cobbler, if I remember aright, but he had thought out this book and by great economy had managed to get it printed. Ordinarily a librarian makes short shrift of book peddlers; but there was something in this case that made me buy the book without any reference to its merits — something in the man himself that forbade me to disappoint him. I watched for notices of it, not being myself a judge of philosophical writings. A long review of it appeared after a time. Imagine the astonishment, that must have been a joy, of the reviewer when he found as he read that this uneducated cobbler who had never read and probably never heard of Spinoza, had worked out a similar philosophy, was as original a thinker, in fact, as Spinoza! Had he been first, he would have been as famous.

This very rare surprise of finding something unusual where one expects the average and the ordinary. . . . There is nothing at such times that one wants to do so much as to get upon a fence or a stone and crow.

Mary Wright Plummer was born March 8, 1856, in Richmond, Indiana. After graduating from the Friends Academy, she took one year of special study at Wellesley College, after which she began teaching in Chicago. She was an avid reader, fluent in German, French, Spanish, and Italian, and she wrote numerous poems that were published in the *Atlantic Monthly* and *Scribner's*.

Mary's writing is from "The Seven Joys of Reading," a paper she read at the New York State Library Association meeting in 1909.

In 1887 the librarian at Columbia College in New York City founded the School of Library Economy. Mary saw the advertisement in a Chicago paper and joined sixteen women and three men in the first class. Upon completion of the two-year program she worked in the St. Louis Library for several years, then took a position on the staff of the Free Library at the Pratt Institute of Brooklyn where she became head librarian in 1894.

Mary had the pleasure of seeing the new library building at the Pratt Institute that she helped design open in 1898. One of her innovations was a special children's room with its own child-size furniture and a children's librarian.

At the age of forty-eight Mary retired as Pratt's librarian to devote her time entirely to the library school. In 1911 Andrew Carnegie donated the money to start a library school at the New York Public Library. She became its principal and remained so until her death.

Mary achieved what she felt was the crowning glory of her career in 1915, when she was elected president of the American Library Association. She died of cancer the following year at her brother's home in Dixon, Illinois.

Margaret Murray Washington

Separation

Chattanooga, Tennessee
July 27, 1892

My Dearest Booker, I have been trying to write you all day but four of the Chattanooga teachers came out at an early hour this morning and they did not leave until tonight. I do not often write you after night for then I am tired and not fresh and I always feel that I should give you the best part of my time. I can not let the night go by and not have a little chat with you. It makes me feel so much nearer you when I write. You can never guess how much I have thought of you today. I can not separate any pleasantry from you. I long to have it so that we can be together oftener. I do get so tired of this constant separation. When I first found that I cared for you, I used to picture myself going on all of your trips with you — but I did not sit down to write a love letter nor to give you an idea that I can not willingly give up this idea.

Margaret's writing is from a letter to her husband, Booker T. Washington, a few months before their marriage. It is included in the Booker T. Washington Papers, Volume 6, *published in 1977 by the University of Illinois Press.*

Margaret Murray Washington was born March 9, 1861, in

Macon, Mississippi, to a free black woman and an Irish father. Her father died when she was seven, and her mother supported the four children as a laundress.

In 1881 Margaret lied about her age, pretending to be four years younger, to further her education at Fisk University Preparatory School. She worked to pay her way and completed the preparatory and college classes in eight years. After graduation, she began teaching at Tuskegee Institute.

The educator Booker T. Washington met Margaret at her Fisk graduation dinner one month after his second wife's death. After her first year at Tuskegee, he promoted her to lady principal with a salary of $500 plus board, and the following year he proposed. They were married in October 1892.

Booker's work kept him very busy and he travelled frequently. Margaret was a member of the fifteen-person executive committee that ran the Institute during Booker's absences. Eventually she became dean of women and continued in that position after his death.

Margaret became involved with the women's club movement and was elected vice president of the National Federation of Afro-American Women in 1895. She sought to improve conditions for young black girls through better personal hygiene, stronger morals, and, above all, education.

In 1920 Margaret and several other club women formed the International Council of Women of the Darker Races, with the aim of helping all women of color. Sadly, the organization dissolved soon after Margaret's death in June 1925.

Mary Mills Patrick

1929

Five years before the end of the reign of Sultan Abdul-Aziz, I became a resident of the Turkish Empire. To me had come a wonderful opportunity to go to the mysterious Orient to teach. This appealed to my love of adventure as well as to the altruism engendered by the atmosphere of my home. I was a young woman of twenty-one and quite unsophisticated. As a matter of fact, I had never been away from home, for even two weeks, before I left for Turkey. . .

When I started on my long journey, in the summer of 1871, my father accompanied me as far as Chicago — a short trip of a few hours. That was not long

*F*arewell

Mary's writing is from her book Under Five Sultans, *published by Century in 1929.*

before the great fire which destroyed so much of the city. I remember the place vaguely as noisy and dirty in the business quarter, with beautiful residences and parks on the shore of Lake Michigan, but I saw little of my surroundings, because my eyes were blinded by the coming separation from my father. He put me into an east-bound train, and as it slowly drew out of the station I looked back and had my last glimpse of him, leaning against a near-by post, wiping away his tears.

Mary Mills Patrick was born March 10, 1850, in Canterbury, New Hampshire. When she was fifteen the family moved to Lyons, Iowa, to try farming. In 1869 Mary graduated from the nearby Lyons Collegiate Institution and applied to the American Board of Commissioners for Foreign Missions. They offered her a teaching position at a mission school in Erzurum, an Armenian section of the Ottoman Empire.

Mary spent four years in Erzurum, during which she mastered both modern and ancient Armenian. She travelled more than 3,000 miles on horseback, touring the countryside during her vacations. She then transferred to the American High School for Girls in Istanbul.

In 1889 Mary became principal of the girls' school, but she dreamed of establishing a college as well. The following year she obtained a charter from the Commonwealth of Massachusetts and opened the American College for Girls. She served as president and earned $440 per year. She was often seen riding around Istanbul on her bicycle, which shocked the conservative Turks.

In 1908 Mary renewed the Massachusetts Charter and purchased land to build a new campus at Arnautkeui on the European shore of the Bosporus. The new buildings were dedicated in a ceremony on June 3, 1914, during which Mary received the Third Order of Shefakat from Sultan Mehmed V. She also received an honorary LL.D. from Smith College and a Litt.D. from Columbia University.

The college thrived despite the Balkan Wars and World War I. Initially formed to educate the Christian minorities of the Ottoman Empire, it expanded to admit Turkish women after the creation of the Turkish Republic in 1923. When Mary retired in 1924, there were more than 400 students from twenty countries. The college is still operating today.

Mary returned to America following her retirement. She published two books on her experiences, one when she was seventy-nine and the last at eighty-four. She died in California in 1940 at the age of ninety and was buried in Canterbury, New Hampshire.

Wanda Hazel Gág

1913

I just got a letter from Phil. It was such a serious one, and I do feel so queer. All I can do is to say "Goodness" at irregular and short intervals. . . . He says I'm not confidential enough, and asks me to be frank and honest in my next letter — that if I don't care for him and his actions he will be willing to listen to me. Goodness. Frankly, here, I like him as well as, and perhaps better than, any other young man of my acquaintance. But goodness, I'm not in love with any-one yet — at least not to my knowledge.

I only hope he isn't terribly serious. I am too young to play seriously with love and — well, I'm so frivolous yet. Perhaps it's only a case of "Distance lends enchantment to the view," only he is a man who gener-ally knows how to read his own heart. That is an accomplishment which I lack.

Wanda Hazel Gág was born March 11, 1893, in New Ulm, Minnesota, a Bohemian, German, and Hungarian settlement chosen by her Bohemian immigrant parents. Neither Wanda nor her six younger siblings spoke any English until they started school.

Wanda's father died when she was fifteen, leaving only their house and a small insurance settlement. Her mother was quite ill, which left Wanda supporting the family. Despite pressure from her neighbors, she decided that all the children including herself must finish high school. In addi-tion to her schoolwork, she managed to contribute drawings to the juvenile supplement of the *Minnesota Journal*, paint and sell greeting cards, and give drawing lessons to children.

In 1910 one of Wanda's drawings won a bronze medal in a statewide contest. After graduating from high school she taught in a rural one-room school until she was awarded a scholarship to the St. Paul Art School in 1913. Her rigorous schedule of working during the day and attending classes at night took a toll on her health and eyesight, but she perse-vered and won another scholarship in 1917 to the Art Students' League in New York City.

Wanda achieved some success drawing fashions for an advertising agency. In 1923 she rented an abandoned farm in Connecticut and concentrated on her art: drawings, litho-graphs, and woodcuts. She held a successful one-woman

Too young for love

Wanda's writing is from her January 17, 1913, journal entry, written when she was twenty. It is included in her autobiography, Growing Pains, *published in 1940 by Coward-McCann Publishers.*

show at the Weyhe Gallery in New York in 1926, followed by a second show two years later. Thereafter her prints were exhibited in graphic arts museums in London, Paris, and Berlin, and she had exhibitions in Sweden, Russia, and Mexico. In 1939 one of her prints was bought by New York's Museum of Modern Art.

In addition to her artwork, Wanda had a second career as a writer and illustrator of children's books. She published her first story, *Millions of Cats*, in 1928, and the public clamored for more. She published five more books, and their simple, folk-tale style made them all classics in children's literature. In 1930 she bought a 125-acre farm in New Jersey, "All Creation," with the royalties from *Millions of Cats*. She lived there with her husband Earle M. Humphreys, a salesman, and a younger brother and sister. She died of lung cancer in 1946 at the age of fifty-three, and her ashes were scattered around "All Creation."

Rebecca Pennell Dean

*F*alse and unreal

1854

To the Trustees of Antioch College

Gentlemen

When I accepted the position to which you elected me, it was with the hope, among others, of being instrumental in assisting you to carry out juster ideas, than had previously been embodied in any educational establishment, with regard to the powers, the duties and the rewards of woman.

Under the circumstances which a vote of yours, passed today, places a Female professor in the Institution, I feel that she would be false to the interests to which I have referred, by continuing in a situation, where her labors are awarded less recompense — just because she is a woman.

In obedience to my convictions of duty, I hereby resign the place I have had the honor to hold.

Should you see fit to appoint me to a situation in the preparatory school, I would very gladly accept it for a time.

Rebecca's letter of resignation, written January 13, 1854, is in the Antiochiana College Library, Antioch College, Yellow Springs, Ohio.

My name would not then be paraded before the world, as a show of any thing false or unreal.

Very respectfully, R. P. Dean

Women's Words, Women's Stories

Rebecca Pennell Dean was born March 12, 1821, in Deerfield, New York. Her father died when she was three and her mother returned to her parents' home in Franklin, Massachusetts, with her four children. Her mother's brother, Horace Mann, was the first secretary of the Massachusetts Board of Education, and he played a major role in Rebecca's education and upbringing.

In 1839 Rebecca enrolled in the first class of the State Normal School in Lexington, Massachusetts, with four other students. After graduating in 1841, she taught for ten years in various towns throughout the state. In 1850 Governor Briggs proclaimed her "the best teacher in the world."

In November 1852 Horace Mann, then a congressman from Massachusetts, revealed his dream for a nonsectarian college in the Midwest that would offer equal education to both male and female students. The following year, Horace and his family, which included Rebecca, began their journey to Yellow Springs, Ohio, to start their great experiment at Antioch College. Rebecca was appointed professor of physical geography, drawing, natural history, civil history, and didactics, the first woman in America to become a college professor.

In January 1854 Rebecca wrote to the college trustees, protesting that male professors earned $800 a year while female professors earned only $500. Although she threatened to resign if conditions did not improve, she actually remained at Antioch until her uncle died in 1859. In 1855 she married the assistant treasurer of the college, Austin S. Dean. Two years later her sister died, and she adopted her nephew Henry Blake.

After Horace Mann died, Rebecca moved to St. Louis to be near her brother and began teaching physiology and natural history at the newly formed Mary Institute, a nonsectarian girls' school. At the age of sixty-eight she travelled to Massachusetts, where she was "one of the most honored guests" at her normal school fiftieth class reunion. While there she was stricken with a serious illness. She died the following year at her sister's home in New York. A dormitory was named in her honor at Antioch.

Janet Flanner

1945

Homecoming

The next day, the first contingent of women prisoners arrived by train, bringing with them as very nearly their only baggage the proofs, on their faces and their bodies and in their weakly spoken reports, of the atrocities that had been their lot and that of hundreds of thousands of others in the numerous concentration camps our armies are liberating, almost too late. These three hundred women, who came in exchange for German women held in France, were from the prison camp of Ravensbrück, in the marshes midway between Berlin and Stettin. They arrived at the Gare de Lyon at eleven in the morning and were met by a nearly speechless crowd ready with welcoming bouquets of lilacs and other spring flowers, and by General de Gaulle, who wept. . . . There was a general, anguished babble of search, of finding or not finding. There was almost no joy; the emotion penetrated beyond that, to something nearer pain. Too much suffering lay behind this homecoming, and it was the suffering that showed in the women's faces and bodies.

Janet Flanner was born March 13, 1892, in Indianapolis, Indiana, to a Quaker family. After graduating from Tudor Hall Preparatory School she travelled throughout Germany for a year with her parents. She then entered the University of Chicago but was expelled for being a "rebellious influence" in the dormitory.

Janet spent several years touring Greece, Crete, Turkey, and Austria until she finally settled in Paris in 1922. She began writing a bimonthly column, the "Paris Letter," in the new magazine *The New Yorker*. Her editor warned her: "I'm not paying you to tell me what you think, I want to know what the French are thinking." Thus for more than fifty years, under the pen name Genet, she wrote what the French were thinking about politics, people, current news, art, opera, and theater, and the word "I" never appeared. During the 1930s she also wrote the "London Letter."

Janet researched her articles thoroughly. Then, shortly before the deadlines, she would seclude herself in her apartment and write night and day until they were completed. She explained her technique: "I keep going over a sentence. I nag it, gnaw it, pat and flatter it." She claimed: "I'm not one of those journalists with a staff. I don't even have a secretary. I act as a sponge. I soak it up and squeeze it out in ink every two weeks."

Janet fled Paris for Manhattan when her beloved city fell to the Germans. She continued to write for *The New Yorker* and worked to rally support for the Free French. She returned to Paris in 1944 and resumed writing her "Paris Letter" for the next thirty years. Those "Letters" were published in three volumes in 1940, 1966, and 1971. She left

Janet's writing is from Paris Journal 1944-1965, edited by W. Shawn and published by Atheneum in 1965.

Women's Words, Women's Stories

France forever in 1974 and moved in with her literary agent, Natalia Murray, in New York City. She died there four years later at the age of eighty-six.

Sarah Flournoy Moore Chapin

1872

Traps of Satan

And now he was indeed alone. In all that seething city he knew no human being. After depositing his valise, he sallied out in search of employment. On the hotel steps he was accosted by a very nice-looking young man about his own age, who asked him if he was not from the South.

Fitz, of course, said he was. The young man seemed delighted to hear it, and claimed to be a Southerner himself, who had been fortunate in getting into business, and he assured Fitz . . . he would soon put him in the way of making money like dirt. "But come," said he, "and let us drink to this new friendship," at the same time leading the way into an elegant building right in front of them.

"No, thank you," said Fitz; "I have only five dollars in the world, and have come here to try and earn a living for the widowed mother and my little brothers and sisters."

"Well, come in, and I'll stand treat this time," said the young man.

"Excuse me," said Fitz; "I never go into a drinking-saloon, no matter how disguised, or by what name called. Rooms like these are 'traps of satan' to beguile unsuspecting youth, as sure as you are born, and this union of trade and 'liquid damnation' must have caused a shout in the regions of the lost. I believe in the judgment, thousands of young men will charge their eternal undoing to the merchants, many of them members of the church, too, who hoodwinked them into thinking that there was no harm in drinking, if you only did so in a so-called respectable place."

"Well, Confed, I did not ask for a sermon; I wanted a drink."

Sallie's writing is from Fitz-Hugh St. Clair, The South Carolina Rebel Boy, *published in 1872 by Claxton, Remsen and Haffelfinger, Charleston, South Carolina.*

Sarah (Sallie) Flournoy Moore Chapin was born March 14, 1830, in Charleston, South Carolina. At seventeen she married Leonard Chapin, a prominent businessman. During the Civil War, Leonard enlisted in the South Carolina Cavalry and Sallie supported the Confederacy as president of the Soldiers' Relief Society. After the war she published her only book, a pro-South novel entitled *Fitz-Hugh St. Clair, the South Carolina Rebel Boy; or, It Is No Crime to Be Born a Gentleman.* Her dual purpose in writing the book was to instill morals in her readers and explain the cause of the Civil War.

Leonard died in 1879, and the next year Sallie attended a temperance convention in New Jersey. She was asked to speak and enjoyed doing it. Thereafter the temperance cause became the focal point of her life. In 1881 she attended the national convention of the Woman's Christian Temperance Union as a delegate, and two years later she was elected president of her state WCTU. She travelled constantly throughout the United States, organizing temperance unions and speaking to large audiences on behalf of her cause.

Sallie lived to see the closing of all saloons in South Carolina in 1893. Two years later, although dying of cancer, she was instrumental in passing a state bill raising the statutory age of consent for women from ten years to sixteen. She died several months later at home in Charleston at the age of sixty-six.

Persia Crawford Campbell

*A*n important role

Persia's writing is from "The Economic Role of the American Housewife," an address she gave at Stern College Month Forum, Yeshiva University, New York, New York, June 4, 1958. It is in the Campbell manuscript collection archives at the Center for the Study of the Consumer Movement, Consumers Union Foundation, Mount Vernon, New York.

1958

As homemakers, you will be responsible for spending a large part of the family income, some of which, of course, you may earn yourself. How are you going to carry out this spending function? How are you going to behave as consumers? Your actions will affect the future not only of your family, but of our society as a whole.

Persia Crawford Campbell was born March 15, 1898, near Sydney, Australia. After graduating from the University of Sydney, she was awarded a two-year fellowship to the London School of Economics. In 1923 she earned a M.Sc. degree and published her first book, *Chinese Coolie Emigration.*

In 1930 Persia began two years at Harvard on a Rockefeller International Fellowship in Economics. She married Edward Rice, Jr., an electrical engineer, and had two children.

Persia's husband died in 1939 leaving her with two small children to support. She joined the Economics Department at Queens College, where she remained until 1965, eventually becoming a full professor and head of the Department of Social Science.

During the early 1940s Persia became concerned with the lack of consumer awareness and determined to organize and educate consumers. She lectured and wrote articles and pamphlets, concentrating initially on women. She perceived women as society's main consumers and believed that millions of educated housewives and professional women could create a consumer voice in government.

In 1954 Governor Averell Harriman appointed Persia the first consumer counsel of New York, and during the late 1950s she had a weekly radio program, "Report to Consumers." She was appointed by President John F. Kennedy, and reappointed by Lyndon Johnson, to the President's Council of Economic Advisers. In 1959 she was elected to the board of directors of Consumer's Union, the publishers of *Consumer Reports*. She spent a great deal of time representing the International Organization of Consumer's Unions at the United Nations.

Persia had a heart attack in 1973, after which she tried to curtail her activities but found it impossible to do so. A colleague recalled: "She was so interested in what she was doing that it made her ill not to be able to keep on doing it." Against her doctor's advice, she attended the first International Organization of Consumer Unions Asian Conference in Singapore in 1974. She later admitted: "I confess that I could not bear not to be present at the birth of the Asian consumer effort, so long gestating. It was that which really overcame me." The next month she collapsed on her kitchen floor and died of a stroke at age seventy-five, having devoted her entire life to "helping people get their money's worth and improve their lives."

Norma Collins Roberts

September 17, 1936

*F*arm life

I own a cow with Napoleon's perseverance for new pastures to conquer. She wrecked yet another peaceful Sabbath morning as she went a mile or so across an old pasture just six steps ahead of me. . . .

A woman's apron is versatile — used for everything

from wrapping a baby to carrying a tasty pie from the oven. I took mine off and tied it across the cow's eyes and she led home very docilely. So if you see a staid New Hampshire farmer hereafter with his wife's apron, know ye he's taken a tip from the Farm Mother.

Norma May Collins Roberts was born March 16, 1891, in Bristol, New Hampshire. Her father was a farmer with a successful grain business.

Norma attended the local Fiske School through the eighth grade, at which point her formal education ended. At sixteen she married Osborn Roberts, a local farmer fourteen years her senior. She had eight children, one of whom died in infancy.

For many years Norma toiled on the farm and raised her family. Her husband was sickly for nineteen years and unable to work for the last eight years of his life, so Norma worked twice as hard. She also found time to read extensively.

In the early 1930s when most of her family was grown and the youngest were teenagers, Norma began writing. She so enjoyed it that she decided to try writing a column for the local newspaper, the *Bristol Enterprise*. Norma submitted her first article, "At the Old Farm by the Farm Mother," in 1935, and it was accepted. Thus began a thirty-year association with the paper. She was paid $1 per inch and would go to the office once a month with her cut-out inches.

In 1939 *Yankee Magazine* published the *Yankee Cookbook*; Norma contributed fourteen of her recipes.

She died in 1975 at the age of eighty-four.

Norma's writings are selections from her weekly column in the Bristol Enterprise.

Clara Morris

A stage entrance

Clara's writing is from her autobiography, Life on the Stage — My Personal Experiences and Recollections, *published by McClure, Phillips and Co. in 1901.*

1901
. . . fate willed after all that I should have an independent entrance for my first appearance on the stage. The matter would be too trivial to mention were it not for the influence it had upon my future. One act of the play represented the back of a stage during a performance. The scenes were turned around with their unpainted sides to the public. The scene-shifters and gas-men were standing about — everything was going wrong.

The tallest and prettiest girl in the ballet had been picked out to do this bit of work, and she had been rehearsed and rehearsed as if she were preparing for the balcony scene of "Romeo and Juliet"; and day after day the stage-manager would groan: "Can't you run? Did you never run? Imagine the house a-fire and that you are running for your life!"

At last, on that opening night, we were all gathered ready for our first entrance and dance. The tall girl had a queer look on her face as she stood in her place — her cue came, but she never moved.

"Are you going on?" cried the frantic prompter.

She dropped her arms limply at her sides and whispered: "I-I-can't!"

He turned, and as he ran his imploring eye over the line of faces, each girl shrank back from it. He reached me — I had no fear, and he saw it. "Can you go on there?" he cried. I nodded. "Then for God's sake go!"

I gave a bound and a rush that carried me half across the stage before the manager caught me — and so I made my entrance on the stage, and danced and marched and sang with the rest, and all unconsciously took my first step upon the path that I was to follow through shadow and through sunshine. . . .

Clara Morris was born March 17, 1847, in Toronto, Canada. She was the eldest of three children; however, her father had a secret second wife and family. When her mother discovered this she placed the two younger children for adoption and fled to Cleveland with Clara. As protection from discovery by her husband, she assumed her grandmother's maiden name, Morrison. At thirteen Clara joined a stock company as a ballet girl earning $3 per week. She did not hear the stage manager ask her name on her first day. Someone answered for her, incorrectly, and she became Clara Morris.

In 1870 Clara moved to New York and was a star at the Fifth Avenue Theatre. She was not beautiful, but she was a gifted, natural performer.

In November 1874 Clara married Frederick C. Harriott, a wealthy New Yorker, who became her agent. Throughout the 1870s and 1880s they toured America with their own company until poor health forced Clara to retire in the early 1890s. Clara then discovered she had a talent for writing and for ten years she wrote a daily newspaper column in addition to numerous articles on acting and the theater for popular magazines. She published many books, including five novels, one children's story, and three volumes of memoirs.

Clara's health and eyesight began to decline until her death in 1925 at the age of seventy-eight.

Marilla Marks Ricker

*R*eal religion

1917

In my opinion we want a religion that will pay debts, that will practise honesty in business life; that will treat employees with justice and consideration; that will render employers full and faithful work without grudging or scrimping; that will keep bank-cashiers true; office-holders patriotic and reliable; citizens interested in the purity of politics and the noblest ideals of the country. Such a religion is real, vital and effective.

But a religion that embraces vicarious atonement, miraculous conception, regeneration by faith, baptism and other monkey business; a religion that promises a heaven of idleness for all those who agree with us, and a hell for those who do not, I regard as barbaric, degrading and unworthy.

Marilla Marks Young Ricker was born March 18, 1840, in New Durham, New Hampshire. She perceived herself as a natural teacher and began teaching in local schools as soon as she herself had graduated at sixteen. During the Civil War she tried to help the Union cause as a nurse, but was rejected because of her age and lack of experience, so she continued as a teacher.

When she was twenty-three Marilla married John Ricker, a wealthy farmer thirty-three years her senior. He died five years later leaving her a substantial fortune. She spent the next four years travelling abroad, learning foreign languages, and absorbing continental ideas on free thought, birth control, and women's rights. She decided on a career in law as her way to help the disenfranchised.

Marilla passed the Washington, D.C., bar in May 1882 with the highest score of all who took the exam with her. She concentrated initially on criminal law and gradually branched out to financial and labor law. In 1882 President Chester Arthur appointed her as a notary public in the District of Columbia.

Due to her concern for Washington-area prisoners and prostitutes, she was called the "Prisoner's Friend." She succeeded in eliminating the "poor convict's law" under which indigent criminals were held indefinitely when they were unable to pay their fines. She also initiated a law giving prisoners the right to send sealed letters to the governor and their lawyers without those letters being opened first by wardens.

Marilla's writing is from I Am Not Afraid, Are You?, *published by the Roycrofters in 1917.*

Marilla was also an ardent supporter of women's suffrage. She voted in 1871, the first woman in the United States to do so, by claiming her right to vote as an "elector" as a taxpayer under the conditions of the Fourteenth Amendment. She was a lifelong member of the National American Woman Suffrage Association and supported Belva Lockwood's attempt to run for president of the United States in 1884.

In her later years she became increasingly involved with the free-thought movement. She published three books condemning organized religion and was hailed as the "high priestess" of the free-thought movement in America. She died in 1920 at the age of eighty, and her ashes were scattered around a favorite apple tree on the New Durham farm where she was born.

Ellen Gates Starr

1919

Now to the momentous subject of my spiritual status. It is astonishing — isn't it? — that, after all these years, when I supposed I had threshed that matter out and settled peacefully down to browsing here and there, where I best liked the pasturage, for the rest of my days, I should find myself being drawn into the current with a pull that is quite different from anything I have ever experienced before. At first I said to myself, "Oh, it's the same old thing; it's due to present itself every now and again — the Roman 'crave.' One weathers it and goes on as before — as one always has." "We can't do it," as you said to me the last time we talked about it. But the other side of it is that maybe we — or I — cannot *not* do it. I grow colder and colder to the Protestant Episcopal Church and warmer and warmer to my devotions at Mass and Benediction in the Church Catholic, Holy, Roman, and Apostolic. Once this summer, in Chicopee, I was kneeling quite alone, on a week day, near the altar, in the Polish church, a large, more or less European-looking structure. That strange feeling came over me of the past and future being confused, — do you know it? — as though at some time before I had knelt there, — or was it something that was to be?

A powerful pull

Ellen's writing on her conversion to Catholicism is from a letter to Professor Charles Henry Wager, Oberlin College. It is included in "A By-path into the Great Roadway," Catholic World, *May-June 1924.*

Ellen Gates Starr was born March 19, 1859, on a farm near Laona, Illinois. As a child she was profoundly influenced by her Aunt Eliza Starr (August 29), a devout Catholic convert and lecturer on Christian art. At her aunt's insistence, Ellen enrolled at Rockford Seminary in 1877; however, her father could only afford tuition for one year, after which she began teaching art appreciation at Miss Kirkland's School for Girls in Chicago.

Ellen opened Hull House, a settlement house in Chicago, with her friend Jane Addams in September 1889.

Ellen was concerned by the lack of art in the lives of the poor settlement dwellers. She organized art history classes, reading clubs, and decorated the walls of Hull House and local schools with reproductions of classical art.

Over the years Ellen came to realize that Chicago's poor needed more than just art to improve their condition. She decided she would have to alleviate the oppressive conditions that stifled artistic creativity and set about combatting child labor and sweat-shops with long hours and low wages. She joined the National Women's Trade Union League and helped organize workers. In 1915 she worked so hard on behalf of striking textile workers that they made her an honorary life member of the Amalgamated Clothing Workers of America.

Ellen had long been dissatisfied with the Unitarian religion. She had experimented with the Episcopal Church before she finally embraced Catholicism in 1920. In 1929 she was left paralyzed from the waist down after an operation to remove a spinal abscess. She moved into the Convent of the Holy Child in New York, where she died in 1940 at the age of eighty and was buried on the grounds.

Cornelia Phillips Spencer

Dark prospects

1863

July 4 — I went with all the children to Mallett's mill pond. The girls all went wading, my girl among them. We sat on the bridge and ate plums. Governor Swain says he doubts if three-fourths of the people in Chapel Hill remember the date. I remember it in great sadness, for a great country torn to pieces and drenched in blood. It will never again be the day it has been to the country. Our children will not be brought up to reverence it. We will have no day for them unless it be the day peace is declared. We are not attached to the

Cornelia's journal writing is included in Old Days in Chapel Hill *by Hope Summerell Chamberlain, published by the University of North Carolina Press in 1926.*

present government and perhaps never will be. The people of North Carolina will never celebrate *secession day*, at any rate. God help us!

Cornelia Ann Phillips Spencer was born March 20, 1825, in Harlem, New York. The following year her father took a job as a math professor at the University of North Carolina, and the family moved to Chapel Hill. Cornelia and her two older brothers were educated at home by their parents until the two boys entered the University of North Carolina. Since women were not allowed to attend the university until 1897, Cornelia had to content herself with studying her brothers' lessons, which she referred to as "crumbs from the college table."

In 1855 Cornelia married James Monroe Spencer, a lawyer, and they settled in Clinton, Alabama. Following his unexpected death in 1861, she returned with her young daughter to her parents' home in Chapel Hill.

Cornelia tried to alleviate her grief through work. She began teaching Greek and Latin and writing articles for the local paper. In 1866 her series on the conditions in the South near the end of the war when the Northern armies marched through was published as *The Last Ninety Days of the War in North Carolina*.

Cornelia loved North Carolina and desired to see her state become the best in the Union. After the University of North Carolina closed in 1871 due to financial need, she began a campaign to reopen it. In 1875 the legislature voted to appropriate the necessary funds, and Cornelia was so overjoyed she climbed the college bell tower and rang the bell.

Cornelia was also responsible for the creation in 1877 of the university's Summer Normal School for training teachers and in 1891 the Normal and Industrial School for Women (later the Woman's College of the University of North Carolina) at Greensboro.

In her later years Cornelia moved to her daughter's home in Cambridge, Massachusetts. She died of influenza in 1908 and was returned to the village cemetery in Chapel Hill for burial.

Alice Henry

1933

The days when I used to pore over Captain Mayne Reid's boys' books, in a quiet way I was looking forward to traveling myself, not to cities, not to London, certainly never to New York or Chicago. For his boy heroes revelled in the South American forests where the cinchona, giver of quinine, could be picked out by the eye in the far distance. I do not think they ever reached Alaska, but they spun along the ice-locked plains of Manitoba in their sledges, with dogs obedient to their whip. And I expected to do the same, for no sex division, still less sex inferiority, obtruded itself on my mental picture. I was a person, a person still under control, and having to await the chances the future might bring. O No! would surely bring. As up till then I had never come in touch with other children, the distinctions between qualities and standing between boys and girls were literally unknown to me, though it was in my hearing that my mother remarked upon it, when a visitor offered a ride upon his pony to my little brother and took no notice of me. That was perhaps my first lesson in feminism.

Alice Henry was born March 21, 1857, in Richmond, Australia, to which her parents had migrated during the 1852 gold rush. She began teaching after graduating from Melbourne High School but quit in 1884 when her first newspaper article was published. For the next twenty years she was a feature writer for the *Melbourne Argus* and its weekly magazine, the *Australasian*.

In 1905 Alice sailed to London as a representative of Melbourne's Charities Organization at an international conference. She tried but failed to find work in London and so left for America the following year. She toured the United States, contacting the leading feminists of the day and lecturing on Australia's suffrage movement. While visiting Chicago's Hull House she befriended the president of the National Women's Trade Union League, who offered her a secretarial position at the Chicago office. For two years she edited league news for the *Union Labor Advocate*. In 1911 impressed by the interest in her writings, the league began its own monthly magazine, *Life and Labor*, with Alice serving as

Alice's writing is from her mimeographed memoirs, edited by Nettie Palmer in 1944, Schlesinger Library, Radcliffe College, Cambridge, Massachusetts.

editor. She blended union and feminist news with national and international news, serialized stories, and household tips, and made the magazine a success.

From 1918 to 1920 Alice was staff lecturer for the league, travelling throughout the country to organize new leagues. In 1921 she established at Bryn Mawr a summer school for women workers. She published two books on women in the labor movement in 1915 and 1923.

Alice retired in 1928 and settled in Santa Barbara, California. However, in 1933 she was forced to return to Australia on family business and remained there until her death in 1943 at the age of eighty-six.

Jessie Sampter

1926

... I am beginning to build my own house. It is a very exciting and happy experience. ... This week we laid the cornerstone ... "we" means Tamar and I ... and although my lot is only about seven minutes' walk from here, I had to take an automobile to go there and carry an easy-chair in the car to sit on there. About thirty or so people came, including the workmen, at eleven in the morning. I put a sealed bottle into the foundation, containing a parchment relating in Hebrew the date, the occasion and the names of the owners, Tamar and I, and that the house is built by Jewish laborers. Some day, it may be an antiquity.

A house in Palestine

Jessie Ethel Sampter was born March 22, 1883, in New York City. Although she was descended from German-Jewish immigrants her prosperous father was a declared atheist, and she did not know that she was Jewish until she was eight. After contracting polio she spent a lonely childhood confined to her bed, where she wrote stories and poems that were published in the children's magazine *St. Nicholas.*

Jessie had an unhappy love affair, and both her parents died when she was in her early twenties. It was during this lonely time in her life that she began searching for a meaningful religion and was initially drawn to the Unitarian church. She held weekly spiritual discussions in her home and published a book on those discussions, *The Seekers*, in 1910. Her Unitarian minister introduced her to the poetry of Hyman Segal, a Jewish poet, and through him she came to

Jessie's letter to a friend, dated February 11, 1926, is included in White Fire: The Life and Works of Jessie Sampter, *by Bertha Badt-Strauss, published by the Reconstructionist Press in 1956.*

identify with the Jewish immigrants who were flocking to New York City from Eastern Europe.

Jessie moved into a Jewish settlement house in the Yiddish-speaking ghetto of New York's East Side. She organized a School of Zionism in 1914 under the auspices of the women's Zionist group Hadassah. She believed she had finally found her congregation, "in the streets, in the tenements, in the crowded 'Pale' of Russia and Poland, in the little agricultural settlements of Palestine. . . . "

In 1918 Jessie had a nervous breakdown, and the following year she moved to Palestine for the remainder of her life. She made toys for war-ravaged children and organized relief work for refugees from Yemen. In 1923, in an attempt to create the family life she longed for, she adopted Tamar, a two-year-old orphan girl.

Jessie became involved with the kibbutz movement and settled in a kibbutz at Givat Brenner in 1933. She wrote poetry, essays, magazine articles, and biographies in both English and Hebrew and translated Hebrew poetry into English. She became ill in 1938, first with pneumonia and later with malaria, and died at Givat Brenner at the age of fifty-five.

Mary Elizabeth Lee

*M*inds can travel

Mary's writing is from a letter to a friend written June 25, 1840. It is included in The Poetical Remains of the Late Mary Elizabeth Lee *by S. Gilman, D.D., published in 1851 by Walker and Richards.*

1840

I have been poring over a book brought me by my friend, Dr. D. The subject is 'Pneumatology;' or should you, like myself, be ignorant of the meaning of this new-fangled word, I will tell you that it means the Science of Ghosts, Spirits, et cetera. Its effect is so powerful on the imagination, that while under its immediate influence, I feel a strong desire to be magnetized and intend sending my mind, on its first excursion, to Walterboro', where, should you prove accessible, we may come into *rapport*, as the term is, and find it just as easy to hold intercourse together, as if we were sitting side by side. What a glorious thing it is to have faith in this new doctrine of magnetism! Steamers, balloons, rail-cars, all move at snail's pace, when compared with the rapidity of mind, and as for travelling at all, what need is there of such wear-and-tear of existence, when one may quietly sit down, and look into the huts

---

of the polar regions, or walk beneath the luxurious forests of the Tropics. Doctor S. Lately magnetized a poor, ignorant, untravelled woman, and had the happiness of gaining from her a most lucid, graphic, and perfectly correct account of the condition, state of morals, et cetera, in Cuba. The only difficulty is, that one can remember nothing.

Mary Elizabeth Lee was born March 23, 1813, in Charleston, South Carolina. A sensitive, introspective child, prone to illness, she did not attend school until her tenth year. She found the pressures of school overwhelming and returned home after two years. She read voraciously and educated herself at home. She learned French alone and mastered German and Italian with some assistance from her pastor. She became so fluent in all three languages that she translated books and essays for publication.

In 1833 Mary submitted some of her poetry to the southern periodical *The Rose Bud*. Initially she signed her work "A Friend" or merely used her initials, "M.E.L." Soon she was contributing to ten popular magazines and gained enough confidence to use her full name.

In 1840 the Massachusetts Board of Education offered a prize for original books in the categories of science, literature, or art. Mary submitted her first and only children's book, *Social Evenings*, or *Historical Tales for Youth*, and won the competition. Her book was placed in the Massachusetts School Library Catalogue and became quite popular.

When Mary reached her early thirties, she was stricken with a mysterious, painful disease. Her right arm became paralyzed, so she began to write with her left. Eventually she had to hire a secretary to assist her. During the last three years of her life she suffered greatly, enduring long periods of debilitating pain, followed by short periods of relief. She was unable to continue her beloved writing career, spending most of her time reading the Bible and other spiritual texts. Mary died at home in 1849 when she was thirty-six years old.

Candace Thurber Wheeler

1918

And so, just now and here, I am beginning the story which my children and friends are always urging me to write — the story of my life.

I fancy that every soul of us could write a book which the world would read, if only we dared to tell the exact truth about ourselves and our happenings, and so give a perfect reflection of one human life.

But who of us does dare to do that? Our ideas about ourselves, our very standards of good or evil, inevitably make us hypocrites. The traits which would be interesting in a life-story, we keep in shadow, or carefully cover up. I am conscious of it in every page I write, and I would no more tell of my own mistakes and tempers than I would parade them as belonging to my dearest friend, not half as soon, indeed, for we find various excuses for relating little accidents of behavior in our friends.

Every human being is new in some of his personal idiosyncrasies to every other human being, and if this difference is brought out with absolute fidelity it is of interest. If we should say what we really thought and tell what we really did in the different befallings of life, we should be considered original, to say the least.

If I tell a pathetic or laughable or interesting tale of something I have seen or experienced in my ninety years of travel along the highways of life some one is sure to say, "You should write that down! You ought to write your life!"

Candace Thurber Wheeler was born March 24, 1827, in Delhi, New York. Her father encouraged her artistic nature, and her mother, well known for her handmade linens, taught her to sew, knit, spin, and weave.

In 1844 she married Thomas C. Wheeler, a bookkeeper ten years her senior. They settled in Brooklyn, New York, and had four children.

Candace's oldest daughter died in 1876. She turned to her art to ease her grief, becoming interested in a project that would offer "decayed gentlewomen" a means to support

Candace's writing is from her autobiography, Yesterdays in a Busy Life, *published in 1918 by Harper and Brothers.*

Women's Words, Women's Stories

themselves through their craftwork. She established the Society of Decorative Art in New York City and the Women's Exchange. Both organizations gave women a place to exhibit and sell their work and offered classes in decorative arts such as embroidery and china painting.

In 1879 Candace joined three male artists in an interior decorating firm. She created textiles and embroideries for many important commissions, including the White House. After four years Candace started her own firm staffed entirely by women.

She organized the exhibition of women's work and decorated the Woman's Building at the Chicago World's Columbian Exposition in 1893.

In her early seventies, Candace transferred her design firm to her son but continued writing books and articles on interior decorating. After her husband's death, she divided her time between her daughter's New York apartment and her winter home in Georgia. She died in New York in 1923.

Maggie Newton Van Cott

1877

Saviour, look in love on me,
Fill my soul with charity;
Keep me from the tempter's pow'r,
Help me in each trying hour.
Jesus, bid my sorrow cease,
Grant my soul a perfect peace;
While, through faith, I look to Thee,
Stamp thine image, Lord, on me.

Perfect peace

Margaret (Maggie) Ann Newton Van Cott was born March 25, 1830, in New York City. When she was seventeen, she married Peter P. Van Cott, the owner of a dry goods store. Two years after their marriage, her husband became seriously ill, and Maggie was forced to assume the management of his business.

In 1857 Maggie had a religious conversion. Soon afterward, she left the Episcopal faith to join the Methodist Episcopal Church. She began leading prayer meetings and Bible study groups at a mission in New York's slums. Her reputation as a fiery preacher grew, and she received invitations from other pastors to conduct revival meetings. In September 1868 she received an "Exhorter's License," and one year later she was given a "Local Preachers License,"

Maggie's writing is from her hymn, "Saviour, look in love on me" which was included in her Praise Book, *published by Oliver Ditson & Company in 1877.*

thus becoming the first woman licensed to preach in the Methodist Episcopal Church in America.

Maggie travelled around the United States preaching, averaging 3,000 to 7,000 miles a year for thirty years. Her reputation preceded her, and wherever she went she attracted large crowds. To increase attendance, she held special meetings for mothers, "old veterans," and children. In 1872 an article in *Zion's Herald* claimed: "She is without doubt today the most popular, most laborious, and most successful preacher in the Methodist Episcopal Church."

The presiding elders of the 1901 Methodist Episcopal New York Conference presented her with $5,000 to help her in her old age. She retired the following year, having converted more than 75,000 people. She died of cancer at home in Catskill, New York, in 1914 at the age of eighty-four.

Bertha Van Hoosen

Self-weaned

1947

Aunt Julia made no effort to conceal her disapproval. She could not have been more disgusted if she found me sucking one of Father's pipes. "I think it is horrid for such a big girl as you to be nursing like a little baby. If you will give it up I will bring you a china cup from Mr. Clemens where I am going today."

With anticipatory speed I agreed, and she brought me a china cup decorated with flowers and an inscription. Mother filled it with milk and I ran to my favorite play spot. . . . only a few delicious possessive moments elapsed before the cup was broken to bits. Bearing the shattered china in both hands I burst into the room where Mother was chatting with some of the neighbors who often dropped in. My wail, "I broke my cup and now I want my titty," was greeted with such deafening laughter that I retired. Never again did I nurse and I boast arrogantly that, if not self-made, I am a self-weaned woman.

Bertha Van Hoosen was born March 26, 1863, on the family farm in Stony Creek, Michigan. She received her A.B. degree from the University of Michigan in 1884 and immediately enrolled in Michigan's medical school. Her parents disapproved and refused to pay her tuition, so she taught school and did obstetrical nursing to pay her expenses.

Bertha's writing is from her autobiography, Petticoat Surgeon, *published in 1947 by Pellegrini and Cudahy when she was eighty-four.*

After completing medical school in 1888, Bertha spent the next four years at various women's hospitals and insane asylums gaining clinical experience. She opened a private practice in Chicago in 1892. In addition to her practice, she taught clinical gynecology for ten years at the Illinois University Medical School. She then taught at Loyola University Medical School from 1918 to 1937 and became the head of the obstetrics department.

Bertha was one of the few American doctors to use scopolamine-morphine anesthesia during childbirth. Also known as "Twilight Sleep," the method was popular in Germany, where it was pioneered; however, some American physicians considered it unsafe. Bertha delivered thousands of healthy babies and called the new method "the greatest boon the twentieth century could give to women." She published her research in 1915 in several articles and a book, *Scopolamine-Morphine Anaesthesia*, and became a hero to many feminists who felt doctors should permit every woman the right to choose a painless delivery.

Bertha was not allowed to join the all-male Chicago Gynecological Society, so in 1915 she founded the American Medical Women's Association and served as its first president. Although some of her colleagues disapproved of separate organizations for the sexes, Bertha stood by her belief that as long as women doctors were being discriminated against, there was a need for a women's organization.

Bertha never lost her drive, performing her last operation in 1951 at the age of eighty-eight. She died of a stroke one year later.

Ruth McCormick Simms

1928

Usually when a candidate announces his candidacy, we read in the paper that owing to the demand of his constituency and the pressure of his friends, he has reluctantly agreed to make this great sacrifice and run for office. In all candor and honesty I must say that nobody asked me to run. I have had no demand upon me from constituents, friends, enemies, neighbors and family, and, as far as I know, nobody wants me to run. But I hope at the end of the campaign that I am going to find a sufficient number of people who think I ought to run.

Candid candidate

Ruth's writing is from the statement she made to open her campaign for Congress, New York Times, January 15, 1928.

Ruth Hanna McCormick Simms was born March 27, 1880, in Cleveland, Ohio. Although she attended private girls' schools, she received most of her education from her father. He sent her to investigate living conditions among streetcar employees when she was sixteen. Later that year he became William McKinley's presidential campaign manager, and she accompanied him on a national tour. In 1898 her father was elected United States senator, and she served as his personal secretary.

Ruth married Medill McCormick, a newspaperman, in June 1903. They settled in Chicago and had three children. Ruth and Medill shared an interest in politics, and she helped him get elected to the United States House of Representatives in 1916 and to the Senate in 1918. In 1919 Ruth was selected as the first chairman of the Women's Executive Committee of the Republican National Committee. In 1924 she then became the Republican National Committee's woman from Illinois and organized a network of statewide women's Republican clubs with several thousand members.

Medill died in February 1925, after which Ruth accelerated her own political involvement. In 1928 she ran for Republican congressman-at-large from Illinois, declaring, "I am no longer a suffragette or a feminist, I am a politician." During her campaign she visited every town in Illinois twice, so residents would feel that they knew her when she returned. She won the election, but after only two months in office she decided to run for senator in 1930. Although she won the Republican primary, she lost the election and never sought an elected position again.

In 1926, in conjunction with her political interests, she bought control of a newspaper in Rockford, Illinois. Four years later, she added a second newspaper and a radio station to her holdings. She also owned a large dairy farm in Byron, Illinois.

In March 1932 Ruth married Albert G. Simms, a retired Congressman from New Mexico whom she had met while serving in the House of Representatives.

After this marriage, Ruth withdrew from politics and became involved in other activities. She founded a girls' school in Albuquerque, New Mexico, and maintained a large sheep and cattle ranch in Colorado. She did return to the political scene after a few years to help Wendell Wilkie's presidential campaign in 1940 and Thomas E. Dewey's in 1944.

Ruth died in December 1944 and was buried in Albuquerque.

Anne Douglas Sedgwick

1925
Never have I spent pleasanter months than these last, tucked away here with Basil, Kay and the new novel; yet of course, in a sense, a novel is a struggle daily renewed; a *delicious* one, however.

I mustn't write much tonight, for the novel is taxing and I have been keeping so well, and instinctively following Monsieur Guillemin's *régime* — as well as my own excellent doctor's, which includes two hours of rest every day, at different times, flat on my back; and I have, for the last three months, written at the rate of 2,000 words a day; (Basil's proud computation; for the number of words means nothing to me); that is to say, I have written a long novel twice over and it is *safely* before me for the final moulding and chiselling. I think it will interest you. There is a wonderful French woman (young and unmarried) in it (at least *I* find her wonderful) called Martha Ludérac. I like her name so much.

Anne Douglas Sedgwick was born March 28, 1873, in Englewood, New Jersey. Her first ten years were spent at the family estate in Irvington-on-Hudson, New York, where she was tutored by a governess. Her father was then hired by a prestigious financial company in London, where she studied with her sisters at an English girls' school. At age twelve she was sent back to America to live with her grandparents in Chillicothe, Ohio, for two years. She later recalled that idyllic period of her life: "Sobriety, sweetness, tradition, are the things that best fit my memories of my grandfather's and grandmother's Ohio home, an Emersonian flavor, a love of books and of nature."

At eighteen after finishing her education in England, Anne began searching for a suitable occupation. She studied painting in Paris for five years, specializing in portraiture. In 1898 she wrote a romance novel, *The Dull Miss Archinard*, as a gift for her younger sisters. Her father found the manuscript and took it to a London printer, who published it immediately. The success of that book encouraged Anne to write five more in the next eight years.

In December 1908, Anne married Basil de Sélincourt, an English essayist. They settled on a country estate, "Far End,"

A delicious struggle

Anne's writing from a letter to her friend James R. Smith is included in Anne Douglas Sedgwick, A Portrait in Letters *chosen and edited by Basil de Sélincourt, published in 1936 by Constable and Company, Ltd., London.*

in the Cotswold district. Except during World War I, when she worked in a hospital in France, Anne remained at home pursuing her hobbies of bird-watching and gardening. She continued writing as well, producing a total of seventeen novels and two volumes of short stories. Her pleasant, romantic fiction enjoyed great popularity, and she was described by one reviewer in the 1924 *Nation* as the "ablest follower of Henry James."

In the mid 1920s Anne became ill with a gradual paralytic disease. In 1931 she was elected to the National Institute of Arts and Letters, and her husband accompanied her on her final visit to America for her induction. She succumbed to her illness in London in 1935.

Caroline Coles Abbott

Nothing to fear

1934

When we lived on the Cob River we were 3 miles from Minnesota Lake and 30 miles from Mankato. Mother had to go to Mankato to get supplies — left me alone for 3 days. One man came to the house. That was the only one I saw. I was about 9. I had to milk and feed cows. I went 2 miles for the cows, did not find them and had to go home in the dark. The last 2 miles was through a strip of timber. The owl hooted. Was I afraid? No! Got home and had to milk 3 cows, and feed 5 calves and strain the milk, and go to bed without a light. There was nothing to be afraid of — no robbers, no kidnappers, no grabbers (nothing to grab), no sewing machines, no washing machines. Mother made men's suits with only a needle and shears, no patterns.

Caroline Coles Abbott was born March 29, 1855, in Juneau County, Wisconsin. She was the youngest of seven children; her father died several months before her birth. Mrs. Coles remarried when Caroline was three, and the entire family set off for Minnesota by ox-cart.

Caroline's writing is from a short, unpublished autobiography she wrote in 1934 when she was seventy-nine. It is among her great-granddaughter Barbara Groves Clark's family papers in Wenham, Massachusetts.

They settled in a one-room sod house in Manterville, Minnesota. There was only one book in the house, the Bible, from which the children learned to read. All supplies were scarce or nonexistent; Caroline recalled fruits being plentiful but having nothing to can them in; and at Christmas their ornaments were eggs with a hole in each end with a string through them.

Caroline walked many miles to school and back. Although she had a pair of shoes handmade by her stepfather, she was told to carry them as much as possible as "feet were more lasting than leather." School was a log structure with a dirt floor with no blackboards or desks, and each student had to carry his or her own bench to sit on. Caroline never missed a day despite the long walk and her many chores at home. When she was sixteen she took a teaching job in a nearby town, where she boarded with a family for $1.50 per week.

Caroline married Isaac Mark Abbott in 1873. Her dowry was two cows and a calf. They settled on 320 wooded acres that had to be grubbed (cut down and burned). Just as her mother had given birth to seven children alone, she had ten children without any assistance from a doctor or nurse. Caroline taught them to read at home before they attended school. Of her eight children who survived to adulthood, all five daughters became teachers, and her sons became an inventor, a preacher, and an attorney.

Caroline died in 1937 and was buried in Paynesville Cemetery, Paynesville, Minnesota.

Franc Johnson Newcomb

1966

The Navaho first-grade pupils who came to my barracks classroom understood only a word or two of English and constantly whispered to each other in sibilant Navaho, giggling behind their hands as they did so. The first graders from ten to fourteen years of age would not admit to understanding one word of English and it was impossible to keep them interested in anything except music, sketching, and clay-modeling. They had been brought by government employees to the boarding school against their own choosing and were simply not going to learn anything more about the three *R's* than they were forced to. It posed quite a problem for a young teacher from the East and I spent many nighttime hours studying new methods of teaching. But it was not until I asked them, one and all, to teach me the Navaho language, that I made any headway. After that things went better and when they completed the year's work they could all read their primers, spell and write the words therein, and equal any white third grader in mathematics.

A teacher's coup

Franc's writing is from Navajo Neighbors, *published in 1966 by the University of Oklahoma Press.*

Franc Johnson Newcomb was born March 30, 1887, in Tunnel City, Wisconsin. Her father died when she was two and her mother when she was twelve, after which she was raised on her grandmother's farm.

In 1912 Franc took a teaching position at the Navajo Reservation at Fort Defiance, Arizona. She earned $25 a month and lived and ate with the students in the dormitory. Franc married Arthur Newcomb, a clerk at the Fort Defiance Trading Post, in June 1914 at the end of the school year.

Franc befriended Hosteen Klah, a medicine man, and he eventually invited her to attend his healing ceremonies. After each ceremony, Franc would paint the sand paintings she had seen from memory and attempt to describe the symbols and their meanings, thereby becoming the first white person to record Navajo symbolism.

During the flu epidemic of 1920, when one-tenth of the Navajo population died, Franc used her knowledge of Navajo religion and healing ceremonies and became a respected medicine woman. She was inducted into the tribe, the first white woman to have such an honor bestowed upon her, and given the name Atsay Ashon.

Franc wrote numerous books about the Navajo. She and her friend Mary Wheelwright established the Museum of Navajo Ceremonial Art in Santa Fe. Franc donated all of her watercolor re-creations of sand paintings, almost 1,000 in all, plus her pottery and basket collections.

Following Arthur's death in 1946, Franc lectured on Navajo religion, history, and rites, and wrote books and poetry on the subject, as well.

In her last years Franc was very ill with diabetes, breast cancer, and arthritis. Her final book, *Navajo Bird Tales*, was due for publication in August 1970, but her health was declining rapidly. A special advance copy was flown to her bedside on July 23, 1970, and, having lived to see her last book in print, she died two days later.

Mary Abigail Dodge
(Gail Hamilton)

MARCH 31

Don't hesitate, write

1863

Any one of you who refrains from writing for fear of ridicule, is a coward. Don't be a coward. . . . The more a man tells you not to write, the more do you write. By this I do not mean to say that you must immediately publish a volume of "Something, and other Poems," though even that I advise you to do, if you feel disposed. . . . It is better than to be talking scandal or making flounces. Would-be critics lament pathetically or satirize mercilessly this "rushing into print." It is mere selfishness on their part. You might rush elbow deep into a batter pudding, or bury heart and soul and mind, beyond all hope of disinterment, beneath a confused rubbish of unmended stockings, or by a letter of recommendation become the fifth wife of some hard-worked, hard-working, broken-down, and worn-out missionary, and they would not lift a finger to prevent. No, girls; no. If your heart is stirred within you to write, write! If you can find an editor or publisher who is willing to print for you, print! Somewhere in the world, a heartstring may tremble to your feeble and unsteady touch, with a strange bliss.

Mary Abigail Dodge was born March 31, 1833, in Hamilton, Massachusetts. Upon graduation from boarding school she began a teaching career, but she quickly tired of teaching and decided to write. In 1858 Mary moved to Washington and adopted the pen name Gail Hamilton. Her shy nature was averse to publicity. Her witty, topical pieces were very popular, and in 1862 she published her first of a series of collected essays.

In 1871 Mary began wintering in Washington at the home of James G. Blaine, the Republican leader and speaker of the house. His wife was Mary's first cousin. She helped James write his speeches and his two-volume memoirs, *Twenty Years of Congress*, published in 1884-1886. After his death she wrote the *Biography of James G. Blaine*. Mary had just verified its final pages when she suffered a stroke. She died the following year.

Mary's writing is from her book, Country Living and Country Thinking, *published by Ticknor and Fields in 1863 under the name Gail Hamilton.*

APRIL

Mary Ursula Burrage

1919

There are lots of ships on the horizon. They say that we are nearing the English coast. I can't tell you what thrills it gives me. Everything is so exciting. I am so afraid I am going to miss something. I haven't been homesick for a moment and don't think I shall be. I always said that I was a hard-hearted creature. This voyage has been so strange, sort of a detached experience. I feel as if I had no connection with my former life and as if there was never going to be any end to it. I have done things that I never dreamed I could do. Hester and I have been out for all the fun going and so we are looked on as sort of organizers and are sought for to start games, songs, etc. I don't believe that you would know me if you saw me. There is nothing like getting rid of Boston and surroundings, which have a preconceived notion of your character and abilities. As Hester says, there is no one who knows us, really, and so we can start in over again, as it were, instead of doing what we think is expected of us and is supposed to be in accord with our characters.

Mary Ursula Burrage was born April 1, 1892, in Chestnut Hill, Massachusetts. She attended a private girls' school and graduated from Radcliffe College in 1914. The following fall she began attending the Simmons College School of Social Work, although poor health limited her to part-time attendance.

Mary's career as a social worker involved work for numerous Boston charities, hospitals, and housing projects. During World War I she worked full time and spent her off hours knitting and sewing for the war effort and entertaining soldiers at the YMCA.

In the spring of 1919 Mary sailed to France with her friend Hester Browne and the Radcliffe Unit to minister to refugees. Her group was affiliated with the French Red Cross, and she spent a year in Vermand, Aisne, as a nurse's aide and ambulance driver. Upon her return to America, she resumed her social work at the Children's Island Sanatorium in Marblehead, Massachusetts; she was appointed its director in 1922.

Mary died of typhoid fever in 1927.

Starting over

Mary's writing is from a letter to her family written at sea, en route to France in 1919. It is in the Mary Ursula Burrage papers, Schlesinger Library, Radcliffe College, Cambridge Massachusetts.

Mary Raymond Shipman Andrews

An alluring job

1935

I was raised in Lexington, Kentucky, in God's own country, the blue grass region, and went to a good school, now extinct, till seventeen. Afterwards studied with my father, a finished scholar, till I managed to marry an innocent young lawyer who developed into a judge in a high court. Then I studied law with him as an adventure and took my examination and since that I have always been after studying something, tho I have not learned very much. I write because it is in my blood to write for generations, and because I think it the most alluring job on earth. Just now I am working out a new and more modern style and should be glad of any prayers offered towards attaining that goal, for it is difficult.

Mary Raymond Shipman Andrews was born April 2, 1860, in Mobile, Alabama. Her father was an Episcopal minister who was transferred often from parish to parish, from Alabama to Kentucky to Wisconsin. In 1877 the family settled permanently in New York City.

On New Year's Eve 1884, Mary married William Shankland Andrews, a recent law school graduate who went on to become a justice of the New York State Supreme Court. They had one son, who followed his father into the law when he grew up, becoming dean of Syracuse University Law School.

The Andrews lived in Syracuse but spent a great deal of time travelling throughout North America, South America, and Europe. They owned a remote camp in the Canadian wilderness where they summered for thirty years. There Mary could indulge in her favorite pastimes of hunting, canoeing, swimming, and horseback riding.

Mary took up writing around the turn of the century, launching a successful literary career that spanned more than two decades. She published over twenty books and many articles, stories, and poems. Her work appeared primarily in *Scribner's Magazine* but could also be found in *Harper's Bazaar, McClure's,* and *The Ladies' Home Journal.* She found a formula that worked and always stuck to it: a familiar setting (the courtroom, the Canadian woods) and a moralistic plot involving romantic characters. *The New York Times* sum-

Mary's writing is from an autobiographical sketch she wrote the year before her death for The Junior Book of Authors, *edited by Stanley J. Kunitz and Howard Haycraft and published by the H. W. Wilson Company in 1934.*

marized her work as "a nice, good, clean story that rolls along charmingly and ends happily."

Mary's most famous book was *The Perfect Tribute*, a sentimentalized tale of Abraham Lincoln. It was published in 1906 and sold more than 600,000 copies. Mary died of cancer in Syracuse at the age of seventy-six.

Elizabeth Wright

1906

I was at Tuskegee only a short time before I made up my mind to try and be the same type of woman as Mr. Washington was of a man. The first week I was there, I was told that Mr. Washington would not let any one stay there who used slang. I had never been told it was unlady-like to use bywords before and decided at once never to say anything that I would be afraid to let Mr. Washington hear.

The talks which he gave us on Sunday evenings in the Chapel did more to mold my character than anything else. I made them a part of me while in school and they stick to me now like lead. His talks influenced me to try to help my fellow men to help themselves, and if a way was not opened for me, I must open it myself. . . .

Inspired

Elizabeth (Lizzie) Evelyn Wright was born April 3, 1872, in Talbotton, Georgia, the seventh of twenty-one children. Her mother was a Cherokee Indian, and her father was a freed black slave. Lizzie's education consisted of a three-month term each year in a district school in the basement of St. Philip's Church. One day, while she was playing with a group of children, the wind blew some newspapers across their play area. An advertisement for Tuskegee Industrial School fell at her feet, and Lizzie read how poor black youths could be educated while working their way through school. She showed the notice to her teacher, and together they made it possible for her to go there.

Lizzie worked as a domestic to earn her tuition and arrived at Tuskegee, run by educator Booker T. Washington, in 1888. Initially she could not afford the day school, so she worked in the school's kitchen and attended classes at night. Lizzie's health suffered from the strain, and Booker T. Washington's second wife, Olivia, also a frail and sickly

Lizzie's writing is from autobiographical notes written a few months before her last illness. They are included in Tuskegee to Voorhees: The Booker T. Washington Idea Projected by Elizabeth Evelyn Wright, *by J. F. B. Coleman, published by R. L. Bryan in 1922.*

woman, took pity on her and arranged for a scholarship. Lizzie and Olivia remained close friends until Olivia's death in May 1889.

Another teacher, Margaret Murray (March 9), who was later to become Washington's third wife, took an interest in Lizzie. She was concerned with Lizzie's, declining health and encouraged her to leave Tuskegee to begin teaching at a school for black children in McNeill, South Carolina, in 1892. Whites burned the school in April 1893, and Lizzie returned to Tuskegee, determined to "build an industrial school patterned after Tuskegee" following graduation.

Lizzie looked at several locations for her school, but racial incidents and threats made it difficult to find a suitable place. Eventually she settled on Denmark, South Carolina, and purchased land with money she had collected from sixty-six churches. She opened the Denmark Industrial School in 1897, and by 1898 there were 236 students and four teachers. Booker T. Washington was very proud of his successful graduate and told the Tuskegee graduating class of 1890: "I want the girls to go out and do as Miss Lizzie E. Wright is doing. I want you to go into the country districts and build up schools."

Lizzie changed the Denmark school's name in 1902 to Voorhees Industrial School in honor of a large donor, Ralph Voorhees. On June 2, 1906, she married Tuskegee graduate Martin A. Menafee. Sadly, she died six months later of chronic gastric catarrh at the age of thirty-four and was buried on the Voorhees campus.

APRIL 4

Mary Ware Dennett

Explaining sex

1930

The needs of my two young sons caused the writing of the pamphlet, *The Sex Side of Life — An Explanation for Young People*. It was in 1915, when one of the boys was fourteen and the other ten years old.

. . . I began a search for the right sort of little book for teen-age children. After weeks of hunting through the bookshops, the Public Library and particularly the excellent library of the American Social Hygiene Association, I began to be discouraged. Many books had to be discarded at once as written on wholly false basis. Many were fine and useful in part but were in the most important parts predicated upon the old

Mary's writing is from her book Who's Obscene?, *published by the Vanguard Press in 1930.*

concept of shame and fear which has been the ruin of so much sex teaching. The result was the decision to write a simple explanation myself which might help my own boys, and possibly other children, too. . . .

Both sons were away for the summer when the paper was done. I mailed it to the older boy, writing that I hoped it would be of some use, by way of supplementing what he already knew. . . . when he arrived home, I was not left in doubt many minutes, though I did not mention the subject myself. After first greetings he betook himself to the shower-bath to tidy up after a transcontinental journey. Above the roar of the water I heard him call. A tousled head was stuck out of the door, and with a most perceiving smile he said, "Hi, mother that paper you sent me was all right." "Did it fill the bill?" I asked. *"It sure did,"* he remarked and disappeared into his bath. That remark spoke volumes, and I would far rather have had those few words from him than all the thousand-dollar prizes in the world, or the approval of any sex-hygiene jurors, no matter how academically distinguished.

Mary Coffin Ware Dennett was born April 4, 1872, in Worcester, Massachusetts. She attended the School of the Boston Museum of Fine Arts and taught design and decoration for three years at the Drexel Institute in Philadelphia.

Mary married William Hartley Dennett, an architect, in 1900 and had two sons. She was happy in the beginning of her marriage, working as an interior decorator, but she became bored and searched for more meaningful activities. She was drawn to the women's suffrage movement and aligned herself with the National American Woman Suffrage Association.

In 1910 Mary moved to New York to head the movement's literature department, which was responsible for distributing millions of pro-suffrage pamphlets throughout the United States. Her husband disapproved of her new life, and they divorced three years later.

Mary believed that sex education was the means to a better understanding of sex and birth control. She had written a sex education pamphlet for her sons in 1915, which was published in 1918 as *The Sex Side of Life*. She mailed out more than 25,000 copies before the postmaster general banned the pamphlet as obscene. In 1928 Mary was convicted and fined $300, which resulted in a great public outcry. The American Civil Liberties Union took up her cause, and the decision was reversed the following year, allowing her to continue her campaign for better sex education. Mary died in a New York nursing home in 1947 at the age of seventy-five.

Fannia Mary Cohn

Rights and status

1945
Our Constitution, our Bill of Rights, never crossed the threshold of a non-union shop. Now, the worker has won the right to bargain collectively, to improve his economic condition. Equally important is the new status he gains as a Union member, a feeling of "belonging," of self-importance, of human dignity. Through the activities of his union, he becomes a functional member of the community and the nation.

Fannia Mary Cohn was born April 5, 1885, in Kletsk, Minsk, Russia. She was privately educated with her four siblings and encouraged to aspire to a career. In 1904 Fannia emigrated to America alone at the age of nineteen. After working for one year as a representative of the American Jewish Women's Committee on Ellis Island, she decided to pursue a career in the trade union movement and took a job in a garment factory.

In 1909 Fannia was elected to the executive board of the Wrapper, Kimono, and House Dress Makers, Local 41, of the International Ladies' Garment Workers' Union. In 1914 she began attending the National Women's Trade Union League's Training School for Women Organizers in Chicago, and in 1915 she led the first successful strike of dress and white-goods workers.

Having established her reputation in Chicago, she returned to New York City and was elected the first female vice president of the ILGWU. In a male-dominated movement, she hoped her position would inspire other women to become more involved. She was appointed executive secretary of the union's Education Department in 1917.

Fannia's writing is from a talk she gave before the National Intercollegiate Christian Council and the Presbyterian Institute of Industrial Relations at the New York Labor Temple in 1945. It was published in booklet form, Labor Unions and the Community, *in 1946 by the Workers' Education Bureau of America.*

Fannia believed that education was the only way to bridge the gap between workers and management. Through her educational programs she hoped to instill union loyalty and to develop future union leaders with "a social conscience." She wrote in a 1934 article, "While organization gives the workers power, purposeful, dynamic education gives them the ability to use that power intelligently and effectively."

However, in the late 1920s and early 1930s the ILGWU

---

lacked the funds to support many of Fannia's endeavors. Never discouraged, Fannia turned her energies to organizing. In 1930 she wrote a friend about her current campaign: "The forty-five thousand dressmakers employed in New York City, under the most miserable sweatshop conditions, the majority being women, are determined to abolish and banish forever the sweatshop from their industry." She continued to work for the union cause for the next thirty years, although as she grew older her duties were reduced. She refused to retire until August 1962, when the union forced her to do so by giving her a surprise retirement luncheon. She died of a stroke four months later.

Martha Moore Avery

1903

*A*n abomination

I have taken upon myself the task of making amends, as far as I may, to my country and to Almighty God for working to give power to that which I now see clearly to be an abomination — to be a blare of false gods which leadeth to destruction rather than to the benign light which leadeth unto wisdom.

It shall now be my pleasure to give over all that I deem necessary to the promotion of industrial equities as against this devil with the specious cry of liberty . . . this devil who denies God and strides towards the temporal throne — this devil who stretches out his hand to grasp the mighty sword of political power in a free land.

Martha Gallison Moore Avery was born April 6, 1851, in Steuben, Maine. When she was in her twenties she opened a millinery shop in Ellsworth, Maine, where she met and married, Millard Fillmore Avery in 1889. He spent much time away from home as a travelling salesman and died in 1890, leaving Martha with a young daughter.

Martha settled in Boston and began working in various socialist organizations. She became close friends with David Goldstein, a cigar maker and socialist. They both left the movement in 1902 after deciding that it was too violent and lacking in religion and morals.

Martha had become interested in Catholicism through the years and sent her daughter to convent school. Both she and Goldstein became Catholics, and Martha spent the rest of her

Martha's writing is from her letter of resignation to the Massachusetts State Committee of the Socialist Party. It is included in Autobiography of a Campaigner for Christ, *written in collaboration with David Goldstein and published by Catholic Campaigners for Christ in 1936.*

life as a pioneer in the Catholic justice movement. She made public speaking appearances for the Catholic Truth Guild until her death in 1929.

Ada Jack Carver

Old at forty

1926

Eugénie Laston was nearly sixty.

When she was in her early forties she had put on deep black — a kerchief tied under her chin at home, and many veils when she went abroad — and had become an old woman. This was the custom among the people with whom she had lived since her marriage, a stocky, blue-eyed peasant folk who, in the days before the war, had drifted to the Louisiana bayous from Burgundy and the north of France. To these people the kerchief and the veils are a symbol: they signify that a woman has forever renounced the world, the flesh, and the devil.

But Eugénie hated her black clothes. They were irksome, distasteful to her. She hated the very smell of black.

Ada Jack Carver was born April 7, 1890, in Natchitoches, Louisiana, to a wealthy Baptist family. As a child her French grandmother told her stories, and when she grew up to become a writer she incorporated these tales into her work.

Ada published her first short story in 1915 in *Southern Women's Magazine*. She wrote for all the popular magazines of the day, including *Harper's Bazaar* and *Century Magazine*. In 1926 she wrote a one-act play that won a literary prize, but mostly she wrote stories about her childhood memories of Natchitoches, a river town with an interesting mixture of French, Spanish, native American, and black cultures.

In 1918 Ada married John B. Snell and moved to Minden, Louisiana. She was never happy in Minden and never used it as a locale in any of her writings. She began work on a novel but never completed it. For some unknown reason, Ada stopped writing altogether in the late 1920s, publishing her last piece in 1928. Thereafter, little is known of her life. All of her letters and personal papers were destroyed at her request upon her death in December 1972.

Ada's writing is from "The Raspberry Dress," published in the November 1926 issue of Century Magazine.

Women's Words, Women's Stories

Elizabeth Bacon Custer

1885

Of all our happy days, the happiest had now come to us at Fort Lincoln. I never knew more united married people than those of our regiment. It will be easily understood that in the close companionship involved in the intimate relationships of that life, either uncontrollable hatred or increasing affection must ensue. If a desperate attack of incompatibility set in out there, the climate, fine as it was, simply had to disagree with the wife, for it was next to madness for both of them if they did not escape from a life where almost every hour is spent with each other. The wife had the privilege of becoming the comrade of her husband in that isolated existence, and the officers seemed to feel that every amusement was heightened if shared by the other sex. That perpetual intimacy was a crucial test of the genuineness of the affection. My husband used to quote a line or two from one of Mrs. Stowe's books that we had read together. The new husband is asked why he knows that he loves his wife: "Because she never tires me; she never makes me nervous." He believed that if husbands and wives bore that proof successfully as time advanced they might count on a happy future.

Elizabeth Clift Bacon Custer was born April 8, 1842, in Monroe, Michigan. She was sent to boarding school at age twelve, following her mother's death.

Captain George Armstrong Custer arrived in Monroe in the winter of 1863 to visit his half-sister. He fell in love with Elizabeth the first time they met. Despite her father's disapproval of Elizabeth becoming an army wife, they were married February 9, 1864.

George and Elizabeth's honeymoon was interrupted by his call to duty with the Army of the Potomac. She pleaded to be allowed to accompany him, and from then on she was "the only woman who always rode with the regiment," joining him on many of his expeditions.

For the next nine years the Custers were stationed in Texas, Kansas, and Kentucky. In 1873 orders came to go to the Dakota Territory, and they departed for remote Fort Lincoln. Elizabeth remained at the fort that summer while George took an expedition into the Black Hills.

Elizabeth's writing is from Boots and Saddles, *one of her books about her husband, published by the University of Oklahoma Press in 1885.*

In May 1876 George returned to Fort Lincoln after testifying in Washington. He immediately joined his regiment to begin the summer Indian campaigns, aimed at dispersing the Sioux and other Indians. Elizabeth and her sister-in-law rode with their husbands to the first camp, twelve miles past the fort. The following day they returned home, stopping en route on a small hill to look down on the marching soldiers. Custer saw them, rode to the head of the column, and waved his hat. This was the last time Elizabeth was to see her husband alive; two months later he was killed at the battle of Little Big Horn.

Elizabeth survived her husband by fifty-seven years and dedicated herself to preserving his memory and defending him to his detractors. She wrote three books about him, and championed his reputation until her death at ninety in 1933.

Harriet Lathrop Winslow

*A*rrival in India

Harriet's writing is from Memoir of Harriet L. Winslow, *edited by her husband Miron and published by the American Tract Society, circa 1840.*

Calcutta
October 24, 1819
My dear Parents, — You will rejoice to hear that after a residence on the water of *one hundred and thirty-three days*, we are in the midst of friends, and on a heathen shore. My emotions on seeing the natives were much as I anticipated. Many of them came to us in boats to sell fruit, or to obtain fire that they might smoke; and two of their boats were attached to our vessel as tenders. The navigation of the river is so dangerous as to make this necessary. Vessels are sometimes lost by being driven on shore by the tide and current.

The dress of the natives, you have often been told, is only a piece of cloth around the waist. Some, however, have a cloth thrown over their shoulders, or wear something like a tunic. Their hair is generally very black and oily. It is cut in various ways, usually most of the head is shaved. We were, of course, a little shocked to see people so nearly naked; but in a moment the recollection of their spiritual degradation filled our minds and hearts to the exclusion of every thought of their external appearance.

Harriet Wadsworth Lathrop Winslow was born April 9, 1796, in Norwich, Connecticut. At the age of twelve she declared a desire to make a "public profession of Christ" by joining the Methodist Church. Her pastor, "knowing my previous fondness for dancing, inquired if I could relinquish that amusement for the sake of my Saviour. I expressed myself willing to make any sacrifice if I might be numbered among God's children." On April 9, 1809, her thirteenth birthday, Harriet, her parents, and a female domestic were admitted into the church.

Harriet soon realized that she "found pleasure in attempting to do good." At eighteen she opened a school for local poor children. In addition to educating them, she ministered to their spiritual needs and cared for them when they were sick.

Harriet married the Reverend Miron Winslow in January 1819. Despite opposition from her family, they set sail for India in June of that year to become missionaries. They settled in Ceylon, where they opened a coeducational school and took several native children into their home as boarders for further religious instruction. Harriet established a women's prayer meeting and a Maternal Society.

The Winslows had four children, three of whom died as infants. Three of Harriet's sisters followed her to Ceylon as missionaries; two of them died while there. Harriet suffered poor health and died in 1835 at the age of thirty-nine. She was buried in Oodooville, Ceylon.

Fanny Davenport

1888

I cannot remember when I did not love the theatre; and a passion for acting seemed born in me. When but ten years old I was constantly engaged in writing scenes (which my younger sisters would never study, much to my annoyance), arranging climaxes for acts, and planning all sorts of things to perform.

The first play I ever remember seeing was *Black-Eyed Susan*, at, I think, Burton's Theatre in New York. My father enacted William. It is with the keenest pleasure I recall this first theatrical experience, — the anticipation, preparation, and almost hysterical feeling with which I took my seat in the private box, with my favorite full dress, and a cherry bow at my throat and on my head, — bits of finery indispensable whenever I "went out." My mother has since told me how I

Her first play

Fanny's writing is from "Some Childish Memories," published in the October 1888 issue of Lippincott's Monthly Magazine.

enjoyed the fun in the piece, and seemed perfectly satisfied with all I saw, until William was sentenced to death. In the scene where he bestowed the gifts upon his messmates and then parted with Susan, I burst into tears, and nothing could induce me to witness the rest of the play. I was not even comforted or convinced when taken behind the scenes to father's knee nor did my sobs cease until, in his arms, and seated upon his knee, I was soothed by his gentle voice and assurances. I clung to him, fearing to lose my hold, dreading those fearful men might never let him return to me. I was about six or seven when this happened.

Fanny Lily Gypsy Davenport was born April 10, 1850, in London to an American father and a British mother, both actors on tour in England at the time of her birth. When Fanny was four the Davenports returned to America, where both parents enjoyed long, successful careers in the theater. All seven of their children pursued the same profession.

Fanny made her stage debut in New York City at age eleven, and thereafter her schooling was frequently interrupted in favor of the theater. In her teenage years she toured the Eastern Seaboard, becoming a leading player at Louisa Lane Drew's Arch Street Theatre in Philadelphia and Augustin Daly's Fifth Avenue Theatre in New York.

Having acted in a wide variety of plays from comedy to Shakespeare, Fanny left Daly's Theater in 1877 to star in and manage her own troupe. In 1883 she had a major success with Victoria Sardou's *Fédora*, after which she specialized in Sardou's melodramatic plays.

Fanny had her first and only unsuccessful theater presentation, *A Soldier of France* (later called *Joan*), in 1897. She lost a large amount of money and retired from the theater brokenhearted. Although she had been married twice to supporting actors in her company, once at twenty-nine and again at thirty-nine, she was now alone. She moved into her South Duxbury, Massachusetts, summer home, where she died in 1898 of heart disease at the age of forty-eight.

Margaret Lea Houston

Raven Hill
June 2, 1849
My beloved

   . . . Dearest, you tell me, that I shall decide whether or not you are to go out with the army. Alas, what has always been my decision, when my own happiness or the good of the country was to be sacrificed? Have I not invariably ascertained your views, and then coincided with them, let my own sacrifices be what they might? And even now, though your personal danger will be far greater than it has been on any previous occasion, since our marriage, I will not express one word of opposition, but I cannot look around upon my widowed hearth and hear my poor boy's plaintive cry, "What makes pa stay so long?" and then tell you that I am willing for you to go. Other trials I have, and must have greater, but these are of such magnitude that the hand of God alone can support me through them. It is true your presence and sympathy would cheer me greatly, but my Heavenly Father alone can sustain me. I have endeavored to write to you as cheerfully as possible on this subject, that the few days of your absence might not be rendered gloomy by any uneasiness about me, but, alas, when I spoke words of comfort, which found no echo in my own heart, I thought that *but a few days* would pass, and then you would be with me, and never, never leave me again.

Margaret Lea Houston was born April 11, 1819, in Perry County, Alabama, to a large, prominent Southern family. In 1836 she was in New Orleans among the crowd of well-wishers cheering Gen. Sam Houston, the hero of the Battle of San Jacinto. She declared then that she would meet him someday. Three years later, she accomplished her goal at a garden party in Mobile.

   Sam Houston immediately began courting Margaret and soon proposed marriage. Margaret was adamant that he travel to her family home to meet her brothers. He put it off for months, knowing the family would disapprove of him. He was twenty-six years older than Margaret and had a reputation as a womanizer and a drunk. Finally, he obliged

Margaret's writing is from a letter to her husband. It is included in the Sam Houston Collection at the Barker Texas History Center, Austin, Texas.

Margaret and appeared at her home. This was enough for her, and despite her family's objections she agreed to marry him.

Margaret was a great comfort to Sam. She was never politically informed, and he teased her about the stacks of unopened newspapers she refused to read. Yet he found solace in her simple grace. She was able to wean him from alcohol to bitters, and through much preaching and reading of the Bible brought religion into his life.

General Houston would often be absent from his and Margaret's Texas home for months, return for a few days, and depart again. Margaret occupied herself with music, religion, and the raising of her children. She gave birth to eight healthy children, the last when she was forty-one.

In 1861 Texas seceded from the Union. All officials were told to take an oath of loyalty to the Confederacy or be removed from office. Sam Houston, then the state's governor, refused to take the oath, resigned, and returned home to Margaret. He mostly stayed in his room, alternately praying, weeping, and sleeping, until his death in 1863.

Margaret and her three youngest children then moved in with her mother. In 1867 she died of yellow fever and was quickly and quietly buried, because of contagion, beside her mother in Independence, Texas.

Lydia Sexton

Loose tongues

1882
Once at a quarterly meeting old Brother Joseph Huffman was presiding elder; and of course it was his duty to "hew to the line," as we say — that is, to arouse every indolent and slothful member to a lively sense of duty. Among other things, the elder said there were some sisters who in prayer or class meeting had never a word to say for Jesus, but only touch politics; and their tongue would run as though it was loose at both ends. I felt guilty before God, and was afraid or ashamed to look up for fear some one was looking at me.

Lydia Sexton was born April 12, 1799, in Sussex County, New Jersey. After her father, a Baptist minister, died when she was a child, she was sent to live with relatives. They arranged a marriage for her when she was fifteen, and to escape the loveless union she ran away to her brother's house in Ohio.

Lydia's writing is from Autobiography of Reverend Lydia Sexton, *published by Garland in 1882.*

Lydia married Isaac Cox when she was eighteen, but he died shortly thereafter, leaving her with an infant son. She worked as a seamstress and weaver to support the two of them. She married Moses Moore, had another son, and was again left a widow within the year. Lydia married for a third time, to a farmer named Sexton, and had two more children.

Sometime in the early 1840s, Lydia "found God" and converted to the United Brethren Church. She also received the "call" to preach, which she tried to avoid due to public disapproval of female preachers. However, she eventually decided that nothing mattered but to teach the word of God. She travelled the countryside from 1846 to 1882, preaching at evangelical meetings.

Lydia preached for equal rights for women, with equal pay for their labor, and against alcohol and slavery. Initially her family and friends disapproved of her ministry, and she travelled alone. After several years, however, her husband joined her. Eventually she was licensed and became the prison preacher at a Leavenworth, Kansas, jail. She retired in 1882 to write her memoirs and died several months later.

Nella Larsen

1928

A discovery

Her thoughts lingered with her mother, long dead. A fair Scandinavian girl in love with life, with love, with passion dreaming and risking . . .

That second marriage, to a man of her own race, but not of her own kind — so passionately, so instinctively resented by Helga even at the trivial age of six — she now understood as a grievous necessity. Even foolish, despised women must have food and clothing; even unloved little Negro girls must be somehow provided for. Memory, flown back to those years following the marriage, dealt her torturing stabs. Before her rose the pictures of her mother's careful management to avoid those ugly scarifying quarrels which even at this far-off time caused an uncontrollable shudder, her own childish self-effacement, the savage unkindness of her stepbrothers and sisters, and the jealous, malicious hatred of her mother's husband. Summers, winters, years, passing in one long, changeless stretch of aching misery of soul. Her mother's death, when Helga was fifteen.

Nella's writing is from Quicksand, *a largely autobiographical novel, published in 1928 by Alfred A. Knopf.*

Her rescue by Uncle Peter, who had sent her to school, a school for Negroes, where for the first time she could breathe freely, where she discovered that because one was dark, one was not necessarily loathsome, and could, therefore, consider oneself without repulsion.

Nella Larsen was born April 13, 1893, in Chicago. Her father, a black West Indian, died when she was a child. Her mother, a Danish immigrant, remarried a white man who disliked Nella and resented her color. Nella felt like an outcast striving to find a place where she belonged.

Nella's attempt to assimilate took her through many schools, several careers, and a broken marriage. She attended Fisk University in Tennessee for one year during her marriage to Elmer S. Imes, a professor there. They soon separated, and she departed for Denmark, where she took classes at the University of Copenhagen. She returned to America, settled in New York City, and graduated from nursing school in 1915.

Nella began her nursing career in Alabama but moved back to New York City after one year. Five years later, she quit nursing to become a librarian, which inspired her to begin writing. She published two novels, *Quicksand* in 1928 and *Passing* in 1929, both of which sold well and earned her a prominent position in the Harlem Renaissance of the 1920s. On the strength of these works, she was awarded a Guggenheim Fellowship in 1930, the first black woman to receive this honor.

Following publication of Nella's story "Sanctuary" in 1930, she was accused of plagiarism. Although exonerated, she never recovered from the scandal. She removed herself from the literary scene and returned to nursing in Brooklyn. She remained there, in obscurity, until her death in 1963.

Anne Sullivan Macy

A little girl

1888

It was touching and beautiful to see Helen enjoy her first Christmas. Of course, she hung her stocking — two of them lest Santa Claus should forget one, and she lay awake for a long time and got up two or three times to see if anything had happened. . . . She was awake the first thing in the morning, and ran to the fireplace for her stocking; and when she found that Santa Claus had filled both stockings, she danced about for a minute, then grew very quiet, and came to ask me if I thought Santa Claus had made a mistake, and thought there were two little girls, and would come back for the gifts when he discovered his mistake. . . . She had a trunk and clothes for Nancy, and her comment was, "Now Nancy will go to party." When she saw the braille slate and paper, she said, "I will write many letters, and I will thank Santa Claus very much." It was evident that every one, especially Captain and Mrs. Keller, was deeply moved at the thought of the difference between this bright Christmas and the last, when their little girl had no conscious part in the Christmas festivities. As we came downstairs, Mrs. Keller said to me with tears in her eyes, "Miss Annie, I thank God every day of my life for sending you to us; but I never realized until this morning what a blessing you have been to us." Captain Keller took my hand, but could not speak. But his silence was more eloquent than words. My heart, too, was full of gratitude and solemn joy.

Anne Sullivan Macy was born April 14, 1866, in Feeding Hills, Massachusetts. After her mother died when Anne was eight, her father abandoned the family. One sister was adopted by relatives, but Anne, who was almost blind, and her brother, an invalid, were sent to the state almshouse.

Anne's brother died soon after arriving at the almshouse, leaving Anne alone and miserable. She had heard of the excellent work being done for the blind at Boston's Perkins Institution for the Blind, and when the chairman of the State Board of Charities visited the almshouse, she implored him to send her there. She arrived at Perkins in the fall of 1880 and graduated six years later as class valedictorian. An eye operation had improved her sight somewhat, so that she was able to read.

The director of the Perkins Institution placed Anne with the Keller family in Tuscumbia, Alabama, as a governess to their daughter Helen who had been left blind and deaf by a childhood illness. Thus began her lifelong association with Helen Keller (June 27) that has since been documented in books, plays, and movies.

Anne had complete control of Helen's education. From 1900 to 1904 they attended Radcliffe College together where Anne spelled the lectures into her hand and spent many hours each day reading textbooks to her in the same manner. Anne's fragile eyesight suffered from the constant strain. In 1903 Helen collaborated on her autobiography with a young Harvard student, John Albert Macy. Although eleven years

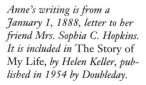

Anne's writing is from a January 1, 1888, letter to her friend Mrs. Sophia C. Hopkins. It is included in The Story of My Life, *by Helen Keller, published in 1954 by Doubleday.*

younger than Anne, he fell in love with her, and they were married in 1905.

Anne, Helen, and John lived together happily for several years. However, the marriage failed, and they were permanently separated in 1913. Helen and Anne began travelling the country, giving lectures.

In her later years, Anne received the recognition she was due for her years of teaching Helen. She and Helen received honorary degrees from Temple University, and the Roosevelt Memorial Foundation gave them joint medals for achievement. Anne became completely blind in 1935. She died at home the following year at the age of seventy.

APRIL 15

Milicent Washburn Shinn

A baby assents

1900

It was about the middle of the twelfth month that the little one added the useful sign of nodding to her means of communicating. She had been taught to nod as a mere trick the month before, and took to it at once, jerking her whole body at every nod and priding herself mightily on it. Perhaps because of this pride and pleasure, it became after a time a sort of expression of approval. . . . So now, when a pleasant suggestion was made, "Would Ruth like a cracker?" "Does Ruth want to go see the kitties?" her nod of approval soon passed into the meaning of assent; indeed, it began now to be joined with the grunt of "E!"

I was nearly taken in at one time by this cheerful nodding and "E!" The little lady used them so intelligently when she was offered something she wanted, and refused so consistently when offered what she knew she did not want, that I began to set down any question as understood if she said yes to it. But presently I had an inkling that when she did not know whether she wanted it or not, she said yes. . . . So I asked her alluringly, "Does Ruth want a course in higher mathematics?"

The rosy baby looked at me gravely, waited with a considering air, as she always did, taking it in, nodded gravely, and said decisively, "E!"

"Does Ruth want to go and be a missionary in Raratonga?"

Milicent's writing is from The Biography of a Baby, *published by Houghton, Mifflin and Company in 1900.*

"E!" with no less decision.

I saved her confidence in my good faith by substituting something else as good, and more immediately practicable, for the mysterious attractions I had offered, and used due caution thereafter in recording her answers.

Milicent Washburn Shinn was born April 15, 1858, in Niles, California. She attended the University of California, taking six years to acquire her A.B. degree because she had to take time off periodically to earn money to continue.

In 1880 Milicent began contributing prose and poetry to *The Californian*. Three years later she assumed ownership of the periodical, changed its name to *Overland Monthly*, and became the editor for the next eleven years. She sold the successful paper in 1894 and gave up her editorship, but continued to submit her essays and poems.

Meanwhile, after the birth of her brother's daughter in 1890, Milicent became interested in child development. She kept a precise record of the baby's mental and physical progress, which was published as *Notes on the Development of a Child*. She returned to the University of California to earn her Ph.D. She was the first woman and only the eleventh person to receive a Ph.D. from the school.

Milicent's psychology work was well received and brought her attention in the United States and abroad. However, after her second book, *The Biography of a Baby*, was published in 1900, she retired to the family ranch in Niles. She lived there quietly for the rest of her life and did no further psychological research. Milicent performed charity and church work and was active in her college alumnae association until her death in 1940.

Dorothy Paulis Lathrop

1934

How I came to write and draw for children I do not know. Perhaps it is simply that I am interested most of all in the things many of them like best — creatures of all kinds, whether they run, fly, hop, or crawl, and in fairies and all their kin, and in all the adventures that might happily befall one in a world which is so constantly surprising and wonderful.

A wonderful world

Dorothy Paulis Lathrop was born April 16, 1891, in Albany, New York. Her mother was a well-known portrait painter who worked in watercolors and oils. As children, Dorothy and her sister Gertrude had the run of their mother Ida's studio and were permitted to pick up brushes and experiment whenever they wished. Their mother's interest and encouragement helped Dorothy to become an illustrator and Gertrude, a sculptor.

Although Dorothy wanted to study only art and writing, her father felt a teacher's diploma was more practical. After graduating from Columbia University's Teachers College, she taught for two years, then studied illustration at the Pennsylvania Academy of Fine Arts and launched her career as an illustrator. From 1918 through the mid 1940s, she illustrated books by many notable authors, including Rachel Field, Sara Teasdale, Nathaniel Hawthorne, and Hans Christian Anderson. In 1938 she won the first Caldecott Medal for *Animals of the Bible*.

In 1931 a friend at the Macmillan Company suggested that Dorothy write her own children's book as well as illustrate it. Her first attempt, *The Fairy Circus*, won the Newberry Honor for 1932. She went on to produce seventeen children's books, and because of her love of animals and skill in drawing them, she became known as an American counterpart of Beatrix Potter. An avid animal lover, she kept nine Pekingese, one poodle, and a monkey as pets and often raised orphaned wild animals such as flying squirrels, mice, or birds to use as live models. She was a vegetarian who "would as soon wear a fringe of fingers as a piece of fur." She tried to pass on her concern for animal welfare to her young readers.

Neither Dorothy nor Gertrude married. They lived at home with their mother and shared a "two-roomed studio building behind the house. This we built when it was increasingly evident that my mother's studio could hardly hold comfortably three working artists at once." Dorothy received the Eyre medal from the Pennsylvania Academy of Fine Arts in 1941 and the Library of Congress Prize in 1946. She worked until she was so frail that she was forced to enter a nursing home with her sister. In her studio she left behind an unfinished woodcut with a poignant note attached explaining that she was physically unable to complete it. Dorothy died at the nursing home in 1980 at the age of eighty-nine.

In 1986 Albany presented a retrospective art exhibit, "The Artists of the Mohawk Hudson Region," to coincide with the city's tricentennial celebration. Works by all three Lathrops — Dorothy, Gertrude, and Ida — were included.

Dorothy's writing is from The Junior Book of Authors, *edited by Stanley J. Kunitz and Howard Haycraft and published in 1934 by the H. W. Wilson Company.*

Women's Words, Women's Stories

Isabel Chapin Barrows

1908

Surgery was the most attractive part of the work to me, but I did not enjoy the "spitballs" which the dignified medical students of Bellevue used to fling at us. The professor laughed at their insults to us, for he had a sneaking desire to do the same, not approving of petti-coats coming to his clinics, as he frankly said. . . . This was long before the day of trained nurses and I wonder now that anyone ever recovered at Bellevue.

*T*aking insults

Katharine Isabel Hayes Chapin Barrows was born April 17, 1845, in Irasburg, Vermont. She graduated from the Adams Academy in Derry, New Hampshire, where she had earned her tuition by making the classroom fires, sweeping, and ring-ing the morning bell. When she was eighteen she married William W. Chapin, a Congregational minister. A few weeks after the ceremony, she stepped on board the *Sydenham*, clutching her beloved cat, to begin the five-month journey to Bombay.

Although the Chapins had planned to do missionary work in India for ten years, William soon succumbed to diphtheria, leaving Isabel a nineteen-year-old widow. She stayed on alone for six months, then returned to the United States to study medicine, so that she could return to India as a medical missionary.

Isabel studied hydropathy under Dr. J. Caleb Jackson and fell in love with a patient, Samuel J. Barrows. Sam and Isabel were married in 1867, and it was decided he would support her while she pursued her medical degree, after which she would support him while he attended Harvard Divinity School to become a Unitarian minister. Isabel attended the Woman's Medical College of the New York Infirmary for Women and Children and spent a year abroad at the University of Vienna, specializing in ophthalmology. Meanwhile, Sam had taken a job in Washington, D.C., as stenographic secretary to Secretary of State William H. Seward. Upon her return to America, Isabel opened a private practice in the capital and taught diseases of the eye at Howard University's School of Medicine. When her husband became ill, Isabel stepped into his position with Seward and thus became the first woman stenographic reporter in Congress, the first woman ever employed by the State Department, and possibly the only female State Department employee to receive the same salary as a man.

Isabel's writing is from "Chopped Straw or the Memories of Threescore Years," a typescript autobiography, 1908, courtesy of William Burnet Barrows, Burnet M. Davis, and June Barrows Mussey.

In 1871 it was Sam's turn to begin his studies, and he left for Harvard. Isabel remained in Washington, doing stenography in addition to her medical practice until shortly before the birth of her daughter in 1873. Upon graduation, Sam served as a minister for four years, after which he resigned to become the editor of the Unitarian weekly, the *Christian Register*. Isabel gave up her medical practice in 1885 and spent most of her days at the *Register* office, serving as unofficial assistant editor. In later years, Sam and Isabel became interested in prison reform and travelled in Europe as delegates of the International Prison Congress.

After Sam's death in 1909, Isabel spent the remainder of her life as a leader in prison reform. She died in 1913 at her daughter's home in Croton-on-Hudson, New York.

APRIL 18

Angna Enters

*A*ffirmation

Angna's writing is from her book Artist's Life, published in 1958 by Coward-McCann, Inc.

1958

Socrates said: "The woods and fields teach me nothing; I get my instructions from men." I am not quite so certain about the woods and fields, but my travels through the nations of men and women have been an endless source of instruction. . . .

Travel for me is a kind of search for something I am not seeking, but something which when I find it, seems to have been within me all the time. Except when I am on specific projects, I do not travel in search of material. In my travels I visit a museum as a spectator. Only interpretive artists who are readily "inspired" can hope to find material this way. I travel, visit museums, for the same reason most people do: to see in the arts and in the life of the world a constant affirmation of the creative spirit of man.

Angna Enters was born April 18, 1897, in Milwaukee, Wisconsin. In 1919 she moved to New York City to study at the Art Students' League. She also began dancing lessons with the Japanese dancer Michio Ito, concentrating on eurythmics and traditional Japanese geisha dancing. Two years later, she became Ito's professional dancing partner.

In 1923 Angna left Ito to tour the United States and Europe with her solo dance program. Entitled "The Theatre of Angna Enters," her repertoire consisted of more than 250 dance-mime compositions. She selected and arranged her own music and designed her own costumes.

In addition to her talent as a dancer, Angna had many other artistic gifts. She published numerous magazine articles, several autobiographies and plays, and co-wrote a novel. Beginning in 1933, she exhibited her drawings and paintings in New York City. She held one-woman shows in the United States, Canada, and Europe, and several of her works hang in the Museum of Modern Art and the Metropolitan Museum of Art.

Angna received a Guggenheim Foundation Fellowship in 1934 and went to Greece to study ancient mime. The following year she was awarded another fellowship, which took her to Egypt and the Near East to study dance. Upon her return she married Louis Kalonyme, the art critic for *Art & Decoration Magazine.*

Beginning in 1940, Angna was employed as a script writer for Metro Goldwyn Mayer. She worked in Hollywood until 1952, when she left to take part in an artist-in-residence program at Baylor University. She subsequently taught at Wesleyan University and Pennsylvania State University. Following her husband's death in 1961, she retired from her grueling touring schedule. She entered a New Jersey nursing home in 1974 and died there in 1989 at the age of ninety-one.

Mary Louise Booth

1875

Do you think women fitted for journalism?

Eminently so; especially in those departments of newspaper discussion which pertain to the family and to the needs of their own sex. Their acute and subtle intuition, and habits of keen observation, readiness of thought, and refined taste, fit them to succeed both as contributors and editors. They know instinctively how to choose what is readable, and to eschew what is tedious to the comfort of their readers. . . .

There are few journals that would not be more interesting for the aid of the feminine mind.

*W*omen journalists

Mary Louise Booth was born April 19, 1831, in Millville, Long Island, New York. In 1844 the family moved to Brooklyn when her father was appointed principal of the Third District School. Mary attended local public schools but was primarily self-taught, particularly in foreign

Mary's writing is from an interview that was included in Views and Interviews on Journalism, *edited by Charles F. Wingate and published in 1875.*

languages, for which she had a remarkable natural aptitude. Her father believed teaching was the only suitable occupation for a woman, so she began teaching at his school when she was only fifteen. She soon rebelled and, desiring a literary career, moved to Manhattan at eighteen to be closer to libraries and newspapers.

For several years, Mary supported herself as a vest maker while studying and writing at night. Eventually she was hired by *The New York Times* as a piece-rate reporter. In 1856 she began her career as a translator, translating more than forty works from French to English during her lifetime. During the Civil War she used her skills to promote the Union cause. She convinced Charles Scribner to let her translate Count de Gasparin's *The Uprising of a Great People: The United States in 1861*. Fearful the war would end before the work could be published, he set a one-week deadline, which Mary met by working twenty hours a day. From 1862 to 1863 she translated four other pro-Union French works, for which she was personally thanked by President Lincoln and Senator Charles Sumner.

In 1867 Harper and Brothers began the weekly magazine *Harper's Bazaar* and hired Mary as its editor. She served in that position until her death twenty-two years later, earning the then-impressive annual salary of $4,000. She was a natural editor with the ability to learn what the public wanted. During her tenure, circulation reached 80,000.

Mary never married, although she was engaged briefly in 1887 while on a trip to Venice. She died unexpectedly of heart disease two years later at the age of fifty-seven.

Caresse Crosby

Cashing in

Caresse's writing about the backless bra she invented is from her autobiography, The Passionate Years, *published by Ecco Press in 1953.*

1953

It wasn't until after I was Mrs. Peabody that I ran into Johnny Field, a famous Yale quarterback, 1913, and a former admirer of mine, and when I asked him what he was doing, he said slyly that he was making "jewel cases." By further inquisitiveness I learned that he worked for Warner Brothers Corset Company in Bridgeport. I told him of my invention and he was so interested that I made an appointment to travel to Bridgeport the following week to show his boss my samples. The long and short of it was that when I produced the Backless Brassière and the patent, the company at once offered fifteen hundred dollars for

Women's Words, Women's Stories

both. To me this seemed not only adequate, but magnificent. I signed on the line and went home in opulence.

Mary Phelps (Polly) Jacob Crosby was born April 20, 1892, in New York City. She met her first husband, Richard Rogers Peabody, when she was fourteen years old. He asked her to marry him in seven years, after his graduation from Harvard, and she said yes.

One evening, while dressing for a debutante ball, Polly became annoyed with her cumbersome, painfully binding corset. She asked her maid to bring her two pocket handkerchiefs, some pink ribbon, and a needle and thread. She stitched together her new, lightweight, yet binding corset and named it the "Backless Brassière." She attributed her talent for invention to the fact that she was descended from Robert Fulton, the inventor of the steamboat, and was quoted as saying, "I can't say that the brassière will ever take as great a place in history as the steamboat, but I did invent it." She obtained a patent and hired two seamstresses to produce them, but had little success until she sold her patent to Warner Brothers Corset Company.

Polly married Dick Peabody in January 1915 and had a son and a daughter. She lived in luxury with her in-laws while he fought in World War I. Upon his return, he was despondent and became an alcoholic. In the spring of 1919 Polly met Harry Crosby as she was leaving her bank. He was twenty-one, dashing in his army uniform, and she was a married woman of twenty-seven. She fell instantly in love, and, in what was a major scandal of the day, soon divorced Dick and ran off to Europe with Harry and her children.

Harry and Polly were married in 1921 and settled in Paris, where they socialized with artists and writers and dabbled at writing poetry. She decided her name was unpoetic and changed it to Caresse.

The Crosbys travelled extensively, always attracting a group of admiring friends. Their life together suddenly came to an end when Harry killed himself in December 1929 in a sensational suicide pact with his lover.

Caresse returned to America in 1935 to marry Bert Young, a dashing young man she had met in Hollywood. They purchased and renovated a run-down estate in Virginia, turning it into a refuge for artists and writers.

Caresse opposed World War II and founded Women Against War to further worldwide peace. She bought a castle in Italy, "Castello de Roccasinibalda," in 1959 to provide a home for pacifists. She died there in 1970.

Abigail Williams May

Fortunate to have a house

1893

Next winter I am to take the housekeeping cares. I have long thought perhaps I ought to do this; but it has not been quite clear that it would be best, and mother has not cared about it. But now it is clear. She is much broken, and everything is an anxiety to her. So I mean to close up some of my outside work, and be more at and do more for home. I do not love household cares. I do not love to be shut up in the house. But, while I am fortunate enough to have one, I ought to be, and believe I am, willing to make some small sacrifice for it.

Abigail Williams May was born April 21, 1829, in Boston. She was educated at private schools in the area. During her childhood she was influenced by her cousins, the noted abolitionist Reverend Samuel May, and Abba May Alcott, mother of Louisa May Alcott. They encouraged her to prepare for a life of charitable service to those less fortunate.

In 1856 Abby joined Boston's Provident Society and taught sewing to "young waifs from the street." During the Civil War she carried on relief work under the auspices of the United States Sanitary Commission. At one point she went to Virginia to travel on board a hospital transport ship so that she could better understand the soldiers' supply needs. After the war she turned her attention to the needs of the freedmen. She joined the New England Freedmen's Aid Society and became a trustee of the Tuskegee Institute.

Abby co-founded the New England Women's Club in 1868. The club's first major campaign was to secure representation for women on the Boston School Committee. Abby and three other women were elected to the committee in 1873 but were refused admission due to their sex. Through the efforts of Abby and other club members, a special act of the legislature was passed permitting women to serve, and Abby took her seat in 1874. As a result of this success, Abby was appointed to the State Board of Education. After her death, the board named a building in her honor at the Framingham State Normal School.

Over the years Abby volunteered much of her time and donated large sums of money to the Massachusetts School Suffrage Association, the Massachusetts Society for the University Education of Women, and the Association for the Advancement of Women. She never stopped believing in the power of the individual to improve social conditions. Abby died in Boston in 1888.

Abigail's letter to her eight-year-old niece is in the Abigail Williams May Collection, Schlesinger Library, Radcliffe College, Cambridge, Massachusetts.

Women's Words, Women's Stories

Ellen Glasgow

*circa
1940*

In the end, as in the beginning, Mr. Collier gave me no encouragement.

"The best advice I can give you," he said, with charming candor, "is to stop writing, and go back to the South and have some babies." And I think, though I may have heard this ripe wisdom from other men, probably from many, that he added: "The greatest woman is not the woman who has written the finest book, but the woman who has had the finest babies." That might be true. I did not stay to dispute it. However, it was true also that I wanted to write books, and not ever had I felt the faintest wish to have babies. Other women might have all they wanted, and I shouldn't object. But I was not made that way, and I did not see why I should pretend to be what I wasn't, or to feel what I couldn't. At that age I suspected, and later I discovered, that the maternal instinct, sacred or profane, was left out of me by nature when I was designed. I sometimes think that a hollow where it might have been was filled by the sense of compassion; but even of this, I am not entirely sure. All I know is that, at any time in my life, it would have seemed to me an irretrievable wrong to bring another being into a world where I had suffered so many indignities of the spirit. After my deafness, this became a moral conviction.

Ellen Anderson Gholson Glasgow was born the eighth of ten children on April 22, 1873, in Richmond, Virginia. She worshipped her mother but rejected her stern father and his Calvinist beliefs. She was a sickly child, shy and prone to headaches, which prohibited her from attending school. During adolescence she began to lose her hearing, which further isolated her and sent her into periodic depressions.

Ellen began writing short stories and poetry at seven and "prayed to become a writer." She completed her first novel at seventeen but destroyed it following a rejection by a New York literary agent. She wrote another novel the following year but destroyed it also when her mother died in 1893.

Why pretend?

Ellen's writing is from her autobiography, The Woman Within, *published by Harcourt, Brace and Company in 1954.*

At last Ellen's first novel was published, anonymously, in 1897. Most of her writing was set in Richmond and described the New South in realistic detail. Ellen fell in love with a married man who died in 1905, her favorite brother committed suicide in 1909, and her favorite sister died in 1911. Unwilling to remain at home alone with her father, Ellen moved to New York until his death in 1916 when she returned to Richmond.

After returning to Virginia, Ellen became engaged to Henry Watkins Anderson. As a result of their first quarrel in 1918 Ellen tried to commit suicide; however, the following year, she and Henry collaborated on a novel. Although they never married, the two remained friends for the next twenty-one years. Ellen helped found the Richmond Society for the Prevention of Cruelty to Animals and served as its president for many years.

In her later years, Ellen received numerous awards and honorary degrees, including the Southern Authors Award and the 1942 Pulitzer Prize for *In This Our Life*. Frequently bedridden for months at a time following a heart attack in 1939, Ellen continued to produce novels while working on her "spiritual" autobiography to be published posthumously. She died at home in 1945 at the age of seventy-two and was buried in Richmond's Hollywood Cemetery.

APRIL 23

Pauline Morton Sabin

Single-issue thinkers

1928

It is interesting to note that those who favor prohibition put that issue ahead of all others. I find this particularly true among women. In almost every instance the woman who is a so-called "dry" judges a candidate entirely upon his stand on that one issue; she will support a man who is so-called "dry" without even taking enough interest to question his stand on other matters, such as National defense, immigration, tariff, and taxation, all of which are of vital importance to our country. She has what some of us call a "one-plank mind."

Pauline's writing is from "I Change My Mind on Prohibition," Outlook, June 13, 1928.

Pauline Morton Sabin was born April 23, 1887, in Chicago. She came from a long line of wealthy, influential citizens, and as a child she inherited millions of dollars from her uncle, the founder of Morton Salt.

Two months shy of her twentieth birthday, Pauline

Women's Words, Women's Stories

married James Hopkins Smith, Jr., and they had two sons. However, the marriage was not a happy one. When he went overseas to fight in World War I, she divorced him and opened an interior decorating business. In 1916 she married Charles H. Sabin, president of Guaranty Trust Company, and settled on an estate in Southampton, New York.

Pauline closed her decorating business to become active in politics. She co-founded the Women's National Republican Club and served as its president from 1921 to 1926. She became New York's first female representative to the Republican National Committee when that organization admitted women in 1924. She constantly encouraged other women to become more involved in politics.

Although Pauline was initially in favor of Prohibition, by 1926 she had reversed her stand and campaigned to have the Eighteenth Amendment repealed. She had come to believe that Prohibition was corrupting elected officials and that children were growing up "with a total lack of respect for the Constitution and for the law." She resigned from the Republican National Committee in March 1929 and formed the Women's Organization for National Prohibition Reform (WONPR). By 1930 she had 100,000 members, and by 1933 there were a million and a half members, three times the membership in the Woman's Christian Temperance Union.

As WONPR's national chairwoman, Pauline testified before Congress, lobbied both parties to secure repeal of the law, and made the cover of *Time* magazine. WONPR was dissolved when the repeal amendment was ratified in December 1933. Pauline had lost her husband in October 1933, and three years later she married Dwight F. Davis, donor of the International Tennis Cup.

Pauline and her new husband resided in Washington, D.C., where she was active in society functions and the American Red Cross. She was a consultant to the Truman administration in its redecoration of the White House. She died in Washington in 1955 at the age of sixty-eight.

Annis Ford Eastman

1884

Into the shadow

Our little story enters here into the shadow from which it will never emerge. Morgan — the blessed, the beautiful, the chosen one, is gone. The child of rarest promise, his mother's chief joy, a boy in whom was no guile, the one upon whom we always looked with perfect satisfaction, who seemed the spiritual prop of the family, how can we walk on through the days that remain without him?

Annis Bertha Ford Eastman was born April 24, 1852, in Peoria, Illinois. Her father's alcoholism and fits of rage created an unhappy home life. Her parents finally separated when the five daughters were teenagers. Following graduation from Peoria High School Annis took the two-year preparatory course at Oberlin College so that she could begin her career as a teacher. While at Oberlin, she fell in love with Samuel Elijah Eastman, a student at the Oberlin Theological Seminary. They were married in August 1875 after he had been ordained as a minister and received his first pastorate at the Congregational church in Swampscott, Massachusetts.

During the early years of their marriage, the Eastmans moved frequently, from Massachusetts to Kentucky to New York. Annis suffered from bouts of depression, and her husband was unable to offer comfort. They had three sons and one daughter, and the death of her eldest son at the age of seven compounded Annis's melancholia.

Samuel's health declined from the stress of his marriage combined with an injury from the Civil War. In 1886 he collapsed and resigned temporarily from the ministry. Within a year, Annis had stepped into her husband's former role and began preaching regularly at the parish church in Brookton, New York. Although she had no formal theological training, she was ordained a Congregational minister in November 1889 at the age of thirty-seven.

In 1893 Annis was asked to address the World's Parliament of Religions at the Chicago World's Fair. The following year, she and her husband moved to Elmira, New York, where they were invited to be assistant pastors at the Reverend Thomas K. Beecher's Park Church. Annis befriended Mark Twain and his wife, who were members of Beecher's congregation. After Mark Twain's death, the family asked Annis to deliver his funeral oration.

In 1903 Annis began attending the Harvard Summer School. Her studies in philosophy made her doubt her religion. In 1907 she changed the Park Church, where she and Samuel had become joint pastors after the death of Reverend Beecher, from Congregational to Unitarian with the consent of the parishioners. However, her involvement with the women's suffrage movement deepened Annis's religious doubts, and she began Freudian analysis in her quest for understanding and inner calm. During the summer of 1910, she finally decided to leave Park Church. She died of a cerebral hemorrhage three months later in October 1910 and was buried in Elmira.

Annis's September 30, 1884, memorial to her seven-year-old son Morgan, who had recently died of scarlet fever, is in the Crystal Eastman Collection, Schlesinger Library, Radcliffe College, Cambridge, Massachusetts.

Margaret Alsip Frink

August 20, 1850

The emigrants are a woe-begone, sorry looking crowd. The men with long hair and matted beards in soiled and ragged clothes, covered with alkali dust, have a half savage appearance. There are but few women; among these thousands of men, we have not seen more than ten or twelve.

The horses, cattle and mules are getting gaunt, thin and weak, almost ready to drop in their tracks, as hundreds of them have already done. . . . The once clean, white wagon tops are soiled and tattered, and grimy with two thousand miles of gray dust. . . . The spokes of the wagons left behind have been cut out to make pack-saddles. The rickety wheels are often braced up with sticks, the hubs wound with wet rags to keep the spokes in, the tires bound with wire, or wedged with chips of wood, to hold them from dropping off. They go creaking along the dusty roads, seeming ready to fall to pieces, drawn by weary beasts hardly able to travel, making up a beggardly-looking caravan, such as never was seen before. The great, splendid trains of fifteen, twenty, or thirty wagons have shrunk to three, four, or at most half a dozen, with three-fourths of their animals missing. . . .

One only hope sustains all these unhappy pilgrims, that they will be able to get into California alive, where they can take a rest, and where the gold which they feel sure of finding will repay them for all their hardships and suffering.

Margaret Ann Alsip Frink was born April 25, 1818, in Frederick City, Maryland. At twenty-one she married Ledyard Frink and settled in Martinsville, Indiana. They lived in the Midwest for ten years until tales of California and the gold to be found there sparked their desire to move west.

The Frinks prepared to depart via the overland route, accompanied by their ward, an eleven-year-old boy, and a neighbor's teenage son.

On March 27, 1850, their journey began. Margaret commenced a diary in which she wrote every day of her five-and-a-half months on the road to California. They travelled alone

Margaret's writing is from her journal, first published in 1897. It was reprinted in Covered Wagon Women, Volume II, *edited and compiled by Kenneth L. Holmes and published by the Arthur H. Clark Company, Glendale, California, 1983.*

or in small groups as far as Saint Joseph, Missouri. There they rented a house for two weeks while they waited for the prairie grass in Kansas and Nebraska to grow enough to feed their horses.

After travelling 2,418 miles of "oppressive heat and intolerable dust," they reached Sacramento. Within one week Margaret met with local ministers to discuss the building of a Baptist church. She and her husband opened a small hotel. Ledyard kept cows, and they gave free milk to their guests, the only hotel to do so and a great treat to those who hadn't tasted milk in one or two years. In October 1851 they bought two adjoining lots and set up a house. They believed California to be "full of promise," and they remained in Sacramento for the rest of their lives. Four years after Margaret's death in 1893, Ledyard published her diary, "owing to the many requests made by relatives and friends for a history of our journey across the plains to California."

APRIL 26   *Alice Cary*

*F*allen fortunes

1852
— it is now twelve or thirteen years since Mr. Harmstead first came to our neighborhood — I remember well the first time I ever saw him. We were coming from school, Rebecca and I, and barefooted rustics we were, when he overtook us, and, adopting what he supposed to be western manners, I suspect, began talking with us: first of our master, then of the village, its scenery, and the character of the people about us. I had never seen any one before who was so well bred, so refined, so gentlmanly as he; and I remember well how mortified I was for our bare feet, and our rustic appearance altogether. Even what I knew, I could not say half so well as though I had been talking with Mr. Hill or Uncle Dale, whom I had always known. In short, my idea of perfection was realized, when I saw him. . . .

Sometimes we saw Mrs. Harmstead, a pale delicate looking woman, but she never smiled or seemed to notice us in any way. She was rather a pretty woman, but in declining health, when I first knew her, or rather when first I saw her. Her dress was of some dark material; and as she walked about the yard and garden,

Alice's writing is from her collection of short stories, Clovernook — or Recollections of Our Neighborhood in the West, *published by Redfield Clinton Hall in 1852.*

she was always enveloped in a crimson shawl. She had been, as rumor said, an heiress, yet through failure of some speculations her husband had lost not only his own estate but the greater part of hers; and their removal to our neighborhood had been in consequence of fallen fortunes, as the loss of wealth involved also the loss of position in their native city.

Alice Cary was born April 26, 1820, in Hamilton County, Ohio, the fourth of nine children. Her education consisted of irregular attendance at the local school and reading and re-reading the six books her family possessed, which included the Bible, tales of Lewis and Clark's travels, and the essays of Alexander Pope.

Alice's mother and two of her sisters died of tuberculosis when she was fifteen. Her father remarried two years later, but the children disliked their stepmother so vehemently that Mr. Cary built a new farmhouse on their property, leaving the old house to Alice and her siblings. She was especially close to her younger sister Phoebe (September 4), who shared her interest in reading and writing.

Phoebe's first poem was published in the Cincinnati newspaper when she was fourteen. Almost simultaneously, Alice's first poem was published in a Cincinnati Universalist Church paper. Their careers were launched, and their work received praise from other well-known poets such as John Greenleaf Whittier and Edgar Allen Poe. In 1850 they were paid $100 for their first volume of collected poems.

After suffering rejection from a man she wished to marry in Ohio, Alice decided to move to New York City in November 1850. Phoebe joined her within six months. Together they earned enough from their writing to purchase a house on Twentieth Street. Their home became a gathering place for writers and other creative people, and for fifteen years they hosted well-attended Sunday evening receptions.

Alice's first book of short stories, about rural life in Ohio, became a best seller. She followed it with two more volumes of short stories, three novels, and five volumes of poetry. She spent her last years as an invalid and died of tuberculosis in 1870. Her sister Phoebe, who had devoted herself to taking care of Alice during her illness, died six months later.

Jessie Redmon Fauset

Living absolutely

Jessie's writing is from a February 16, 1905, letter to W. E. B. DuBois, editor of The Crisis, *the influential journal of the National Association for the Advancement of Colored People. It is included in* The Correspondence of W. E. B. DuBois, *edited by Herbert Aptheker, University of Massachusetts Press, 1973.*

1905

I saw your article "Credo" sometime ago in either the *Outlook* or the *Independent* — I have forgotten which. At that time I meant to write you to tell you how glad I was to realise that that was your belief, and to ask you if you did not believe it to be worthwhile to teach our colored men and woman *race* pride, *self*-pride, self-sufficiency (the right kind) and the necessity of living our lives as nearly as possible, *absolutely*, instead of comparing them always with white standards. Don't you believe that we should lead them to understand the reason we adopt such and such criteria which are also adopted by the Anglo Saxon, is because these criteria are the *best*, and not essentially because they are white?

Jessie Redmon Fauset was born April 27, 1882, in Fredericksville, New Jersey. Her father was a minister in the African Methodist Episcopal Church. After Jessie's mother died when she was a toddler, her father remarried, and they relocated to Pennsylvania. Jessie graduated with honors as the only black pupil at the Philadelphia High School for Girls. Despite her academic success, she was denied admission to a local teacher's college. Her father intervened, and she was eventually accepted at Cornell University, where she became the first black woman elected to Phi Beta Kappa.

After being refused a teaching position in Philadelphia because of her race, she moved to Washington, D.C., to begin teaching French and Latin at the M Street High School. She remained there for the next fourteen years and was widely respected as an inspirational teacher. One of her students later recalled that she was the first person he had heard use the word "ubiquitous" in conversation.

In 1912 Jessie began contributing book reviews and articles to W. E. B. Du Bois's magazine *The Crisis*. From 1919 to 1926 she served as the journal's literary editor and was responsible for showcasing many of the writers in the Harlem Renaissance. She chose the poetry and fiction for the magazine and served as a mentor to the authors, prompting black novelist and poet Langston Hughes to comment that she had "midwifed the so-called New Negro literature into being."

Jessie wrote her first novel in the early 1920s because of her dissatisfaction with the inaccurate portrayals of blacks in fiction. She wrote about the hopes, dreams, and daily existence of middle-class blacks who encountered prejudice but did not let it defeat them.

In 1927 Jessie resumed teaching French at the DeWitt Clinton High School in New York City. Two years later, at the age of forty-seven, she married Herbert Harris, an insurance salesman. They were separated from 1931 to 1932, when he was named a correspondent in a divorce suit, but she eventually took him back. They stayed together until his death in 1958.

Jessie and Herbert lived for many years with her sister Helen in an apartment on Seventh Avenue in Harlem. After her sister's death in 1936, Jessie established a memorial to her, the "Helen Lanning Corner," in the library at the school on West 127th Street where she had taught. Jessie set it up to "contain books only about colored people, especially colored children." Eventually she expanded the memorial to ten other libraries throughout the United States.

Jessie died at her brother's home in Philadelphia in 1961 at the age of seventy-nine.

Bernie Babcock

1911

Dollie had said with a strange light in her sad, big eyes, "Forget yourself! Strangle your conscience! If your soul stirs, drown it with whisky! If you think of your mother, drink whisky! When you catch the infection drink whisky. When disease is eating you up, drink whisky! When life is one long death, load up on morphine! Take enough so they can't pump it out and a slab Morgue will be your Heaven!"

Bernie Smade Babcock was born April 28, 1868, in Unionville, Ohio. Her family relocated to Russellville, Arkansas, where she attended public schools. After graduating from Little Rock University, she married William Franklin Babcock, a railroad auditor, in 1886. They had three daughters and two sons.

William died in 1898, leaving Bernie with five young children to support. She felt it was her "blessed duty" to stay home and mold the characters of her children. "She mixed the gingerbread with her hands while mixing the grueling fictional characters with her mind"; then in the evening, as her babies slept, she wrote.

*W*here whiskey leads

Bernie's writing is from With Claw and Fang: A Fact Story in a Chicago Setting, *published in 1911 by Clean Politics Publishing Company.*

Bernie published her first novel when she was thirty-two, two years after her husband's death. It sold more than 100,000 copies in six months. During her thirty-year career as an author, she published twenty-five novels and one book of poetry. Her most popular novel was the love story of Abraham Lincoln, *The Soul of Ann Rutledge*. It ran into fourteen editions with a first reprint of 10,000 copies. For children she wrote *Little Abe Lincoln*, which was listed among the 100 best books for school libraries. Her books based on the life of Lincoln brought her the French medal, Arts et Belles Lettres.

Bernie was active in Arkansas charities that helped the poor and especially in the Woman's Christian Temperance Union. She wrote gripping morality stories, such as *With Claw and Fang: A Fact Story in a Chicago Setting*, that portrayed the wretchedness awaiting those who drank.

Her strong faith and belief in life after death led Bernie to study psychic phenomena, especially the fourth dimension and sixth sense. She hoped to find scientific proof of immortality.

She died at her home on Petit Jean Mountain, Arkansas, in 1962 when she was ninety-four.

Margherita Arlina Hamm

Suicide for money

1895

Some years ago General Liu Ming Shan, then Governor of Formosa, started a railway. It was a source of wonder and delight to the people, who patronized it liberally and crowded the road in every town and village to watch the trains go by. In due course of time the news got abroad that the wonderful iron horse was as common as ordinary equine quadrupeds among the "foreign devils," and that the law of railroads required them to pay heavy damages to the family of any one they ran over. Shortly after that an old man was killed on the track, and then an old woman was seen to throw herself under the wheels of the train. The families promptly demanded indemnity for the loss, and received, say, two hundred dollars from the authorities, accordingly. People kept on being run over until the railroad officials became tired. They made an investigation and found that in every case the victims had discussed the matter with his or

Margherita's writing is from "The Mongol Triad," Overland Monthly, February 1895.

her household, and had agreed to offer up life beneath the wheels so that the kindred could obtain damages from the road.

The grievance was reported to the Governor, who immediately published a new law. It made loitering or being near a railway with suicidal intent a capital offense and prohibited any indemnity for a death under such circumstances.

Margherita Arlina Hamm was born April 29, 1867, in St. Stephen, New Brunswick, Canada. The family moved to Bangor, Maine, when she was a child. In the late 1880s Margherita took her first job as a reporter for the *Boston Herald*. In 1890 she moved to New York City and continued to freelance for several of the city's daily papers.

Margherita married William E. S. Fales, a lawyer and vice-consul to Amoy, China, in 1893. They travelled extensively throughout Japan, Korea, and China and were trapped in Korea during the Sino-Japanese War in 1894. Margherita sent articles home on the attempted assassination of the Queen of Korea and attacks on the palace. Upon her return to the United States she lectured on her experiences and continued to publish articles on the Orient.

Margherita held positions with various magazines and New York newspapers. In 1898 she went to cover the civil war in Cuba and head the nursing staff of the women's auxiliary of the National Guard. The president of Cuba presented her with a medal for her efforts. She also covered Edward VII's coronation in England in 1901.

Margherita married fellow journalist John Robert McMahon in 1902, two days after her divorce from William Fales became final. They had one daughter. Five years later she died of pneumonia at the age of forty.

Louise Beatty Homer

1910

*O*pera's tongues

I am for English opera unequivocally, but I am not for doing away with opera in the tongues in which the music was composed. That would be a great step backward. True, on the continent of Europe most operas are translated and sung in the vernacular. But we are too big for that. Our Metropolitan Opera House is easily first in its cosmopolitanism. For one thing, we

should lose the privilege of hearing some great singers. Foreigners do not find it easy to sing in English. Americans are much better linguists. Yet even many of them fail to achieve the pronunciation that the French, German and Italian public demands.

The demand for opera in the vernacular comes from the public, which insists that it shall understand the text as well as hear the music. Do you think it would be content to listen to broken English, improperly phrased?

Louise Dilworth Beatty Homer was born April 30, 1871, in Shadyside, Pennsylvania. As a child she sang in the church choir, and at fourteen she made her public debut singing in a cantata. After her father's death, she wanted to contribute to her family's income and took up stenography. She worked as a school secretary and court stenographer, taking singing lessons on the side.

In 1893 Louise moved to Boston to study voice seriously with several teachers. Her theory and harmony teacher, the composer Sidney Homer, took her to her first opera, which changed her life. They were married in January 1895 and left the following year for further study in Paris.

Louise obtained her first singing contract in 1898 for the summer opera season at Vichy. For the next two years, she was steadily engaged at opera houses in Paris, London, and Brussels. In 1900 the manager of the Metropolitan Opera in New York gave her a three-year contract, and she returned to America.

From 1900 to 1919 Louise was a principal force at the Metropolitan, singing all the major contralto parts. She sang opposite Enrico Caruso and Arturo Toscanini on the nights of their debuts, and presented *Madame Butterfly* to American audiences for the first time while Italian opera composer Giacomo Puccini listened from the house. During this time she also recorded for the Victor Company and had numerous hit records, not only with opera but with her husband's songs and hymns.

Louise sang with the Chicago Opera Company from 1922 to 1926, then returned to the Metropolitan in 1927. Although her voice was still in fine form, she retired in 1929 to be with her ailing husband. Despite her long and busy career, she had always maintained a happy home life and had raised six children. She received honorary degrees from Smith, Tufts, Russell Sage, Middlebury, and Ohio's Miami University, and in 1923 was named one of the twelve greatest living American women in a League of Women Voters poll. After her retirement, she and her husband spent half the year in Lake George, New York, and the other half in Winter

Louise's writing is from "English Opera at Stake, Says Louise Homer, at Friday Night's Trial at the Metropolitan," an interview with Sylvester Rawling in The Evening World, *March 12, 1910.*

Women's Words, Women's Stories

Park, Florida, where they worked with young musicians at Rollins College. The death of her youngest daughter dealt Louise a blow from which she could not recover, and she died six months later in May 1947.

MAY

Cecilia Beaux

1930

Strange is the existence in which there is no memory of
a mother; no vestige of even a momentary, vague,
child-impression. This was my fate, and, although it
was so, there has been no stronger reality in my life
than the reality of my mother's person and influence....

Sometimes chests were opened, and cloaks, dresses
she had chosen and worn were taken out and refolded.
There was an exquisite fan or two; a bit of frilled ribbon, and, above all, the square white box edged prettily
with gold, in which lay her wedding veil and the
wreath, the narrow satin slippers, and a pair of short
white kid gloves, with lace at the wrists.

The glamour and awe which lay about these relics
was one of the great emotions of my childhood. Their
elegance was to me a positive possession, a sort of
patent of nobility, I would not have parted with for the
most longed-for and special personal adornment of my
own.

I was proud, too, of not being thought worthy to be
called in any ordinary way by her name; that name
which was pronounced by the last breath upon her
dying lips, as the name to be given to me, the newly
born she hardly knew herself.

After two years these names were formally given to
me in baptism, and I walked up a long aisle between my
grandmother and my father, to receive them; but my
father could not endure to hear her child called by his
wife's name for years, after her death, and I was always
called "Leslie."

Cecilia Beaux was born May 1, 1855, in Philadelphia.
Following her mother's death when she was twelve days old,
Cecilia and her sister were raised by their grandmother and
two aunts. As a child, Cecilia showed promise as an artist and
was enrolled in drawing lessons.

At seventeen Cecilia began attending Dutch artist Adolf
Van der Whelen's Philadelphia Art School. After two years
of private instruction with the painter William Sartain, she
opened her own studio.

A mother's influence

*Cecilia's writing is from her
autobiography,* Background
With Figures, *published by
Houghton, Mifflin and
Company in 1930.*

Cecilia's first full-length portrait, a painting of her sister and nephew, was exhibited in 1885 at the Pennsylvania Academy of Fine Arts, where it received the Mary Smith Prize for "best painting by a resident woman artist." It was later accepted in Paris for showing at the Spring Salon.

Cecilia's fame as a portrait artist continued to grow. She received the Mary Smith Prize two more times, and in 1895 she was appointed the first female instructor at the Pennsylvania Academy of Fine Arts.

During World War I Cecilia painted portraits of all the European leaders: one of eight American artists commissioned by the National Art Committee to record prominent Allies. In her later years she received many honorary degrees and was twice named one of America's twelve greatest living women. She died in 1942 at her summer home, "Green Alley," in Gloucester, Massachusetts.

Hedda Hopper

An open door

1963

My sister Margaret was my father's pet. He and I didn't get on well. He thought women should be the workers; I believed my brothers should share the burden. Mother was ill for six years after Margaret's birth, and I took on her duties as well as my own, since my older sister Dora had married. I had to catch a brother by the scruff of the neck to get any help, but they all helped themselves three times a day to the meals I prepared. I also did the washing, ironing, cleaning and helped Dad in his butcher shop.

When I couldn't take any more, I ran away — to an uncle in New York. I found a stage door that was open, walked in, and got a job in a chorus, which started a career.

Hedda Hopper was born Elda Furry on May 2, 1885, in Holidaysburg, Pennsylvania. The family moved to Altoona, Pennsylvania, where her father owned a butcher shop, when she was three. After the shop went bankrupt, he ran away to Canada's Klondike region, leaving his sons and daughters to support the family by working and attempting to collect the debts owed to the butcher shop. Elda later recalled that she was "the fightingest fourteen-year-old bill collector in Altoona."

Hedda's writing is from her autobiography, The Whole Truth and Nothing But, *published in 1963 by Doubleday.*

Elda's feisty, independent spirit led her to quit school after the eighth grade and run off with a theatrical troupe. During a 1908 performance of the musical comedy *The Pied Piper*, at New York's Majestic Theatre, she met W. DeWolf Hopper, a small-time actor twenty-seven years her senior. In May 1913 she became his fifth wife.

In 1915 Elda gave birth to her only child, W. DeWolf, Jr. Soon after, the family departed for Hollywood, where she took her first film role for the Fox Company. In 1918 she changed her name to Hedda upon the advice of a numerologist. Hedda's movie career progressed, and by 1920 she was earning $1,000 a week. Meanwhile DeWolf's career was floundering, and he was engaged in numerous affairs. She finally divorced him in 1922 and signed a $250-a-week contract with Metro Goldwyn Mayer as security for raising her son. She made at least twelve movies a year for more than ten years and was called the "Queen of the Quickies."

In 1937 MGM executives were searching for a rival for gossip columnist Louella Parsons, and they selected the flamboyant Hedda. Her column, "Hedda Hopper's Hollywood," debuted in February 1938. As she knew nothing of grammar or spelling and did not care to learn, she dictated her column to her staff, who then prepared it for printing. She realized early what the public wanted, stating in her autobiography, "The minute I started to trot out the juicy stuff, my phone began to ring." Always dressed elegantly and wearing her trademark elaborate hat, she carried on a bitter feud with Louella Parsons as they tried to scoop each other for the latest gossip. Hedda used informants ranging from beauticians to morticians, milkmen to obstetricians, to produce her daily columns and radio broadcasts. Always conservative in her views, she lambasted those she felt were liberals or communist sympathizers and was able to make or break many a career. By 1942 she was a household word, and she bought a Beverly Hills mansion that she sarcastically referred to as "The House That Fear Built."

After Louella's retirement in 1964, Hedda reigned alone as Hollywood's gossip queen. In 1965 she was sued by British movie actor Michael Wilding for $3 million in a libel suit that was settled out of court. She died the following year at the age of eighty and was buried in Los Angeles.

Georgia Madden Martin

In praise of cabbage

1924

I was in my teens when I discovered that cabbage and its near of kin, cauliflower and Brussels sprouts, were recognized and reputable adjuncts to civilized man's gustatory pleasures. My father, who did not like them himself, did not so consider them. In his household, with its otherwise plentiful table, we never had them. What the man of the family sent home in that market basket each day, this his household — adults, servants, and minors — received, prepared, and ate.

Georgia May Madden Martin was born May 3, 1866, in Louisville, Kentucky. A sickly child, she was primarily tutored at home and at various Southern resorts where she was sent for her health.

Georgia married local Louisville businessman Attwood Reading Martin in June 1892. Soon after her marriage she joined the Author's Club, a group of ladies who met weekly to discuss and critique each other's writings. Georgia took George as her pen name and continued using it for the rest of her life. Her first story was published in *Harper's Weekly* in 1895, and her first novel followed two years later. She wrote a total of ten novels which were serialized in *McClure's, American Magazine*, and other popular periodicals of the time.

During World War I George wrote for the *Red Cross Magazine* and thereafter became less interested in fiction and turned her attention to social reform. Her liberal views regarding Negroes were very advanced for conservative Louisville. In 1919 she co-founded the Commission of Interracial Cooperation and served on its board for fourteen years. She tried but failed to have Negro history taught in Kentucky schools, and she was chairman of the Association of Southern Women for the Prevention of Lynching.

George died at home in 1946 at the age of eighty.

George's writing is from her article "American Women and Paternalism," published in the June 1924 Atlantic Monthly, *Volume I, Number 6.*

Hulda Minthorn Hoover

1865
W. Branch, Iowa

Dear Friend,

Last evening I received a very welcome letter and hasten to reply for I like prompt answers and wish to set a good example. I think by thy tell, your summer has been very different from ours for it has been very wet. I spent my summer and fall with sister Ann. I had a pleasant time through the summer, spent my time herding sheep on the prairie all alone several miles from home or sight of house or tree. . . .

Miranda I wish I could see thee and have a good long chat. This dreary day; it is raining and quite cold; the girls have all gone to meeting and Mother and I are here alone. . . .

Hulda Minthorn Hoover was born May 4, 1848, on a farm in Ontario, Canada. When she was eleven her father moved their large family of seven children to Iowa. They purchased the Lone Tree Farm near West Branch, a young Quaker settlement.

Hulda attended Iowa State University at Iowa City for several semesters before beginning her teaching career in West Branch. She married Jesse Clark Hoover when she was twenty-two, and they had two sons and a daughter. Her eldest son died in childhood but her second son, Herbert Clark Hoover, became the thirty-first president of the United States.

Hulda was ordained a minister of the Society of Friends in 1881 following the death of her husband. She sold the farm, placed the money in trust for her children, and became a travelling minister. However, her ministry was cut short by her untimely death in 1882 when she was thirty-four. Although Herbert was only eight when his mother passed away, she left a strong mark on his religious and secular education. He recalled having spent many days at the polls with her during early temperance crusades.

To a friend

Hulda's writing is from a letter to her childhood friend Miranda Stover in Canada. The original is in the Herbert Hoover Presidential Library Collection, West Branch, Iowa.

Elizabeth Cochrane Seaman (Nellie Bly)

Her idea

Nellie's writing is from Nellie Bly's Book: Around the World in Seventy-Two Days, *published in 1890 by the Pictorial Weeklies Company, New York, New York.*

1890

It was my custom to think up ideas on Sunday and lay them before my editor for his approval or disapproval on Monday. But ideas did not come that day and three o'clock in the morning found me weary and with an aching head tossing about in my bed. At last tired and provoked at my slowness in finding a subject, something for the week's work, I thought fretfully:

"I wish I was at the other end of the earth!"

"And why not?" the thought came: "I need a vacation; why not take a trip around the world?" . . . .

I approached my editor rather timidly on the subject. I was afraid that he would think the idea too wild and visionary.

"Have you any ideas?" he asked, as I sat down by his desk.

"One," I answered quietly.

He sat toying with his pens, waiting for me to continue, so I blurted out:

. . . "I want to go around in eighty days or less. I think I can beat Phileas Fogg's record. May I try it?"

To my dismay he told me that in the office they had thought of this same idea before, and the intention was to send a man. However he offered me the consolation that he would favor my going, and then we went to talk with the business manager about it.

"It is impossible for you to do it," was the terrible verdict. "In the first place you are a woman and would need a protector, and even if it were possible for you to travel alone you would need to carry so much baggage that it would detain you in making rapid changes. Besides you speak nothing but English, so there is no use talking about it; no one but a man can do this."

"Very well," I said angrily, "Start the man and I'll start the same day for some other newspaper and beat him."

"I believe you would," he said slowly.

I would not say that this had any influence on their decision, but I do know that before we parted I was made happy by the promise that if any one was commissioned to make the trip, I should be that one.

Elizabeth Cochrane Seaman (Nellie Bly) was born May 5, 1865, in Cochran's Mills, Pennsylvania. Elizabeth was educated at home with the exception of one year spent at boarding school.

In 1855 Elizabeth responded to an anti-suffrage editorial, "What Girls Are Good For," in the *Pittsburgh Dispatch*. The editor was so impressed with her writing talent that he hired her as a reporter. Elizabeth took the pen name Nellie Bly from the Stephen Foster song and began her adventures as a newspaperwoman.

Nellie Bly's most famous adventure occurred in 1889 when newspaper publisher Joseph Pulitzer sent her around the world by "train, steamer, ricksha and sampan" to challenge the fictional record in Jules Verne's *Around the World in Eighty Days*. The *World* published her exotic tales regularly, and upon her return (in seventy-two days) she was greeted by parades in her honor.

In 1895 Nellie met a wealthy New York businessman, Robert Seaman, while returning by train from an assignment in the Midwest. Although he was seventy-two and she only twenty-nine, they were married after a few days' courtship. They lived in New York City until his death in 1910. She died of bronchopneumonia in 1921 at the age of fifty-six and was buried beside her husband in New York's Woodlawn Cemetery.

Phebe Coffin Hanaford

1890

A new preacher

The death of a sister and brother, and other near relatives and friends, led me to examine more closely the foundations of the theological beliefs I had adopted. I read the Bible through from Genesis to Revelation, both included, carefully and prayerfully. . . . Finally, after long and conscientious struggle, I came out into the light and joy of liberal Christianity, I became a Universalist. That was the only liberal church in the town where I was then residing. Still I did not think of preaching, till, in 1886, being on a visit to my island

Phebe's writing is from her article "Twenty Years in the Pulpit," which appeared in the December 27, 1890, issue of The Woman's Journal.

birth-place, at the request of my father I prepared and delivered two sermons in the little school-house at Bisconset, where, when I was sixteen years of age, I had been the public school teacher. They were sermons right out of my own heart experiences. In the midst of sorrows and trials I had found consolation, and that comfort I strove to impart to others. My first audience was composed of my dearest relatives and others, many of whom had known me from a babe. The little school-room was crowded. It was summer time, and men stood outside leaning in at the open windows to hear my gospel message. Though tears were on many faces, yet I believe the sunlight of truth entered their souls. Twice I preached on that memorable Sunday, and then I did not intend to be a preacher when I began to preach. I was caring for my children still, and using my pen.

Phebe Ann Coffin Hanaford was born May 6, 1829, on Nantucket Island, Massachusetts. Her cousin, Lucretia Coffin Mott, a Quaker preacher, was an inspiration to her.

Phebe graduated from local schools and began her teaching career at sixteen. When she was twenty, she married Dr. Joseph Hibbard Hanaford, a homeopathic physician and teacher ten years her senior. They had two children. She commenced writing for publication, producing poems, prose, and children's stories for popular periodicals.

Over the years, Phebe had abandoned her Quaker faith for her husband's Baptist theology. The deaths of her brother and sister caused her to examine her beliefs further, and she joined the Universalist church. She began preaching in Nantucket at her father's request in 1865, and the following year she substituted for the Reverend Olympia Brown (January 5) at her church in Canton, Massachusetts. Phebe was ordained in 1868.

Phebe separated from her husband in 1870 and moved to New Haven, Connecticut, where she was minister of the First Universalist Church. She became active in the women's suffrage movement and in later years officiated at the funerals of her friends, Elizabeth Cady Stanton and Susan B. Anthony (February 15). She died at her granddaughter's home in Rochester, New York, at the age of ninety-two.

Harriet Starr Cannon

1891

I truly believe that as you surrender your whole being more perfectly and entirely to the Divine Will, so your vocation will become clearer to you and you will marvel at the hesitation and the holding back of the past. We may not look for perfect unity of opinion in a Community: there must be diversity; it is impossible that all should think alike on minor points, and even in graver matters there will be differences. On general principles there must be agreement. With a loving heart I say, my very dear Sister, come back to us, and with us "fight manfully unto your life's end."

*Y*our clear vocation

Harriet Starr Cannon was born May 7, 1823, in Charleston, South Carolina. Both parents died of yellow fever when Harriet was a little more than a year old, and she and her sister were taken to an aunt in Bridgeport, Connecticut. She moved to Brooklyn, New York, in 1851 after her sister's marriage and supported herself by singing in the Grace Church choir and by giving music lessons.

In 1855 Harriet was preparing to join her sister and her husband in California, but on the eve of her departure her sister died unexpectedly. This was a tremendous emotional blow for Harriet, and a few months later she entered the Episcopal Sisterhood of the Holy Communion as a probationer. For two years she worked as a nurse in an eighteen-bed infirmary until St. Luke's Hospital was completed, after which she was head nurse of a forty-bed ward.

Harriet's order was not a traditional convent but more a service organization. Harriet was searching for "a contemplative life of prayer and devotion" in addition to "an active life of labor." Eventually, she and four other sisters left St. Luke's. At the request of Bishop Horatio Potter, the five women took over the House of Mercy, a rehabilitation home for prostitutes. Impressed by their success, Bishop Potter granted their wish to form a traditional convent community, and in 1865 Harriet and four other sisters became the first members of the Community of St. Mary. Harriet was elected Mother Superior, a position she held until her death more than thirty years later.

Mother Harriet and her order also assumed management of an orphanage, the Sheltering Arms, and of St. Barnabas' House for homeless mothers and children. In 1870 they

Harriet's writing is from a letter written August 14, 1891, to a member of her order and is included in Harriet Starr Cannon, First Mother Superior of the Sisterhood of St. Mary, *by Morgan Dix, published by Longmans, Green, and Co. in 1896.*

established the St. Mary's Free Hospital for Poor Children. During a trip to England in 1867, Harriet became interested in convent schools, and the following year she opened St. Mary's School on New York's West Fifty-sixth Street. Others followed in Peekskill, New York; Memphis, Tennessee; and Kenosha, Wisconsin. Harriet spent the last twenty years of her life at the Peekskill school and was buried at the convent there after her death in 1896. At her death she left ninety-one working sisters at thirteen different Community of St. Mary projects. There is a window in her honor at the Bishop's House in Washington's National Cathedral.

Lucretia Longshore Blankenburg

An improper person

1925

As a child I experienced some persecution because my mother was a doctor: at school one of the teachers advised the children not to play with me because my mother was an improper person. That it was considered improper and vulgar for a woman to study anatomy and physiology, in fact to know anything about the human body and its ailments, seems strange to us today.

Lucretia Longshore Blankenburg was born May 8, 1845, on a farm near New Lisbon, Ohio. When she was six months old the family returned to their Quaker roots in rural Pennsylvania. Five years later, they moved to Philadelphia when her mother enrolled in the first class at the Female Medical College. Police had to be called in for her graduation, fearing a demonstration, and even during her years as Philadelphia's first practicing female physician she encountered prejudice. Lucretia, named for the Quaker reformer Lucretia Mott, witnessed this discrimination firsthand and decided as a child to work for women's rights.

Lucretia graduated from the Friends' Central School and Bryant and Stratton Commercial College. To please her parents, she attended the Woman's Medical College (formerly the Female Medical College) but quickly discovered she had no aptitude for medicine and quit after one semester. She was married in April 1867 to Rudolf Blankenburg, a young German immigrant. Lucretia helped her husband get his start in business, working by his side at his yarn, linen, and notions store. His business was so successful that after three years he opened a textile manufacturing company.

Lucretia's writing is from her book, The Blankenburgs of Philadelphia, *published by the John C. Winston Company in 1929.*

Lucretia had three daughters who all died as children. After the death of her last daughter of diphtheria in 1878 she threw herself into charity work. She joined the New Century Club and the Society for Organizing Charitable Relief, and through these organizations she implemented many civic improvements. In 1884 she befriended Susan B. Anthony (February 15), who invited her to join the suffrage movement. She was elected president of the Pennsylvania Woman Suffrage Association in 1892 and served in that capacity for sixteen years. Miss Anthony coached her in public speaking, and she often testified before congressional committees.

In 1908 Lucretia resigned from the Woman Suffrage Association when she was elected auditor of the General Federation of Women's Clubs. Her goal was to win over the women's club movement to the suffrage movement. After much lecturing, she succeeded in 1914 in persuading the federation to adopt a formal resolution endorsing women's suffrage.

Mr. Blankenburg was elected mayor of Philadelphia in 1911 with a large percentage of the female reform vote. Lucretia worked closely by his side and was referred to as the "co-mayor." Even as she aged she never slowed down, taking a solo automobile trip across the United States at the age of seventy-five. She died of pneumonia in Philadelphia in 1937 at the age of ninety-one.

Elizabeth Garver Jordan

1938

*I*n a convent garden

That beautiful old convent garden, the size of a squared city block inside its high brick walls, was a favorite haunt of my own. The etiquette of the occasion, when one encountered Mother Caroline there, was to bow and pass on. But one May evening, when she and I happened to be the only human figures against that enchanting background, she shook my young heart by stopping to speak to me. After we had chatted a few minutes she drew me to a bench beside the big fountain, and we sat there together while she asked me about my routine studies and my music.

I was only fourteen, and in addition to the academic course I was giving two hours a day to piano practice, as I had done since I was eight.

Elizabeth's writing is from her autobiography, Three Rousing Cheers, *published in 1938 by D. Appleton-Century Company, Inc.*

Elizabeth Garver Jordan was born May 9, 1865, in Milwaukee, Wisconsin. She graduated as valedictorian in 1884 from St. Mary's High School at Notre Dame Convent. Her dream of becoming a nun was vehemently opposed by her mother, who wanted her to be a concert pianist. As she had shown talent as a writer and had already had several stories published in local newspapers, her father encouraged her to try journalism. He contacted family friend George W. Peck and secured a position for her as editor of the woman's page of *Peck's Sun*. In 1890 she left for New York City to take a job at the *World*.

Elizabeth had been working at the *World* only a short time when she scored a major triumph: an exclusive interview with President Benjamin Harrison's wife Caroline. The Harrisons were vacationing at Cape May, New Jersey, and many journalists had tried to obtain an interview but were turned away. Elizabeth charmed her way past the butler and made friends with Mrs. Harrison's grandson. Thereafter, Elizabeth's talent as an interviewer and her knack for human interest stories led her to write the weekly "True Stories of the News," which actually were fictionalized tales of prisoners, Chinese immigrants, insane asylum inmates, Appalachian Mountain people, and the like. In 1893 she had a double success with her coverage of Lizzie Borden's trial and a series on New York's tenements entitled "The Submerged Tenth."

After her father lost his fortune in the panic of 1893, Elizabeth became the family's sole supporter. She began writing short stories to supplement her income and published her first book in 1895. Two years later she was promoted to assistant Sunday editor at the *World*.

Elizabeth left the *World* in 1900 to become editor of *Harper's Bazaar* magazine. Beginning in 1913 she also worked at Harper and Brothers Publishing Company as a literary adviser. She discovered and promoted many new authors including Zona Gale (August 26), Dorothy Canfield Fisher (February 17), and Sinclair Lewis.

Elizabeth left Harper and Brothers in 1918 to work as an editorial director for Goldwyn Pictures. She was unsuccessful in this venture and returned to writing novels, producing one a year. From 1922 to 1945 she wrote theater reviews for the Catholic weekly *America*. During her long and busy career, she was also an avid sportswoman and travelled to Europe more than thirty times. She continued writing until two years before her death. She died in 1947 at the age of eighty-one.

May French Sheldon

1892

...when all the preparations possible to make before reaching Aden were completed, and a myriad of boxes and a bewilderment of nondescript packages — my tent, gun, table, chairs, pistols, photographic apparatus, and personal effects — had been sent by steamer to meet me at Naples, and for the first time I felt I was without doubt actually bound for East Africa. Gruesome remarks were intermingled with inspiring words of faith in my success: "Well, you have my prayers for safe return." "*If* you return alive, what a story you'll have to tell!" "Do be reasonable, and abandon this mad, useless scheme." "Brave woman, you'll accomplish all you aim to; we owe you a vote of thanks for your courage and self-sacrifice." And A. Bruce, the sturdy son-in-law of the great Livingstone, thrust into my hands a long-range field glass, as if to bid me be far-sighted. "Remember, nothing is accomplished without giving yourself up to the work at whatever sacrifice, and that honest failure is not defeat. We believe you will succeed." His true words were branded on my brain indelibly, and echoed through my thoughts time out of number. Around me pressed lovely girl friends, sentimental hero-worshippers, who set the seal of admiration upon my lips by their farewell kiss, and whispered, *"How I wish I could go with you!"* Sedate man friends looked compassionately at my husband, and involuntarily calculated that the time would be brief ere he should regret his consent, which I had flouted widely, as evidence that when he sanctioned my undertaking, it was not irrational. We were off midst cheers, pelting of flowers, and the usual half-hysterical, frantic commotion attending a departure where a friend's life seemed at stake.

May French Sheldon was born May 10, 1847, in Beaver, Pennsylvania. Her mother, a physician, was her role model.

May married Eli Lemon Sheldon, an American banker living in London, in 1876. In 1890 her friend Henry Stanley returned to England after spending years exploring Africa.

Thrilling departure

May's writing is from the first pages of her book, Sultan to Sultan: Adventures Among the Masai and Other Tribes of East Africa, *published in 1892 by Arena Publishing Company, Boston.*

She was fascinated by his stories and decided to mount an expedition to Africa herself.

Everyone except her husband was opposed to May's journey. In Mombasa the British authorities refused to help her, so she went directly to the sultan of Zanzibar to appeal for aid. He outfitted her with 103 porters and a letter of introduction. Her goal was to meet the sultans of every African tribe.

May set out on foot, at the head of the group, carrying a walking stick and a banner inscribed "Nolime Tangere." She brought a bright red silk evening gown, with a train covered with costume jewelry, which she dutifully donned each time she was presented to a sultan.

In all, May visited thirty-five tribes. On the return trip, she was severely injured when the porters carrying her across a pole-bridge slipped and dropped her to the river twenty feet below. The porters rushed the rest of the way back to Mombasa, where she boarded a ship for England. In time she recovered and wrote a book about her experiences.

May toured Europe and America giving travel lectures. She continued travelling and lecturing into her eighties, until her death in London in 1936.

Mari Sandoz

*I*ndians and their children

1952

One morning the summer I was eight a playmate from an Indian camp across the road tapped shyly at our kitchen door.

"Ahh! I have a brother too, now!" she whispered, her dark eyes on the baby astride my hip. "He is just born. Come see!"

In the dusky interior of a smoky old canvas tipi an Indian woman bent over the new baby on her lap. At the noise of our excited entry, the tiny red-brown face puckered up. The mother caught the little nose gently between her thumb and forefinger, and with her palm over the mouth stopped the cry soundlessly. When the baby began to twist for breath she let go a little, but only a little, and at the first sign of another cry she shut the air off again, crooning softly a Cheyenne growing song to make the son straight-limbed and strong of body and heart.

Mari's writing is from "What the Sioux Taught Me," Empire Magazine, *February 24, 1952.*

Women's Words, Women's Stories

I already know why none of my small Indian friends made more than a whimper at the greatest hurt. An old grandmother had told me that Indian mothers always shut off the first cry of the newborn, and as often after that as necessary. . . .

But I knew . . . that never in this new baby's life would he be touched by a punishing hand. He would be made equal to the demands of his expanding world without physical chastisement. I remember the stern faces of the Sioux when in the swift heat of temper my father whipped us. These Indians still consider the whites a brutal people who treat their children like enemies that must be bribed or punished or coddled like fragile toys.

Mari Sandoz was born May 11, 1896, in Sheridan County, Nebraska. At nine, speaking only German, she began school, walking three miles each way. At ten she had her first story published in the *Omaha Daily News* and decided to become a writer despite her father's belief that artists and writers were "the maggots of society."

Mari began teaching school at the age of sixteen and two years later married homesteader Wray Macumber. She divorced him after five years and never spoke publicly about her marriage. Soon after her divorce she enrolled as a special adult student at the University of Nebraska, taking courses in English and writing.

In 1933 Mari submitted her completed manuscript *Old Jules* to the *Atlantic Monthly*, but it was rejected. She gave up her dream of being a writer, burned more than seventy-five of her stories, and retreated to her family's Nebraska home in a severe state of depression. After one and a half years she resubmitted *Old Jules* to the *Atlantic Monthly*. This time it won a $5,000 prize for distinctive nonfiction and was published by the Book-of-the-Month Club.

Old Jules was the first of six books in Mari's Trans-Missouri series, which captured "the hardship, the violence and gaiety" of frontier life on the plains. In 1941 she began teaching creative writing courses during the summer at various Midwestern universities.

Mari worked hard to finish her last two books, a personal recollection of her life and a novel about the Battle of Little Big Horn. She succumbed to cancer in March 1966 and was buried, as she requested, in the Nebraska sandhills.

Mary Fife Emerson

Be strong

1906

My good friend and true. . .

Here's my real hardness. I love power, physical, intellectual and spiritual. I remember once at home in Peterboro, a dear boy was visiting us. He was completely run down and as he lay on the hammock, I felt a sort of repulsion. I think it was terrible. Naturally you might have expected that the weakness would have made an appeal to my sympathies. . . . Weakness in a man is not the same as in a child to me, and when I have to make like allowances, he loses his position for he is not a child. . . .

Mary Fife Emerson was born May 12, 1874, in Ontario, Canada. Her father was a physician, and as a young girl she often accompanied him on his house calls.

After completing the education course at the University of Ontario, Mary taught high school for three years. She then attended Radcliffe College, Cambridge, Massachusetts, and received her master's degree in British history and literature. She remained in Massachusetts for another year teaching at Miss May's School in Boston. One of her co-workers invited her to a tea at Harvard one afternoon, where she met Eugene Emerson, a philosophy graduate student.

Soon after, in June 1904, Mary departed for a year-and-a-half tour of Europe with her mother and sister. Eugene wrote her long letters discussing everything from books and philosophy to current fashions and Cambridge gossip. Mary asked him to please number his pages as they read like "a Chinese puzzle." Eugene often shared his innermost thoughts in his letters to her, yet Mary's letters to him were more impersonal. In one of his letters of January 1905 Eugene asked why her letters were so "chilly" and requested that she write more about her thoughts and feelings. She apologized, but there was little change in her ability to share her feelings with him. However, Eugene persevered. In his letter of January 1906 he announced abruptly, "I love you; how deep I cannot fathom." He received little encouragement from Mary but remained optimistic and kept pursuing her. He finally won her heart, and they were married in July 1907.

Mary and Eugene lived in Ann Arbor for four years, where he taught psychology at the University of Michigan. They

Mary's writing is from a letter she wrote from Kenora, Ontario, to Eugene a year before their marriage. The original is among his papers at the Harvard Medical School Library.

returned to Cambridge in 1911 when he was appointed to head the Psychology Department at Massachusetts General Hospital, a position he held for the next twenty-five years. The couple had two sons and two daughters.

Mary tutored, taught Sunday School, and was an active contributor to the social and academic life of Cambridge and Boston. She believed as her mother had that "Christianity included hospitality." Her home was a happy gathering place for her many friends, her husband's colleagues, and her children's friends. Eugene died in 1939. Mary lived on for twenty-six years in the home they had shared, and died there in 1965.

Mary Devereaux Clarke

1854

Fancy's joys

Nemo Semper Felix Est

Oh! there are moments when my soul
    From common things would soar away,
To wander free from all control,
    Beneath the light of Fancy's ray.
Often when this spell is o'er me
    Till my heart with joy's opprest,
Riseth up those words before me —
    "Nemo semper felix est."

Slowly then my wandering mind
    Yields to reason's sterner sway,
Leaveth Fancy's joys to find
    Peace in duty's rugged way.
Calmer thoughts will soon succeed,
    And my troubled soul find rest,
What tho' its wounds awhile may bleed —
    "Nemo semper felix est."

Mary Bayard Devereaux Clarke was born May 13, 1827, in Raleigh, North Carolina. She had ten brothers and sisters. Following her mother's death when she was nine, a governess was hired to tutor the children. Mary was permitted to study her brothers' college courses, and she became fluent in French, German, and Spanish.

Mary married Capt. William John Clarke, a veteran of the Mexican War, in April 1848. They had three sons and a daughter. Two years before their marriage, her husband had

Mary's poem "Nemo Semper Felix Est," from which these two stanzas are taken, is included in Wood-Notes or Carolina Carols: A Collection of North Carolina Poetry, Volume II. *The collection was compiled by Tanella (Mary's pen name for her poetry) and published by Warren L. Pomeroy in 1854.*

published a poem lamenting "the paucity of poetic production" in Raleigh. Mary tried to fill that void by writing poetry herself and by editing the first anthology of North Carolina verse.

In 1855 Mary spent the winter in Havana, Cuba, to improve her health. The Clarkes moved to San Antonio, Texas, the next year in search of a dry climate. With the outbreak of the Civil War, William joined the Confederate Army, and Mary returned to Raleigh with the children. During the war years, she produced many patriotic poems, several of which were published in the *Southern Illustrated News*.

William became a colonel. He spent several years in a Northern prison. Mary was forced to write to support the family. She published poetry in Southern magazines and wrote fiction under the pen name Stuart Leigh. She also translated French novels, composed an opera, and sold Sunday school hymns for $5 apiece.

Mary continued to write prolifically until she suffered a stroke in 1883. She died in 1886 when she was fifty-eight years old.

Minerva Parker Nichols

Delight of design

1893

The chief charm of any house is its individuality. There are many things which houses or people possess in common; but the thing which charms us is the thing peculiar to a certain house or a certain person.

Women often seem so helpless when they come to design their own houses that the mere thought of a specification to be read or an inspection of the plans, is enough to deprive the poor architect of their society for days. I assure you, French novels will seem dull compared with the delight of threading your way through the translation of plans, when you have once mastered the mechanical part of the drawing.

Minerva's writing is from "An Uncultivated Field," which appeared in the June 10, 1893, issue of Housekeeper's Weekly.

Minerva Parker Nichols was born May 14, 1861, in Chicago. Her father fought for the North in the Civil War and died in a field hospital. Her mother moved to Philadelphia to open a boarding house for medical students. Minerva's maternal grandfather had been an architect, and she felt drawn to his profession.

Minerva graduated from the Philadelphia Normal Art School in 1882 and took a drafting job in the prestigious firm of Frederick G. Thorn, Jr. When he retired six years later, she opened her own office and completed his remaining projects.

Minerva enjoyed a successful and varied architectural practice. Although she preferred to design private homes, she also did two notable spaghetti factories and two women's clubs. In 1893 she entered a competition for the Queen Isabella Pavilion at the World's Columbian Exposition and won first place. Minerva used many different styles ranging from Moorish to Renaissance to Colonial. She recommended a separate style for each room to reflect the rooms' different purposes and the owner's personality. She was unique in that she not only designed buildings but supervised their construction as well, prompting one contractor to remark, "She knows not only her business, but mine, too."

In December 1891 Minerva married William Ichabod Nichols, a Unitarian minister. They had four children, and in 1896 moved from Philadelphia to Brooklyn, New York. After the move Minerva designed buildings only when specifically requested by friends and family. These included the main building at Cambridge's Brown and Nichols School, which her brother-in-law co-founded, and her final work, a home for her daughter in Connecticut. Minerva died there in 1949 at the age of eighty-eight.

Margaret Sloan

April 27, 1902

Undecided

Heard from Willard Friday, he said this trouble between us had caused his Father to alter his life insurance, making Eva the beneficiary instead of him.

He wants to know if I come back if I am going to be suspicious of him, Jealous of every woman, etc, makes the terms as hard as he possibly can, but I will fight this out I believe.

Monday, April 28, 1902

Well I answered Willards letter and I reversed things, refused to accept his terms and stated mine, it is left to him now, he is to decide whether I return and the world be none the wiser that a tragic under current exists, or whether it is all to be made public, and I go out to fight my way.

Margaret's writing is from the published edition of her journal, The Shattered Dream, *edited by Harold Woodell, University of South Carolina Press, 1991.*

My letter will probably end it all between us, for he will be furious at my telling him I knew who had circulated reports to injure my character and disgust him, and that if any other than C.S. Thomson asked him laughingly about those charges I was bringing against him, he or Mrs. T. — had told him, and had him ask him for *effect*.

I would much prefer going back if he would do right, but I can't promise to be deaf and blind to any kind of a life he may choose to lead, and unless he promises to treat me as he knows I have a right to be treated, then I can't get the consent of my mind to go back. God knows best, and will lead me through this vale of sorrows I trust, and teach me the *way*.

Margaret Sloan was born May 15, 1874, in Calhoun, Tennessee. From childhood she planned for her ultimate goal — to marry a wonderful man and live happily ever after by his side.

Margaret met her future husband, Willard Leland, an army sergeant, in 1898. They were married in June 1900 and took up residence in a boarding house in Asheville, North Carolina. Margaret soon discovered that Willard travelled frequently in his job while she was left alone, lonely and bored. Worse than his absences were his cold indifference when he was home and his blatant flirtations with other women. After discovering Willard's affair with another woman at the boarding house, Margaret returned to her family in Tennessee.

Margaret returned to her husband to try again in Douglas, Arizona, where he was working for the railroad. They had a son, Raymond, in 1905, but she was unable to tolerate Willard's philandering. She left him permanently in 1915. After residing with her sister for several years Margaret moved to Knoxville, Tennessee, with Raymond when he opened a business there. She served as a paid companion to an elderly heiress for many years. Margaret died in a convalescent home in 1960 when she was eighty-five.

Margaret Dwight Hitchcock

1897

As we were announced, the Empress came forward to
meet us and, of course, we made a curtsey when we
entered the room and then another when she gave us
her hand. She asked us to come and sit down. Really
she was simply lovely. Quite a large woman with lovely
dimples and complexion and very pretty. She looks like
an English woman and has a tiny German accent but
very little. Of course, she asked us when we came? If
we liked it. What kind of a trip we had etc. . . .

I have lost my heart to her. She was a little embarrassed at first but it soon wore off. Then when she was
through with us, she bowed her head, and we rose and
she rose. We curtseyed and bent over her hand and
then bowed again, before leaving the room. Of course,
backing out.

But I must tell you what kind of dress she had on, as
I was more observant than Father. It was a dark blue
moiré with a stripe of the same color. Made with a vest
and lapels of white lace over blue and trimmed with
sable round the edge. When we came out, the other
ones were taken in. I feel sorry for her; it must be such
a dreadful bore.

Meeting the empress

Margaret (Peg) Dwight Hitchcock was born May 16, 1878, in
St. Louis, Missouri, where her father was a prominent businessman. In July 1897 President William McKinley
appointed Mr. Hitchcock minister plenipotentiary to Russia
in the hope that a businessman would help foster trade
between Russia and the United States.

Peg, her sister Anne, and her parents departed for Russia
in the fall of 1897. Six months after arriving in St.
Petersburg, Mr. Hitchcock was promoted to ambassador.
Peg, her sister, and mother spent much of their time and
energy entertaining.

President McKinley recalled the Hitchcocks from Russia
in 1898. The family returned to America where Mr.
Hitchcock assumed his new position as Secretary of the
Interior. Peg lived with her parents in Washington, D.C.,
but found the life too restrictive. Eventually she left for Paris
to study music. She never married and remained in Paris for

*Peg's December 17, 1897, let-
ter to her married sister Sarah,
describing her presentation to
the empress of Russia, is among
the personal papers of her niece,
Mrs. Anne Sims Morison of
Cambridge, Massachusetts.*

the rest of her life with only an occasional visit home. She died of pneumonia in France in 1927 at the age of forty-nine.

Olivia Shipp (Olivia Porter)

A budding musician

1979

My first musical instrument was a comb and tissue paper. My sister and I celebrated my father and mother each evening after dinner, getting all conceivable harmonies and rhythms. As for the keyboard, the family acquired an old pump organ from a local minister's wife. They were moving to a country assignment and didn't have the money to move the organ. I got the gist of the thing and proceeded to teach myself. . . .

I didn't come up just given things. I worked hard; I sacrificed. I had good teachers. For my lessons, I would take something out of my home and pawn it, because study was important to me. I never worked at anything but music.

Olivia Sophie L'Ange Shipp was born May 17, 1880, in New Orleans, Louisiana. Both Olivia and her sister, May Kemp, had musical talents that were nurtured by their parents. As children they sang in the church choir and learned to play several instruments. May grew up to perform in the Black Patti Troubador Company and eventually had her own vaudeville act, "Bob and Kemp."

Olivia joined her sister in New York around 1900. Until her marriage in 1920 to Mr. Shipp, a black athlete, she changed her last name to Porter out of respect for her father because of show business' bad image. She began working in vaudeville shows to earn money to live and for piano lessons. Her piano teacher took her to a performance of a British cello and piano team, and she decided the cello was "the sweetest instrument ever heard."

Olivia eventually bought her own cello and began taking lessons with a well-known Hungarian. When he moved away she continued studying with black cellist Leonard Jeter, a member of the Shuffle Along Orchestra. She served as his assistant at the Martin-Smith Music School and played in the school's orchestra.

In 1921 Olivia joined the Lafayette Theatre Ladies' Orchestra as a string bassist. She also substituted when needed with the top male bands in New York City because

Olivia's recollections, from an interview with D. Antoinette Handy, are included in Black Women in Bands and Orchestras, *by D. Antoinette Handy, The Scarecrow Press, Inc., Metuchen, New Jersey, and London, 1981.*

she "played like a man and played bass like a cello." In the late 1920s she organized her own band, Olivia Shipp's Jazz-Mines Famous Female Orchestra, which played "music for all occasions." Several years later, with the assistance of Local 802 of the American Federation of Musicians and state Representative Fiorello La Guardia, she founded the city's first civic orchestra, the Negro Women's Orchestral and Civic Association. When visiting performers came to New York and needed a band, Olivia would fill the spaces with members of her Civic Association. She worked steadily until her retirement in the early 1950s.

Olivia died in New York City in 1980 at the age of 100. One year before her death she reminisced, "I played the best of shows; I worked with the best of them."

Annie Trumbull Slosson

1889

We fell into talk at once, Ralph and Waldo rushing eagerly into questions about the fish, the bait, the best spots in the stream, advancing their own small theories, and asking advice from their new friend. For friend he seemed even in that first hour, as he began simply, but so wisely, to teach my boys the art he loved. . . . But it is not of these practical teachings I would now speak; rather of the lessons of simple faith, of unwearied patience, of self-denial and cheerful endurance which the old man himself seemed to have learned, strangely enough, from the very sport so often called cruel and murderous.

The art of fishing

Annie Trumbull Slosson was born May 18, 1838, in Stonington, Connecticut. She attended local schools until 1852 when the family moved to Hartford, where she completed her education.

In 1867 Annie married Edward Slosson, a lawyer, and settled in New York City, but he died four years later. Her sister Mary, married to William Prime, editor of the New York *Journal of Commerce*, died a few months after Edward. Annie and William comforted each other in their losses and became very close friends.

At the age of forty Annie turned to writing and published her first book, *The China Hunter's Club*, which wove a series of stories around pieces of old china found in New England

Annie's writing is from Fishin' Jimmy, *published in 1889 by Anson D. F. Randolph and Company, New York.*

homes. Although she published this work anonymously as "The Youngest Member," it was illustrated by her brother Gurdon with an introduction by her brother-in-law William, so there was little doubt as to its authorship. Thereafter, she used her own name.

Annie and William shared a summer house together in Franconia, New Hampshire. All of her writings were set either in Connecticut or New Hampshire and usually concerned eccentric or outcast characters. She captured the spirit of New England and its residents, always rugged and independent. Annie published fifteen short story collections between 1878 and 1918 in addition to contributing frequently to *Harper's* and the *Atlantic Monthly*.

Annie began spending more and more of her time in Franconia and the surrounding White Mountains. She became a respected amateur entomologist, contributing articles on her findings to *Entomological News* and *Among the Clouds*, the weekly paper published on the summit of Mount Washington. Beginning in 1900 she spent seven consecutive summers on Mount Washington, collecting more than 3,000 species of insects. The Connecticut scientific community recognized her achievements by attaching her name ("slossoni") to two types of regional wasps.

Annie and William's New Hampshire cottage was on the grounds of the famous summer resort, the Mount Lafayette House. Eventually Annie bought the hotel, although she spent more of her time at the Summit House on top of Mount Washington. In the early 1900s she lost three of her brothers, and her beloved brother-in-law William died in 1905. Three years later the Summit House burned to the ground, which she likened to the loss of another human friend. She wrote of her "loved shrine" that, "Of late years it had been my home, my HOMIEST home. . . . Dear old house! I loved every timber, every clapboard of it." Annie sold the Mount Lafayette House and returned to New York City. Shortly before her death in 1926 at the age of eighty-eight, she divided her extensive insect collection, more than 35,000 specimens, between New York's Museum of Natural History and the Harvard Museum of Comparative Zoology.

Agnes Boyle O'Reilly Hocking

1898
Friday, May 6th. Now I must tell you about Thursday.
. . . They were learning the "Ballad of the Thrush."
You know it? Austin Dobson.

Spirit of the thrush

> "Across the narrow street
> I hear him careless throw
> One warning utterance, sweet."

They really understood it and loved it. Mary
Gallagher raised her hand four times to tell us she
"wished she was a bird" . . . and Frank Wasanwitz, who
usually sits rolled up in his own thoughts except during
arithmetic, woke up enough to say he "hated a man
who hurt a bird." And they grasped the inner meaning
of it too, for I tested them by saying that the thrush
reminded us of some one, a little girl we'd heard of . . .
and they all saw in a flash and called out "Pippa,
Pippa." We'd learned bits of "Pippa Passes."

But Mary liked it more than all the rest; she kept
raising her hand to say, "Let's say the end line over
again, 'Sing on, Sing on, O Thrush'". . . .

Monday, May 9th . . . Everyone was overflowing
with interesting news about Sunday. Sara Butler could
have run on for half an hour in her little nut-meg-
grater voice about "Cousins in Chelsea." . . .

Charles McLeod said they had talked of thrushes at
Sunday School. . . .

Then they said the "Ballad of the Thrush" in a way
that would have done Austin Dobson's heart good. I
am so glad I taught it to them and I was goose enough
at first to think it might be too old. Father was right;
give everyone the best you've got without any scrupu-
lous anxieties about its being over their heads.

Agnes Boyle O'Reilly Hocking was born May 19, 1878, in
Charlestown, Massachusetts. Her father, the poet and writer
John Boyle O'Reilly, passed on to his children the love of
books and learning. There was frequent reading aloud in the
family circle during her childhood.

*Agnes's writing is from a May
9, 1898, letter to her sisters
Elizabeth and Blanid. The
letter is among the personal
papers of her son, Richard Boyle
O'Reilly Hocking of Madison,
New Hampshire.*

Agnes received her early schooling at the Convent of the Sacred Heart in Providence, Rhode Island. Her first teaching position upon graduating from Boston Normal School was as a volunteer at the George Jr. Republic School, an experimental reform school for boys in Freeville, New York.

She married William Ernest Hocking, a philosophy professor at the Andover Theological School, in 1905. Ernest's career took them from Andover to the University of California at San Francisco for two years and then to Yale in 1908.

The local public school in New Haven was not up to the standards that Agnes wanted for her son, Richard. With the encouragement of her husband, Agnes became the guiding force in organizing a small cooperative school with other parents. She had the most teaching experience of any in the group, having taught in New York and the Boston public schools before she married. Classes were held in a large tent with a wooden floor and a wood-burning stove.

In 1914 Ernest received an appointment at Harvard, and the couple moved to Cambridge with their three children. Agnes found upon their arrival in Cambridge that its local public school had problems, too. She again started a cooperative school with other parents. This time it was held on the Hockings' enclosed but unheated back porch with ten children. This small beginning grew into what today is the well-known Shady Hill School.

Agnes loved poetry and history, and she transmitted her enthusiasm to her pupils much as her father had with her. She regarded poetry not as an ornamental way of saying things but rather as a way of expressing faith without dogma. In her view, the conveying of faith was a school's most important obligation.

Agnes died at her home in Madison, New Hampshire, in 1955 when she was seventy-seven.

MAY 20

Antoinette Louisa Brown Blackwell

In praise of exertion

1868

Utterly ruinous is it for old people to fall into the monotony of quietude, which is without care, and therefore without interest. When I see an aged person thus settling himself, to sleep away the remainder of life, it affects me with something of the horror one feels on seeing an infant fed upon narcotics. Certain heathen nations formerly exposed their old people in the wilderness, that their wearisome lives might be sooner ended. We beguile ours into idiocy, by withdrawing all social and moral pressure towards further exertion. Mistaken kindness, how much it will have to atone for!

Antoinette Louisa Brown Blackwell was born May 20, 1825, in Henrietta, New York. At nine she made a public declaration of faith and was accepted as a church member by the elders of the Congregational society.

After graduating from the literary course at Oberlin College, Antoinette decided to follow in her brother's footsteps and pursue a theological degree at Oberlin. She met with strong opposition from family and faculty, and although she was reasoned with and pleaded with, she never wavered from her decision to become a minister. Oberlin permitted her to attend classes but did not award her a degree. Despite her lack of a diploma she was ordained a minister of the First Congregational Church in Wayne County, New York, in September 1853, thus becoming the first ordained woman minister in America.

After preaching for only one year Antoinette found her growing religious liberalism was at odds with the Congregationalists, and she severed all ties to become a Unitarian. She spent the following year administering to the needs of prisoners and slum-dwellers in New York City.

Antoinette was married in January 1856 to Samuel Blackwell, the brother-in-law of her best friend, the feminist Lucy Stone. For the next two decades she retired from public service to raise her five daughters, although she made certain she averaged "three hours of daily habitual brain work, not including daily papers and miscellaneous light reading."

Antoinette returned to the ministry in 1901 following her husband's death. She lived with two of her daughters and founded the All Souls' Unitarian Church in Elizabeth, New Jersey. From 1908 until her death she served as pastor emeritus, preaching her last sermon in 1915 at the age of ninety. She was delighted, at the age of ninety-five, to be able to vote for the first time. She died the following year and was buried in Elizabeth, New Jersey.

Antoinette's writing is from her article "A Plea for the Afternoon" in the March 1868 issue of the Atlantic Monthly.

Amy Fay

A musician's wish

New York
April 12, 1911
Dearest Cater,

. . . I am just *crazy* to go abroad this summer, and I ought to be on hand for the grand celebration of Liszt's centenary, which will be at Heidelberg in August, I believe. There will be a gathering of the clans among the famous musicians. Busoni will be there and I should suppose Paderewski and perhaps Safonoff might be. Safonoff has an engagement to conduct six orchestral concerts in Rome in *June*, at the Exposition. My former pupil, Nora Smith, is living in Rome now, and it would be so nice to go there with *her* as a guide. Miss Read has engaged her passage on the Venezia for July 1st and I would give anything to accompany her! I see no prospect of my being able to do so, however, and keep asking my brain how I could earn five hundred dollars the next two months! With my playing and my writing, it seems a pity I can't *make it pay!* I could write another book if only I could get across the big pond and have some experiences worth describing!

Amelia (Amy) Fuller Fay was born May 21, 1844, in Bayou Goula, Louisiana, the fifth of nine children. Her father, an Episcopal priests, had left New England for Louisiana to establish a parish there. When she was four, the family returned to St. Albans, Vermont, where she began to play music by ear on the piano. Her mother, an excellent self-taught pianist, took up her instruction and continued until her death when Amy was twelve.

In 1862 Amy moved in with her older married sister in Cambridge, Massachusetts. She studied Bach with a Harvard professor in addition to her classes at the New England Conservatory. However, her dream was to study with the masters in Germany.

When Amy was twenty-five she departed for Berlin to become a concert pianist. She remained in Germany for six years, working with various teachers. The high point came in the summer of 1873, when she was able to study with Franz Liszt.

Amy made her concert debut in May 1875 in Frankfurt. She was a great success and returned to America soon after to

Amy's writing is from a letter to her sister, who subsequently lent her the money for her trip. It is included in More Letters of Amy Fay: The American Years, 1879-1916, *selected and edited by S. Margaret William McCarthy and published by Information Coordinators in 1986.*

perform and to teach. She settled and lived for the next twenty years in Chicago, where she founded the Artist's Concert Club. She also served as the first president of the Women's Philharmonic Society in New York City.

In 1881 Amy published *Music Study in Germany*, with the help of her friend Henry Wadsworth Longfellow. Her family had saved all the letters she had written home during her student years in Germany, and these were presented in book form. The book was very popular in the United States, as well as in Great Britain, and was translated into French and German. It is credited with influencing thousands of young students to seek a musical education in Germany.

Amy died in 1929 when she was eighty-three.

Bertha Honoré Palmer

1890

Ladies: I feel deeply the honor of being called upon to preside over this Commission. My humility never asserted itself more strongly than now, as I stand among so many distinguished women of national fame, whose brilliant careers have been a matter of pride to the entire country.

A new president

One well-known and generous friend has flatteringly put me in nomination, and another has most cordially and eloquently seconded this nomination. They have shown by their words not my worth, but the qualities of their own generous hearts. The kindness expressed to me personally by the ladies of the Board, in placing this great responsibility in my hands, has greatly touched me.

My position differs slightly from that of your temporary Chairman in this, that while I have no enemies to punish, I have many friends to reward — all of this Board. I regret, after such a mark of confidence, that I have to ask indulgence for my inexperience in presiding. I hope that when we have been holding meetings as long as the other sex, a knowledge of parliamentary law will be taken as a matter of course in every woman's training.

Bertha's writing is from remarks she made in Chicago on November 20, 1890, upon accepting the presidency of the Board of Lady Managers of the World's Columbian Commission. It is included in Addresses and Reports of Mrs. Potter Palmer, President of the Board of Lady Managers, World's Columbian Commission, *published by Rand McNally and Company in 1894.*

Bertha Honoré Palmer was born May 22, 1849, in Louisville, Kentucky. When she was six the family moved to Chicago

where she attended fashionable private schools. At twenty-one she married Potter Palmer, a wealthy businessman twenty-three years her senior. Initially they lived at Palmer House, one of his many real estate holdings and famous the world over as one of America's finest hotels. After the births of two sons, they moved to an elaborate castle on Lake Shore Drive that included a seventy-five-foot-long art gallery, which housed their extensive art collection. Bertha was instrumental in popularizing the French impressionist movement in America, and upon her death left $100,000 worth of paintings to the Chicago Art Institute.

The wealthy and influential Palmers were leaders in Chicago's society, and Bertha was known as "the Mrs. Astor of the Middle West." She volunteered at Hull House, served as a trustee at Northwestern University, and helped organize Chicago's millinery workers through her affiliation with the Women's Trade Union League. She scored a major triumph as chairman of the Board of Lady Managers of the World's Columbian Commission, established to organize women's participation in the World's Columbian Exposition of 1896. She organized exhibits from forty-seven nations at the Woman's Building, which emphasized the importance of women as a social and economic force.

When the Chicago Civic Federation was established in 1893 to improve conditions within the city, Bertha served as its first vice president. In 1900 she was appointed by President William McKinley as the only female member of the United States Commissioners at the Paris Exposition. Following her husband's death in 1902 Bertha spent eight years abroad and then returned to America, settling in Florida. She built a large country estate near Tampa and was a leader in the development of Florida's west coast. During the sixteen years she survived her husband, she more than doubled her $8 million inheritance through shrewd investments and real estate developments. She died of cancer in 1918 and was buried in the family mausoleum in Chicago.

Kate Barnard

A consecration

1912

Another day I stood at the mouth of a burning coal mine. Fire leaped high through the only entrance. Fifteen men were hopelessly cut off below. The smell of their burning flesh came up to us on the crest of the flame. A woman, clothed in only one garment, with three children clinging to it, and a babe in her arms, peered down into the pit. Her husband was below. She cried out, and, going suddenly insane, tried to leap down to join him.

There was only one reason why that mine should have but one entrance; it would cost money to provide another. Then and there I determined to consecrate myself to the remedy.

Kate Barnard was born May 23, 1875, in Geneva, Nebraska. After her mother's death when she was eighteen months old, she was left with relatives in Kansas until 1889, when she rejoined her father in the Oklahoma Territory. They lived on a remote 160-acre ranch, and although she attended parochial school in the new town of Oklahoma City, she spent considerable time alone while her father was away on long surveying trips.

When Kate was seventeen she became a schoolteacher. She taught for three years and then became a stenographer. In 1901 she was appointed clerk and stenographer for the Democratic minority in the territorial legislature at Guthrie. In 1904 she was sent to work for the Oklahoma Commission at the St. Louis World's Fair, where she witnessed for the first time some of the problems of big-city living: unemployment, slums, and low-paying jobs with terrible working conditions. She returned home determined to pass legislation to protect Oklahomans from the same poor labor conditions.

Kate's first success came in 1906 at the Shawnee Convention, a meeting of the Oklahoma Farmers' Union, the American Federation of Labor, and four railway brotherhoods. As a delegate of the AFL, Kate urged the group to abolish child labor and support compulsory education. Democratic party leaders adopted Kate's reform proposals for their platform at the constitutional convention later that year. They also, at her suggestion, created the elective office of Commissioner of Charities and Corrections. Kate campaigned eagerly for the position and won, becoming the first woman to win a statewide elective office in the United States.

During her two terms in office Kate created a lasting body of reform legislation. She improved conditions for the mentally ill, convicts, child and adult laborers, and widows.

Kate launched an investigation into the Indian land scandals, the practice of white "guardians" defrauding dependent Indian minors of their timber, oil and gas, and farmlands. She met with much opposition and harassment and decided not to seek re-election in 1914. She retired from public life in 1914 and spent the rest of her life managing rental properties left to her by her father. She resided at the Oklahoma City Hotel where she died of a heart attack in February 1930.

Kate's writing is from "Through the Window of Destiny — How I Visualized My Life Work," Good Housekeeping, November 1912.

Lillian Moller Gilbreth

A shocking vision

Lillian's writing is from her chapter "Women in Industry" in American Women: The Changing Image, *edited by Beverly Benner Cassara and published by Beacon Press, Boston, in 1962.*

1962

The status of women employed to help in the home has changed enormously with the years. I can well remember the women who helped in our household when I was growing up, and I remember the work they did and the long hours they labored. I can remember with amusement the shock it was to the ladies of my mother's generation when I said that I hoped to live to see the day when every domestic servant would live in her own home, and be able to ask and get adequate wages, good working hours and a choice of other occupations if she had the capacity and the wish for it.

Lillian Evelyn Moller Gilbreth was born May 24, 1878, in Oakland, California. She was tutored at home until she was nine, at which time she entered the Oakland Public Schools. Against her parents' wishes she enrolled in the University of California at Berkeley, graduating in 1900 with a B.Lit. degree. She was the first woman to be chosen as the university's commencement speaker.

After earning her master's degree in English from Berkeley, Lillian departed in 1903 on a trip to Europe. On a stopover in Boston she met Frank B. Gilbreth, a cousin of her travelling companion. He was one of New England's leading building contractors, an early advocate of the speed-building technique known as motion study. Lillian and Frank were married in October 1904, after which Lillian became a partner in his rapidly expanding motion study business.

Lillian had twelve children. With the assistance of her mother-in-law and hired help, she managed to earn a Ph.D. in psychology from Brown University in 1915. One of her children, Frank, Jr., grew up to write a best-selling book about their childhood, *Cheaper by the Dozen*, published in 1948. Lillian and her husband opened Gilbreth, Inc., in Montclair, New Jersey. Their company pioneered the application of motion study in industry. Using motion pictures as the main form of analysis, they consulted with major industries around the country.

After Frank's death in 1924, Lillian continued their work alone and put all of her eleven surviving children through college. She shifted the emphasis of motion study from industry to the home.

From 1935 to 1948 Lillian was a professor of management at Purdue University where she established a time and motion study lab. She became a consultant at the Institute of Rehabilitation Medicine at New York University Medical Center, where she developed a model kitchen adapted to the needs of the handicapped.

Lillian continued to do research into her seventies and lectured and published books into her eighties. She received more than twenty honorary degrees and numerous awards. Lillian died of a stroke in 1972 at the age of ninety-three. A fellowship in her memory was established by the Society of Women Engineers as a tribute to her lifelong encouragement of women to become engineers.

Elizabeth Rogers Mason Cabot MAY 25

June 11, 1860

A Boston wedding

Walter came at 11. At 12 we were standing in front of the minister. People say it is over in a few moments: to me it seemed endless. We stood with our backs to the people so that as I hoped I hardly realized their presence, and only saw Mother who was in front of me. But at first my knees shook so violently that I was frightened, and could think of nothing but not to fall; this passed off partially, and then I could feel the service with my whole soul. . . . Dr. Gannett was very solemn but also not too long, just as I liked. For a few moments after it was over I almost lost my self-control; but Mrs. Cabot, dear old lady, came and stood right in front of me, and in a few moments I was safe.

Elizabeth Rogers Mason Cabot was born May 25, 1834, in Boston. Her father was a prominent lawyer. Elizabeth was tutored at home and later in a small class at a friend's house. She took lessons in French, Italian, and German.

In 1844 when she was not quite ten, Elizabeth began keeping a diary and continued it for the next sixty-two years. Her diary was her friend and companion in which she shared all her thoughts and confidences. She wrote, "When my heart seems bursting from long suppressed yearning for sympathy, I take up this my ever-constant friend."

At the age of sixteen Elizabeth met Walter Cabot, a Harvard student, at a dance. After Harvard, he left for several years to train as an engineer in Europe. Elizabeth also went to Europe on a sixteen-month tour with her parents. Upon her return she began teaching a Sunday School class and worried about her "old age and decrepitude at twenty."

Elizabeth's diary entry is from More Than Common Powers of Perception — The Diary of Elizabeth Rogers Mason Cabot, *edited by P.A.M. Taylor and published by Beacon Press, Boston, 1991.*

She and Walter became reacquainted in 1857 and were married in 1860.

Elizabeth and her husband lived in Boston during the early years of their marriage but eventually moved to nearby Brookline, where Walter farmed and Elizabeth brought up five children. When her children were grown, Elizabeth raised money for Radcliffe College and worked for the Children's Aid Society.

Walter died in 1904 leaving Elizabeth alone for the last sixteen years of her life. She donated $50,000 to Harvard in Walter's name to enhance the salary of a deserving professor.

In one of her final diary entries she explained why she had kept her diary so faithfully: "I write this for my children and grandchildren, that the picture may not become dimmed. If life continues and is renewed in death, the past will be ineffaceable — I would say, 'Alas' but are not the mistakes, even the sins a ladder to climb by if we will?" Elizabeth died in 1920 at the age of eighty-six. Her diary was published in 1991.

Myra Fairbanks Eells

*A*mong the Indians

1838
Indians on every side of us. Their clothing is principally skins and blankets. Their hair is cut short, except a narrow strip straight over the top of their heads. They are abundantly painted and ornamented. Their ears are filled with tin and pewter jewels, their ears having been bored all through, many of them are tied in with red ribbon. Their features are large. They would come around our tent to watch us like great dogs. Our dog grabbed one, who was nearly naked, Mr. Eells called him off, whipped him, and then tied him. . . . Feel that I have been preserved through dangers seen and unseen. Will God give me grace and wisdom and knowledge and strength equal to my day; make me useful in life, happy in death, and in eternity. Mr. Eells is so tired that he says a bed of stones would feel soft.

Myra's writing is from her April 28, 1838, diary entry. It is included in The First White Women over the Rockies — Volume III, *edited by Clifford M. Drury, Arthur H. Clark Co., 1963-1966. A copy of her diary is on display at the Oregon Historical Society in Portland.*

Myra Fairbanks Eells was born May 26, 1805, in Holden, Massachusetts, the oldest of eight children. When she was eighteen, she became interested in becoming a missionary through her pastor, who had just returned from India. She joined the Gentlemen's and Ladies' Missionary Association to

Women's Words, Women's Stories

prepare for her future. A young theological student, Cushing Eells, began teaching part time in Holden in the mid-1830s. He was also interested in becoming a missionary and asked Myra to marry him and "join him in the life of a foreign missionary." In 1837 they were appointed by the American Board of Missionaries to live among the Zulus in East Africa. A tribal war prohibited them from going, however, and they were asked to go to Oregon instead.

Myra and Cushing were married March 5, 1838, and the next day they departed for Oregon. As a wedding present, she was given a diary in which she faithfully recorded every detail of her transcontinental journey. Her first entry read "left home, Father, Mother, Brothers, and Sisters, and all near and dear by the ties of nature and affection, with the expectation of never seeing them again in the world."

The Eells travelled with two other missionary couples. After completing the first part of the journey from New York City to Independence, Missouri, they rested, bought supplies, and repaired their tents. On April 23 they began the second leg, the 1,900 miles from the beginning of the Western Frontier across the Rockies to the Columbia River, with "twenty-five horses and mules, nine yearling heifers and four fresh milk cows, a dog named King, and a light wagon." Four months later they arrived at their destination.

Myra and her husband remained in Waiilatpu, Oregon, for the next fifty years, although little is known of her life during that period. Just as she had predicted in her diary, she never was able to return to the East to see her family. She died in 1878 at the age of seventy-three.

Julia Ward Howe

1896

April 8. . . . I asked in my prayer this morning, feeling miserably dull and weak, that some deed of help and love might be given me to accomplish to-day. At noon came three gentlemen, Hagop Bogigian, Mr. Blanchard, and Mr. Breed, of Lynn, praying me to make an appeal to the women of America for their Armenian sisters, who are destroying themselves in many instances to avoid Turkish outrage. The funds subscribed for relief are exhausted and some new stimulus to rouse the public is much needed. . . . I felt that I had had an answer to my prayer. . . .

*A*n answered prayer

Julia's writing is from her diary. It is included in Julia Ward Howe 1819-1910, Volume II, *by Laura E. Richards and Maud Howe Elliott and published in 1915 by Houghton, Mifflin and Company.*

Julia Ward Howe was born May 27, 1819, in New York City. The Ward family was relatively well off financially, and Julia and her six siblings were educated at home by governesses and at local private schools. In 1841 on a visit to Boston Julia met Samuel Gridley Howe, the forty-year-old head of the Perkins Institution for the Blind. They were married in April 1843 and spent a year's honeymoon abroad, during which time their first daughter was born. After their return to Boston, they took up residence near Perkins in a home Julia referred to as "Green Peace" due to its isolated location. Three more daughters and one son followed in quick succession. However, her sixth child, a son, died as an infant.

Julia wanted to help her husband with his work at Perkins, but he was opposed to married women in public life. The differences between them led immediately to problems in the marriage, and in 1850 Julia separated from her husband for a year. They considered divorce several times, but they always reconciled and remained married until his death in 1876. Reflecting in her journal on twenty years of marriage, Julia wrote: "In the course of that time I have never known my husband to approve of any act of mine which I myself valued. . . . Everything had been contemptible in his eyes because not his way of doing things. . . ."

Julia's sadness and loneliness in her marriage caused her to turn inward. She read constantly, studied foreign languages, philosophy, and religion, and began writing plays and poetry. Her first volume of poems, *Passion-flowers*, was published in 1854, followed by *Words for the Hour* in 1857. Her first play, *Leonoro or the World's Own*, was presented at New York City's Lyceum Theatre in 1857. However, its racy plot concerning a woman who tries to kill her lover but fails, and then commits suicide, was condemned by critics as "offensive, immoral, and indecent" and was closed after one week.

In February 1862 the *Atlantic Monthly* published Julia's poem "The Battle Hymn of the Republic," which was to change her life. It was set to the tune of "John Brown's Body" and within two years became the rallying cry of the North. It is said that President Lincoln wept the first time he heard the song. At first, Julia was unsure how to handle her new-found fame, but by 1868 she had decided to join the women's movement. She became a leader in the American Woman Suffrage Association and found companionship among her new woman friends. She later wrote in her autobiography, "One of the comforts which I found in the new association was the relief which it afforded me from a sense of isolation and eccentricity."

In *Heroines of Modern Progress*, Adams and Foster wrote that Julia in her old age "became a kind of an institution, a repository for the spirit of a vanished age. . . . People came on pilgrimage to see her, as they might a historic monument."

In 1908 she was the first woman elected to the American Academy of Arts and Letters, and no other woman was admitted for another twenty-two years. She died at home in 1910 at the age of ninety-one. The governor of Massachusetts led the dignitaries at her memorial service in Boston's Symphony Hall, where 4,000 people sang "The Battle Hymn of the Republic" and hundreds more were turned away for lack of space. She was buried at the Mount Auburn Cemetery in Cambridge.

Frances Leigh

1882

... in January 1876 I was taken very ill, and for five days lay at the point of death, during which time the anxiety and affection shown by my negroes was most profound, all work stopped, and the house was besieged day and night by anxious inquirers. My negro nurse lay on the floor outside my door all night, and the morning I was pronounced out of danger she rushed out, and throwing up her arms, exclaimed, "My missus'll get well; my missus'll get well! I don't care what happens to me now." And when at last I was able to get about once more, the expressions of thankfulness that greeted me on all sides were most touching.

*D*ear people

Frances Butler Leigh was born May 28, 1838, in Philadelphia. Her father owned several cotton and rice plantations in Georgia. Her mother, an actress, wrote a popular book describing the horrors of slavery she had witnessed on the family plantations. Her parents' opposite views on slavery resulted in their divorce in 1849.

Frances and her sister remained close to both parents and divided their time between them. With the outbreak of the Civil War, Frances volunteered for hospital work in Philadelphia, although her allegiance was with the Confederates. After the war she accompanied her father to the Butler plantations, where they attempted to reclaim their abandoned property.

Mr. Butler died in 1867, but Frances remained in the South, determined to continue her father's efforts. She managed the plantations successfully, planting the rice crops and supervising the laborers, who were now paid a weekly wage. In exchange for her workers' loyalty, she provided them with a hospital, store, and school on the plantation grounds.

Frances's writing is from Ten Years on a Georgia Plantation, *published in 1883 by R. Bentley and Sons.*

In 1870 Frances journeyed to London, where she became acquainted with James Wentworth Leigh, a British clergyman. They were married the following year, and she turned over the management of the plantations to him. In 1883 she published a book based on her journal, describing the ten years she managed the plantations on her own. She died in Hereford, England, in 1910 at the age of seventy-two.

Leila Mechlin

Not beautiful

1915

It seems remarkable that there could be any disagreement concerning what constitutes beauty or ugliness; but there is. Not a little so-called "modern art," that art which it is claimed is most advanced is positively ugly. One may stand before such a painting today representing ugly misshapen forms — absolute deformity — and showing inharmonious, jarring color, and be told that it is beautiful. If the observer does not agree that it is beautiful then he is told that the fault is with him. . . .

Leila Mechlin was born May 29, 1874, in the Georgetown district of Washington, D.C. She inherited her artistic interests from her mother, a portrait painter, and her grandfather, an etcher and engraver who helped found the United States Bureau of Engraving and Printing.

After graduating from Washington High School, Leila attended the Corcoran School of Art. In 1900 she began her career as art critic for the Washington *Evening* and *Sunday Star*, a position she held for the next forty-five years. She selected journalism because she felt it was "that branch of literature closest to the masses" and "because she was persuaded that the guidance of popular taste was a constructive vocation." Her views were traditional and conservative. She had little interest in novelty art but preferred serious art that would make an enduring contribution to the world. She firmly believed that people developed the best in themselves through a love of art.

In 1909 Leila co-founded the American Foundation of Arts to "increase and diffuse knowledge and appreciation of art." She organized many travelling exhibitions and opened a "channel for the expression of public opinion." Her most important duty was as editor of the Federation's official magazine *Art and Progress*, which was first issued in 1909.

Leila's writing is from "Beauty or Ugliness?," published in the November 1915 issue of Art and Progress, *the magazine she edited for twenty-two years.*

The magazine changed its name in 1915 to the *American Magazine of Art*, and Leila remained editor through 1931. It was the United States' first periodical devoted to art.

In 1932 Leila assisted the chairman of the Olympic Fine Arts Committee in selecting 1,200 works from thirty-five countries for display at the Xth Olympiad games in Los Angeles. During the 1930s she also served as art adviser to the Telfair Academy of Art in Georgia, the Mint Museum of North Carolina, and the Universities of North Carolina and Virginia. She was awarded honorary degrees from the University of Nebraska and George Washington University, and in 1940 she was elected a Fellow of London's Royal Society of Arts. She died in 1949, having devoted her entire life to spreading a love of art, and was buried in Georgetown's Oak Hill Cemetery.

Zilpah Polly Grant Banister M A Y   3 0

1872

My Dear Life-long Friend . . . Since the first of last November I have had in my room a class of intelligent young ladies for Bible study, and have been greatly refreshed by the manifestations of mind and heart in their young and vigorous life as sweetly expressed in their countenances and speech. In the vanishing of many of their difficulties I have seen an illustration of the text, "The entrance of thy word giveth light."

Zilpah Polly Grant Banister was born May 30, 1794, in Norfolk, Connecticut. She lived with her mother through her twenties, her father having died in a farm accident when she was two. Despite poor health (she suffered from pleurisy), she began teaching at fifteen to bring in added income for the family.

Zilpah's mother remarried in 1820, after which Zilpah moved to the Byfield Female Seminary in Byfield, Massachusetts, an institution run by the free-thinking Reverend Joseph Emerson, a leader in women's education. In 1824 she was offered the position of principal at the newly chartered Adams Female Academy in Londonderry, New Hampshire.

Soon after her arrival in Londonderry, her mother committed suicide, and an accident left Zilpah on crutches for several years. However, her strong religious beliefs sustained her, and she worked hard to build Adams Academy's

A Bible class

Zilpah's writing from a May 8, 1872, letter to the Reverend Mr. Marsh is included in The Use of a Life: Memorials of Mrs. Z. P. Banister, *compiled by L. T. Guilford and published by the American Tract Society in 1885.*

reputation. In 1828 the trustees decided to put less emphasis on religious training and more on secular studies such as music and dance. Zilpah disapproved of the changes and departed for Ipswich, Massachusetts, where "the leading men" of the town asked her to organize a seminary. Many of her teachers and pupils accompanied her to the new school, the Ipswich Female Seminary.

In 1835 Zilpah's assistant principal, Mary Lyon, left Ipswich to found Mount Holyoke College. Four years later, Zilpah's poor health forced her to retire from teaching. She married William Bostwick Banister, a lawyer twenty years her senior, in September 1841. She moved into his large home in Newburyport, Massachusetts, where she founded the American Women's Educational Association, a group formed to enlist missionary teachers for the West.

Zilpah's husband died in 1853. In 1874 on her eightieth birthday, former students gathered to celebrate and gave money to establish a room in her name at the Home of Woman's Board of Missions in Constantinople. She died of a heart attack later that year and was buried in Newburyport.

Kate Kennedy

The pigeon

circa 1890

I consider it needless to offer any apology for comparing intelligent human beings to pigeons. Had I likened them to gulls, the comparison might be deemed uncomplimentary, for the gull is the emblem of invincible stupidity; but the pigeon, though simple and unsuspicious to an incredible degree, is nevertheless capable of a very high moral and intellectual development, as is proved by the records of history. In the far-off pagan times, it was sacred to the goddess of Love and Beauty, and was reverenced as the type of innocence and purity, while the Christian dispensation presents it to its votaries as the symbol of spiritual enlightenment.

Kate's writing is from Doctor Paley's Foolish Pigeons and Short Sermons to Workingmen, *published posthumously in 1906 by Cubery & Co.*

Kate Kennedy was born May 31, 1827, in Gaskinstown, County Meath, Ireland. After graduating at the top of her class from the local convent school, she assumed responsibility for teaching her five younger sisters. Her father's death in 1841 and the great famine of 1846-1847 left the family destitute. In 1849 Kate sailed for New York with one brother and one sister.

Kate and her sister began working in New York City's garment district. The rest of the family arrived in 1851. Drawn by tales of wealth and opportunity in California, the entire Kennedy clan moved to San Francisco. Kate began her thirty-year teaching career in the San Francisco school system and gained a reputation as a superior teacher. In 1867 she was appointed principal of the North Cosmopolitan Grammar School, but because she was a woman her salary did not reflect her promotion. She began an "equal pay for equal work" campaign that concluded in 1874 when the state legislature passed a bill that stated, "females employed as teachers in the public schools of the State shall in all cases receive the same compensation as is allowed male teachers for like services when holding the same grade certificate."

As a result of the years she had spent in the New York sweatshop, Kate had strong pro-labor beliefs. She joined the Knights of Labor and the Land Reform League and participated in labor strikes. In 1886 she was nominated state superintendent of public instruction at a labor party convention. However, school officials could not tolerate her political activities, and she was demoted to a smaller school with a lower salary. She was dismissed altogether when she refused the transfer. She waged a three-year battle against the school board, finally winning in 1890 when the State Supreme Court wrote an opinion regarding teacher tenure. By then, however, her spirit and health were broken and she died a few months after the court decision. In 1911 the Kate Kennedy Schoolwomen's Club was founded to further teachers' rights, and a San Francisco school was named in her honor.

JUNE

Caroline Seabury

April 24th, 1857
Nearly four lonely months have passed & today a new field of duty seems opened for me. Columbus is thoroughly roused by a case of small-pox. A poor boy son of a widow has come up from Mobile sick — the physicians pronounce it smallpox — which has electrified the town with fright. This morning I met the Dr. attending who told me no one could be found who would go or send a servant to his mother's assistance. . . . I am in no danger from the disease — A solemn vow was made while I was suffering from it, & on what I supposed must be my death-bed, that if then my life were spared — in gratitude for all the care & kindness I then received, I would do all in my power to return it — when & wherever I could. That was in Mass — now in Miss, I have first to test my sincerity in making that resolution. *I will go.*

April 25th
I have tied up my bundle, a change of old clothes, for I promise to bring nothing away, and in a few minutes start for the house.

Fulfilling a vow

Caroline Seabury was born June 1, 1827, in Southbridge, Massachusetts, the eldest of six children. In 1850 eight family members died of consumption, including her father. Her mother committed suicide from grief. Only Caroline and two of her siblings survived the epidemic.

Caroline moved to Brooklyn, New York, to live with her uncle and his wife. Aware that she needed to support herself, she turned to teaching, one of the few professions open to women at that time. In 1854 she accepted a position at the Columbus Female Institute in Columbus, Mississippi. She purposely chose a school far from all that she had known. She explained in her diary, "I was leaving a sad gloomy sorrow marked past — going to an untried future, and could only 'let the dead past bury its dead,' hoping for a brighter future, of contented usefulness at least."

As a "Yankee teacher," Caroline was appalled at the horrors of slavery that she witnessed but was forced to keep quiet to maintain her job. Despite her silence, she was let go in 1862 when the principal at the Columbus Female Institute decided to employ only Southerners. She remained in

Caroline's writing is from her diary and is included in The Diary of Caroline Seabury, *edited by Suzanne L. Bunkers, University of Wisconsin Press, 1991.*

Mississippi one more year as a tutor for the daughters of a Confederate colonel. In July 1863, after the Union forces had broken through Confederate lines, Caroline decided it was time to return north.

In 1866 Caroline moved to St. Paul, Minnesota, to live with her brother Channing. She kept house for him, helped raise his children after his wife died, and did the bookkeeping for his wholesale grocery business. She died on March 18, 1893, and was buried in the Seabury family plot in St. Paul.

Marjorie Hill Allee

Quaker girlhood

Marjorie's writing is from an autobiographical sketch she wrote a few years before her death. It is included in The Junior Book of Authors, *edited by Stanley J. Kunitz and H. Haycraft and published by H. W. Wilson in 1951.*

1941

I was born on June 2, 1890, which has always seemed to me an admirable date; in the first place, June is the best possible month for birthday celebrations, and in the second place I can always remember how old I am without elaborate mathematical calculations.

I grew up on the farm my great-grandfather had bought in the early days of the state, near Carthage, Indiana, in a community of self-respecting Quakers. . . .

My sister and I walked a mile to a one-room district school which had been called the "Rabbit Hash School" for three generations, and there were still rabbits in the brush piles of the surrounding woods.

Marjorie Hill Allee was born June 2, 1890, near Carthage, Indiana. Her family, Quakers from the South, had migrated north to avoid the evils of slavery. Marjorie attended the local "Rabbit Hash" grade school, then "drove our horse and buggy four miles to town and back every day" to attend high school. After two years at Earlham College in Richmond, Indiana, she returned to teach all eight grades at "Rabbit Hash."

Marjorie aspired to become a writer, and to further her goal she enrolled at the University of Chicago. There she "found another Quaker, Warder Clyde Allee, who had also migrated from his ancestral farm, and we were married and have lived happily ever afterward in various parts of the country wherever he happened to be teaching zoology." Through the years they lived in Illinois, Utah, Oklahoma, and Massachusetts.

In 1925 Marjorie collaborated with her husband on her first book, *Jungle Island*, a nonfiction children's book describing the plants and animals on an island in the Panama Canal. Marjorie enjoyed writing for children, and between 1929 and 1945 she published fourteen juvenile novels. Six of her novels were about the Quakers, and most of her work concerned young women beginning to confront fast-approaching adult problems. In 1931 she won the Newberry Honor Award for *Jane's Island*, about dedicated young marine biologists in Woods Hole, Massachusetts.

Marjorie received the annual award of the Child Study Association of America for her next-to-last novel, *The House*, which dealt with racial intolerance. Her citation read, "A book which faces with honesty and courage real problems in our children's world; a realistic picture translating democratic ideals into everyday terms." She published her last book in early 1945 and died on April 30, one month short of her fifty-fifth birthday.

Hannah Kent Schoff

1915

Time for a rescue

One morning in May, 1899, the Philadelphia papers gave an account of the arrest and imprisonment of a little girl for setting fire to a house. Her picture was published, and with startling head-lines she was heralded to the world as "A Prodigy of Crime." Motherless since she had been two years old, an inmate of an orphanage and then a drudge in a city boarding-house, with no companionship save that of ignorant servants, there had been little opportunity for her to develop any moral responsibility. Friendless she was, arrested, imprisoned, tried in a criminal court and sentenced to a House of Refuge, and only eight years old! When asked why she had started the fire she frankly said, "To see the fire burn and the engines run."

Branded as a criminal and sentenced to the companionship of girls guilty of crimes of far greater menace to character, what hope could the future hold for her? The injustice in the treatment of this poor child led me to the determination to rescue her if possible, and to do for her what I should wish some one to do for my own little girl were she in a similar position — as she might have been had she been motherless and friendless at such a tender age.

Hannah's writing is from her book The Wayward Child, *published in 1915 by the Bobbs-Merrill Company.*

Hannah Kent Schoff was born June 3, 1853, in Upper Darby, Pennsylvania. She married Frederic Schoff, an engineer from Massachusetts, when she was twenty. They settled in Philadelphia and raised seven children.

In 1897 Hannah attended the First National Congress of Mothers, representing her local women's club. She rose quickly in the new women's club movement, serving as the national organization's vice-president and later president until she retired in 1920. Under her administration, membership swelled to 190,000 in thirty-seven state branches. She travelled and lectured extensively to promote her goal of establishing parent-teacher organizations in the schools.

Hannah organized the International Conference on Child Welfare held in Washington, D.C., in 1908. Two more conferences followed in 1911 and 1914. She was particularly interested in juvenile court and probation reform, drafting several bills to establish juvenile courts and detention homes plus a new probation system designed for children.

From 1901 to 1923 Hannah served as president of the Philadelphia Juvenile Court and Probation Association. She attended almost all sessions of the new court, studying thousands of cases. She assisted in creating juvenile court systems in three other states and was the first woman to address the Parliament of Canada, where she helped train probation workers for their new juvenile court system there.

Hannah published two books on children and the legal system. She died in 1940 and was buried in the Schoff plot in Newton, Massachusetts.

JUNE 4

Catharine Waugh McCulloch

Excessive punishment

1935

One of these men teachers punished whisperers by putting a stick about an inch long between our jaws and put us up in the front of the whole school. For once my father interfered and asked the teacher to devise some other punishment as he did not want my mouth stretched. Perhaps this humorous suggestion or other complaints ended that system of torture. That's the only time I remember being punished in school.

Catharine's writing is from a 1935 autobiographical sketch that is in the Catharine Waugh McCulloch and Grace H. Harte Papers, Schlesinger Library, Radcliffe College, Cambridge, Massachusetts.

Catharine Gouger Waugh McCulloch was born June 4, 1862, on a farm near Ransomville, New York. Her family relocated to a farm in Illinois when she was five. Her father was very intelligent, and although untrained in law, assisted his neighbors with their legal problems. Catharine was very close to her father, as she recalled years later in a newspaper interview: "I was my father's 'little lawyer' and he aided and abetted me in my fatal tendency." In 1885 she enrolled at the Union College of Law in Chicago.

Catharine passed the Illinois bar and opened a practice in Rockford. In May 1890 she married Frank H. McCulloch, a lawyer from Mason City, Iowa. She joined her husband's firm, which was renamed McCulloch and McCulloch. She had three sons who all became lawyers and a daughter who married a lawyer.

Over the years Catharine became involved in the women's suffrage movement. In 1893 she drew up a bill providing for women's suffrage in presidential and certain specific local elections and presented it, unsuccessfully, to the state legislature for the next twenty years. Each year she travelled to Springfield with a group of supporters to lobby on its behalf. It was finally enacted in 1913, the year after her retirement as legislative superintendent of the Illinois Equal Suffrage Association.

Catharine played many roles in the women's movement. In 1901 she drafted a bill passed by the Illinois legislature granting women equal rights with their husbands in the guardianship of their children. Four years later, she helped pass another bill raising the age of consent for women from fourteen to sixteen. In 1910 she conceived the idea of the "suffrage auto tour," which organized motorized teams of women who travelled throughout the state, speaking from open automobiles. The following year she wrote a feminist play that was performed successfully before groups of suffragists.

Following the adoption of the federal suffrage amendment in 1920, Catharine turned her attention to the League of Women Voters and the Woman's Christian Temperance Union. She served as legal adviser to both organizations and as president of the Women's Bar Association of Illinois for five years. In 1940 she and her husband were named "Senior Counselors" of the Illinois Bar Association in recognition of their long years of legal practice. Catharine died of cancer in 1945 at the age of eighty-two and was buried in Chicago's Graceland Cemetery.

Ruth Fulton Benedict

Terrible to be a woman

1912

So much of the trouble is because I am a woman. To me it seems a very terrible thing to be a woman. There is one crown which perhaps is worth it all — a great love, a quiet home, and children. We all know that is all that is worth while, and yet we must peg away, showing off our wares on the market if we have money, or manufacturing careers for ourselves if we haven't. We have not the motive to prepare ourselves for a "life-work" of teaching, of social work — we know that we would lay it down with hallelujah in the height of our success, to make a home for the right man.

And all the time in the background of our consciousness rings the warning that perhaps the right man will never come. A great love is given to very few. Perhaps this make-shift time filler of a job is our life work after all.

Ruth Fulton Benedict was born June 5, 1887, in New York City. Her father died when she was only twenty-one months old, and her mother returned to her parents' farm in upstate . New York. Ruth had a morbid fascination with death and was subject to severe tantrums and vomiting as a child, which evolved into long periods of depression as she grew older. Despite her mental handicaps, she excelled at school and graduated Phi Beta Kappa from Vassar College in 1909.

In June 1914 Ruth married Stanley Rossiter Benedict, a biochemistry professor at Cornell Medical School. She occupied herself with social work and began writing a book, but by Christmas 1916 she realized she could not achieve personal happiness merely by being a wife. Thereafter, through the late 1920s she saw her husband only on weekends, and from 1930 on they ceased meeting altogether. Neither of them remarried, however, and Stanley left his entire estate to her when he died in 1936.

Ruth began taking anthropology courses at the New School for Social Research in 1919. She earned her doctorate in 1923 from Columbia University, studying under the famous anthropologist Franz Boas. From 1922 to 1931 she made repeated field trips to the West and Southwest to study various Indian cultures, which resulted in two books on the folktales and mythology of the different tribes.

During her frequent fits of depression, Ruth wrote highly

Ruth's writing is from her journal and is included in Anthropologist at Work: Writings of Ruth Benedict, *compiled by Margaret Mead and published by Columbia University Press in 1959.*

personal poetry which she published under the pseudonym Anne Singleton. In 1931 Franz Boas appointed her as an assistant professor at Columbia, after which her depression lifted permanently and she ceased writing poetry.

In 1934 Ruth published what is still considered the definitive introduction to anthropology, *Patterns of Culture*.

Ruth's most important work, *The Chrysanthemum and The Sword: Patterns of Japanese Culture*, published in 1946, firmly established her as one of the leading female anthropologists of her day. She outlined the various obligations of the Japanese to themselves, their family, and their emperor, and drew conclusions regarding the best ways to assimilate the Japanese into a peaceful world community. A few months prior to her death in 1948 Columbia fulfilled her dream by appointing her a full professor.

Lucile Wolf Heming Koshland

JUNE 6

1946

A role in history

This is the promised P.S. to my letter, to tell you what I'm doing here. It's a wonderful experience to be in at the birth of a great experiment. I can't help wondering what our children's children will say about all this. The National Commission is pretty impressive, yet the spirit of these people is humble and at the same time not overawed by the fantastic job assigned to us.

The State Dept has put on this show in an impressive setting. We meet in the newly remodeled international Conference Room, in the War Manpower Building on Penn. Ave., air-conditioned, sound proofed, with grey walls, lovely drapes, rug and Venetian blinds, comfortable chairs — covered in material made of spun glass (I'm told). We sit around a beautiful horseshoe table, with microphones and thermos jugs before us, and little name placques like Bank officers have on their desks. It gave me an odd feeling — that I should pinch myself to see "MRS. C. E. HEMING" in black letters on the shiny white placque.

Lucile Wolf Heming Koshland was born June 6, 1898, in New York City. She attended private schools and graduated Phi Beta Kappa in 1919 from Barnard College with a degree in American History. A year before graduation she married Charles E. Heming, a stockbroker.

Lucile's writing is from a September 26, 1946, letter to her family while she was in Washington, D.C., attending meetings of the National Commission for UNESCO. It is among the personal papers of her daughter Delia Heming Cantor, Scarsdale, New York.

Lucile was widowed in 1929, and although she had four children to raise, she became very active in civic organizations. In 1939 she was the first female grand juror. She served on the National Commission for UNESCO (United Nations Educational, Scientific, and Cultural Organization) for two years and on the National Child Labor Committee for twenty years. She was president of the New York State Chapter of the League of Women Voters and later a member of the league's national board.

Following Carrie Chapman Catt's death in 1947, the league decided to create a fund to honor her memory. The Carrie Chapman Catt Memorial Fund was established to help women in foreign countries attain responsible citizenship by teaching them the most effective use of the vote. Lucile was elected first president of the fund and remained on the board through 1966. In 1953 she received the Commander's Cross of the Order of Merit from the Federal Republic of Germany in recognition of the fund's program of democratic education for German women.

In 1959 when she was sixty-one years old, Lucile married Daniel Koshland, a widower with three grown children. In the late 1960s her friends set up a scholarship fund for students at San Mateo College in Lucile's name as a birthday present. Over the years she remained in contact with the students, and on her birthday in 1973 eleven of the exchange students arrived at her home to celebrate. Lucile died in California in 1978 at the age of eighty.

JUNE 7

Janet Ayer Fairbank

A skating party

1932

Miss Wentworth agreed to chaperon the skating party, and after tea they all went down to the pond. The moon was riding high in the sky suffused with light; all about the edge of the cleared space the heaped snow shone like silver. Jeremiah put on Abby-Delight's skates and bound the straps about her ankles. He pulled her to her feet and took both her mittened hands in his. His legs were so long that he swept her away with him in great swoops, which made her laugh.

"You skate well."

"Everyone can skate," Abby-Delight replied modestly.

"No — not everyone." Was it an accident that his

Janet's writing is from her book The Bright Land, *published by Houghton, Mifflin and Company in 1932.*

Women's Words, Women's Stories

eyes rested on Sally, who was at the moment being held on her feet by two delighted young gentlemen? They were all laughing, and Abby-Delight marveled at Sally's being amused when she was doing something so badly. That complete lack of self-consciousness was one of the things she most admired in her friend.

"Sally is learning," she said loyally.

"Can you grapevine?"

"Yes." In an instant they were weaving an intricate pattern across the pond, in and out among the skaters, and Abby-Delight was agreeably aware of causing admiring attention. They had barely passed when someone else came up and asked her to skate.

Miss Wentworth was having a good time, also. Jeremiah Everett went to skate with her when he was free; she could see him swinging her along in his swaying, effortless stride. . . . All the boys skated with Abby-Delight; those from the Academy coming up to be introduced, so that they might ask her. She played crack the whip with them; it reminded her of rough games with Amos on the pond at home.

Jeremiah walked back with her and carried her skates.

"I have had a delightful evening," Abby-Delight told him. She could see his face very clearly in the bright light, as he smiled down at her.

Janet Ayer Fairbank was born June 7, 1878, in Chicago. She attended local private schools and graduated from the University of Chicago. She married Kellogg Fairbank soon after graduation in 1900.

Janet published her first novel in 1910. She continued writing through 1936, publishing ten more novels. All of her books were set in Illinois with strong characters, especially women, combatting the trials of everyday life. Current history and politics were also worked in. Janet's older sister M. A. Barnes was also a novelist, and they collaborated on a book in 1935.

In addition to her writing career, Janet also worked for the cause of women's suffrage. A Democrat, she served on the Illinois Democratic National Committee and as a delegate to the 1932 Democratic National Convention. She served on the board of the Chicago Lying-in Hospital for twenty-four years.

Janet died at her Chicago home in 1951 at the age of seventy-three.

Marian Anthon Fish

Young idlers

1915

There is nothing sadder than the growing class of rich young idlers in America and throughout the world. If the great war now in progress does something toward stopping that, and it seems reasonable to believe that that may be another of its indirect results, it will not have been an unmixed evil.

Marian Graves Anthon Fish was born June 8, 1853, on Staten Island, New York. Her father was one of the best-known criminal lawyers of the time. One week shy of her twenty-third birthday, she married Stuyvesant Fish, the son of President Ulysses Grant's secretary of state, Hamilton Fish.

Marian and Stuyvesant had four children, although the eldest son died at six months. They lived in a beautiful Manhattan townhouse and often spent weekends at the Fish family country estate, "Glenclyffe," in Garrison-on-Hudson. Marian quickly adapted to the life of a wealthy socialite. She became famous for her lavish dinner parties. When Newport, Rhode Island, was proclaimed America's most exclusive summer resort, she built "Crossways," a grand Colonial Revival mansion, and began giving parties there. Stuyvesant, although he loved his wife, disliked such an active social life and usually summered at "Glenclyffe."

Marian found herself bored at the customary two- to three-hour dinners given by her social counterparts, Mrs. Astor and Mrs. Vanderbilt, so she introduced society to the fifty-minute dinner. Champagne flowed while footmen speedily served the food. After dinner, guests were treated to performances by opera singers, Japanese dancers, or vaudeville actors. Mrs. Fish became known as a colorful personality who consulted clairvoyants and enjoyed playing practical jokes. Once, when a Newport neighbor had a dinner for the Grand Duke Boris, she gave a rival dinner for the Czar to draw the guests to her house instead. Of course, her Czar was an impostor.

In 1913 Marian became interested in the working women on strike in the wrapper and kimono industry in New York's garment district. She made several trips to the Lower East Side to talk with the women in their tenement homes to see what could be done to help them.

Marian died of a cerebral hemorrhage at "Glenclyffe" in May 1915 at the age of sixty-one.

Marian's writing is from "Mrs. Stuyvesant Fish Decries Hard Up Hysteria," the New York Times, *January 17, 1915.*

Helen Marot

1918

A friend of mine, in describing the Russian people as he observed them in their present revolution, said it was possible for them to accept new ideas because they were uneducated; they did not, he said, labor under the difficulty common among educated people of having to get rid of old ideas before they took on new ones. I think what he had in mind to say was that it is difficult to accept new ideas when your mind is filled with ideas which are institutional.

New ideas

Helen Marot was born June 9, 1865, in Philadelphia to a Quaker family. She was educated at home and at local Friends' schools and was raised to be independent. Her father always admonished her, "I want you to think for your-self — not the way I do."

Beginning in 1893, Helen took several positions as a librarian in Philadelphia and Wilmington, Delaware. After four years, she opened a small library of her own in Philadelphia for "those interested in social and economic problems." The library became a gathering place for liberal thinkers. As Helen described it in an interview, "People of all shades of radicalism come there — Single Taxers, Socialists, Philosophical Anarchists — attracted by the unusual books and periodicals and no less by the opportunity for discussion."

In 1899 Helen was hired by the United States Industrial Commission to investigate the custom tailoring trades in Philadelphia. What she discovered about the poor working conditions, especially for women and children, changed her from a peaceful, studious librarian into a militant activist. She went to New York City in 1902 to uncover child labor problems there, which resulted in the formation of the New York Child Labor Committee. The following year, she helped push the Compulsory Education Act through the New York legislature.

Helen was elected secretary of the Women's Trade Union League of New York in 1906, a position she held for the next seven years. During that time she lectured on the benefits of unions to countless members of the garment trade and orga-nized a new union for bookkeepers, stenographers, and accountants. Her research helped persuade the United States Supreme Court to uphold the constitutionality of a law limit-ing working hours for women.

From 1909 to 1910 the League, under Helen's supervision,

Helen's writing is from the introduction to her book Creative Impulse In Industry — A Proposition for Educators, *published in 1918 by E. P. Dutton.*

led the great waist and dressmaker's strike. The strike brought attention to workers' plight, empowered women, and began an industrial revolution in the garment industry that led to the formation of the International Ladies' Garment Workers' Union. Exhausted from her efforts in the strike, Helen took an extended European vacation and returned renewed. In 1914 she turned her attention to writing, publishing pamphlets and magazine articles promoting her socialist views. She worked as an editor for the radical magazine, *The Masses*, until it was shut down in 1917 for its antiwar policy, after which she joined the staff of *The Dial*.

After retiring in 1920, Helen divided her time between Greenwich Village and her summer home in West Becket, Massachusetts. She died in 1940, six days short of her seventy-fifth birthday, and her ashes were scattered over Long Island Sound.

JUNE 10

Marion Florence Lansing

A good story

Marion's writing is from The Junior Book of Authors *by Stanley J. Kunitz and Harold Haycraft, published by H. W. Wilson in 1934.*

1934

One day the little girl, who was Marion Lansing, went with her mother into Boston to see Mr. Ginn, who was publishing these Stickney readers. He took her on his knee and said to her, "Will you make books for me when you grow up?" And she answered, as any five-year-old would, "Yes." But the best part of that story for the girl, who was myself, was that she did.

Marion Florence Lansing was born June 10, 1883, in Waverly, Massachusetts. When she was a child, her family moved to Cambridge, where she remained for the rest of her life. Her mother worked for Ginn & Company Publishing House, compiling children's readers. Marion later reminisced, "I learned to read on my mother's page proofs and was barely five when I committed myself to a writing career." After graduating from Cambridge Latin School, she enrolled in Mount Holyoke College. Although the college's founder, Mary Lyon, died before Marion began attending the school, she was deeply influenced by her. In 1937, on the 100th anniversary of the college's founding, she edited a book, *Mary Lyon Through Her Letters*, honoring her as a pioneer in women's education.

After graduating from Mount Holyoke, Marion spent a year at Radcliffe College studying history. Her professor encouraged her to begin writing history texts. She took several extended trips to South America which resulted in her book *Liberators and Heroes of South America*. It was followed a few years later by *Liberators and Heroes of Mexico and Central America*. She went on to produce numerous children's history books about explorers, knights, patriots, and scientists. Her characters came alive through the magic of her pen, stimulating the imagination of her young readers and offering them fascinating glimpses of history. One critic called her an important "channel of international understanding of youth."

Marion died at home in February 1966 at the age of eighty-two.

Jeannette Pickering Rankin

1917

*A*gainst war

Mr. Chairman, I still believe that war is a stupid and futile way of attempting to settle international difficulties. I believe that war can be avoided, and will be avoided, when the people — the men and women — in America as well as in Germany, have the controlling voice in their Government.

To-day special privileged commercial interests are controlling the world. When we declared war on Germany, we virtually declared war on Germany's allies. The vote we are now to cast is not a vote on a declaration of war. If it were, I should vote against it. This is a vote on a mere technicality, in the prosecution of a war already declared. I shall vote for this as I voted for money and for men.

Jeannette Pickering Rankin was born June 11, 1880, on the Grant Creek Ranch in Montana Territory. She attended Missoula public schools and graduated in 1902 from the University of Montana with a biology degree. Two years later her father died, and she returned home to help take care of her six younger siblings.

In 1910 Jeannette joined the suffrage movement while studying at the University of Washington. She was determined to combine the quest for peace with the suffrage platform. She spent the next few years lobbying for suffrage in fifteen different states and was a major force in acquiring the vote for women in Montana in 1914. In 1916 she campaigned for Congress as a Republican, endorsing prohibition, suffrage, child protection laws, and "preparedness that will

Jeannette's writing is from her speech given in the House of Representatives during the debate on the declaration of war on Austria-Hungary, December 7, 1917. It is in the Congressional Record of that date.

make for peace." She won the election, becoming the first woman in the House of Representatives. Four days after her arrival in Washington in April 1917, she voted against United States entry into World War I. Fifty-six congressmen voted with her, and although it was falsely reported that she cried as she cast her vote, in fact several of the men did cry.

Having lost a bid for election as a Montana senator, Jeannette finished out her term as a congresswoman and moved on to the Women's International League for Peace and Freedom. In 1924 she built a second home in Athens, Georgia, where she established the Georgia Peace Society. From 1929 to 1939 she was an organizer and lobbyist for the National Council for the Prevention of War. In 1939 she again ran for Congress from Montana. With the support of women, labor, and citizens against the war, she was able to defeat her liberal Democratic opponent.

The day after Pearl Harbor, December 8, 1941, Jeannette cast the only opposing vote to America's entry into World War II, earning her the distinction of being the only member of Congress to oppose both World Wars. After losing her bid for re-election in 1942, she began travelling extensively abroad to study pacifism in other countries. She was especially fascinated by Ghandi's work and made seven trips to India between 1946 and 1971.

Out of the limelight for twenty years, she re-emerged in 1967 with the Jeannette Rankin Brigade, an organization opposed to the Vietnam War. She decided, at eighty-eight, to run for a third term in Congress but was unable to carry out her plans due to unexpected surgery. She died of a heart attack in California in 1973, one month short of her ninety-third birthday.

Sukey Vickery Watson

Beware of rakes

1803
It seems to gratify the pride of some weak females to be admired by a rake, especially if his figure is pleasing. Those fellows are generally polite, tender and attentive, and they have such a smooth, artful, insinuating address, that they persuade those whom they flatter, to believe they are angels, while they are only endeavoring to sink them below the dregs of creation. It is amazing to me how any girl in her right senses can listen to such men.

Sukey's writing is from her novel Emily Hamilton, *published by Isaiah Thomas, Jr. in 1803.*

Sukey Vickery Watson was born June 12, 1779, in Leicester, Massachusetts. Her father, a tailor, had relocated there from Boston four years previously in search of work. At nine Sukey began attending Leicester Academy, where she studied Latin, Greek, and logic in addition to the regular subjects.

After graduation, Sukey became a part of the social life of that period, attending church socials, dancing parties, and making the occasional shopping trip to Boston, forty miles away. Unbeknownst to her friends, however, Sukey wrote poetry. Her first poem was published in 1801 in the periodical *The Massachusetts Spy* under the pen name Fidelia. Over the next two years, she published many poems in *The Spy*, mostly with patriotic or religious themes and all very flowery and sentimental.

On September 15, 1802, *The Massachusetts Spy* printed an announcement that a book was soon to be published by a "Young Lady of Worcester County," the first ever to be published in that county. *The Spy* advertised for advance subscriptions to the book at seventy-five cents a copy, and if six were ordered the seventh was free. Sukey's largely autobiographical book, *Emily Hamilton*, appeared in June 1803. However, it was not a big seller, and she never wrote anything again.

On October 14, 1804, Sukey married Samuel Watson, a local clothing shop operator. In 1805 she had the first of nine children, seven girls and two boys. In 1810 she co-founded the Leicester Female Society with the purpose of self-improvement through social contact, reading, and needlework.

Sukey died in June 1821 at the age of forty-two. Although her husband married twice after her death, he chose to be buried in Leicester beside Sukey, the wife who had borne his children and helped him in the early days of his business.

Francis Sawyer

May 26, 1852

Indian fight

A large party of Pawnee Indians passed us this morning going on to their hunting grounds after buffalo, and this afternoon we met them returning. They had met a party of Sioux, and the result was a battle took place. The Sioux had whipped them, killing and scalping two of the party and wounding several others. . . . I met some ladies that saw the fight, and they said they were scared almost to death themselves. The Pawnees had made a poor fight. . . . When we came to where the battle had been fought, Mr. Sawyer and I drove off the road a short distance to see one of the Indians who had been killed. It was the worst horrible sight I ever saw. Four or five arrows were sticking in his body and his scalp was gone. . . .

I am sorry I went out to look at him. . . . We are in camp with a large company of emigrants, to-night, and have out a strong guard. So we women are safe and secure from danger, and may rest in peace and comfort, if we don't dream of dead Indians.

Francis Lamar Sawyer was born June 13, 1831, in Cloverport, Kentucky. Her father had hoped for a son. Therefore, he spelled his daughter's name "Francis" rather than the feminine version, "Frances."

In her late teens she married Thomas Sawyer, a local boatman who worked on the river. He had dreams of moving west and went to California via the Overland Route in 1849, returning in the fall of 1850. In the spring of 1851 he left again and "went out by water, by way of New Orleans and the Isthmus." He was accompanied by Francis's brother and another man from Kentucky. He "soon got homesick again" and returned home in the fall of 1851.

During Tom's absence, Francis had given birth to their first child, Henry, but he died at the age of nine months. Soon after the child's death, Tom began making plans to move to Oregon permanently with his wife. He bought a wagon and some mules, and on April 25, 1852, they left Louisville by steamer for St. Louis.

Francis began a diary on the day of her departure and kept it faithfully every day until she arrived at their destination. There were four in their party, Francis and her husband and two other young men, neighbors from Hancock County, Kentucky. She meticulously noted the weather, road conditions, and distance travelled each day, which varied from six to thirty miles.

On June 20 they passed the famous Independence Rock in Wyoming. She wrote, "This rock is a great curiosity, standing, as it does, here on the level plain, single and alone, hundreds of miles from any companion. It should have been named Emigrant's Register, as it contains thousands of names on its surface, some being carved, some being placed there with paint, and others with tar. . . ." On the following day she wrote, "We went to the big rock this afternoon, and placed our names on it."

Along the way Tom changed his mind about their final destination, deciding on California instead of Oregon. On

Francis's diary entry is from Covered Wagon Women — Volume IV, *edited and compiled by Kenneth Holmes and published by the Arthur H. Clark Company in 1985.*

August 16 the Sawyers parted company with their two travelling companions who remained in Placerville, California, to
try their luck at mining. On August 17 they reached
Sacramento City, and that was the last day Francis wrote in
her diary.

Francis and Tom spent the next twelve years in California,
where she gave birth to three daughters and two sons. In
1864 they returned to their "Old Kentucky Home" in
Cloverport. Three more daughters were born in Kentucky,
and Tom supported the family as a painter. In 1937 one of
their children, Nancy Wills, donated her mother's diary to
the Bancroft Library of the University of California at
Berkeley.

Cornelia Peake McDonald

1875

I never in my heart thought slavery was right, and having in my childhood seen some of the worst instances
of its abuse, and in my youth, when surrounded by
them and daily witnessing what I considered great
injustice to them, I could not think how the men I most
honored and admired, my husband among the rest,
could constantly justify it, and not only that, but say
that it was a blessing to the slave, his master, and the
country; and, (even now I say it with a feeling of
shame), that the renewal of the slave trade would be a
blessing and benefit to all, if only the consent of the
world could be obtained to its being made lawful.

Cornelia Peake McDonald was born June 14, 1822, in
Alexandria, Virginia. Her father, a physician, lost a large part
of his fortune when she was a young child by "acting surety
for friends." Embarrassed to reduce his standard of living
before his friends and associates, he moved the family to
"Waterfall," a plantation near Haymarket, Virginia.
Cornelia's two older sisters, although only fourteen and sixteen, opened a school to augment the family's income, and
Cornelia was enrolled as a pupil.

In 1835 Dr. Peake decided to seek his fortune out West,
and they departed with "the family in carriages, brother
William riding his own horse, the Negro men walking, while
the women and children rode in wagons." They settled in
Palmyra, Missouri, but within a short period of time almost

A feeling of shame

Cornelia's writing is from A
Diary with Reminiscences of
the War and Refugee Life in
the Shenandoah Valley,
1860-1865, *edited and published by her son Hunter
McDonald in 1934.*

all of their 100 Negroes had died of malaria, and two nieces who had accompanied them had died of consumption. After her mother's death in 1837, the family moved again to Hannibal, Missouri. There, Cornelia met Angus McDonald, a widower with four children. Following their marriage, Cornelia and Angus returned to Winchester, Virginia, where he practiced law and she had nine children.

During the Civil War, Angus joined the Confederate Army as a colonel. He was taken prisoner early, so Cornelia spent most of the war alone, trying to keep her family together and her home in her possession. After the Union Army occupied Winchester in 1862, she was evicted and became a homeless war refugee. During this difficult time she kept a diary, which was later published by her son.

After the war Cornelia travelled to meet her husband upon his release from prison, but he died before she arrived. She continued to struggle on, a widow with many small children, in war-torn Virginia. She raised her family and was active in the Episcopal church. Cornelia died in March 1909 at the age of eighty-six, and was buried beside her husband in Richmond's Hollywood Cemetery.

JUNE 15

Malvina Cornell Hoffman

A test of memory

Malvina's writing is from her book Yesterday is Tomorrow, *published by Crown Publishers in 1965.*

1965

Perhaps the most surprising and significant lesson I ever had was in Rodin's studio soon after I had begun my studies under his direction. One day he led me into a room adjoining his salon and showed me five or six portraits in marble and bronze. "Choose one of these," he said, "and examine it carefully while I look over some letters. I will return in twenty minutes." He left and closed the door.

In half an hour he returned and told me to follow him into the next studio, where he pointed to the clay bin and said: "Now show me how accurate your observations were. Model for me the head you selected in the other room, from memory, about half the size of the original. . . . So saying he closed the door and locked it from the other side. . . .

As a test of memory this was it. My heart was pounding, and I knew I had to burn through my fog of panic. Memory is both illusive and piercingly bright.

Once started, I was carried along by some inner sight that re-created the forms that had impressed their planes upon my mind. Gradually the face took on the look of the gaunt and severe personality I had selected without knowing who it was. The expression of the eyes and general outline of the head were so unusual that my memory had caught them, but when it came to other details I found that they had not registered.

Rodin returned, asking me if I had completed my task. I said Yes, as far as my memory would guide me! He took the clay head and examined it from all sides. *"Pas mal, mon enfant!"* (Not bad, my child!) He led me back to the original bronze in the little gallery. "Now," he said, "in five minutes check your mistakes and bring it to me. Then I will take you to lunch at l'Avenue's!" Before we left, he placed the clay on a high shelf in a closet so that it might dry and harden. . . . "I want you to keep it for a reminder. You will never forget this lesson, for most people *look* at things without *seeing* them, and very few know the value of cultivating memory. But you will need to do this *all your life*! Don't forget it."

Malvina Cornell Hoffman was born June 15, 1885, in New York City. After graduating from a private girls' school, Malvina studied painting and modeling but soon concentrated on sculpting. In 1909 she went to Paris with her mother, determined to study with sculptor Auguste Rodin. After viewing her work, he recognized her talent and accepted her as a pupil.

In 1924 Malvina married Samuel B. Grimson, an English violinist whom she had met fifteen years earlier while sculpting his bust. Malvina held her first major exhibit in 1929 at the Grand Central Art Gallery in New York. The 105 pieces of sculpture then travelled to museums all over the United States for the next five years. In 1930 she received the largest commission ever given for sculpture: more than 100 separate bronze statues depicting all the races in the world, to be exhibited at the Field Museum of Natural History in Chicago.

To complete this commission Malvina travelled for two years with her husband to remote places in Asia, Africa, Europe, the Pacific Islands, and the Americas, studying and sketching various racial types.

Malvina wrote two autobiographies and a textbook on sculpture and received five honorary degrees and numerous awards, including the National Sculpture Society's Gold Medal of Honor. She succumbed to a heart attack at her New York studio in 1966.

Alma Bridwell White

Unbearable sights

1914

By the time I reached the top of the long flight of steps, I was so ill I feared that I would never reach the bottom again in safety. But the officer kept his eye on me and told me afterwards that he thought perhaps he would have to come to my assistance. I had one glimpse of the hogs and could bear no more. I saw them stuck with a knife and pitched into the boiling water, and the sight will remain with me as long as I live. Still dizzy and staggering, I was conducted to the place where the cattle were killed and without going into details, will say that the sight of the blood that was flowing in streams, nearly caused me to faint. . . .

After reaching my room, I was so burdened over the cruelty I had seen, that I felt I could never eat any more meat.

Alma Bridwell White was born June 16, 1862, in Kinniconick, Kentucky, the seventh of eleven children. She described her early life as "toilsome." She was unable to attend school as she had to work in the family tannery, although she taught herself to read and write. She decided to become a teacher to escape the drudgery of the tanning vats, and she took her first job when she was seventeen. In 1882 she moved in with her aunt in the frontier settlement at Bannack, Montana, where she organized a community school.

As early as her sixteenth year, Alma had felt a strong conviction that she had been called by the Lord to preach the gospel. She was discouraged by the Methodist hierarchy from trying to become a preacher and was told to marry a minister and make her contribution through him. On December 21, 1887, she married Kent White, a recently ordained minister.

Kent permitted Alma to lead the hymns and prayers. Occasionally, she preached a sermon, never preparing it in advance but waiting for "heavenly dynamite to explode." She discovered that she had a powerful gift and could bring people to their knees crying or make them skip through the aisles

Alma's writing is from Why I Do Not Eat Meat, *published in 1914 by the Pentecostal Union, Zarephath, New Jersey.*

singing. She experienced a "second blessing" in 1893, after which she was no longer satisfied with merely assisting her husband and began leading her own revival meetings.

Alma met with opposition from the Methodist hierarchy, whom she denounced as "agents of Satan." After she was forbidden to preach from Methodist pulpits, she convinced her husband to resign his pastorate to accompany her around the country conducting camp meetings. In 1901 she organized her own independent sect, the Methodist Pentecostal Union, which she changed to the Pillar of Fire Church in 1917. Her membership grew over a thirty-year period from 230 to 4,044 in forty-six separate congregations. She often preached three to four times per day and crossed the Atlantic forty-eight times to organize congregations abroad. She purchased two radio stations, one in Colorado and one in New Jersey, to be able to reach a larger audience, and by 1936 her church-owned property was valued at $4 million. Alma established seven schools that combined Bible study with vocational skills such as typesetting and carpentry, and in 1921 the Alma White College was authorized by the state of New Jersey to award degrees in arts and sciences. Somehow, she also managed to find time to write more than 200 hymns and publish several books of poems.

Alma became involved with the Ku Klux Klan after World War I, calling it "the greatest moral and political movement of the generation." Although she could not be a member because she was a woman, she lectured on the group's behalf and wrote a book, *The Ku Klux Klan in Prophecy*, in which she quoted passages from the Bible that proved the Klan was endorsed by God. She claimed that the Apostles and the Good Samaritan were Klansmen.

Alma kept up her hectic pace until the end. She took up oil painting at the age of seventy, producing more than 300 landscapes in six years. She died in 1946 at the age of eighty-four. Following services in the Alma Temple in Denver, she was buried in the Fairmont Cemetery.

Chrystal Katharine Herne

*circa
1925*

A vivid picture

Having been born, practically, on the stage, with my father and mother both actors, I cannot remember the first play I ever saw. It probably was when I was quite a mite of a baby girl. . . .

The first play I remember almost broke my little

heart. It was "Drifting Apart," and my father and mother played the leading parts. I was a little girl, not more than seven or eight, I am sure, and the place was Boston.

The story of "Drifting Apart" is sad and though I knew it was only a play, and that my mother and father were only acting, I could not keep my heart from filling with grief, and my eyes from flooding with tears. The impression of the sight of father and mother apparently unhappy was so vivid it was days before I could get the picture out of my mind.

Chrystal Katharine Herne was born June 17, 1882, in Dorchester, Massachusetts. Her father had been a stage manager in San Francisco when he married a young Irish actress during her engagement at his theater. In 1879 he made a great deal of money from a play, *Hearts of Oak*, which he wrote with another man. With his sizable earnings, he moved to a comfortable home in the suburbs of Boston. Chrystal was named for the character her mother played in *Hearts of Oak*.

When she was sixteen Chrystal made her stage debut in a play written by her father. The following year, she and her sister Julie joined a touring company in Sag Harbor with Lionel Barrymore. After her father's death in 1901, Chrystal continued to land good roles as she slowly made a name for herself in the American theater. In 1905 she starred in a play written by her sister, after which she spent a year on the London stage.

In 1914 Chrystal married Harold Stanley Pollard, the chief editorial writer of the *New York Evening World*. Not wanting to leave her husband while on long theater tours or filming in Hollywood, Chrystal remained at their home, "Herne Oaks," in Southampton, Long Island, and limited her theater work to Manhattan. In 1925 she played her most famous role, the lead in *Craig's Wife*. Her character was selfish and unsympathetic, yet she was praised by critics and audiences alike for her convincing portrayal. In 1926 the play was awarded the Pulitzer Prize.

Chrystal retired from the stage in 1936 at the age of fifty-three. She became ill with cancer in August 1950 and died the following month at Massachusetts General Hospital.

Chrystal's writing is from a newspaper article, "Drifting Apart" (date and source unknown), which is in the clipping file at the Harvard Theatre Collection, Widener Library, Cambridge, Massachusetts.

1850

I trust you will write that life of Poe. I will do as you wished: — I will write, as far as is proper, in a letter to you, my reminiscences of that year, and try to make it interesting and dignified, and you in introducing it by one single sentence can put down at once my envious calumniators. . . .

I never thought of him till he sent me his Raven and asked Willa to introduce him to me, and immediately after I went to Albany, and afterwards to Boston and Providence to avoid him, and he followed me to each of those places and wrote to me, imploring me to love him, many a letter which I did not reply to until his wife added her entreaties to his and said that I might save him from infamy, and her from death, by showing an affectionate interest in him.

Frances Sargent Locke Osgood was born June 18, 1811, in Boston. She was educated primarily at home, and at fourteen had her first piece published in *Juvenile Miscellany* magazine. She met Samuel Stillman Osgood, a local artist, in 1834 and he asked her to sit for a portrait. They were married in October 1835.

The Osgoods sailed to England for a long honeymoon abroad. Samuel painted portraits while Frances wrote poetry and gave birth to a daughter, Ellen, in July 1836. Frances published two volumes of poetry in 1838, *The Casket of Fate* and *A Wreath of Wild Flowers from New England*, which were well reviewed in the London papers. The actor Sheridan Knowles was impressed with her writing and requested that she write a play for him to perform. She complied; however, the death of her father forced her to return to America before it could be produced on stage.

Back in New York, Frances contributed prose and poetry to all the popular magazines of the day and published several collections of poems, establishing her reputation as an author throughout the United States.

Frances was introduced to Edgar Allan Poe in 1845 when he asked her opinion of his poem, "The Raven." Thereafter they met often, privately and publicly, and developed a close friendship that lasted until his death in 1849. There was much public speculation as to whether or not they had a romantic liaison, which neither would confirm or deny. They

Frances's writing is from a letter to Rufus W. Griswold, Poe's biographer, in reply to his request that she provide him with information about her relationship with Edgar Allan Poe. It is included in The Correspondence and Other Papers of Rufus W. Griswold, *published by Griswold Publishers in 1898.*

both used the rumors of their affair to bolster their reputations as writers and to boost sales of his literary magazine, *The Broadway Journal.* Frances used the pen names Ellen, Clarice, Kate Carol, and Violet Vane and wrote poems "To _____" with lines such as "We shall never part again! Our souls are one forever!," which were published in the *Journal.* Poe would respond with a poem of his own, all the while driving their readers wild with speculation.

Frances gave birth to her third daughter, Fanny, in June 1846, which helped to quiet the gossip concerning her relationship with Poe. However, Poe's wife Virginia was gravely ill, and she was tormented in the last year of her life by anonymous letters alleging that Edgar and Frances were adulterers. After Virginia's death in 1847, Poe asked Frances to elope with him; but she refused, and from then on their relationship consisted only of the exchanging of letters and poems. After Edgar's death, Frances wrote one final poem for him, "The Hand that Swept the Sounding Lyre," which she placed at the end of her book *Poems*, published in 1850.

Samuel left for California in 1849 in search of new portrait commissions. When he returned the following year, he found his wife dying of tuberculosis at the age of thirty-eight. She died in May 1850 and was buried in Cambridge's Mount Auburn Cemetery. The following year, Samuel remarried and returned to California. Although two of Frances's poems, "I Have Something Sweet to Tell You" and "Call Me Pet Names, Dearest, Call Me a Bird" were set to music and enjoyed some degree of popularity, she is mostly remembered for her relationship with Poe.

Beatrix Jones Farrand

Campus trees

1931

Deciduous trees have been used on the campus because nature struck the keynote, and we have tried to play in tune with her. The red and pin oaks both seem patient under cultivation; the white oak is not so useful because it is moved with great difficulty after it becomes large enough to make an effect that even the most indulgent alumnus would consider satisfactory. American elms are mainly used since these seem to be the consecrated college trees. Memory recalls them in many a New England intervale or on many a northern roadside, and they seem just as much at home on the campus where

Beatrix's writing is from "Landscape Gardening at Princeton," published in the Princeton Alumni Weekly, *May 29, 1931.*

their splendid strength, delicate grace and high droop-
ing limbs give a feeling of airy space beneath them.

Beatrix Jones Farrand was born June 19, 1872, in New York
City. Her wealthy family was of English and Dutch descent.
Her grandmother had the first espaliered fruit garden in
Newport, Rhode Island, which led Beatrix to comment that
she was "the product of five generations of garden lovers."
   Beatrix grew up in the sheltered world of New York society. She was tutored at home and travelled abroad frequently
with her mother and aunt, the novelist Edith Wharton.
Edith continued to support Beatrix after her parents were
divorced when she was twelve.
   When she was nineteen Beatrix moved to Boston to live at
"Holm Lea," the home of Charles Sprague Sargent, the
founder and first director of the Arnold Arboretum. He
encouraged her to become a professional landscaper, advising
her "to make the plan fit the ground and not twist the ground
to fit a plan." She heeded his advice and became known for
her beautiful and subtle combinations of formal plantings
with wild and native materials.
   In December 1913 Beatrix married Max Farrand, chairman of the Yale University History Department. She
designed the Graduate College gardens at Princeton in 1916
and the Memorial Quadrangle gardens at Yale in 1923. In
addition to her work at Princeton and Yale, she served as a
landscape consultant to Vassar College, Oberlin College, and
the University of Chicago. Some of Beatrix's finest work can
still be seen at "Dunbarton Oaks," an estate in Washington,
D.C. She spent more than twenty years, beginning in 1920,
designing various formal and informal gardens, which have
survived as she designed them.
   Beatrix worked out of a small office in New York City but
travelled between garden sites, supervising the development
of her garden designs. She received the Garden Club of
America Medal of Achievement in 1947 and the New York
Botanical Garden Distinguished Service Award in 1952.
After her husband Max's death in 1945, Beatrix spent most of
her time in Bar Harbor, Maine, working on the gardens at
her family's estate, "Reef Point," where she died in 1959 at
the age of eighty-six.

Elizabeth Blair Lee

Mrs. Lincoln's grief

Washington
April 20, 1865

My dear Phil I did not leave Mrs. Lincoln until after six when her two children had returned from the obsequies of their father — I was so weary from 24 hours of unflagging watching that I undressed & went to bed — & slept until late this morning. I am quite refreshed & the Secy of the Navy has just left me — saying Mrs. Welles wishes me to relieve her — so I am off in a few moments. . . .

Washington April 22, 1865

My dear Phil . . .

Mrs. Lincoln is better physically and her nervous system begins to rally from the terrible shock — I thought her mind had recovered in part its tone — but her grief is terrible and altogether for her husband as her all in life — this makes her sorrow doubly touching. I am surprised to find so far that she has not uttered a word of resignation — or religious submission. She had her hand on his arm when he was shot he never quivered — the flash of the pistol made her hold him tighter. . . . She addresses him in sleep and in her delirium from raging fever in terms and tones of the tenderest affection — She constantly refers to his religious faith — but never to her own — I shall return there again this evening and shall continue to go as long as I find I can stand it — or be of any use —

Elizabeth Blair Lee was born June 20, 1818, in Frankfort, Kentucky. Her father helped get Andrew Jackson elected president in 1828, and two years later the family was called to Washington. Elizabeth, bright and personable, was a favorite of the president, and she often assisted him in transcribing letters and documents. He was so fond of her that he gave her his late wife Rachel's wedding ring.

In 1836 Mr. Blair purchased a home across the street from the White House. Blair House was constantly filled with politicians, visiting dignitaries, and Washington's intelligentsia, and Elizabeth was a gracious hostess to them all.

Elizabeth blossomed into a popular society belle. While vacationing in White Sulphur Springs, West Virginia, she

Elizabeth's writings are excerpts taken from two letters she wrote to her husband. They are included in Wartime Washington, The Civil War Letters of Elizabeth Blair Lee, *edited by Virginia Jeans Laas, University of Illinois Press, 1991.*

met and fell in love with Lt. Samuel Phillips Lee, a poor relation of the Lees of Virginia. After a four-year courtship, they were married.

Phillips Lee, a naval officer, was away at sea for long periods at a time, during which Elizabeth stayed at her parents' home. She promised her husband she would write him every day they were apart, and she kept her vow. He cherished her letters and saved them all. Elizabeth also wrote to all absent family members and friends, believing her correspondence to be a "family institution" that bound everyone together.

Elizabeth had her first and only child when she was thirty-nine. Phillips retired from the navy in 1873, and they spent twenty-four years together at their Silver Spring, Maryland, farm. Following his death in 1897, she went to live with her son, a United States senator from Maryland, until her death in 1906.

Mary Cutler Fairchild

The Sunday readers

1889
Besides the people who need to be enticed to a library on Sunday, there is a large number of intelligent working men, who have already begun the work of self-improvement, who find Sunday the only time for carrying out their plans; do not deny them a Sunday afternoon in a quiet place, relieved from the distractions of the home. Perhaps you have no *right* to deny them on their only day of leisure that which they are taxed to pay for as a common good.

Mary Salome Cutler Fairchild was born June 21, 1855, in Dalton, Massachusetts. She graduated from Mount Holyoke Seminary in 1875 and remained there as a teacher for the next three years. In 1884 she applied to the well-known librarian of Columbia University, Melvil Dewey, for help in finding work as a librarian. He hired her himself as a cataloger. She was promoted to head cataloguer the following year and remained in that position until 1889.

Dewey opened the first library school in America at Columbia in 1887, and Mary joined the staff as an instructor in cataloguing. He resigned suddenly in 1889 and opened the New York State Library School in Albany. Mary transferred to Albany with her mentor and served as vice-director of the school. She was instrumental in creating the course list and soon made a college degree mandatory for admission. She

Mary's writing is from "Sunday Openings of Libraries," published in the May-June 1889 issue of The Library Journal.

took the students to other libraries to observe their practices and set up an apprenticeship program.

Mary married Edwin Milton Fairchild, a Unitarian minister, in July 1897. She tried to balance her duties at work with her duties as a housewife, but the pressure became too much for her. In 1905 Dewey resigned after being accused of anti-Semitism; Mary had a nervous breakdown and retired. Thereafter she occasionally lectured or wrote on library issues but mostly led the life of a semi-invalid. She died in 1921 at Washington Sanitarium in Takoma Park, Maryland.

JUNE 22

Harriet Stone Lothrop

Love of Norway

1906

During a long, leisurely, delightful cruise in the summer of 1905 through the fjords of Norway, from Bergen to the North Cape, then on to Spitzbergen, the marvellous scenery held full possession of me, as is naturally the case with every wanderer into that wonderful region. However carefully prepared by study one may be for the journey, nature's surprises concealed here cannot properly be disclosed except by actual survey.

But the marvels revealed under the spell of the Midnight Sun, through a cruise made almost wholly in superb weather under kindly skies, became after all a source of interest to be divided with another kind of study. This was connected with the people living in the midst of these wonderful fastnesses of nature, only to be seen at their best in their own setting. This study was fascinating, yielding a rich harvest.

Too much in approval cannot be said of these people. It was a constant delight to find unfolding before one's eyes the best qualities of human nature that a student of his kind fondly looks for wherever he goes. Truth, honor, honesty, — all the rugged and simple virtues that ought to control a man, — here were the daily accompaniments of the Norwegian life, regardless of the fear or favor of onlookers. Truly, the sight was pleasant, and gave a special zest to the journey.

Harriet's writing is the preface of Two Little Friends in Norway, *published by Lothrop, Lee, and Shepard in 1906.*

I was rejoiced that I cruised here during that period when Norway was in the throes of a final decision as to the political fate of the country. I could enter into sympathy with her people as at no other time, and understand her better.

And the children — I could not withstand them! And in Brita, wholly (as is every other Norwegian character set forth on these pages) a creature of my imagination, I hope to show to others what I learned to love while there, — the dear little children of Norway.

Harriet Mulford Stone Lothrop was born June 22, 1844, in New Haven, Connecticut. Her father taught architecture at Yale. As a child she longed to write, but her father disapproved of women writing for publication. When she began publishing stories and poems in magazines and newspapers, she used the pen name Margaret Sidney so as not to offend him.

In 1877 Harriet wrote "Polly Pepper's Chicken Pie" for *Awake*, a Boston-based children's magazine. That was the beginning of her timeless Five Little Peppers series. *Five Little Peppers and How They Grew* was first published in 1880. Over the years she wrote eleven more volumes, ending with *Our Davie Pepper* in 1916.

Daniel Lothrop, the publisher of *Awake*, travelled to New Haven in 1881 to meet Harriet. They were married the following October and moved to Concord, Massachusetts. They bought "The Wayside," the former home of Nathaniel Hawthorne and before that, the Alcott family. In 1904 Harriet organized the Hawthorne Centenary at "The Wayside," a four-day celebration.

Following the death of her husband, Harriet took many trips to Europe with her daughter Margaret. They eventually settled in California, where Margaret taught sociology at Stanford University. Harriet died when she was eighty, and her body was returned to Concord for burial on Author's Ridge in Sleepy Hollow Cemetery. During her lifetime, more than 2 million copies of her books were sold, many of which continue to be popular with today's children.

Jennie Kimball

1869

I have just read your notice of me in the Clipper and I feel very bad about it for you have been represented to me as being a gentleman and a just whole souled man and I am Positive had you known the circumstances you would have been more lenient towards me. . . .

My songs and can can were all encored and in what way I have been broad and vulgar I cannot imagine. If you have seen me and can tell me of my faults I will consider it a great favor if you will be friend enough to me to inform me of them. . . .

May I ask if you will be kind, as to keep this letter private as I feel much grieved at the way I have been treated in this city. The Herald and Tribune have given me very good notices. I believe they are the only ones that have been friendly to me.

Jennie Kimball was born June 23, 1851, in New Orleans, Louisiana. She made her stage debut in 1865 at the Boston Theatre, singing a minor role in *Bluebeard*. Her manager suggested that she take a year off to study drama and music, after which she returned to the Boston stage in *The Black Crook* at the Continental Theatre.

In 1868 Jennie toured the country as Oberon in *A Midsummer Night's Dream* and singing the lead in *The Grand Duchess*. She returned to the East and joined the Florence Burlesque Opera Company as its star singer, followed by a move to New York City to perform in John Broughham's Opera Company.

Jennie married D. Doane while on a tour of the South, and they had one daughter, Corinne. Doane died when Corinne was only two, and Jennie married Thomas Flaherty, a Boston piano dealer, in 1878. Jennie retired from singing in 1879, when she organized a children's opera company with Corinne as the star. Although the company was successful, the New York Society for the Prevention of Cruelty to Children brought suit. The subsequent trial brought a great deal of publicity to Jennie and Corinne.

After the trial Jennie regrouped and founded the Kimball Opera Company. It opened at the Bijou Opera House in New York City for four weeks followed by a nationwide tour. Thereafter Jennie devoted all her efforts to establishing Corinne as a major star. She handled all aspects of the business, including booking performances, designing costumes, and writing advertising copy.

Thomas Flaherty died in 1892, and the following year Jennie married Arling Schaeffer, a banjo player in her company. He joined Jennie and Corinne in their mansion in Philadelphia, which they had purchased years earlier. Jennie died in March 1896, leaving a personal fortune of more than $600,000. The Kimball Opera Company cancelled its dates for two weeks to honor its founder while Corinne accompanied her mother's remains to Boston for interment at the Forest Hills Cemetery.

Jennie's writing is from a March 11, 1869, letter to a Mr. Brown at The Clipper. *It is in the Harvard Theatre Collection Archives, Widener Library, Harvard University, Cambridge, Massachusetts.*

Women's Words, Women's Stories

Rebecca Harding Davis

Misery in the mills

1861

Deborah groped her way into the cellar, and, after considerable stumbling, kindled a match, and lighted a tallow dip, that sent a yellow glimmer over the room. It was low, damp, — the earthen floor covered with a green, slimy moss, — a fetid air smothering the breath. Old Wolfe lay asleep on a heap of straw, wrapped in a torn horse-blanket. He was a pale, meek little man, with a white face and red rabbit-eyes. The woman Deborah was like him; only her face was even more ghastly, her lips bluer, her eyes more watery. She wore a faded cotton gown and a slouching bonnet. When she walked, one could see that she was deformed, almost a hunchback. She trod softly, so as not to waken him, and went through into the room beyond. There she found by the half-extinguished fire an iron saucepan filled with cold boiled potatoes, which she put upon a broken chair with a pint-cup of ale. Placing the old candlestick beside this dainty repast, she untied her bonnet, which hung limp and wet over her face, and prepared to eat her supper. It was the first food that had touched her lips since morning.

Rebecca Harding Davis was born June 24, 1831, in Washington, Pennsylvania. When she was five, the family settled in Wheeling, Virginia (later West Virginia), one of several mushrooming steel towns in the country.

Rebecca was educated at home until she was fourteen, when she was sent to three years of finishing school at the Washington Female Seminary. She complained that there was little of substance that she was able to learn there. Upon her return home in 1848, she pursued her studies on her own. When her brother went to college, she eagerly studied his courses as well.

From the age of seventeen to her early thirties Rebecca stayed at home, helping her mother with the household and the younger children. She felt trapped in Wheeling, stifled by the lack of intellectual companionship and cursed with "an education one cannot use." From her front window, Rebecca could see the mule trains hauling pig iron and the workers who, day after day, year after year, trudged by en route to

Rebecca's writing is from "Life in the Iron-Mills," first published anonymously in the April 1861 Atlantic Monthly.

their fourteen hours in the steel mills. One day Rebecca decided to write about what she saw.

The *Atlantic Monthly* published her story "Life in the Iron-Mills" in 1861. It was grim and realistic, portraying the true hopelessness, poverty, and degradation of life in Wheeling. The following year she published her first book, *Margaret Houth*, about the empty life of an office clerk at an Indiana mill.

After reading "Life in the Iron-Mills," Lemuel Clarke Davis, a lawyer, began writing to Rebecca to express his admiration for her and her work. He eventually came to Wheeling to court her, and they were married in March 1863.

Rebecca and Lemuel moved to Philadelphia and had three children. Rebecca continued to write, but her family was her first priority. She produced several novels, but primarily wrote children's stories, historical essays, and Gothic romances for popular magazines. None of her later work, however, measured up to "Life in the Iron-Mills," which stands today as a landmark in the history of American literature. She died in 1910 at her son's home in Mount Kisco, New York.

Crystal Eastman

Letter to mother

1899

. . . whenever I pray, my thoughts go to you before they go to God. Do you think that's wrong? Then my thoughts seem to go in a circle from myself, through a vast conception of infinite good, to you. Sort of an electric current conveying good from me to you and from you to me. I suppose I ought to feel that way about all the world. . . .

Crystal Eastman (Catherine Crystal) was born June 25, 1881, in Marlborough, Massachusetts. Both her parents were Congregational ministers, and she was strongly influenced by her mother's work and beliefs about women's rights.

Crystal's writing is from an October 27, 1899, letter to her mother. It was written soon after she entered Vassar College and is included in the Catherine Crystal Eastman Collection, Schlesinger Library, Radcliffe College, Cambridge, Massachusetts.

Crystal graduated from Vassar College in 1903 and went on to receive a master's degree in sociology from Columbia University. While in New York City, she decided her career as a social reformer would be enhanced by a law degree. She graduated from New York University Law School in 1907 and immediately joined the Pittsburgh Survey team. The survey was funded by the Russell Sage Foundation to study the effects of industrialization on workers. She studied more than 1,000 industrial accidents and published her findings in 1910 in *Work Accidents and the Law*. Her research did much to promote the passing of workmen's compensation laws.

In May 1911 Crystal married Wallace Benedict, an insurance agent . They settled in Milwaukee, Wisconsin, where she co-founded the Congressional Union for Woman Suffrage. She tried unsuccessfully to get women's suffrage approved on the Wisconsin ballot in 1912.

Crystal believed in total equality for women and therefore opposed laws that favored women as well as those that favored men. When she divorced her husband after five years of marriage, she refused support, saying, "No self-respecting feminist would accept alimony. It would be her own confession that she could not take care of herself."

Crystal was remarried in 1916 to Walter Fuller, a transplanted Englishman. Together they embraced the peace movement and worked to avoid America's entry into World War I. Later, during the war, she co-founded the Civil Liberties Bureau to assist conscientious objectors.

Walter and Crystal moved to England in 1921 with their two children. She continued to work for women's rights abroad and joined the National Woman's Party. In 1927 she took a trip to America to promote child welfare laws. After her arrival, she received word of her husband's death. Her own health declined, and she died of nephritis the following year at her brother's home in Pennsylvania, two weeks after her forty-seventh birthday.

Jessie Field Shambaugh

Wheaton, Iowa
October 4, 1910

A country teacher

Dear Daddy: — Well, the first month has gone and I surely do think that teaching country school is the best work in the world. The country is beautiful these early autumn days. The corn is tall and straight, with the ears hanging down as though they were quite weary of their own weight. I wish you were here. Shut your eyes and think of hills and valleys covered with rows of corn; with grain and alfalfa fields between and — here and there — pretty white houses and red barns. Daddy, doesn't the sight do your heart good?

Celestia Josephine (Jessie) Field Shambaugh was born June 26, 1881, in Shenandoah, Iowa. She began teaching while

Jessie's writing, from a letter to her father is included in The Corn Lady, *published by A. Flanagan Co., in 1911.*

still attending Western Normal College. Following graduation from Tabor College in 1903, she taught locally for two years until she was appointed principal of the Jefferson School in Helena, Montana.

Jessie soon formed the first Boys Corn Club and Girls Home Club to teach her students new farm techniques and to increase their self-confidence. These clubs were the precursors to the 4-H clubs she would later develop.

In 1906 Jessie was elected superintendent of schools in Page County, Iowa. Three years later, she published the popular *Farm Arithmetic*, a book intended to make math more applicable to farm youth. She established a Boys Corn Club and a Girls Home Club in each of the 130 schools in her district. Her students won many prizes at local fairs, including a blue ribbon at the 1909 Omaha International Corn Show.

Fifteen superintendents of southern schools visited Page County in 1909 and declared Jessie a "genius" and "a prophet in her own country." Her clubs received national attention in educational journals and newspaper accounts. In 1910 she designed a three-leaf clover pin to be given as a club award to attract more student participation. The letter H was inscribed on each leaf, symbolizing "Head," "Hands," and "Heart." Later a fourth H was added for "Health," and the 4-H clubs were launched. The clubs eventually became a national organization sponsored by the United States Department of Agriculture.

Jessie became concerned that "the city continues each year to claim an immense number of the best country people." In an attempt to rectify this situation, she moved to New York City in 1912 to become national YWCA secretary for small town and country work. She believed the YWCA could counteract the rural exodus by improving the social, domestic, and religious lives of women living on farms and in small towns.

Jessie married Ira William Shambaugh in 1917. She remained active in 4-H work until her death in 1971 at the age of eighty-nine.

Helen Keller

Experiencing Rodin

1937

At three o'clock Mr Borglum came with the gratifying news that permission had been obtained through the American embassy for me to touch Rodin's works. . . .

The first sculptures shown in the museum were "Victor Hugo" and "Grief." A chair was placed against the base so that I might reach the mighty figure of the Liberator, gazing with divine compassion upon anguish-bowed Grief, extending his hand, entreating her to be quiet and hear Freedom's trumpet call ringing from land to land. . . .

Mr Borglum led me to where "The Thinker" sat, primal, tense, his chin resting on a toilworn hand. In every limb I felt the throes of emerging mind. As I said to Mr Borglum, I recognized the force that shook me when Teacher spelled "water," and I discovered that everything has a name and that the finger motions were the way to whatever I wanted. Often before had my deliverance caused me to wonder, but not until then had I perceived clearly how Teacher hewed my life bit by bit out of the formless silent dark as Rodin hewed that mind-genesis out of the rock. What loneliness enveloped the first thinker and the outer world lying at his feet with no power except his brawn, no motive save his will!

Helen Keller was born June 27, 1880, in Tuscumbia, Alabama. An illness at nineteen months left her blind, deaf, and mute. She grew up a spoiled, willful, wild, and destructive child, locked in her own lonely world. When she was seven, her parents hired Anne Sullivan (April 14) to be her teacher and governess. After four weeks of constant, repetitive work together, Helen at last realized that Miss Sullivan was spelling the word "water" in her hand when she held her hand under an open faucet and water flowed across it.

Miss Sullivan, forever referred to as "Teacher" by Helen, remained by her side for the next forty-nine years, until her death in 1936. They attended several schools together, culminating in Helen's graduation cum laude from Radcliffe College in 1904. Helen worked to improve conditions for the blind; she was appointed to Massachusetts' first State Commission for the Blind. A socialist, she supported many reform movements, such as the abolition of capital punishment, the birth control movement, and the NAACP.

Helen fell in love at thirty-six with her secretary, Peter Fagan, also a socialist. Sadly, her mother and Teacher terminated their relationship. Thereafter, Helen said, she turned her "energy into channels of satisfying sympathy and work." She made a movie in Hollywood about her life and toured for four years on the Keith vaudeville circuit. In 1924 Helen brought the American Foundation for the Blind to the attention of the American public and raised a great deal of money in addition to promoting legislation for the blind.

Helen's description of her visit to the Louvre in Paris is taken from her January 20, 1937, journal entry. It is included in Helen Keller's Journal 1936-1937, *published by Doubleday, Doran and Company, Inc., in 1938.*

Helen spent World War II touring military hospitals, lecturing to improve morale. This she referred to as "the crowning experience of my life." Helen died in 1968, just short of her eighty-eighth birthday.

JUNE 28   *Lydia Lucretia Mossman Martin*

Language problem

1883
We are the only family with white faces within a distance of nearly thirty miles, and no one around us can talk in English. If they could only speak Urdu we would not mind it so much, but this Dogar is a rough dialect. I do not get along in it yet as with the people ten or twelve miles south, who speak a different Punjabi dialect.

Lydia Lucretia Mossman Martin was born June 28, 1838, on a farm near Kinsman, Ohio. She was awarded two state lifetime teaching certificates, one for Ohio and one for Pennsylvania. She was teaching at the Jamestown Pennsylvania Seminary when she met her future husband, Samuel Martin, a student at Pittsburgh Theological Seminary.

Lydia and Samuel were married on September 27, 1866. They decided to become missionaries and set sail within the year for India, where the Mission Board of the United Presbyterian Church had assigned them to work near Lahore in the Punjab. They set up a permanent mission in Sialkot and began their lifelong efforts with the natives.

The Martins worked primarily with the Churhas, India's lowest caste, the "untouchables." While her husband preached and sought converts, Lydia set up schools for the women and young girls. She was a talented linguist, mastering Hindustani, Urdu, Persian, and several local dialects. After just one year she had 150 pupils. She proudly wrote in a letter home, "The girls in the day school are reading for the first time. There is no such thing to be found as a Hindustani dictionary, so I am obliged to make my own dictionary as I go along. They are now reading in First Samuel."

The summer months were so hot that they were confined indoors during the day. Lydia wrote in July 1875, "We are having a nice cool day today, with the thermometer down to 85 degrees. We have killed this summer, in the house, seven centipedes and more than a hundred scorpions." During the winter they travelled the countryside, establishing small missions and as always, searching for converts. It is estimated

Lydia's writing is from a March 1883 letter to her parents from Zafarwal, India. It is included in A Father to the Poor, *a short, privately printed biography of Lydia's husband, Dr. Samuel Martin, by their daughter E. Josephine Martin. It is among the personal papers of Lydia's grandson, G. Lloyd Martin, Brick, New Jersey.*

Women's Words, Women's Stories

that over his long career as a missionary, Dr. Martin baptized more than 7,000 people, possibly as many as 15,000.

After eleven years in India, the Martins returned to the United States with their five daughters and two sons on a two-year furlough. They settled in New Concord, Ohio, where Dr. Martin taught mathematics at Muskingum College. When they returned to Sialkot in 1880, they left their four oldest girls behind to attend school in America. Sadly, this would be the last time Lydia would see them. Eventually, all seven children graduated from Muskingum College.

By March 1886 Lydia had twenty-nine schools in operation with others ready to open in the district. In the fall of 1885 they departed as usual on their yearly evangelical journey. Although Lydia came down with a severe cough and cold, she insisted on continuing. Pneumonia developed, and she was carried many miles on a stretcher to the Ladies' Mission House in Narowal, where nothing could be done for her. She died on December 3, 1886, and was taken back to Sialkot for burial. Twenty-four years later, her husband was laid beside her. Three of their daughters, Mary, Josephine, and Jane, became missionaries to India. It was written in a 1940 publication by the United Presbyterian Board of Missions, "The Martin family gave individually a total of one hundred and sixty-two years of service to our India Mission . . . a record in the annals of United Presbyterian Foreign Missions."

Eloise Bibb Thompson

1927

And so when Paupet, the whitest octoroon that she had ever seen, came to the Quarter, she showed her preference for him at once. When, after their marriage, in the course of time their first born was expected she was like an experimentalist in the mating of cross-breeds, painfully nervous and full of the greatest anxiety over the outcome of a situation that she had been planning so long. . . .

To the midwife too she communicated her hopes and expectations, dwelling at great length upon the future of the child the whiteness of whose face would be a charm against every prevailing ill. Such optimism augured ill to the midwife who rarely vouchsafed her a

A child's face

Eloise's writing is taken from "Masks," her short story about crossing the color line, published in the October 1927 issue of Opportunity.

word. When at length the child was born, the midwife tarried a long time before placing it into Julie's arms. It was sympathy upon her part that caused the delay. But Julie could not understand it. In the midst of her great sufferings she marvelled at it, until at length she caught a glimpse of her child's face. Then she screamed. With horror she saw that it was identical with the one in the locket about her neck. It was the image of her chocolate-colored mother.

Eloise Bibb Thompson was born June 29, 1878, in New Orleans, Louisiana. When she was only seventeen, she published her first volume of poetry. For someone so young, she wrote about a broad range of topics: love, history, and religion.

Five years after her poetry book was published, Eloise returned to school to become a teacher. After teaching in New Orleans public schools for two years, she again enrolled in school for more courses. In 1908, following her graduation from Howard University Teachers' College, she assumed the position of head of the Social Settlement at Howard.

In 1911 Eloise married Noah Thompson, a Catholic journalist who had been recently widowed and left with a young son. They moved to Los Angeles, where Eloise began writing for the *Los Angeles Tribune* and the *Morning Sun*. She continued writing poetry for magazines and began lecturing to local Catholic women's clubs in an attempt to foster understanding and acceptance of the Negro race.

Eloise turned to playwriting in 1915 to express her beliefs on racial issues. She wrote *Reply to Clansmen* to counteract Thomas Dixon's novel *The Clansman*, which was pro-Ku Klux Klan. D. W. Griffith was interested in the movie rights to Eloise's play, but he failed to live up to his oral agreement. He bought the rights to Dixon's book instead and turned it into *The Birth of a Nation*.

Eloise wrote three more popular plays. She described the 1922 production of her play *Africans* as the "first time in Los Angeles theatre history that a drama about an African country, written by a black author and intended for a black audience had been realized by an all black cast."

Eloise's Catholic faith and her concern for the improvement of her race were constants in her life and her writing. Unfortunately, her career was cut short at the age of fifty by her sudden death on January 8, 1928.

1943

I remember once writing a sophomoric piece that I entitled "The Literary Interregnum," in which I tried to point out that there are usually "between periods," or periods of transition, in which the literary product is weak and uncertain. Old themes and patterns are dying and the new is not yet born. My reference was mainly to poetry. The nineteenth-century poets had passed and their successors had not yet come to the foreground. But I felt pretty sure of the future and of my word "interregnum." I was sure that it would end and that new literary kings would be crowned. They will be, of course, but they seem more likely to be kings of prose than kings of verse.

Louise Pound was born June 30, 1872, in Lincoln, Nebraska. Her mother felt the public school curriculum was "too stereotyped," so she educated her three children at home. In 1888 Louise enrolled at the University of Nebraska. During her four years of college she was the associate editor of the school paper, class orator and poet, and women's state tennis champion. She was also the university tennis champion in both men's singles and doubles, for which she received a man's varsity letter.

Louise began teaching English at the University of Nebraska in 1894 in addition to serving as a member and coach of the university's winning women's basketball team. She also took part in several "century runs," which required bicycling 100 miles in twelve hours. As a redhead, she founded the Order of the Golden Fleece to which only natural redheads could belong.

Louise went to Germany in 1898, where she obtained her Ph.D. from the University of Heidelberg in only two semesters instead of the usual seven. In 1900 she returned to the University of Nebraska, where she was to teach for the next forty-five years, becoming a full professor in 1912. She specialized in American language and literature at a time when most university departments offered only English literature. She established the scholarly study of American speech and folklore, examining changes in the English language as it was spoken in the United States. She founded the journal *American Speech*, and served as its editor from 1925 to 1933. Her interest in American folklore focused on Nebraska and

Louise's writing is from "The Future of Poetry," a paper she wrote in 1943. It is included in Selected Writings of Louise Pound, *published by the University of Nebraska Press in 1949.*

the Midwest. In 1915 she published *Folk-Songs of Nebraska and the Central West: A Syllabus, Nebraska Folklore*, which was published posthumously in 1959. In 1955, at the age of eighty-two, she was elected the first woman president of the Modern Language Association.

Louise gave up tennis in her fifties because "bi-focal glasses wrecked my ground strokes," but she was a ranking woman golfer for more than twenty-five years, as well as an accomplished ice skater. In 1955 she was the first woman to be elected to the Nebraska Sports Hall of Fame. She wrote to a friend: "First woman again — life has its humors." She died at home in Lincoln in 1958, two days before her eighty-sixth birthday.

JULY

Susan Keating Glaspell

1927

I was going away. It was the last evening we would
have together for — we did not know how long. We
met at Black Hawk's Watch Tower — a few hours
together on that bluff of Rock River, where the old
Indian Chief had watched in other days, where Indian
lovers, too, had known the sweetness and no doubt at
times the pain and terror. It seemed now that life was
driving us apart, and out of the anguish of that, from
the rending of much we had held dear, in the crash that
was the years, glowed a love which gave life to the love
of vanished women for men long in their graves. We
knew who we were, we knew what it all was, and that is
why I murmured: "I wish we could die now. . . ."

Nor did the years take that moment. We talked of it
one night in Delphi, when for him death was only two
weeks away, a night of strange beauty when daylight
found us still talking — of love, of death; and he said
then, after looking into the years of his life: "When
you said, 'I wish we could die now' — that is the greatest beauty I have known on earth."

The glow of love

Susan Keating Glaspell was born July 1, 1876, in Davenport,
Iowa. She began publishing short stories while still in college
at Drake University in Des Moines. After graduation, she
took a job as a reporter for the *Des Moines Daily News*, but
returned home after two years to write novels and short
stories. Her first novel was published in 1909, and she spent
the royalties on a year abroad in Paris.

After Susan's return to Davenport in 1911, she joined the
Monist Society, a group of young radical free-thinkers.
Through the society, she met George Cram Cook, a Harvard
graduate and local eccentric, and in 1913 she became his third
wife.

The Cooks spent summers in Provincetown,
Massachusetts, where they founded the Provincetown Players,
a theater group dedicated to producing original plays by
American authors, primarily Eugene O'Neill and herself. She
wrote numerous one-act plays and four full-length plays for
the group. After a presentation of O'Neill's *The Emperor
Jones* made them financially viable, George rejected their
success, and the couple moved to Greece, where they lived as

*Susan's writing is from her
biography of her husband
George Cook,* The Road to
the Temple, *published in
1927 by Frederick A. Stokes
Company.*

peasants at Delphi on Mount Parnassus. Following his death in 1924, the Greek government took a piece of the Temple of Apollo as his gravestone.

In 1925 Susan returned to America and married the author Norman H. Matson. However, they were divorced after five years. She resumed her life in Provincetown and continued to write, publishing four more novels and a total of fifty short stories. In 1930 she won the Pulitzer Prize for her play about Emily Dickinson, *Alison's House*. She died in 1948 at the age of seventy-two and was buried on Cape Cod.

Lucy Sprague Mitchell

The real world

1953

I began going to Hull House by myself. I had fallen under the spell of Jane Addams, that great and gracious woman who lived there — a spell which never lost its hold on me. She became for me a symbol of the "real" world — a world of work and of people that I longed to reach but could not. I felt I was a "pampered darling" bound by my father's wealth to a world of people whose standards I could not accept. My adolescent conflict of loyalties became acute. I developed a sense of shame and guilt at being rich which has never completely left me.

Lucy Sprague Mitchell was born July 2, 1878, in Chicago. Eight years earlier, her parents had moved west from Vermont. Her father, together with his brother and another Vermont farmer, Ezra Warner, started the Sprague-Warner Company, which grew to be one of the largest wholesale grocery businesses in the world.

Lucy was educated at home by a private tutor until she was twelve. She was then enrolled in a local private girls' school, but she had to leave because she became too nervous whenever she went to class. She stayed at home, reading every book in her father's library and writing stories in secret notebooks.

Lucy's family was among the financial supporters of Jane Addams' (September 6) Hull House, and she did volunteer work there. Exposed to the poverty of working girls, she became uncomfortable with her own wealth.

Lucy's writing is from Two Lives, The Story of Wesley Clair Mitchell and Myself, *published in 1953 by Simon and Schuster.*

In 1896 Lucy enrolled in Radcliffe College, graduating with honors in philosophy in 1900. After graduation she returned to California to nurse her ailing parents, but left after a few months when friends offered to take her to Europe.

In 1906 Lucy was offered the position of dean of women and assistant professor of English at the University of California at Berkeley, one of the first two women to hold a faculty position at the university. Despite her lack of training, she was an excellent dean, and during her six-year tenure she did much to expand social and educational opportunities for women students.

Lucy resigned from the university in May 1912 to marry Wesley C. Mitchell, an economist. They moved to New York City, where they adopted two children and had two of their own. After years of observation and studying the progressive education movement, Lucy developed her own ideas about proper teaching methods. In 1931 she co-founded the Cooperative School for Teachers to train the "whole teacher." Her approach to education combined a "scientific attitude with the attitude of the artist."

In 1938 Lucy established the Writer's Workshop to help authors of children's books understand the needs and interests of children. She herself wrote twenty books for children. After Wesley's death in 1948, Lucy suffered from loneliness. She retired from her educational endeavors and moved to Palo Alto, California, to be near one of her children. She died of heart disease in 1967 at the age of eighty-nine.

Ella Elgar Bird Dumont

1928

It was rather lonely for me. The men all left early in the morning, each on his line, and they did not return until later in the afternoon. . . .

One day after they had all gone I was looking around the place. I noticed some large-sized goods boxes. We had been using two of those large benches for a dining table. I made up my mind I would make a table. . . . The baby was asleep, so I went to work. I had good luck with it. Everything measured out, and by the middle of the afternoon, I had a first-class table on foot with a large drawer for cold victuals. For knobs on the drawer I sawed a large spool in two and attached [the halves] with two horseshoe nails in each, and I bradded them on the inside of the drawer. All was

Making a table

Ella's writing is from An Autobiography of a West Texas Pioneer — Ella Elgar Bird Dumont, *edited by Tommy J. Boley and published in 1988.*

complete, and I was rather proud of the job if I did do it myself.

That afternoon when the men came in, Mr. Sullivan was the first. He asked who had been here.

I said, "No one at all."

He asked, "Where did the table come from?"

"I made it," I said.

He laughed rather incredulously, as he thought I was joking. I could hardly convince him that I really did make it. He examined the drawer and everything and said it beat anything he had ever seen made by a woman. He went out and brought in Mr. Savage to look at it. He would hardly believe it either at first. He said there was not a man in the country that could do half as good a job. They gave me such a "blow-up" that I rather got plagued out and almost wished I had not made it.

Ella Elgar Bird Dumont was born July 3, 1861, in Guntown, Mississippi. Her father died of typhus during the Civil War, after which her mother remarried in Memphis. Two years and two children later, her stepfather also died. Like many of their neighbors, her mother and grandmother went west with the family to Texas in 1867.

Ella's family settled in Johnson County in the Texas Panhandle. At fifteen she met James Thomas (Tom) Bird, a cousin of her sister's husband, visiting from southern Texas. He asked her to marry him and returned for her the following year. For several years they led a nomadic life, travelling in all directions from their base camp, hunting buffalo and other game. Ella practiced shooting and became a crack shot. She also took up carving local gypsum rock and made many beautiful statues and vases. Tom and Ella were mostly alone and quite lonely. She complained that "there were months and months that I did not see the face of even one woman," and Tom later recalled he would have been "proud to see even one of our old neighbors' dogs come in."

Ella loved to sculpt, and she regretted that she did not do more of it, believing she had "buried a talent on those broad barren prairies of the Texas Panhandle." Instead, she raised two children and earned extra money with her beadwork. She "made many fringed and beaded vests of buckskin for which I received twelve dollars each. The beaded gauntlet gloves were seven dollars each."

In 1886 Tom died, probably of a ruptured appendix, while out on a roundup. In 1889 Ella received a letter from an old friend, Auguste Dumont, pledging his love. She wrote back that she would prefer to remain friends. However, they were married six years later. Dumont was the deputy sheriff, postmaster, and dry goods merchant of Paducah, Texas, where they lived in "six nicely plastered rooms" on the lower story of the jail. They had one son who died of whooping cough as an infant, and a second son was born in 1900. Ella raised flowers and poultry and collected cacti, boasting a garden of more than 400 varieties.

Ella's daughter Bessie Bird died in 1904 after a fall from a horse. Ella never recovered from her grief and wore black the rest of her life. In 1915 Dumont died after twenty years of marriage. Ella wrote her memoirs, completing them in 1928, and spent the next thirteen years trying unsuccessfully to find a publisher. (They were published posthumously in 1988.) She died in 1941 at the age of eighty-one and was buried beside her husband, daughter, and infant son in Paducah. Her tombstone reads: "A Frontier Woman Buffalo Hunter/A West Texas Pioneer."

Edmonia Lewis

Rome
May 3, 1868
Dear Mrs. Chapman,

It seems almost I was going to say, impossible that not one of my many kinds of friends have not written to me some word about the group, Forever Free — Will you be so kind as to let me know what has become of it? and has Mr. Sewall got the money for it yet or not. I am in great need of the money. What little money I had I put all in that work with my *heart*. And I truly hope that the work of two long years has not been lost. Dear Mrs. Chapman I been thinking that it may be that you have met with some who think that it will ruin me to help me — but you may tell them that in giving a little something towards that group — that will not only aid me but will show their good feeling for one who has given all for poor humanity. I have written to Mr. Sewall some time ago but as yet I have not heard from him — Will you dear Mrs. Chapman be so kind as to see Mr. Sewall and if he has been paid the Eight hundred dollars ($800) will he be so kind as to send to me the same as I am in need of it very much —

Artist in need

Edmonia's letter to her patron, the abolitionist Maria Weston Chapman, concerning payment for her composition Forever Free, *is in Rare Books at the Boston Public Library.*

I beg you will excuse the liberty I have taken in sending
this letter but my belief that you will receive it without
offence — should you honor me by a reply to this
application, a letter would reach me, addressed to care
of Mr. Freeborn and Co.

Rome, Italy

Your obedient Servant, Edmonia Lewis

Mary Edmonia Lewis was born July 4, 1845, in Greenbush,
New York. Her mother was Native American, and her father
was a black gentleman's servant.

Edmonia's Chippewa name was Wildfire. Her older
brother, Sunrise, had gone west and prospered in the
California gold rush. He sent money home, which enabled
her to enroll in Oberlin College. She thrived at college, but
her education was cut short after three and a half years when
her two best friends, white girls, were poisoned. Edmonia
was accused of murder, and although she was acquitted after a
lengthy trial, she fled to Boston.

One day in 1863 she saw the statue of Benjamin Franklin
in front of Boston City Hall and declared, "I, too, can make a
stone man." After a few lessons in modeling technique,
Edmonia began sculpting, eager to make up for lost time.
One of her first works, a Civil War colonel leading his troops
to battle, sold 100 copies, providing her with enough capital
to move to Rome.

Edmonia soon achieved both professional and social
acclaim abroad. One of her best-known pieces, called *Forever
Free*, depicted two slaves overcome with joy at the news of
their emancipation.

Edmonia had converted to Catholicism soon after her
arrival in Rome. One of her proudest moments occurred
when Pope Pius IX visited her studio and blessed her work.
She died at home in Italy in 1911.

Frances Christine Fisher Tiernan

*R*eunited

1871

". . . there is but one person alive who would have
tended me thus, or been to me what she has — more
than friend and sister. Brother, she is there! Have you
no word of thanks for her?"

He turned; and almost, as it were, against her will,
Valerie rose from her seat, and stood before him — her

---

face shining upon him fair and pale as a star. Maurice recoiled a step in astonishment; for, though he knew that she was there, he had not expected to see her so soon. Then they stood and looked into each other's eyes. Both were sadly changed — upon the faces of each sorrow and care had laid stern signet — but what of that? They looked into each other's eyes, and they read there the love and faith that had never faltered with either, and were forever beyond the things of Earth and Time. Maurice opened his arms with one cry:

"Valerie!"

After that, there was never any need of explanation.

Frances Christine Fisher Tiernan was born July 5, 1846, in Salisbury, North Carolina. Her mother died when she was very young, and her father, president of the Western North Carolina Railroad, was killed at the first battle of Bull Run in 1861. Frances and her two siblings moved in with a spinster aunt, an eccentric recluse. Aunt Christine taught the children at home and instilled in them a love for reading and writing.

Frances converted to her aunt's religion, Roman Catholicism, in 1868. She began writing under the pen name Christian Reid. She published her first novel, a romance set in the antebellum South, in 1870. It sold more than 8,000 copies, which gave her encouragement to continue. She published thirteen books during the next nine years.

Frances took an extended European journey in 1879, which provided her with material for her next three novels. At the age of forty-one, she met and married James Marquis Tiernan. They settled for ten years in Mexico, where he operated mines. They travelled throughout the West Indies before returning to North Carolina to live in 1897.

During her long career, Frances produced forty-five books, all with heavy Catholic overtones designed to instill morals in her readers. She claimed her "purpose has always been to inculcate high standards of living, to influence none to do wrongly." She died in Salisbury, her birthplace, in 1920 at the age of seventy-four.

Frances's writing is from her first novel, Valerie Aylmer, *written under her pen name* Christian Reid, *published by D. Appleton and Co., in 1871.*

Katherine Westcott Tingley

Point Loma

1914

I told him this story, this fairy story; that in the golden land, far away, by the blue Pacific, I thought as a child that I could fashion a city and bring the people of all countries together and have the youth taught how to live, and how to become true and strong and noble, and forceful royal warriors for humanity. "But," I said, "all that has passed; it is a closed book, and I question if it will ever be realized."

"Well," he said, "the city you have described is a place that I know exists." And he then told of Point Loma. He was the first to name the place to me.

Katherine Augusta Westcott Tingley was born July 6, 1847, in Newbury, Massachusetts. She briefly attended a convent school in Montreal but left in 1867 to marry Richard Henry Cook, a printer. However, the marriage lasted only two months. In 1880 she married George W. Parent, an investigator for the New York Elevated Railway, but they also divorced after a few years.

At the age of forty-one Katherine married Philo B. Tingley, a mechanical engineer ten years her junior. Although they remained married, he played only a minor role in her life. To earn money, she gave "psychometric readings," which led to her involvement with the Theosophy movement. Theosophy was an occult religion that dealt with the mystical apprehension of God, based on elements of Buddhism and Brahmanism.

William Judge, one of the founders of the Theosophical Society and Katherine's friend, left the original society and formed the Theosophical Society in America. He served as president for one year until his death. Katherine persuaded the other leaders of the society that she had received spirit messages from Judge that he intended her to take over as "Outer Head" of the society's Esoteric Section.

Katherine began a world tour in 1896 with five other American Theosophists, visiting ancient holy places and seeking converts from Europe, the Middle East, and the Orient. During her world crusade, she envisioned a "'white city,' an ideal community which would serve also as the Society headquarters and a place where the theosophical way of life could be realized." In 1900 she opened her new headquarters in Point Loma, California, a beautiful setting overlooking San Diego Bay, one of the most unusual and elaborate utopian communities in America.

Katherine's writing, in which she relates a conversation she had with General Fremont, is from the June 1914 issue of The Theosophical Path.

Women's Words, Women's Stories

Point Loma attracted musicians, artists, and writers who performed concerts and plays for the 600 residents. They had their own printing plant that published Theosophical literature; a forestry and horticulture division that planted flower gardens, orchards, and citrus groves; and a "Woman's Exchange and Mart" that produced clothing and fabric.

Katherine was injured in May 1929 in a car accident in Germany. She died two months later at the Theosophical community in Visingsö, Sweden. Her cremated remains were divided for burial in Sweden and at Point Loma. Without Katherine, Point Loma gradually declined, and by 1951 the few followers left had relocated to Pasadena.

Lillien Jane Martin

1930

Fiftieth reunion

I feel that a college can be measured only long after its students have gone out in the world. We have been out fifty years. We have had a long time in which to observe, and my observation is this: that no institution in this country can compare with Vassar in initiative and leadership. This, I believe, is the most important thing for women today. . . .

I want to make a wish, and that wish is that all the people here, when they approach eighty, will find, as I am finding, that that is the best, the most interesting, the most satisfactory period of life.

Lillien Jane Martin was born July 7, 1851, in Olean, New York. After her father deserted the family, her mother saw to it that she received a proper religious and secular education. She began attending the Olean Academy at the age of four. When she was sixteen, her mother took a position as a matron in a college in Racine, Wisconsin, and Lillien began teaching in a nearby Episcopal girls' school to earn money for her college tuition. Finally, in 1876 when she was twenty-four years old, she was able to begin her studies at Vassar College.

Lillien had befriended the librarian at Vassar and after graduation obtained a job from her brother, David Starr Jordan, teaching chemistry and physics at Indianapolis High School. She remained there for nine years, until she was offered the position of vice-principal and head of the Science Department at the Girls' High School of San Francisco.

Lillien's writing is from a talk she gave to the trustee's luncheon at her fiftieth reunion at Vassar in 1930.

After five years in San Francisco, at age forty-three, she suddenly decided to become a psychologist.

Lillien studied at the University of Göttingen in Germany and received her Ph.D. degree in 1898, followed by a year's study in a Swiss psychiatric hospital specializing in hypnotism. Meanwhile, Jordan, her old friend and mentor, had become president of Stanford University. In 1899 he cabled her abroad to offer her an assistant professorship in psychology. She was promoted to full professor in 1911, and in 1915 she became Stanford's first woman department head. Unfortunately, she turned sixty-five the following year and was forced to retire.

Lillien did not enjoy retirement, so she moved to San Francisco and opened a private practice. While counseling one of her patients, a problem child, she became acquainted with his mentally imbalanced grandmother, which accidentally thrust her into the field of gerontology. She opened the first old-age counseling center and devoted the rest of her life to researching the rehabilitation of old people who had become public liabilities.

Lillien herself never slowed down and was an inspiration to the older generation. She travelled to Russia alone at seventy-eight, accompanied a friend on a cross-country auto trip at eighty-one, spent six months trekking through South America at eighty-seven, and learned to drive at ninety. She earned numerous honorary degrees and awards that recognized her contribution to the field of psychology, the most amusing being her inclusion in the book *American Men of Science*, with a star beside her name denoting distinction. She died of bronchopneumonia in San Francisco in 1943 at the age of ninety-one.

Ella Reeve Bloor

*F*or the movement

Ella's writing is from her autobiography, We Are Many, *published in 1940 by International Publishers, New York.*

1940

It has been said, I know, that when one begins to write an autobiography it is time to send for the undertaker. I hasten to say, however, that never have I felt so far from the end of life as I do today, as I begin this story. I am strong and vigorous at the age of 78 and I would really much rather talk about plans and dreams for the future than to delve back into the past. But my life has been a part of so many phases of the workers' and farmers' struggle for freedom in this country that my experiences really do not belong to me alone.

Ella Reeve Bloor was born July 8, 1862, on Staten Island, New York, the oldest of ten children. She married a distant cousin when she was nineteen and had six children. She began her long career as a political activist by organizing Philadelphia streetcar workers in the early 1890s.

Following her divorce in 1896, Ella and her children moved to the utopian community of Arden, Delaware, which had been established by socialists. There she met and married Louis Cohen, a fellow socialist, and had two more children. That marriage also failed, after which Ella threw herself wholeheartedly into her radical political activities. Although a member of the Woman's Christian Temperance Union and a tireless worker on behalf of women's suffrage, it was labor organization that interested her most. She spent twelve years organizing labor unions and rallying support for strikers.

The author Upton Sinclair, Ella's friend and fellow socialist, asked her to investigate further the Chicago meat packing industry, which he had exposed in his book *The Jungle*. She was accompanied by a young Socialist Party member, Richard Bloor, and she took his name to avoid the scandal of an unmarried investigative team. After a brief romantic fling, they separated permanently, although she retained his name for the rest of her life.

Ella became disillusioned with the socialists, and in 1919 she helped found the United States Communist Party. Two years later, she took the first of several trips to the Soviet Union. At the age of sixty-three, she hitchhiked across the United States, recruiting new members for the party. In North Dakota she met Andrew Omholt, a Communist party candidate for Congress, who became her third husband.

Ella was an honored guest in the Soviet Union in 1937 at the celebration of the twenty-year anniversary of the October Revolution. At home she continued to be a popular speaker, despite threats and harassment by police. She was arrested more than thirty times, including once at the age of seventy-two for assault and inciting to riot. She retired when she was seventy-six, moving with Andrew to an apple farm in Pennsylvania, which she described as her "first real home." She died in Pennsylvania in 1951 at the age of eighty-nine.

Clara Louise Kellogg

*H*ard to stop

1913

I never formally retired from public life, but quietly stopped when it seemed to me the time had come. It was a Kansas City newspaper reporter who incidentally brought home to me the fact that I was no longer very young. I had a few grey hairs, and after an interview granted to this representative of the press — a woman, by the way — I found, on reading the interview in print the next day, that my grey hairs had been mentioned.

"They'll find that my voice is getting grey next," I said to myself.

I really wanted to stop before everybody would be saying, "You ought to have heard her sing ten years ago!"

It was not easy to stop. When each autumn came around, it was very difficult not to go back to the public. I had an empty feeling. There is no sensation in the world like singing to an audience and knowing that you have it with you. I would not change my experience for that of any crowned head. The singer and the actor have, at least, the advantage over all other artists of a personal recognition of their success; although, of course, the painter and writer live in their work while the singer and the actor become only traditions. But such traditions!

Clara Louise Kellogg was born July 9, 1842, in Sumterville (now Sumter), South Carolina. In 1855 the family moved to New York City when her father took a job as a salesman for Pitman's shorthand system.

Both of Clara's parents played instruments, and she began piano lessons when she was five. After the move to New York, she started taking singing lessons with several renowned voice teachers. Clara's operatic debut was as Gilda in Verdi's *Rigoletto* at the New York Academy of Music in February 1861.

In 1863 Clara sang the part of Marguerite in Gounod's *Faust*, which became America's favorite opera and her most popular role. Over the next twenty years, she sang more than forty roles in Italian, French, and English. Yet Marguerite remained her greatest triumph.

Clara's writing is from Memoirs of an American Prima Donna, *published in 1913 by G. P. Putnam and Sons.*

Clara enjoyed a successful career in the United States and abroad. She spent the 1880-1881 season at the Russian Imperial Opera in St. Petersburg. Upon her return to America, she continued to tour for a few years until her marriage in 1887 to a young opera singer, Carl Strakosch, the nephew of her former manager. They built a home, "Elpstone," in New Hartford, Connecticut, and divided their time between Connecticut and Italy. Clara died of cancer at "Elpstone" in 1916 and was buried in the Town Hill Cemetery.

Mary McLeod Bethune

1949

I attended the funeral services held in the East Room of the White House on April 14th and found it impossible to restrain my feelings. I wept openly like a little child. I looked at the flag-draped bier and my mind went back to the time when we first met, and I had moved him to tears by my impassioned plea for my people's rights. I recalled holding his hands and looking into his fine, strong face, and telling him how much the common people depended on him.

Sad recollection

Mary McLeod Bethune was born July 10, 1875, to former slaves near Mayesville, South Carolina. She realized at a young age the importance of education and devoted her life to offering educational opportunities to others, regardless of race or economic background.

Mary married Albertus Bethune in 1898. In 1904 she started the Daytona Educational and Industrial School for Training Negro Girls, which merged with Cookman Institute in 1923 to become Bethune-Cookman College. Mary was head of the school until 1942.

She was elected to the Executive Board of the National Urban League, served as vice-president of the National Association for the Advancement of Colored People, and founded the National Council of Negro Women. President Herbert Hoover invited her to the White House several times to discuss issues of housing and child health. During Franklin D. Roosevelt's administration, Mary was director of the Division of Negro Affairs in the National Youth Administration. She enjoyed close working and personal relationships with FDR, as well as with his mother and his wife.

Upon her death at eighty, Mary left behind an inspiring

Mary's writing is from "My Secret Talks with Franklin D. Roosevelt," in the April 1949 issue of Ebony *magazine.*

will. She felt her worldly possessions were few but her experiences many, so she drew up a list of principles and policies to pass on to black people everywhere. She concluded with the statement, "Faith, courage, brotherhood, dignity, ambition, responsibility — we must cultivate them and use them as tools for our task of completing the establishment of equality for the Negro. . . . The Freedom Gates are half a-jar. We must pry them fully open. . . . I pray now that my philosophy may be helpful to those who share my vision of a world of Peace." She died in Daytona, Florida, in 1955.

Millie-Christine McKoy

None like me

circa 1870

'Tis not modest of one's self to speak;
But daily scanned from head to feet,
I freely talk of everything,
Sometimes to people wondering.

Some persons say I must be two,
The doctors say this is not true;
Some cry out, "Humbug" till they see,
Then they say, "Great mystery."

Two heads, four arms, four feet,
All in one perfect body meet;
I am most wonderfully made,
All scientific men have said.

None like me since the days of Eve,
None such perhaps shall ever live.
If marvel to myself am I
Why not to all who pass me by?

I'm happy quite, because content,
For some wise purpose I was sent;
My Maker knows what he has done,
Whether I'm created two or one.

This poem was written and often recited by Millie-Christine. It was published in the November 29, 1925, edition of The News and Observer, *Raleigh, North Carolina.*

Millie-Christine McKoy was born July 11, 1851, on a plantation near Whiteville, North Carolina. Although actually a pair of Siamese twins, joined at the spinal cord, she considered herself one person and always referred to herself as such. From the waist up she was distinctly separate, but from the waist down, although she had four legs, she could walk on two if she wished, and if one sister's foot was pricked the other sister could feel it as well.

Millie-Christine was born to slaves on the Jabez McCoy plantation. The white family spelled its name "McCoy," but the slaves used the spelling "McKoy." Mr. McCoy sold Millie-Christine at ten months for $1,000 plus 25 percent of the profits from exhibiting her. She was sold again at age two and displayed at agricultural fairs throughout the South for a 50-cent admission charge. Professor Millar bought her when she was four and took her on tour in England and Scotland.

In 1857 Millie-Christine was reclaimed in British court by a former owner, Joseph P. Smith, and her natural mother. She continued to tour the United States until the Civil War forced her temporarily to retire. After the war, she resumed touring with Mr. Smith, but thereafter she received 25 percent of the profits.

Millie-Christine was very intelligent and musically gifted. She spoke three languages, sang, danced, and played the guitar. Queen Victoria particularly enjoyed her and gave her lavish gifts each time she visited. As an adult she often toured with Chang and Eng Bunker, the first joined siblings to be called Siamese twins and forty years her senior. Interestingly, Chang and Eng were not compatible like Millie-Christine and often argued violently.

Millie-Christine used her earnings to buy the Jabez McCoy plantation one acre at a time for her family, which consisted of seven older and seven younger siblings. She donated large sums to black charities and schools. On October 8, 1912, Millie died of tuberculosis, and Christine died the following day. They had twin headstones, one for Millie-Christine and one for Christine-Millie, which read, "A soul with two thoughts. Two hearts that beat as one."

Lucy Fitch Perkins

Evanston
July 14, 1890

A piece of news

I don't know where you are but I know where I wish you were. Right here in Evanston where I could talk to you instead of writing. I have a piece of news that I shall not have to tell you of, in every letter. I have promised to marry Dwight Perkins. . . . It came sooner than I expected. Sunday night we undertook to discuss our differences and found so much sympathy in our spiritual experience that we were both surprised at ever having felt afraid of each other. And so it is settled and I am quietly content.

Lucy Fitch Perkins, children's book writer and illustrator, was born in Maples, Indiana, on July 12, 1865. Lucy obtained her early education at home. The family moved to Kalamazoo, Michigan, when she was fourteen. From her youngest years she had loved to draw, and when she was sixteen some of her cartoons were published by the *Kalamazoo Gazette*.

After she graduated from high school, Lucy was able to go on to the Museum of Fine Arts School in Boston because of the generosity of relatives who banded together to raise her tuition money. She worked for the Pang Educational Company after graduation from college and later taught at the Pratt Institute of New York.

After her marriage in 1891 to Dwight Perkins, Lucy had a studio room in her home where she illustrated children's books. She had a son and a daughter.

In 1911 she published *The Dutch Twins*, the first of her twenty-six Twin Books. They were very popular, with sales of more than 2 million copies, and were translated into many languages.

Lucy believed that anyone who wanted to write success-fully for children must first learn to draw. She drew the illustrations for her books before she wrote the text. She was still writing at the time of her death in 1937 when she was seventy-two.

Lucy's writing is an excerpt from a letter she wrote to her friend Florence Walker in 1890 and is included in Eve Among the Puritans: A Biography of Lucy Fitch Perkins, *written by her daughter Eleanor Ellis Perkins and published in 1956 by Houghton, Mifflin and Company.*

Mary Allen West

*B*lessed homes

1887

It is not a book of sermons or didactic teachings, but one that has grown naturally out of the rich soil of a thousand homes. During twelve years my work took me constantly into the homes of the people; hundreds of homes scattered far and wide over the entire country opened to me hospitable doors and took me into their very hearts. . . . Not all that goes to make up an ideal home is found in any one family circle, for Heaven has not yet come down to dwell among men, yet each pos-sesses some of the elements that, combined, make the

---

perfect whole, and from each have been taken tints for the picture I have tried to paint of what childhood should be.

Mary Allen West was born July 13, 1837, in Galesburg, Illinois. Education was stressed in her home, as her parents were among the founders of Knox College. Mary enrolled in the college at an early age. She graduated when she was seventeen and immediately began her teaching career.

Mary was elected superintendent of schools in Knox County, one of the first women to hold such a position in Illinois. She resigned after nine years to become president of the Illinois Woman's Christian Temperance Union. She never returned to teaching, devoting herself instead to the temperance cause full time. She spent many years organizing the women of Illinois, eventually moving to Chicago to become editor of the *Union Signal,* the newspaper of the WCTU. She was able to reach a large audience through the paper, which had a circulation of more than 100,000.

In addition to her temperance work, Mary was active in the Chicago Woman's Club, the Illinois Woman's Press Association, and the Protective Agency for Women and Children. In 1892 she travelled to California and then on to the Sandwich Islands and Japan on behalf of the temperance cause. She died while in Kanazawa, Japan, in December of that year.

Mary's writing is from her introduction to Childhood: Its Care and Culture, *published in 1887 by R. S. King Publishing Co., Chicago.*

Florence Bascom

1925

The women lacked gymnasium drill or any form of organized athletics, except that sometime in 1878 or 1879 at the instigation of Will Anderson, of grateful memory, and with him as instructor, the inadequate University gymnasium (by custom ceded to the men exclusively) was opened to the women a few hours every week. This was far from sufficient exercise and the women suffered from lack of regular exercise unless they indulged individually in swimming, boating, or riding. There was little enough of this, but the feat of swimming from Picnic Point to our boat-house (a good seven-eighths of a mile) was accomplished by a woman in my class. It is an interesting manifestation of the attitude of certain public critics toward change, that

*I*n need of exercise

Florence's writing is from "The University in 1874-1887," published in The Wisconsin Magazine of History, *March 1925.*

when the collegiate training of women was first on trial there were clamorous complaints that the health of young women was being wrecked; now the same class of public critics are loudly complaining that college women are "Amazons."

Florence Bascom was born July 14, 1862, in Williamstown, Massachusetts, where her father was a professor at Williams College. The family moved to Madison, Wisconsin when she was twelve, her father having been named president of the University of Wisconsin. Florence enrolled in the university at sixteen and earned two bachelor's degrees in 1882, one in letters and one in arts. She took additional courses after graduation and received a bachelor of science degree in 1884.

Florence's special interest was geology. She studied with two of America's finest geologists for three years and received her master's degree in 1887. After teaching for two years, she returned to school to study at Johns Hopkins University, which awarded her its first Ph.D. to a woman in 1893.

In 1895 Florence joined the faculty at Bryn Mawr College, where she would remain for the next thirty years. She began as a reader in geology and worked her way up to lecturer, assistant professor, and finally full professor in 1906. She introduced geology as an undergraduate major and eventually as a graduate program, despite the objections of the college's president, who felt science should be only an elective in a women's college. Starting with nothing, Florence begged and bought rock and mineral collections and in 1899 obtained a petrographic microscope, which enabled her to teach a course in petrography.

Florence was the first woman to be appointed a geologist with the United States Geological Survey. She spent her summers touring the Piedmont Mountains on horseback, collecting specimens and writing reports. She also served as associate editor of the *American Geologist* from 1896 to 1905. Florence died of a cerebral hemorrhage at the age of eighty-two and was buried in the Williams College Cemetery.

Saint Frances Xavier Cabrini

1891

Our mode of work is to go right down into the Italian quarters and go from house to house, from apartment to apartment. We are recognized by all Italians, and many of them are glad to see us. We try to learn about all the Italian children we meet, whether they have proper homes and proper schooling. I have said that we are especially anxious about the girls just now, and the reason must be apparent. The temptations that a big city like this offers to poor, ignorant girls of any nationality are very great, and to abandoned Italian girls, who have no means of livelihood and are ignorant even of the language of those around them, they are terrible. . . .

Saint Frances Xavier Cabrini was born July 15, 1850, in Lombardy, Italy. She was the youngest of thirteen children, of whom only four survived childhood. Her uncle, a priest, was a major influence on her, and she later recalled that at her confirmation at age seven she knew she would always serve God.

In 1874 her pastor asked her to accompany him to the village of Codogno to work in the House of Providence orphanage. She took her religious vows three years later and was named mother superior of the orphanage by Bishop Gelmini. In 1880 she began an institute of missionary sisters with seven young women from the orphanage, and the Missionary Sisters of the Sacred Heart was officially ordained.

Within seven years Mother Cabrini had established seven convents, a school, and a nursery. In 1888 she met with Pope Leo XIII, who described her as "a woman of marvelous intuition and of great sanctity." He officially recognized and blessed her work. Bishop Scalabrini and the Pope were concerned for the Italian immigrants settling in New York City, and they asked Mother Cabrini to go to America. In 1889 she arrived in New York with six nuns and opened the first American motherhouse of the Missionary Sisters of the Sacred Heart on East Fifty-ninth Street.

From 1890 to 1892 Mother Cabrini travelled constantly, opening schools, orphanages, and hospitals throughout North America, South America, and Europe. In 1909 she became a United States citizen, and in 1910 she was made superior general of her order for life, presiding over sixty-five houses with more than 1,500 nuns.

Anxious

Mother Cabrini's writing is from a letter to Mother Savaré, June 26, 1891, and is housed in the Cabriniana Room, Cabrini College, Radnor, Pennsylvania.

Although Mother Cabrini was never physically strong or healthy, she refused to slow down or indulge in self-pity, saying, "With one ounce of love of God one bears burdens silently and joyfully." In April 1917 she had a recurrence of the malaria she contracted years earlier in South America. Several months later, she collapsed at an altar during mass and died soon after. In 1931 Pope Pius XI pronounced her "Venerable," and in 1938 she was beatified and named "Blessed." She was canonized in 1946, the first American to achieve sainthood.

Ida Bell Wells-Barnett

A fighter

Ida's writing is from her autobiography, begun in 1928. Edited by her daughter Alfreda M. Duster, it was published in 1970, thirty-nine years after her death, by the University of Chicago Press.

1928

When the train started and the conductor came along to collect tickets, he took my ticket, then handed it back to me and told me that he couldn't take my ticket there. I thought that if he didn't want the ticket I wouldn't bother about it so went on reading. In a little while when he finished taking tickets, he came back and told me I would have to go in the other car. I refused, saying that the forward car was a smoker, and as I was in the ladies' car I proposed to stay. He tried to drag me out of the seat, but the moment he caught hold of my arm I fastened my teeth in the back of his hand.

I had braced my feet against the seat in front and was holding to the back, and as he had already been badly bitten he didn't try it again by himself. He went forward and got the baggageman and another man to help him and of course they succeeded in dragging me out.

Ida Bell Wells-Barnett was born to slaves on July 16, 1862, in Holly Springs, Mississippi. She was attending the local freedmen's high school when her parents and three siblings died of yellow fever. Although only fourteen, she pretended to be eighteen to get a teaching position to support her five younger siblings.

In 1884 Ida moved to Memphis and taught in the city's Negro school while taking courses herself at Fisk University. Her minister, a leader in the black Baptist community, urged her to take up writing. She contributed articles to black-run newspapers, and, because some of her articles were critical of the poor educational opportunities available to blacks, her Memphis teaching contract was not renewed. Ida then turned to journalism full time and became the co-owner of the *Memphis Free Speech*.

In March 1892 three close friends of Ida's were lynched in Memphis. She wrote a series of anti-white articles and urged blacks to move to the West. While on a short business trip to New York, her paper's offices were destroyed by an angry mob, and she never returned to Memphis.

Ida began a one-woman crusade against lynching. She lectured around the United States and Great Britain and organized anti-lynching societies and Negro women's clubs. After her marriage in 1895 to Ferdinand Lee Barnett, she settled in Chicago and continued to lecture and organize. She published *A Red Record*, an account of all the lynchings in the South during a three-year period. In 1898 she took a group of protesters to see President William McKinley to demand justice for the lynching of a black postmaster in South Carolina.

While raising her four children, Ida travelled less and turned to aiding the black population of Chicago. She founded several women's clubs and the Negro Fellowship League to provide social centers for blacks. She started the Alpha Suffrage Club of Chicago, the first black suffrage organization, and served for years as the director of the Cook County League of Women's Clubs. From 1913 to 1916 she was a probation officer for the Chicago municipal court. In 1918 she visited East St. Louis, Illinois, after the race riots. Upon returning home, she wrote a series of articles for the *Chicago Tribune* warning the city "to set the wheels of justice in motion before it is too late." A few weeks later, the city erupted in racial violence with forty deaths and hundreds injured.

Ida died at home in 1931. In 1940 the Ida B. Wells housing project in Chicago was dedicated in her name.

Linda Anne Eastman

1929

Dr. Roland Marcel was away from Paris on his vacation, and consequently my reception at the Bibliothéque Nationale was very different from what it would have been had he been there. It was in fact anything but pleasant — an example of how things should *not* be done in a library. At first I was told that I could not even look inside the library proper, and only my persistent statement that Dr. Marcel would wish me to see it finally resulted in my being shown the general reading room and the stack room adjoining, but only after I had filled out a card giving considerable biographical data, and had it exchanged for a second card at the desk, which latter card was checked carefully and taken up as I went out. The young woman who was finally detailed to show me these rooms explained the complicated system of catalogs, and said that it usually took at least an hour to get a book to a reader after he had found it in the catalog and put in his written request for it; also that a reader needed to make about ten visits before he could understand the catalogs sufficiently to really use them intelligently.

Linda Anne Eastman was born July 17, 1867, in Oberlin, Ohio. Following graduation from high school and one year at normal school, she began teaching fourth grade. She was pleasantly surprised by her pupils' desire to read and decided she could help more children by becoming a librarian.

Linda had met William Brett, the head of the Cleveland Library, when he assisted her in finding a book when she was a schoolgirl. She began working for him in 1892, and he appointed her head librarian of a branch library two years later.

Linda became Brett's protegé. Together they founded the Ohio Library Association and the School of Library Science at Western Reserve University. She established libraries in hospitals and sanitoriums, created a separate children's room within Cleveland's public library, and started a Braille collection and blind reading group.

Brett passed away in 1918, and Linda was elected as his successor. In 1925 she opened the city of Cleveland's new six-story library and initiated many innovative services. When she retired thirteen years later, the library staff had grown from eighteen to 1,100, and she had increased the number of books from 57,000 to more than 2 million.

Linda died at the age of ninety-five, having received many awards and three honorary degrees. The Eastman Branch of the Cleveland Library and the Eastman Reading Garden were named for her.

Linda's writing about the Bibliothéque Nationale in Paris is from a September 1929 letter she wrote to her family from Interlaken, Switzerland. It is in the Schlesinger Library, Radcliffe College, Cambridge, Massachusetts.

Women's Words, Women's Stories

Clara A. Swain

1870

The latter part of our voyage was very rough and I was too sick to write, and I had five sick ones to look after besides myself as there was no stewardess or ship doctor. I cannot bear to think of the sea, it treated me so badly.

We were met at Bombay by Rev. Mr. Bowen, a missionary who took us to lunch and arranged for our journey up-country. We were detained at Nagpur over a week waiting for our trunks. . . . Our trunks came at last and we left Nagpur on the evening of the 17th of January in one of those delightful "dák gáris" which Mr. Coffin describes so perfectly in his book, *A New Way Around the World.* We appreciated his experience more fully when one of the horses lay down in the road and the men tried for an hour to get it up; when they succeeded they left us alone in the conveyance while they went back three miles for another pair of horses. All around us in the jungles we could see fires built by the natives to keep tigers away from their huts.

We made ourselves as comfortable as possible with blankets and shawls, closed the doors of the conveyance and lay down for a nap, weary and I fear a little discouraged.

Clara A. Swain was born July 18, 1834, in Elmira, New York, the youngest of ten children. When she was fifteen she lived for a year in Michigan with an aunt and taught at the local school. In 1856 she moved in with another aunt in Canandaigua, New York, where she studied for a year in a seminary and then returned to teaching. Although she taught for seven more years, she longed to become a doctor. In 1865 she began working at the Castile Sanitarium in Castile, New York, alternating work with study at the Woman's Medical College of Pennsylvania until she graduated in 1869.

In November 1869 Clara was sponsored by the New England branch of the Woman's Foreign Missionary Society and was sent to Bareilly, India, to teach medicine at an orphanage as well as treat women.

Clara was accepted by the local Indian women, who called her "Dr. Miss Sahiba," and she soon had more patients than

A trip to India

Clara's writing in a letter to her sister from Bareilly, India, January 25, 1870, is included in A Glimpse of India: Being a Collection of Extracts from Letters of Dr. Clara A. Swain, *published in 1909 by J. Pott, New York.*

she could handle. Clara built a six-room dispensary in 1873 and a hospital in 1874, where she treated 1,600 patients in the first eight months. With each prescription she also gave the patient a verse of scripture printed in Hindi, Persian, and Urdu.

From 1876 to 1880 Clara returned to Castile to rest and repair her health from the long years of treating thousands of patients. She resumed her work in Bareilly in 1880, and in 1885 was asked to become palace physician for the wife of the Rajah of Rajputana. She also rode her own elephant throughout the surrounding countryside, treating patients who were unable to come to her. She spent ten happy years with the Rajah and his wife, retiring in 1896.

Upon her retirement, Clara returned to Castile to work on her book, *A Glimpse of India*. She died in Castile on Christmas Day 1910 at the age of seventy-six.

JULY 19

Mary Ann Ball Bickerdyke

Defying death

Mary Ann's writing is from a letter to a friend from Farmington, Georgia, in 1862. It is included in Cyclone in Calico: The Story of Mary Ann Bickerdyke *by Nina Brown Baker, published by Little, Brown and Company, 1952.*

1862
One day a coffin was brought in the ambulance with a sick man. I said, "What have you got that thing for?" The driver replied, "Oh, we had it on hand, and as he is so nearly dead we thought we'd bring it along." "Well, you take care of your coffin and I'll take care of the man," I said. And Frank — good fellow that he was, he could swear a little on occasion as well as pray — said "I'll split that thing up for kindling wood, and d-n the fellow who'd put a man in a coffin before he is dead!" And he was as good as his word.

Mary Ann Ball Bickerdyke was born July 19, 1817, in Knox County, Ohio. Following her mother's death when she was just eighteen months old, she was shuttled between various relatives. As a result, she received only the most basic education.

In April 1847 Mary Ann married Robert Bickerdyke, a widower eleven years her senior with three children. After ten years of marriage, they left his children with relatives in Kentucky and went to Galesburg, Illinois, with their two sons, aged six and eight. Robert died suddenly three years later, and Mary Ann began supporting the family by practicing "botanic" medicine, which she had studied in Cincinnati before she was married.

During a church service in the spring of 1861, Mary Ann

was horrified to hear her pastor's description of the neglect of Illinois volunteers sick with typhoid and dysentery at a Union Army camp in nearby Cairo. She organized a relief fund and took it to Cairo for disbursement. Upon her arrival, she found the situation even more squalid than the minister had described, with filthy, crowded, unsanitary conditions and barely any food. Without stopping to seek anyone's permission, she began cleaning, feeding, and nursing the sick men, thus beginning her four-year career helping the Civil War's sick and wounded both at the front and behind the lines.

Mary Ann left Cairo after nine months for a hospital established after the Battle of Belmont. In 1862 she made five trips to the battlefield at Fort Donelson to evacuate the injured to various hospitals. This experience convinced her that she was most needed at the front, so she began following General Grant's army as it moved up the Tennessee River toward the Confederate stronghold in Mississippi. As she worked at Union field hospitals, usually tents hidden in the woods, she washed clothes, prepared food, distributed supplies, and tended the wounded. She was known and loved by the men as "Mother Bickerdyke."

She accompanied Grant to Vicksburg and Sherman to Chattanooga and was the only woman present at the battles of Lookout Mountain and Missionary Ridge, where she worked in freezing rain and deep mud to care for the 1,700 Union wounded.

Mary Ann was in Beaufort, North Carolina, when the war ended, and she followed Sherman's victorious army into Washington, D.C., where she was given a place of honor in the May 24, 1865, Victory Parade. She spent the years immediately after the war relocating veterans to Kansas. In 1876 she moved to San Francisco and was awarded a clerkship at the mint by her wartime friend, Gen. John Logan, by then a senator from Illinois. She spent her last years with her son in Kansas, where she died in 1901 at the age of eighty-four. She was buried in Galesburg, and the town erected a statue in her memory.

Anne Ryan

1931

Fiesta

My darling Sitty. . . . Did you have a nice time at Thanksgiving? I want to tell you about the beautiful fiesta I had — we all went to Jed's house. I arrived early in order to make a pie. You have no idea of that fine old, old, kitchen, copper pots, hand-carved utensils, high chopping block on three legs (exactly the kind you see in fairy tale books) and a lattice door on the pantry — a pantry filled with old peasant plates, chuggy brown casseroles, huge wine bottles encased in plaited straw and such a delicious smell — cinnamon, orange & anise. Only their little maid knew how to tend the queer charcoal stove — she stood in front of it with a fan and a beatific expression! . . . Jed had a whole baby pig cooked at the bakers (thank Heaven!) There were strange Mallorcian vegetables and artichokes and apple sauce — (I made it with orange!) and lobster salad and stuffed eggs and wonderful candied coconut, and fat fat almonds (much fatter than we get home). The pig I'll never forget. He was borne to the table by the older and more important maid, an apple in his mouth and three beautiful roses (just picked in the garden) on his back. Oh! Of course there was good wine, you never tasted such nectar and at last yellow Chartreuse in thimble glasses. We took coffee before the fire which was lit just for looks but the long doors were open to the wide fields & a distant view of the water. And there we sat, ten of us, writers, people just down from Paris, people from Dorsetshire, — hours we sat. We decided everything, who were the best writers today, the best poets, and of course, all over again about Emily. We played again & again the Cesar Frank symphony records. At dusk the sheep who live two walls away from Jed's rooms were driven past, they sounded all their little bells so singly, it is such a tender, tinkling, hidden, sunken in fur! When the night really came we went out into the back garden. A jagged range of naked stone is beyond, and the moon came up. We sat on the low-well curb and in long wicker chairs. The music was brought out. It sounded much clearer in that space. The old old walls, the tired ancient roof was mellowed in that light. The squat cross on the special little chapel which belongs to Jed's house was cut against a low cluster of stars. We sat there a long time.

Anne's November 1931 letter to her daughter Elizabeth, written from Majorca, is in the Anne Ryan Papers at the Archives of American Art, Washington, D.C.

Anne Ryan was born July 20, 1889, in Hoboken, New Jersey. Her mother committed suicide when she was twelve, and her father died the following year, after which she was raised by her grandmother. She graduated from St. Elizabeth's

Convent and went on to St. Elizabeth's College, but left in 1911 to marry William J. McFadden, a law student.

Anne and William had twins in 1912 and a son in 1919, but they were permanently separated in 1923. Anne, anxious to be more than a housewife, resumed her maiden name and began writing poetry, essays, and a novel. She published her first volume of poetry, *Lost Hills*, in 1925. In 1931 she placed her children in boarding school and departed for a two-year sojourn on the Mediterranean island of Majorca. She wrote poems and articles for American magazines and worked on a biography of Fra Junipero Serra, which she never completed. Upon her return to America, she took up residence in Greenwich Village and socialized with artists she met through the Federal Arts Project and the American Artists Group. At fifty, with her artist friends' encouragement, she took up painting and turned out a series of pleasing engravings and woodblock prints.

However, Anne had a major artistic revelation in 1948 when she first saw the collages of German artist Kurt Schwitters. From then on, she worked solely in that medium, producing numerous abstract collages of fine paper and textiles. She participated in many New York exhibitions, including the Whitney Annual and the Brooklyn Museum Print Annual. Although she continued to write poems and short stories, it is as a collage artist that Anne left her mark on American art. She died of a stroke in 1954 at the age of sixty-four at her son's home in New Jersey.

Louise Blanchard Bethune

1891

Out of the question

The future of woman in the architectural profession is what she herself sees fit to make it. It is often proposed that she become exclusively a dwelling house architect. Pity her, and withdraw the suggestion. A specialist should become so from intrinsic fitness, not from extrinsic influence. Furthermore, the dwelling is the most puttering and worst paid work an architect ever does. He always dreads it, not, as someone may have told you, because he must usually deal with a woman, but because he must strive to gratify the conflicting desires of an entire household, who dig up every hatchet for his benefit and hold daily powwows in his anteroom, and because he knows he loses money nearly

Louise's writing is from "Women and Architecture," Inland Architecture and News Record, March 1891.

every time. Dwelling house architecture, as a special branch for women, should be, at the present rate of remuneration, quite out of the question.

Louise Blanchard Bethune was born July 21, 1856, in Waterloo, New York. As a student at Buffalo High School, she already showed great aptitude in planning houses and various other structures. She allowed two years following graduation to prepare for entering Cornell's newly opened architecture school. However, during that time she was offered a job as a drafter by Buffalo architect Richard A. Waite.

Louise read Waite's entire library of architecture books and learned techniques of drafting and architectural design. In October 1881 she opened the Blanchard and Bethune architectural firm with a Canadian, Robert A. Bethune. Two months later they were married and changed the company's name to R. A. and L. Bethune.

The Bethunes did not specialize in any type of building but rather pursued a wide variety of projects in the Buffalo area, including an Episcopal church, a brick factory, a grandstand at a baseball park, a bank, a hotel, the Seventy-fourth Regiment Armory, and the East Buffalo Live Stock Exchange. In addition, Louise designed numerous homes, apartments, stores, and eighteen schools. In 1880 she was elected the first woman member of the American Institute of Architects, and the next year she became the first woman Fellow of the Western Association of Architects. She held very strong feminist views and demanded "equal pay for equal service."

In 1890 the Bethunes took on a third partner, William L. Fuchs, and Louise semi-retired. She spent her leisure time raising her son and investigating her family's genealogy. She felt the body of work she designed during her career had proved that a woman could understand the "practical questions of actual construction" and could be a successful architect. She died of kidney failure in 1913 at the age of fifty-seven.

JULY 22 | *Margery Williams Bianco*

Love of surprise

1925

To engage children's interest in anything you have to be keenly interested in that thing yourself; if you are not, if you are merely pretending or playing up to them, they will promptly catch you out.

There are two things the storyteller can always count on with some degree of certainty, love of adventure and love of surprise — the kind of surprise that is really an open secret between the inventor and the listener, something which the listener has all the joy of expecting beforehand and can await trustfully, knowing that after whatever suspense of complication it will unfailingly appear, at just the right moment and with all the accumulated dramatic effect. Children love to be taken, as it were, into the writer's confidence. However often the miracle appears, it will never miss fire. The author of *Swiss Family Robinson* realized this to perfection. He knew that the child mind would follow him faithfully through pages of tedious moralizing, through veritable morasses of instruction, solely for the joy of seeing the needle-and-thread tree perform its useful little stunt just at the very moment when it becomes imperative for the boys to have new trousers.

Margery Williams Bianco was born July 22, 1881, in London, England. Her father believed that children should be taught to read very early, then left alone to read as much as possible until they were ten. Margery, six years younger than her nearest sibling, spent much of her childhood reading alone in her room.

When Margery was nine her mother took her to the United States after the death of her father and sister. Margery was at last permitted to attend school, graduating from the Convent of the Holy Child in Sharon, Pennsylvania. In 1901 the family returned to London, where Margery started to write. Her first novel was published the following year. She joined a writer's club where she met Francesco Bianco, an Italian working in London as a book binder and dealer in rare books. They were married in 1904 and had two children.

The Biancos spent the next seventeen years travelling between homes in London, Paris, and Turin, Italy. In 1921 they moved to New York City. With the exception of a short travel guide of Paris, Margery put aside her writing while raising her family. After their arrival in America, she decided to resume writing, publishing her first children's book, *The Velveteen Rabbit*, in 1922. This classic modern fairy tale is still popular today and established her immediately as a leader in children's literature. She published eight more children's books between 1925 and 1944, several of which were illustrated by her daughter, Pamela. She also translated stories from French and frequently contributed to *Horn Book Magazine* for children. Her career was cut short in September 1944, when she died suddenly from a cerebral hemorrhage.

Margery's writing is from "Our Youngest Critics," The Bookman, *November 1925.*

Florence Guertin Tuttle

Presents from beaux

1948

My beaux in New York — we never called them boy friends then — used occasionally to send me five pound boxes of Maillard's candies. My Mother and sister used to sit down and devour them. We all watched for the old slow white horse who brought the express. One swain sent me a gold watch on my birthday. Mother made me return it. "He'll be buying you clothes next," she said — and that was the present to end presents.

Florence Guertin Tuttle was born July 23, 1869, in Brooklyn, New York. She attended the Nassau Institute until her father lost his fortune in bad Wall Street investments. She spent one year at public school until Myra Hotchkiss approached her parents and offered Florence free tuition at Nassau. She graduated as valedictorian and received nineteen bouquets from admiring beaux.

As a teenager, Florence became engaged to a Yale student named Dexter. He died of typhoid fever before they could be married, and Florence went into mourning for years. She turned to writing "partly for diversion, partly because I loved it, and largely to help our financial status." She recalled in her autobiography, "I was born with inky fingers. Never can I remember the time when I did not write diaries, stories or very bad poems." At sixteen, her first short story submitted to *McClure's* magazine won a $100 prize. This was the beginning of a lifelong pattern of successful firsts for Florence. Her first play was produced on the B. F. Keith circuit, her first poem was "copied widely and preached upon from pulpits," and her first book of essays was accepted by the first publisher who saw it.

In her late twenties, Florence met Frank Day Tuttle, a Yale student, while she was writing a Sunday column for the *Brooklyn Daily Eagle*. He was one of her many suitors until she picked up the *New York Sun* at breakfast one day and read the headline, "Frank Day Tuttle shot by a burglar." He was confined to bed in a dark room for weeks as the gunpowder had to be slowly and painfully picked from his face, during which time Florence corresponded with him. When he was well, he asked her to his first social outing, the Yale Ball, and "within a week he had proposed to me and invited me to go to London on our honeymoon, to see the Yale crew row at Henley." It was too soon for Florence, and she refused him.

Florence began studying Greek and Latin in order to

Florence's writing is from her unpublished autobiography, "I Travelled Hopefully," written in 1948 when she was seventy-nine. The manuscript is in the Florence Guertin Tuttle Papers, Sophia Smith Collection, Smith College, Northampton, Massachusetts.

understand the derivation of words to help her with her writing. She asked Frank Tuttle to recommend a Latin teacher, and he offered to tutor her himself. She later recalled, "We got through Caesar, Cicero, and began Virgil as we became engaged. Frank said, 'Thank God for dead languages.'" They were married in 1898 and had two sons.

In 1914 Florence joined the Woman's Peace Party after realizing that "Peace must be organized, as war had to be organized, to win." She published *Women and World Federation* in 1918 with a foreword by ex-President William Howard Taft, a plea to all women to work for organized world peace. Florence and Frank travelled to Geneva in 1923, arriving on the day Mussolini bombarded Corfu. They stayed for a month and visited the Fourth Assembly of the League of Nations. When she returned to America, Florence became the chairperson of the Women's Pro-League Council.

Florence remained active in the peace movement until her death in 1951. She was buried in the family plot in Brooklyn.

Amelia Mary Earhart

1928

Bill made a skilful mooring in a protected harbor and we were rowed ashore. There were six policemen to handle the crowd. That they got us through was remarkable. In the enthusiasm of their greeting those hospitable Welsh people nearly tore our clothes off.

Finally we reached the shelter of the Frickers Metal Company office where we remained until police reinforcements arrived. In the meantime we had tea and I knew I was in Britain.

Twice, before the crowd would let us get away, we had to go to an upper balcony and wave. They just wanted to see us. I tried to make them realize that all the credit belonged to the boys, who did the work. But from the beginning it was evident the accident of sex — the fact that I happened to be the first woman to have made the Atlantic flight — made me the chief performer in our particular sideshow.

With the descent of reporters one of the first questions I was asked was whether I knew Colonel Lindbergh and whether I thought I looked like him.

Celebrity

Amelia's writing is from 20 Hrs. 40 Min. — Our Flight in the Friendship, published in 1928 by G. P. Putnam's Sons, New York.

Gleefully they informed me I had been dubbed "Lady Lindy." I explained that I had never had the honor of meeting Colonel Lindbergh, that I was sure I looked like no one (and, just then, nothing) in the world, and that I would grasp the first opportunity to apologize to him for innocently inflicting the idiotic comparison.

Amelia Mary Earhart was born July 24, 1897, at her grandparents' home in Atchison, Kansas. Mr. Earhart repeatedly lost jobs due to his fondness for alcohol, and as a result the family travelled from Kansas to Iowa to Minnesota to Illinois.

After graduating from high school in Chicago, Amelia maintained the family's nomadic style. She spent the war years in Toronto, assisting the Red Cross at a military hospital. She then found herself enrolled as a premedical student at Columbia University. It was in Glendale, California, at the age of twenty-three, that Amelia took her first airplane ride, and it was an event that would change her life.

Amelia finally had found something that held her interest. She took flying lessons from Neta Snook, a pioneer woman pilot, and bought her first plane — a Kinner Canary — when she was twenty-five. She soon set a woman's altitude record of 14,000 feet.

In 1928 Amelia became the first woman to cross the Atlantic by air, which thrust her instantly into the public eye. She was fêted in England and greeted in New York City by a ticker tape parade down Fifth Avenue.

Amelia married George Palmer Putnam in 1931. He encouraged her to write and promoted her name through a line of sports clothes and luggage. In 1932 she completed a solo crossing of the Atlantic in fifteen hours. In 1935 she won a $10,000 prize by flying solo from Honolulu to the mainland.

In March 1937, Amelia and her crew left Oakland, California, for Honolulu. On July 2, they left New Guinea for a tiny landing strip on Howland Island, but they never arrived. Extensive searches failed to turn up any trace of the plane or aviators. Rumors persisted for years that she was still alive, either stranded on an island or a prisoner of war, but no proof was ever found.

Flora Adams Darling

St. Charles Hotel, New Orleans, L.A.
Jan. 1861

My own dear Father:

I am really very fond of my new friends.
Southerners have not the reserve and dignity of
Northerners, but are so kind and hospitable that one
can easily pardon many little things that at one time
seemed unpardonable in my eyes. A gentleman often
appears in his shirt sleeves in a lady's presence smoking
a pipe, and will tip back in a chair, and the majority eat
with their knives, and yet I condone the offences
against etiquette, and think they are splendid. You will
smile at the smallness of my charge and wonder if these
are the only "crimes" I have to bring against the South.

Flora Adams Darling was born July 25, 1840, in Lancaster,
New Hampshire. When she was twenty, she married Edward
Darling and moved to his home in Louisiana. He died during
the Civil War, and Flora was arrested by Union officers as
she tried to return to New England. She was released after a
few days, but she discovered that her trunk had been emptied
of her cash, jewelry, and Confederate bonds. She fought for
more than thirty years to receive compensation from
Congress and was finally awarded $5,683 in 1903.

Flora started to write in the late 1880s, hoping to support
herself and her son. However, she produced only sugary
novels about Southern society and short stories that were
accepted by lesser magazines. Her best effort was *Mrs.
Darling's Letters, or Memories of the Civil War*, which was
notable as one of the few works by a Northerner to endorse
slavery.

Flora would have died in obscurity had she not formed the
women's hereditary patriotic society known as the Daughters
of the American Revolution. She issued invitations to the
first meeting on October 11, 1890, and served as vice-president general until she was forced out of the organization due
to her autocratic nature.

A view of the South

*Flora's letter, written ten
months after her arrival in the
South, is included in* Mrs.
Darling's Letters, or
Memories of the Civil War, *
published by J. W. Lovell in
1883.*

Ella Alexander Boole

*F*louting the law

Ella's writing is from Give Prohibition Its Chance, *published in 1929 by the National Woman's Christian Temperance Union.*

1929

Most states forbade the sale of liquor on Sunday, but side-doors were open on that day and often front doors as well, until it was said, "They'll sell anyway. Why not license them?" There were laws forbidding the sale of liquor to minors; yet children were sent to the saloons for beer, and it was sold to them openly in defiance of the law.

On one occasion I was addressing the Sunday school of the church in New York City of which my husband was pastor. In order to point a moral, I told the story of a woman who had worked hard all day, and when she got home, sent her little boy across the street for a pint of beer. "Five times she sent him," I explained. "Now, that beer was seven cents a pint." All over the room the children called out, "No, eight cents a pint." They knew from experience, far better than I, what was the current price of beer.

Ella Alexander Boole was born July 26, 1858, in Van Wert, Ohio. After attending local public schools, she received her A.B. and A.M. degrees from the College of Wooster. She taught at Van Wert High School and the First Presbyterian Church Sunday School.

At a teacher's conference in 1883, Ella met William Boole, a twice-widowed Methodist minister thirty-one years her senior. They married and settled near his pastorate in Brooklyn, New York. Ella had one daughter and raised the three daughters from William's previous marriages.

Ella joined the Woman's Christian Temperance Union and within several years was vice-president of the New York state chapter. She was a skilled public speaker with good organizational skills and was often sent to Albany to lobby for the cause. After William's death in 1896, she devoted most of her time to the WCTU. She was elected president of the New York WCTU and held the position from 1898 to 1925, when she became president of the national WCTU.

In 1920 Ella ran for the Senate on the Prohibition party ticket. She felt compelled to challenge the incumbent, who had voted against prohibition, women's suffrage, and child labor laws. Although she lost, she did get over 150,000 votes. She ran twice more, in 1922 and 1926, campaigning tirelessly with the slogan, "Send a mother to the Senate," but those bids were also unsuccessful.

Ella waged an uphill battle in the late '20s and early '30s to retain prohibition. Public support was waning, and although she gave her 1933 annual address on radio in an attempt to reach more people, she realized that defeat was imminent. She retired soon after as president of the national WCTU, although she remained president of the world organization. Her last achievement before complete retirement at eighty-eight was to obtain recognition of the world WCTU by the United Nations. She died in 1952.

Lucy Maynard Salmon

1897

A call for careers

. . . it seems not unreasonable to consider marriage on its practical side as a business partnership to which the woman as well as the man is to contribute. If she contributes a practical knowledge of housekeeping, the business agreement is a fair one; if she does not contribute this knowledge, but brings a knowledge of other things as valuable, it is also a fair arrangement; but if she brings no knowledge of household affairs, and no equivalent for it, the partnership on its business side is unfair. There should be a definite understanding when a woman marries whether she is to keep house or not, and if so, that she knows how. The time ought to come when, in case she marries and boards, she will be willing and able, and society will allow her, to contribute her share in a business capacity to the life partnership.

Lucy Maynard Salmon was born July 27, 1853, in Fulton, New York. After her mother died when she was seven, she spent an unhappy childhood with a stepmother. Concerned for her mental and physical well-being, her parents sent her to stay with relatives in Illinois and Michigan. One of her cousins in Detroit was planning to attend the University of Michigan and urged her to do the same. She entered the university in 1872 at a time when there were only fifty females in the school.

After graduation, Lucy spent several unsettled years unsure of what she wanted to do. She taught high school in a small Iowa town, but she disliked country life and returned to

Lucy's writing is from her historical study Domestic Service, *published by the Macmillan Company in 1897.*

the University of Michigan for her master's degree. After four more years teaching in Indiana and Pennsylvania, she became the first history professor at Vassar College.

Lucy loved Vassar and remained there her entire career. As chairman of the history department, she introduced many new ideas and new courses. She was also instrumental in the drive to build a new, larger school library. In 1884 she became a founding member and first female member of the American Historical Association.

Lucy somehow evaded the mandatory retirement age and continued teaching into her seventies. In 1926, when she was seventy-three, the Lucy Maynard Salmon Fund for Research was created by alumnae to further her scholarly endeavors. She died of a stroke in 1927 and was buried near Vassar in the Poughkeepsie Rural Cemetery.

JULY 28

Louise Smith Clappe

The right sort

1851

To-day I called at the residence of Mrs. R. It is a canvas house containing a suite of three "apartments," as Dick Swiveller would say, which, considering that they were all on the ground-floor, are kept surprisingly neat. There is a barroom blushing all over with red calico, a dining-room, kitchen, and a small bed-closet. The little sixty-eight-pounder woman is queen of the establishment. By the way, a man who walked home with us was enthusiastic in her praise. "Magnificent woman, that, sir," he said, addressing my husband; "a wife of the right sort, *she* is. Why," he added, absolutely rising into eloquence as he spoke, "she earnt her *old* man" (said individual twenty-one years of age, perhaps) "nine hundred dollars in nine weeks, clear of all expenses, by washing! Such women ain't common, I tell *you*. If they were, a man might marry, and make money by the operation."

. . . and he looked at me as if to say, that, though by no means gloriously arrayed, I was a mere cumberer of the ground, inasmuch as I toiled not, neither did I wash. Alas! I hung my diminished head, particularly when I remembered the eight dollars a dozen which I had been in the habit of paying for the washing of

Louise's writing is from one of her letters that is included in The Shirley Letters from California Mines in 1851-52, *printed by Thomas C. Russell in 1922.*

Women's Words, Women's Stories

linen-cambric pocket-handkerchiefs while in San Francisco. But a lucky thought came into my mind. As all men cannot be Napoleon Bonapartes, so all women cannot be manglers. The majority of the sex must be satisfied with simply being mangled. Reassured by this idea, I determined to meekly and humbly pay the amount per dozen required to enable this really worthy and agreeable little woman "to lay up her hundred dollars a week, clear of expenses." But is it not wonderful what femininity is capable of? To look at the tiny hands of Mrs. R., you would not think it possible that they could wring out anything larger than a doll's nightcap; but, as is often said, nothing is strange in California. I have known of sacrifices requiring, it would seem, superhuman efforts, made by women in this country, who, at home, were nurtured in the extreme of elegance and delicacy.

Louise Amelia Knapp Smith Clappe was born July 28, 1819, in Elizabeth, New Jersey. When Louise was thirteen, the family moved to Amherst, Massachusetts. Her father died shortly after, and her mother followed five years later, leaving Louise and her six siblings wards of a local attorney.

In 1839 on a trip through Vermont, Louise met Alexander Hill Everett, an author and diplomat. They became good friends and he served as her literary mentor for the next ight years. They carried on lengthy correspondence, even while he was ambassador to China. It was Everett who suggested that she start writing as a "new and inexhaustible source of comfort and satisfaction." Although twenty-nine years her senior, Alexander would have liked to marry Louise, and their friendship came to an abrupt end when she announced her engagement to Fayette Clappe.

Fayette, a medical student, and Louise were married in 1849. Soon after, he was enticed by the possibility of striking it rich in the California gold rush, and they set sail for San Francisco via Cape Horn. Fayette departed for a mining camp on the Feather River, high up in the Sierra Nevadas, while Louise waited for him in Marysville. Her first California writings were published in the *Marysville Herald* under the pen name Shirley.

After six months, Fayette sent for Louise and she joined him at a remote mining camp on the Feather River. She began writing in earnest, using the letter as her literary device, describing every detail of life in the camp through its heyday in 1851 to its decline in 1852 with the failure of the fluming operation. Her writings, known as the *Shirley Letters,* were published serially in a new California magazine, *The Pioneer*. Her work influenced many other western writers, most notably Bret Harte.

When the mine closed, Louise and Fayette returned to San Francisco; they separated and later divorced. Louise remained in San Francisco and taught high school for the next twenty-four years. She also established evening classes for working men and women and held a weekly salon, the "first salon the Golden West ever knew," where she entertained local and visiting intellectuals.

Poor health forced Louise to retire from teaching in 1878. She settled on the East Coast, where she travelled and lectured. She spent her last years at an elderly women's home in New Jersey run by two of Bret Harte's nieces. She died there in 1906 at the age of eighty-six.

Eunice Tietjens

Awakened

1938

After dinner on this vital evening we repaired to the little room which was Floyd Dell's study. There Margery and Floyd curled up on the sofa. . . . the talk ran on poetry. For the first time in the many years of my long sleep I heard what had been like a secret vice with me brought out boldly into the open, with no apology, as though it were indeed one of the great facts of existence. . . .

Afterwards I walked home through the dark streets of Evanston. And I walked on air. . . . Poetry, I cried to myself, is not a dead thing, something that is shut in books to dress library shelves and is taught to school children, something to be given away at Christmas or bought shyly and read in one's own room as one might take drugs, and never, never spoken of because nobody cares. Poetry is a live thing. I am not alone in the world today. . . . Poetry is alive! And I danced in the streets and sang to myself . . . from that evening some floodgate had broken in me and I was beginning to be awake.

Eunice's writing is from The World at my Shoulder, *published in 1938 by the Macmillan Company.*

Eunice Hammond Tietjens was born July 29, 1884, in Chicago, the eldest of four children. Her sister Louise became a missionary to China; her other sister, Elizabeth, became a concert cellist; and her brother Laurens became an inventor, best remembered for his Hammond electric organ. After their father died in 1897, Mrs. Hammond took the family on a lengthy tour of Europe. Eunice attended schools in Geneva and Paris and graduated from the Froebel Kindergarten Institute of Dresden.

In 1904 Eunice married Paul Tietjens, the American composer, whose best-known work was the score for the stage version of *The Wizard of Oz*. The couple separated in 1910, and Eunice returned to her mother's home in Illinois with her three-year-old daughter, Janet. She befriended Harriet Monroe, the founder and editor of *Poetry* magazine, who published several of her poems. In 1913 she joined the staff of *Poetry* "as office girl and general nuisance," an association that was to last in one form or another for the rest of her life.

Eunice and her mother went to China in 1916 to visit Louise at her mission in Wusih. The country's "strange blend of sordidness, tragedy, beauty, and humor" affected her deeply. The result was her first book of poetry, *Profiles from China*, published in 1917.

Eunice spent World War I in France as a correspondent for the *Chicago Daily News*. Upon her return to America, she spent two years writing a novel that conveyed "all the sense of human pain and futility that the war had roused in me." In February 1920 she married the playwright Cloyd Head. They went to Europe in 1923, and after spending time in France and Italy they settled in Hammamet, Tunisia. During the following years, it became the couple's pattern to alternate stays in exotic locales such as North Africa and Tahiti with periods of intense work in America, which produced books of poetry and prose about their travels.

The Heads spent their later years in Florida. Eunice published her last book, her autobiography, in 1938. During a trip to Scandinavia in 1939, she was diagnosed with cancer and died five years later at the age of sixty.

Elizabeth Ross Haynes

1923

Employers apparently feel that a majority of the women beyond the ages of 45 and 50 have become too set in their ways, somewhat cranky, and largely unable to do general housework. The most frequent objections of employers to young girl domestic workers are: They are untrained and inexperienced; they are unwilling to sleep in; they are saucy; and their interest in men company causes them to neglect their work.

The older Negro women in domestic service, realizing that with their advancing years their possibilities for employment become less, often hesitate and even fail to give their correct ages when applying at employment agencies for positions. For example, a New York City agency registered a woman who gave her age as 34, but whose written references, yellowed with age, showed that she had worked for different members in one family for fifty years. Frequently an older woman registrant when asked her age hesitates and ends by saying "just say 'settled woman.'"

Elizabeth Ross Haynes was born July 30, 1883, to former slaves in Mount Willing, Alabama. Her father had served with the Union Army and used his bounty to purchase property in Alabama. Through years of hard work, he eventually owned a 1,500-acre plantation.

Elizabeth was class valedictorian at the state normal school in Montgomery and received a scholarship to Fisk University. After graduation in 1903 she taught high school in Galveston, Texas, for several years, taking courses in graduate school at the University of Chicago during the summer.

From 1908 to 1910 Elizabeth worked for the Student Department of the National Board of the YWCA, travelling from college to college assisting black students. In 1910 she resigned to marry George E. Haynes, whom she had met at Fisk years earlier. They returned to Nashville to live when George was appointed to the Fisk faculty. Their only child, a son, was born in 1912.

In 1918 George was elected director of the Negro Economics Division of the Department of Labor in Washington, D.C., and Elizabeth served as his assistant director. She reorganized the Domestic Service Section of the United States Employment Service and helped set the minimum wage.

Elizabeth returned to the YWCA in 1922 after she was named to the newly formed Council on Colored Work. She served on the board through 1934. She and her husband then moved to New York City, where she was elected in 1935 as co-leader of New York's Twenty-first Assembly District. Two years later, Governor Herbert H. Lehman appointed her to the New York State Temporary Commission on the Condition of the Urban Colored Population. She worked hard to improve schools, libraries, and health services in Harlem. She died in 1953 at the age of seventy, having devoted her adult life to promoting the advancement of her race and interracial tolerance.

Elizabeth's writing is from "Negroes in Domestic Service in the United States," Journal of Negro History, *October 1923.*

Josephine Washington

1893

Think of the many noble single women of your acquaintance who are bravely fighting the battle of life alone. . . . The prince has not come to them. Some have grown old in life's struggle and will go through the remainder of their years without the halo of love, without tender home ties of their own; but they will have fought a good fight, and in many cases they have given of their strength and courage to some weak wife or mother, bowed down with the burdens and responsibilities of a position too often lightly and thoughtlessly assumed.

Josephine Turpin Washington was born July 31, 1861, in rural Goochland County, Virginia. She was tutored at home until the family moved to Richmond, where she graduated from Richmond High School and the Richmond Institute (later the Richmond Theological Seminary). She received her bachelor's degree from Howard University in 1886.

Josephine began her writing career at sixteen with the publication of her first literary piece in the *Virginia Star*, the state's only black newspaper. Her article, "A Talk about Church Fairs," was a protest against the selling of wine at church social functions. She also wrote about women's problems and racial issues for various periodicals. She was an ardent feminist and advocated education for women to "increase earning power, become better mothers, expand their job opportunities beyond the limits of domestic service, and develop communication skills which would improve their ability to relate to men."

In 1888 Josephine married Samuel H. H. Washington, a physician, and moved to his home in Birmingham, Alabama. She was active in the State Federation of Colored Women's Clubs, which organized activities to help foster racial pride. She also helped organize the curriculum at Selma University, which specialized in training teachers and ministers. Little is known of Josephine's later life or the details of her death.

Josephine's writing is from the introduction to Women of Distinction: Remarkable in Works and Invincible in Character, *by L. A. Scruggs, published by L. A. Scruggs in 1893.*

AUGUST

Angela Diller

1958

My name was originally Mary Angelina. I changed it to Angela. Angela Diller! It sounds like perfumery, but at least it has a rhythm. I can't remember when I didn't play the piano. I began to read music when I was three; before that I played by ear. When I was eight, I wanted to take German lessons at school. They were a rather expensive extra, and we weren't rich, but the teacher said I could have them free if I'd play the piano when the other children sang songs in class, so I did. German folk songs. The first one I played was 'Die Lorelei.' I began to teach when I was twelve, before anyone had taught *me*.

Angela Diller was born August 1, 1877, in Brooklyn, New York. Her father was a church organist and choirmaster who encouraged his children to develop their musical talents. As a young girl, she started playing the piano by ear and later was taught to read music by her older sister.

In 1894 Angela took a teaching position at St. John the Baptist School for Girls, in New York City. She taught music and composition while furthering her own music education with courses at Columbia University and Barnard College. From 1899 to 1916, she was head of the Music Theory Department at the Music School Settlement, a New York City school that provided musical education for underprivileged children.

In 1921 Angela co-founded the Diller Quaile School of Music with Elizabeth Quaile, a teacher she had befriended at the Settlement School. They taught children and adults in addition to training music teachers. The two women published the Diller Quaile instruction book of folk tunes for the piano, which led to an impressive series of more than forty instructional books.

Angela admitted that she would "rather teach teachers than anyone else." From 1920 to 1950 she travelled throughout Europe and America, lecturing at conservatories and universities. In 1953 she was given a Guggenheim Foundation award to write a book about her teaching experiences, *The Splendor of Music*. In later years her eyesight and hearing began to fail, although she continued teaching until her death in 1968 at the age of ninety.

A young pianist

Angela's words are from an interview, "Teacher's Teacher," The New Yorker, September 20, 1958.

Alice Gerstenberg

*N*ot collegiate

1950

My mother too, had wanted to be an actress. (In fact, I discovered later almost all the mothers of that era had once wanted to be actresses.) Of course then, it had not been the "thing to do." So they exhausted their talents on china painting. (I have magnificent plates of mother's painting.)

But I compromised for a few years and went to Bryn Mawr. Now Bryn Mawr has a most beautiful campus, and a very high standard, but I was not a collegiate type. I highly disapprove of sending artistically inclined girls to any academic institution. It may harden them up, but it tortures the spirit. My early travels to Europe, Canada, all over the United States, my home background of music and the arts, and interesting guests, had destroyed any juvenile amusement in the rah-rah of green youngsters on a campus.

I played the game and wrote home glowing letters about it all to please my parents, but I didn't really care. My only real excitement came when my class had to produce a play.

Alice Gerstenberg was born August 2, 1885, in Chicago. She graduated from Bryn Mawr College and began her career as a writer, publishing her first novel in 1908. Her love of the theater inspired her to write her first play in 1915, a three-act version of *Alice in Wonderland* that debuted at the Booth Theater in New York City.

Alice's best-known play, *Overtones*, was a psychological drama about two women and their search for love and money. She employed a unique approach: Harriet and Margaret spoke in the present tense, while their subconscious thoughts were expressed by their alter egos, Hetty and Maggie. The play was acclaimed as a breakthrough in theater technique, and many playwrights, including Eugene O'Neill, were influenced by her work.

Alice's writing is from a long autobiographical letter she wrote to her friend Nancy Cox-McCormack Cushman when she was sixty-five. It is among the Nancy Cox-McCormack papers, Schlesinger Library, Radcliffe College, Cambridge, Massachusetts.

Alice was very involved in the little theater movement. She was an original member of the Chicago Little Theater, the first little theater in the United States. She also co-founded the Chicago Junior League Theater for children and the Playwright's Theater of Chicago. Alice wrote many one-act plays that were easy to stage in a small area, for little theaters.

Occasionally, Alice would act in her own plays. She also wrote articles for theater magazines. In 1938 she was presented the Chicago Foundation for Literature Award. She continued writing her entire life, publishing her last work at the age of eighty-four. Three years later she died at home in Chicago.

Helen Adelia Manville

1874

I wonder if she'll have a name
 In that blest country far away,—
The little blue-eyed one, who came
 To us, and went away to-day?
If so, I hope the angels will
 Give her as sweet a one as we
To her had given had she lived!
 I wonder what her name will be?

Named by angels

Helen Adelia Wood Manville was born August 3, 1839, in New Berlin, New York. On her mother's side she was related to Alice Cary (April 26) and Phoebe Cary (September 4), child poets who were popular in the early 1800s, and she claimed to have inherited her writing talent from them.

After the death of her mother when Helen was a child she accompanied her father, Col. Artemus Wood, to Farmington, Lacrosse County, Wisconsin. She was married on Christmas Eve 1854, at the age of fourteen, to Marvin M. Manville, a local businessman.

Helen began writing poetry and had her first poem published in *The Lacrosse Independent Republican* in 1864. Thereafter she contributed poetry and prose to local newspapers and periodicals under the pen name Nellie A. Mann. She wrote more than 2,000 poems and published more than 1,500. In 1875 she published her only book, a volume of 128 poems, entitled *Heart Echoes*.

Helen had one daughter, Marion, also a gifted poet. She died in 1912 while visiting her daughter at her home in Buenos Aires, Argentina. Ten years later, her body was returned to Lacrosse for burial beside her husband.

Helen's writing is from the first verse of her poem, "Baby's Drawer," which was inscribed "to my dear and only sister, Mrs. Louise Wither." It is included in her book of poetry, Heart Echoes, *published in 1875.*

Marjorie Barstow Greenbie

Civil ceremony

circa 1970

. . . we set out to be married, there in New York City, by a Justice of the Peace. For I had yielded to Sydney's objections to a religious marriage, so often expressed in his letters, and was ready to be content with a civil ceremony. . . .

We arrived at City Hall only a few minutes ahead of the twelve o'clock Saturday closing hour, and plunged desperately into the end place of a long waiting line which filled up behind us, many of them Negro couples. It was hot and smelly in City Hall, that malodorous grime that clings to all municipal buildings in New York. A uniformed guard kept pushing us along, "Get along. Get along." We found ourselves in front of a tired, perspiring greasy faced man. He mumbled something of which I understood only "One dollar, please," and the guard pushed us out and the next couple in place.

Outside in the spring air, fresh with coming rain, Sydney looked at me. "I don't feel married, do you?"

I said doubtfully, "A church would have been cleaner."

He answered thoughtfully, "A padre is usually a gentleman."

The word padre suggested a solution. . . . I said, "Sydney, you know the church of England service — "

"Yes," he said decisively. "We will be married again and by a padre."

Marjorie Barstow Greenbie was born August 4, 1891, in Jersey City, New Jersey. After graduating Phi Beta Kappa from Cornell University in 1912, she was awarded a graduate fellowship at Yale. She earned her Ph.D. in only two years at a time when few women were attending graduate school

Marjorie moved to New York City and took a job as an editor at *Harper's* magazine. The United Methodist Church hired her on the side to write some promotional material. They liked her writing so well that they sent her to Asia in 1918 to gather material for a pageant to celebrate 100 years of Methodist missionary work. While watching the Gion

Marjorie's writing is from an autobiographical sketch which she wrote in her eighties at her son Barrie's urging. It is among his personal papers in Amherst, Massachusetts.

Matsuri Festival in Kyoto, Japan, she met her future husband, Sidney Greenbie, a historian and author of books on the Far East.

Sydney and Marjorie were married in May 1919 and had one son and one daughter. In 1920 Marjorie published her first book, *In the Eye of the East*, the story of her trip to China and Japan and her courtship with Sydney. She co-authored several children's history books with her husband and published historical books and plays of her own. Her most popular book, *American Saga*, which told the story of the development of America through the eyes of immigrants, was on the best-seller list in 1939.

Marjorie was one of the first self-help authors, producing a series of books that offered advice on how to get the best out of life. Some of her titles included *The Arts of Leisure, In Quest of Contentment*, and *The Art of Living in Wartime*. In addition to writing, she taught English at the University of Kansas, Vassar College, Connecticut College, and Mount Holyoke.

The Greenbies spent World War II in New Zealand, where Sydney held a diplomatic post. Upon their return to America he joined the United States Department of the Interior, and Marjorie resumed writing and teaching. After her husband's death in 1960, she divided her time between homes in Florida and Maine. She was director of the drama workshop at the University of Tampa and director of outdoor theaters in Clearwater, Florida, and Castine, Maine. She died in Maine in 1976 at the age of eighty-four.

Mary Ritter Beard

1931

Shared pleasures

The ordinary woman who has functioned in accordance with nature's laws does not hate man or exaggerate his importance; most of the time she is as indifferent to him as he is to her; but with respect to the amenities and enjoyments of life the sexes are one. Love, joy, and beauty are bound up in their relations. As Aristophanes could say twenty-three centuries ago, "there is no pleasure for a man unless the woman shares it," so the modern feminist will soon discover, if she has not already, that there is no pleasure for a woman unless the man shares it.

Mary's writing is from the introduction of her book, America Through Women's Eyes, *published in 1933 by the Macmillan Company.*

Mary Ritter Beard was born August 5, 1876, in Indianapolis, Indiana. At sixteen she enrolled in DePauw University, the same school her father and five siblings had attended. She graduated in 1897 and three years later married Charles Austin Beard, a fellow student.

The Beards spent two years at Oxford while Charles studied history. It was in England that Mary first became involved in the women's suffrage movement. After their return to New York City, she joined the Women's Trade Union League and became editor of the suffrage publication *The Woman Voter*. Her main concern was social reform for the working woman, and she published two books on the subject in 1915 and 1920.

Mary's gift to the women's movement was her talent as a writer, and she wrote numerous books, articles, and speeches. She believed women's contributions to society were as important as men's. She drew a connection between woman's role as childbearer and caregiver and woman's potential as an agent for progressive social change. In an attempt to bolster women's confidence, she wrote several historical studies on the importance of women in society. She sought to correct the impression that "all history is but the story of the 'man's world.'"

During the 1930s Mary established a World Center for Women's Archives in New York City, to preserve records of women's lives. The project failed, however, due to lack of funds. She continued to write and lecture well into the 1940s, publishing her best book, *Woman as a Force in History*, at seventy. After Charles' death she retired to Arizona, where she died in 1958 at the age of eighty-two.

AUGUST 6

Edith Kermit Roosevelt

The fiancé

Edith's writing is from a June 8, 1886, letter to her fiancé, Theodore Roosevelt. It is included in Edith Kermit Roosevelt, Portrait of a First Lady, *by Sylvia Jukes Morris, published by Conard, McCann and Geoghegan in 1980.*

1886

London is perfectly lovely now, everything is so bright and gay. Last night we heard your cousin Mr. Scovell, poor Marcia Roosevelt's husband, sing in *Carmen*. He is middle aged, ugly and uninteresting with not enough voice to redeem his bad acting. His one idea of making love is to seize the prima donna's arm and shake her, violently. I am so glad it is not your way. It is such fun driving in the park and seeing all the people. You may not believe it, but I never used to think much about my looks if I knew my dress was all right; now I do care about being pretty for you, and every girl I see I think

Women's Words, Women's Stories

"I wonder if I am as pretty as she is," or "At any rate I am not quite as ugly as that girl."

Edith Kermit Carow Roosevelt was born August 6, 1861, in Norwich, Connecticut. She grew up in an affluent atmosphere on Union Square in New York City. Her mother supervised her education, which included frequent trips to museums, concerts, and plays.

As a child, Edith's closest friend was Corinne Roosevelt. She was always attracted to Corinne's older brother Theodore and was devastated when he married in 1880. Three years later his wife died during childbirth, and he and Edith resumed a tenuous courtship.

Edith had moved to London with her mother and sisters following her father's death in 1883. Edith and Theodore were married there in December 1886. They had five children, and in 1901 they moved to the White House when Theodore was elected president.

Edith was an excellent first lady, assisting her husband with advice as well as being a gracious hostess. Theodore Roosevelt died in 1919 after which Edith spent most of her time at the family estate, "Sagamore Hill," in Oyster Bay, New York. She occasionally travelled in Europe but mostly stayed near home with her children and grandchildren.

Edith died in 1948 at the age of eighty-seven and was buried beside her husband in Young's Memorial Cemetery in Oyster Bay. Following her death, *Life* magazine eulogized her as "one of the strongest-minded and strongest-willed presidential wives who ever lived in the White House."

Paulina Wright Davis

Liverpool
May 25, 1873
Dear Husband,

Your letter was duly received from Barings. Our fare is settled our seats at table secured and we leave sometime on Thursday 29th. This will be in a day or two before us I trust. . . I was sorry you did not send the money as proposed, for I made the purchases for Mrs. Peckham desired, paid all bills and then found myself bankrupt again. But sister Mary has let me have 20 pds. which I hope you will remit to her at once as I fear she could not let me have it without inconvenience. . . .

Think of me

Paulina's letter to her husband is in the manuscript collection at Schlesinger Library, Radcliffe College, Cambridge, Massachusetts.

Who knows but this may be the last letter I shall ever write you. The great deep lies before me and I have never in my life before shrank from trusting myself to its bosom. Now a terror seems to hang over me. I do not fear sudden death the spirit world seems very near and dear to me but I shudder and dread suffering if it should come to me and to Maybelle [her adopted daughter]. But it's no use to be anxious if I never reach you think of me loveingly and hold our children first and dearest to you.

Ever your loving wife, Paulina

Paulina Kellogg Wright Davis was born August 7, 1813, in Bloomfield, New York. She was raised by a strict, overly religious aunt following her parents' deaths when she was seven. Constantly forced to participate in church activities she discovered her feminist awareness as a teenager, when she objected to a church discussion on whether or not women should be allowed to speak during religious meetings with men present.

Paulina's aunt was preparing her to become a missionary in Hawaii, but she ran off at age twenty to marry Francis Wright, a wealthy local merchant. Following Francis's death in 1845, Paulina travelled the United States with a female mannequin, lecturing to women about hygiene and health reforms.

While lecturing in Providence, Rhode Island, Paulina met Thomas Davis, a state representative who shared her anti-slavery and pro-feminist views. They were married in 1849 and adopted two daughters. Three years later he was elected to Congress, and they moved to Washington, D.C.

Paulina, elegant and well-spoken, was an able representative of the women's rights movement. She helped organize the first National Woman's Rights Convention held in Massachusetts in 1850. In 1853 she began publishing, at her own expense, the monthly periodical *UNA*, one of the first women's rights publications. In 1868 Paulina co-founded the New England Woman Suffrage Association and the Rhode Island Suffrage Association.

Despite crippling rheumatism, Paulina worked for women's rights until her death in 1876. Her husband continued her work for nearly twenty years afterward and was honored as a friend of the cause by the national suffrage convention.

Florence Merriam Bailey

1896

A new bird world

"Climb the mountain back of the house and you can see the Pacific," the ranchman told me with a gleam in his eye; and later, when I had done that, from the top of a peak at the foot of the valley he pointed out the distant blue mountains of Mexico. Then he gave me his daughter's saddle horse to use as long as I was his guest, that I might explore the valley and study its birds to the best advantage. Before coming to California, I had known only the birds of New York and Massachusetts, and so was filled with eager enthusiasm at the thought of spending the migration and nesting season in a new bird world.

I had no gun, but was armed with opera-glass and notebook, and had *Ridgway's Manual* to turn to in all my perplexities. Every morning, right after breakfast, my horse was brought to the door and I set out to make the rounds of the valley. After dinner I would take my camp-stool and stroll through the oaks at the head of the valley, for a quiet study of the nearer nests. Then once more my horse would be brought up for me to take a run before sunset; and at night I would identify my new birds and write up the notes of the day. What more could an observer crave? The world was mine. I never spent a happier spring. In my small valley circuit of a mile and a half, I made the acquaintance of about seventy-five birds, and without resort to the gun was able to name fifty-six of them.

Florence Augusta Merriam Bailey was born August 8, 1863, in Locust Grove, New York. Her interest in nature began as a child at her parents' country estate; and by the time she entered Smith College, she was specializing in ornithology.

Florence published her first book, *Birds Through a Looking Glass*, in 1889. In 1893 she headed west in search of a milder climate for her tuberculosis. She spent the next three years travelling through Utah, Arizona, and California, observing western birds. After returning home, she turned her experiences into three more bird books.

Through her brother, the director of the United States Biological Survey, Florence met and fell in love with one of

Florence's writing about her experiences in California is from her book A-Birding on a Bronco, *published by Houghton, Mifflin and Company in 1896.*

his employees, Vernon Bailey. Soon after their wedding in December 1899, Vernon began the first of many journeys to New Mexico for the Survey. In 1902 Florence published the classic *Handbook of Birds of the Western United States*. Six years later she was honored when her name was given to a California chickadee, the *Parus gambeli baileyae*.

The Baileys spent more than thirty years walking and riding throughout the Dakotas, the Southwest, the Pacific Northwest, and Texas, collecting and identifying specimens. Florence was the first woman to receive the Brewster Medal of the American Ornithologists Union, and in 1933 she was given an honorary LL.D. degree from the University of New Mexico.

Vernon and Florence lived in Washington, D.C., when not on the road exploring nature. Florence was active in the local Audubon Society, which she had helped found, and initiated classes in both field and laboratory ornithology. Florence died when she was eighty-five and was returned to Locust Grove for burial at the old Merriam homestead.

Janie Porter Barrett

Needed

1915
My dear Dr. Frissell, . . .

I want to thank you also for the many helpful and encouraging things you have said in your annual letter this year. It makes me feel that I must try harder than ever to be helpful.

A letter from Mrs. Washington asking me to come to Tuskegee and take charge of the girls makes me wish that I could be in two places at once. I should be glad to serve at Tuskegee but I know I am going where I am needed and though the undertaking is most difficult it isn't impossible and if the friends will stand by me this Home School will be, in time, a tremendous power for good. May the new year bring to you all the rich blessings you deserve.

Sincerely yours, Janie Porter Barrett

Janie's writing is from a December 25, 1915, letter to Dr. Hollis P. Frissell, president of the Tuskegee Institute, in which she declines his offer of a job as dean of women. It is in the Harris and Janie Porter Barrett Collection in the Hampton University Archives, Hampton, Virginia.

Janie Porter Barrett was born August 9, 1865, in Athens, Georgia, to former slaves. Her mother Julia worked as seamstress and housekeeper for the Skinner family, where Janie was accepted as one of the family and received the same education as the three Skinner children. After Julia married a railway worker and had two more children, Janie continued to live in the "big house" with her "other" family. Janie was light-skinned, and when she was fifteen, Mrs. Skinner wanted to become her legal guardian and send her to a northern school where she could live as a white person. Her natural mother, however, disagreed and felt that Janie should live as a black person in a black environment. She severed ties with the Skinners and enrolled her daughter at the Hampton Institute in Virginia.

Janie decided to make a career out of helping to better her race. Following graduation from Hampton in 1884, she taught school for several years in Georgia and Virginia. In 1889 she married Harris Barrett, Hampton's cashier and bookkeeper. She opened her home to a group of neighborhood girls for a sewing class and soon realized the need for other classes in cooking, gardening, child care, and livestock raising. The Barretts took money they had set aside for house renovations to build a small clubhouse on their property.

In 1908 Janie helped found the Virginia State Federation of Colored Women's Clubs and served as president for twenty-five years. Through her club she raised the funds for a much-needed rehabilitation center for black female juvenile delinquents. In 1914 she purchased a 147-acre farm eighteen miles north of Richmond and opened the Virginia Industrial School for Colored Girls. Her husband died the following year, leaving her a widow with four children. She was offered the position of dean of women at the Tuskegee Institute but felt she could be more useful at the Industrial School.

Janie moved into the Industrial School as its resident superintendent. She was skilled at fundraising and soon was able to build several residential cottages. She viewed the school as a "moral hospital where each girl is studied and given individual treatment." The school was run on the honor system with no bars on the windows and no corporal punishment. After a two-year training program, girls with good records were released on parole and placed with families.

By 1920 the Russell Sage Foundation ranked Janie's Industrial School among the top five institutions of its type in the nation. In 1929 she received the William E. Harmon Award for Distinguished Achievement among Negroes, and the next year she was invited to the White House to participate in the Conference on Child Health and Protection. She retired in 1940 and died eight years later of complications from diabetes and arteriosclerosis. Ten years after her death, her beloved Industrial School where she had spent twenty-five years of her life changed its name to the Janie Porter Barrett School for Girls.

Anna J. Cooper

*W*omen can think

1892

I was asked a few years ago by a white friend, "How is it that the men of your race seem to outstrip the women in mental attainment?" "Oh," I said, "so far as it is true, the men, I suppose, from the life they lead, gain more contact; and so far as it is only apparent, I think the women are more quiet."

But I am sure there is another reason which I did not at that time see fit to give. The atmosphere, the standards, the requirements of our little world do not afford any special stimulus to female development.

It seems hardly a gracious thing to say, but it strikes me as true, that while our men seem thoroughly abreast of the times on almost every other subject, when they strike the woman question they drop back into sixteenth century logic. They leave nothing to be desired generally in regard to gallantry and chivalry, but they actually do not seem sometimes to have outgrown that old contemporary of chivalry — the idea that women may stand on pedestals or live in doll houses, (if they happen to have them) but they must not furrow their brows with thought or attempt to help men tug at the great questions of the world. I fear the majority of colored men do not yet think it worth while that women aspire to higher education.

Anna Julia Haywood Cooper was born August 10, 1859, in Raleigh, North Carolina. Her mother was a slave, and her father owned the plantation. An exceptional child, Anna was awarded a scholarship to the St. Augustine Normal School & Collegiate Institute at the age of nine.

After graduation, Anna remained at St. Augustine's as a teacher. She met and married George A. C. Cooper, a fellow teacher, in 1877. George died two years later, and Anna never remarried.

Anna's writing is from A Voice From the South: By a Black Woman from the South, *published in 1892 by the Aldine Printing House, Xenia, Ohio.*

Anna enrolled in Oberlin College and earned a B.A. in 1884 and an M.A. in mathematics in 1887. She began teaching math and science at the Washington, D.C., Preparatory High School for Colored Youth, where she served as principal from 1901 to 1906.

In 1914 Anna began her doctoral studies at Columbia

University. She finished her coursework in three years but was unable to complete the residency requirement because her nephew's wife died suddenly, leaving him with five young children. Anna returned to Washington and purchased a large home where she could raise the five orphans. Still determined to receive her degree, she continued to study during the summers and had her credits transferred to the Sorbonne in Paris. In 1925 at the age of sixty-six, she presented her dissertation and received her Ph.D., the fourth black American woman to do so.

From 1929 to 1944 Anna was president of Frelinghuysen University in Washington, D.C., which served older, working adults.

On her 100th birthday, Anna received a congratulatory letter from President Dwight Eisenhower. She died in 1964 at the age of 105 and was buried beside her husband, whom she had outlived by eighty-five years.

Eliza Hart Spalding

1836

August 6 — Yesterday my horse became unmanageable in consequence of stepping into a hornets nest. I was thrown, and notwithstanding my foot remained a moment in the stirrup, and my body dragged some distance, I received no serious injury. I have suffered but little inconvenience in riding to day in consequence of being thrown from my horse yesterday. The hand of God has been conspicuous in preserving my life thus far, on this adventurous journey. Surely the Lord is my Shepherd, and I shall have nothing to fear, if I will but repose my whole trust in Him.

*P*reserved by God

Eliza Hart Spalding was born August 11, 1807, near what is now Berlin, Connecticut. Her early education concentrated more on homemaking than on book learning. On August 20, 1826, she joined the Presbyterian church and surrendered completely to "the will of Christ."

Eliza received a letter from a friend in Plattsburg, New York, telling her of a twenty-seven-year-old student, Henry Harmon Spalding, who wished to correspond with a pious young lady. They corresponded for over a year before they met. When Henry left for Western Reserve College in Ohio in the fall of 1832 Eliza accompanied him. She took courses

Eliza's writing is from her August 6, 1836, diary entry. It is included in The First White Women Over the Rockies — Volume I, *edited by Clifford M. Drury, published by Arthur H. Clark Company, 1963-1966.*

that were "requisite in order to become prepared for the usefulness in the service of my Redeeming Lord."

Henry and Eliza were married in October 1833 and
moved to Cincinnati, where Henry was a member of the
inaugural class at Lane Theological Seminary, a Presbyterian
institution.

Dr. Marcus Whitman and his wife Narcissa Prentiss
Whitman were planning to go to Oregon as missionaries and
invited the Spaldings to accompany them. On February 1,
1836, the Spaldings said farewell to Eliza's family, whom she
was never to see again, and began their westward journey.
Eliza and Narcissa travelled mostly on horseback, riding
sidesaddle. On July 4 they crossed the Continental Divide
and became the first white American women to go over the
Rockies. They, "alighting from their horses and kneeling on
the other half of the continent, with the Bible in one hand
and the American flag in the other, took possession of it as
the home of American mothers, and of the Church of
Christ."

The Whitmans settled among the Cayuse Indians at
Waiilaptu near Fort Walla Walla, and the Spaldings established a mission among the Nez Perce at Lapwai, near what is
now Lewiston, Idaho. Eliza quickly learned the language of
the Nez Perce. She opened a school that was attended by up
to 100 students. In addition to English, she taught sewing,
weaving, and spinning. Henry taught the Indians to farm,
planting peas, potatoes, and apple orchards. Lapwai became
the most successful of the four Oregon missions established
by the American Board of Commissioners for Foreign
Missions.

Eliza died of tuberculosis in 1851 at the age of forty-three.
In 1913 her body was moved and placed beneath a granite
monument beside her husband at their old mission at Lapwai.
There is also a monument at the South Pass of the
Continental Divide commemorating Eliza and Narcissa's
historic crossing.

AUGUST 12   *Elizabeth Oakes Smith*

*E*arly reader   *1924*

I cannot remember a time when I could not read. I had
a sister two years older than myself, who was sent to a
school in the neighborhood, where she was regarded as
a phenomenon. I missed her so much at home that an
arrangement was made for me at two years to go with
her.

The good teacher let me lie upon her bed for my daily nap. When my sister stood up for her lesson, I used to stand beside her and listen with amazed interest to the mystery of A B C. I never opened my mouth to pronounce a word, but with my two little hands tucked under my arm-pits, stood with intent and solemn eyes fixed upon the book until the lesson was done. No one supposed I was learning anything; but one day when my mother was exulting over the proficiency of my sister, I quite astonished the family by saying, "I can do that, too;" and all laughed. I took the book and read with perfect ease.

At first it was thought mere imitation, but on further trial it was found I could read as well as my sister. I do not think this altogether pleased my mother, who had a natural love and pride in her first-born and did not like to see her eclipsed. I saw this, and had a feeling of shame, as if I had surreptitiously obtained book knowledge. . . .

Elizabeth Oakes Price Smith was born August 12, 1806, in North Yarmouth, Maine. Her father, a ship's captain, was lost at sea when she was a toddler. Her mother remarried and settled in Portland, Maine. Elizabeth was so intelligent that she could read by the age of two, but she was pushed to achieve and had a breakdown when she was six. She was sent to rest and recuperate at her grandfather's farm and eventually had a complete recovery.

After graduation from private high school, Elizabeth hoped to open a school of her own. However, her mother had other plans for her, and she was married when she was sixteen to Seba Smith, the thirty-one-year-old editor of the *Portland Eastern Argus.* They had five sons.

Seba Smith went bankrupt in 1837, after which the family relocated in New York City. Elizabeth took up writing to help supplement their income, publishing her first children's book in 1838. She wrote numerous poems and stories for *Godey's Lady's Book, Graham's Magazine, The Ladies' Companion,* and other popular magazines. She used the pen names Ernest Helfenstein and Oakes Smith. She liked the name Oakes Smith so much that she legally changed her sons' last name to Oaksmith.

In 1851 Elizabeth went on the lyceum circuit, lecturing on women's rights and encouraging women to develop their talents to the fullest. In 1860 the Smiths relocated to Patchogue, Long Island, where she began writing "dime novels" to help augment the family income. Two of her sons

Elizabeth's writing is from The Autobiography of Elizabeth Oakes Smith, *edited by Mary Alice Lyman and published in 1924 by the Lewiston Journal Company.*

and her husband died in the early 1860s, after which she moved in with her eldest son in Hollywood, North Carolina. In 1878 and 1879 she represented North Carolina at the National Woman Suffrage Association conventions. She died in 1893 at the age of eighty-seven and was buried in Patchogue in the family plot.

Phoebe Ann Moses (Annie Oakley)

Love of shooting

1913

I believe I was born with a fondness for shooting. My earliest recollections are of the times I would smuggle my brother's musket away to the woods and shoot game, and I feel certain that I shall never lose that fondness. I am, too, quite sure that I have a preference for game shooting, a sport that seems to increase as I grow older. . . .

. . . I made up my mind to show the world that shooting was a healthful exercise and pastime that might be followed with benefit to health and without detracting from a lady's qualities.

Phoebe Ann Moses (Annie Oakley) was born August 13, 1860, near Woodland, Ohio, the fifth of eight children. After her father died from exposure in a snowstorm when she was four, the children were separated and placed with various relatives. At nine Phoebe was sent to an orphanage, where she learned to hate her name when the other children teased her and called her "Moses Poses." At ten she was placed with a farm family who wanted an extra worker. Two years later she ran away and tracked down her mother, by then remarried and living in northern Ohio.

Phoebe lived with her mother and stepfather for four happy years, learning to ride and hunt. She was given an old cap-and-ball rifle and taught herself to shoot, discovering that she had amazing hand-eye coordination that made her a natural sure-shot. She supported the family and paid off the mortgage by selling game birds at markets in Cincinnati. During one of her trips to Cincinnati at age fifteen, she went to a shooting club and won a match against professional marksman Frank Butler. They were married two months shy of her sixteenth birthday.

Phoebe legally changed her name to Annie Oakley, Oakley being the name of a Cincinnati suburb. She and her husband toured the country in a shooting act billed as "Butler and

Annie's writing is from Annie Oakley — A Brief Sketch of her Career and Notes on Shooting, *a booklet in the rare books collection, Hamilton College Library.*

Oakley." Frank taught Annie to read and improved her self-confidence and marksmanship.

Annie and Frank joined the Sells Brothers Circus in 1884. Frank left the act after a year to manage his more talented wife. In 1885 she joined the Buffalo Bill Wild West Show as a featured performer. Although she was under five feet and weighed only 100 pounds, she made quite an impression as she raced around the arena. One of her specialties was to shoot the flames of a revolving candle wheel as she galloped by on her pony. A punched ticket containing a lot of holes became known in the vernacular as an "Annie Oakley" after her habit of shooting a playing card repeatedly in mid-air.

Annie toured with the Wild West Show for sixteen years making numerous trips abroad, where she was more famous than Buffalo Bill. Her career ended in 1901 when the show train had an accident and she was seriously injured. Thereafter she gave shooting demonstrations and lessons at summer resorts and army camps. In 1922 she was left partially paralyzed from a car accident. In 1926 she and Frank returned to her native Ohio, where she soon died of pernicious anemia. Frank died three weeks after Annie's death, and they were buried beside each other in Brock, Ohio, near her birthplace.

Ellen Spaulding Reed

March 19th, 1856

A letter home

There was a man here yesterday to look of the land. and I hope he will take it, for we want to be off somewhere, where there is wood and water. We have given up expecting you out here and I do not know when we shall come there. I think Grandmas dress is very pretty. When you write I wish you would send me a lot of patterns for working skirts and pantiletts. I have got a girl now that has to be worked around the edges you know. I am pieceing me a comfortable, called Boneparts retreat. Mrs. Harris has got another baby. Babies are as thick out here as flies in the sumer, but poor folks like us cannot afford it.

Ellen's writing is from a letter home to her parents in Vermont. It is included in Pieced From Ellen's Quilt — Ellen Spaulding Reed's Letters and Story, by Linda Otto Lipsett, published by Halstead and Meadows, 1991.

Ella-Elizabeth (Ellen) Spaulding Reed was born August 14, 1835, in Ludlow, Vermont. In the spring of 1854 her first cousin, J. Willard Reed, stopped at the house to visit for a few days enroute to Wisconsin. As Willard was departing he asked Ellen to marry him, and she accepted. He went to Wisconsin and cleared his land, built a small log cabin, and then returned for Ellen. They were married September 5, 1854.

Ellen and Willard departed for Wisconsin by train the day after the wedding. She brought with her only one large steamer trunk and a hatbox. Inside the trunk was her most cherished possession, the friendship quilt her sister Leonora had made for her as a wedding present. Each square had the signature of a friend or neighbor embroidered on it.

Life in Wisconsin was very hard. Ellen suffered terribly from loneliness, and wrote long letters home to her parents and sister imploring them to come for a visit. After a while, she began to despair that her family would ever take the long trip to Wisconsin, and her health steadily declined.

Ellen's parents finally arrived in April 1858 and were shocked to find her near death and living in terrible poverty. She had never mentioned either condition in her letters, but had kept her communications optimistic and cheerful in hopes of bringing them west. In July, three months after her mother and father arrived, Ellen died of consumption. She was twenty-three.

Several times in the last days before Ellen died, she had pleaded with her father to take her home to Vermont. After burying her in a nearby cemetery, her heartbroken parents stayed on for five months, waiting for winter weather so that they could reopen the grave and take her body back to Vermont. She was finally buried in Mt. Pleasant View Cemetery in Ludlow, Vermont.

Ellen's bridal friendship quilt, her one prized possession, was returned to her sister Leonora. It was passed as a cherished heirloom to Leonora's son, then to his only son. When he died in 1965, it was left to an aunt who asked her daughter to sell it for her. Linda Otto Lipsett bought it in California. Starting with the names embroidered on the quilt, she spent twelve years researching its story and the story of Ellen's life.

Eliza Lee Cabot Follen

A pleasant stroll

1838
The three hours passed rapidly with the friends, as they strolled along, chatting by the way, just as when they were girls; with this difference, that what was then a fancy or a golden dream, was real now; and that joys, which were then unthought of, formed the groundwork of their hopes.

Before they came to the old bridge, they met Mr. Roberts. His face beamed with pleasure, at the sight of his wife with the beloved friend of her childhood.

"Do you want me now, Fanny?" said he, gaily.

"Yes, we do," said she. "We have nothing more to say about you."

Eliza Lee Cabot Follen was born August 15, 1787, in Boston, the fifth of thirteen children. As a member of the prominent New England Cabot family, she received the best educational opportunities available. She was active in the Federal Street Church, led by the well-known Unitarian minister William Channing. In 1826 while she was teaching Sunday School, her best friend and fellow author Catharine Sedgwick (December 28) introduced her to her future husband, Charles T. C. Follen.

Charles was a German political refugee nine years younger than Eliza. At the time of their wedding in September 1828, he was Harvard's first German professor. Eliza's brother Samuel and several of his friends subsidized a Harvard professorship for Follen for five years. During those happy years, Eliza gave birth to their only child, Charles Christopher.

Eliza had published her first book, *The Well-Spent Hour*, a collection of children's stories, the year before her marriage. During the early 1830s she produced several works, both for children and adults in addition to translations from the French. Harvard did not renew Charles's faculty appointment at the end of the five years, most likely because of his anti-slavery activities and encouragement of student activism. After several uncertain years, he accepted the invitation of a small liberal group in Lexington, Massachusetts, to become its pastor. In 1839 he designed and supervised the building of an octagonal church that still stands today. The following year he died in a shipboard fire, while returning from a lecture in New York.

After her husband's death Eliza resumed writing in earnest out of financial need. As she was already tutoring her son to prepare him for Harvard, she added to her income by tutoring some of his friends. In 1841 she published a biography of her husband and a collection of his sermons. From 1843 to 1850 she was editor of the children's magazine *Child's Friend*, and in 1858 she completed her twelve-volume set of *Twilight Stories*. As a member of Boston's literary set, she was acquainted with the current authors of the day and was mentioned in James Russell Lowell's poem "Letter from Boston," in which he described her face as "bright with the inward grace."

In her later years, Eliza served on the executive committees of both the Massachusetts and the American anti-slavery

Eliza's writing is from Sketches of Married Life, *a guideline for matrimonial happiness, which she dedicated to her husband. It was published in 1838 by Hilliard, Gray and Company.*

societies. She died at home in 1860 at the age of seventy-two, and was buried in Cambridge's Mount Auburn Cemetery.

Leila Davidson Simpson

A novel celebration

At sea one day out from Saigon, French Indochina
July 3, Wed. 1924
Dearest Bill, Nell and Family. . . .

We took dinner in the Raffles Hotel and as it was "The Glorious Fourth" we celebrated by doing it up right! We sailed just before the evening meal at 6:30 and while ashore we bought flags in red, white, and blue paper and decorated our "dining room" and had another celebration on board. We had two speeches by Mr. Genso (of Korea, a missionary there) and Mr. Rhodes — one to Coolidge and one to the French President. We drank to the health of back home with our only beverage *water* and the French enjoyed the humor of it all. Their tables of course, are always lined with wine bottles! All of us have refused wine so systematically that our bottles have now been removed!! They have found that we Americans stand for prohibition whether in America or out of it!

I would always enjoy celebrating "The Fourth" on a French boat, in an English port — it was a novel thing for Americans to do.

Leila Fayssoux Davidson Simpson was born August 16, 1881, near Fish Dam in Union County, South Carolina. Her father was a colonel in the Confederate Army, and her great-uncle founded Davidson College.

As a teenager Leila met Mr. Charles N. Crittenton, the founder of the Florence Crittenton homes, and through him she became interested in welfare work. After the death of her first husband, William J. Simpson, she immersed herself in charitable activities, and with the onset of World War I she volunteered for overseas work with the army.

Leila was accepted for service abroad but while waiting to receive her orders was asked by Mr. Charles Coker to assume management of his day nursery. He had opened a nursery in Hartsville, South Carolina, for the children of mothers who were working in his mill while their husbands fought in the war. Leila decided that caring for these children would be

Leila's writing, from a July 3, 1924, letter to her family, is in the South Carolina Historical Library, Charleston.

her way of serving her country, and she remained at Hartsville until the war ended.

In September 1920 she set sail for Anking, China. She taught in the Episcopal Mission School there for four years. After she left China, she travelled throughout the Orient, North Africa, and Europe.

Upon her return to America Leila taught kindergarten and worked in an orphanage library. Although she never returned to China, she described her feelings in an interview: "I enjoy life in my own country, but somewhere in my innermost soul I often hear the 'Call of the East' and long for rickshas, sail boats, the jade and amber temples and pagodas, and the smell of incense. They have something in their old world civilization that we young Americans know nothing of."

In 1933 Leila took courses in kindergarten work at Winthrop College. Upon completion of her studies she opened her own kindergarten in Charleston, South Carolina. She and retired businessman James W. Wilkinson were married in 1942. Leila died in 1970 and was buried in South Carolina.

Gene Stratton-Porter

1904
When day after day the only thing that relieved his utter loneliness was the companionship of the birds and beasts of the swamp, it was the most natural thing in the world that Freckles should turn to them for friendship. He began by instinctively protecting the weak and helpless. He was astonished at the quickness with which they became accustomed to him and the disregard they showed for his movements, when they learned that he was not a hunter and that the club he carried was used more frequently for their benefit than his own.

*F*riends in nature

Gene Stratton-Porter was born August 17, 1863, on Hopewell Farm, near Wabash, Indiana, the youngest of twelve children. She was taught to read and write by her older siblings and did not attend school until she was eleven. Much of her youth was spent wandering in the woods, where she developed a love of nature that eventually led to her career.

In 1863 Gene married Charles Darwin Porter, a druggist twenty years her senior. They settled in Geneva, Indiana,

Gene's writing is from Freckles, *her novel about a crippled orphan boy, published in 1904. Ten thousand copies were sold in the original edition and over a million in a later, less expensive reprint.*

and had one daughter. In 1889 oil was discovered on their land, and they were suddenly wealthy. Gene designed a fourteen-room house, which she called "Limberlost Cabin" after the swamp outside of town.

Around 1895 Gene began experimenting with nature photographs and had many of her photos published in *Recreation* and *Outing* magazines. Encouraged by her initial success, she decided to try writing fiction. She submitted her first story to *Metropolitan* magazine, renting a secret post office box to hide rejection. However, it was accepted and published in September 1901. Her husband supported her wholeheartedly, and from then on they took meals at the village hotel to free up her time for writing.

Gene's first novel, *The Song of the Cardinal*, was published in 1903 and enjoyed moderate popularity. Her second novel, *Freckles*, published the following year, was a tremendous success. The hero, a poor boy, befriends the animals in the wild and protects the timber in Limberlost Swamp from poachers. In this book, as in all her subsequent books, humans are seldom virtuous, but the animals exemplify moral virtue. Even her snakes showed fairness by rattling before they struck, while humans destroyed nature and wildlife without reason or warning.

During her long career Gene produced nineteen novels that sold between 8 and 9 million copies, and earned her more than $2 million. She believed the values of country life should be presented to city dwellers, and her intent was "to carry to workers inside city walls, to hospital cots, to those behind prison bars, and to scholars in their libraries, my story of earth and sky."

In 1919 Gene visited California and became so enamored of the climate that she bought a house on the outskirts of Los Angeles and moved there permanently. Charles remained in Indiana and visited occasionally. In 1922 she organized her own film company to make movies based on her stories, believing they could "exert a wholesome influence on family life." Gene was fatally injured in a car accident in Los Angeles in 1924.

Selma Kronold

1899
A hidden talent

. . . when I was a very small girl, in a convent in Poland, it was thought that my talent was for instrumental music. I played the piano very well for so young a child, but the sisters declared that I was their worst pupil in singing. The secret was that I was timid and was afraid to open my mouth, and so at the convent they never discovered that I had any voice at all.

Selma Kronold was born August 18, 1861, in Kraków, Poland, to a musically gifted family. Her cousin was a well-known pianist and composer, and her brother Hans became a cellist and composer. Selma began piano lessons at convent school and went on to study voice at the Royal Conservatory in Leipzig and with a private tutor in Paris.

At the Leipzig conservatory Selma began her long collaboration with the conductor, Anton Seidl. From 1882 to 1883 she toured Europe with him, and when he was hired as conductor of German opera at the Metropolitan Opera in New York, she went with him. She made her American debut at the Thalia Theatre in 1885 and spent the next five years there singing German operas.

In 1890 Selma married Jan Koert, a Dutch violinist in Seidl's orchestra. She briefly changed her name to Koert-Kronold, but the marriage ended in divorce after a few years due to their "conflicting careers."

Selma occasionally appeared at the Metropolitan but she established her American reputation by touring the country and performing with opera companies in Philadelphia, Boston, and other major cities. She spent the 1898 season as the prima donna soprano of the Italian Opera Company at the Teatro National in Mexico City. In 1900 she joined Henry Savage's opera company, which introduced operas sung in English to the American public. Selma had a repertoire of forty-five operas in four languages. She traced her talent to her Polish roots, formed by "the tragic history of the lost country." She explained in an 1899 newspaper interview, "There is a sadness deep in the heart of every Pole, be he peasant or aristocrat, that never may be quite forgotten; and it is this national sorrow that has brought out the sentimental and dramatic qualities for which my countrymen are famed."

Selma retired from her operatic career in 1904 and devoted the rest of her life to charitable and religious causes. She founded the Catholic Oratorio Society to train young

Selma's writing is from "A Chat with Selma Kronold," which appeared in the New York Dramatic Mirror, *November 11, 1899.*

singers, and she occasionally performed with them at church services at St. Patrick's Cathedral. She was fifty-nine when she died in 1920 of pneumonia and chronic nephritis.

Mary Belle Harris

In the open air

1936

I asked among other things that a part of the lawn be fenced in as an outdoor exercising place for the women. Although sentences at the Workhouse did not exceed six months, that is a long time for an active, well person to be pent up in one building. The women who worked in the laundry went outdoors to hang up clothes, and sometimes sat in the laundry yard. The cell bucket procession in the morning enabled one woman from each cell to get out of doors for a few minutes; and the squads which went to clean the hospitals had a short walk in the open air. Most of our six hundred inmates, however, did not breathe the outdoor air for months at a time. When the playground or "yard," as it was called, was completed, a schedule was arranged permitting everyone to be in the open air at least an hour a day, and many of the "sitters," the unoccupied women, did their sitting there.

Mary Belle Harris was born August 19, 1874, in Factoryville, Pennsylvania. Her mother died when she was six and her father, a Baptist minster, and later president of Bucknell University, remarried after one year. Mary, her two brothers, and six half-brothers graduated from Keystone Academy, a Baptist school established by their father.

By 1895 Mary had earned an A.B., an A.M., and a music degree from Bucknell. She soon enrolled in the University of Chicago, receiving a Ph.D. in 1900 in Sanskrit and Indo-European Comparative Philology. She then taught Latin for ten years in Chicago and Baltimore while pursuing her own studies in archaeology and numismatics at Johns Hopkins University. From 1910 to 1912 she served as teacher-chaperone at the American Classical School in Rome, so that she could study Roman coins in Italy and Germany.

When Mary returned to America her old friend from the University of Chicago, Katharine Bement Davis, had become commissioner of corrections in New York City. She offered

Mary's writing is from her book, I Knew Them in Prison, *published in 1936 by the Viking Press.*

Mary a job as superintendent of women and deputy warden at a workhouse on Blackwell Island. Although Mary had no experience in prison administration, she accepted the position and began a long and successful career.

The workhouse was a short-term prison with more than 700 women serving terms from three days to six months. Many of the opportunities available at regular prisons, such as a library and an outdoor exercise area, did not exist at the workhouse, and Mary worked to establish them. After three and a half years, she was forced out with the election of a new mayor. She then became superintendent at the State Reformatory at Clinton, New Jersey.

Kate McPhelim Cleary

1883

May passed. And many Mays passed. It would be a loving eye, indeed, which could now discern beauty in Marjorie Grant's face. It had grown thin and colorless and haggard. It looked aged and ungirlish. There were pathetic wrinkles where had been velvet dimples. In the village they had come to regard her with a sort of complacent pity. When the flashy, over-dressed bride whom Pierre Lechesne had brought home from Ottawa noticed her, and inquired concerning her, her husband smiled and tapped his forehead significantly with his finger.

*F*aded beauty

Kate McPhelim Cleary was born August 20, 1863, in Richibucto, Kent County, New Brunswick. Her parents had emigrated from Ireland to establish a prosperous lumber business. Her father died when she was two, leaving her mother with three small children to raise. Her mother believed strongly in the importance of education and invested her savings in her children's schooling. Kate attended the Sacred Heart Convent School in St. John, New Brunswick.

Kate had her first literary piece published when she was fourteen and from then on wrote to support herself. In February 1884 she married Michael T. Cleary, a lumber salesman from Hubbell, Nebraska, and they had four children. She continued her literary career, publishing poetry and prose in current magazines and newspapers that included the *New York Ledger*, the *Fireside Companion*, *Puck*, *St. Nicholas*, the *Chicago Tribune*, and the *Detroit Free Press*. In

Kate's writing is from her short story, "At Dawn O'Day," published in the June 13, 1883, issue of The Continent.

1894 she wrote a novel about Nebraska with the town of Hubbell thinly disguised as "Bubble."

The Clearys moved to Chicago in 1897 and separated four years later. Michael gained custody of the four children, and Kate was allowed to contribute to their support with the understanding that her husband would bring the children occasionally to see their mother. She was confined for a short while in the Elgin Asylum for the Insane. In early 1905 Michael brought her into court again in another attempt to prove her insane, but he was not successful. Ten days later, he brought the two younger children to see their mother at her residential hotel. Michael and Kate got into an argument, and Kate turned very pale and was given restoratives from the hotel drug store. She started upstairs to her room with her seven-year-old son Teddy, and just as she reached her door on the third floor she collapsed dead at her son's feet.

Ethel Eyre Valentine Dreier

*T*ravelling alone

Ethel's writing is from a paper she wrote in the summer of 1941 about her trip to California. It is in the Ethel E. Dreier Papers in the Sophia Smith Collection, Smith College, Northampton, Massachusetts.

1941

My trip to the West last June took me through seventeen states in all. I travelled a little less than 7,000 miles in my Ford car, alone and unmolested. I started out with the intention of seeing as many birds, animals and plants as possible and for this purpose the perfect arrangement was that I go without a companion. It worked out beautifully and I was able to enjoy to the fullest extent every moment of this wonderful vacation. My thoughts were my own and I stopped when and as often as I pleased. I could back up for a snake or stop to pick wildflowers and seed or watch birds with no thoughts of boring or detaining a comrade.

Ethel Eyre Valentine Dreier was born August 21, 1874, in Brooklyn, New York, the oldest of five girls. She graduated in 1895 from the Packer Collegiate Institute and went on to found the ASACOG (All Sorts and Conditions of Girls) Club, Brooklyn's first social settlement. Ethel served as president for several years until the club merged with the United Neighborhood Guild and the People's Institute of Brooklyn.

In April 1901 Ethel married H. Edward Dreier, the proverbial "boy who lived next door." They remained in Brooklyn and had two sons and two daughters. From 1913 to

1917 she was chairman of the Women's Suffrage Party of Brooklyn. After suffrage was won, she continued her leadership in the movement as chairman of the League of Women Voters.

Ethel joined the Women's City Club of New York and was president from 1924 to 1930 and from 1932 to 1936. Through the club, she was able to bring pressure for better city government and improved conditions in the city. She inspired club members to take more civic responsibility. She was made an honorary president for life in recognition of the club's growth and influence under her leadership. Ethel was also a member, and later vice-president, of the Brooklyn Committee for Better Housing. In 1928 she was instrumental in the creation of the Brooklyn Garden Apartments, the first racially integrated project under the New York State Housing Law.

In 1941 Ethel and Edward moved permanently to Fort Salonga on Long Island, which had previously been their summer home. Not content to grow idle, she joined the Garden Club and served on the local school board. She died in 1958 at the age of eighty-four and was buried in Brooklyn.

Maud Powell

1898
I have never had anything to complain of in American audiences. . . . They have always been very kind to me. But an audience here is quite different from an audience abroad. An American audience cannot give way. Perhaps they are not sure of themselves, though that may not be true of a musical audience. But there is a certain Puritanism about Americans: they cannot give way and allow their feelings full sway. It is the same with a player. One of the first things an American musician has to learn is to let himself go, to throw himself out. It is that certain Puritanism. And there is something in the climate, too. Foreigners speak of it. When I came home after my trip abroad with the Arion Society I felt the difference immediately. I played the same music and I was surrounded by the same old friends, but I could not play.

Maud Powell was born August 22, 1868, in Peru, Illinois. Showing musical talent as early as age four, she was

A curiosity

Maud's words are from an interview, "Fiddle and the Fiddler, A Story of Maud Powell's Transition from Baby Instrument Up to the 'Strad' Period," which appeared in the March 20, 1898, edition of the New York Times.

supervised and encouraged by her mother, an amateur composer. By the age of eight she was playing Mozart's violin sonatas, and at nine she toured the Midwest for six weeks with the Chicago Ladies' Orchestra.

With the generous financial assistance of local townspeople, Maud was sent to Europe at age twelve to study piano and violin. After one year in Leipzig, she was one of six students chosen from a group of eighty to study at the Paris Conservatory. In 1883 she moved to London, followed by two years of study in Berlin. In 1885, at the age of seventeen, Maud returned to America and made her debut with the New York Philharmonic Society, playing a violin concerto by Bruch.

Maud missed the liberal artistic atmosphere of Europe and felt discriminated against as a woman violinist. However, she persevered and earned a reputation in her field. In 1892 she toured Germany and Austria with the New York Arion Society, and the following year she was invited to play at the Chicago World's Fair.

In 1894 Maud's interest in chamber music led her to form the Maud Powell String Quartet. She toured continuously throughout America, Europe, Russia, and South Africa. She presented many violin concertos for the first time, including works by Saint Saëns, Dvořák, and Sibelius. She debuted Tchaikovsky's *Concerto*, which later became known as a masterpiece, in New York City in January 1889.

Maud married her manager, H. Godfrey Turner, in September 1904. When she was not on tour, they divided their time between homes in Great Neck, Long Island, and New Hampshire's White Mountains. In later years she lectured at schools and colleges, and during World War I she entertained troops at army training camps. Maud was the first violinist to record with the Victor Talking Machine Company. In January 1920 she collapsed in Uniontown, Pennsylvania, while on a concert tour. She died of a heart attack in her hotel room at the age of forty-one.

Sophie Kerr Underwood

Dining alone

1953

I have often reflected as I sat at dinner alone, how much more interesting the food is than when I am giving my very grandest party. French fried onions, for instance, crisp golden wisps of incomparable pungency — I do not offer these at parties and yet I know that if I did most of the company would shout for joy. Suppose

I gave a dinner at which there was nothing but a great platter filled with ground beef patties, crusty brown outside, and juicily, temptingly pink within; a mountain peak of French fried onions; a gallon of cole slaw dressed with a sauce of cream and lemon juice and celery seed; and afterward an enormous dried-apple-and-raisin pie and large cups of devilishly black hot coffee. It sounds wonderful and it would taste even better. But do I ever give a dinner like that? No, not to anyone but myself and perhaps one or two people who regard French fried onions as I do, the most delicious way in which a most delicious vegetable can be served.

Sophie Kerr Underwood was born August 23, 1889, in Denton, Maryland. She learned a love of cooking from her mother and a love of plants from her father, a nurseryman. She graduated from Hood College and received a master's degree from the University of Vermont.

Sophie married John Underwood when she was twenty-four, but they were divorced four years later. She took up writing as a means of supporting herself and contributed to all the popular magazines of the day, including the *Saturday Evening Post* and *Ladies' Home Journal.*

Sophie published her first novel in 1916 and continued to publish through 1951, producing thirty works of fiction and drama. In 1934 she collaborated on *Big-Hearted Herbert,* which was made into a film the following year. All of Sophie's writing was sentimental and romantic; virtue triumphed over wrongdoing and happy endings were guaranteed.

Sophie died in 1965 at the age of eighty-four at her home in New York City.

Sophie's writing is from The Best I Ever Ate: A Practical Home Cookbook, *published in 1953 by Rinehart and Company, Inc.*

Madeleine Zabriskie Doty

1914

On Monday, November 3, 1913, I awoke with beating heart. That day was the day. But suppose something should prevent the adventure? Then I laughed. To be fighting to get behind prison-bars with as much determination as the man caught in a misdeed struggles to escape was amusing. A queer topsy-turvy world, with its continual battle for that which is denied.

Getting into prison

Madeleine Zabriskie Doty was born August 24, 1879, in Greenfield, Massachusetts. After graduating from Smith College, she went to Harvard to study law, although women were strictly barred. She attended four lectures dressed as a man, in a tailored suit with a hat hiding her hair, before she was discovered by the professor. She argued her case before the faculty but was not allowed to continue. She completed her law degree at New York University, and although she passed the bar she did not like to try cases and turned to social reform work instead. She worked in the juvenile court system until she was appointed to the New York State Commission on Prison Reform in 1912, beginning her long career in public service.

In 1913 Madeleine decided that the best way to determine needed prison reforms was to put herself in the convict's place. With the cooperation of the warden and chief matron, she was incarcerated for four days as "Maggie Martin" in the women's penitentiary at Auburn on a trumped-up forgery charge. Upon her release, she wrote a scathing exposé for the *New York Sunday Post*, describing the deplorable conditions and her poor treatment.

Madeleine was engaged in 1918 to Roger Baldwin, the future founder of the American Civil Liberties Union. As a conscientious objector, he had to serve a year in prison for refusing the draft before they could be married in August 1919. They lived together in Greenwich Village until 1924, when Madeleine was selected as the international secretary of the Women's League for Peace and Freedom, based in Geneva, Switzerland. With the exception of an occasional visit to New York or Florida, she spent the rest of her life abroad. In her mid-fifties, she returned to school and obtained her Ph.D. degree in international relations from the University of Geneva. In addition to her duties as league secretary, she managed a home maintained by the league for thirty-five years and served as director of the Smith College Junior Year Abroad Program.

Even after their divorce in 1935, following ten years of separation, and his subsequent remarriage, Roger and Madeleine remained close friends and always corresponded. It was Roger who met Madeleine at the plane when she returned to America for the last time in 1963, at the age of eighty-four, confined to a wheelchair. She had made plans to spend her last days at a retirement hotel in the Berkshires. A few months later, she died peacefully during a massage and was buried in Greenfield, Massachusetts.

Madeleine's writing is from "Maggie Martin, #933, A Woman's Voluntary Week in Prison," which was published in the October 1914 Century *Magazine.*

Nora Antonia Gordon

1889

Christ's preciousness to me makes me feel that I wish my feet had wings, that I might hasten to take the Bread of Life to the poor heathen. I have counted the cost of missionary service, and my love for Christ makes me willing to bear the many peculiar trials through which I am confident I must pass. . . .

Love for Christ

Nora Antonia Gordon was born August 25, 1866, in Columbus, Georgia. Her parents, former slaves, had taken their name from their master, General Gordon. Nora attended Spelman Seminary in Atlanta for six years, graduating in 1888. Her graduation essay, "The Influence of Women on National Character," presented her personal beliefs on the importance of women: "Let no woman feel that life to her means simply living; but let her rather feel that she has a special mission assigned her, which none other of God's creatures can perform."

Shortly after her graduation, the secretary of the Society of the West wrote to Spelman, seeking someone to assist Miss Fleming, a missionary in Palabala in the Congo. Nora was chosen and set sail for Africa in March 1889. The missionaries' early attempts to bring Christianity to the natives were often very humorous. She later recalled her first church service: "The worker, after speaking to a crowd of heathens, asked them all to close their eyes and bow their heads while he would pray to God. When the missionary had finished his prayer and opened his eyes, every person had stealthily left the place."

Nora remained at Palabala for two years, teaching school and caring for the young children. She then moved on to Lukungu to assist Clara Howard, another Spelman graduate, at the mission there. Poor health forced Nora to return to America in 1893. However, she brought two young African women with her. This started a tradition at Spelman, and she brought five other women to be educated in the next two years.

In 1895 Nora married Reverend S. C. Gordon while he was home on leave from the English Baptist Mission at Stanley Pool, also in the Congo. They returned together to the mission, which was older and more established than her two previous assignments. Soon after their arrival, however, officials of the Belgian Congo drove them out. They went into the French Congo, but there they were prohibited from preaching to Africans.

Nora's writing is from a talk she gave at Spelman College in 1889 prior to leaving for missionary service in Africa. It is included in Progress of a Race or the Remarkable Advancement of the American Negro, *by J. W. Gibson and W. H. Crogman, published in 1969 by Mnemosyne Publishers, Inc., Miami, Florida.*

In 1900, after the death of their second child, Nora and her husband returned to the United States. Nora died at Spelman six months later at the age of thirty-four. In his 1919 book *Women of Achievement*, Benjamin Brawley wrote: "No larger mission could come to a young Negro in America trained in Christian study than to make his or her life a part of the redemption of the great fatherland. The salvation of Africa is at once the most pressing problem before either the Negro race or the Kingdom of Christ. Such a worker was Nora Gordon. It is to be hoped that not one but thousands like her will arise."

AUGUST 26

Zona Gale

A four-leaf clover

Zona's writing is from a letter she wrote to her good friend, Laura Chase. It is included in her biography, Still Small Voice, *written by August William Derleth and published in 1940 by D. Appleton-Century Co.*

1926

Tonight I drove to the cemetery — she always loved that hour up there, the shadows, the buds, the river. And so dear a thing happened. The grass is greening, the little Judas tree overhanging our lot is budding, the robins were singing. I knelt to uproot some little creeping mossy weed which runs in the grass and right high up, above the dear breast, was a tiny baby four leaf clover, perfect. So many many times since I was a little girl I have heard mother say that she never found a four leaf clover. "It is no use for me to search," I have heard her say, "I never found one, I have never found one." And there it was, an April four leaf clover from her. I left it there — but it was as if she had smiled, had looked. I could see her dimpling with it. I felt warm — Her *spirit* was like substance.

Zona Gale was born August 26, 1874, in Portage, Wisconsin. As an only child, she received abundant attention and encouragement from her parents. They fully supported her decision, at age eight, to become a writer. In later years, Zona acknowledged that her parents were the most important influences in her life.

While in school, and later at the University of Wisconsin, Zona wrote continuously — mostly short stories and romantic poetry — but none of it was published. After graduation she took a job as a newspaper reporter, first in Milwaukee, then at the *Evening World* in New York City in 1901. During a visit home to her mother and father in Portage, she looked at her hometown in a new light; in 1905 she began writing folksy tales about middle-class rural life in her Friendship Village series.

From 1908 to 1919 Zona published four volumes in the Friendship Village series and achieved broad popularity. Following a failed engagement to a poet in New York, she returned to Wisconsin permanently in 1911 to live with her parents. At the same time, she received a $2,000 prize in a contest sponsored by *Delineator* and began publishing a book a year.

Zona produced her most popular book, *Miss Lulu Bett*, in 1920, another in her series of observations of small-town life. She turned it into a play as well, for which she received the 1921 Pulitzer Prize for drama.

Zona was married at fifty-three to a wealthy Portage businessman she had admired since childhood. She continued to write prolifically: novels, poetry, essays, plays, and one biography. Her happy marriage was cut short after only ten years by her sudden death from pneumonia at sixty-four. She was buried in the Silver Lake Cemetery in her beloved Portage.

Rosalie McClendon

1927

I cannot say that all my life I wanted to act. I had seen so many things badly done in churches that I wanted always to teach children what to do and when to do it; so when the chance came to study under the late Franklin Sargent of the American Academy of Dramatic Arts, I jumped at it. I studied with him for three years and before I knew it I was doing one of the leading roles in Butler Davenport's "Justice."

A new actress

Rosalie Virginia Scott McClendon was born August 27, 1884, in Greensville, South Carolina. When she was six, her parents moved to New York City, where they had jobs as coachman and housekeeper for a wealthy family. In 1904, after graduating from public school, Rosalie married Dr. Henry Pruden McClendon. Although he was a licensed chiropractor, he was unable to earn a living as such and spent most of his time as a Pullman porter for the Pennsylvania Railroad.

In 1916 Rose received a scholarship to the American Academy of Dramatic Art at Carnegie Hall in New York City. After studying for three years, she made her debut with the Bramhall Players at the Davenport Theatre on East

Rose's writing is from "Dramatis Personae, Rose McClendon," which appeared in The Crisis, *April 1927.*

Twenty-seventh Street. For the next fifteen years, she appeared in all the important dramas about Negro life that were produced on the New York stage. She believed the Negro theater was the best way to present an honest picture of black American life.

In 1926 Rose appeared on Broadway in *Deep River*, a "native opera." She played an aging mulatto, the "proudly withered madam" that made her famous. A reviewer in the *New York Post* described her as an "unforgettable picture," and Ethel Barrymore called her performance "one of the memorable, immortal moments in the theatre."

After *Deep River* Rose starred in the Pulitzer Prize-winning play *Abraham's Bosom*, for which she received an acting award from the *Morning Telegraph*. She next appeared in *Porgy*, the play on which George Gershwin based his opera *Porgy and Bess*. *Porgy* ran for 217 performances in New York, followed by an extensive tour of the United States and Europe. An all-black cast in a successful play about blacks was a major breakthrough in the late 1920s.

In 1935 John Houseman and Countee Cullen were working on a project to showcase Rose's talents. They were reworking Euripides' *Medea* with Medea as a black woman with two mulatto children. The project fell through due to financial problems and Rose's illness. Her last appearance was in *Mulatto* by Langston Hughes, the first full-length play by a black author to be presented on Broadway. She was forced to withdraw from the cast due to ill health, and she died six months later at the age of fifty-one. At the time, there was a reluctance to admit to having cancer, so her cause of death was listed as pneumonia.

Belle Jennings Benchley

A strange visitor

1940

On another occasion, while I was watching an evening motion-picture show in the city, a call for Mrs. Benchley was flashed on the screen. I rushed out to the box office, called the number, which was that of the police department, and learned that a seal had apparently escaped from the zoo for one had appeared at a house on Ninth Street occupied by two unmarried sisters. They had heard a tapping on their door and had gone to open it. When they did, in walked a seal. For a moment the ladies did not know what to do with such a strange but apparently friendly visitor. Thinking that

Belle's writing is from My Life in a Man-Made Jungle, *published in 1940 by Little, Brown and Company.*

their bathtub might be the solution they led the way into the bathroom; the seal, dominated by curiosity, followed. When they had filled the tub with water, he climbed in and they rushed out, shutting the door behind them. After that they phoned the police and the police called me.

Belle Jennings Benchley was born August 28, 1882, in Pratt, Kansas. When she was four her family moved to Point Loma, California, when her father became sheriff of San Diego County.

Belle received her teaching certificate from the San Diego State Normal School. She married William Benchley in 1905, and they had one son. In 1922 they were divorced, leaving her with a son to support. After completing a book-keeping course in 1925, she answered an ad to fill in for the vacationing bookkeeper for Dr. Harry Wegeforth, founder and director of the San Diego Zoo.

The zoo had between 600 to 800 animals housed on 150 acres with ten employees when Belle first started. When she retired twenty-six years later, it had grown to 3,000 animals on 200 acres with 200 employees. During her first week at the zoo, she would report to Dr. Wegeforth with suggestions for improvements, and his answer invariably was, "Well, do something about it." She had a wolf moved to a larger cage, solicited funds from San Diego's wealthy community, wrote promotional articles for the newspaper, and on her days off visited local grocers to ask for food donations. Belle was hired permanently after the regular bookkeeper returned from vacation. In 1927 she was made executive secretary and director of the zoo.

Belle spent several weeks when she took over as director doing the jobs of her employees to better understand the operation of the zoo. She cleaned the elephants' cages, nursed a sick emu, and patrolled the grounds as a night watchman. She believed the zoo was there for the animals, not the people. She would not tolerate any abuse or neglect of the animals, warning her keepers always to use "a soft word instead of a club, a gentle twinkle of the eye instead of a whip."

Belle was the first to use moats as natural barriers for bears and big cats. She made certain every cage had a private place, out of view of the public, as a retreat. In 1931 she obtained two gorillas, out of only five in the country, and in 1938 she opened the largest bird cage in the world for birds of prey, complete with a real hill with cliffs and trees. She was very proud of the zoo hospital, the first in the United States, and of the zoo's highly successful captive breeding program.

She believed that women had a special inner sense in caring for animals and that there should be more women working in zoos. She opened the field to them by hiring some of the first female keepers in the country.

In 1952 Belle announced her plans to retire to a reluctant board of directors, who replied, "Mrs. Benchley, the San Diego Zoo without you is unthinkable." Her last day, December 10, 1953, was declared "Belle Benchley Day" in the city and county of San Diego. Eight hundred guests attended her farewell dinner. She was presented with a gift of a three-month trip around the world, so that she could fulfill her dream of visiting the world's zoos. Summing up her career, she said, "I have known the thrill of having a rattlesnake cuddle trustfully in my arms, and the soft touch of a gorilla's tongue on my cheek. Hairy, scaly, leather-covered — they are all mine and I love them, every one." Belle died in December 1973 at the age of ninety-one, but her zoo lives on as a monument to her beliefs.

Eliza Allen Starr

A welcome

1857

When I arrived in this busy Western city I had no acquaintances, no friends to go to, a stranger in a strange land; I put up at a hotel, which I soon learned was opposite St. Mary's Cathedral, Wabash Avenue and Madison Street. On the following morning, Sunday, I went to first mass, and found the attendance enormous; the pews, the aisles, and vestibules were crowded with worshipers, and I could only obtain a kneeling spot inside the vestibule. I went to second mass, but the crowds were equally as great. . . .

I knelt this second time near the confessional on the Epistle side of the door. After the sermon, the collection was taken up, and the gentleman who took up the collection in the aisle I occupied, looked closely at me when I placed my small contribution on the plate. After he had passed the plate into the sanctuary gate, he came down to where I was kneeling, and respectfully beckoned me to follow him, when he conducted me to a pew near the altar, which I saw was his. When mass was over he turned to me and said, "I see you are a stranger. You may occupy a seat in my pew whenever

Eliza's writing is from a letter written soon after her arrival in Chicago in 1857. It is included in The Life and Letters of Eliza Allen Starr *by James J. McGovern, published by Lakeside Press in 1905.*

you come to this church." Such was my first welcome in Chicago among strangers.

Eliza Allen Starr was born August 29, 1824, in Deerfield, Massachusetts. She began studying painting at Deerfield Academy, and in 1845 she moved to Boston to study with Mrs. Caroline Hildreth, a well-known miniaturist.

While in Boston, Eliza began a nine-year struggle with the Unitarian faith she had been reared in, which culminated in her conversion to Catholicism in December 1854. In 1848, while on a visit in Philadelphia to her cousin George Allen, a former Episcopal clergyman and recent Catholic convert, she met Bishop Francis Kenrick. Both men played an important part in awakening her new religious beliefs. After spending three years in Natchez, Mississippi, as a tutor for the children of a wealthy plantation owner, Eliza returned to Boston and was baptized by Bishop John B. Fitzpatrick.

Two years after her conversion, Eliza moved to Chicago, where she opened an art studio and started teaching children to paint. After her studio burned in the Chicago fire of 1871, Eliza moved in with the Sisters of the Holy Cross at St. Mary's Academy near South Bend, Indiana. She founded an art department there and used the school as her home base.

Eliza travelled throughout Europe from 1875 to 1877. Upon her return, she moved into a new residential studio built for her during her absence by friends, which she christened St. Joseph's Cottage. She published several books on Catholic art and a book of poems, *Songs of a Lifetime*, in 1887. She received the Laetare Medal from Notre Dame University and a special gold medal from the Catholic Congress at the Chicago World's Columbian Exposition. In 1899 she was presented with a medallion from Pope Leo XIII for her book *The Three Archangels and the Guardian Angel in Art*. She died two years later at the age of seventy-seven while on a visit to her brother Caleb. She was buried in a Dominican habit that had been given to her by the nuns at the Third Order of St. Dominic.

Evelyn Maurine Carrington

1975

*A*lways busy

Hannah Elizabeth "ate not the bread of idleness." She rose early and worked late to supply food and clothing for her family and household. She saw that a flower garden was planted, shared her wisdom and religion with her children, gave prestige to her husband, and helped the poor and needy. Some way or other, she found time to do fine handwork. . .

During the Civil War, there were many deprivations. One fall when her grandsons needed new suits, Hannah Elizabeth had only a bolt of bed ticking from which to fashion these. She sent the boys to gather huckleberries. Using the berries, she dyed the material. Then she cut and sewed the suits.

Evelyn Maurine Carrington was born August 30, 1898, in Austin, Texas. Following graduation from Austin public schools, she received her A.B. and Ph.D. degrees from the University of Texas. After a year of postdoctoral work in educational psychology at Columbia University, she returned to Texas and began her career as an associate professor of education at Sam Houston State Teachers' College in Huntsville.

Dr. Carrington gained a reputation over the years as one of the most respected authorities on educational psychology in Texas. She was a delegate to the President's Conference on Aging, a member of the Advisory Committee of the Hogg Foundation of Mental Health, and president of the International Council of Women Psychologists.

The Children's Development Center of Dallas was founded in 1951 to aid brain-injured, mentally retarded, and emotionally abused children of the area who were not eligible for public school education. Evelyn was appointed as the first administrative director of the nondenominational, nonprofit, state chartered day school. She set up a program with Southern Methodist University to bring to the center student teachers from the university's speech, art, and physical education departments. The center was very successful, and many of its pupils were able to "graduate" to the public school system.

Evelyn spent her later years in private practice and as staff psychologist at the Children's Medical Center in Dallas. She died in October 1984 at the age of eighty-seven and was buried in Austin.

Evelyn's writing is from the story of her great-grandmother, "Hannah Elizabeth Denny (1807-1903)." It is included in Women in Early Texas, *edited by Evelyn and published in 1975 by the Jenkins Publishing Company, Pemberton Press, Austin, Texas.*

Elizabeth Stuart Phelps Ward

1895

A successful venture

The name of the story was "A Sacrifice Consumed." It was a very little story, not covering more than four or five pages in print. I sent it to "Harper's Magazine," without introduction. . . . It was immediately accepted, and a prompt check for twenty-five dollars accompanied the acceptance. Even my father knew nothing of the venture until I carried the letter and enclosure to him. The pleasure on his expressive face was only equaled by its frank and unqualified astonishment. He read the story when it came out, and, I think, was touched by it, — it was a story of a poor and plain little dressmaker, who lost her lover in the army, — and his genuine emotion gave me a kind of awed elation, which has never been repeated in my experience.

Elizabeth Stuart Phelps Ward was born August 31, 1844, in Boston. She was baptized Mary Gray Phelps but took her mother's name after her mother died when she was eight. Her father, a Congregational minister, took an active interest in Elizabeth's education. She attended Abbott Academy and Mrs. Edwards' School and studied theology with a professor from the Andover Seminary. From 1848 to 1878 her father taught at the seminary, giving Elizabeth access to the school's library and private tutors.

Elizabeth fell in love with a student at the Andover Seminary. After he died in October 1862 in a Civil War battle, she vowed to remain single forever and became a writer. She had already published stories in *The Youth's Companion* and other juvenile magazines, starting at the age of thirteen. She published her first adult story in *Harper's* in 1864.

Elizabeth's father remarried in 1858, and Elizabeth disliked her stepmother. She gave her no encouragement in her aspirations as a writer, and Elizabeth was forced to do her writing in the attic or the barn. After the publication of her successful first book, *The Gates Ajar*, in 1864, her family rewarded her by giving her a small summer house to use as a study.

The Gates Ajar was a fictionalized story about the magnificence of heaven where all loved ones are once again reunited. She argued that, "If the Bible tells us there will be harps in heaven, why should we not also hope for pianos?" Although

Elizabeth's writing is from her autobiography, Chapters in a Life, *published by Houghton, Mifflin and Company in 1895.*

the book was attacked as heretical theology, it enjoyed tremendous popular success, and Elizabeth received thousands of letters thanking her for the comfort she had given her readers. Her book's promise of a glorious reunion in a perfect heaven consoled many who had lost family and friends during the Civil War.

Elizabeth married Herbert Dickinson Ward, an author and son of a family friend, in October 1888. She was forty-four and he was twenty-seven, and although they collaborated on three books, their marriage was never happy. Elizabeth contributed countless poems and articles to magazines and published fifty-seven books during her lifetime. In her later years, she took up the causes of anti-vivisection and temperance, and could often be seen lecturing local fishermen on the evils of alcohol near her summer home in Gloucester, Massachusetts. She suffered from nervous disorders and insomnia and was an invalid for several years before her death in 1911 at the age of sixty-six.

SEPTEMBER

Emma Stebbins

1878

I am really stronger then I feel. I am satisfied that Dr. Mitchell has got hold of a bottom fact, in making patients take absolute rest of body, it is what we all need sooner or later, I know it is the thing for me — but what do you suppose he does with the unquiet restless spirit? Enforced idleness is more trying to me than any amount of hard work — I have been a busy worker all my life, and it is almost an impossibility for me to be entirely idle — There in my own little den, which I wish you could see, I putter about and busy myself endlessly with little writings — seeing such Vistas of things I want to do. . . .

The unquiet spirit

Emma Stebbens was born September 1, 1815, in New York City, the sixth of nine children. As a child, her drawings of friends impressed the leading portrait painter in the city, and he began giving her lessons in oil. She also worked with watercolors and crayons. One of her first major accomplishments was a book of poetry, *The Book of Prayer*, which she illustrated.

In 1843 Emma was elected an associate of the National Academy of Design. She participated in the academy's annual exhibitions in addition to those at the Pennsylvania Academy of Fine Arts. She went to Rome in 1857 to study portraiture but soon switched to sculpture. She studied with several Italian masters and after two years received her first commission, for statues representing "Commerce" and "Industry" for a Pennsylvania coal mine. Some of her more famous pieces include a bronze statue of Horace Mann in front of Boston's State House, a bust of her brother in the New York Mercantile Library, and the Bethesda Fountain in Central Park.

Emma was commissioned in 1860 to create a bust of the actress Charlotte Cushman, which was donated to the Handel and Haydn Society in Boston. Emma and Charlotte became close friends and left Italy together in 1870 to return to America. They spent the last six years of Charlotte's life at her Newport, Rhode Island, estate. Emma survived Charlotte by six years. She died in New York City in 1882 at the age of seventy-three.

Emma's writing is from a September 2, 1821, letter to her friend, Anne Whitney (September 2), Wellesley College Archives, Wellesley, Massachusetts.

Anne Whitney

A sunny home

1871

Twelve years ago, then, with bandbox, box, and bundle I appeared at your front door, and you opened it and let me in. I remember you cordially welcomed the way-farer, and your mother too, and father no less. I think Aunt Elizabeth [Manning] thought, "Well, I don't know how this is going to answer — a boarder!" but she came round, the good heart that she is, and would have taken a further-away cousin — a kangaroo perhaps — had one laid any claim to her kindness. How well at home I felt. Blest the days and doubly blest the evenings! A good warm, sunny home! into whose interior workings I looked with interest; and the sun of it radiated on through all these years, and still vibrates.

Anne Whitney was born September 2, 1821, in Watertown, Massachusetts. Except for one year spent at Mrs. Little's Select School for Young Ladies in Bucksport, Maine, when she was thirteen, Anne was educated at home by private tutors. After graduation, she taught school and dabbled at writing poetry, publishing a volume of poems in 1859.

Anne's real interest and talent lay in sculpting, which she discovered accidentally after a watering can overturned in her greenhouse and she began molding the wet sand. She went to Philadelphia and New York in 1858, studying sculpture as well as anatomy at the Brooklyn Hospital. She entered her first piece, a marble bust of a child, in an 1860 exhibit at the National Academy of Design in New York. That piece is now in the National Collection of Fine Arts.

The Civil War cancelled her plans to go to Italy for further study, so she remained at the family home and worked in her small studio nicknamed "the shanty," paid for by her brother. During that period she exhibited several large works in New York and Boston.

In 1867 Anne was finally able to study in Rome, where she remained for four years. Soon after her return to America, she was commissioned to create a life-size statue of Samuel Adams for the Statuary Hall in the Capitol in Washington, D.C. For the next twenty years, she worked out of her Beacon Hill studio, creating works that still stand in Boston's Museum of Fine Arts, at Wellesley College, and on the Commonwealth Avenue Mall in Boston.

Anne's writing is from an 1871 letter written to her lifelong companion Adeline Manning, Wellesley College Archives, Wellesley, Massachusetts.

In her seventies, Anne made a sculpture of Leif Ericson for the Smithsonian and contributed several busts to the Chicago World's Columbian Exposition in 1893. Her last work, completed when she was eighty, was a reworking of a memorial to Charles Sumner, which she had entered in a competition in 1875. She won first place but was denied the commission when the judges discovered that she was a woman. This annoyed her the rest of her life; she was finally appeased when she was allowed to complete the statue in 1902. It can be seen today in the center of Harvard Square. Anne died of cancer in 1915 at the age of ninety-three and was buried in Cambridge's Mount Auburn Cemetery.

Prudence Crandall

Canterbury
March 14, 1833
Mr. Garrison,

Allow me to tell you My dear friend, my soul is sick with every day's report of wrong and outrage with which "Canterbury" is filled. And were it not for the confidence I have in the hand of The Omnipotent hence I should fall like the fading leaf before the northern blasts. Last week on Thursday the committee composed of the *select men* and civil authority of the town promptly fulfilled their appointment and informed me that the town unanimously united in disappropriating the school I am about to establish and also they were authorized to advise me to desert from my purpose. I gave them my answer in writing which is as follows, Gentlemen, I have listened attentively to all you have said, will duly consider it, — will consult my friends and abide by their advice.

On Saturday last I visited Rev. Mr. May. I told him the answer I gave the committee and his reply was if I was not afraid to proceed to go on and if I was he would advise me to give it up. I assured him I was not apprehensive of any danger either on my own account or that of my scholars, therefore I remain as firm to my purpose as ever. . . .

Prudence Crandall was born September 3, 1803, in Hopkinton, Rhode Island. From 1825 to 1830 she attended

*U*nafraid

Prudence's writing is from a March 14, 1833, letter to William Lloyd Garrison, Rare Books and Manuscripts Department, Boston Public Library.

the New England Friends' Boarding School in Providence, after which she taught school in Plainfield, Connecticut.

As a teenager Prudence's family had moved to Canterbury, Connecticut. When the Quaker townspeople heard of Prudence's success as a teacher in Plainfield, they asked her to return home to open a girls' school in one of the large houses on the town green. She operated her school successfully for several years until the daughter of a respected Negro farmer applied for admission, as she wished to become a teacher herself. Prudence decided to accept the young black girl, but she was met with threats and vehement opposition from the parents of her Quaker students. She closed the school and wrote to William Lloyd Garrison, editor of the *Liberator*, that she was "determined if possible during the remaining part of my life to benefit the people of color." She announced her plan to recruit students from the leading black families of New England and New York with the intention of reopening her school in one year as a boarding school for Negro girls.

The people of Canterbury reacted quickly, passing a "black law" that prohibited any school from teaching out-of-state Negroes. Local merchants refused to sell Prudence food and supplies, and she was arrested for defying the black law and placed in the county prison. Although she eventually won her case and received much publicity in the *Liberator* and other anti-slavery magazines, Prudence was still confronted by angry townspeople upon her return. She endured vandalism, the polluting of her well, and an attempt to burn down the school. However, after a mob attack in September 1834 she finally gave up her long struggle. She had recently been married to Reverend Calvin Philleo, a Baptist minister sixteen years her senior with three children, and they departed Canterbury forever.

Prudence and her husband settled at first in upstate New York and later moved to rural Illinois. Although she always dreamed she would some day open a school for black girls, she had to be content with running a school for white girls out of her home. Following her husband's death in 1874, she went to live with a brother in Elk Falls, Kansas, where she was active in the temperance and women's suffrage movements. She died in June 1890 at the age of eighty-six and was buried in Elk Falls.

Phoebe Cary

1865
But if any young man needs advising,
  Let me whisper a word in his ear:
Don't talk of the lady that's absent
  Too much to the lady that's near.

My kindness is disinterested;
  So in speaking to me never mind;
But the course I advise you to follow
  Is safe, as a rule, you will find.

You may talk about love in the abstract,
  Say the ladies are charming and dear;
But you need not select an example,
  Nor say she is there, or is here.

When it comes to that last application,
  Just leave it entirely out,
And give to the lady that's present
  The benefit still of the doubt!

The lady that's absent

Phoebe Cary was born September 4, 1824, in Mt. Healthy, Ohio, the sixth of nine children. The Cary family was susceptible to tuberculosis, and by the time she was eleven Phoebe had lost two sisters and her mother. There was much work to be done on the farm and little time for education. The Carys owned no more than six books, and Phoebe received most of her literature from the "Poet's Corner" in a Universalist paper, the *Trumpet*.

Phoebe and her older sister Alice both began writing poetry as children, not surprisingly with themes of illness and death. At fourteen, Phoebe submitted a poem to a Boston paper at the same time Alice had a poem published in a Cincinnati paper, thus beginning their long and popular careers as poets.

In 1849 works by both sisters were included in *The Female Poets of America*, and the following year a publisher paid them $100 for *Poems of Alice and Phoebe Cary*. In 1850 Alice moved to New York City to further her literary career, and Phoebe joined her six months later. Within six years they had earned enough to purchase a home on Twentieth Street, where they lived for the rest of their lives. They began a tradition of

Phoebe's writing is from her poem "Up and Down," which appeared in The Poetical Works of Alice and Phoebe Cary, *published in 1865 by Houghton, Mifflin and Company.*

Sunday evening receptions where, over the next fifteen years, countless intellectuals came to sip sweetened milk and water and join in topical discussions.

Phoebe published two more volumes of poetry, in 1854 and 1868. Devoted to her sister, she rejected several marriage proposals in order to continue living with Alice. Alice developed tuberculosis and spent the last years of her life as an invalid under Phoebe's care. Alice's death in February 1871 was too much for Phoebe to endure, and she died five months later. The sisters were buried beside each other in Brooklyn's Greenwood Cemetery.

Hannah Chaplin Conant

The martyr

1856

On Friday, the sixth of October, 1536, William Tyndale was led forth to die. Having been bound to the stake, he was first strangled and his dead body then burned to ashes. His last words, "uttered with fervent zeal and in a loud voice were these: 'Lord, open the King of England's eyes!'"

Thus perished, a victim to priestcraft, the purest of England's patriots and the crown of her martyrs — the best and greatest man of his time!

Nothing is more common with the enemies of truth than to suppose, when the champion of a great principle is struck down, that the principle itself is dead. Especially does the history of Bible translation abound with exemplifications of this remark. Every step of progress in this foundation work of Christian philanthropy — without which all others are but as blossoms without a root, and out of which all others spring by an inevitable law — has been marked with martyrs. Not all martyrs at the stake, like Frith and Tyndale; but martyrs as to their peace, their reputation, the good will and respect of their fellow-men.

Hannah's writing is from what is believed to be her most important work, The English Bible: History of the Translation of the Holy Scriptures into the English Tongue, *published in 1856 by Arthur Hall, Virtue, London.*

Hannah O'Brien Chaplin Conant was born September 5, 1809, in Danvers, Massachusetts, the eldest of ten children. Her father, a Baptist minister, moved the family to Waterville, Maine, in 1818 when he became the head of a small Baptist school (later Colby College).

Hannah attended public schools in Maine but received

additional instruction from her father. She became proficient in French, German, Hebrew, Greek, Latin, and Oriental languages. At twenty, she married Thomas Jefferson Conant, a language professor.

The Conants settled in Hamilton, New York, where Thomas taught at Hamilton Literary and Theological Institution (later Colgate University). Hannah began their family, which eventually numbered ten children, and edited the *Mother's Monthly Journal* of Utica. She also wrote articles on religion for newspapers and magazines and published her first book, a German translation, in 1844. She wrote or translated numerous books and was praised in a *New York Times* review as a "vigorous and graceful writer."

In 1857 the Conants moved to Brooklyn, New York, following Thomas' retirement. He was working on a revised translation of the Bible, and Hannah was at work on another translation of a German theological study, when she died unexpectedly in 1865 at age fifty-five. Henry Ward Beecher wrote a eulogy in the *Watchman* that described her as a "scholar in the best sense of the word, working almost as regularly as her husband, and at the same tasks."

Jane Addams

1910

... the most painful episode of the winter for me came from an attempt on my part to conform to carefully received instructions. A shipping clerk whom I had known for a long time had lost his place, as so many people had that year, and came to the relief station established at Hull-House four or five times to secure help for his family. I told him one day of the opportunity for work on the drainage canal and intimated that if any employment were obtainable, he ought to exhaust that possibility before asking for help. The man replied that he had always worked indoors and that he could not endure outside work in winter. I am grateful to remember that I was too uncertain to be severe, although I held to my instructions. He did not come again for relief, but worked for two days digging on the canal, where he contracted pneumonia and died a week later. I have never lost trace of the two little children he left behind him, although I cannot see them

A painful blunder

Jane's writing is from her book Twenty Years at Hull House, *published in 1910 by the Macmillan Company.*

without a bitter consciousness that it was at their expense I learned that life cannot be administered by definite rules and regulations; that wisdom to deal with a man's difficulties comes only through some knowledge of his life and habits as a whole; and that to treat an isolated episode is almost sure to invite blundering. . . .

Jane Addams was born September 6, 1860, in Cedarville, Illinois. Her mother died when she was two, and five years later her father remarried. She graduated at the head of her class at Rockford Female Seminary in 1881.

The years immediately following graduation were troubled for Jane. Her father died, after which she toured Europe for two years with her stepmother. Her initial encounter with the indigent in London's East End was her first experience with the urban poor, and it had a profound effect upon her. Later, during another European trip with her friend Ellen Gates Starr (March 19) in 1888, she decided to open a settlement house in America to attempt to alleviate the human suffering caused by industrialization.

In September 1889 Jane and Ellen moved into the dilapidated Hull mansion in Chicago's Nineteenth Ward, which teemed with Italian, Russian, German, and Greek immigrants. Hull House was to remain Jane's home for the remaining forty-six years of her life. She received financial support primarily from wealthy women of Chicago, and more than 2,000 people used the facilities each week.

Hull House became a leader in social reform after it became apparent that community services alone were not enough to heal the neighborhood's suffering. The influence of Hull House extended to political fights for child labor laws, labor unions, compulsory school attendance, welfare projects, and safety in the workplace. In 1899 Chicago became the first city in America to have a juvenile court, primarily due to the efforts of Jane and others at Hull House.

Jane wrote magazine articles and published her first of several books in 1902. Her autobiography, published in 1910, sold more than 80,000 copies during her lifetime and continues to be popular today. In 1910 she was the first woman to receive an honorary degree from Yale, and the following year she was named head of the National Federation of Settlements.

In addition to her work at Hull House, Jane was active in the women's suffrage movement and the peace movement. She spoke against America's entry into World War I, and after the war served as president of the Women's International League for Peace and Freedom. In 1920 she co-founded the American Civil Liberties Union. Her efforts were officially recognized in 1931 when she shared the Nobel Peace Prize with a professor from Columbia University.

Jane's health began to fail following major surgery in 1931 and a heart attack two years later. She died in May 1935 at the age of seventy-four. Her body lay in Hull House for two days as most of Chicago filed by, as many as 2,000 per hour. Following funeral services at Hull House, she was buried in Cedarville.

Anna Mary Robertson ("Grandma" Moses)

1952

When I was quite small my father would get me and my brothers white paper by the sheet, it was used for newspapers. He liked to see us draw pictures, it was a penny a sheet and it lasted longer than candy. . . . I would draw the picture, then color it with grape juice or berries, anything that was red and pretty in my way of thinking. Once I was given some carpenter's red and blue chalk, then I was rich, children did not have so much in those days, we appreciated what we did get.

Father was not well that winter, he had pneumonia. One day he said to mother, "Margaret, how would you like me to paint the walls?" And mother said she did not care, just so they were clean. So he commenced in one corner of the room and painted a scene he had seen the spring before up at Lake George. It was so pretty, mother told him to do some more, so he painted different scenes all around the room. . . . Underneath the clock shelf there was a square space, and father told aunt Maria she could have that to paint a picture on it . . . . I did not like the picture she'd painted, I could do better than that, and I commenced to paint on sticks of wood. Next summer I would get pieces of slate and window panes. Then I had some pretty pictures. That was the time they made fun of me, I had some "very pretty lamb scapes," as my brothers said I called them, they had some brilliant sunsets, and father would say, "oh not so bad." But mother was more practical, thought that I could spend my time other ways.

Anna Mary Robertson "Grandma" Moses was born September 7, 1860, to a large farm family near Greenwich,

Budding artist

Grandma Moses's writing is from Grandma Moses, My Life's History, *published by Harper & Brothers in 1952.*

New York. She had no formal schooling other than a few months at a local one-room country school.

Anna left home at twelve to earn her keep as a domestic servant. After fifteen years as a paid housekeeper, she married Thomas Salmon Moses, a farm worker. They settled in Virginia, where she bore ten children, five of whom died as infants.

The Moses family returned to New York state in 1905. When Anna's arthritis became too painful for her to do fine handwork, she turned to painting. Her first work was done in exterior house paint on "an old piece of canvas which had been used for mending a threshing machine cover."

Anna placed several of her paintings for sale with her other craftwork at the local drug store. A vacationing New York City art collector bought them all and went to her farmhouse to purchase fifteen others. He placed three of them in the 1939 "Contemporary Unknown American Painters" show at the Museum of Modern Art. The following year she had a one-woman show at a well-known gallery, and at the age of eighty became an overnight success. Entirely self-taught, "Grandma" Moses was often unable to explain her techniques, but her primitive style and familiar subjects were appealing and reasonably priced.

Grandma Moses painted well into her nineties, producing more than 1,000 pictures. She died in 1961 at the age of 101.

SEPTEMBER 8 *Ida Henrietta Hyde*

A curiosity

Ida's writing is from "Before Women Were Human Beings," Journal of the American Association of University Women, *June 1938.*

1938

At the time the European Fellowship was awarded, it was not known to my professors nor to me that universities in Germany were not coeducational institutions, and that women had never studied in the University of Strassburg; in fact, that they had not been permitted to matriculate in any German university. Therefore we on this side did not appreciate the full significance and importance of the departure, when Professor Goette, director of the Zoology Department in the University of Strassburg, graciously invited a woman student of Bryn Mawr College to work in his department.

It was not until I had worked many days in the splendid laboratory assigned to my private use that it dawned upon me that I was occupying a unique position, and that I was regarded by the students, faculty members, and their wives as a curiosity. In the university circle the news quickly spread that an American "woman's rights" freak, a blue stocking and what not, had had the boldness and audacity to force entrance into the college halls.

Ida Henrietta Hyde was born September 8, 1857, in Davenport, Iowa. After teaching for years in the Chicago school system, she enrolled in Cornell University and received her B.S. degree at the age of thirty-four. She then began her career as a physiological scientist, despite the popular opposition to women in science.

Ida's career commenced at Bryn Mawr College, first as an assistant and then as a fellow in biology. Her experiments were noticed by a zoology professor at Germany's University of Strassburg, who invited her to work with him. In 1896 she received a Ph.D. in physiology, magna cum laude superavit, from the University of Heidelberg, the first woman to receive a doctorate from that institution.

In the fall of 1896 Ida returned to America and spent one year as Irwin Research Fellow at Radcliffe College. She then received an appointment as assistant professor at the University of Kansas. In 1905 she was made a full professor of physiology. She remained at the University of Kansas for more than twenty years. In addition to teaching, she continued her research and published two definitive textbooks on physiology.

Ida was elected the first female member of the American Physiological Society in 1902. To assist other women scientists with their educational pursuits, she established scholarships at the University of Kansas and at Cornell. Shortly before her death, she donated $25,000 to create the Ida H. Hyde Woman's International Fellowship of the American Association of University Women. She retired from teaching in 1920 and died in 1945 of a cerebral hemorrhage, two weeks before her eighty-eighth birthday.

Rebekah Kohut

1925

... despite a year of preparation for the great work I was to undertake, certain misgivings came to me as we neared New York after the honeymoon. Success, I had felt, depended upon me alone, and if I did my share, all would be well. Suddenly now fear took possession.

Nine lives

There were eight children awaiting me, eight individuals, each with a different temperament, soul, desires, likes and dislikes. . . .

How different the reality! My fears proved to be phantoms. . . . Such heart-warming greetings as I received when we arrived in New York were beyond my expectations. We started our life together, and continued it, in a spirit of mutual affection; and I felt that nothing could go wrong.

Rebekah Bettelheim Kohut was born September 9, 1864, in Kaschau, Hungary. Her father was a rabbi and a physician, and her mother was the first female Jewish schoolteacher in Hungary. She influenced Rebekah to "seek out all kinds of less sheltered activities."

When Rebekah was three the family emigrated to America, settling in Virginia. Three years later, her mother died. After her father remarried and moved to San Francisco, Rebekah attended public schools and the University of California at Berkeley. She realized while at college that her vocation lay in a "career of service," and she began working for social welfare within her community.

In 1887 Rebekah married Alexander Kohut, a well-known Hebrew scholar and rabbi twenty-two years her senior. A widower, he had recently arrived in the United States from Hungary with his eight children. Rebekah threw herself into her role as the rabbi's wife and mother to his children.

For several years, especially those following Alexander's death in 1894, Rebekah had less time for her community service work while raising eight children. She did serve as president of the New York branch of the National Council of Jewish Women and set up several scholarships at Yale in her husband's name to promote Jewish scholarly research.

During World War I, Rebekah volunteered her skills to the government, becoming a "Dollar-a-Year" patriot. She was a member of the Women's Committee for National Defense, the National League for Women's Service, and Woodrow Wilson's Federal Employment Committee. After the war, she made numerous trips abroad to organize relief efforts for Jewish refugees.

Rebekah's writing is from her autobiography, My Portion, *published by Thomas Seltzer, Inc., 1925.*

Franklin D. Roosevelt, then governor of New York, appointed Rebekah to the New York State Advisory Council on Employment in 1931. She continued to take an active part in her many clubs and committees until her death in 1951 at the age of eighty-six.

Women's Words, Women's Stories

Georgia Douglas Johnson

1927

If I might ask of some fairy godmother special favors, one would sure be for a clearing space, elbow room in which to think and write and live beyond the reach of the Wolf's fingers. However, much that we do and write about comes just because of this daily struggle for bread and breath — so, perhaps it's just as well.

Georgia Blanche Douglas Camp Johnson was born September 10, 1877, in Atlanta. Her paternal grandmother was English, her maternal grandfather was black, and her maternal grandmother was an American Indian. In her autobiography, Georgia referred to herself as a "hybrid" and "a little yellow girl," and her mixed heritage became a dominant theme in her adult writings.

Georgia's childhood was lonely. She later claimed that Atlanta's University Normal School was the "first real homey sympathetic atmosphere" she had experienced. She dreaded graduation when she would have to leave her "haven." Music was her "first and strongest passion, composition mainly," but she feared she could not make a living through music and so turned to teaching.

In September 1903 Georgia married Henry Lincoln Johnson, a prominent attorney. Her first poem was published in the June 1905 issue of *Voice of the Negro*. Her first book of poems, *The Heart of a Woman*, was published in 1918, followed by two more in 1922 and 1928. Although some of her poetry concerned race issues, she wrote primarily on universal themes. She explained in a letter to a friend, "Whenever I can, I forget my special call to sorrow and live as happily as I may. Perhaps that is why I seldom elect to write racially."

Interestingly, while Georgia's poetry was raceless, her plays were completely the opposite. In 1926 her play *Blue Blood* won a prize in an *Opportunity* magazine competition. It portrayed two black women at a wedding, the mothers of the bride and groom, bragging about how much "blue blood" their children had, only to discover that they shared the same father, a wealthy white banker. She used humor to dramatize the age-old problem of white men taking advantage of black women.

After her husband Henry's death in 1925, in recognition of her literary ability Calvin Coolidge appointed Georgia commissioner of conciliation for the Department of Labor, a position she held from 1925 to 1934. Unfortunately, her time was "too much taken up with making a living to give

The daily struggle

Georgia's writing is from "The Contest Spotlight," which was published in the July 1927 issue of Opportunity.

much of it to literary work," although she did write a syndicated weekly newspaper column, "Homely Philosophy," from 1926 to 1932. During the late 1930s and 1940s, she resumed writing in earnest, publishing poems and short stories in magazines. Her poem "Tomorrow's World" was set to music and became very popular during World War II. It was read on the Senate floor and published in the *Congressional Record*. She published her last book of poetry, *Share My World*, in 1965 and died the following year at the age of eighty-nine.

SEPTEMBER 11

Anna Palmer Draper

A work continued

1883

. . . The only interest I can now take in life will be in having Henry's work continued, yet I feel so very incompetent for the task that my courage sometimes completely fails me — I understand Henry's plans and his manner of working, perhaps better than anyone else, but I could not get along without an assistant and my main difficulty is to find a person sufficiently acquainted with physics, chemistry, & astronomy to carry on the various researches — I will probably find it necessary to have two assistants one for the Observatory and one for the laboratory work, for it is not likely that I will find any one person with the varied scientific knowledge that was peculiar to Henry. I am willing to pay good salaries, so as to secure first class men, but I should want men willing to identify themselves with the work already commenced and develop it. . . . I want to be careful not to publish anything that Henry did not consider ready. He wished to get the spectra of several of the winter stars, and this we intended doing this winter. It is so hard that he should be taken away just as he had arranged all his affairs to have time to do the work he really enjoyed, and in which he could have accomplished so much. I cannot be reconciled to it in any way.

Anna's writing is from a January 17, 1883, letter to her husband's friend Edward C. Pickering, director of the Harvard College Observatory. Her letters are in the Harvard University Archives Collection, and several are included in "Mrs. Henry Draper and the Harvard College Observatory — 1883-1887," by Lyle G. Boyd, Harvard Library Bulletin, January 1969.

Mary Anna Palmer Draper was born September 11, 1839, in Stonington, Connecticut. She married Dr. Henry Draper, a science professor with an interest in astronomy, in October 1867. Although untrained as a scientist, she immediately became his research assistant.

Anna assisted her husband in his efforts at nebular and lunar photography. In addition to participating in his astronomy projects, she served as his hostess, entertaining co-workers and visiting scientists in their home. In November 1882 she gave a dinner for the forty members of the National Academy of Sciences. Henry developed pleurisy right after the meal and died two days later at forty-five.

Following Henry's death, Anna became obsessed with continuing her husband's research, especially his attempts to photograph stellar spectra. She considered building an observatory, but after four years of unsuccessful attempts, she decided to affiliate herself with Harvard College Observatory. She donated her husband's telescopes and a great deal of money to establish the Henry Draper Memorial. She began a thirty-year working relationship with Edward C. Pickering, director of the Harvard Observatory, who shared her interest in photographing the spectra of stars. Anna visited Harvard frequently, observing the work in progress.

In addition to her Harvard affiliation, Anna remained a lifelong member of the National Academy of Sciences. She died of pneumonia at home in New York City at seventy-five.

Florence Kelley

1926

Dismal ideas

Father had taught me to read when I was seven years old, in a terrible little book with woodcuts of children no older than myself, balancing with their arms heavy loads of wet clay on their heads, in brickyards in England. They looked like little gnomes and trolls, with crooked legs, and splay feet large out of all proportion to their dwarfed frames. The text told of the hardships they were then suffering, nearly two decades after Lord Shaftesbury's bill to shorten the working hours of women and children in English factories had been enacted by Parliament. When my mother and grandmother remonstrated with him for darkening the mind of a young child with such dismal ideas, he replied seriously that life can never be right for all the children until the cherished boys and girls are taught to know the facts in the lives of their less fortunate contemporaries.

Florence's writing is from "My Philadelphia," The Survey, *October 1, 1926.*

Florence Kelley was born September 12, 1859, in Philadelphia. Her early schooling occurred primarily at home. After graduating from Cornell University in 1882, she applied to the University of Pennsylvania Law School but was refused because she was a woman. The next year, while on a trip to Europe, she met M. Carey Thomas, who was the first woman to receive a doctorate from the University of Zurich. Florence enrolled in the University of Zurich and was quickly converted by the "new wildfire of socialism."

In June 1884 Florence married Lazare Wischnewetzky, a Russian medical student and fellow socialist. They returned to America the following year, settling in New York City, where Florence immersed herself in party work. The socialist labor leaders did not trust Florence, and she and her husband were expelled from the party in 1887. Shortly thereafter Florence and her three children moved to Illinois, where she obtained a divorce.

Florence and her family, which now included her mother, settled at Chicago's Hull House, where she began to work for the enactment of child labor laws.

Discouraged at the difficulties she encountered in prosecuting cases against major corporations, Florence obtained a law degree from Northwestern University in 1894. Three years later, however, she was dismissed from her job as factory inspector by the incoming governor. She relocated to New York City, where she became the general secretary of the National Consumers' League.

Florence held her position with the National Consumers' League until her death thirty-three years later. During that time she organized sixty leagues in twenty states and participated in two international conferences. She worked to establish a minimum wage, and by 1913 nine states had introduced some form of minimum wage legislation. Although she had some successes regarding child laborers, she was discouraged that not enough was being done to help them. She spent her last years campaigning for a child labor amendment to the Constitution. She died in Philadelphia in 1932 at the age of seventy-two and was buried near her summer home in Maine.

SEPTEMBER 13   *Maud Ballington Booth*

No one cared

1903

Many, many letters have I received, I remember one especially. It was written just after my first visit to Joliet State Prison and was in the natural unrestrained language of one who had never learned the art of deftly turning sentences. He began with an apology for bad spelling and poor writing in which he explained that it was the first letter he had attempted to write in seven years, for he had no one in the world who cared whether he lived or died. Then he thanked me for what I had said to them Sunday, adding, "You said you loved us. Nobody ever said that to me before in my whole life and I hardly know what the word means."

Maud Ballington Booth was born Maud Elizabeth Charlesworth, September 13, 1863, in Limpsfield, Surrey, England. In 1881 her mother took her to a Salvation Army meeting led by Ballington Booth, the son of General W. Booth, the founder of the organization. A year later her mother died, and she joined the group. She and Ballington's sister Catherine went to France and Switzerland to establish Salvation Armies there. Upon her return she went to the training home for women officers in London. She rejoined the "slum sisters," a group of women who lived in the slums while trying to reform them.

In September 1886 Maud married Ballington Booth and assumed both of his names. They departed for New York City to supervise the Salvation Army in America. They became citizens in 1895, but the next year they were recalled by General Booth. They resigned from the Salvation Army and started their own organization, the Volunteers of America. Many former Salvationists joined the new religious and humanitarian group, and by 1953 they had ninety-two posts.

After the Volunteers of America was firmly established, Maud left the administration to her husband to concentrate her efforts on prison reform. She started a similar organization, the Volunteer Prison League, whose goal was the religious rehabilitation of prisoners. While the Volunteer Prison League administered to prisoners' needs, the Volunteers of America took care of their families on the outside and helped secure employment for them upon their release. Maud opened "Hope Halls," homes for newly discharged prisoners in Flushing, New York, Chicago, and several other cities. Her concept of rehabilitating prisoners rather than punishing them was implemented with prison education programs, both academic and vocational. She achieved a very high rate of successful rehabilitation.

After Ballington's death in 1940, Maud, at the age of seventy-five, was elected general and commander-in-chief of the Volunteers of America. For the next seven years, she travelled across the country, visiting and lecturing at the organization's widely scattered posts. She died at the age of eighty-two at her daughter Theodora's home on Long Island.

Maud's writing is from her book After Prison — What?, *published by F. H. Revell Co. in 1903.*

Margaret Sanger

Liberty in marriage

1927

All I want is a little more freedom. That is not much to ask, but I must be able to feel that I can waste a whole night or day or week if I feel it good for me to do so without explanation or asking. I'm too grown up & too developed to not be free. My actions so far have been tempered with intelligence & I can't go back to chattel slavery. For that is what it really is dear when a woman is not made to feel that she can act without asking her husband's consent. Outside of financial affairs (which is & should be a joint affair between them) there should be utter liberty for both parties to enjoy tastes & friendships utterly free from the other. You will never see this I am certain, but until you can see it there will be no real happiness for the modern woman.

Margaret Louise Higgins Sanger was born September 14, 1879, in Corning, New York. Her mother bore and raised eleven children and died at the age of forty-nine. Margaret always blamed her mother's death on her excessive fertility and determined at a young age to become involved in women's fight for birth control.

Following a brief stint as an elementary school teacher, Margaret enrolled in nursing school at White Plains, New York. She completed two years of practical nursing and was about to begin a three-year degree program when she married William Sanger instead.

After the birth of her third child Margaret returned to nursing, becoming a home nurse on New York's Lower East Side. She soon discovered there was a serious need for information regarding birth control, sex education, and venereal disease. She started publishing articles on the subject for the socialist weekly, *The Call*. In 1913 her article on syphilis was deemed unmailable by the U.S. Post Office. The following year, another article on birth control was declared unmailable, and Margaret fled to Europe to continue her work.

Margaret's writing is from a letter written September 27, 1927, to her second husband, J. Noah Slee. It is included in Hear Me for My Cause, Selected Letters of Margaret Sanger, 1926-1927, *by Elizabeth S. Duvall, published by the Sophia Smith Collection, Smith College, Northampton, Massachusetts, in 1967.*

After witnessing numerous women's deaths from self-induced abortions, she decided to establish advice centers throughout the nation where women could receive birth control information. She spent time in the Netherlands studying their advice centers, which were run by midwives, and learning how to fit the new spring-loaded vaginal diaphragm.

Margaret returned to America in 1915 and opened her

Women's Words, Women's Stories

first birth control clinic with her sister Ethel in the Brownsville section of Brooklyn. She was only in business for ten days before the police closed her down, but during that short time she gave advice on contraception to 488 women.

Margaret divorced Sanger in 1920 and two years later married J. Noah Slee, the millionaire manufacturer of Three-in-One Oil. In 1923 she opened the Birth Control Clinic Research Bureau in New York City, the first such clinic in the United States to be staffed by physicians. Hundreds of doctors came to the clinic to learn about contraception, which was not taught in medical school at that time. Misinformation, such as that diaphragms did not work and only caused cancer and madness, was clinically disproved.

By 1938 Margaret had established more than 300 birth control clinics throughout the United States. She was forced to smuggle European-made diaphragms until 1925, when she convinced a friend to begin production in America with money provided by her husband. In 1936 the government reversed its 1873 decision that classified birth control as an obscenity, which allowed the American Medical Association to recognize contraception as a subject that should be taught in medical schools.

In the early 1940s Margaret and her husband moved to Tucson, Arizona. She curtailed her activities considerably, but never altogether. She introduced the work of biologist Gregory Pincas in 1952 to a wealthy female friend who funded his experiments with birth control pills until they were eventually marketed in 1960. Margaret died of heart failure in a Tucson nursing home in 1966 at the age of eighty-six.

Nancy Gardner Prince

1850

Sanctimony

My mother was not satisfied, and came after me. I would not go to Gloucester. She left me at a friend's, and this woman had a daughter, who came home from service, sick. I took her place, and thought myself fortunate to be with religious people, as I had enjoyed the happy privilege of religious instruction. . . .

There were seven in the family, one sick with a fever, and another in a consumption; and of course, the work must have been very severe, especially the washings. Sabbath evening I had to prepare for the wash; soap the clothes and put them into the steamer, set the

Nancy's writing is from her autobiography, A Narrative of the Life and Travels of Mrs. Nancy Prince, *published in 1850 by the author.*

kettle of water to boiling, and then close in the steam, and let the pipe from the boiler into the steam box that held the clothes. At two o'clock, on the morning of Monday, the bell was rung for me to get up; but, that was not all, they said I was too slow, and the washing was not done well; I had to leave the tub to tend the door and wait on the family, and was not spoken kind to, at that.

Hard labor and unkindness was too much for me; in three months, my health and strength were gone. I often looked at my employers, and thought to myself, is this your religion? I did not wonder that the girl who had lived there previous to myself, went home to die. They had family prayers, morning and evening. Oh! yes, they were sanctimonious! I was a poor stranger, but fourteen years of age. . . .

Nancy Gardner Prince was born September 15, 1799, in Newburyport, Massachusetts. Her father died when she was three months old. Her mother remarried and eventually produced eight children with four husbands. When Nancy was thirteen, her stepfather died, and she began a life of drudgery as a domestic to support her family.

Nancy was angry at the stifling racism in America, where she felt she could never be anything but a servant. In 1822 she quit her job to learn a trade (sewing clothes) with the intention of leaving the United States.

Nero Prince was a freeborn black man from Massachusetts, a sailor who had remained in St. Petersburg, Russia, since 1812 to serve as one of the twenty hall sentries at the czar's palace. Nancy met him in 1824 during his brief visit home, and she saw him as her ticket out of the country. They were married within two months and set sail for St. Petersburg.

Nancy lived in Russia for ten years and experienced "no prejudice against color." She mastered the language, was active in the Protestant church, and helped start an orphan asylum in St. Petersburg.

Nancy returned to America in 1833 following Nero's death and devoted herself to community service. She was searching for just the right humanitarian project, which she found at a lecture about emancipated slaves in Jamaica.

In 1840 Nancy departed for Jamaica where she established a Free Labor School. Nothing is known about her life after 1856, when she wrote in the preface to the third edition of her autobiography that her health was deteriorating and she had lost the use of her arms.

Karen Danielsen Horney

1911

Oskar simply takes a person as he is and in his great kindness lays more weight on the good in him with regard to his capacity for development than on the other, I am always quickly there with value judgments, trying to give opinions like "valuable" and "inferior" a definable or applicable content. Even with people I know, I avoid rather than seek association, here mostly with the idea that it is only a waste of time, nothing worthwhile would come of it. That this does in fact very often turn out to be so — at least from my point of view — is again in most cases my own fault. It is just as if I were afraid the conversation might go deep, especially that it might become too personal. A typical example of this was my attitude toward Frau H. I have a sincere sympathy for her, and at times when I longed to have a friend, I certainly thought she and I could be good friends. She has an open, simple, natural personality. She came to see me recently — and I managed to talk with her for 2 hours without our coming one bit closer. Apparently there was a repression there that brought about this behavior despite an honest wish to be close. . . .

Karen Danielsen Horney was born September 16, 1885, near Hamburg, Germany. At the age of twelve she was determined to become a doctor, and she and her mother united to combat her father's opposition to her attending college.

Karen married Oskar Horney, a law student, in 1909. Two years later she graduated with her M.D. degree from the University of Berlin and gave birth to her first daughter. Two more daughters were born during the next four years while she completed her residency and wrote her doctoral thesis.

In 1911 Karen began seeing a psychiatrist, one of Freud's Berlin disciples. Although unhappy with her treatment, she was nonetheless convinced of the benefits of psychoanalysis. In 1919 she became allied with the Berlin Psychoanalytic Clinic and Institute, where she lectured as well as treated patients.

Karen remained with the institute for twelve years, during

Her own fault

Karen's writing is from a January 2, 1911, entry in her diary. Her diaries were hidden and discovered posthumously by her daughter Renate. She, too, kept them hidden for twenty years until it was revealed to her in a dream that she possessed a "buried treasure." The diaries were published as The Adolescent Diaries of Karen Horney, *by Basic Books, Inc., in 1980.*

which time she separated from her husband. Karen rejected Freud's theories that emphasized female inferiority.

Karen moved to America in 1932 hoping for more freedom of expression and to avoid the Nazis, who condemned psychoanalysis. In 1941 she established the American Institute for Psychoanalysis, where she served as dean and edited a journal until her death.

From 1937 to 1950 Karen published five textbooks which were translated into thirteen languages. In November 1952, she discovered that she had cancer. It spread quickly, and she died within two weeks.

Mary Morris Talbert

The call

1914

Clear and insistent is the call to the women of my race to-day — the call to self-development, and to unselfish Service. We cannot turn a deaf ear to the cries of the neglected little children, the untrained youth, the aged and the poor. Wherever you have established a kindergarten, a day nursery, a Home of any sort, or a School; wherever you have stretched out a helping hand or spoken a kindly word or given a smile, you have answered nobly and well. Women of the Negro race, we must continue with ever-increasing intelligence and courage and zeal and faith, aye if need be, with our lives, to answer "the call of the hour."

Mary Morris Burnett Talbert was born September 17, 1866, in Oberlin, Ohio, the youngest of eight children born to free black parents. Her father had purchased land in Oberlin in 1860 and hoped to move his family there from North Carolina because of its excellent educational opportunities. The Civil War delayed his plans until 1865 when the family was finally able to relocate.

Mary's parents were successful in Ohio, her father as a barber and her mother as the proprietor of a restaurant and boarding house that catered to the Oberlin College community. Mary went to local public schools, was active in church, and took piano lessons. She enrolled in Oberlin College and received her S.P. degree in 1886 and her B.A. degree in 1894.

Mary's writing is from the November-December 1914 issue of National Notes, *the National Association of Colored Women's Clubs' publication.*

Mary's first job was as a mathematics, history, and Latin teacher in the segregated school system of Little Rock, Arkansas. Although she was aware of the insults and inequities suffered by blacks, she herself never encountered prejudice until her arrival in Little Rock. She taught for four years until her marriage in 1891 to William Talbert, a wealthy city clerk from Buffalo, New York.

For several years Mary took care of the household and raised her daughter Sarah. In 1899 she co-founded the Phillis Wheatley Club, a major force for change in Buffalo's black community. She organized meetings at her home with speakers such as Booker T. Washington and W. E. B. Du Bois. In 1905 she established the Buffalo chapter of the National Association for the Advancement of Colored People (NAACP) and served as its director.

Although Mary believed that black women had come far in recent years, she knew they could go farther. Black women, she observed, had to endure a "simultaneity of oppression" that included race, class, and sex discrimination. She saw this oppression worldwide, wherever black people lived.

From 1916 to 1920 Mary served as president of the National Association of Colored Women (NACW). In 1918 she began travelling throughout the South, establishing NACW branches in Texas and Louisiana. She purchased and restored the Frederick Douglass home in Washington, D.C., as a tribute to Douglass and black achievement. The home became NACW's national headquarters.

Mary spent World War I in France as YMCA secretary and Red Cross nurse. Fluent in several languages, she lectured on the conditions of black Americans and was the guest of Queen Wilhelmina of the Netherlands and Lady Aberdeen of Scotland. She died in 1923, soon after her return to Buffalo at the age of fifty-seven.

Mary Ann Farlow Vincent

1878

*O*verpowering surprise

My Dear Mr. Bowditch in attempting an expression of gratitude for your very great kindness to me I feel so agitated that my heart beats and my hand trembles almost as wildly as they did the other night when I received the basket of flowers you had so beautifully arranged for me. The surprise was overpowering and when I saw the pretty vase and its shining contents I shed tears of joy and happiness.

Such a tribute would have been delightful had I been a young woman but at my age away from home without any relatives near me it possesses a value that few can

Mary Ann's writing, from a February 25, 1878, letter to Dr. Vincent Y. Bowditch, is in the theater collection at Harvard University's Widener Library.

imagine. May God bless you for your kindness and restore it to you a thousand fold.

Mary Ann Farlow Vincent was born September 18, 1818, in Portsmouth, England. After she became an orphan at the age of four she was raised by her grandmother and aunt. At sixteen she ran away to the Isle of Wight and made her stage debut as a chambermaid in a George Colman comedy. She married the actor James R. Vincent and toured with him for several years throughout the British Isles.

In 1846 the Vincents moved to Boston to join the acting company of the National Theatre. James committed suicide four years later but Mary Ann, known professionally as Mrs. J. R. Vincent, remained at the National until it burned down in 1852. She then joined the Boston Museum Theatre Company. Except for spending the 1861-1862 season in Washington, D.C., where she was greatly admired by President Lincoln, she remained with the Boston Company until her death.

Mrs. Vincent established her reputation as a character actress. Her roles varied from classical comedy to French melodrama to Shakespeare. She was also known as somewhat of a character herself, renting out rooms to struggling actors in her rambling house which was filled with an assortment of dogs, cats, and birds. Once she almost missed a performance because she was out in the street waving her umbrella at a teamster who was working a lame horse.

On April 25, 1885, the Boston Museum Theatre Company celebrated Mrs. Vincent's fiftieth anniversary on the stage by presenting *She Stoops to Conquer* at the matinee and *The Rivals* in the evening, with Mrs. Vincent starring in both. Two years later she became ill after her performance in *The Dominie's Daughter*. She died of a stroke several days later at the age of sixty-eight. After her death her many fans, mourning the death of Boston's "dear old lady," raised funds to build a hospital in her honor. Vincent Memorial Hospital was dedicated in 1891, and the Vincent Club was formed to help maintain it. The club is still in operation today. It stages annual theatrical performances to raise funds for the hospital.

Rosetta Sherwood Hall

1890

Buddhism has been placed under ban by the reigning King, and though the lower class have some forms of demon worship and the upper class are influenced by Confucianism, yet Korea has no recognized religion. Her people seem waiting for the 'Good News' that the missionaries of Christ bring. Indeed you are sometimes stopped upon the street and thanked for coming so far to tell *'Chosen saram'* about God and Jesus Christ, His Son. They are an extremely grateful people, always anxious to do something in return for any favor shown them. The other day in the hospital a poor woman said she wanted to sell her body to get me a present for making her little son well.

I like my work in Korea and I thank the Lord for sending me here. He is so good. In Seoul there are scarcely twenty-five missionaries, counting missionaries' wives. What are they among a million people? But among the remaining eleven millions of Korean people outside of the capital there is no missionary, though there are three ports open to foreigners. . . . *The harvest truly is great, but the laborers are few.*

A missionary

Rosetta Sherwood Hall was born September 19, 1865, in Liberty, New York. After graduating from State Normal School in 1883, she taught for three years until she heard a lecture on medical missions in India and decided to become a doctor. After graduating from the Woman's Medical College of Pennsylvania, she began working at a Methodist Mission Dispensary in New York City. There she met and fell in love with William James Hall, the medical superintendent at the dispensary.

In August 1890 Rosetta was sent to Seoul, Korea, to a small women's hospital run by the Methodist Woman's Foreign Missionary Society. William went over the following year and they were married in June 1892. Two years later, William contracted typhus fever and died, leaving Rosetta pregnant. She and her young son returned to her parents' home in Liberty, New York, where she gave birth to her daughter four days after her arrival.

Rosetta refused to abandon her missionary career and returned to Korea in 1897. Her daughter died of amoebic

Rosetta's writing is from a letter to her family dated October 10, 1890, and is included in With Stethoscope in Asia: Korea, published in 1978 by MCL Associates, McLean, Virginia.

dysentery in May 1898, but her son grew up to become a doctor in Korea and later, India. Rosetta remained in Korea for thirty-five years. She established several hospitals, the Women's Medical Training Institute, and the Institute for the Blind and Deaf.

Rosetta returned to America after her sixty-eighth birthday. She took care of her sick stepbrother and practiced medicine for another ten years in upstate New York. She retired to a New Jersey rest home for Methodist missionaries in 1943 and died there of pneumonia in 1951. Her ashes were buried beside her husband and daughter in Seoul.

Isabel Mack Willson

A brazen stranger

1939

Overloaded as usual, mostly the passengers were men, but back in the corner was a slim young girl, with smooth brown hair and a witching smile in her eyes. The men piled out, each one as he did so jockeying for a position where he could assist the young lady to alight. Their gallantry was lost, however, for she looked right past them all to where her aunt and uncle were standing. "Uncle Finley," she called, reaching out her arms. Two minutes later "Mollie" was in her Aunt Martha's embrace, and they were all laughing and crying with joy, amid home chatter and her account of the long and exciting journey. But what had happened as she was about to jump down from the stage? Who was the tall blond person with jingling spurs on his boots, a wide-brimmed black hat, bright blue handkerchief knotted at his throat? Who indeed was this brazen creature that had caught her in his arms, lifted her down from the stage and carried her a few steps to set her down by her Aunt Martha, then instantly vanished into thin air?

Isabel Mack Willson was born September 20, 1865, in Kingston, Ohio. Her father had served for three years in the Union Army until he suffered a permanent injury when a cavalry horse fell on him. Her mother died when she was five, after which her father enrolled in the Episcopal Theological School in Nashota, Wisconsin.

After her father became an ordained minister, Isabel

Isabel's writing is from her autobiography Cabin Days in Wyoming, *privately printed in 1939.*

travelled with him on his missions to the Indians of northern
Wisconsin. She later reminisced: "I 'helped' by playing the
chants and a few hymns, mostly with one hand, on a little
organ he took with him wherever possible. Our cathedral was
the great forest of towering pines, a most appropriate setting
for these primitive people of the open spaces."

In 1886 Isabel graduated from Wolfe Hall in Denver.
Three years later she graduated from nursing school in
Chicago. That July she married Eugene B. Willson, a long-
time resident of Wyoming and well-established rancher and
stockman. They lived at the Running Water Ranch near
Lusk, Wyoming, and had four children.

After ten years on the ranch the Willsons moved into the
town of Lusk to be closer to the public school system. Isabel
was glad to be in town "because of the association with
women and their activities, which during the early ranch days
was impossible." She joined the Eastern Star Organization,
the Niobrara County War Mothers' Association, and was first
Chairwoman of the Lusk Red Cross. At her death she was
serving as state chairwoman of the Committee for the
Marking of Old Trails.

Ethel Percy Andrus

*circa
1955*

*W*hen learning stops

Some persons tragically cease to be curious at twenty;
others regretfully at forty, many — and these are the
fortunate ones — never cease to be till death. Yet there
are others who cease to look for new experiences.
When this happens, senility approaches and the oldster
tends to live in his memories to exalt the past. The
doctors call it *misoneism*, a dislike of and a distaste for
something new. This is the cardinal symptom of
senility. After it appears and is recognized, it may be
already too late to do anything about it. The Chinese
proverb tells us, "Learning is like rowing up stream;
not to advance is to drop behind."

Ethel Percy Andrus was born September 21, 1884, in San
Francisco. Soon after her birth, the family moved to
Chicago, so that her father could complete his law degree at
the University of Chicago. After attending local public
schools, Ethel received her bachelor's degree from the
University of Chicago in 1903. For the next seven years, she

*Ethel's writing is from "The
Aged and the Retired," which is
included in* The Wisdom of
Ethel Percy Andrus, *a collec-
tion of editorials she wrote
through the years for the
National Retired Teachers
Association Journal and
Modern Maturity. The collec-
tion was edited by her niece,
Dorothy Crippen, and others
and was published by the
NRTA and AARP in 1968.*

taught English and German at the Lewis Institute (later the Illinois Institute of Technology) while studying for a B.S. degree.

Ethel moved to California in 1910. In 1916 at the age of thirty-two she became the principal of Abraham Lincoln High School in East Los Angeles, the first female principal in the state.

When Ethel arrived at Lincoln High School it had 2,500 students of varied backgrounds with a high delinquency rate and a reputation for "lawlessness." She decided that the role of the school was to help each pupil find fulfillment according to his or her unique nature. To overcome community hostility and involve parents in their children's education she established an evening Opportunity School, which offered a variety of courses. The neighborhood crime rate dropped noticeably, for which she received a special citation from the East Los Angeles juvenile court in 1940.

Ethel was forced to retire in 1944 to take care of her mother. Her state pension was only $60 a month, and although she had other income, she realized many other teachers worked their entire lives only to end by struggling to survive on their tiny pensions. In 1947 she founded the National Retired Teachers Association (NRTA). In 1956 after years of fighting for low-cost insurance for retired teachers, she helped establish the first health insurance plan for people over sixty-five. Two years later, pressured by retired people in all walks of life, she founded the American Association of Retired Persons (AARP) which helped to extend the benefits she had won for teachers to a broader population. Ethel gave older people a voice, and the AARP continues to operate today as a powerful lobbying force in Congress.

Ethel's second career as a spokeswoman for the aged was as rewarding as her first career. She encouraged retired people to remain active and begin a second career, for which she founded several Institutes of Life Long Learning around the United States to offer classes geared to retirees' needs. Ethel died in Long Beach, California, in 1967 at the age of eighty-two.

Anna Maria Green Cook

1864

For three weeks I adhered to my resolution and purposes about air castle building &c. but during the past week my thoughts have again been dreams of love. Bryan Thomas has been at home, I am not in love with him for I do not know him sufficiently, but still two . . . schoolmates have been married in the past month, and . . . I long for one manly heart to love and care for me, and Bryan Thomas is handsome and I think a man I could admire, but still it is unmaidenly to write this and my face burns. . . .

Mr. Gesner came out to see me last Monday evening I enjoyed his visit very much though terribly frightened from several remarks he made indicating his fancy for me. . . . I was not as much frightened as I expected, but he did it in such an indirect manner. After my telling him this morning that I would not correspond with him and no gentleman unless engaged he asked me this afternoon to [agree to] those conditions. I merely said I could not.

Of course I would not marry Mr. G. — a widower with four children. . . . I should regret the circumstance much more did I think Mr. G. was in love with me, but I do not think his affections are at all enlisted — he is seeking a mother for his children, a mistress in his home. In courting me the argument that shall win must be I love you. Tis what I long for, the key to my heart is that simple word love. . . .

Anna Maria Green Cook was born September 22, 1844, in Milledgeville, Georgia, the seventh of eight children. Her mother died in 1860. The following year Anna Maria enrolled in the Southern Masonic Female College at Covington. After graduating with honors, she returned home with the sole purpose of finding a husband.

Anna Maria attended parties, read popular fiction, and took music lessons. The Civil War provided an endless stream of army men through the area, and she dated six different soldiers in six years. At the end of the war, she became engaged to Adlai Osborn Houston, widower of her late oldest

Love is the key

Anna Maria's writing is from her January 30, 1864, journal entry. Her journal is in the Green-Cook Collection of the University of Georgia Library and is included in The Journal of a Milledgeville Girl, *edited by James C. Bonner and published by the University of Georgia Press, 1964.*

sister. Although she did not love him, she felt she could be a mother to his children.

Anna Maria probably would have married Adlai out of duty, but he became ill and died. She was at his bedside through his illness and death. She returned home and soon after met her future husband, Samuel Austin Cook. Samuel was a patient of her father's who was being treated for alcoholism. He was one of the twenty percent of paying clients at the County Insane Asylum, and due to his family's wealth and prominence, he was allowed to roam the facility freely and often played the piano in the Greens' parlor.

Anna Maria married Samuel Cook on December 31, 1867. They had ten children, four of whom died in infancy and two others in their teens. Anna Maria survived her husband, all of her siblings, and most of her children. A devout Methodist, she prayed to be allowed to die on the Sabbath. She passed away at the age of ninety-two on a Sunday, in the same room and at the same hour as her husband had passed away twenty-five years earlier.

Mary Church Terrell

Barred by color

Mary's writing is taken from her autobiography, A Colored Woman in a White World, *published by Ronsdell, Inc., in 1940.*

1940
Uncle Tom's Cabin was to be played at one of the theatres. I wanted my girls to see it, and they were eager to see it also. But it was produced at a second-rate theatre whose accommodations for white people were none too good and whose arrangements for colored people were simply out of the question. That was the first time I had to explain to them that we would have to be very careful indeed because colored people were not allowed to sit in the good seats in the desirable part of the theatre where I hoped to buy tickets for them. There are few things more heart-breaking for a colored mother than to be obliged to explain to her children that they can not go where children of other racial groups may go, and they can not see what those favored children may see.

Mary Eliza Church Terrell was born September 23, 1863, in Memphis, Tennessee. Her father, a former slave, opened a saloon after he was freed by his master, who was also his father. During the yellow fever epidemic of 1878-1879 he invested all his money in bargain-priced real estate as people fled the city, becoming the South's first black millionaire. Mary's parents divorced when she was six, and she was sent to board with a family in Ohio.

Mary attended Oberlin College where she took the four-year men's course instead of the two-year ladies' curriculum. Being light-skinned she could pass for white, but she was proud of her race and determined to prove that a black student could excel academically.

In October 1891 Mary married Robert Heberton Terrell, one of the first black graduates of Harvard. They settled in Washington, D.C., where she began a long career in community service. She served for eleven years on the District of Columbia Board of Education and was president for life of the National Association of Colored Women. She joined the suffragist cause and lectured at the 1898 convention of the National American Woman Suffrage Association on "The Progress of Colored Women." Beginning in the 1920s Mary served as an advisor to the Republican National Committee, assisting black women with their newly won right to vote.

Mary had a successful thirty-year career as a lecturer on such topics as racial injustice, black history and culture, and the black woman's advancement since Emancipation. She also wrote for newspapers and magazines, ending with the publication in 1940 of her autobiography, *A Colored Woman in a White World.*

At the age of eighty-seven Mary staged a sit-in at a Washington restaurant in an attempt at desegregation. Her efforts failed, so she sued and took her case all the way to the Supreme Court, where she was victorious. Mary died just short of her ninety-first birthday.

Frances Watkins Harper

1858

Oh, how I miss New England, — the sunshine of its homes and the freedom of its hills! . . . Do you know that two of the brightest, most sunshiny (is not that tautology?) years of my life, since I have reached womanhood, were spent in New England? Dear old New England! It was there kindness encompassed my path; it was there kind voices made their music in my ear. The home of my childhood, the burial place of my kindred, is not as dear to me as New England.

Now let me tell you about Pennsylvania. I have been travelling nearly four years, and have been in

The meanest place

Frances's writing is from a letter published in The Liberator, *April 23, 1858.*

every New England State, in New York, Canada and Ohio: but of all these places, this is about the meanest of all, as far as the treatment of colored people is concerned. I have been insulted in several railroad cars. The other day, in attempting to ride in one of the city cars, after I had entered, the conductor came to me, and wanted me to go out on the platform. Now, was not that brave and noble? As a matter of course, I did not. Some one interfered, and asked or requested that I might be permitted to sit in a corner. I did not move, but kept the same seat. When I was about to leave, he refused my money, and I threw it down on the car floor, and got out, after I had ridden as far as I wished. Such impudence! . . .

I have met, of course, with kindness among individuals and families; all is not dark in Pennsylvania; but the shadow of slavery, oh how drearily it hangs!

Frances Ellen Watkins Harper was born September 24, 1825, in Baltimore, Maryland, the only child of free black parents. Following their deaths when she was not yet three, she was raised by an uncle at his school for free blacks.

Frances's first book of prose and poetry was published in 1845. Soon thereafter she took a teaching job in Pennsylvania, but her anti-slavery beliefs caused her to speak out repeatedly on behalf of the black race. She gave her first abolitionist lecture in New Bedford, Massachusetts, in 1854. For the next six years she travelled throughout New England, New York, New Jersey, Pennsylvania, and Ohio as a lecturer for the Anti-Slavery Society.

In 1854 Frances published a book of anti-slavery verse, *Poems on Miscellaneous Subjects*, from which she often quoted in her lectures. She contributed to all the black periodicals of the day and in 1859 produced the first published short story by an American black. She donated much of her income to assist fugitive slaves.

In 1860 Frances married Fenton Harper and settled on his Ohio farm. After his death four years later she returned to the lecture circuit. Her main themes were blacks' need for education, high moral standards, and temperance. She became a leader in both the National Women's Christian Temperance Union and the American Association of Education of Colored Youth, and she continued to write, publishing several new volumes of poetry. Frances died in Philadelphia in 1911 at the age of eighty-five.

1888

I heard the bell toll twice distinctly, as she swayed on
the uprooted bridge, and then came the horrible crash
and the fierce hissing of the stream as tender and
engine went down in twenty-five feet of water, told the
nature of the fate that had overtaken them. The shock
seemed to shake the earth. "Oh, Mother," I said, "it is
No. eleven. They have gone down Honey Creek
Bridge." It seemed as still as death; as silent as the
grave. The storm and all else was forgotten and I said
that I must go to the help of the men, and to stop the
passenger train that would soon be due at Moingona,
the midnight train from the West. Remonstrance was
of no avail — I felt I had to go. I believe that God
makes strong the weakest, and makes the poorest of us
able to endure much for his merciful purposes. When
they found that I was not to be dissuaded, Mother said
"Go then in the name of God, and do what you can." I
had on an old skirt and jacket. I caught up an old straw
hat, improvised a light by hanging a little miner's lamp
in the frame of an old lantern. I filled the little lamp,
and for a wick cut a strip from an old felt skirt and
started out into the night and the storm, to do what I
could, and what I thought was my duty, knowing that
Mother and the children were praying God to keep me
from every harm.

Kate Shelley was born September 25, 1865, in Ireland.
Before her first birthday the family emigrated to America.
Her father bought a farm in Moingona, Iowa, and took a job
with the Chicago & Northwestern Railroad which ran within
sight of their house.

    Kate's father and brother died when she was thirteen. Her
mother never totally recovered from her grief, forcing Kate to
assume the responsibilities of head of the household. One
evening when she was fifteen years old Kate heard a train
plunge through a nearby bridge during a severe wind and rain
storm. She ran through the night, across treacherous terrain,
to reach the station at Moingona. Station officials alerted the
approaching passenger train in time, saving all 200 people on
board. Next, Kate led them to the crash site where they were

Into the night

*Kate's writing is from a lecture
she gave in 1888. A photostatic
copy of the original manuscript
is in the files of the Order of
Railway Conductors and
Brakemen Records at the Labor
Management Documentation
Center, Cornell University.*

able to rescue two of the four trainmen, who were clinging to trees in the rushing water.

Kate became an instant popular heroine. Her exploits were covered in major newspapers, songs and poems were written, and numerous awards were bestowed upon her. The state of Iowa presented her with $200 and a gold medal designed by Tiffany. The Chicago & Northwestern Railroad gave her food, coal, $100, a gold medal, and a life-time pass to ride the railroad. As a special bonus, whenever she rode the train it would stop and let her off in front of her home.

Kate grew up and became a teacher. Twenty years after her ordeal she was proud to bring along her class when a new iron bridge was dedicated in her honor.

In 1903 Kate assumed the position of railroad station agent at Moingona, a position she held proudly until her untimely death nine years later at the age of forty-seven. Today there is a Kate Shelley Memorial Park and Railroad Museum at Moingona, and the lantern she carried that stormy night is enshrined at the Iowa Museum of the State Department of History and Archives.

SEPTEMBER 26

Adelaide Johnson

*W*ithout her glasses

1907

In 1866 the making of a portrait bust of Miss Anthony was suggested to her and to me by Ellen H. Sheldon.... So it was now twenty-one years ago my first model of the portrait bust — and I believe the very first — of Susan B. Anthony, was made, for which she gave unstinted sittings. . . . At the annual Woman Suffrage Convention at Washington, in 1887 the general impression and frequent remark was, "Well, Yes, that is Miss Anthony, if only the glasses were there" — as Miss Anthony had, since early childhood worn glasses, and was, therefore only known to her friends, with them.

Adelaide's writing is from a speech she delivered February 15, 1907, at the United States Capitol before her sculpture of Susan B. Anthony. The speech was included in the March 10, 1934, issue of Equal Rights *Magazine.*

Adelaide Johnson was born September 26, 1859, in Plymouth, Illinois. She studied at the St. Louis Art School, and went to Chicago to study further, supporting herself by woodcarving. While in Chicago she accidentally fell down an elevator shaft at the Central Music Hall, sued, and used her $15,000 settlement to pay for a trip abroad to study sculpture.

Adelaide spent a year in Dresden, Germany, followed by eleven years in Rome studying with Giulio Monteverde. An ardent feminist, she decided the women's movement was "the mightiest thing in the evolution of humanity" and took it upon herself to immortalize the leaders of the movement through her sculptures. In 1893 she exhibited busts of Lucretia Mott, Elizabeth Cady Stanton, and Susan B. Anthony at the Woman's Pavilion of the World's Columbian Exposition in Chicago.

In January 1896 Adelaide married an English businessman, Alexander F. Jenkins. Although he was twenty-five and she was thirty-six, she altered her age on the marriage certificate to twenty-four. They were married by a woman minister in Adelaide's studio with busts of Elizabeth Cady Stanton and Susan B. Anthony serving as "bridesmaids." He took her name, becoming Mr. and Mrs. Johnson, as "the tribute love pays to genius." However, she came to feel that they had lost the "spiritual consciousness" they had shared, and they were divorced in 1908.

Adelaide dreamed of establishing a museum of the history of the women's movement and of placing a women's monument at the United States Capitol. She approached the National American Woman Suffrage Association for funding, but Susan B. Anthony preferred to place the statue at the Library of Congress, and a rift ensued. She received assistance instead from the National Woman's Party. On February 15, 1921, Susan B. Anthony's birthday, Adelaide's seven-ton marble sculpture, "The Woman's Movement" was presented to the nation on behalf of American women. Her work gave historical significance to the women's movement and remains to this day the only national monument to the movement.

Adelaide's career declined during the 1930s although her sculpture of Anthony was used as a model for the 1936 three-cent postage stamp. She refused to sell her work, finding the prices offered "an affront," and she was threatened with the loss of her home for failure to pay taxes. In 1939 devastated by the realization that her women's museum would never materialize, she defaced many of her sculptures after inviting the press to witness the destruction. Having made herself twelve years younger in 1896, she made herself twelve years older in the late 1940s and celebrated her "one hundredth through one hundredth and eighth" birthdays with fanfare and publicity. She died of a stroke in 1955 at the actual age of ninety-six.

Aubertine Woodward Moore

Better than cosmetics

1919

A young woman asked me recently what cosmetic I used to keep my skin pure, clear, and unwrinkled. She evidently did not believe me when I said I used none. If you keep the body wholesome within and without and the spirit serene, you will require no outward lotion beyond plenty of pure clear water and a moderate amount of pure soap, to make the skin clean and wholesome. The admonition of my mother's Aunt has always been with me. "Trust in God, and possess the soul in peace. Then all will go well with thee." It is the serenity of spirit that banishes wrinkles and scowls and sullen looks.

Aubertine Woodward Moore was born September 27, 1841, near Philadelphia. She attended local public schools and studied music, giving piano concerts along the East Coast.

During the 1870s, Aubertine became interested in foreign literature and began translating novels from the German and French. In 1877 she translated the *Nibelungenlied*, a German epic poem based on Teutonic myths. As German myths were similar to Norse myths, her publisher put her in touch with Rasmus Bjórn Anderson, a professor of Scandinavian languages at the University of Wisconsin. He invited her to move into his home in Madison, Wisconsin, to help him popularize Norwegian literature in America.

Aubertine moved to Madison in 1879, learned Norwegian, and published her first translation the following year. In 1880 Anderson was asked by Houghton, Mifflin and Company to translate seven of Bjórnstjerne Bjórnson's novels to commemorate his visit to the United States. Although Anderson got the credit, it was actually Aubertine who did the work. In 1866 she translated nine essays from the Danish, again under Anderson's name.

Aubertine's writing is from a 1919 essay "How I Keep Fit," which she submitted to a "Keep Fit Contest" sponsored by the Physical Culture Publishing Company. It is in the Aubertine Moore Collection, State Historical Society of Wisconsin Archives, Madison, Wisconsin.

Aubertine married Samuel H. Moore, a Madison building contractor, in 1887 at the age of forty-six. Thereafter she returned to her original love, music, teaching from 1900 to 1912 at Madison Musical College. She gave lectures and recitals on the history of Scandinavian music, translated numerous essays and songs from Norwegian, and published in 1881 the *Norway Music Album*, a collection of traditional dances, folk songs, and contemporary music. She died at home in 1929, five days before her eighty-eighth birthday from complications from a fall. She was buried in Madison's Forest Hill Cemetery.

Kate Douglas Wiggin

1923

The journey to California was taken after waiting many weeks in Maine for a proper duenna. One was never found, and my parents, being anxious that I should join them, consented at length to the only available escort, a newly resigned Lieutenant of the Navy, going as far as Utah to the ranch he had recently bought. I knew him well, and so did all my elderly friends. He was an engaged man, which rendered him in their minds as safe as a man is ever likely to be, even under the most favorable circumstances, and he was to be joined in Albany by a younger brother who was to share his ranching experiences, so that we should be a party of three.

Never could a girl of seventeen be chaperoned more imprudently, safely, and delightfully than by two gentlemen aged respectively thirty-eight and twenty-two. Both were like big brothers; both were knights of chivalry. . . . We were very sad when we parted at Ogden, for I had to make the rest of my journey alone, until I met my stepfather in San Francisco.

A trip west

Kate Douglas Smith Wiggin was born September 28, 1856, in Philadelphia. Her father died when she was a toddler, and her mother remarried a man from Maine. When Kate was seventeen the family moved to California, seeking a healthier climate for her ailing stepfather. His death three years later left them financially destitute, forcing Kate to take up writing to earn money.

Kate submitted her first story to *St. Nicholas Magazine*; it was immediately accepted for publication. Despite this early success she turned away from writing in favor of working with children.

In 1878 Kate was asked to run the first free kindergarten in California, located in "the wretchedest of slums" in San Francisco. She relinquished the job to her sister Nora three years later when she married Samuel Bradley Wiggin, a lawyer. They moved to New York City where she continued her kindergarten work and resumed writing.

Kate's writing is from her autobiography, My Garden of Memory, *published posthumously in 1923.*

After only eight years of marriage, Samuel died suddenly. Kate spent much of her time at her mother's home in Maine. She published several children's books as well as three popular adult books, and earned extra money by giving public readings.

At the age of thirty-eight Kate married George C. Riggs, a New York City businessman. She described his support and pride in her literary endeavors as a "sustaining force" in her life. Her most popular novel, *Rebecca of Sunnybrook Farm*, appeared in 1903.

Kate died of bronchial pneumonia in 1923 while on a trip to England as a delegate to the Dickens Fellowship. As she had requested, her ashes were returned to America to be scattered over the Saco River near the family home in Maine.

SEPTEMBER 29

Gertrude Barnum

The striker

1905

It was during the Fall River strike, and Mary was one of the hundred and thirty mill girls brought to Boston by our League to enter domestic service. She had wrenched herself from her forlorn family after a sleepless night of dread. She had braved her first journey to a great bewildering city to begin life all over at thirty-four. She sat in a dark and crowded room, herded with a hundred other "domestics." The old "rounders" and the timid, green Irish and Nova Scotia girls were eyeing her as a "striker," with curiosity and hostility. The pasteboard dress box and bundle at her feet were the worse for wear and for the rain. She might have been forty-five from her appearance — round shouldered, anaemic and nervous. The strained eyes behind their glasses were excited and alert.

"I can't write," she whispered, as I gave her a record blank to fill. "I never got much schoolin'." There was something peculiarly pathetic in her mortification at this admission and in her efforts to cover her bursting bundles with her dress skirt.

Gertrude's writing is from "Story of a Fall River Girl," published in the February 2, 1905, issue of The Independent.

Gertrude Barnum was born September 29, 1866, in Chester, Illinois. Her father was a prominent judge and leading Democrat in Chicago. As she matured and became aware of the poverty in Chicago's slums, she gradually rejected her family's wealth and social status, even refusing to participate in her debutante party.

During the late 1890s Gertrude worked at Jane Addams' (September 6) Hull House, and from 1902 to 1903 at the Henry Booth House, another Chicago settlement. She decided to devote herself to the labor movement to eradicate the need for charity and settlement houses. She joined the National Women's Trade Union League and served as an organizer, supervising strike activities. She assisted in the strikes of female textile mill operators in Fall River, Massachusetts; laundry workers in Troy, New York; and corset workers in Aurora, Illinois. She concentrated on publicizing the strikes and their causes so as to inform the public and win their sympathy.

From 1911 to 1916 Gertrude worked as an organizer and publicist for the International Ladies' Garment Workers' Union. She approached New York City's civic leaders, socialites, and college students, demanding that they get involved and contribute money. She believed that "Society is in disgrace for its apathy under conditions which threaten the very lives of the future mothers of the race. The leisure class should not be outdone by the workers in courage and self-sacrifice."

Gertrude was appointed in 1914 as special agent for President Woodrow Wilson's United States Commission on Industrial Relations. From 1918 to 1919 she served as director of the investigation service of the Department of Labor. She retired from all labor reform activities in 1919 and settled in Berkeley, California. She died in Los Angeles in 1948 at the age of eighty-one.

Anne Henrietta Martin

1920

The oppressed

What is the remedy? Will the live-stock interests subdivide their holdings? Will pigs fly? The stockman's motto is "What I have I hold," down to the last drop of water. I have seen large quantities of it overflowing the ditches and running to waste on the fields and roads of company ranches producing a rich crop of willows and tules after irrigating the wild hay lands. Across the road were the scattered "dugouts" and cabins of settlers who under great difficulties had cleared a few acres of sage-brush land. They were struggling to "prove up" and sustain life for their families and themselves on a

Anne's writing is from "Every Woman's Chance to Serve Humanity," Good Housekeeping, February 1920.

"dry" farm, as their entire water supply was from a well. Staring at us through the sage-brush or clinging to their mother's skirts were two or three eerie little children, timid as jack-rabbits, growing up without school or toys, in ignorance even of children's games. Sooner or later these settlers are starved out, as Nevada is literally the "driest" State in the Union (as regards rainfall), and dry-farming is hopeless. These failures please the large owners; they do not want homesteaders "fussing about," fencing the land on their own government range, and breaking the continuity of their holdings.

Anne Henrietta Martin was born September 30, 1875, in Empire City, Nevada. She graduated from the University of Nevada at nineteen and received a master's degree in history from Stanford University, studying under Mary Sheldon Barnes. She was a tennis champion at both schools as well as an excellent horseback rider, golfer, and mountain climber.

After graduation Anne founded the History Department at the University of Nevada and became its first head. She resigned after her father died in 1901 because her inheritance enabled her to travel extensively throughout Europe and Asia. She spent two years in England where she joined a group of militant suffragettes and was arrested several times for demonstrating. Upon her return to the United States in 1912, she was elected president of the Nevada Equal Franchise Society. Within two years she saw her state suffrage amendment win at the polls to become law.

Anne next turned her attentions to the national suffrage movement. She served on numerous committees, attended many conventions, and became vice-chairman of the National Woman's Party. In 1917 she was arrested for picketing the White House. In 1918 she became the first Nevada woman to run for state senator, and she resigned all positions to return to Nevada to concentrate on her campaign. Although she lost two elections, Anne was a role model for other women. She chose to ignore the established, male-dominated political parties to run as an independent. Her platform supported aid to mothers and children, farmers, miners, and other oppressed laborers.

In 1921 Anne moved with her mother to California, where she wrote feminist essays for American and British magazines. She urged women to challenge men's control, run for office themselves, or support women who were running for office. She was impatient with the inequality between the sexes, stating, "Equality for women is a passion with me." She continued writing and lecturing to women's groups until her death in 1951.

OCTOBER

Fannie Moore Richards

1915

There never was a day when I wasn't glad to go to the children — when I did not really enjoy what I had to do. For years before I came into the system, you know, there had been separate schools for the colored and the white children, but though I was the first colored teacher in Detroit I never felt the least discrimination against me. So kindly were all the teachers with whom I worked and the children whom I taught that I actually had to look in the glass to realize that I was colored. I loved my boys and girls, Negro, Jew, and German, as they came to me in the many changes that 44 years in one district will bring. The mixture was interesting to watch in the class room, for while the Jewish children led in arithmetic, and the German children were the best thinkers, the colored children were the best read-ers, almost orators, I might say. The colored boys and girls had the feeling and the voices for expressive read-ing and no one takes keener pleasure in the progress that the Negroes have made in an educational way in Detroit than I have.

In the classroom

Fannie Moore Richards was born October 1, 1840, in Fredericksburg, Virginia. Her father was of noble black ancestry. He was born in Guadeloupe, educated in London, and moved to Virginia in search of a milder climate for his health. Her mother was a free black woman from Toronto.

Virginia laws forbade anyone to sit or stand to teach a black. Fannie and her older siblings attended a clandestine school in a private home. So as not to be discovered sitting or standing in violation of the law, teachers often reclined on couches while instructing. They also kept wood splinters handy so they could pretend to be teaching the children to make matches.

The Richards family moved to Detroit in 1851 after the death of Mr. Richards. Fannie attended local public schools and graduated from normal school in Toronto. She took postgraduate courses in Germany, where she was introduced to the new concept of kindergarten. In 1863 she returned to Detroit and began teaching at Colored School 2, becoming the first full-time professional black teacher in the city. At the time, whites received twelve years of schooling while

Fannie's words are from an interview, "Colored Teacher Loved Children and Enjoyed Forty-four Years in Service," published shortly after her retire-ment, in the June 20, 1915, Detroit News Tribune.

blacks received only six. Fannie helped lead the crusade for desegregation, which went all the way to the state Supreme Court. When a favorable court decision was handed down, Fannie Richards and her pupils cheered. They formed a circle, held hands, and danced around the room.

For more than forty years Fannie taught at Detroit's Everett Elementary School, part of the time as the city's first kindergarten teacher.

In 1898 Fannie helped start the Phillis Wheatley Home, an organization that cared for elderly black women. Over the years Fannie regularly gave half her annual salary to the home, which remained in operation until 1967.

Fannie retired in June 1915. She died seven years later at the age of eighty-one. In 1970 artist Carl Owens presented a portrait of Fannie to the Detroit Historical Commission, and the Detroit Public Library presented an exhibition about her work. The mayor of Detroit declared October 1, 1975, Fannie Richards Day. Fannie firmly believed, "It is through education that blacks are going to make their mark."

OCTOBER 2

Hannah Adams

Growing old

Hannah's writing is from A Memoir of Miss Hannah Adams, Written by Herself. *She wrote her memoirs to earn money for her sickly younger sister, and they were published by Boston, Gray and Bowen a year after her death in 1832.*

1810

Old age is upon me, and some of its infirmities; my memory is much impaired, and my mind, in temporal things and subjects, becomes very desultory. Not so in spirituals: I think, I not only hear and read with more intense attention; and prompt application; but my mind is more disposed to meditation; and though I cannot remember much of the sermons I hear, yet my mind is often furnished with happy and profitable thoughts on the same subjects; and I find myself instructed, without remembering the instructions.

Hannah Adams was born October 2, 1755, in Medfield, Massachusetts. A shy, sickly child, she rarely attended school and preferred instead to stay in her room reading poetry and fiction. Financial need forced the family to take in boarders, one of whom taught Hannah Greek and Latin, and another, religion.

Hannah became fascinated with the world's religions and spent her spare time studying them and taking notes. She earned a meager income from tutoring and from weaving bobbin lace until it occurred to her to publish her notes. *An Alphabetical Compendium of the Various Sects* was published in

Women's Words, Women's Stories

1784. The book was reprinted four times in the United States and three times in England, earning enough money for Hannah to pay her debts and start a savings account. She became the first American woman to support herself by writing.

She had several influential mentors among Boston's intellectuals. William S. Shaw, director of the Boston Athenaeum, gave her reading privileges at the Athenaeum, making her the first woman to be allowed to study there. James Freeman, minister of King's Chapel, gave her help in getting her work published, and the Reverend Joseph Buckminster allowed her to use his 3,000-volume collection of theological works. Hannah wrote several historical volumes, most notably *A Summary History of New England*, *History of the Jews*, and *Letters on the Gospels*.

Hannah never married. In her later years she was thought to be an eccentric. She often talked to herself, and in conversation frequently punctuated her sentences with a pinch of snuff. She died in 1831 at the age of seventy-six.

Clara Thompson

1964

There is also the woman of fifty, who hopes, by dyeing her hair, having her face lifted, and wearing youthful clothes, to have the sexual charm and allure of a woman of thirty. She is doomed to failure in her attempts at salvaging her misspent life. People sometimes come to analysis for miracles. One must first face and come to terms with the fact that one can never make up for lost years. One can only hope to live from now on. And for that, middle age is not too late to begin.

Clara Thompson was born October 3, 1893, in Providence, Rhode Island. She attended Classical High School and declared at fifteen that she was going to be a medical missionary in India. Thereafter she concentrated on her studies, graduating in 1912 with the highest honors. She began pre-medical courses at Pembroke College, the women's school at Brown University. Due to family pressure, she gradually abandoned her dream of being a missionary and settled on medicine alone.

Clara entered Johns Hopkins Medical School in 1916 after refusing to marry a major in the Army Medical Corps who demanded that she give up her medical aspirations. At

*F*rom now on

Clara's writing is from Interpersonal Psychoanalysis: The Selected Papers of Clara M. Thompson, *edited by Maurice R. Green and published by Basic Books, Inc., 1964.*

medical school, she studied under William Alanson White and decided on a career in psychiatry and psychoanalysis. She began her three-year residency at the Henry Phipps Psychiatric Clinic at Johns Hopkins. However, in 1925 she underwent psychoanalysis herself, which was not viewed favorably by the university community. As a result, she left Phipps and opened a private practice in Baltimore.

In the late 1920s Clara went to Budapest to study psychoanalysis under Sandor Ferenczi. She returned to America in 1933 and opened a practice in New York City. She established the Zodiac group in her home, a weekly meeting of American and visiting European psychoanalysts for the purpose of intellectual discussion. In 1943 she resigned from the American Institute of Psychoanalysis in support of her friend Erich Fromm and opened her own training institute, the William Alanson White Institute of Psychiatry, Psychoanalysis and Psychology. She and Fromm were co-directors for the next ten years.

Clara spent summers in Provincetown on Cape Cod, where she met the Hungarian artist Henry Major in the late 1930s. They spent every summer together until his death in 1948 despite the fact that he was married and returned to his wife each winter. Clara died of cancer in her New York apartment in 1958 and was buried beside Major in Provincetown.

OCTOBER 4

Miriam Van Waters

*C*hildren need privacy

1927

Parents who have allowed themselves no privacy cannot be expected to value it for their children. Privacy, however, is as necessary as sunlight for growing children. Yoemans, author of *Shackled Youth*, has pointed out that nothing is more needed in our times than opportunity for being alone. There are two kinds of a good time, the fun one has in comradeship, — and the joy one experiences in solitude. It is a sin of modern architecture that each member of the family is audible and visible to all the others, every hour of the day. If homes cannot supply privacy children must be sent away to seek it.

Miriam's writing is from her book, Parents on Probation, *published in 1927 by New Republic, Inc.*

Miriam Van Waters was born October 4, 1887, in Greensburg, Pennsylvania. When she was an infant her father, an Episcopal minister, moved the family to Portland,

Oregon, where he began establishing churches throughout the Northwest.

Miriam graduated from the University of Oregon in 1908 with honors in philosophy and two years later received an A.M. degree in psychology. She received a Ph.D. from Clark University in Worcester, Massachusetts, in 1913.

Miriam's career began in 1913 with her appointment as an agent of the Boston Children's Aid Society. She was in charge of assisting young girls in juvenile court, many of whom were charged with sexual offenses and were viewed by the public as "morally insane." Miriam improved health care services for these girls and sought to place them in foster homes. She returned to Portland in 1914 to head the county juvenile detention center, but she was forced to retire for three years after she was diagnosed with tuberculosis.

In 1919 Miriam was appointed head of El Retiro, an experimental home for delinquent girls in Los Angeles. She introduced vocational training, paid wages, and allowed the girls to govern themselves to a large degree. She called the home a "preventorium" and established drama clubs, libraries, and a halfway house to ease the girls' re-entry into society.

Miriam succeeded Jessie Hodder in 1923 as superintendent of the Massachusetts Women's Reformatory in Framingham. She referred to the inmates as "students" and over the years introduced many innovations, such as work furloughs and allowing women to keep their children at the institution's nursery. After a prisoner committed suicide in 1947 Miriam was investigated by the commissioner of corrections, who disliked Miriam for her vocal opposition to capital punishment. She was fired in 1949, but public support resulted in a special governor's commission that reinstated her. She returned to Framingham triumphantly as an inmate choir sang "Te Deum," and she remained superintendent until 1957. After her retirement, Miriam resided in Framingham near the reformatory and continued to write articles and give speeches. She died in 1974 at the age of eighty-six.

Grace Espy Patton

1895

One's own thinking

Men like to dictate to their wives, and their wives — many of them — seem to like to be dictated to: There is no responsibility in having someone other than self to do one's thinking. Whenever a human being reaches the state when he needs some outside assistance

in order to move his mental machinery, the time has come when he should separate the soul from the body and begin the process of transmigration; and he should begin low down in the scale of the animal creation in order to be in his proper sphere of intelligence. — He might choose his first abiding place in the shell of an oyster, provided, of course, the oyster should offer no objection.

Grace Espy Patton was born October 5, 1866, in Hartstown, Pennsylvania. When she was ten her family moved to Fort Collins, Colorado, where her father became mayor. She graduated in 1885 with high honors from the state agricultural college and was immediately hired to teach English and sociology. At the same time, she pursued her own studies and received her M.S. degree in 1885.

Grace wrote literary and political articles for newspapers in Denver and Fort Collins, as well as the *Chicago Tribune*. In 1894 she initiated her own monthly magazine, *The Tourney*, with the intention of focusing on "the intellectual energy of the West in general, and of Colorado in particular, upon the questions of the day, and to promote an independent public opinion thereon."

Since Colorado's women had won the right to vote in 1893, Grace was able to use her magazine as a political forum and gain personal recognition and influence. She was elected president of the Colorado Woman's Democratic Club. In January 1895 she moved her magazine to Denver, changing the name to *The Colorado Woman*. She announced that the new magazine's scope would be broader than that of *The Tourney*. She experimented with a weekly format for several months, but by November 1895 her interests had changed, and she closed the magazine to enter politics.

In 1896 the Democrats nominated Grace as state superintendent of public instruction. At the time of her nomination she had not yet reached the minimum age requirement of thirty, although she would turn thirty a month before the election. Despite her petite and youthful appearance she came to be known as "the little professor" and won the election by a large margin of votes.

As superintendent, she served in the state teachers' association, on the board of trustees of the state normal school, and as president of the State Board of Education. During her administration she raised qualification standards for teachers and established kindergartens, vocational training programs, and libraries.

Grace's writing is from "The New Voters vs. The Purifying Process," published in the January 1895 issue of The Colorado Woman.

On April 9, 1898, Grace married Lt. Warren Hayden Cowles, an Army officer on loan to the Military Science Department at the state agricultural college. She retired from

Women's Words, Women's Stories

public office and journalism to travel with her husband to his new military assignments, and her name disappeared from Colorado records after 1898.

Caroline Gordon

1957

I have an aunt who disapproves of adultery. She does not hold with incest, either, or mayhem, rapine, or murder. Whenever I publish a novel I receive from her a letter whose contents seldom vary — a letter of stern rebuke, written, she maintains, in my best interests. She is convinced, she says, that I myself have never committed any of the crimes that occur so often and so lamentably in my novels, that I am, indeed, incapable of committing them. But how, she concludes plaintively, are other people to know that? As long as these crimes abound in my novels, people who do not know me personally are apt to form a poor opinion of my character. She usually ends up urging me to mend my ways.

*W*hen crimes abound

Caroline Gordon was born October 6, 1895, on her mother's ancestral farm, "Merimont," in Kentucky tobacco country. She was educated at home until she was ten by her father, a teacher and part-time preacher. He founded a boys' preparatory school, Gordon's University School, in Clarksville, Tennessee, in 1905 which Caroline attended as the only female pupil.

Mr. Gordon chose Bethany College in Bethany, West Virginia, for his daughter because of its affiliation with the Campbellites, who required daily attendance at chapel, and because the town was "free from saloons, wicked resorts and other influences all too common in other college towns." Caroline thrived at the college where she was a member of a sorority, a drama group, and a literary society.

After graduating in 1916 Caroline taught science, French, and agriculture at Clarksville High School for four years. However, she did not enjoy it and was looking for a way to leave home to escape her tense relationship with her mother. In 1920 she took a job in Chattanooga as a journalist for the *Chattanooga News.*

In 1923 Caroline wrote an article about the growth of little magazines in the Chattanooga area, one of which was *The Fugitive*, a product of Vanderbilt University faculty and

Caroline's writing is from her book, How to Read a Novel, *published in 1957 by the Viking Press.*

students. While doing her research she met Allen Tate, a staff member at *The Fugitive*. The following summer he called on her while she was visiting her parents in Kentucky, and they were married in the fall. The Tates spent the first few years of their marriage travelling abroad on a Guggenheim Fellowship. Upon their return to America, Caroline took a job as Ford Madox Ford's literary secretary. In 1931 she published her first book, *Pennally*, which Ford declared was "the best novel that has been produced in modern America." She was a prolific writer and went on to publish ten novels and several volumes of essays and short stories.

After her divorce in 1950 Caroline continued to write, as well as teach. She was a professor and writer-in-residence at various colleges. She was teaching at the University of Dallas in 1975 when her health began to deteriorate, but she did not retire until two years later at the age of eighty-two. Caroline died at her daughter's home in Mexico in 1986 at the age of ninety.

Abby Maria Hemenway

Golgotha

Abby's writing is from "Mystical Rose," which she included in Poets and Poetry of Vermont, *published in 1860 by Brown, Taggard & Chase.*

1860

Golgotha trembles with the living surge
That round its fastness of rock hard press,
And echoes back the fiendish roar that swells
Like sullen soundings from a storm-lashed sea, —
Grim lictors stretch their Victim to His cross,
Maddened to scoffing that no groan they wring
From lips, sweet-breathing, still, *"Father forgive!"*
"Oh, God! and are these men! Has earth
No human left?"

Abby Maria Hemenway was born October 7, 1828, in Ludlow, Vermont, the fourth of ten children. She began teaching in a local public school when she was only fourteen, while simultaneously furthering her own education at the Black River Academy.

In her early twenties Abby went to Michigan to teach. She remained there three years, although she was miserable and terribly homesick. Her loneliness inspired her to write poetry, and upon her return to Vermont she placed ads in "various county papers" to acquire the work of other poets. She selected 110 pieces, and these plus her own sentimental verse were published in 1858 in *Poets and Poetry of Vermont*.

Buoyed by the success of her first book, Abby decided to

write a complete history of Vermont, county by county. She began with Addison County, home of Middlebury College, which had the only county historical society in the state. The faculty at Middlebury warned her that her plan was "not suited for a woman," but she ignored them. She toured the area by wagon and stagecoach selling copies of *Poets and Poetry of Vermont* along the way to raise money.

Abby published three volumes of her Vermont history in 1867, 1871, and 1877. Although she received a modest stipend from the state legislature, she was deeply in debt. Her fourth volume, published in 1882, was immediately attached by the printer for unpaid bills. She moved to Chicago to escape her debts and began working on volume five. A fire destroyed all her work in 1886; but she persevered and not only began volume five again, but began collecting material for volume six as well.

Abby died suddenly in Chicago at sixty-one of apoplexy, leaving numerous debts to private creditors and three printers. Her sister completed volume five, but volume six was destroyed in another fire just as the Vermont Historical Society was negotiating its publication.

Emily Blackwell

1850

I have been reading quietly by my fire and thinking, I have just read over some of Eliz's letters, how calm and steady and free from moods her disposition is. I think if it were not for the terrible ill success that pursues my efforts I should have something of that too, but when my most earnest efforts fail so completely there rises such a terrible self doubt in my mind and I ask myself whether I am of the stuff that reformers must be made of. I will strive to retain my faith in myself. If I cannot be a fine teacher I will strive to be a noble woman.

Emily Blackwell was born October 8, 1826, in Bristol, England. The family emigrated to America when she was five, settling with friends in Cincinnati on the grounds of Lane Theological Seminary. Emily was inspired by her older sister Elizabeth (February 3), one of the first women to receive a medical degree in the United States, and decided to follow her into medicine. To earn money for her schooling she took a teaching position but confided to her diary: "Oh,

Emily's writing, from her October 18, 1850, journal entry, is included in the collection of her writings at the Schlesinger Library, Radcliffe College, Cambridge, Massachusetts.

for life instead of stagnation. I long with such an intense longing for freedom, action, for life, and truth."

Emily was rejected by eleven medical schools, including her sister's alma mater in Geneva, New York. She was finally accepted in 1852 at Chicago's Rush Medical College, but the state medical society censured Rush for admitting a woman and she was asked to leave at the end of her first year. She joined her sister at her charity dispensary in New York City and gained as much practical experience as she could. Happily, she was then accepted at the medical college of Western Reserve University in Cleveland.

After graduating from Western Reserve with honors, Emily went to Scotland for further study with Sir James Simpson, a pioneer in the use of chloroform during childbirth. Upon her return to America she rejoined her sister, who had recently established the New York Infirmary for Women and Children as a teaching clinic for women doctors, and a place where women could consult physicians of their own sex. In 1858 Elizabeth left for a year to study abroad leaving Emily in control of the infirmary.

In 1860 the infirmary moved to larger quarters. The sisters established an on-site nursing school and medical college. For thirty years Emily served as dean of the medical school and professor of obstetrics and gynecology. The Blackwells felt that their school was no longer needed after 1898 when Cornell began accepting women students. During its thirty-one years of operation the Woman's Medical College had graduated 364 women doctors.

Emily retired in 1900 and died in September 1910, three months after her sister. The New York Infirmary for Women and Children is still in operation today. One of Emily's former pupils reminisced years after her teacher's death, "She inspired us all with the vital feeling that we are still on trial and that, for women who meant to be physicians, no educational standards could be too high. I think not many of us realized that we were going out into the world as test cases, but Dr. Blackwell did."

Elaine Goodale Eastman

Helping the Sioux

circa 1887

There was a great deal of sickness, whole families succumbing to the plague of tuberculosis, against which no precautions were taken. Medical service was hardly more than a gesture in most cases, since the govern-

---

ment physician was not supplied with transportation and rarely visited the homes. . . .

We not only administered medicines but prepared suitable food for our sick, carried it to their homes, and personally saw it consumed. We commanded them to stop in bed with fever, instead of dashing out of doors to cool off. Sometimes the present of a doll would keep a little girl quiet. Little babies perished in droves from exposure in winter, and in summer of dirt and improper feeding. If we banished the medicine man and the patient died, we, of course, were bitterly reproached. No attempt was made to penalize his well-paid activities. . . .

After all the children had recovered I came down with measles myself, and was rather seriously ill with that and an ulcerated ear. The only real hardships of those days must be laid to the combination of extreme cold and insufficient fuel. The first winter we burned green cottonwood in the schoolroom and I was often compelled to teach in my heavy coat, fur tippet, and arctics! In spite of everything I was happy.

Elaine Goodale Eastman was born October 9, 1863, at Sky Farm in the Berkshire Hills of Massachusetts. She was not permitted to attend local schools but was taught instead by her mother, who emphasized music and poetry. Elaine, named for Tennyson's lovelorn heroine, was very close to her younger sister Dora.

Elaine left home at eighteen to begin teaching at the Hampton Missionary School in Virginia. The school was divided into three separate sections: one for white students, one for blacks, and one for Indians. She quickly became committed to helping the Indians and asked to be transferred to the Sioux Agencies in the Dakota Territories.

In 1886 Elaine moved into the White River Lodge where the closest white person was eight miles away. She studied the Dakota language and became fluent. She had fifty students between the ages of six to sixteen, none of whom could read or speak English.

After three years Elaine returned to Massachusetts to write newspaper articles and lecture on behalf of the Indians. The Secretary of the Interior created a new office, "Supervisor of Education in the Two Dakotas," and appointed Elaine as the first person to hold the position. She returned to the Dakotas, where she had sixty schools in her jurisdiction. She travelled the plains in a horse-drawn wagon, unarmed to show trust, inspecting and improving the schools.

Elaine's writing is from Sister to the Sioux — The Memoirs of Elaine Goodale Eastman, *edited by Kay Graber and published in 1978 by the University of Nebraska Press.*

Elaine married Dr. Charles Eastman, a Sioux who had been raised off the reservation and had attended medical school in Boston. They had six children and returned to Massachusetts where they could better educate their family.

Elaine also wrote for newspapers on current Indian affairs and reviewed books about Indians until her death in 1953.

OCTOBER 10

Caroline Maria Hewins

The joy of reading

circa
1919
I can date my first reading of a novel by the place where I read it. When the little sister, seven and a half years to a day younger than I, was a few weeks old I was left with her and my mother, with instructions to call someone if they needed anything. As an inducement to be very quiet, *The Lamplighter*, then new, was given me to read. The woes of little Gerty, her years in the old part of Boston when the kind lamplighter took her home, her life with the Grahams after his death, her journey up the Hudson, her heroic conduct and the romantic ending to the tale made a deep impression on me.

Caroline Maria Hewins was born October 10, 1846, in Roxbury, Massachusetts, the first of nine children. As the eldest she was often called upon to care for her siblings. She read her favorite classics to them over and over and developed a love of books that would shape her future career.

Following a year at normal school Caroline began teaching in a private academy. She was sent to the Boston Athenaeum on a research assignment and was so impressed that she took a job there as a library assistant. She realized that library work was her chosen vocation, so she enrolled in Boston University to earn her degree.

In 1875 Caroline took a position as librarian at the Young Men's Institute in Hartford, Connecticut, where she would remain for the next fifty-one years. Under her direction, membership increased and services expanded. In 1893 following an earlier merger with the Hartford Library Association, the institute officially became the Hartford Public Library.

Caroline's writing is from her recollections of her childhood, A Mid-Century Child and Her Books, published by the Macmillan Company in 1926.

Caroline's major focus as a librarian was teaching children to love to read. In 1882 she was asked by the editor of *Publisher's Weekly* to compile a list of suggestions for children's reading. Her *Books for the Young: A Guide for Parents and Children* was reprinted many times, sponsored by the American Library Association.

In 1925 Caroline's friends honored her fiftieth year as a librarian by establishing the Caroline M. Hewins Scholarship for women studying to be librarians. She passed away the following year at the age of eighty. In 1946 the editor of *Publisher's Weekly* endowed a lectureship in her name.

Clara Dargan Maclean

1891

There she stood, a wedded wife. How far the years seemed since her mother had called her from dreams to daily drudgery! This cool, hazy autumn day, the sunlight glinting through the quaintly-latticed windows of the little parish church, recalled to her, with strange persistency, one morning ten years ago, when she sat crouched under an old cherry-tree, reading Schiller, and suddenly came the sound of that gentle, weary voice close beside her, saying, "My daughter, leave these idle fancies. There is work for you to do." How ungraciously she had gone to her homely tasks, ended now forever!

Yes, forever! For was not she the bride of Charles North, whose name was a synonym for unlimited credit in the commercial world? True, he was her senior by a full score of years; he was a man who scarcely comprehended the meaning of the word "sentiment"; but honor, truth, justice — these were engraved as by a pen of steel upon his straight, stern features. The slight figure beside him thrilled with the conviction. Here was a human creature who could not deceive. To Christine Trescot this was all in all.

Clara Victoria Dargan Maclean was born October 11, 1841, near Winnsboro, South Carolina. Following her graduation from the Salem Female Academy, she began teaching at local schools. In 1862 she took a position as tutor with the Weatherly family in Bennetsville, South Carolina. However, she left after one year for a similar job with another family because the eldest Weatherly son was smitten with her, and she was not interested.

*A*ll is well

Clara's writing is from her novel, Light O'Love, *published in 1891.*

Jack Weatherly courted Clara for years to no avail. In 1867 she broke off an engagement with a suitor named John Boner because he had "turned radical." Several other men tried to win her hand, including a lawyer from Alabama and a French musician. Finally, in 1870 she married Joseph Adams Maclean and settled in Yorksville, South Carolina.

Prior to her marriage Clara had published poems and short stories in Southern periodicals, and she produced a novelette in 1862. Later she put her literary career aside to concentrate on raising her son, born in 1872. In 1883 Clara separated from her husband. She travelled the United States, residing in New York and Virginia and singing in church choirs.

Clara published her only novel in 1891, and little is known of her after that time. She passed away in Florida in 1921.

OCTOBER 12

Sarah Jane Foster

Slander and faith

Saturday, January 27, 1866
I am in trouble tonight. I have been slandered by the mob til Mrs. Hokes dares not board me. I can hardly blame her and yet it cuts me deeply. Mr. Brackett has come up to see about it. They say that I have walked night after night arm in arm with Colored men. It is a lie, and yet how can I prove it. God help me. . . . Rode out with Mary Hopewell tonight on the Winchester pike and around town a little. Could not help it. Said "yes" without thought when she asked me and then felt I must go. Called at Mr. Brown's and three other Colored families today. Elisha went to show me one of them. I somehow begin to renew my faith. God is at work here. Oh Father let me stay. I cannot give it up now.

Sarah Jane Foster was born October 12, 1839, in Gray, Maine, the second of seven children of a shoemaker. From an early age, Sarah determined to improve herself through reading and studying in her spare time. She read history books, Shakespeare, and poetry, and she taught herself French. One of her goals was to earn enough money to purchase her own books.

In 1860 Sarah took a job as a domestic. Although good at her work she regarded it as taking valuable time away from her reading and writing. She had begun to write religious

Sarah's writing is from her diary, which she kept from 1864 to 1868. It is included in Sarah Jane Foster, Teacher of the Freedmen, *edited by Wayne E. Reilly and published by the University Press of Virginia, 1990.*

Women's Words, Women's Stories

essays and short stories, several of which were published in the *Home Monthly* and *Zion's Advocate*, a newspaper of the Baptist church.

Through her affiliation with the local Freewill Baptist Church, Sarah became interested in missionary work and applied to become a teacher of former slaves in the South. She began teaching in Martinsburg, West Virginia, in November 1865.

Although the citizens of Martinsburg were mostly pro-Union and endorsed the education of freemen, they remained prejudiced and disapproved of social mixing of the races. Sarah was caught in the middle of this dilemma, and it cost her job. Often she was taunted and called "nigger teacher," so she got in the habit of having one of her students walk her home at night for safety's sake. She was accused of fraternization and was evicted from the family with whom she was boarding. Her contract with the Freewill Baptist Home Mission Society was not renewed for the following year.

Sarah returned to Maine for the summer, humiliated and despondent. However, she believed in her calling, and she found the strength to apply to the American Missionary Society. She was accepted and returned to the South to teach on a remote, black-operated farm in Charleston Neck, South Carolina.

Sarah taught for one successful year in South Carolina, all the while writing articles for *Zion's Advocate*, describing her experiences and asking for donations for needed school supplies. On the advice of her superiors, she closed her school a month earlier than town schools to avoid the fever that threatened her Ashley River district. She returned to Maine tired and with a bad cold, but on June 19, 1868, she wrote in *Zion's Advocate* that she was resting and recovering. On June 25 she died of yellow fever.

Della Fox

1900

A hard lesson

I am as one who has been snatched by a miracle from the grave, or, worse, from the madhouse.

I weighed ninety-four pounds when I entered the sanitarium. I left today weighing 125 pounds. My mind is clear as a bell. The world looks bright and cheerful and is filled with sunshine. Life is again worth living.

I am strong enough to work hard and long without resort to drugs or liquors hereafter. The lesson has been dearly learned.

The real trouble began with my illness last autumn, although the way had doubtless been paved by over-fondness for the gaieties of life. When given up for dead I pulled through. The convalescence was slow, and for months people who should have known better gave me stimulants, drugs and liquor.

I should have been removed to the country and kept there for months. Instead, with nerves racked and ruined, and suffering in body and mind, I determined to return to the stage.

I accepted an engagement in vaudeville because the salary was alluring, and, suffering all torments, I determined to finish it. I resorted to stimulants to pull me through. Then I found myself lost in an unconquerable desire for drugs and drink.

I would not listen to friends. My will was gone. I cared most for drugs which were administered by a physician. I knew that my mind was weakening, but I did not care.

Finally I was taken away.

Della May Fox was born October 13, 1870, in St. Louis, Missouri. Her professional acting career began at the age of twelve when she was chosen to play Editha in *Editha's Burglar*, a one-act farce adapted from Frances Hodgson Burnett's story. She toured the United States and Canada in the role from 1883 to 1885, after which she graduated to soprano roles in light operas.

In 1894 Della opened in New York City in the operetta *The Little Trouper*. She received superb reviews and was regarded as a rising star. During the late 1890s, her hairdo, the "Della Fox curl," was popular throughout the United States. A *New York Times* reviewer wrote that she recalled "irresistibly that little girl who had a little curl in the exact centre of her forehead and could on occasion be so very, very good."

After forming her own company in 1897, Della toured America in the musical *The Little Host*. She was reported to be the highest paid performer at the time. She was forced to leave the stage in the spring of 1899 after suffering an attack of peritonitis. The following year she was committed to a sanitarium following a nervous breakdown that resulted from her addiction to alcohol and drugs.

Della's writing is from a message to her public that she submitted to The Boston Herald *in June 1900.*

Women's Words, Women's Stories

After her release from the sanitarium, Della retired from the theater to marry Jacob David Levy, a New York diamond broker and theatrical entrepreneur. She died of an intestinal obstruction at age forty-two and was returned to St. Louis for burial in the Bellefontaine Cemetery.

Lillian Gish

1969

I have never forgotten the color and pageantry of the elevation of a cardinal. It took place at dawn, and all ambassadors to the Holy See attended in full regalia. Two of our actors, Barney Sherry and Charles Lane, were more than six feet tall, white-haired, and so distinguished-looking in their white ties and tails that they were mistaken for ambassadors and taken in with the highest in the Church. They held up their heads as they passed us but managed to wink. Cardinal Bonzano must have been greatly loved, for tears flowed as he received his honor.

When we were filming in Rome, the atmosphere was spiritual. Years later, when Helen Hayes and Clark Gable were making a new version of *The White Sister*, Helen called me long-distance. She was dissatisfied with the rushes [first cut on film]. Clark was a good actor, but he was subtly wrong for the part. She asked me how, in our original film version, we had achieved certain effects.

"How is it on the set between scenes?" I asked her.

"Oh, you know, the usual stories and jokes," Helen replied.

"Then you're not going to get it," I was obliged to tell her. "You cannot set up a camera and take a picture of faith."

*F*ilming in Rome

Lillian Diana Gish was born October 14, 1893, in Springfield, Ohio. Her father, a candy salesman, deserted the family when Lillian was five and her younger sister Dorothy was three. Their mother performed with a troupe of actors in New York City to support them, and both daughters began taking children's parts to earn a few dollars. Taught that acting was a shameful profession, they never used the name Gish in the early years so as not to disgrace the family.

Lillian's writing is from her autobiography, Lillian Gish, the Movies, Mr. Griffith and Me, *published in 1969 by Prentice-Hall, Inc.*

In 1912 Lillian's life changed forever after a chance meeting with the director D. W. Griffith. The sisters stopped at his Manhattan office to visit their friend, child actress Gladys Smith (who later changed her name to Mary Pickford). Griffith liked the way the girls used motion and gestures, not just words, and he hired them on the spot as extras in his current film. Lillian went on to make more than sixty silent films with D. W. Griffith, becoming the first movie "star" after her performance as Elsie in *Birth of a Nation* in 1915.

With the advent of talkies Lillian moved to Metro Goldwyn Mayer where she clashed with Louis B. Mayer, who was looking for sexy women, not the vulnerable innocence that Lillian projected. She told him that she couldn't do it, that she was "not a sexpot." He threatened to ruin her, so she simply quit and returned to the stage. She starred in more than forty plays, including *Uncle Vanya*, *Camille*, and *Hamlet*, in which she played Ophelia opposite John Gielgud.

She convinced D. W. Griffith to donate his films to the Museum of Modern Art, marking the beginning of film preservation in the United States. In 1987 Miss Gish went on location to Maine for her last movie, *The Whales of August*, with Bette Davis. One day after viewing the rushes the director told Miss Davis that Lillian's closeups had gone well, and she answered, "It should — she invented them."

Lillian died in her sleep in her New York City apartment in February 1993 at the age of ninety-nine.

OCTOBER 15   *Fannie Veale Beck*

Cowboy gallantry

1937

I have a high regard for all cowboys; I was brought up with them — went to school with them. A cowboy was my first beau, and I had other good friends, who were men of honor and integrity, whose lives were spent on the range, and I felt perfectly safe in their company. Many a night I have spent out on some lonely ranch dancing all night because the distance was too great to get back to town and there was no provision made for sleeping at the ranch. A group of us girls with our beaux would ride out on horseback, have supper at the house where the party was given, then dance the hours away until daylight, eat breakfast, and go home. John (her brother) was usually along on these all-night parties, but I would have felt perfectly safe if he had not

Fannie's writing is taken from the book she wrote for her children, On The Texas Frontier, Autobiography of a Texas Pioneer, Britt Publishing and Printing Company, St. Louis, 1937.

been; for a woman's honor was a sacred thing and sacredly guarded by these young gallants, even though they were lacking in a good many niceties demanded by polite society in later years. There was no chaperone except the hostess in the home where the dance was given. The young people paired off and rode in couples on horseback. There was no love-making, no drinking, no foolish and questionable conversation. We just had a good time, and felt none the worse for the all-night "carousal."

Fannie Davis Veale Beck was born October 15, 1861, in Dresden, Texas. She was the eldest daughter of a large family of early Texas pioneers. Her father, Judge William Veale, was a self-made man who educated himself for the law while teaching in little country schools. When Fannie was sixteen her family moved to Beckenridge, Texas, and it was there that she met Henry Beck, her future husband. Henry, an architect, had gone to Beckenridge from Morning Sun, Iowa, on an adventure trip. He stayed and built the first department store. He was active in the same Presbyterian church Fannie attended. Henry was the choir master, and she played the organ.

Fannie and Henry were married in 1885 in New Orleans while attending the Cotton Exposition. It was Fannie's first trip outside Texas. They returned to Bosque County, Texas, and started their married life together living in a tent until their ranch house was built. Henry was frail and he suffered from rheumatism and stomach problems. Fannie worked very hard doing much of Henry's work as well as being responsible for her own domestic chores. The couple had eleven children, three of whom died in infancy. For most of her life, Fannie was an active member of the Presbyterian church and a devoted Sunday school teacher.

In an autobiography that she wrote at her children's request, Fannie described the early years of pioneer life on the Texas frontier. She described nights of fear when the Comanche and Tonkaway Indians were on the warpath, and the suffering of near-starvation and lack of water during the terrible drought years of the late 1800s.

In 1935 on their 50th wedding anniversary Fannie and her husband were given a large celebration by their friends and family in Morning Sun, Iowa, where they had settled after the early years in Texas. Everyone in the town of Morning Sun attended. In her autobiography she recalled the party, "Everyone was kind and attentive, and all our guests made us feel that their presence was a mark of real esteem and affection. It was a wonderful occasion, something for us to dream about and live over again with happiness."

Fannie died in Morning Sun when she was ninety-four.

Elizabeth Haven Appleton

A passion for Trollope

Elizabeth's writing is from her lecture "The Trollope Family," written in 1884. It is included in, In Memory of Elizabeth Haven Appleton: Selections from Her Lectures, *published by Robert Clarke & Co. in 1891.*

1884

. . . I have a passion for Anthony Trollope's books, and a great many people laugh at me and call them stupid. They are no more stupid than any other society gossip, and they have this advantage over society gossip, that they never do any harm; on the contrary, they do good. Mr. Trollope says no more than the truth about his books when he claims that "no girl has risen from the reading of his pages less modest than she was before, and that some may have learned from them that modesty is a charm well worth preserving."

Elizabeth Haven Appleton was born October 16, 1815, in Wavertree, England. Her parents came from Baltimore, but at the time of her birth they were temporarily residing in England while her father worked as an agent for American merchants. They returned to Baltimore in 1816, where her five younger siblings were born.

The Appletons moved to Cincinnati in 1832. Mrs. Appleton died the following year, leaving the care of the house and younger children to Elizabeth. In 1835 the family moved to Boston when Mr. Appleton married his cousin. Elizabeth did not get along with her stepmother, and she left home forever in 1840.

Elizabeth taught school for two years in New Bedford, Massachusetts, after which she received an invitation to teach at Mr. Morison's School for Girls in Baltimore. She remained there for six years, then moved back to Cincinnati. From 1855 to 1875 she operated Miss Appleton's School for Girls. Elizabeth began to study French when she was forty-six and became so fluent that she was able to translate several books.

Elizabeth closed her school in 1875 and spent her first year of retirement in Europe. She returned to Cincinnati and began volunteering at the Cincinnati Historical Society. She found rooms filled with boxes of books, pamphlets, letters, and other historical material. She spent the next ten years cataloging and arranging the contents of the boxes until the task was completed.

From 1877 to 1886 Elizabeth was one of two secretaries of the Women's Art Museum Association, an affiliate of the Cincinnati Art Museum. She died in 1890. In her will she left her books and pictures and $500 to the museum.

Halle Johnson

Montgomery, Alabama
August 20, 1891
(To Booker T. Washington)

Hoping to succeed

Dear Sir, Have just come in to my dinner & find your note. Am glad to know you are all interested in my success. It certainly is pleasant to me when far from home to find friends, such as I have been fortunate to make since my stay here. I am getting along well. Try to keep before myself the possibility of failing but unless something harder and more complex than anything they have given me yet I feel that I can not, but, if they mark me fairly will get thro. . . .

Yesterday evening a man in the Capitol stopped me & demanded in rough voice "what my business was at the Capitol every day." I told him to "ask Dr. Cochran and he would tell him," just now I met the same man on the corner of Union & Washington streets, he glared at me, I don't suppose it amounts to any thing but confess it sort of bothers me.

I am really trying to do the best that I can in my studies & hope to succeed.

Again thanking you all for thinking occasionally of me.

I remain Sincerely, Halle T. Dillon

Halle Tanner Dillon Johnson was born October 17, 1864, in Pittsburgh. Her parents took an active interest in their seven children's education and cultural development, and as a result they all achieved success far beyond that of the average black family of that era.

Halle attended the Woman's Medical College in Philadelphia at the age of twenty-four. Booker T. Washington, president of the Tuskegee Institute of Alabama, had been looking for four years for a black resident physician for his school. He offered the position to Halle at $600 per year

Halle's letter to Booker T. Washington was written while taking her medical exams. The original is in the Booker T. Washington Collection, Library of Congress, and is included in The Booker T. Washington Papers, edited by Louis R. Harlan and published by the University of Illinois Press, 1974.

plus board, providing she could pass the state medical exam.

Halle passed the exam and became the first black woman to practice medicine in Alabama. Halle enjoyed her position at Tuskegee from 1891 to 1894. She retired to marry the Reverend John Quincy Johnson, whom she met during his year teaching math at Tuskegee. She had been married briefly in 1886 to Charles E. Dillon, but he died soon after, and little is known of that marriage.

Halle and John settled in Nashville, where he was pastor of St. Paul's African Methodist Episcopal Church. Halle bore three sons but died at the age of thirty-seven during childbirth complicated by dysentery. She was buried in the Greenwood Cemetery, Nashville.

OCTOBER 18

Fannie Hurst

Strangely exultant

1958

Are you a sorority girl?

I hated his asking me a question which was still difficult for me even to discuss. Are you Jewish? I hated his asking that, even more.

Yes.

I can't tell you how happy that makes me, he said.

What difference does it make? I told myself.

But inside me it was making a difference. All the difference in the world. Suddenly he had less to explain to me, and I had less to explain to him. We were knowing each other with our blood. In a strange way, I felt exultant. For the first time, pride of race, which my snide snobbery had so long denied me, stirred. I don't know what of this may have been telegraphed to him, but he leaned over intensely.

Fannie, he said, using my given name for the first time, I want to see much of you. I had better not go on, or I will say too much — too soon.

Fannie's writing is from Anatomy of Me, A Wanderer in Search of Herself, *published in 1958 by Doubleday.*

Fannie Hurst was born October 18, 1889, on a farm in Hamilton, Ohio. Her parents had emigrated to America from Bavaria in 1869, and she was raised in a "middle-western world of assimilated Jews." After graduating from Washington University in St. Louis in 1909 she moved to New York City to "study people" for her chosen career as a writer. To learn about the "small people," she worked as a

Women's Words, Women's Stories

waitress, shop clerk, and actress and spent time wandering the streets and sitting in on night court sessions.

Initially, Fannie's writing was not accepted for publication; she received thirty-five rejections from *The Saturday Evening Post* alone. Finally, in 1912 she sold a story for $30 followed by another for $300. In 1914 she published her first book of short stories, and by 1925 she was one of the three highest-paid writers in America. She became known as the "sob sister" of American fiction because her work often championed the causes of labor, women, homosexuals, and displaced Jews.

Fannie was married to the pianist Jacques Danielson in 1915. She did not reveal the marriage until 1920. She kept her maiden name, and she and Jacques maintained separate residences. She believed that "nine out of ten marriages were merely sordid endurance tests overgrown with the fungi of familiarity," and she was determined that her marriage "should not lessen my capacity for creative work or pull me down into a sedentary state of fatmindedness." Despite public criticism of her lifestyle, including a scathing editorial in *The New York Times*, Fannie and Jacques were happily married for thirty-two years.

Fannie published her last novel in 1964 and died four years later at the age of seventy-eight. She left behind a solid body of work that included seventeen novels, nine volumes of short stories, and three plays. She also collaborated on several movies and was the hostess of a television talk show. She left $1 million to Brandeis University and $1 million to Washington University to establish creative writing professorships.

Annie Smith Peck

1932

In 1903, when I sailed for South America to climb one of the great peaks of the Andes, I did not dream of ever flying over or around them. . . .

. . . about the time in 1908 that I climbed the north peak, 21,812 feet of Peru's highest mountain, Huascarán, a flight of one hour was accomplished. In 1909, I ventured to call on Wilbur Wright at the Hotel Vanderbilt a day or two before he was to fly up the river for the Hudson Fulton Celebration. Mr. Wright received me with much courtesy, but to my inquiry if I could go with him he responded that he would take me

An urge to fly

if anyone; but he would make the flight alone.

To be the first woman to fly had seemed worth taking a chance; but why be the thousandth? No joy-rides for me! though in later years an invitation from Colonel Lindbergh for an hour's flight would have been promptly accepted. Had he been aware that I had climbed higher on my two feet than he in his airplane, perhaps he would have asked me.

Annie Smith Peck was born October 19, 1850, in Providence, Rhode Island. She graduated in 1872 from the Rhode Island State Normal School. After two years of teaching in Providence public schools she was selected for the position of preceptress of the Saginaw, Michigan, high school.

Annie first became interested in mountain climbing in 1885 when she saw the "frowning walls" of the Matterhorn while travelling abroad. Her first important climb came three years later when she ascended Mount Shasta in California. As a child she had always been in competition with her three older brothers and as a result had developed the courage and physical stamina she later needed as a mountain climber.

In 1895 Annie climbed the Matterhorn and achieved instant acclaim, not only because she was a woman but also for her climbing costume of knickerbockers, long tunic, and felt hat with a veil. Two years later she climbed an 18,314-foot-high mountain in Mexico, the highest peak ever climbed by a woman.

Annie hired a professional manager in 1900 and started on a circuit, which was to be her major source of income for the rest of her life. She alternated mountain climbing with lectures about her climbs, illustrated with stereopticon slides she made from her own photographs. She was petite, attractive, and feminine, which always took her audiences by surprise.

After climbing the major mountains in Europe, Annie moved on to unexplored areas of South America in her quest to reach "some height where no MAN had previously stood." In 1904 she broke her previous height record when she mastered the 21,300-foot-high Mount Sorata in Bolivia. She tried twice and failed to reach the summit of the twin-peaked Huascarán in Peru, but she was successful on the third attempt in 1908 with the help of two expert Swiss guides. For her achievement she was awarded a gold medal from the Peruvian government, and a silver stirrup from the Lima Geographical Society. In 1927 the society named the north peak of Huascarán the "Cumbre Aña Peck" in her honor.

Annie continued to climb mountains, give lectures, and write books despite advancing age. At sixty-one she became the first woman to climb Mount Coropura in Peru. As a

Annie's writing is from her book, Flying Over South America, *published by Houghton, Mifflin and Company in 1932.*

statement of her support for women's suffrage she planted a "Votes for Women" pennant on its summit. She climbed her last mountain, Mount Madison in New Hampshire, at the age of eighty-two. She died two years later and was buried in the North Burial Ground in Providence.

Sara Murray Jordan

1936

When I was still young, and my parents were approaching middle age, an old family friend warned me secretly that I must be prepared for the "breaking up" process which was bound to occur in people of that age. "Very few men and women keep their health through middle life." This dire prediction was a bug-a-boo to me for many years, until I suddenly realized that my parents and most of my friends' parents had passed merrily from middle age to old age, without experiencing much more than the usual wear and tear of common colds and gall bladder operations. My secret fears had been folly.

Needless fears

Sara Claudia Murray Jordan was born October 20, 1884, in Newton, Massachusetts. She graduated from Radcliffe College in 1904 and went on to the University of Zurich for a doctorate in classical philology and archaeology. In January 1913 she married Sebastian Jordan, a German lawyer she had met at the university. Their daughter Mary was born the following year.

Sara's father pressured her to return to America for the duration of World War I. She complied and never saw her husband again, obtaining a divorce in 1921. Sara enrolled in Tufts College Medical School in 1917 and graduated four years later at the head of her class.

Dr. Frank Lahey chose Sara during her second year of medical school to assist him in a patient study at New England Deaconess Hospital. Their research resulted in a paper, written together, on treatment of diseases of the thyroid. Lahey was so impressed with Sara that he arranged for her internship in Worcester, followed by special training in gastroenterology in Chicago.

In 1922 Sara joined Dr. Lahey, another surgeon, and an anesthesiologist at the newly opened Lahey Clinic in Boston. She quickly established herself as an authority on diseases of

Sara's writing is from her article, "Cheerio — Middle Age! By a Middle-Aged Female Medic," The Radcliffe Quarterly, May 1936.

the gastrointestinal tract. She advised, "every businessman over 50 should have a daily nap and nip — a short nap after lunch and a relaxing highball before dinner."

In 1951 Sara co-authored a cookbook, *Good Food for Bad Stomachs*. She advocated medical over surgical intervention whenever possible and recommended a healthy diet, rest, and recreation for all her patients. To set an example, she gave up smoking and played golf several times a week with her husband Penfield Mower, whom she married when she was fifty-one.

Sara received numerous awards from her peers and was elected the first woman president of the American Gastro-enterological Association in 1942. She retired from her practice in 1958 and wrote a syndicated newspaper column, "Health and Happiness." The following year she diagnosed her own cancer of the colon. She died several months later at the age of seventy-five.

Mabel Buland Campbell

Time on stage

1912

In Elizabethan plays, a single scene is frequently so presented that events of a few minutes' duration appear to cover an entire night. An actor may announce that it is midnight, and ten minutes later without the intervention of a single interval to help the imagination to bridge the space that the dawn is breaking. . . .

Such is the illusion which Marlowe produced in the last scene of *Doctor Faustus:* While Faustus speaks a six-minute soliloquy the clock strikes eleven, the half-hour, and twelve, the emotional tension of the scene being so severe that the audience readily accepts this fearful rapidity in the flight of time.

Mabel Buland Campbell was born October 21, 1885, in Greenwood, Wisconsin. Her father, a physician, relocated the family to Castle Rock, Washington, when she was a young child. She graduated from the Castle Rock public school system and the University of Washington and attended Columbia University for graduate study. In 1912 she received a Ph.D. in philosophy from Yale, one of the first women admitted to a Yale graduate school.

Mabel returned to Washington after obtaining her Ph.D. and began teaching at Whitman College in Walla Walla. In

Mabel's writing is from her doctoral dissertation, "The Presentation of Time in Elizabethan Drama," published in 1912 by Henry Holt and Company.

1915 she married George N. Campbell, a banker who later became president of the Kalama State Bank. She had a son, George, and a daughter, Catharine.

The Campbells settled in Kalama. Mabel eventually resigned from her teaching position at Whitman to become superintendent of the Kalama school system. She was a member of the Daughters of the American Revolution, the Woman's Christian Temperance Union, and the Round Robin Study Club. From 1929 to 1931 she served as president of the State Federation of Women's Clubs, and from 1934 to 1935 as president of the Western Federation of Women's Clubs. Always interested in furthering women's educational opportunities, she was chair of the Committee on Scholarships and Loans of the General Federation of Women's Clubs from 1935 to 1938. For many years she held the position of chair of the State Library Board, and she was the first president of the local League of Women Voters. After her death the *State Library News Bulletin* wrote, "Her keen mind and her fine intellect made her an important adjunct to any group she contacted and she was frequently in demand as a speaker in various places in Washington and Oregon. But beyond that, her warm personality and her great capacity for friendship endeared her to all who knew her."

Mabel spent the last three years of her life travelling throughout Mexico, South America, Egypt, and the Holy Land. She died in January 1961 at the age of seventy-five, leaving most of her estate to the Kalama Public Library.

Harriet Chalmers Adams

1916

Peru may be likened to a tall, gray-stone house with a steep flight of steps leading up to the roof. From this bleak roof rise the highest chimney peaks of the Americas — mountains perpetually snow-crowned, their imperial heads glistening in the sunlight like a Titanic chain of diamonds. Behind this chilly, drab house lies nature's loveliest gardens; but no well-built stairway leads down to it. The traveler, bound for the vine-hung wonderland of the tropics, risks his life and — slides off the roof.

We slid.

Never have I seen such a steep, slippery trail; it was

A steep descent

Harriet's writing is from "Sliding off the World's Roof," which appeared in the November 1916 edition of the Ladies' Home Journal.

in the bed of a brook, which tumbled down the mountain side to a cañon far below. The wet mist enshrouded me, screening the rider ahead; the rain fell in torrents. My dejected white horse tripped over rolling boulders, hurling me to and fro in the saddle, and finally pitched me, heels over head, into the stream. There I lay until the men came to the rescue — looking, I am sure, like a wet mummy, for my costume that day was wonderful to behold.

Harriet Chalmers Adams was born October 22, 1875, in Stockton, California. In 1899 Harriet married Franklin Pierce Adams, an engineer who shared her love of adventure. They soon set off on a three-year tour of Central and South America. Although she eventually visited every continent, her main interest was in the primitive peoples of Spanish-speaking countries.

Between journeys, Harriet wrote magazine articles and gave lectures. She often wore an evening gown when she spoke, and her delicate elegance was a sharp contrast to her tales of crossing the Andes on a llama or travelling the Amazon in a dugout canoe. In 1907 she began a twenty-eight-year association with *National Geographic*, publishing more than twenty-five articles illustrated with her own photographs. In 1925 she founded the Society of Woman Geographers and served as its first president.

In 1927 Harriet fell off a sea wall on the Balearic Islands, breaking her back. Although she was told she would never walk again, she spent two years strapped to a board and upon her recovery she immediately set off alone to Spain, North Africa, and Asia Minor.

In later years, Harriet concentrated on studying South American cultures, especially the women in those cultures. Harriet and her husband retired to the south of France in 1934. She died there three years later and was buried in her hometown of Stockton.

1904

To the uninitiated or uninterested observer, all small, dull-colored birds are "common sparrows." The closer scrutiny of the trained eye quickly differentiates, and picks out not only the Song, the Canada, and the Fox Sparrows, but finds a dozen other familiar friends where one who "has eyes and sees not" does not even suspect their presence. Ruskin says, "Hundreds of people can talk for one who can think, but thousands can think for one who can see. To see clearly is poetry, prophecy, and religion — all in one."

Neltje Blanchan De Graff Doubleday was born October 23, 1865, in Chicago. After graduating from the Misses Masters' School in Dobbs Ferry, New York, she married Frank Nelson Doubleday, who ten years later was to found the publishing house that still bears his name. They maintained homes in Manhattan and Oyster Bay, Long Island, and had three children.

Probably encouraged by her connections with the publishing world, Neltje took up writing under the pen name Neltje Blanchan. She published her first book, *The Piegan Indians*, in 1889. Although she always maintained her interest in Indians and occasionally wrote magazine articles on Indian handcrafts, she soon turned to her first love, nature, for literary inspiration.

Neltje revealed her knowledge and love of birds in her next book, *Bird Neighbors*, published in 1897, followed by a companion volume, *Birds That Hunt and Are Hunted*, in 1898. Both books were elegantly printed and bound and contained fifty color photographs of mounted birds. Although she held a few misconceptions, for example that eagles carry off children, for the most part she was scientifically correct and was an early conservationist who hoped for "the ultimate passage of protective laws in every state of the Union."

In 1900 Neltje published *Nature's Garden* about wildflowers, followed by *The American Flower Garden* in 1909. Both books revealed her enthusiasm for gardening, combined with lavish full-page color photographs. She published what was to be her last book, *Birds Worth Knowing*, in 1917 and departed soon after with her husband to undertake Red Cross work in China. She died suddenly on February 21, 1918, of unknown causes while in Canton and was returned for burial on Long Island.

*T*o see clearly

Neltje's writing is from her preface to Bird Neighbors, an Introductory Acquaintance with One Hundred and Fifty Birds Commonly Found in the Gardens, Meadows, and Woods About Our Homes, *published in 1897 by Doubleday.*

Belva Bennett Lockwood

A well-trodden road

Belva's writing is from "My Efforts to Become a Lawyer," Lippincott's Magazine, *February 1888.*

1888

The colleges of the country were closed to women. What could a simple country-girl do against the prejudices of centuries? There was only one avenue open to her, and that the one for which the American girl had been educated all of the years of the past century, — marriage. The daughter of a poor farmer, I followed the same well-trodden road, and was soon united in *marriage* to a promising young farmer of my neighborhood. . . .

A babe soon gladdened my household, but my married life was short, as my husband sickened soon after my marriage and died of a lingering consumption during the fifth year, leaving me, without fortune, to make my way in the world.

Belva Ann Bennett McNall Lockwood was born October 24, 1830, in Royalton, New York. After attending local country schools she had to begin teaching at fifteen to help support the family. When she was eighteen she married her neighbor, Uriah H. McNall. He died after five years of marriage, leaving her with a young daughter to support.

Belva resumed teaching while pursuing her own studies, receiving a B.S. degree with honors from Genesee College in 1857. Soon after graduation she assumed the position of preceptress of the Lockport Union School in Lockport, New York. She introduced many innovations at the school including nature walks, public speaking, gymnastics, and ice skating.

In 1866 Belva moved to Washington, D.C., and opened her own school, the first private coeducational school in the city. At the age of thirty-seven she married Ezekiel Lockwood, a sixty-four-year-old dentist. He assisted her in running the school until she closed it due to his poor health, followed by his death in 1877. Meanwhile, beginning in 1871, Belva had been preparing for a law career. After being denied admission to several universities because of her sex, she was finally accepted at the newly formed National University Law School. Although she graduated in 1873 her diploma was delayed, and she received it only after petitioning President Grant, the school's ex-officio president. In 1876 she was denied permission to argue a case before the United States Supreme Court due to established custom. Belva lobbied Congress and saw the passage of a bill in 1879 that allowed female lawyers to pursue legal matters through the highest courts in the country. On March 3, 1879, she became the first woman to appear before the United States Supreme Court.

An early feminist, she was instrumental in pushing through legislation in 1872 that guaranteed female government employees equal pay for equal work. In the 1880s, believing that women had made great progress in lifting restrictions that hampered them, she turned her attention to the peace movement. She ran for president of the United States in 1884, nominated by the National Equal Rights Party, and received 4,149 votes.

Belva spent her later years practicing law in Washington, D.C. In 1906 she argued a case before the Supreme Court on behalf of the Eastern Cherokee Indians which resulted in a $5 million settlement. She died in Washington in 1917 at the age of eighty-six and was buried in the Congressional Cemetery.

Irene McCoy Gaines

1957

A leader's words

Living and working in today's world is a challenge to all women of good will. Negro women have particularly heavy demands on them to express love, understanding, and right living and acting.

We have to break down barriers of hate and prejudice. We must do so without violence, but with love for all. We can go far toward our goal by raising standards for all Negroes in health and sanitation, housing, education, and working conditions.

Irene McCoy Gaines was born October 25, 1892, in Ocala, Florida. After her parents' divorce in 1903 she moved with her mother to Chicago, where she attended local public schools. After graduating from Fisk Normal School in Nashville in 1910, she returned to Chicago to take a position as typist in the complaint department of the juvenile court.

Irene married Harris Barrett Gaines, an attorney, in 1914 and had two sons. Once her children were in school she began her career as a social worker in the Cook County Welfare Department. For fourteen years she served as president of the Chicago Council of Negro Organizations. Under her leadership the organizations established the first integrated

Irene's words are from "Negro Women See Progress," Christian Science Monitor, *December 2, 1957.*

nursery school in Chicago and opened a home for pregnant teenagers.

In 1941 Irene organized the first march on Washington. She led a group of fifty Chicagoans who joined other marchers from around the country to protest discrimination against blacks in employment.

Irene's most important contributions were made through her affiliation with the National Association of Colored Women's Clubs (NACWC). From association headquarters in Washington, she organized nationwide programs of neighborhood improvement to end slums. In 1956 she obtained a grant from the Sears Roebuck Foundation to sponsor a neighborhood beautification contest. She wrote: "Alleys were cleaned, unsightly buildings torn down, streets and sidewalks built, homes rehabilitated, and grounds landscaped." For her efforts she received the George Washington Honor Medal from the Valley Forge Freedom Foundation.

During her years of leadership in NACWC, Irene established nursery schools and day care centers, opened eighty-five boarding homes for working girls, and created numerous industrial training schools and homes for delinquent boys and girls.

Fisk University presented Irene with its Distinguished Alumni Service Award in 1959, and she received an honorary degree from Wilberforce University in 1962. She died of cancer two years later and was buried in Chicago.

OCTOBER 26

Elizabeth Payson Prentiss

A pious dog

Elizabeth's writing is from a letter to her eldest son, George. It is included in her husband's The Life and Letters of Elizabeth Prentiss, *published by A. D. F. Randolph & Co. in 1882.*

1878

H. is full of a story of a pious dog, who was only fond of people who prayed, went to church regularly, and, when not prevented, to all the neighborhood prayer-meetings, which were changed every week from house to house; his only knowledge of where they would be held being from Sunday notices from the pulpit! I believe this the more readily because of Pharoah's always going to my Bible-reading at Dorset and never barking there, whereas if I went to the same house to call he barked dreadfully.

We are constantly wondering what you boys will be. Good men, I hope, at any rate. Good-night, with a kiss from your affectionate mother.

Women's Words, Women's Stories

Elizabeth Payson Prentiss was born October 26, 1818, in Portland, Maine, the first of eight children. Although her father, a dramatic revivalist preacher, died when she was nine, he was a major influence on her religious and intellectual beliefs.

When Elizabeth was twenty she opened a school in her mother's home, and two years later she left for a teaching position at Mr. Persico's school for girls in Richmond, Virginia. She was plagued her entire life by poor health, which included headaches, fainting, and a recurring pain in her side — so much so that she was quoted in later years as saying, "I never knew what it is to feel well." She suffered from spells of "severe nervous excitement," after which she would retreat for periods of religious introspection.

In the spring of 1845 Elizabeth married George Lewis Prentiss, a recently ordained Congregational minister. They had six children, two of whom died in infancy.

In 1853 Elizabeth published her first Little Susy book, which began her career as a popular children's writer. She followed with two more Little Susy books, attracting a large following in America, Great Britain, and France. Her most successful book, *Stepping Heavenward*, was published in 1869 and sold more than 100,000 copies in the United States and was translated into French and German.

In later years Elizabeth's writings included religious poems and hymns. Her hymn, "More Love to Thee, O Christ," is still included in modern hymnals. She died in 1878 at her summer home in Dorset, Vermont, and was buried in nearby Maplewood Cemetery.

Sharlot Mabridth Hall

1910

In 1883, when I was twelve years old, my parents moved from Barbour County, Kansas (in which state they had been among the earliest pioneers), to Yavapai County, Arizona. We started on the third day of November with two covered wagons drawn by four horses each. I rode a little Texas pony and drove a band of horses.

We followed the old Santa Fe Trail nearly all the way. In many places the deep ruts worn by the old caravans could still be seen; rocks and cliffs were marked by names, painted or cut into the stone, and all along the roadside were sunken graves, mostly unmarked and

Santa Fe Trail

Sharlot's writing is from the introductory notes for her poem "The Santa Fe Trail." They are included in her poetry collection, Cactus and Pine, published in 1910 by Sherman French Company, Boston.

nearly obliterated. Often I would slide out of my saddle, as I drove the band of young horses behind the wagons, and try to read and brace up with rocks some rotting bit of board that had once told who rested there.

The metre of this poem was suggested by the turning wheels of the big wagons used in the old caravans, the middle rhyme being the chug of the huge wooden brake-blocks, to the regular rhythm of which I often listened.

Sharlot Mabridth Hall was born October 27, 1870, in Barbour County, Kansas. In 1882 she and her family crossed the plains in horse-drawn wagons bound for the Arizona Territory. Sharlot drove a large group of thoroughbred horses to establish a herd in the new land. They settled on the Orchard Ranch on lower Lynx Creek, twenty miles outside of Prescott, Arizona.

Sharlot's education was informal, but her mother taught her to love literature. She began writing poetry when she was twelve, progressing to short stories and historical articles as she matured. Her talent did not go unnoticed, and by the time she was thirty she was editor of *Out West Magazine*.

Out West Magazine was based in Los Angeles, so Sharlot made the journey back and forth, staying in California for several months at a time until she could return to her real love, the ranch.

In 1909 Sharlot became the first woman appointed to public office in the Arizona Territory when she began serving as Arizona's historian. In 1928 she bought the Old Governor's Mansion in Prescott and moved in with her extensive collection of Arizona artifacts. She soon opened it as a museum, and her enthusiasm inspired others to donate items related to early Arizona history.

Sharlot died in 1943 and was buried beneath a native granite boulder in the Prescott Pioneer's Cemetery. Her dream, the Sharlot Hall Museum continues as a state institution. She was named to the Arizona Women's Hall of Fame in 1981 for her contribution to the literature and history of Arizona.

Katharine Curran Brandegee

1890

A young doctor is not usually overrun with patients, and as a member of the California Academy of Sciences in San Francisco, with considerable time on my hands, I began to make myself useful, especially about the herbarium, which was in a shocking condition.

I began to collect plants in 1882 and the next year was offered the curatorship which I accepted, giving up my small practice and devoting the succeeding ten very active years to the service of the Academy. My botanical trips are too numerous to catalogue. By the aid of the railway companies I enjoyed a general pass on the roads which allowed me to ride from Pullman to engine. Later this was somewhat restricted and confined to the state, but it was of the greatest value in allowing me, without too great expense, to utilize the time of the short desert blooming season.

Mary Katharine Layne Curran Brandegee was born October 28, 1844, in western Tennessee, the second of ten children. She married Hugh Curran, an Irish immigrant, in 1866, but was left a widow eight years later. In 1875 she enrolled in the University of California at San Francisco Medical Department and earned her M.D. degree. A botany professor took a special interest in her, and as a result she became a botanist, although she admitted that she "would have preferred the study of birds or more strongly still, the study of insects."

In 1883 Kate became the curator of the California Academy of Sciences herbarium, a position she held for twenty years. In 1889 she married fellow botanist Townshend S. Brandegee, and they spent their honeymoon walking 500 miles from San Diego to San Francisco collecting plant specimens. In 1893 while she was returning by boat a month earlier than her husband from a botanizing trip to Baja, California, the ship broke up on the rocks of San Pedro. Upon hearing of the shipwreck, her husband was concerned only whether she had saved all their plant specimens, which indeed she had.

The Brandegees lived for ten years in San Diego where they established their own herbarium and botanical library. Kate had numerous pets, including a guinea hen and a wild sickle bill thrasher, who came to her call. In 1906 the couple

Traveling botanist

Kate's writing is from a few notes about her life that she wrote at the request of staff members of the University of California Department of Botany. They were published after her death in the university's Publications in Botany, *Volume XIII, 1926.*

moved to San Francisco and devoted the rest of their lives to the University of California herbarium. They donated their library and their collection of 75,000 plant specimens to the university. In 1913 Kate made her last trip to observe botanical centers on the East Coast. She died in 1920 at the age of seventy-five.

Fanny Brice

*A*ll she had

1936

I appeared on the program at nine-thirty, the crux of the evening, when the audience was swimming in boredom because of the show's lack of rhythm and gait.

I was sheathed in a white satin gown that fitted like a silk stocking. When the signal came for my appearance, it wasn't a stage I was on — it was a magic carpet! After about eight encores of "Lovie Joe" the audience was still so enchanted with me that I decided they should have all I had.

I was painfully thin and my dress fitted like a vise. The last roar that met my ears came when I pulled my skirt up over my knees and then, peering down on legs that looked like two slats, put my hand over my eyes in one despairing gesture and stalked off. . . .

When the tumult and the shouting died, nothing further was said about my not going to New York.

Fanny Brice was born October 29, 1891, in New York City. The family moved to Newark, New Jersey, where her father operated several saloons. While her mother Rose ran the business, her father Charlie spent the profits gambling. Eventually Rose divorced her husband, settled in Brooklyn, and became successful in the real estate business.

Fanny won her first amateur talent contest at the age of fourteen, after which she quit school to devote herself to the theater. She changed her last name from the harsh-sounding Alsatian Borach to that of family friend John Brice. She soon realized that she was too tall and skinny to be a chorus girl and learned to rely on her talent for comedy.

Irving Berlin spotted Fanny in 1910 while she was touring with the Columbia burlesque circuit. He gave her a Yiddish parody, "Sadie Salome," to sing. She wore a starched sailor suit that was too small, which caused her to squirm and grimace as she sang. The audience thought she was hilarious,

Fanny's writing is from an interview with Palma Wayne, "Fanny of the Follies," which was published in Cosmopolitan, *February 1936.*

and from then on she built her act around physical humor, parody, and different dialects. She never embarrassed herself by exploiting her sex to get a laugh, but rather used her "talent for sly dissection of all that is fake and preposterous."

Fanny made her debut with the Ziegfeld Follies in 1910, received twelve encores her first night and went on to be Flo Ziegfeld's greatest star. She became famous for her renditions of such songs as "My Man" and "Second Hand Rose." She also made six feature films, including *The Great Ziegfeld* in 1936 and *Zeigfeld Follies* in 1946, and she had her own radio show from 1944 until her death.

Fanny's personal life was not as successful as her stage career. At nineteen she was briefly married to a barber from Massachusetts. From 1918 to 1927 she was married to the love of her life, the gambler Jules "Nick" Arnstein. Their two children were raised by nannies because of the demands of Fanny's career. Eventually Fanny divorced Nick (although she still loved him) because she could no longer tolerate his infidelities. Her marriage to producer Billy Rose in 1929 lasted ten years.

Fanny died of a stroke in Los Angeles shortly before her sixtieth birthday. The director George Cukor eulogized her as "one of the great, great clowns of all time."

Gertrude Atherton

1932

The women of the United States, admirably organized, were now engaged in a nation-wide campaign to win the franchise. I took no active part in it, for that would have meant making speeches, than which I could think of nothing I'd hate more, and I had my own work to do. . . .

I had an inspiration to do something for the cause in my own way. I would write a novel on this burning theme and endeavor to make the movement attractive to the hostile or indifferent. Hitherto I had written for my own pleasure and the public could take it or leave it; I had regarded the propaganda novel as an insult to art, but now I was fired with a holy enthusiasm to do something for my downtrodden sex! . . . All my adverse critics had been men, and they had displayed an almost childish sex-enmity; I had succeeded in spite of them, and it was up to me to use what influence I might

A burning theme

Gertrude's writing is from her Adventures of a Novelist *published in 1932 by Liveright. Inc., New York.*

have to help liberate those unequipped by nature to conquer life for themselves.

Gertrude Franklin Horn Atherton was born October 30, 1857, in the exclusive Rincon Hill area of San Francisco. Her parents were divorced when she was two, and her mother remarried three years later. Most of Gertrude's early upbringing came from her grandfather, who raised her "with a prayer book in one hand and the *Atlantic Monthly* in the other." As a result, she developed a strong dislike of religion and a desire to be a writer.

Gertrude was sent to finishing school in Kentucky when she was seventeen. Upon her return she found her mother about to marry her third husband, George Henry Bowen Atherton. However, George soon switched his affections to Gertrude; and after forever alienating her mother, they were married on Valentine's Day, 1876.

Gertrude's marriage was unhappy. She felt confined by George's strait-laced family, and he jealously objected to any attempt to broaden her horizons. He did not even approve of her reading books. However, Gertrude persisted with her writing, locking herself in her room at night to work. She published her first novel in serial form in the *Argonaut*, infuriating the entire Atherton family. Fortunately for her sanity and her literary career, George died in 1887 on a ship bound for Chile.

Gertrude never remarried but dedicated the rest of her life to writing. She travelled throughout the United States and Europe in search of locales for her next book, usually averaging one novel a year. At her death at ninety-one she left behind more than fifty books and countless articles. Just prior to her death in 1948 she was awarded two honorary degrees, and the city of San Francisco acknowledged her ninetieth birthday with a gold medal.

OCTOBER 31

Lillian Weston Hazen

*T*ough standards

1922
I used to be an intellectual snob myself, but close intercourse with brave, patient, good-hearted working men and women cured me.

A Montana rancher must be "all man" to hold down his job, and his wife must be a real helpmate; I lost my pride in intellect and culture when I saw what my neighbors could do, dare, and suffer, without a murmur, and realized that I was inferior, measured by their standards of courage and endurance.

But I did know how to cook; I tried my best to gratify the appetites of those laboring men, and experienced quite a thrill when the dexterous wielder of knives, after eating a generous helping of soft molasses cake piled high with whipped cream, leaned back in his tipped chair and said it was the nicest stuff he had ever tasted.

Lillian Weston Hazen was born October 31, 1864, in Medford, Massachusetts. Her father was a "professional pedestrian," which kept him away from home for long periods at a time. He would take long walks, such as the 1,326 miles from Portland, Maine, to Chicago, after which he would write an article about the journey. At seventy-one he walked from Santa Monica, California, to New York City in seventy-six days.

When Lillian was fifteen she accompanied her father on a walking tour of England before beginning the fall term at a convent school in Paris. She remained in Paris following graduation, taking courses at the Sorbonne and the French National Art School.

Lillian returned to America in 1887 and began a career as a freelance writer. She published a weekly column of news and gossip, "Lillian's Letters," in *The New York Sunday Herald*. In 1895 she married Frank Hazen, a Dartmouth graduate. The couple had two children.

Lillian had always been fascinated with the West, so she was pleased when her husband took a job as bookkeeper in a Montana mining camp in 1889. They settled in a three-room cottage overlooking the town of Gilt Edge.

In 1903 Frank was elected clerk and recorder of Fergus County, and the family moved to the small town of Lewistown, "the Gem of the Judith Basin." Two years later, their contentment was shattered by the death of their daughter from pneumonia. To ease her grief, Lillian began writing poems and articles about her beloved Montana.

The Hazens joined the Montana land rush in 1916, purchasing 1,200 acres near Acushnet. Although initially successful they never fully recovered from a three-year drought and returned to Lewistown in 1931. Thereafter they wintered in California, but always returned to Montana in the spring. Lillian died in 1949 at the age of eighty-five.

Lillian's writing is from "A Ranchwoman's Guests," Scribner's Magazine, *July-December 1922.*

NOVEMBER

Tamsen Donner

1846
We are now 450 miles from Independence. — Our
route at first was rough and through a timbered country which appeared to be fertile. After striking the
prairie we found a first rate road; and the only difficulty
we had has been crossing creeks. In that, however,
there has been no danger. I never could have believed
we could have travelled so far with so little difficulty.
The prairie between the Blue and Platte rivers is abundant beyond description. Never have I seen so varied a
country — so suitable for cultivation. Every thing was
new and pleasing. The Indians frequently come to see
us and the chiefs of a tribe breakfasted at our tent this
morning. — All are so friendly that I cannot help feeling sympathy and friendship for them.

A happy start

Tamsen Eustis Dozier Donner was born November 1, 1801,
in Newburyport, Massachusetts. Her father was a mariner
and she was raised in a well-to-do environment. After graduating from a private girls' school, Tamsen took a teaching
position at a small academy for girls in Elizabeth City, North
Carolina. She married Tully Dozier and had two children,
but her entire family died during the winter of 1831.

Tamsen returned to her family in Newburyport. Her
brother William had moved to Illinois and invited her to live
with him, and help raise his children after he was widowed in
1836. In May 1839 she married George Donner, an older
man twice widowed with two grown children.

George and Tamsen had three daughters of their own,
Frances, Georgia Ann, and Eliza. They became interested in
the stories of the good life in California. Although they were
advanced in years, he sixty-two and she forty-five, and could
easily have remained in their comfortable midwestern life,
they decided to go west.

In April 1846 the Donners, George and Tamsen and their
three little girls under the age of six, joined his brother's family and set off from Springfield, Illinois, for Independence,
Missouri, where they joined twenty other wagons. Tamsen
had sewned their life savings into a quilt and had brought
along many books, as she hoped to open her own school in
California.

George was elected leader of the wagon train of seventy
people. After an uneventful crossing of the plains, a sudden,

*Tamsen's writing is from a
June 16, 1846, letter to a
friend in Springfield, Illinois.
It was first published in the
June 23, 1846, Springfield
Sangamo Journal and is
included in Covered Wagon
Women, Diaries and Letters
from the Western Trails
1840-1890, edited and com-
piled by Kenneth L. Holmes,
The Arthur H. Clark
Company, 1990.*

unexpected blizzard trapped them in the Sierra Nevadas, and forty-one of the seventy travellers perished. Finally, a rescue party was able to reach "Starved Camp" and lead the survivors to safety. George was near death and too weak to travel. Tamsen could have gone with the rescuers but chose to stay with her dying husband.

She offered what money she had to Mr. Eddy, one of the rescuers, to take her children. His two children had already perished in the camp, and he refused her money but agreed to save the children. There were no provisions to leave with Tamsen, and as the rescuers departed it was evident that she would perish. Her last audible words were, "Oh, save, save my children!"

Tamsen's body and her diaries were never found. Her children did survive, and her youngest daughter, Eliza, published a book about her experiences, *The Expedition of the Donner Party and Its Tragic Fate*, in 1920. Several books and plays have been written about Tamsen, and her hometown of Newburyport has established the Tamsen Donner Fund to support women's history projects.

NOVEMBER 2

Alice Brady

The actress' nose

1919

The directors used to hold conferences about my nose. They wanted me to cut it off, or have an operation or do something to make it more regular. I used to cry every time I saw my nose in a film. I would weep real tears and the directors would swear to themselves. But I am getting over that. The audience is, too. As more and more regular actresses came on the moving picture screen the audiences looked less and less for features and more and more for acting. Now I don't care a bit about my nose.

Alice Brady was born November 2, 1892, in New York City. Her mother, a French dancer, died when she was two so she was raised by her father, a theatrical and movie producer. After graduating from the Convent of St. Elizabeth in Madison, New Jersey, she enrolled in the New England Conservatory of Music in 1910 to study opera. After a year and a half she was told she needed at least five more years of preparation, which "seemed like an eternity" to the impatient young Alice. She quit the conservatory and embarked on her career in light opera and musical comedies.

Alice's words are from an interview, "Prefers the Stage to the Screen," that appeared in the Boston Globe, November 23, 1919.

Women's Words, Women's Stories

Alice convinced her father in 1910 to let her play a small part in his revival of *The Mikado*. She did so well that the next year she made her formal debut in the musical *The Balkan Princess*. Initially, she concealed her identity as Marie Rose to avoid connection with her father and charges of nepotism.

Alice spent a year playing in a series of Gilbert and Sullivan operettas followed in 1917 by her first dramatic role, Meg, in *Little Women* in 1917. She then toured the country for a year with Hedda Hopper's (May 2) husband, DeWolf Hopper, bringing light opera to rural America. In 1914 she made her first motion picture, commencing a movie career that would last twenty-five years. Thereafter she alternated between stage and screen, becoming one of the country's most successful and versatile actresses in light opera, serious drama, and comedies, in silent as well as talking films.

In May 1919 Alice married the actor James Lyon Crane; they had one son. Although she made numerous movies she always preferred the theater because of the presence of a live audience and the absence of long delays between scenes, allowing her to maintain concentration. She did not make any movies between 1923 and 1933, devoting herself exclusively to the New York stage. She returned to the big screen in 1933 and received an Academy Award in 1937 for her portrayal of Mrs. O'Leary in *In Old Chicago*. Two years later she died of cancer at the age of forty-six and was buried in the Sleepy Hollow Cemetery in Tarrytown, New York.

Lucy Crump Jefferson

1965

Negroes had to be taught to use Negro funeral directors. They were just simply something the public was not used to. We were an oddity and doomed to early failure so thought many of our friends. W. H. Jefferson had to keep his job on the railroad to help pay expenses so that the late J. H. Jefferson, father of the present owners, took charge of the business. An embalmer from Memphis, Tennessee, was hired to do the embalming. Within five years the firm was on the way to financial success. This was done through the support of many friends who have remained loyal to our business down through the years.

Funeral success

Lucy's words are from an interview published posthumously in the Vicksburg Evening Post, *April 16, 1965.*

Lucy Crump Jefferson was born November 3, 1866, in Jackson, Mississippi. She was one of two children of Alice Crump, a former slave, and an unknown father. Her family settled in Vicksburg where she attended local public schools.

When she was twenty-three Lucy married W. H. Jefferson, the well-to-do son of a Virginia freedman. Five years later they founded the W. H. Jefferson Funeral Home, the first funeral home for blacks in Mississippi, and the first business in the state owned and operated by blacks. In 1914 they expanded to include the Jefferson Burial Association, which was staffed with grief counselors and professionals able to explain the complicated insurance plans available to clients.

Following W. H. Jefferson's death in 1922 Lucy continued to manage the funeral home with the assistance of her father-in-law. She believed strongly in education for blacks and established the Lucy C. Jefferson Scholarship, which she presented to a graduating high school student each year for more than forty years. She also served as a trustee at Campbell College in Jackson, Mississippi. As president of the Mississippi Federation of Colored Women's Clubs from 1928 to 1934 she oversaw numerous philanthropic projects, including the establishment of the Margaret Murray Washington (March 9) Home for Delinquent Boys and Girls.

Lucy died of cancer in 1953 at the age of eighty-six and was buried in her beloved Vicksburg. Thirteen years after her death an all-black junior high school was built and named in her honor.

NOVEMBER 4

Sarah Hall Boardman Judson

To a young son

Sarah's poem, written in 1835 in Burma to her young son George in America, is included in Memoir of Sarah B. Judson of the American Mission to Burmah by Emily C. Judson, published by Lewis Colby in 1848.

1835

For my darling Georgie.
You cannot see your dear mama,
  But think of her, my love;
Nor can you see your dear papa,
  For he's in heaven above.

Your sister Sarah, too, is gone,
  And little brother dear; —
But still, my child, you're not alone,
  For God is ever near.

Sarah Hall Boardman Judson was born November 4, 1803, in Alstead, New Hampshire, the eldest of thirteen children. Although she briefly attended a local female seminary, financial difficulties forced her to return home to assist in the care and education of her younger siblings. She was deeply religious, a devout member of the First Baptist Church.

In 1823 Sarah attended a talk given by Ann Hasseltine Judson, wife of Adoniram Judson, the first American missionary to Burma. Ann's lecture sparked in Sarah an interest in missionary work.

Sarah wrote a poem in honor of James Colman, a missionary who had died in Burma. A young college student, George Dana Boardman, read her poem and began a correspondence with the author. They discovered that they had much in common and were married in July 1825.

Two weeks after their wedding the Boardmans set sail for Calcutta. They were detained, however, for more than a year because of the Anglo-Burmese War. Sarah used that time to study the Burmese language, becoming fluent in it. Finally, in the spring of 1828 they reached the American Baptist Mission in Amherst, Burma, with their newborn daughter, Sarah.

The Boardmans were soon sent to Tavoy, a small village on the Bay of Bengal. Together they established day and boarding Christian schools for the natives. They also worked with the Karens, a jungle people who were badly treated by the Burmese. Sarah gave birth to a son, George, in 1827 and another son, Judson Wade, who died as an infant in 1830.

Their daughter Sarah died of dysentery in 1829 and her husband died a few months later of heart disease and exhaustion.

Sarah decided to remain in Burma to carry on the work with the Karens, for whom her husband had given his life. In 1834 she married Adoniram Judson, whose first wife Ann had died eight years previously.

Sarah decided she needed to send her son George back to America. She wrote in her journal, "My reason and judgement tell me that the good of my child requires that he should be sent to America." Little George was sent off alone on the ship *Cashmere* to return to Boston where other missionaries would select suitable parents to raise him. His mother gave him two letters, one for him full of sentimental and religious advice, and one for his future guardians instructing them in certain aspects of his upbringing. She implored them to "let him often be reminded of us; and let the love which he now feels for us be carefully cherished. I could not bear to be forgotten by the little one." Her fondest wish was that "at some future day he might stand in his father's place, and preach among the heathen the unsearchable riches of Christ." He did indeed grow up to become a well-known Baptist minister.

Sarah and Adoniram had eight children, five of whom survived infancy. She helped her husband in all aspects of his work and translated the New Testament and other religious writings into Burmese and the local dialect of the Peguans. After the birth of her last child in December 1844, Sarah became very ill. Adoniram accompanied her on the ocean voyage to return to America for medical treatment, but she died en route on September 1, 1845, at the age of forty-one. She was buried on the island of St. Helena in the South Atlantic.

Ann Raney Coleman

Ladies in Texas

Ann's writing is from her journal, which she gave to her niece in 1889. It appeared in 1971 as Lady on the Texas Frontier — the Journal of Ann Raney Coleman, *edited by C. Richard King and published by the University of Oklahoma Press.*

1832

The country was full of bachelors, but very few ladies. When bedtime came we were ushered into a room where there were several beds. We did not like this much, as we expected a room to ourselves, but on being told that the gentlemen slept on one side and the ladies on the other side of the room, I opened both my eyes and ears and looked again at my hostess, who did not seem to be jesting. Presently several more ladies came in to go to bed. They went through the undressing operation quickly and were all in bed before we had got over our surprise at this new fashion of sleeping. We soon undressed but did not divest ourselves of all our garments, keeping on outside garments which were calico wrappers. We had been in bed about an hour when the gentlemen came in one by one until all had retired. I watched with breathless suspense the coming of the last one. This was something we were not accustomed to, and it was several nights before I could sleep — not until nature was completely exhausted and overcome with watching.

The ladies all laughed at us and said, "By the time you have been in Texas a few months, if you travel in the country, you will have to sleep with the man and his wife at the house you visit," as houses were only log cabins with two rooms, one for the house servants, the other for the family.

Ann Raney Coleman was born November 5, 1810, in Whitehaven, England. In 1829 her brother emigrated to Texas, where he died after six months. Her father had

---

suffered heavy financial losses, and after filing for bankruptcy he followed his late son to America.

Ann and her mother and sister remained in England until 1832 when they set sail for New Orleans to reunite the family.

Ann married John Thomas in the first public wedding in Brazoria, Texas. During the war between Texas and Mexico they were forced to flee their home when they heard that Sam Houston and his troops were retreating. They resettled on a plantation in Bayou Grosse Tête, Louisiana, near Baton Rouge.

Ann and John prospered in their new location. They had three children, two sons and a daughter, and made a comfortable living farming the plantation. Their happy life together ended in 1847 with the deaths of John and their two sons.

Ann married again, to John Coleman, in haste; she soon realized that she had made a mistake. In 1854 she left Louisiana, returning to England for a year to visit old friends and relatives. Upon her return to America she filed for divorce and went back to Texas. She supported herself by teaching in local schools.

In 1875 Ann wrote to her niece that she was writing a book about her life as she had suggested. Ann had kept a detailed journal since her ocean voyage to America forty-three years earlier. She worked on her book for the next fourteen years until 1889, when she at last declared to her niece that it was finished. However, she could not afford to pay the publishing costs.

Ann died in Texas in 1897 at the age of eighty-seven.

Helen Thompson Wooley

1923

*I*nner strength

Her teacher's first view of Jean was at home, where a family of eight people occupied two rooms, and here is her comment: "She was standing in a wretched dirty basement among a lot of unkempt little brothers and sisters, attending to her business of caring for them. She looked strong and rugged and happy." Jean's parents were illiterate. The father proudly told the principal of the school that he himself had never been in jail. He worked as a teamster for the support of his family of eight children.

Helen Bradford Thompson Wooley was born November 6, 1874, in Chicago. After attending Chicago public schools she enrolled in the University of Chicago. She received her Ph.B. degree in 1897 and her Ph.D., summa cum laude, in 1900. After a year of studying abroad she began teaching psychology at Mount Holyoke College.

Helen married Dr. Paul Gerhardt Wooley, head of the Serum Laboratory in Manila, in 1905. They spent three years in Manila and Siam, then returned to the University of Cincinnati where Paul was a professor of pathology, and Helen resumed teaching as an instructor in philosophy.

In 1911 Helen was appointed director of the newly formed Bureau for the Investigation of Working Children following passage of the 1910 Ohio child labor law. She then began her extensive study of schoolchildren versus working children. She completed a five-year follow up study of 750 children who had left school at fourteen to go to work, compared with the same number of workers who had finished school, which resulted in the passage in 1921 of the Bing Law for compulsory school attendance.

The Wooleys moved to Detroit in 1921 when Paul was offered a position at the Detroit College of Medicine. Helen joined the staff of the Merrill-Palmer School as a professor and school psychologist. She taught courses to both undergraduate and graduate students and set up one of the first nursery schools to serve as a laboratory for the study of child development. Her work resulted in her writing several books on the personality and mental development of three-year-olds.

Paul and Helen were separated in 1924. He moved to California, and she went to New York City as a professor of education at Columbia University's Teachers College. She was very unhappy living alone, and when she learned that her separation from her husband would be permanent, she became ill and took a leave of absence from the university. She returned to work in the fall of 1929 but had lost her teaching skills and was asked to resign. With her professional career over, Helen spent her remaining years with her daughter in Havertown, Pennsylvania, where she died in 1947 at the age of seventy-three.

Helen's writing is from "Diagnosis and Treatment of Young School Failures," a bulletin she wrote for the Department of the Interior, Bureau of Education. It was published by the Government Printing Office, Washington, D.C., in 1923.

Eleanor Medill Patterson

1930

All kinds of people ask me if I intend to change the policies of *The Washington Herald.*

I would not if I could. I could not if I would. . . .

Dozens of other inquiries have come in as to how a woman proposes to boss an office full of men. But why should it be a worse job to boss men in the office than to boss them in the home? Men have always been bossed by women anyway, although most of them don't know it.

Still others want to know what ideals, if any, are peculiar to the female editor. The ideal of all true newspaper folk, regardless of sex, is to keep a paper interesting, inspiring, honest and successful. . .

The new boss

Eleanor Medill Patterson was born November 7, 1881, in Chicago. She was educated at private schools in Boston and Farmington, Connecticut. At twenty-one, Eleanor, nick-named Cissy, joined her uncle abroad where he was the American envoy in Vienna and later St. Petersburg. At one of the Romanov balls she met Count Josef Gizycki, a Polish nobleman twice her age with a reputation as a womanizer and gambler. They were married at the family mansion on Dupont Circle in Washington, D.C., in April 1904.

Although it was soon discovered that his "castle" in Moravia was a dilapidated wooden shack and that he had married Cissy only for her money, she remained with him and had a daughter, Felicia. In 1908 however, she left him while on a European trip after he beat her when she objected to his interest in another woman. He kidnapped Felicia, but Cissy's father influenced President-elect Taft to contact Czar Nicholas II. After one and a half years Cissy was finally able to return to America with her daughter.

Cissy suffered from a series of nervous illnesses so she moved to Jackson Hole, Wyoming, to seek relief in the wilderness. She camped, fished, rode horseback, and in 1921 was the first woman to take the 163-mile boat trip through the Salmon River rapids.

Cissy returned to New York City in 1923 and two years later married Elmer Schlesinger, a successful corporate lawyer. They travelled between homes in Manhattan, Long Island, and Washington, D.C., and she became renowned as a social hostess. After Elmer's death in 1929 she resumed her maiden name, calling herself Mrs. Patterson.

Eleanor's writing is from the biography, Cissy, *by Ralph Martin, published in 1979 by Simon and Schuster.*

Although wealthy, Cissy was lonely and bored and searching for something to give meaning to her life. A family friend convinced William Randolph Hearst to hire Cissy as editor and publisher of the morning *Washington Herald;* and although she knew nothing about running a paper she began her career in August 1930.

In 1939 Cissy bought the *Herald* and the evening *Times* and merged them into the successful *Times-Herald. Collier's* magazine called her "the most powerful woman in America," and *Time* called her "the most hated woman in America" because of her power. She often received threatening letters and began carrying a pistol in later years. She died of a heart attack at her Maryland estate in 1957 when she was sixty-six.

Eartha Mary Magdalene White

Only a step

1933

I fell from the walk between the sidewalk and the car, striking and fracturing my right arm on the running board. . . .

I was a "shut in" for weeks, but friends came to see me, bringing fruit and flowers, and doing everything they could to make me comfortable. But while confined in bed my thoughts were centered on plans for the further improvement and building up of my work, the Mission.

A thought came to me that the day before my mother died, she made this expression "death is only a step." I began to ponder that thought in my heart. . . .

Eartha Mary Magdalene White was born November 8, 1876, in Jacksonville, Florida, to Mollie Chapman, a young black woman, and an unidentified white man. Clara White, a friend of Mollie's, adopted Eartha shortly after her birth and raised her as her own.

Eartha attended local public schools until 1893 when Jacksonville was put under quarantine for yellow fever. Clara sent her to live with friends in New York City where she studied at Madame Thurber's National Conservatory of Music. She joined the Oriental American Opera Company, the country's first black opera company.

Eartha toured America, Europe, and Asia with the opera company but returned to Jacksonville often on visits. During one of these visits she fell in love with James Jordan, a railway

Eartha's writing is from a small eight-page booklet, "Some Sayings of My Mother," which she wrote in memory of Clara White. It was printed in 1933 and used to raise funds for her mission. It is in the Eartha White Collection, University of North Florida Library, Jacksonville.

worker. They set their wedding date for June 1896, but while she was still on tour in May she received news of his death. She ended her singing career and returned to Jacksonville. Clara advised her to "Do all the good you can, in all the ways you can, in all the places you can, for all the people you can, while you can," and for the next seventy-eight years that is exactly what she did.

In 1901 Eartha started buying real estate at low prices and then selling at a profit. By 1905 she had saved enough for a dry goods store that catered to black people. She then went on to own several other businesses. She reinvested her considerable wealth in the black community in the form of Boy's and Girl's Clubs, recreation centers, and parks. She operated the only orphanage for black children in the state of Florida and conducted weekly Bible classes at the county prison. She was most proud of the Clara White Mission, named for her adoptive mother, which offered food and shelter to the homeless and destitute.

Although confined to a wheelchair in later years, Eartha remained active. A few years before her death she obtained a federal grant to begin construction of the Eartha M. White Nursing Home, a 120-bed facility for welfare patients.

She received numerous honors, including the Lane Bryant Award for "the person in America considered to have made the most outstanding voluntary contribution to his or her community during the past year," and in 1971 she was a guest of President Richard Nixon at the White House. She was referred to as "an institution in Jacksonville," and for the last years of her life her birthday was celebrated in the city's civic auditorium. Eartha died in January 1974 at the age of ninety-seven and was buried in the old Jacksonville city cemetery.

Harriot Kezia Hunt

1856

*He*r birth

There had been a preparation for my birth in mother's life. . . . She was then thirty-five years of age. Children had been repeatedly offered her for adoption; to each offer she would say, "If the Lord wills me to sustain that relation, he will give me a child." The Lord willed it.

The birth of her first-born was an event, not only in the family, but in the neighborhood; and it even excited interest among strangers. Severe, sorrowful, anxious hours dragged by; still the physicians tarried, and

Harriot's writing is from her autobiography, Glances and Glimpses, *published by John P. Jewett Co. in 1856.*

uncertainty became resolved into anguish as the news spread that both mother and child could not live. After three days of intense anxiety — surgical skill being demanded — a baby was born and laid away as lifeless. But the joy was great, for the wife was saved!

A careful, capable aunt, my mother's eldest sister, who herself had a family, took this baby, — this child of so many prayers, hopes, and aspirations, — and exerted all her skill for its preservation. She rubbed, and chafed, and breathed upon its apparently lifeless body; and it revived — it moved — a cry escaped. How many times I have been told of that cry! The tidings broke upon my parents like an electric shock. They had a daughter! Never was a child more gladly welcomed — never was an anxious mother more devoted — never was more true love breathed on an infant!

Harriot Kezia Hunt was born November 9, 1805, in Boston. She and her younger sister Sarah were educated at local private schools. In 1827 Harriot opened a small school of her own.

Sarah became ill in 1830 and was subjected to a long but unsuccessful treatment that included leaches, blisters, prussic acid, and calomel. In 1833 an English couple by the name of Mott arrived in Boston and began treating patients. Under their care Sarah achieved a complete recovery.

Harriot closed her school and with her sister studied with the Motts for two years. In 1835 the Hunts opened their own practice primarily treating women and children, often succeeding where other doctors had failed. They stressed cleanliness, healthy diet, rest, and exercise. They received calls from all over the Boston area for "given up cases" and "chronic diseases of the aggravated character." They often found the causes of "physical maladies growing out of concealed sorrows" and therefore treated patients' mental as well as physical health.

Sarah retired in 1840 after her marriage, but Harriot continued alone. In 1847 she petitioned Dr. Oliver Wendell Holmes, dean of Harvard Medical School, for permission to audit lectures. Although he was in favor of admitting her the governing board overruled him, calling it "inexpedient." Three years later she was granted permission to attend lectures, but the senior class staged a protest that was reported in the Boston papers and she decided to withdraw.

Harriot joined the women's suffrage movement and lectured frequently on the importance of admitting women to the medical profession. Each year for twenty years, Harriot paid her taxes with an accompanying note protesting the taxation of a woman's property when she was not allowed to vote. She died of Bright's disease in 1875 at the age of sixty-nine. She was buried in Cambridge's Mount Auburn Cemetery beneath the statue of the goddess Hygeia, which she had commissioned years earlier by the black sculptress, Edmonia Lewis (July 4).

Mabel Normand

1920
One of the secrets of being a comedienne is in knowing jazz, because when you know the syncopated tunes, you know the songs to which the average heart responds, and so, in a way you know humanity. To be a comedienne you've got to be human. That's the truth of the matter. You've got to be able to appreciate that side of people which is queer, ridiculous, and yet lovable.

The comedienne

Mabel Ethelreid Normand was born November 10, 1893, in Boston. The family moved to Staten Island, New York, soon after her birth. Mrs. Normand sent Mabel to the Butterick Company where young girls were being employed in the pattern department. The head of the pattern department said, "You're too pretty to work in this department," and sent her to the art department where she was hired as a model.

After several years of modeling she went to work at D. W. Griffith's Biograph Studio. She was hired to hold the skirt of a noblewoman in one of Griffith's films. She later recalled, "While I was rehearsing I noticed a stocky, red-faced Irishman leaning against the wall and grinning. I remembered his face and years later I made a tremendous fortune for that Irishman. His name was Mack Sennett."

When Mack Sennett left New York for California in 1912 to start his own Keystone Film Company, he took Mabel with him. They made a series of slapstick comedies together, and her gifts for pantomime and mimicry made her very popular. Previously, comediennes had been homely, awkward buffoons, but Mabel was "the first *beautiful* girl who could produce an earthquake of laughter in the darkened theatres of the world simply by walking out before the camera and standing still!" as Sidney Sutherland described her in *Liberty*, September 6, 1930.

Charlie Chaplin joined Keystone in 1913 and made eleven pictures with Mabel. His famous tramp character debuted in *Mabel's Strange Predicament*. She also made many "Fatty and

Mabel's writing is from "How to be a Comedienne," New York Dramatic Mirror, *June 19, 1920.*

Mabel" films with W. Roscoe Arbuckle, and she is credited with being the first person to throw a pie in someone's face for laughs.

Mabel's film *Mickey*, released in 1918, was popular all over the world and became her best-known role. She left Keystone soon afterward and made sixteen movies in three years for Samuel Goldwyn. Her salary, reportedly four figures a week, was spent lavishly on clothes, jewelry, wild parties, and drugs. On February 2, 1922, she was the last person to see William Desmond Taylor, a well-known director, minutes before he was shot to death. His murder was never solved, but it was thought that he died protecting her from blackmailers who were going to expose her drug addiction. Public outrage, especially from women's clubs, was strong, and for a while her films were banned.

Mabel made two more movies, but scandal struck again on New Year's Day 1924, when her chauffeur shot Courtland S. Dines, a wealthy oil magnate, during a jealous argument over Mabel. Her career could not survive this second catastrophe, and she never worked again. In 1926 at 3 a.m., after a drunken party, she married Lew Cody, an actor she had worked with years earlier in *Mickey*. She died alone, four years later, of tuberculosis in a private sanatorium in Monrovia, California.

Leonel Ross O'Bryan (Polly Pry)

Her new creation

1903

I read a very nice story the other day, written by a particularly nice man, who is a friend of mine. It was all about this little paper — and me.

It was not exactly a true story, that was the reason I liked it, probably, but it was intended to help me out and therefore I am grateful.

The man said, among other things, that my friends were all millionaires, and that I had "touched" them, to the modest tune of Fifteen Thousand Dollars.

I didn't mind that; it was kind of him to think that I had "Savey" enough to do it. The only thing that broke my heart was, that it wasn't true. . . .

I wanted this paper, truly, and I wanted it pretty badly — well — here it is, my friends, in its best and only bib-and-tucker, making its initial bow to you. It is not exactly a howling beauty, but for that you can

Leonel's writing is from the first issue (September 5, 1903) of her weekly magazine Polly Pry.

blame my "millionaire friends," it is as lovely as I could afford to make it, that is my first and only apology. The contents I am responsible for.

I hope they will please you, if not, then I hope they will seriously displease you, as, in either event, the result will be the same — i.e. You will read the paper.

Leonel Ross Campbell Anthony O'Bryan was born November 11, 1857, on a Mississippi plantation. She attended private school in St. Louis, but when she was fifteen she climbed over the wall to elope with George Anthony.

In 1878 Leonel left her husband and arrived in New York City, where she asked a family friend for a position at *The New York World*. She did such a good job that she was sent to Panama as the Latin American correspondent. Twenty years later she moved to Denver to be near her parents and began writing for *The Denver Post*. She took the pen name Polly Pry, a rhyming tribute to her role model Nellie Bly (May 5), a world-travelling journalist.

While writing an article on Colorado prisons, Polly Pry met Alfred Packer, who had been given the death penalty for killing and eating five prospectors to save himself from starvation during a blizzard. Although his sentence had been reduced to forty years in prison on a technicality, Polly Pry took up his cause, arguing that he had not killed them but had only eaten them after they died as an act of self-preservation. She was able to secure his release in 1901.

Leonel started her own liberal feminist magazine named *Polly Pry*. In January 1904 she opened the door to her home only to be shot at twice by an unknown assailant. Luckily the bullets missed her. She claimed it was organized labor trying to silence her, although others said she had staged the event to increase her magazine's sales.

Leonel ran out of funds and closed her magazine in 1905. In 1910 she married Denver lawyer Harry J. O'Bryan, but he died four years later while she was on assignment in Mexico doing a story on Pancho Villa. She spent World War I in Greece and Albania as director of publicity for the Red Cross. After the war Leonel settled in Denver where she did public relations work for the Red Cross. She died in Denver in 1938 when she was eighty-one years old.

Electa Kellogg

Chord of memory

*circa
1865*

His private worth, how he excell'd in all
The kind amenities in social life,
As husband, father, friend — e'en now I seem
To feel the pressure of his hand upon
My head; I see the fond, paternal smile,
And hear the words, "My daughter," from his lips.
That word awakes one chord, one strain alone,
Alas! alas! my father, thou art gone!

Electa Washburn Kellogg was born November 12, 1805, in
New Haven, Connecticut. Her father, the Reverend
Ebenezer Washburn, was a minister in the Methodist
Episcopal Church. Although she occasionally attended private school in New York City her fragile health usually kept
her at home. She received most of her education from her
father, and they became very close. She often accompanied
him on his rounds, "sharing his thoughts and ministrations."

Electa married S. H. Kellogg, and the couple lived in
Connecticut for several years before deciding to move to the
wilderness of Wisconsin. Together they built a log cabin and
eventually had ten children, two of whom died as infants. On
the first Sunday after settling into their cabin Electa "gathered the settlers' children around her, and organized the first
Sabbath School in the country, which was continued without
interruption for fifty years at the place known as 'Kellogg
Corners.'"

In 1860 the Kelloggs moved to the town of Janesville,
Wisconsin, where Electa continued to be active in the local
church. The young people in her parish regarded her as a
living encyclopedia of universal knowledge. After her husband's death in 1867 Electa travelled around the state visiting
her children. She spent time with her son in Milwaukee then
went on to Racine to see two of her daughters. Her
youngest, Belle, was pregnant for the first time, and Electa
hoped to be present at the delivery. However, she became ill
and her last words were: "Could I but see 'round this one little turn for you, dear, I should die content." She died in
September 1868, before the birth of Belle's twin boys, and
was buried beside her husband in Janesville.

*Electa's writing is from her
poem, "The Moaning Harp,"
written in memory of her
father. It was included in*
Woman in Sacred Song,
*compiled by Eva M. Smith and
published by D. Lothrop and
Co. in 1885.*

Annie Lowry

1966

I am a half-breed. That means I live on the fringe of
two races. My white friends think I am just a plain old
Paiute, while the Indians say I think I am better than
they because my father was a white man. When the
time came to make a choice between the Indians and
the white race, I made up my mind to be an Indian. At
that time I felt resentful toward my white father
because he was not fair to my mother. I was determined that no white man would ever make me suffer as
Jerome Lowry, my father, a white man, made my little
Indian mother suffer. I know I was right to choose the
Indians for my people because I loved them more.
Anything Indian I learned quickly, but to the white
teaching my mind was closed.

Annie Lowry was born November 13, 1866, near Lovelock,
Nevada. Her mother was a Paiute Indian named Sau-tau-
nee, also known as Susie. Her father, Jerome Lowry, was a
white man who was often away from home for long periods.
While he was away, she and her mother reverted to Indian
ways, but when he was around he insisted that everyone speak
English and discouraged all Paiute talk. He enrolled Annie in
the Lovelock School, the first Indian in the area to go to
school with white children and possibly the first Paiute to go
to school at all.

Eventually, Mr. Lowry grew prosperous. His Indian
family became an embarrassment so he deserted them, never
to return. When he died years later friends urged Annie to
travel to Oregon to make a claim for her inheritance. She
refused, not wishing to cause trouble for her two brothers
who were living as whites. After her father's departure Annie
gave up her white heritage and returned to Indian ways.

Annie did housework, the only work available to Indian
women, for $1.50 per week. She married a local Indian
named Sanny in the traditional Paiute ceremony that took
five days. They had nine children, five of whom survived
infancy.

In 1910 Sanny died of typhoid fever and Annie was left
penniless. She refused to send her children to the government Indian orphanage, for she was determined to keep her
family together. To make ends meet she worked two jobs a
day, seven days a week. At night she took in sewing, which

Choosing her people

Annie's writing is from
Karnee, A Paiute Narrative,
*by Lalla Scott, University of
Nevada Press, 1966.*

she did by lamplight after the children were in bed. Eventually she met and married John S. Pascal, an English-speaking Paiute.

Annie taught her husband to read, which was a great comfort to him in later years after he was run over by a runaway team of horses and left unable to walk. After he died Annie tore off the wing of the house containing their bedroom, an Indian custom, and moved into the rest of the house. In 1925 she was stricken with a mysterious illness that left her paralyzed on one side and unable to see. Doctors in Reno were not able to help her, so she turned to the local Indian doctor for help. He ministered to her for five days and nights, and on the fifth day she was well. Annie lived another eighteen years in perfect health. She died in 1943.

Claribel Cone

Companionship

1910
I am glad you are having (I shall not say "have had") such happy days with Bertha alone. Of course — no third fourth or fifth person can enter the complete circle of two people — and leave it complete — that goes without saying — it does not matter who the 3rd 4th and 5th etc people are — they are intruders — and when they are not people of whom one quite approves they are intolerable intruders. Any person who enters and interferes with the friendship — the companionship of two people — is de trop — I sometimes feel that some people who enter the company of one person is de trop —

There is a sort of intolerable loneliness in being with people you do not like a loneliness much greater than that of being alone — for in being alone there are the possibilities of all sorts of other companionships — when you have time to think of them — whereas a bad companion is an actual unpleasant fact.

Claribel Cone was born November 14, 1864, in Jonesboro, Tennessee, the fifth of thirteen children. Her parents had emigrated from Germany eight years before her birth. Her father worked his way up from street peddler to proprietor of a country grocery store to wealthy owner of a wholesale grocery business.

The newly affluent Cones settled in Baltimore, where

Claribel's writing is from a June 22, 1910, letter to her sister Etta of Frankfurt, Germany, it is in the Archives of American Art, Smithsonian Institution, Washington, D.C.

Claribel graduated from Western High School for girls. She then attended the Woman's Medical College of Baltimore, graduating at the top of her class. Following her internship at Philadelphia's Blockley Hospital for the Insane, she returned to Baltimore to pursue her special interest in pathology.

Claribel worked in Dr. William A. Welch's pathology laboratory, publishing two articles about her research on tuberculosis. She joined the board of trustees at the Woman's Medical College and began teaching pathology there in 1894.

After Mr. Cone's death in 1897, Claribel and her younger sister Etta began travelling throughout Europe, purchasing art. While in Paris in 1904 the sisters visited friends from Baltimore, Leo Stein and his sister Gertrude, where they were introduced to the work of post-impressionist artist Paul Cézanne. The Steins also collected antique Renaissance furniture which they used to offset their art collection, and the Cones began to do the same.

Claribel met artist Henri Matisse in 1906 and they became good friends. His work formed the core of her collection. After the Woman's Medical College closed in 1910 Claribel retired from medicine and devoted the rest of her life to collecting art. In 1921 she and Etta rented a seven-room apartment in the building where they lived in Baltimore, which they turned into a museum.

Claribel and Etta spent summers purchasing art abroad and winters in Baltimore working on their museum displays. Claribel died suddenly of pneumonia in Lausanne, Switzerland, in 1929. She left her entire art collection to her sister, suggesting that she eventually leave it to the Baltimore Museum of Art "if the spirit of appreciation of modern art in Baltimore becomes improved." Apparently, Etta felt Baltimore was deserving and did leave the collection to the museum along with $400,000 to build a wing to house it in. The Cone collection remains one of the most important private collections of the twentieth century.

Sara Josephine Baker

1939

*F*rom the heart

My impulse to try to do things about hopeless situations appears to have cropped out first when I was about six years old, and it should be pointed out that the method I used was characteristically direct. I was all dressed up for some great occasion — a beautiful white lacy dress with a blue sash and light blue silk

stockings and light blue kid shoes — and inordinately vain about it. While waiting for Mother to come down, I wandered out in front of the house to sit on the horse block and admire myself and hope that someone would come along and see me in all my glory.

Presently a spectator did arrive — a little colored girl about my size but thin and peaked and hungry looking, wearing only a ragged old dress the color of ashes. I have never seen such dumb envy in any human being's face before or since. Child that I was, I could not stand it; it struck me right over the heart. I could not bear the idea that I had so much and she had so little. So I got down off the horse block and took off every stitch I had on, right down to the blue shoes that were the joy of my infantile heart and gave everything, underwear and all, to the little black girl. I watched her as she scampered away, absolutely choked with bliss. Then I walked back into the house, completely naked, wondering why I had done it and how to explain my inexplicable conduct. Oddly enough both Father and Mother seemed to understand pretty well what had gone on in my mind. They were fine people, my father and mother.

Sara Josephine Baker was born November 15, 1873, in Poughkeepsie, New York. Her father and only brother died when she was sixteen, and she decided then to become a doctor. After a year's private study she was accepted at the Woman's Medical College of the New York Infirmary for Women and Children.

Josephine graduated second in her class of eighteen and opened a private practice in New York. However, after earning only $185 her first year, she became an inspector for the city health department. Although she maintained her private practice she became involved in public health work with a special concern for lowering the infant mortality rate.

At the beginning of the twentieth century the infant mortality rate in New York City was very high — often 1,500 deaths per week during the heat of the summer. In 1908 Josephine tackled this problem with a team of thirty nurses. They went door to door, advising mothers on breastfeeding, cleanliness, and good ventilation. The mortality rate dropped considerably, which resulted in the establishment of a Bureau of Child Hygiene with Josephine as director.

Josephine was a pioneer in preventive medicine and public health education. She lectured throughout the United States

Josephine's writing is from her book, Fighting for Life, *published by the Macmillan Company in 1939.*

on child hygiene and published five popular books on the subject in addition to more than 250 magazine articles. In her lifetime and largely through her efforts, Dr. Baker saw the infant mortality rate in New York City drop from 111 to 66 per 1,000 births.

Josephine spent her retirement at her farm in New Jersey. She died of cancer at the age of seventy-five and was buried in the Rural Cemetery in Poughkeepsie.

Minnie Hauk

1925

My *début* — the first of any American singer in Vienna — passed off brilliantly before an immense audience. It seems that I took the severe and critical Viennese by storm. I was enthusiastically called before the curtain and cheered, and next day my name was on everybody's lips. To this sudden popularity I contributed, quite unawares, by a slight slip of the tongue. When Faust, on meeting Gretchen in the market place of Nuremberg, offers his arm to her, she replies in confusion:

> *Bin weder Fräulein, weder schön,*
> *Kann unbegleitet nach Hause geh'n.*

Then she walks quickly off towards the back of the stage. In doing so, I heard the intense stillness broken by general tittering, followed by wild applause. Of course, I did not realize the cause of this hilarity, for I had sung the phrase to the best of my ability, and was somewhat disconcerted. Arriving behind the scenes, I was told that instead of "*unbegleitet*," which means "unaccompanied," I had inadvertently pronounced that word so that it sounded like "*unbekleidet*," meaning "undressed." Of course, that was something for the gay Viennese. The story made the rounds of Vienna, and everybody wanted to see the American who could go home *unbekleidet*. My following appearances at the opera were witnessed by immense audiences.

Minnie Hauk was born November 16, 1851, in New York City. The family moved to New Orleans when she was nine,

A brilliant début

Minnie's writing is from her autobiography, Memories of a Singer, *published in 1925 by A. M. Philpot, Ltd.*

where she started singing lessons. After hearing her sing once, her teacher refused to accept any payment for instructing her.

Minnie and her mother returned to New York in 1862. She continued her singing lessons and made her operatic debut when she was fifteen at the Brooklyn Academy of Music. She became well known touring the states during the next two years until a loan from a wealthy music publisher enabled her to go to Europe in 1868. Minnie debuted in Paris the following year and went on to sing operas in England, Holland, Russia, and Austria. In 1874 she moved to Berlin, where she was one of the Royal Opera's principal singers for the next three years.

Minnie married Baron Ernst von Hesse-Wartegg, an Austrian journalist, in 1881. She continued to tour Europe and America singing with all the major opera companies. In 1884 she sang for President Chester Arthur at the White House. She gave her final U.S. performance in 1893 and her ·final European performance in 1895, after which she travelled throughout China, Japan, India, and South America with her husband.

The baron lost most of his fortune during World War I. Following his death in 1918 Minnie was almost blind and without funds. A handful of American opera patrons raised money to support her, so that she was able to remain at her villa in Lucerne until her death in 1929.

Grace Abbott

*B*etrayal

Grace's writing is from her book, The Immigrant and the Community, *published by The Century Company in 1917.*

1917

Promise of marriage may, of course, be a factor in cases of the betrayal of American girls, and the foreign girl, whose village experience has not prepared her for the easy way in which men can disappear in the United States, is more easily victimized through her affections. . . .

It is the same story of the desire for affection, together with loneliness, lack of knowledge of herself, and long hours of hard, monotonous work. The difference between the temptations which meet the American country girl who comes to the city and those of the immigrant girl is, in the main, one of degree and not of kind.

Grace Abbott was born November 17, 1878, in Grand Island, Nebraska. She attended Brownell Hall, a girls' boarding school in Omaha, and went on to receive a Ph.B. degree from Grand Island College in 1898.

Grace moved to Chicago in 1907 and received her master's degree at the University of Chicago in 1909. She took up residence at Hull House from 1908 to 1917 and began her career as a social worker.

In 1917 Grace accepted an invitation to join the staff of the Federal Children's Bureau. She served as head of the Child Labor Division, investigating offenders of the child labor law. After the Supreme Court declared the child labor law unconstitutional, Grace resigned but spent the rest of her life lobbying for a Constitutional amendment prohibiting child labor.

Grace spent the next four years working with the Illinois State Immigrants' Commission and the Immigrants' Protective League. She then returned to the Children's Bureau, moved to Washington, D.C., and began administering the Sheppard-Towner Act of 1921, a new law to assist states in combatting infant and maternal diseases and mortality. She directed the opening of more than 3,000 prenatal and pediatric care centers around the United States. The cooperation between federal and state governments in creating these centers laid the foundation for modern-day welfare programs.

As Grace's health began to decline she became eager to return to the Midwest. In 1934 she took a position as professor of public welfare at the University of Chicago's School of Social Service Administration, where she was reunited with her sister Edith, who had become dean. She published her last book, *The Child and the State*, in 1938. Although she never saw the child labor amendment ratified, she was partially satisfied with the Fair Labor Standards Act of 1938. She died the following year of acute anemia at the age of sixty.

Elizabeth Meriwether Gilmer (Dorothy Dix)

1939

The seducer

I get an increasingly large number of letters from girls who tell me that they are in love with men who offer them only a free-love union. These men tell them that marriage is an outmoded convention that soon will be entirely and universally obsolete; that the only real bond between a man and a woman is mutual affection and that nothing kills love so quickly as the sense of being bound. . . .

In former days any man making such a proposition to a girl would have been called a seducer and held up to the scorn of all decent people, and her father would have gone after him with a shotgun, which was a good old American custom.

Dorothy Dix was born Elizabeth Meriwether Gilmer on November 18, 1861, at "Woodstock," the family farm in Montgomery County, Tennessee. She educated herself primarily by reading all the books in her grandfather's library. She did attend Hollins Institute in Virginia for one semester but was miserable and quickly returned home.

After her mother's death, her father married a cousin. In November 1882 Elizabeth married her stepmother's brother, George O. Gilmer, an inventor ten years her senior. Although he was able to earn some money by developing new methods for distilling turpentine, he was plagued by mental and physical problems, and the marriage was always difficult. Eventually, he was committed to a mental institution where he died in 1929.

Reacting to the stress of coping with her husband, Elizabeth herself had a nervous breakdown in 1892. Her father took her to Bay St. Louis, a Mississippi Gulf Coast town, to recuperate. There she met and befriended Eliza Nicholson, owner and editor of the *New Orleans Daily Picayune*. Eliza offered her a job, and in 1894 she moved to New Orleans to start her career as a writer. She began by writing recipes and obituaries, but was so talented that within the year she had her own weekly column. She used the pen name Dorothy Dix, which she took as her own name for the rest of her life.

In 1901 William Randolph Hearst sent Dorothy to Kansas to cover Carry Nation's hatchet crusade. He was so impressed with her work that he hired her as a crime reporter for the *New York Journal*. For the next sixteen years she covered all the scandalous murder cases. Her column ran five days a week, and she received an enormous amount of reader mail which she felt obligated to answer personally. Although she had no formal training, her common sense and sympathetic understanding led her to begin an advice column which developed a large national following.

Dorothy retired from the *Journal* in 1917 to concentrate full time on her advice column. She moved back to New Orleans, where she received 400 to 500 letters a day and earned $100,000 a year. In June 1928 the city of New Orleans declared a Dorothy Dix Day. She was fêted by thousands in a public park, and she received many tributes,

Dorothy's writing is from How to Win and Hold a Husband, *published in 1939.*

Women's Words, Women's Stories

including an especially meaningful one from a factory worker who told her that more than 500 women at the factory read her column daily. The writer declared, "Nobody knows how much she means to us. More than anything else she keeps us going."

Dorothy wrote her advice column until April 1949. She suffered a stroke one year later and died in New Orleans in December 1951 at the age of ninety.

Mary Hallock Foote

circa 1920

*A*n intimate bond

And there at the ferry entrance stood James D. Hague, my new brother-in-law, coolly waiting till the last handshakes and hopes to meet again were over — we made more of our fellow travelers on overland trains in those days. Crushed as I felt by my own appearance, I was the more impressed by his: I thought him appallingly well dressed and handsome. We broke the news at once that my wretched trunks were a day behind. He took me in with one of his strong penetrating looks and changed our arrangements at once, despatching A. uptown to borrow a tide-me-over outfit from his sister Mary, and he took charge of me and my domestic retinue himself as far as the Occidental where our rooms had been engaged. And when, that evening, I came into the hotel parlor to be presented to my lovely sister-in-law, I was dressed self-consciously in her own clothes, but her eyes met mine without a glance at what I had on. She had selected a black silk dress made in a fashion that commended her taste to my taste, adding a little black lace jacket to save the fit — and everything else a woman seven days on an overland train should need, with the fragrance of her bureau drawers included. And the whole incident in its intimacy and awkwardness brought us together as nothing else could unless I had fainted in her arms.

Mary's writing is from her reminiscences written in the 1920s. They are included in A Victorian Gentlewoman in the Far West, *edited by Rodman W. Paul and published in 1972 by the Huntington Library, San Marino, California.*

Mary Anna Hallock Foote was born November 19, 1847, in a Quaker settlement at Milton, New York. She discovered her artistic talents while attending the Poughkeepsie Female

Collegiate Seminary and persuaded her parents to send her to the Cooper Institute School of Design (later Cooper Union) in New York City when she was not quite seventeen.

After graduation Mary immediately began work as an illustrator for the Fields, Osgood & Co. publishing house. She also drew for popular magazines, including *Harper's Weekly* and *Scribner's Monthly*.

When Mary was twenty-eight she married Arthur De Wint Foote, a civil engineer, who took her to a mining camp in Leadville, Colorado. Initially Mary continued her career as an illustrator, sending back interesting drawings of western mining scenes to *Scribner's*.

Mary switched to a writing career and published her first novel in 1883, followed by fifteen more novels plus numerous short stories and magazine articles.

The Footes settled near Boise, Idaho, for ten years, during which time her husband lost all their money speculating on a scheme to irrigate the Boise River Valley. After the Idaho failure, they moved to a mining community in Grass Valley, California, where they lived for the next thirty-five years. All the while Mary was writing books and stories that incorporated the various locations and experiences of her life.

When Arthur and Mary were in their late sixties, he lost all their money again trying to build a road to a mine high in the Sierra Nevadas. Mary died in 1938 at the age of ninety; her ashes were scattered in Grass Valley.

NOVEMBER 20

Rose Pesotta

May Day

Rose's writing is from her autobiography, Days of Our Lives, *written in 1958 and published by Excelsior Publishers, Boston.*

1958

We had decided to take part in the big labor parade next day, which was staged by labor and fraternal organizations, our own local union among them. When the boss got wind of this, he delivered an ultimatum. "Everybody must come to work tomorrow. Whoever doesn't show up is fired." We answered with a shrug of our shoulders. In the morning we met as agreed in front of the shop, and marched in a body to the *Jewish Daily Forward* Building in Rutgers Square and Stewart Park where the procession was to start.

En route we came to the scene of the tragic Triangle Shirtwaist Company fire at Greene and Washington Place, just behind the New York University, in which 146 workers, mostly teen-age girls, died in 1911. The building was still scorched, and we shuddered as we visualized that horror. Many of the victims had leaped to death from the eighth, ninth, and tenth floors when trapped by the flames, because all the exit doors had been locked to keep out union organizers (in those days they were known as troublemakers). Two girls from Derazhnya, schoolmates of mine, were among the dead. My sister Esther had worked there the previous season.

Rose Peisoty was born November 20, 1896, in Derazhnya in the Russian Ukraine. To avoid an arranged marriage when she was seventeen she followed her older sister Esther to America, where their last name was changed to Pesotta. Rose began working in a Manhattan shirtwaist factory and joined Local 25 of the International Ladies' Garment Workers' Union.

The ILGWU was to remain a focal point of Rose's life for the next fifty years. In 1915 she helped set up an education department within the union and was soon elected to the Local 25 Executive Board.

The ILGWU recognized Rose's organizational talents and enlisted her to organize women garment workers. In 1933 they sent her to Los Angeles to organize in a traditionally anti-union city, and her success there resulted in her election as vice president of the ILGWU the following year. For a decade Rose travelled from state to state, encouraging workers to "avoid ruling from the top" by training "the workers to take care of themselves." She travelled to Boston, San Francisco, Seattle, San Juan, and Montreal and gained a national reputation.

Rose eventually grew angry that despite the fact that eighty-five percent of the union's 305,000 members were women, she was the only female representative on the union's Executive Board. In 1944 she refused to run for a fourth term as vice-president and returned to her old shop as a sewing machine operator. She took up residence in the union's cooperative apartments in New York City and wrote two autobiographies in her spare time. After learning that she had terminal cancer she moved to Miami, Florida, where she died in 1965.

Martha Perry Lowe

A memory

1884
His memories of his childhood, as we recall them from his lips, always showed unconsciously a delicate sympathy with others' troubles, or the patient endurance of his own. He remembered all his youth the expression of disappointment on his little sister's face, because the birthday china mug had her name spelled wrong on it. Neither spoke, so implicit was the habit of reticent obedience. But what a photographer is the memory to make much lasting impression upon the mind and heart!

Martha Perry Lowe was born November 21, 1829, in Keene, New Hampshire. Her parents sent her away when she was fifteen to Madame Sedgwick's School for Girls in Lenox, Massachusetts. Following graduation she moved to Boston to study music.

Martha spent the winter months of 1850 in the West Indies. The next year she went to Madrid to visit her brother who had married Carolina Coronado, the poet laureate of Spain. She enjoyed European life and remained with her brother for several years. Soon after her return to America she married the Reverend Charles Lowe at the age of twenty-eight.

Martha published her first volume of poetry, *The Olive and the Pine*, in 1859. The first part of the book contained poems about Spain, while the poems in the second half were set in New England. Her second book, *Love in Spain*, was a long, dramatic poem about her fascination with everything Spanish.

Martha was forty-five when her husband died in 1874. For the next ten years she labored over his diaries and letters to produce a memoir of his life. Martha settled in Somerville, Massachusetts, to be near her two married daughters. She died there in 1902 at the age of seventy-three.

Martha's writing is from her Memoir of Charles Lowe, *published by Cupples, Upham, and Company in 1884.*

1955

In 1952 I suddenly realized what an old lady I was, and that in November I would be ninety-five. I didn't feel old; I always kept very busy about something in connection with the Colony, but to my astonishment a great deal of attention was called to the fact that I was going to be ninety-five. Many people were thinking of this, and more particularly my close friends in Peterborough.

All sorts of plans were being made for a day in August in which to celebrate my birthday, as in the New England climate we dared not have this occur in November.

Now I am three years older, but though my body is worthless, my mind seems to be the same it has been ever since I started what was considered a hopeless project. Now here we are, an institution which has been called one of the most important art institutes anywhere.

Marian Griswold Nevins MacDowell was born November 22, 1857, in New York City. After her mother's death when she was nine, Marian helped her father raise her two younger sisters.

Marian showed talent on the piano, and in 1880, after four years of studying with her Aunt Caroline, she went to Germany. She studied for two years with Edward Alexander MacDowell, an American composer residing abroad. They were married in July 1884 and lived in Germany until 1888, followed by eight years in Boston. In 1896 they moved to New York, where Edward became the first professor of music at Columbia University. During these years Marian put aside her own music career to further her husband's. In addition to her duties in the home she served as his secretary, copyist, and critic.

Edward resigned from Columbia in 1904 after a dispute with the president and board of trustees. He had contracted syphilis, and his mental and physical health began to deteriorate rapidly until his death in 1908. Marian used the $30,000 that had been raised for him by the Mendelssohn Glee Club of New York to establish the Edward MacDowell Association. It fulfilled his lifelong dream of creating a summer retreat at

Here we are

Marian's writing is from an unpublished autobiographical sketch, "Story Told by Mrs. MacDowell of Her Last Three Years" transcribed when she was ninety-eight. It is among her papers in the Manuscript Division, Library of Congress, Washington, D.C.

his Peterborough, New Hampshire, property where com-
posers, authors, and artists could live and work in a nurturing
setting. For the next fifty years Marian gave concerts of
Edward's piano music and lectured throughout the country to
raise funds for the MacDowell Colony. By the 1930s the
colony had become a major influence in America's artistic
community, attracting such notables as Aaron Copland,
Dubose Heyward, Thornton Wilder, and Willa Cather
(December 7).

Under Marian's guidance the colony grew from 135 acres
to 700 acres, which housed twenty-four studios, three dormi-
tories, a recreation center with dining area, and a library. She
left the colony in 1945 at the age of eighty-eight and, nearly
blind, moved in with a companion in Los Angeles. She died
there ten years later and was buried beside her husband in a
two-grave woodland plot near the colony. The colony is still
in operation today.

Katharine Coman

*O*ur faith

1913

As we carried the dear body to Cedar Hill Cemetery, a
lovely woodland place out beyond the town, the birds
were singing, and as we reached the spot where our
grandparents and our father and Harriet and the two
little brothers were buried, a redbird sang a song of joy
and triumph. The grass was growing green, and the
buds were swelling, and the sun shone bright on the
ponds in the meadow below. Everything spoke of the
renewal of life.

On Easter Sunday we came home to an empty
house, but the morning text spoke our faith, "It was not
possible that he should be holden of death."

Katharine Coman was born November 23, 1857, in Newark,
Ohio. She attended Steubenville Female Seminary for several
years until her father got into a dispute with the principal.
He believed in equal education for males and females and was
dissatisfied with the courses at Steubenville. Katharine transferred to the high school of the University of Michigan for
her senior year, after which she attended the university. She
received her Ph.B. degree in 1880.

After graduation Katharine joined the faculty of Wellesley
College as a professor of rhetoric. Seven years later she

Katharine's writing is from
Memories of Martha
Seymour Coman, *published by*
Fort Hill Press in 1913.

became a professor of economics and sociology, her chosen field. Her textbook, *The Industrial History of the United States*, published in 1905, went through several printings and was widely used in American schools. To gather research for her book *Economic Beginnings of the Far West*, she travelled throughout the West interviewing old fur traders, railroad men, and other settlers.

Katharine was an English history scholar and published several books on the subject, including *A History of England for High Schools and Academies*, and *English History Told by English Poets*.

In 1890 Katharine joined the College Settlements Association and was chairman of the Boston Settlement Committee. The committee opened Denison House, a settlement house in Boston's South End in 1892. She also developed an exchange program that allowed college graduates to spend up to a year at one of the association's settlement houses across the country. Denison House also served as a meeting place for young working girls and a center for labor organizing activities.

Katharine retired from Wellesley in 1913. Although she was ill with cancer she spent most of 1914 travelling throughout England, Spain, Sweden, and Denmark, studying their social insurance programs. She died at home in Wellesley in January 1915 at the age of fifty-seven. Her research on insurance was published posthumously as *Unemployment Insurance: A Summary of European Systems*.

Anna Louise Strong

1935

*I*maginary worlds

There was a period, but whether it lasted weeks or months I cannot recall, when the world I built came continuous with new structures added nightly in the interval before sleep. Once when a girl chum spent the night with me, we both admitted in the sheltering dark that we spent long hours in a quite different world, a much more exciting world than our ordinary life, but a world of which we would tell nobody. When after many pledges of mutual disclosure and secrecy, she admitted that she thought of boys and I that I thought of heaven, I am not sure which was the more ashamed. I was younger than she; I had not begun to think of boys. I privately thought her very silly, but I thought myself sillier still for having told.

Anna's writing is from her autobiography, I Change Worlds: The Remaking of an American, *published by H. Holt and Company in 1935.*

Anna Louise Strong was born November 24, 1885, in Friend, Nebraska. After obtaining her A.B. from Oberlin College in 1905 and her Ph.D. in philosophy from the University of Chicago in 1908, she moved to Seattle with her father to work at urban social reform.

In 1915 Anna ran unsuccessfully for the Washington state legislature, but she was elected to the Seattle School Board. However, she was soon dismissed from the board due to her openly expressed views on socialism and her opposition to the draft. In 1919 she published an editorial in the *Seattle Union Record* that was a major cause of the Seattle General Strike. This launched her lifelong interest in the support of revolutionary activities throughout the world.

Anna departed for Poland in 1921 to assist famine victims. She soon moved on to Moscow, anxious to take part in the Russian revolution. She befriended Trotsky, taught him English, and began chronicling the revolution in numerous articles. She was not allowed to join the Communist Party, and she eventually realized she would always be an outsider. She concluded that, "I would organize no more . . . but I could always write." She spent the next forty-five years "roving to revolutions and writing about them for the American press."

During her long career Anna covered the Mexican Revolution, the Spanish Civil War, and the German invasion of Russia during World War II. Her strongest ties, however, were to China and Russia. In 1930 she founded the English-language paper *Moscow News* with the approval and assistance of Stalin. Two years later she married Joel Shubin, a fellow communist sympathizer and editor of the *Moscow Peasant's Gazette.* Her travels back and forth from Russia to America to China often kept them apart, and the German invasion of Russia in 1941 prevented her from being with him at his death the following year.

Anna lived in China from 1946 to 1947 and recorded in an interview Mao Tse-tung's famous statement that all reactionaries were paper tigers. She returned to Russia at his urging to publicize the revolution, but the Russians were suspicious of her Chinese affiliations. She was accused of being a spy and deported in 1949. She returned to China permanently in 1958, residing in Peking, where she published a newsletter, *Letter from China.* Mao Tse-tung honored her on her eightieth birthday, and the Red Guards made her an honorary member. She died there in 1970 at the age of eighty-four and was buried in Peking's National Memorial Cemetery of Revolutionary Martyrs.

Josephine Clifford McCrackin

1916

Busy as I am, I still have time to make myself disagreeable to people who have no love for any of the Creatures God gave us to protect, the wild life of the forest, or the animals who serve us and guard us. In other words I belong to every protective society and league, and believe myself to be working for the best interests of California.

A protector

Josephine Woempner Clifford McCrackin was born November 25, 1838, in Petershagen, Westphalia, Germany. She and her family emigrated to St. Louis when she was eight.

In January 1864 Josephine met and married James A. Clifford, a lieutenant in the army's Third Calvary Regiment. They were assigned to Camp Bayard, Arizona, and Josephine travelled with the company by mule-drawn wagon from Fort Leavenworth, Kansas, to Arizona.

She loved the West and her life as an army wife, but her husband began suffering from paranoid delusions. Years before he had been implicated in a murder, and he became obsessed with the fear that his wife would turn him in. After months of death threats she finally fled Camp Bayard to join her family in San Francisco.

In 1869 Josephine submitted her first story to Bret Harte's magazine, *Overland Monthly*. He was so impressed that he encouraged her to write more, especially concerning army life and her impressions of the Southwest.

Josephine married Jackson McCrackin, a transplanted Southerner, in 1882, and they settled on a ranch in California's Santa Cruz Mountains. She described the next eighteen years as the happiest of her life, until a fire caused by thoughtless lumbering practices destroyed her home and a surrounding grove of ancient giant redwoods. She later said, "It was this sudden calamity to myself that awakened me to the great necessity of inaugurating a movement to preserve the forest groves of the State from fires of this character." She helped found the Sempervirens Club of California (later the Save-the-Redwoods League) and the Ladies' Forest and Song Bird Protective Association, and was the first female member of the California Game and Fish Protective Association. She was instrumental in pushing the state to purchase 3,800 acres of redwood forest in Santa Cruz County to create California Redwood Park.

Josephine's writing is from "Reminiscences of Bret Harte and Pioneer Days in the West," Overland Monthly, January 1916.

Following her husband's death in 1904 Josephine settled in a furnished bungalow in Santa Cruz that was given to her by a local women's club. She wrote for the *Santa Cruz Sentinel* and remained active in conservation work until her death in 1920 at the age of eighty-two.

Ellen Gould Harmon White

Gather the roses

1921

Many, walking along the path of life, dwell upon their mistakes and failures and disappointments, and their hearts are filled with grief and discouragement. While I was in Europe, a sister who had been doing this, and who was in deep distress, wrote to me, asking for some word of encouragement. The night after I had read her letter, I dreamed that I was in a garden, and one who seemed to be the owner of the garden was conducting me through its paths. I was gathering the flowers and enjoying their fragrance, when this sister, who had been walking by my side, called my attention to some unsightly briers that were impeding her way. There she was, mourning and grieving. She was not walking the pathway, following the guide, but was walking among the briers and thorns. "O," she mourned, "is it not a pity that this beautiful garden is spoiled with thorns?" Then the guide said, "Let the thorns alone, for they will only wound you. Gather the roses, the lilies, and the pinks."

Ellen Gould Harmon White was born November 26, 1827, in Gorham, Maine. When she was seventeen she became a devout follower of William Miller, a travelling preacher who was awaiting the Second Coming of Christ. After he predicted the end of the world in the fall of 1844, and the time came and went without incident, Ellen had the first of many visions that explained to her why his prediction had failed.

Ellen married James White, another "Millerite," in 1846. Inspired by Ellen's visions they travelled the country preaching their beliefs: the existence of the devil, the fallacy of Roman Catholicism, the Second Coming of Christ, and the need to observe the Sabbath on the seventh day of the week, Saturday. Eventually she established in 1863 the Seventh Day Adventist church based on those beliefs.

Ellen's writing is from her book, Steps to Christ, *published by Pacific Press Publishing Association in 1921.*

Following James's death in 1888 Ellen increased her speaking dates. Believing Christianity could be used as a tool for social reform she lectured her followers on health, education, and the need for temperance. She advocated taking the "plain path" of life, recommending the wearing of comfortable, loose-fitting clothing and the avoidance of tobacco, coffee, alcohol, sugar, and meat.

Although she had only a third-grade education Ellen wrote more than 100,000 pages of doctrines. She attributed her writing proficiency, despite a lack of schooling, to God's vision and His divine plan for her. She strongly urged Seventh Day Adventists to seek an education, recommending equal opportunities for both sexes, even in home economics. She wrote, "Boys as well as girls should gain a knowledge of household duties. . . . it is a training that need not make any boy less manly; it will make him happier and more useful."

Ellen died in 1914, leaving behind a well-established Seventh Day Adventist church with thousands of followers and its own system of schools, hospitals, and sanitariums.

Mabel Wheeler Daniels

1905

Just a line before I go to sleep to tell you that everything went off beautifully at the concert to-night. In one way it was an awful experience — awful, dearest of friends, in its most literal sense. This was not on account of the hall, I assure you, although it looked marvellously great and high as one stepped out of the dressing-room; nor was it because of the imposing audience, nor the crowds of pupils, who stood with critical attention around the sides of the room. Each of these factors may have its individual influence in striking terror to the heart of the timid performer, but they are all as nothing, absolutely nothing, I say, in comparison with that austere, black-coated, solemn-visaged line of professors who occupy the front row. You cannot imagine anything more terrifying than to stand on the platform and look down on this human barricade which shuts one off, as it were, from all that is friendly and encouraging. . . .

The moment after I made my very quaint, very German courtesy — a ceremony insisted on by the

The pupil's concert

Mabel's writing is from her book, An American Girl in Munich, Impressions of a Music Student, *published by Little, Brown and Company in 1905.*

Frau Professor — I suddenly became terribly conscious of the fact that I was an American, that all these people before me were German, and that I was about to sing to them in Italian. . . . But, dear me! I forgot all about that and everything — yes, even the depressing effect of the front row — when once I got to singing. And when it was over I could have hugged the fellow who cried "Bravo! Amerika! Amerika!" What mattered it that it was only an unpretentious pupils' concert? I could not have felt any prouder if it had been my début in grand opera. . . .

Mabel Wheeler Daniels was born November 27, 1878, in Swampscott, Massachusetts. She was given an early appreciation of music by her parents; her father had a beautiful singing voice and her mother was a skilled pianist.

Mabel attended Radcliffe College, where she began composing and conducting operettas and singing in the glee club. After graduating magna cum laude, she pursued her musical talents at the New England Conservatory and the Royal Conservatory of Munich. Upon her return to America she became music director at Simmons College, directed the Radcliffe glee club, and sang with the Cecelia Society.

Mabel gained popularity as a composer, creating a variety of musical compositions. She achieved many firsts for a woman: the only woman to have three pieces played by the Boston Symphony, the only woman composer at the Carnegie Hall Festival, and the only woman whose work was chosen by the Boston Symphony Orchestra to record.

During her lifetime Mabel received numerous awards and honorary degrees. She composed music well into her eighties, producing her last work in 1960. She died at home in 1971 at the age of ninety-three.

Harriet Chalmers Ford

A few inches of calm

1923
The blizzard begins shortly after we clear the city. There is a nice shut-in-ness to a train ride in a storm that far surpasses the cozyness of a mere stationary seat by a fireside. There is an exhilarating difference between withdrawing into a substantial shelter and rushing through a swirling world, with only a few inches of magical intimate calm surrounding you.

Harriet Chalmers Bliss Ford was born November 28, 1876. After graduating from Smith College in 1899, she began her career as an editor, or "literary butcher" as she referred to herself at *Century Magazine*. She held the position of associate editor at the magazine from 1899 until her marriage in 1912 to George Burdett Ford.

Soon after the outbreak of World War I the Fords sailed for Paris, where George served as deputy commander of the American Red Cross. Harriet organized the Women's War Relief Corps under the auspices of the Red Cross.

Upon their return to America in 1920 the Fords resided in Manhattan. Harriet worked for the National Board of the YWCA. For twelve years she organized the YWCA's publicity, conferences, conventions, and pageants.

Harriet's real devotion was to her alma mater, Smith College. During an interview for *American Magazine*, she credited her professional success wholly to Smith, and she admitted that the "bitterest words that ever fell from her lips about an individual were, 'Even Smith could do nothing for her.'" In 1923 she joined the college's board of trustees. As director of the Alumnae Association she inaugurated the Alumni Fund and served as first fund chair. After her husband's death in 1930 she became the first and only resident trustee in the history of the college. She lived on campus from 1931 to 1936, during which time she drafted a twenty-five-year plan for the development of the school and gave more than 100 lectures in thirty-eight states. She moved to a house in Northampton near the college in 1941 and continued to work for the school in various roles until her death in February 1964 at the age of eighty-seven.

Harriet's writing is from "Snow-Shoes and Things Like That," published by The Woman's Press, March 1923.

Adella Prentiss Hughes

NOVEMBER 29

1947

One evening in 1889, a young Yale friend of mine came to call. I always played the piano for my friends. We had been talking music, and I started to show him how Liza Lehmann's Persian Garden went, and then said longingly how wonderful it would be to hear that work done by celebrated artists in Cleveland. He answered, "Why don't you bring them here?" I laughed back, "Why don't I?" But those three words came back to me when I went to bed, and I started thinking that, if I did, how would I do it? The result was that I wrote a letter to my friend Mrs. Ford in New York, asking her

Her first concert

Adella's writing is from her autobiography, Music Is My Life, *published by World Publishing Company in 1947.*

if she would get me options on Marguerite Hall, Mackenzie Gordon, and David Bispham for a concert in Cleveland. . . . And then I had to tell the family. My personal bank account at that time was fifteen dollars. I had signed contracts for $750. My mother was alarmed. My father, a clear-sighted lawyer, looked at me gravely and then said, "I think you can do it, daughter."

The motives back of this undertaking were threefold. I wanted to hear beautiful music beautifully performed. I wanted to advertise the fact that I was an accompanist available for engagements; and I needed to earn money, for the family had had serious reverses. My friends rallied around me and I had a fine patrons' list in no time. . . . I was my own publicity agent, and took care of every detail of the concert, in spite of the fact that I had obsequious offers of assistance from a man who was trying to be a manager of miscellaneous events in Cleveland at that time.

The net proceeds of this first concert amounted to $1,000. It was invested in a Steinway piano which is still my dear delight after forty years of use.

Adella Prentiss Hughes was born November 29, 1869, in Cleveland, Ohio. She always loved music and could play the piano by ear, even before she started taking lessons when she was six. At Vassar College she was very active in the music programs including the glee club and banjo club. Following graduation she toured Europe with her mother, taking in numerous concerts and studying piano and voice in Berlin.

After returning to America Adella began her career as a professional accompanist. In 1894 she became a charter member of the Fortnightly Musical Club, an organization whose purpose was to bring orchestras and well-known musicians to Cleveland.

Over the years, Adella brought many talented artists to Cleveland. She started a symphony program with regular concerts by visiting orchestras. In addition to the symphony, she brought ballet, opera, and chamber music to Cleveland.

Adella married the singer Felix Hughes in 1904, but their separate careers kept them apart too much, and they divorced in 1923. Meanwhile, Adella continued with triumph after triumph: she founded the Cleveland Orchestra and served as its manager for fifteen years; established a music program in the public schools; began summer "pops" concerts; and was a major force behind the building of Severance Hall, a world-

class concert auditorium. She died in 1949 at her home in
Cleveland Heights.

Cassandra Morris Small Blair

1863
Lat has been twice to the battlefield — while they were
fighting on Thursday and Friday; his descriptions were
awful!
. . . He returned on Friday evening and went back
again Saturday with five ladies as nurses, and an
immense wagon filled with provisions for the wounded.
Since then hundreds of wagons have gone with all sorts
of things, as the Gettysburg people are nearly starving.
. . . Lat and his party returned at midnight Sunday;
said it was no place for ladies then. But yesterday the
ladies went again; said they could prepare niceties for
the wounded. They took a large supply of things
including shirts and drawers.

Cassandra Morris Small Blair was born November 30, 1828,
in York, Pennsylvania. She came from a wealthy, prominent
family of mill owners who were active in the local Presbyterian church.
    During the summer of 1863 Confederate troops occupied
York. Cassandra was thirty-four, unmarried, and living at
home with her parents. She wrote several letters to her
cousin Lissie Latimer in Delaware, describing in vivid detail
the events that were transpiring in the area as well as the feelings of the townspeople. The Rebels took over the town for
several weeks, ransacking homes, stealing provisions, and
damaging the local hospital. Cassandra wrote, "Oh, it was
too humiliating — almost more than human nature could
bear, to see such a ragged horde marching up our street and
know that they were our enemies — panting to revenge
themselves." After the troops had eventually moved on, she
said, "I could fill sheet after sheet with all their audacious
villainies. It is a matter never to be forgotten by us."
    Cassandra's brother Latimer and several friends were busy
travelling back and forth to the battlefield at Gettysburg to
deliver food and supplies to the wounded. Cassandra wrote
to Lissie, "We haven't been to the battlefield yet. . . . Several
who went up (strong, hearty women) have been sick in bed
since their return. We think it is caused by the terrible
smell!"

No place for ladies

*Cassandra's letter to her cousin
Lissie Latimer is in the York
Historical Society, York,
Pennsylvania.*

Following the war, Cassandra married Dr. Alexander R. Blair, whom she met while he was an assistant surgeon at the United States Military Hospital near York. He maintained a practice in York, and they had one child, Phillip. Cassandra died in August 1891 at the age of sixty-two and was buried in York's Prospect Hill Cemetery. Sixty-five years after she wrote her Civil War letters, they were found in a small wooden box in the Latimer attic by a descendant.

DECEMBER

Ann Preston

1843

How clearly we can trace the symbols of our own
"inner world" in the changes of the outward. The sunshine and shadow, — the spring time and autumn what
are they but types of the infinite, yet ever changing
spirit? and when we learn to trace the similitude, what
instruction and hope do we gather from all around us.
Sunshine breaks through clouds, — calm succeeds the
storm — Spring follows winter; "hope on, hope ever,"
is nature's universal language.

*H*ope

Ann Preston was born December 1, 1813, in West Grove,
Pennsylvania, a Quaker settlement near Philadelphia. She
attended a Friends' boarding school in Chester, Pennsylvania,
until her mother's poor health forced her to return home to
help care for her six younger siblings. She was active in the
local anti-slavery society and the temperance movement.

When the youngest Prestons no longer needed her care,
Ann began teaching. She became interested in physiology
and recognized the public's need for more information on the
subject, so she initiated classes in female physiology and
hygiene for women and girls.

In 1847 Ann began a two year apprenticeship with Dr.
Nathaniel Moseley in Philadelphia. After completing her
apprenticeship she applied to four medical colleges in
Pennsylvania but was rejected because of her sex. In 1850 the
Woman's Medical College of Pennsylvania was founded by a
group of Quakers to meet the needs of the many women who
were seeking a career in medicine. Just shy of her thirty-sev-
enth birthday Ann enrolled in the first class with seven other
women.

Ann remained at the Woman's Medical College after
graduation as a professor of physiology and hygiene. In 1858
she started a fundraising campaign to build a woman's hospital in connection with the college to provide hands-on clinical
instruction. Although the college was closed during the Civil
War, Ann continued to move forward with her hospital plans.
When the college reopened in 1862 the new adjoining hospital also opened.

In 1866 Ann was appointed dean of the Woman's Medical
College, the first woman to hold the position. She applied
for permission for her students to attend general clinics at the
Philadelphia Hospital but was met with demonstrations by
male medical students protesting the impropriety of edu-

*Ann's writing is from an
October 8, 1843, letter to her
friend Lavinia Passmore and is
in the Chester Historical
Society, West Chester,
Pennsylvania.*

cating men and women in medicine together. Her reply was published in the November 15, 1869, Philadelphia newspapers: "Whenever it is proper to introduce women as patients, there also it is but just and in accordance with the instincts of the truest womanhood for women to appear as physicians and students."

Ann continued her work as dean and professor of physiology and consulting physician at the Woman's Hospital until her premature death in 1872, at the age of fifty-eight.

Ruth Draper

How to be happier

Ruth's writing is from a June 10, 1932, letter to her nephew, William D. Carter. At the time, he was struggling with the recent death of his twin brother, and she was mourning the tragic death of her lover Lauro de Bosis.

1932

We must be patient with ourselves, kindly — slightly humorous — trying always to look at things in the large, not concentrating too much on any one thing. It helps often when one gets in a jam of introspection and worry to make little outward gestures — give a penny to a child — take a rose to Mrs. Thorndike — I remember once, more than once, giving some grass to a sad looking horse waiting with a load — and it made me so happy and somehow simpler and freer inside!

Ruth Draper was born December 2, 1884, in New York City. She was educated primarily at home by a tutor but was always more interested in the theater than in formal schooling. As a child she entertained friends and family with her short dramatic sketches and impersonations. When she was nineteen she made her stage debut with a one-woman show consisting of assorted character sketches.

Over the years Ruth constantly studied and experimented to improve her craft. She was influenced by Beatrice Herford, the British actress who popularized the monologue as a theater form. She also borrowed from Chinese theater, which emphasised words and gestures over elaborate scenery.

Ruth was a close friend of the pianist Ignace Jan Paderewski and the author Henry James, who encouraged her in her avant-garde theater projects. James wrote a monologue specifically for her to perform. In 1916 she staged a one-act play by August Strindberg and appeared in a Broadway play, both of which were unsuccessful. Thereafter she concentrated on expanding her own characters and monologues, and never appeared with any other actors or used material other than her own.

In 1921 Ruth played for President Warren Harding at the

Women's Words, Women's Stories

White House, and in 1928 she performed for nineteen consecutive weeks at New York's Comedy Theatre. Although she used only a table or chair for scenery and wore only a shawl for a costume, she enthralled audiences with the illusion that a complete play was being performed by numerous actors. Her repertoire consisted of thirty-five different sketches she had composed herself.

Ruth never married but had a long affair with the Italian poet Lauro de Bosis. He wanted to marry her but she kept procrastinating in favor of her career. He was killed in a plane crash in 1931 while dropping anti-fascist pamphlets over Rome, and Ruth always felt guilt and regret that she had not married him when he asked her.

Ruth received many awards and honorary degrees and in 1951 was made a commander, Order of the British Empire. She was most proud, however, of the fact that during her long career she had missed only one performance. Ruth died in 1956 at the age of seventy-two after a show in New York. As she had requested, her coffin was draped with all the shawls she had used to create her characters.

Ellen Henrietta Swallow Richards

1870

Very mysteriously God leads us, doesn't he? He grants us our wishes, often tho in different ways from what we expect. You will know that one of my delights is to do something that no one else ever did. I have the chance of doing what no woman ever did and the glimpse I get of what is held out to me makes me sober and thoughtful. . . . To be the first woman to enter the Massachusetts Institute of Technology, and so far as I know, *any scientific* school, and to do it by myself alone, unaided, to be welcomed most cordially, is this not honor enough for the first six months of post-collegiate life?

Ellen Henrietta Swallow Richards was born December 3, 1842, in Dunstable, Massachusetts. After her parents moved to Westford, Massachusetts, in 1859 she attended Westford Academy and assisted her father in his little neighborhood store.

In 1868 Ellen entered Vassar College, where she concentrated on chemistry and astronomy. She planned to teach astronomy in Argentina after graduation but was prevented

To be the first

Ellen's letter to a friend, dated December 25, 1870, was written two weeks after learning of her acceptance to MIT as a special student in chemistry. It is included in The Life of Ellen H. Richards, *by Caroline L. Hunt, published by Whitcomb and Barrows in 1912.*

from going by civil war in that country, so she applied to the Massachusetts Institute of Technology (MIT), instead. She was accepted "without charge" as a special student in chemistry.

While at MIT, Ellen met Professor Robert Hallowell Richards, a leader in establishing the school's mining and metallurgical engineering labs. He proposed to her in the chemistry lab, and they were married in June 1875. Ellen assisted him as his chemist in his two-year project experimenting with methods of concentrating copper ore, for which she became the first woman elected to the American Institute of Mining and Metallurgical Engineers.

Ellen was concerned with further science education for women, and she asked the Woman's Education Association of Boston to fund a women's laboratory at MIT. She operated her lab for eight years, from 1875 to 1883 teaching chemical analysis, industrial chemistry, mineralogy, and biology. She closed the lab after MIT began accepting her students full-time, complaining that she felt as though her children had grown and left home, leaving her without "anything to do or anywhere to work."

In 1884 MIT established a chemical lab for the study of sanitation with Ellen as first assistant. She was appointed as a professor in sanitary chemistry, a position she held for the next twenty-seven years. In 1890 she joined MIT's Department of Sanitary Engineering, the first in the country. Her students became leaders in public sanitation throughout the United States.

From 1890 on, Ellen's main focus was on what came to be called the home economics movement. She felt the home was the "civilizing center of society," but that the skills to manage a home were not being taught in schools. In 1899 at Boston's Woman's Educational and Industrial Union, she organized a school of housekeeping, which combined dietetics and household skills with elements of sociology and economy. She later transferred the school to the newly founded Simmons College. It became the first home economics department in an American college.

Ellen maintained her busy schedule until her death from heart disease in 1911, at the age of sixty-eight. She had just finished writing her address for MIT's semicentennial celebration. She was eulogized as the person who opened the scientific professions to women, and as the creator of the study of home economics, having been "for twenty-five years its prophet, its interpreter, its inspirer, and . . . its engineer."

1893

*W*earing work

We now number fifty-seven — not a great number, but they require much care and prayer, much teaching, training, and nursing. . . . In addition to my duties here in the Asylum, I now have six village schools, three Sunday-schools, and six pupils in their homes in the village. I am to visit three of the schools every week and the homes every week. In order to reach all the schools, I must ride, walk, and climb steps a total distance of forty miles, and superintend the teaching of two hundred boys and girls, as well as teach the teachers how to teach. I *enjoy* the work, though it is wearing in addition to all else I find to do.

Mary Reed was born December 4, 1854, in Lowell, Ohio. At sixteen she had a religious revelation, and thereafter was very active in her local Methodist church. She taught school for ten years at the Kenton, Ohio, district school from 1874 to 1884, when she suddenly decided she wanted to be a foreign missionary.

Mary set sail for India in November 1884 under the auspices of the Methodist Woman's Foreign Missionary Society. At first she was stationed at Pithoragarh in the Himalayan foothills to observe other missionaries at work, and to learn Hindustani. She was then assigned to the Girls' Boarding School at Gonda.

In 1890 Mary was sent home to the United States to recoup her health. She was experiencing strange symptoms, which included a constant pain in her right forefinger and an odd spot on one cheek, and she began to suspect that she had contracted leprosy during a visit to a leper colony in Chandag. A skin doctor in New York City confirmed her diagnosis. Mary interpreted this as a sign from God that she was intended to minister to the needs of the outcasts who suffered from the disease.

Mary returned to India in 1892, and Bishop Thoburn of the Methodist church appointed her superintendent of the leper asylum at Chandag. Under her leadership the unsanitary, dilapidated huts were replaced with comfortable houses, and she built a chapel and a hospital. She acquired forty-eight additional acres from the Indian government for animal pastures and gardens for the residents. While she was ministering to their physical problems, she converted many Hindus to Christianity.

Mary's writing is from an October 3, 1893, letter to Mr. and Mrs. Wellesley C. Bailey from a leper colony near Pithoragarh, India. It is included in Mary Reed: Missionary to the Lepers, *by John Jackson, published in 1900 by Fleming H. Revell.*

Mary did not treat her own leprosy, preferring to trust God's will. By 1895 her symptoms had disappeared. In 1897 and 1899 she travelled to the annual Methodist missionary conferences, but after 1906 she never left the leper colony. She died in 1943 at the age of eighty-eight and was buried beside the chapel she had built. The Mary Reed Memorial Hospital opened at Chandag in 1949 and is still in operation today.

Rose Wilder Lane

Being in love

1928

It's the great joy of being in love, that logic flies out the window. Little by little, as I sit gazing upon the few inadequate words that my typewriter has stammered out . . . memories return to me. To find one curve of one cheek the loveliest line in the world, to see in the mirrors of two eyes the very best you are or ever hoped to be — and to believe that they are not mirrors at all, but clearest glass — to have a heart that will start, and stand still, and leap again, at the sound of just one step, just that one only step, of all the steps of all the feet in all the world . . . To know, to *know*, never to doubt, that this one thing that you have is good, is the best, is the one thing always to hold to, to keep, forever and forever, against all the winds of time and chance — By gosh, enthusiasm stirs once more in my old bones! Yes, you're right. Being in love is something to thank God for.

(There's also a great deal to be said for being out of love. But never mind. . . .)

Rose's writing is from a January 10, 1928, letter to Dorothy Thompson, who was just beginning her romance with Sinclair Lewis. It is included in Dorothy Thompson and Rose Wilder Lane: Forty Years of Friendship Letters, 1921-1960, *edited by William Holtz and published by the University of Missouri Press, 1991.*

Rose Wilder Lane was born December 5, 1886, on her parents' homestead in what is now South Dakota. She was their only surviving child. Her parents, Almanzo and Laura Ingalls Wilder (February 7) are known to generations of children through the Little House series of books and the television series.

The Wilders moved to Mansfield, Missouri, in the Ozarks soon after Rose's birth, seeking a milder climate for Almanzo's health. She was educated in the local one-room schoolhouse. Following graduation she took a job as a telegrapher, a field that had recently been opened to women. In

Women's Words, Women's Stories

1909 she married Gillette Lane, but they were divorced eight years later.

After her divorce Rose moved to San Francisco, where she sold real estate and began writing for the *San Francisco Bulletin* and *Sunset* magazine. She published her first book, a biography of Henry Ford in 1917, followed by a biography of Herbert Hoover in 1920. In 1920 she began the first of several annual trips to Albania. There she lived in a primitive hut in the mountains and was often the first foreign woman any of the natives had ever seen. She wrote *The Peaks of Shala* in 1923, about her experiences in Albania.

Rose was very close to her mother and encouraged her to write her recollections of her early life on the midwestern plains. Laura Ingalls Wilder wrote her first book, *Little House in the Big Woods*, in 1931. It was followed by seven books in the best-selling Little House series. Rose assisted her mother as her agent and editor in addition to helping her with the actual writing. Rose herself published two books similar to her mother's in theme, but from an adult point of view.

In her later years Rose became increasingly anti-government. She retired to her farm in Danbury, Connecticut, in 1943 until "the American scene produced a politician who'll stand up and tell the truth." She especially abhorred Franklin D. Roosevelt and the New Deal. In 1944 she ceased writing altogether to avoid paying taxes to finance the New Deal. She died at home in 1968 at the age of eighty-one.

Margaret Morse Nice

circa
1960

*He*r best nests

My "personally taken" collection of nests was augmented by a windfall. My mother had taken me to call upon two elderly ladies who had a number of nests; upon seeing my admiration, they then and there presented them to me. I arranged all my best nests on a shelf above my bed — the greatest prizes being a bunch of glued twigs of a Chimney Swift and a few straws laid by a Mourning Dove on top of an old Robin's nest. I gloated over my treasures, and every evening, for fear I might forget their identity, I recited their names. . . .

Margaret Morse Nice was born December 6, 1883, in Amherst, Massachusetts, where her father was a history professor at Amherst College. Her parents encouraged her early

Margaret's writing is from Research is a Passion With Me, *published after her death in 1979 by Consolidated Amethyst Publications.*

interest in wildlife, especially birds. She spent hours studying their habits and collecting samples.

Margaret received her A.B. degree from Mount Holyoke College in 1906, and began taking graduate courses in biology at Clark University. In 1909 she married Leonard Blaine Nice, a graduate student she met at Clark.

Blaine and Margaret moved to Norman, Oklahoma, in 1913, where he ran the physiology department at the University of Oklahoma. In addition to raising her five daughters, Margaret also raised captive birds that had been injured or removed from their nests. She used these birds as live research subjects, resulting in thirty-five magazine articles on the state's birds. In 1924 she published *The Birds of Oklahoma*, the first complete study of the subject.

The Nices moved to Columbus, Ohio, in 1927 and Margaret began her most important work, the life history of the song sparrow. By placing colored bands on the birds she followed their individual behavior patterns from birth to death. She published the two-part *Studies in the Life History of the Song Sparrow* in 1937 and 1943, which established her reputation as one of the world's foremost ornithologists and behaviorists.

In 1936 the Nices moved again, this time to Chicago. Margaret spent most of her time working at her desk, as field research was impossible in the city. She sadly wrote to her daughter, "A great city is no proper home for me." She was an ardent conservationist and wrote stirring pleas to ban the use of pesticides in America. From 1935 to 1974, except for three years during World War II, she was an associate editor of *Bird-Banding* magazine.

In 1969 the Wilson Ornithological Society created the Margaret Morse Nice Grant-in-aid for self-trained researchers in recognition of her special contribution to the field. The society noted: "Her career demonstrated to countless others that a housewife without a doctorate, raising children, could, by studying the birds in her own backyard, make the outstanding contribution of the present quarter-century to ornithological thinking in America."

Margaret died in Chicago in 1974 at the age of ninety.

Willa Cather

June 2, 1927

Dear Mr. Jones,

The first time I was ever confronted by myself in print was one Sunday morning (please don't append an editorial note here, stating just how many years ago it was) when I opened the *Sunday Journal* and saw, stretching out through a column or two, an essay on "Some Personal Characteristics of Thomas Carlyle," which Professor Hunt had given you to publish, quite without my knowledge. That was the beginning of many troubles for me. Up to that time I had planned to specialize in science; I thought I would like to study medicine. But what youthful vanity can be unaffected by the sight of itself in print! It had a kind of hypnotic effect.

Youthful vanity

Willa Sibert Cather was born December 7, 1873, in the Back Creek Valley of Virginia. She spent the first nine years of her life as a tomboy at her grandparents' farmstead, "Willow-shade." She was uprooted in 1883 when the family relocated to the vast, unsettled plains of Red Cloud, Nebraska. In later years when Willa wrote about the immigrants she befriended there she noted that she felt a kindred spirit with them, because she, too, was so painfully homesick.

Willa attended the University of Nebraska. A professor secretly sent one of her stories to a Boston magazine, which published it. This early success encouraged her to become a writer. In 1903 Willa published her first book — a volume of poetry for which she had to pay half the publishing costs. Her father loved her poetry and urged her to pursue it, but Willa disagreed and felt her talents were more suited to fiction. She moved to New York City in 1908 to become the editor of *McClure's* magazine. She left the magazine four years later to write fiction for the rest of her life.

All of Willa's novels were immensely popular. She published *O Pioneers!* in 1913 and *My Antonia* in 1918. *My Antonia* was translated into twenty-eight languages. In 1922 she received the Pulitzer Prize for *One of Ours*. In 1924 Warner Brothers bought the rights to *A Lost Lady* and made a silent film. Willa disliked movies and agreed to the sale only because she wanted to make a large donation to the Red Cloud Hospital building fund. In 1934 without consulting her, Warner remade the movie with sound. She disliked the

Willa's letter is to Will Owen Jones, one of her many lifelong friends and correspondents. He was the city editor of the Nebraska State Journal, the newspaper that offered Willa her first job. The letter is included in Willa Cather in Person — Interviews, Speeches and Letters, *selected and edited by L. Brent Bohlke and published by the University of Nebraska Press, 1986.*

way the studio handled her story and vowed never to let it happen again. By placing a clause in her will she prevented any of her books from ever being made into a movie.

Willa spent her later years in New York City and New Hampshire. Although her family had strong ties to Nebraska, she and her brother Doug decided they did not want to be buried there. When he died in 1938 Willa angered her family by upholding his wish. Her brother's coffin was on a train bound for Nebraska, but she intervened and had him returned to his desired resting place in California. Willa chose to be buried in New Hampshire beside a close friend's little boy who had died as a child. As he was dying, Willa had promised him that she would never leave him, and so she was buried in the Osterman family plot in Jaffrey, New Hampshire, when she died at the age of seventy-three.

DECEMBER 8

Mary Kimball Morgan

*T*eacher and pupil

Mary's writing is from "Educational Reforms," published in the January 25, 1910, issue of The Principia Alumnus.

1910

One of the chief difficulties encountered with pupils who enter a school above the primary grade is a false sense of relationship between teacher and pupil. This is one of the first obstacles to successful teaching and successful learning. When a school succeeds in proving to a child that all its efforts are in his behalf, that all the teachers are his friends and helpers, half the battle is won. Upon the basis of friendship, a teacher can gain ground rapidly.

Mary Kimball Morgan was born December 8, 1861, in Janesville, Wisconsin. When she was six the family moved to St. Louis, where her father joined an established wholesale hardware business. She had hopes of attending college, but poor health prevented her from going past the twelfth grade. She was active in the Union Methodist Church where she met William Edgar Morgan, a dry goods salesman twelve years her senior.

William and Mary were married in December 1885. Her already frail health took a turn for the worse soon after her wedding. She turned to Christian Science and found her health improved considerably. The Morgans then founded a group of worshippers that grew into the first Christian Science church in St. Louis. In 1896 Mary became an authorized Christian Science practitioner.

Mary believed that character education should be included

in the educational process. She felt it was lacking in the public school system, so she refused to send her two sons. Instead, she developed a "moral plan" for instruction and tutored them at home. Word spread among her church members and she was besieged by requests from other parents to teach their children, also. In October 1898 she officially opened her home school, teaching the younger students herself and hiring an assistant for the older ones.

Mary named her school The Principia, and although it was not officially affiliated with the Christian Science church it was endorsed by the church's founder, Mary Baker Eddy in 1899. Within four years the school comprised an entire block of buildings. In 1910 Mary added a two-year college course, creating one of the first junior colleges in America. In 1932 the college expanded to four years and moved to a beautiful site on top of the Mississippi palisades in Elsah, Illinois, twenty-five miles north of St. Louis.

Following William's death in 1935 Mary moved to the Elsah campus permanently. Three years later her son Frederic succeeded her as president, and her other son, William, took over as vice-president and headmaster of the high school. She died at the college in 1948 at the age of eighty-six.

Emma Abbott

circa 1880
my dear father,

How much pleasure it always gives me to get a letter from your dear hand, and how I thank God for keeping you strong and well.

You don't know how deeply I love you dear Pa, or how I long to see you again. Just think how many years have passed since we last met. But separation nor time cannot alter my deep love for you.

As to my business affairs, they are "mixed" enough, to thoroughly perplex anyone who relies upon himself, but you know my old belief that God loves and guides me and I feel perfectly sure that all the troubles I have had, have been sent me as experiences and that they will be proven in the future to have been necessary to my development.

Love and faith

Emma's letter to her father is included in The Life and Professional Career of Emma Abbott, *by Sadie E. Martin, published in 1891 by L. Kimball Printing Company.*

God bless and guard you my dear father, is the prayer of your loving daughter.

Emma

Emma Abbott was born December 9, 1850, in Chicago. Soon after she was born her family moved to Peoria, where Mr. Abbott was a music teacher. Emma was also musically talented and began performing when she was quite young. She sang and played the guitar for appreciative audiences who left voluntary donations. As the family was quite poor, Emma's earnings represented a valuable contribution.

In 1867 the famous singer Clara Kellogg (July 9) heard Emma in Toledo and brought her to New York to study. She practiced for four years, singing in two church choirs, until her professional debut at a benefit concert in 1871. The following year the congregation at one of her churches took up a collection to send her to Milan and Paris for further study.

Emma made her operatic debut at London's Covent Garden in 1876. Although a success, her contract was soon terminated when she refused to sing *La Traviata* because she felt it was immoral. She returned to the United States and performed in Baltimore, Washington, Philadelphia, and New York.

Emma had secretly married Eugene Wetherell, a New York pharmacist, while in Europe. Together they formed the Emma Abbott English Opera Company and began touring the country. Her goal was to introduce opera to the common man; she presented lavish stage productions with elaborate costumes, and as the operas were sung in English they were easier to follow.

Emma's opera company was quite successful earning several thousand dollars per week, and she became known as "the people's prima donna." In 1878 she began a two-year tour of the West, commencing in Iowa and ending in Ogden, Utah. She developed pneumonia from an unheated dressing room in Ogden, and died in 1891 at the age of forty. Having invested her earnings in real estate and bonds, Emma left a considerable estate which she gave in her will to various charities, and to the twelve churches she had attended during her lifetime.

1918

*T*o capture the truth

I assure you it is great fun chasing all these historical facts, when it is possible visiting the places where they happened — following the smallest clue descriptions — portraits — manners and customs — for I try to be true to every part of my story: The atmosphere those people radiated in their manner of living and thinking — as well as the number of buttons on their military coats and the size and shape of their flint-lock guns.

Jennie Augusta Brownscombe was born December 10, 1850, in a log cabin near Honesdale, Pennsylvania. As a child she was encouraged by her mother, a poet, to develop her artistic talents, and her paintings won ribbons each year at the Wayne County Fair. After her father died in 1868 she taught school for three years, until she enrolled at the Cooper Institute School of Design (later Cooper Union) in New York City. She supported herself as an illustrator for *Harper's Weekly* and other periodicals. In 1876 she sold her first painting, *Grandmother's Treasures*, at the Art Students' League annual exhibition.

From 1882 to 1895 Jennie established a pattern of studying abroad alternating with periods of work at her New York studio, and extended visits to her mother in Honesdale. During one of her European trips in 1890 she met George Henry Hall, a successful still life painter. Their romance lasted more than twenty years during which time he instructed her in painting techniques, and improved her style and use of color. From 1908 until his death in 1913 they shared a studio each summer in the Catskill Mountains.

During the late 1890s Jennie turned to historical subjects for inspiration. She researched her characters and their time period for her historically accurate imaginary scenes. She painted Betsy Ross sewing, Dolly Madison entertaining at a ball, and fifteen pictures of George Washington engaged in various activities. Printing companies discovered Jennie's art and began mass producing her work as calendars, magazine illustrations, and inexpensive prints. More than 100 of her prints were copyrighted.

Jennie continued working through her seventies. At seventy-six she illustrated a children's book, *Tales of the Mayflower Children*. Despite suffering a stroke in 1931 she completed one last painting, *Children Playing in an Orchard*, as a gift to the grade school she had attended in Honesdale. She

Jennie's writing is from a July 29, 1918, letter to Mr. Edwin Callaway. It is in the Wayne County Historical Society, Honesdale, Pennsylvania.

died in 1936 at the age of eighty-five, and was buried in the Brownscombe family plot at Glen Dyberry Cemetery in Honesdale.

Eliza Azelia Williams

*A*board ship

Eliza's writing is from a September 7, 1858, journal entry. It was her first day of a three-year voyage to the Indian and Pacific Oceans aboard her husband's whaling ship. Eliza's journal is included in One Whaling Family, *edited by Harold Williams and published in 1964 by Houghton, Mifflin and Company.*

1858
Now I am in the place that is to be my home possibly for 3 or 4 years; but I can not make it appear to me so yet it all seems so strange, so many Men and not one Woman beside myself; the little Cabin that is to be all my own is quite pretty; as well as I can wish, or expect on board of a Ship. I have a rose geranium to pet, that Mrs. Fish has been kind enough to send me, and I see there is a kitten on board. I think it will not all be as pleasant as it is today; the motion of the Ship I shall be a long time getting used to. . . . I shall be lonely, though not alone, for I have a kind Husband with me.

Eliza Azelia Griswold Williams was born December 11, 1826, in Wethersfield, Connecticut. At the age of twenty-four she married Capt. Thomas W. Williams, captain of a whaling ship. During his long absences at sea she was left in charge of his business affairs. Not only was she lonely, but she did not like having to collect his debts and then reinvest the money. She decided that she was going to accompany him on future voyages.

Eliza set sail on her husband's whaling ship, the *Florida*, on September 7, 1858, despite the fact that she was five months pregnant. She kept a detailed journal of her first voyage, which was to last more than three years. She did not adapt immediately to ocean life. Her entry for September 10, 1858, reads, "It is quite rugged today, and I have been quite sick; these three or four words I write in bed." The next day she wrote, "It remains rugged and I remain sea sick. I call it a gale, but my husband laughs at me and tells me that I have not seen a gale yet. If this is not one I know I do not want to see one."

Eliza's maiden voyage lasted thirty-eight months, from September 1858 to October 1861. Her son William was born in January 1859, followed by a daughter Mary in February 1861. Her second voyage was eighteen months long and subsequent trips were limited to a year in length.

In 1868 the Williams family moved to Oakland, California. They set off on a whaling expedition soon after their arrival in California, and their daughter Flora was born somewhere in the Japan Sea. In 1873 their oldest, William, joined the crew as a boatsteerer, or junior officer. Their last voyage was in 1874, after which Captain Williams opened a carriage business and the children attended school in Oakland. After Captain Williams died in California in August 1880, Eliza returned to Wethersfield, Connecticut, with Mary. She died there in February 1885 at the age of fifty-eight, and was buried beside her husband in the Village Cemetery.

Rachel Crothers

1911

*A*ll wrong

I was not directing rehearsals myself, so I had the exquisite torture of sitting by and seeing it all go wrong while I dug my nails into my flesh by way of self-control. In the first place the play — my play — was all wrong — and also the people were wrong. They were not in the least suggestive of the aristocratic old family they were supposed to be and had no power of making themselves such. The sets were wrong. The fine old New York mansion, which was supposed to have kept the air of the Old World, looked like a boarding-house on upper Lexington Avenue, with the most hideous red plush furniture it has ever been my misfortune to see. Some of the wall-paper was so hideous that at the eleventh hour I rebelled and it was repainted, so that on the opening night the audience got a bracing smell of fresh paint as the curtain rose.

Rachel Crothers was born December 12, 1870, in Bloomington, Illinois. Although the theater was foreign to her conservative family, she was interested in it from the age of thirteen when she wrote her first play. At the age of forty her mother discarded tradition by studying medicine and becoming central Illinois' first female physician. Rachel gained strength from her mother's courage and independence, and maintained her passion for the theater despite her family's objections.

Rachel almost died of typhoid fever when she was eighteen, and her illness delayed her high school graduation until she was twenty-one. After graduation she founded the Bloom- ington Dramatic Society as a means to present her plays. After a few years she moved to New York City to

Rachel's writing is from "Troubles of a Playwright," Harper's Bazaar, January 1911.

study drama at the Stanhope-Wheatcroft School of Acting. Although she acted occasionally and directed several productions her main love was playwriting. In 1902 her first play, a one-act comedy, opened at the Madison Square Theatre.

From 1902 to 1937 Rachel wrote thirty-eight plays and produced at least one a year on Broadway. She wrote comedies and dramas, but all her plays had a strong, independent woman as the heroine, combatting life's injustices with will power and love.

In 1933 Rachel won the Megrue Prize for *When Ladies Meet*, and in 1937 the Theatre Club's gold cup for *Susan and God*. During World War I she founded the State Women's War Relief Fund, serving on the board until it dissolved in 1951. During World War II she co-founded the American Theatre Wing, which was responsible for such wartime services as the Stage Door Canteen. She died at home in Connecticut in 1958 at the age of eighty-seven.

Frances Newman

A shocker

1926

Apparently the Virgin has worked love out of my system. Atlanta, by the way, is shocked almost into convulsions over it, and I haven't a particle of character left. Lots of people apparently think I've done everything in it, and although I point out that Hawthorne was never the mother of an illegitimate daughter and that Dreiser has never been electrocuted and that Kipling wasn't brought up by an elephant — it doesn't do any good. However, all of it sells the book, I gather, so I try to bear up.

Frances Newman was born December 13, 1883, in Atlanta. Her father was a United States District Court judge for northern Georgia. Frances wrote a novel when she was ten, but destroyed it when she heard her sister and her boyfriend laughing about it. She later recalled, "I gathered that he and my sister found it very comical. And after I had wept for a few minutes on a bed of mint in my family's garden, I gave up literature."

Frances studied languages at the University of Tennessee, and graduated with a degree in library science from the Carnegie Library School in Atlanta. After graduation she spent one year as librarian at the Florida State College for Women in Tallahassee, which she referred to as "a year of

Frances's writing is from a November 30, 1926, letter to her friend Mabel Gieberich, shortly after the publication of her first novel, The Hard-Boiled Virgin. *The letter is included in* Frances Newman's Letters, *edited by Hansell Baugh and published in 1926 by Boni and Liveright.*

bondage in a strange land." In 1914 she left Florida for an extended tour of Tuscany, Greece, Algiers, and Egypt with her sister Isabel.

Upon her return to America, Frances joined the catalog and circulation department at the Carnegie Library. At Carnegie, she began writing book reviews for library bulletins and local newspapers. Her caustic, highly critical style attracted the admiration of James B. Cabell and H. L. Mencken, who encouraged her to pursue a literary career. Her first short story was published in 1924 in Mencken's *American Mercury* magazine and received the O. Henry Award.

Two years later Frances published her first novel, *The Hard-Boiled Virgin*. Its shocking title and tale of a woman who had many affairs caused much controversy, and the book was banned in Boston. Her second novel, published in 1928, had an equally shocking title: *Dead Lovers Are Faithful Lovers*.

Frances travelled to Paris in the spring of 1928 to research a French author whose work she was translating. That fall she returned to America where she collapsed, unconscious, in her New York hotel room while on a visit to her publisher. She died two days later at the age of forty-five, probably of a ruptured cerebral aneurysm, and was buried in Atlanta's West View Cemetery. It is widely believed that had her career not been cut short, she would have become one of America's major female writers.

Catherine Paine Blaine

1853

My dear mother,

. . . We have written what a fine warm winter we are having, but the present weather gives the lie to all that. The present week is the coldest known within the memory of the oldest white inhabitant. Yesterday the family that has been living in the back room of this house moved out, taking the windows with them. The two rooms are not wholly separated and the cold wind comes in making itself disagreeably felt. Our one room is so open that we can look out through the cracks on every side. It freezes not six feet from the stove when we have as much fire as we can get into the little thing. . . . we console ourselves with the thought that this will not last long. Indeed, it is already growing warmer. It

Thoroughly cold

is now near midnight. David is asleep. I am sitting up to bake my bread. The yeast became chilled so that my bread was a long time in rising and this detained me. . . .

Catherine Paine Blaine was born December 14, 1829, in Seneca Falls, New York. She married David Edwards Blaine, a Methodist minister, in 1853. Two months after their wedding the couple left on the long journey west to establish the first Christian church in Seattle.

The Blaines left New York City by steamer through the Isthmus of Panama to San Francisco. They travelled from San Francisco to Olympia, Washington, on a small barge and completed the journey in a canoe, "manned by a crew of Indians who kept time with the stroke of their paddles by a sing-song refrain peculiar to their race." When they arrived in Seattle they found only a dozen white families.

The Blaines were given a rent-free, sixteen-by-thirty-foot building for use as a church until one could be built. Catherine organized a Sunday School and a Thursday evening prayer meeting. She also established the first public school in Seattle and taught there from 1854 to 1856.

In late 1855 the Indian War began, placing Seattle under military regulation. Hostile Indians attacked on January 26, 1856, just three days after Catherine had given birth to her first child. The Blaines escaped to the warship *Decatur* in the harbor, and within the month departed Seattle for Portland.

The Blaines resided in Oregon and later New York for many years. In 1882 they returned to Seattle permanently. On the eve of her husband's funeral, Catherine opened the door to the basement, believing in her grief that it was a closet. She took a terrible fall down the stairs, fracturing several bones. She was able to attend the funeral but was unable to go to the cemetery. Catherine died in 1908 at the age of seventy-eight.

Catherine's writing is from a letter to her mother written in December 1853 from Seattle, Washington Territory. It is included in Memoirs of Puget Sound — Early Seattle 1853-1856 — The Letters of David and Catherine Blaine, *edited by Richard A. Seiber, Ye Galleon Press, Fairfield, Washington, 1978.*

Vida Dutton Scudder

Fiftieth reunion

1937

Time passed; and we went, five of us, to Smith College, entering in 1880, the autumn after the first class, 1879, had been graduated. The institution seemed venerable to us.

By chance — if such thing there be, which I doubt — I came to writing this part of my story just as I returned from the fiftieth reunion, in Northampton, of my own college class, 1884. In the candle light of our class supper, each of us old women — gayer by a long shot than in our youth — confronted a photograph of her girlish self, in a stand enwreathed by our class flower, forget-me-not. We were graduated forty-two; twenty-six were living; we sat down sixteen to that supper, plus half a dozen who had been with us a year or more. We joked and chatted; we sang the old songs rather feebly, and intoned spoken responses to the young groups serenading us:

"Let us speak; we can not sing;
But we love the songs you bring."

I thought how much nicer my classmates were than ever I had realized. . . . electric currents of affection ran through the group at that table. I think we were surprised to find how much we meant to each other. Group-consciousness, so real and unique a thing, was flowing free, bearing us back into a past happier than we had known.

Vida Scudder was born Julia Davida December 15, 1861, in Madura, India. Her father, a Congregationalist minister, drowned when she was an infant and her mother immediately returned to her family in Auburndale, Massachusetts.

In 1880 Vida enrolled at Smith College, her first and only separation from her mother. After graduating she joined the English department at Wellesley College, choosing Wellesley over Smith to be near her mother. As a student of John Ruskin, her social conscience had been awakened; she had become aware of the "plethora of privilege" in her life, and that it was "privilege unshared" by much of the rest of the world. Thus began her lifelong conflict between her teaching career and her personal views on the need for social reform.

Her radicalism often put her at odds with the administration at Wellesley, culminating in her vocal opposition to a donation by the Rockefeller family in 1900. She had a nervous breakdown in 1901, followed by two years of travel in Europe. She returned more committed than ever to her social reform causes, eventually joining the Socialist party in 1911.

Vida initially supported World War I, but by the war's end she had become a dedicated pacifist. After her retirement from Wellesley in 1928 she published her most famous book, *The Franciscan Adventure*, establishing her as one of the foremost Franciscan scholars. Throughout her eighties and early nineties, Vida wrote and lectured extensively on Christian social reform. She died at her Wellesley home in 1953, two months before her ninety-third birthday.

Vida's writing is from her autobiography, On Journey, *published in 1927 by E. P. Dutton.*

Elizabeth Johnson Harris

The good news

1922
I was a constant visitor to the churches, in company
with my dear old grandmother and sometimes with
Grandpapa and with mother and father when on a visit
to them. I was always taken near the front seat, I
enjoyed class meetings, and prayer meetings. I joined
the church on a Thursday night at a great Love-Feast
meeting. The church was crowded and the Holy Spirit
seemed to have had full control of the house. I was a
small figure in the large crowd, but at the appointed
time, I arose willingly and stood before, or in the midst
of the great crowd, and fearlessly related the fact of my
conversion and the good news that God had given me
to tell. *"Blessed be the Lord."*

Elizabeth Johnson Harris was born to ex-slaves on December
16, 1867, in Augusta, Georgia. Her mother gave her to her
grandparents to raise when she was eleven months old. In
1874 they relocated when her grandfather was given a lifetime right to three acres in Summerville, Georgia, by a member of the family he had served as a slave.
　Elizabeth attended the local public school for colored children, which was located in a church building. The church
became the center of her life; she was an active member of
the Black Christian Methodist Episcopal Trinity Church for
sixty-seven years.
　Elizabeth married Jacob Walker Harris, whom she
described as an "ordinary laboring man," on July 5, 1883.
They had nine children, two of whom died as infants.
　Music was always important to Elizabeth. As a child she
had learned to play the piano from a friend who was taking
lessons. As an adult she played piano and organ for her
church, and served as its choir directress. She passed her love
of music on to all of her children, especially to her son
Charles, who became head of the music department at South
Carolina State College.
　Elizabeth survived her husband by twenty-six years; she
died in Augusta on September 14, 1942.

*Elizabeth's writing is from her
handwritten memoirs, which
are in the Special Collections
Department, William R.
Perkins Library, Duke
University.*

Deborah Sampson

1802

May 5. When I entered the hall, I must say I was much pleased at the appearance of the audience. It appeared from almost every countenance that they were full of unbelief — I mean in regard to my being the person that served in the revolutionary army.

Some of them which I happened to overhear swore that I was a lad of not more than eighteen years of age. I sat some time in my chair before I rose to deliver my address. When I did, I think I may with much candor applaud the people for their serious attention and peculiar respect, especially the ladies.

A female soldier

Deborah Sampson was born December 17, 1760, in Plymouth, Massachusetts. Following her father's death her mother was unable to provide for her six children, so she dispersed them to various families. Deborah lived with a pastor's family from age five to age ten, when she was bound as a servant to the Thomas family of Middleborough.

Deborah performed numerous household chores in addition to tending the animals and plowing the fields. She was fortunate in that she received an education during her stay with the Thomases. She became an avid reader of daily newspapers and other periodicals, which developed her interest in local current events.

Deborah was thirteen at the time of the Boston Tea Party. She followed the news of the American Revolution until she was twenty-one, when, having finished her period of indenture to the Thomases she was free to join the Continental Army. Deborah disguised herself in men's clothing and enlisted under the name Robert Shurtleff.

"Robert" fought in the battles of White Plains, Tarrytown, and Yorktown. She was shot in the shoulder at Yorktown, and later developed brain fever from which she was not expected to recover. The doctor who treated her never revealed her sex enabling her to be discharged honorably from the army.

Deborah returned to Massachusetts in 1783 and settled with an uncle. She was soon married to Benjamin Gannett, and had three children. Herman Mann wrote a lecture for her on her wartime adventures, which she adapted to her liking. She then toured New England, telling her story for profit.

In 1792 Deborah received a soldier's pension from the

Deborah's writing is from a diary she kept from May 1802 to January 1803. It is in the archives of the Sharon (Massachusetts) Public Library.

state of Massachusetts. In 1804 Paul Revere was instrumental in acquiring a federal pension for her services to the nation. She died in 1827 when she was sixty-seven; the back of her tombstone reads, "Deborah Sampson Gannett, Robert Shurtleff, The Female Soldier: 1781-1783."

Miriam Davis Colt

Gathering storm clouds

June 5th, 1856

The Indians have gone away now on their hunt; it seems quiet and good to have our fear removed for a time. The people say we have had our hardest time here, but it does not seem so to me. I often ask myself, "Why do I have so many presentiments of coming sorrow?" The dark storm-clouds, (to my mind's eye,) are gathering in our horizon, and even now they flap their cold, bat-like wings about my head, causing my heart to tremble with fear. I am so impressed some nights with this feeling, that I sit up in bed for hours, and fairly cringe from some unknown terror. I tell my husband, "We are a doomed ship; unless we go away, some great calamity will come upon us; and it is on me that the storm will burst with all its dark fury." Sometimes a voice speaks to me in thunder tones, saying, "Rise, rise! flee to the mountains, — tarry not in all the plain. Haste away! Destruction's before thee, and sorrow behind;" and, "you never will be a happy family again." I call Willie to me, put my hand on his head, and weep and weep, and say, "O, Willie! Willie! Willie!" My husband says, "Miriam, don't feel so; I am afraid you will go crazy. I think it is your imaginings, caused by our disappointments and discomforts." I answer, "I hope it is, but I don't know why I should be so overpowered with such feelings; they come to me without being invited, and I cannot help giving them expression sometimes."

Miriam's writing is from her book Went to Kansas; Being a Thrilling Account of an Ill-Fated Expedition to that Fairy Land and Its Sad Results, *published in 1862 by L. Ingalls & Company.*

Miriam Davis Colt was born December 18, 1817, in Crown Point, New York, the twelfth of sixteen children. Miriam began teaching in local schools when she was twenty. Two years later she met and fell in love with William H. Colt, a fellow teacher. He soon departed for a teaching position in

Montreal, and they carried on their romance via letters and an occasional visit for five years.

Miriam and William were finally married in 1845. For the next seven years they settled in Montreal, where they both taught school. Their first child, Miriam, was born in 1847, and their son, William, was born in 1853, soon after their return to upstate New York.

Mr. Colt, a vegetarian, became involved with the Neosho Colony in Kansas, organized by the Vegetarian Settlement Company. The company promised to build a sawmill and grist mill, schools, and a temporary boarding house there for the families to stay in until their homes were built.

In April 1856 the Colts headed west with all their possessions. When they arrived in Kansas they discovered that nothing had been built as planned, and that the colony consisted of a few tents. Miriam feared the Indians, the snakes, and the threats of illness and death to her family. By September they realized that no amount of labor could establish them in Kansas, and they departed for New York. However, Miriam's premonitions came true: her son died en route from an illness contracted in Kansas, and her husband died a week later. After a few months in shock and mourning, Miriam resumed her journey home with her daughter.

Miriam lived with her daughter until her second marriage in 1866. She spent her last years with two of her brothers, until her death in 1899 at the age of eighty-two.

Clara Temple Leonard

1874

I have thought of nothing but our campaign since my return. How glorious it was to see the enemy routed. I feel deeply, more than ever, that voting would be the ruin of our sex. We should be completely demoralized and unfitted for our duties. I see the effect now, upon myself, of a taste of political life.

*O*pposed to voting

Clara Temple Chapman Leonard was born December 19, 1828, in Greenfield, Massachusetts. She attended Miss Leavitt's dame-school and the Misses Stone Boarding School.

Clara's father became ill when she was twenty-three, and although she had no medical experience she spent several months nursing him. She fired her father's physician who was bleeding and blistering him and hired a homeopathic doctor instead. Her father made noticeable progress until

Clara's writing is from a June 29, 1874, letter to her friend Mrs. Poor. It is included in Clara Temple Leonard — A Memoir of Her Life, *by her daughter, published in 1908 by Loring-Axtell Co.*

one day he asked for pen and paper to write an important business letter; the strain was too much, and he suffered a stroke and died.

In 1853, despite the objections of her impoverished family, Clara set off for the South, where she had obtained a position as governess for the children of a wealthy plantation owner. Unfortunately, the "Blake children were numerous and wholly untaught and ungoverned. Their mother, an invalid, had no idea of discipline but to cuff them right and left when troublesome. They could none of them read." Clara was staunchly anti-slavery, but she thought she would be able to keep her opinions to herself. After six weeks she could no longer tolerate the abuses of slavery or Mrs. Blake, and she hastily returned home to Massachusetts without receiving any salary.

Clara began teaching at Mr. Bent's Boarding and Day School in Worcester. On August 3, 1856, she married Nehemiah Leonard, a successful lawyer in Springfield. In September 1863 she gave birth to their third daughter, who died after a few days. Clara's grief was so overwhelming that she became ill and depressed. Her minister tried to interest her in outside activities to take her mind off her grieving. He asked her one Sunday to go to the county jail as a Sunday school teacher. For the next nine years she went regularly each Sunday to minister to the needs of the female prisoners. She was not a suffragist and believed it was best that women didn't vote.

In February 1865 Clara and several other women organized the Home for Friendless Women and Children. It was a place where discharged prisoners could go "for a brief time to pull themselves together and receive assistance and guidance for the future." Clara was elected manager of the home in 1867, a position she held until 1876.

Following her husband's death in 1890, Clara occupied herself primarily with church-related activities and struggled with declining health. Twelve days before her death she asked for her diary. A nurse opened it and turned it to the correct date, but she turned it ahead several days to her birthday and wrote, "My seventy-sixth birthday, and I am still alive. I feel very old and feeble." She never wrote in it again and died three days after her birthday in 1905.

Jessie Hubbell Bancroft

1941

One of the two private school openings in New York was with Miss Koues on West Ninety-fifth Street, who offered a fourth floor room and board in exchange for two mornings a week of physical training for her private school. The other was a visiting position in the well-known school of Miss North on Madison Avenue in Harlem. After some months I received from Miss North a criticism which became a corner stone in all my future practice. "You are a graceful performer," she said, "and an effective leader and commander; but you do not teach. You see only the class and not the individuals in it. You do not correct faults." That difference between teaching and leading was one that I not only had to master myself, but in which I had to train every assistant who ever came to me in after years. . . .

A helpful critique

Jessie Hubbell Bancroft was born December 20, 1867, in Winona, Minnesota. In the early 1880s she attended a lecture on hygiene, diet, and exercise that was to change her life. She later recalled in her autobiography, "The adolescent years were a period of invalidism for me, and it was for my own health that I first became interested in physical training." In 1888 she enrolled in the Minneapolis School of Physical Education, where she studied physiology, anatomy, gymnastics, and techniques for leading group exercise classes.

After two years of teaching exercise at clubs and churches in the Midwest, Jessie enrolled in Dr. Sargent's Summer School of Physical Education at Harvard. She then moved to New York City, and became a special instructor in physical education at several institutions. In 1893 she was appointed director of physical training of the Brooklyn public school system. She was promoted in 1904 to assistant director of physical training for the entire greater New York City school system. Her book, *Games for the Playground, Home, School, and Gymnasium*, published in 1909, was regarded as the most complete game book published in English.

Jessie wrote in her autobiography, "During forty years of professional work I can recall only one summer that was not devoted mainly to writing, lecturing, teaching or research; so also was the major part of most Christmas and incidental holidays." Her research included testing the sight and hearing of her pupils and taking the "measurements of thousands of children in different racial groups." Among the many results of

Jessie's writing is from "Pioneering in Physical Training — An Autobiography," Research Quarterly, *October 1941.*

this latter research was the revision of tables for the adjustment of school furniture, so that little Italian legs were not dangling in the air, or tall German or Old-stock American backs rounded over desks too low."

In 1941 Jessie founded and was president of the American Posture League. Her work "changed the design of men and boys clothing for more freedom of movement." She designed seats on new principles that were adopted for New York subway cars.

Jessie spent her later years travelling in Europe. She died of a heart attack in 1952.

DECEMBER 21

Mary Hawes Terhune

Learning to cook

1871

When I took possession of my first real home, the prettily furnished cottage to which I came as a bride, more full of hope and courage than if I had been wiser, five good friends promised me with as many cookery-books, each complete, and all by different compilers. One day's investigation of my ménage convinced me that my lately-hired servants knew no more about cookery than I did, or affected stupidity to develop my capabilities or ignorance. Too proud to let them suspect the truth, or to have it bruited abroad as a topic for pitying or contemptuous gossip, I shut myself up with my "Complete Housewives," and inclined seriously to the study of the same, comparing one with the other, and seeking to shape a theory which should grow into practice in accordance with the best authority. I don't like to remember that time! The question of disagreeing doctors, and the predicament of falling between two stools, are trivial perplexities when compared with my strife and failure. . . .

Mary Virginia Hawes Terhune was born December 21, 1830, in Dennisville, Virginia. She was educated at home by private tutors, and both parents encouraged her to read and use the library frequently.

Mary's writing is from her book, Common Sense in the Household, *published by C. Scribner's Sons in 1871.*

Mary began writing as a child, hiding her work in the bottom of a trunk. In 1853 a literary weekly, *The Southern Era*, offered a $50 prize for the best serial on a temperance theme. Mary submitted a story, using the pen name Marion

Harland that she would use for the next seven decades, and won the prize. Delighted with her success she went on to write twenty-five novels and three volumes of short stories.

Mary was already a successful writer in 1856 when she married Edward Terhune, a Presbyterian minister. They had six children, three of whom survived to adulthood and also became authors.

In the 1870s Mary's focus changed from fiction to domestic advice. Her first such effort, *Common Sense in the Household*, became a best seller and was translated into French, German, and Arabic.

Mary outlived her husband by fifteen years, remaining vital and productive until the end. Her last book, a novel, was published when she was eighty-nine. She died in New York City in 1922.

Aline Frankau Bernstein

1926

My dear . . .

I had your two letters with me, and read them both over this morning before I got up. I hope there is another on its way. You say you do not want my heart to ache, you want it to be faithful. It is faithful, and it aches. At times I am completely overcome with the thought that you are gone from me forever. I want to cry out to you and how can I? Do you know, I had an intense feeling to call up your telephone number, NU 4961 tonight. But I didn't do it.

Tom dear do you think I am utterly mad? Here I am every day charged to the utmost with love for you. I must write some of it. My fear is that some day one of these letters will come to you and you will not want it. I wonder if you are trying at all to release yourself. You used to tell me you would "pull out" some day. I go deadly cold at the thought —

Aline Frankau Bernstein was born December 22, 1880, in New York City. Her father named her Hazel at birth, but her mother later changed her name to Aline. After both parents died when she was a teenager Aline became the ward of her aunt, a drug addict. Luckily a family friend, who was one of the directors of the New York School of Applied

Anxious love

Aline's writing is from a letter to Thomas Wolfe. It is in the Willard B. Wisdom Collection, Houghton Library, Harvard University.

Design, recognized Aline's artistic talent, and arranged for her to attend the school on a scholarship.

In November 1902 Aline married Theodore Bernstein, a stockbroker, and soon had a son and a daughter. For several years she concentrated on portrait painting until her friends, the Lewisohn sisters, opened the Neighborhood Playhouse, modeled after the popular European art theaters. From 1915 to 1934 she designed costumes and sets for most of the Lewisohn's productions.

In 1925 Aline met the writer Thomas Wolfe, twenty years her junior, and began a five-year affair. She became his financial supporter and unofficial agent as well. During a 1929 trip to Europe, he took Aline's suggestion and put aside his unsuccessful attempts at playwriting to begin his first novel, *Look Homeward, Angel*. When their relationship ended in 1931 Aline was distraught, and it is rumored that she attempted suicide. Ten years later Wolfe published two books whose central character, Esther Jack, was based on Aline. She, in turn, published a short story in the volume *Three Blue Suits* (1933) and a novel *The Journey Down* (1938) based on the early days of their affair.

Despite Aline's dalliance with Wolfe, her marriage survived and her career flourished. In 1928 she became the resident designer at Eva Le Gallienne's Civic Repertory Theatre. During the Depression she invented a money-saving set using a skeletal frame that could be adapted to any play with the addition of doors, windows, and inserts. After the Neighborhood Playhouse and the Civic Repertory Theatre closed in 1934, Aline worked for independent producers and was paired with Lillian Hellman for her first play, *The Children's Hour*. They enjoyed working together and did four more plays as a team over the next fifteen years.

From 1943 to 1949 Aline taught costume design at Vassar College's Experimental Theatre. In 1949 at the age of seventy, she received the Antoinette Perry Award for her costumes for the opera *Regina*. Aline retired from the theater in 1953, but continued as president of the Costume Institute of the Metropolitan Museum of Art, which she had founded years earlier with Irene Lewisohn. She died at home in New York in 1955, three months shy of her seventy-fifth birthday.

Sarah Breedlove Walker

1919

The Negro in the south has up to the time of his induction into the army, been denied the use of fire-arms and in the timid and coward-like condition forced upon him, he has been no match for the fiends and brutes who have taken advantage of his helplessness and heaped every iniquity upon a practically defenseless and friendless people.

But in the meantime their country called them to defend its honor on the battle-fields of Europe and they have bravely, fearlessly bleed and died, that that honor might be maintained. And now — they will soon be returning. To what? Does any reasonable person imagine — to the old order of things? To submit to being strung up, riddled with bullets, burned at the stake, etc.? No! A thousand times — No! And what good friend, even of humanity, would wish it so. . . .

*N*o more submission

Sarah Breedlove Walker was born December 23, 1867, in northeastern Louisiana, the daughter of former slaves. She married Mr. McWilliams when she was fourteen and had a daughter, A'Lelia. Following McWilliams's death six years later, she moved with her child to St. Louis, where she found work as a laundress.

In 1905 Sarah had a dream that revealed to her the formula of a pomade to straighten Negro hair. She mixed the ingredients herself in washtubs and sold it door to door. Buoyed by her success, she moved to Detroit to be near her brother and continued selling door to door. She married Charles J. Walker, a newspaperman, and although the marriage was unsuccessful she kept his name, and "The Walker Method" was born.

Sarah built a factory and recruited sales agents, who dressed in starched white shirts and long black skirts and took Walker products to homes all over the United States and the Caribbean. They were called "beauty culturists" or "scalp specialists" and were never allowed to use the term "hair-straighteners." Sarah organized her 3,000 employees into social and philanthropic clubs, and held national conventions attended by delegates from these clubs. She rewarded employees for high sales and those who did the most charity work.

Sarah's writing is from a letter to Col. William J. Schieffelin, treasurer of the Welfare League of an all-black infantry unit. It is part of the Walker Collection maintained by her granddaughter, A'Lelia Bundles, of Alexandria, Virginia.

By 1910 Sarah had become a millionaire and one of the best-known black women in America. She donated large sums to black and Christian charities and endowed scholarships for women at Tuskegee Institute. In 1913 she built a beautiful townhouse, including a beauty school and salon, on West 136th Street in New York City. Several years later she built a twenty-room mansion, "Villa Lewaro," on the Hudson River. She hoped her lavish homes would inspire other blacks to strive for achievement.

Sarah died of kidney disease at "Villa Lewaro" in May 1919 and was buried at Woodlawn Cemetery in the Bronx. The Madam C. J. Walker Manufacturing Company continues in business today as a major producer of ethnic hair products.

Octavia Rogers Albert

Joyful reunion

1890

This colored man, I learned, was the Rev. Dr. Col. Lee, pastor of a prominent church in Louisiana. I was so delighted with his speech, and felt so proud of him, that I forced my way through the crowd to shake his hand and to thank him, in the name of his race, for the honor he had reflected upon himself and his race. After congratulating him I said:

"Your name is Dr. Lee?"

"Yes," said he; "my father was a white man, and he would not let me be called by his name. So mother gave me her name, which was Lee, and so I have kept it right along."

Said I, "Is your mother living?"

Said he, "The Lord only knows. She was sold from me when I was only four or five years old. . . . "

"Pray tell me, sir, what was her name?"

"Her name was Jane Lee, who originally was sold to Louisiana from Virginia."

"Well, well!" thought I; and just as I was about to tell him about Aunt Charlotte, and what she told me of Aunt Jane Lee, there came a woman apparently about fifty or sixty years of age, who, upon hearing him, rushed wildly, and, throwing her arms around his neck, cried out, amid tears of great joy,

"My long-lost son, my long-lost son! my son, my son!"

Octavia's writing comes from her book, The House of Bondage, *published in 1890 by Hunt and Eaton, New York.*

Women's Words, Women's Stories

Every body turned around to see what was the
matter, only to unite in praise to God for the wonderful
reunion that he had thus vouchsafed to this long-
separated mother and son.

Octavia Rogers Albert was born to slaves on December 24,
1853, in Oglethorpe, Georgia. Following emancipation she
attended local schools and graduated with a teaching degree
from Atlanta University.

Octavia taught for a year in Montezuma, Georgia, where
she met her future husband, the Reverend A. E. P. Albert.
They were married in 1874 and had one daughter.

In her forties Octavia began interviewing former slaves
and recording their conversations. After her untimely death
at forty-six, her daughter Laura published these tales in serial
form in the *Southwestern Christian Advocate*, the magazine of
the Methodist Episcopal church. Letters of appreciation
poured in to the editor. As a result, the conversations were
published in book form, *The House of Bondage*, in 1890.

Clara Barton

1910

In such a family I had no playmates. My [older] brothers and sisters became school teachers. Naturally
among so many teachers my education commenced not
entirely systematic, as you will observe. Each instructor followed the bent of his or her own taste. My
sisters, — beautiful girls that they were, — took charge
of all ordinary studies.

My father drilled me in military tactics; we mar-
shalled large armies, laid in ambush, and fought san-
guinary battles. My elder brother, a fine student and
business man, taught me mathematics and book-
keeping; while the younger brother, a skilled horseman,
taught me to ride wild horses, like a little Mexican, and
my practical mother complained that among them all,
her prospects of making a good housekeeper of me,
were not hopeful. Still faithful to her blessed memory
and patient efforts I have "kept a moderate tight grip
on the handful of things" she did tell me.

Clara Harlowe Barton was born December 25, 1821, in

Plenty of teachers

*Clara's writing is from an
address she gave at her
nephew's church in Oak Park,
Illinois, on May 8, 1910, when
she was eighty-eight. It is
among the Clara Barton papers
in the Sophia Smith Collection,
Smith College, Northampton,
Massachusetts.*

North Oxford, Massachusetts. Most of her education came from her family, especially her four older brothers and sisters. She later wrote, "I had no playmates, but in effect six fathers and mothers." From age eleven to age thirteen she nursed her brother David through a serious illness, laying the foundation for her future career.

Clara taught school for many years in Massachusetts and Bordentown, New Jersey. She received three marriage proposals during this time but refused them all. In 1854 she resigned from teaching and moved to Washington, D.C., where she was appointed a clerk in the Patent Office, one of the first female civil servants. In the early months of the Civil War she began ministering to the needs of displaced Massachusetts soldiers. At the Battle of Bull Run she observed firsthand the lack of medical facilities and supplies. She placed an ad in the *Worcester Spy* and received shipments of food, medicine, and bandages, which she distributed by mule team to makeshift hospitals on the battlefields. She was present at many of the Civil War's major battles. She described in a letter home how she had to wring the blood from the bottom of her clothes because they became so weighted down that it was hard to step. Although others assisted her and she was loathe to accept all the glory, it was Clara whom soldiers remembered as the "Angel of the Battlefield."

In 1865 Clara, with the cooperation of the War Department and approval of President Lincoln, opened an office to help families locate missing soldiers. At the same time she travelled the country, giving more than 300 lectures on her wartime experiences. By 1868 she was exhausted and had lost her voice. She went to Europe on the advice of her doctor to recuperate. While abroad she learned about the International Committee of the Red Cross, which had been ratified by eleven countries in the Geneva Treaty. Clara worked with the International Red Cross during the Franco-Prussian War and the Russo-Turkish War, after which she returned to the United States to wage a five-year campaign to ratify the Geneva Treaty and organize an American Red Cross society.

Initially Americans were disinterested in the Red Cross as they did not anticipate future wars. After she expanded the concept to include relief in domestic disasters, and after years of lecturing and writing articles, the Geneva Treaty was signed by President Chester Arthur in March 1882. Clara served as president of the American Association of the Red Cross until 1904, during which time she provided relief in twenty-one disasters, including forest fires, floods, hurricanes, and a yellow fever epidemic. She never drew a salary and often contributed her own savings when needed.

When Clara was seventy-seven she was still in the field,

delivering supplies by mule wagons in the Spanish-American War. By 1902 there was dissension in the organization as younger women wanted to take over with more modern, efficient ways. Clara was eventually forced to resign in 1904. She died in 1912 at the age of ninety and was buried in her birthplace, North Oxford, Massachusetts.

Eva March Tappan

1923

A new school

The last day of school arrived. Ella went through the exercises almost in a dream. She began to realize that she was going into a strange new school, and she was half afraid. After the day was over and the guests had gone, the whole class wrote their names on the board with "Graduating Class of 1869. Good-bye."

On the following morning a long procession of boys and girls wound its way up the hill to the high school. They were distributed among the different rooms. Each room was in charge of a teacher, and Ella was delighted to find the assistant standing by the door in her room, ready to welcome her. The place of honor was given to arithmetic; first written, then mental arithmetic. It was "mental" indeed, for not one figure was allowed to be written. The pupils did the examples in their minds as best they could, then set down the answer; and they had had so much practice in keeping the example as well as the work in mind that it seemed to them hardly more than play when a good clear printed copy of the questions lay before them.

Eva March Tappan was born December 26, 1854, in Blackstone, Massachusetts. After her father died when she was six, her mother took a teaching job at the Smithville Seminary in Rhode Island, so that Eva could continue to live with her and receive a good education.

In 1871 Eva enrolled in Vassar College, where she was elected to Phi Beta Kappa. She was so poor that she was forced to spend most of her vacations at the school. Although she showed writing talent as editor of *The Vassar Miscellany*, she began a teaching career following graduation in 1875. She taught at Wheaton College and later at a private academy in New Jersey. While in New Jersey, she commuted across

Eva's writing is from Ella, A Little Schoolgirl of the Sixties, A Book for Children and for Grown-ups who Remember, *published by Houghton, Mifflin and Company in 1923.*

the river to the University of Pennsylvania in Philadelphia, where she took graduate courses in English literature. She earned a master's degree in 1895 and a Ph.D. the following year.

In 1897 Eva was hired as head of the English department at English High School in Worcester, Massachusetts, where she took a special interest in the large immigrant student population. She helped the students master the language by casting them in school plays, which she directed.

Eva published her first children's book, about the author Charles Lamb, in 1896. She quickly published nine others concentrating on the lives of historical figures such as Queen Elizabeth, Alfred the Great, and Robin Hood. Believing she could reach far more students through her writing, she retired from teaching in 1904 and published at least one book a year thereafter through 1928. Most of her books were social histories, although she also translated folktales from foreign countries.

In her later years Eva became deaf and somewhat of a recluse. She died in 1930 at the age of seventy-five. Her will provided a generous endowment for a scholarship fund at Vassar for women from Worcester County.

Rose Guggenheim Winslow (Jane Burr)

*A*lone

1949

Somewhere in one of your letters you said you wish you knew whom Mary Margaret McBride referred to in her note hastily scribbled with red pencil. It was her dead mother. When my mother died I lost my only real friend. I wrote to Mary M that now she had lost her only real friend and that there would be no more for either of us. Oh, lots of people around if we wanted them but no real friends. My mother used to carry my verse around in her pocket-book. She clipped everything and saved everything and so did Mary Margaret's mother. I expect no more real understanding. I wrote her that she might as well not expect any for it would not arrive.

One learns to walk alone.

Rose's writing is from an August 17, 1949, letter to her friend Margaret Grierson, Sophia Smith Collection, Smith College, Northampton, Massachusetts.

Rose Guggenheim Winslow (Jane Burr) was born December 27, 1882, in Cleburne, Texas. When she was eighteen she married Jack Punsch, an older man, just "to get away from home." She began attending Washington University in St. Louis, the first married woman ever to go there. She later wrote in her memoirs, "I had no education when I was young. I had no time for school. Never read a book till I was eighteen. Then the desire for learning came like an avalanche." Over the years she attended many universities as a special student, and when she died she left her memoirs and other papers to Smith College.

In 1905 Rose divorced her husband and took her first job as a reporter for the *St. Louis Star*, using the pen name Jane Burr. On an assignment out west in 1907, she was stricken with appendicitis and became one of the first patients at the newly formed Mayo Clinic. Years later she joked, "Everything I ever owned is out there in bottles of formaldehyde."

Rose soon began publishing novels and volumes of poetry, also under the name Jane Burr. Her best-known books were *The Queen Is Dead* and *Marble and Dust*.

Rose had established her reputation as an American novelist by 1922, when the United Press sent her on a five-year, around-the-world assignment. Her task was to study the position and condition of women all over the world and to send a weekly article to be syndicated in the United States.

Upon her return to America in 1927, Rose had her own radio program and continued to publish novels. She married for a second time to Horatio Winslow, also an author. In 1938 they moved to an estate, "Patches," in Woodstock, New York. She opened an antique store, the "Anteekery," in her barn and gave free tea and cigarettes, scintillating conversation, and autographed copies of her books to her customers. She had a rule that no one was permitted to buy anything on the first visit. They could take something for free from the "Don't ask it Basket," but they couldn't make a purchase until they returned a second time.

In 1949 Rose was bedridden with rheumatoid arthritis. She became morbid and began writing her memoirs and her will, preparing for her end, which she felt was imminent. She died at home in February 1958 at the age of seventy-five.

Catharine Maria Sedgwick

Links of a chain

May 5th, 1853

My Dear Little Alice, — About two years since your father wrote me an eloquent note persuading me to write for you some memorial of my life, and what I knew of your forbears and mine. If you live to be an old woman, as I now am, you may like to rake in the ashes of the past and, if perchance, you find some fire still smouldering there, you may feel a glow from it. It is not till we get deep into age that we feel by how slight a tenure we hold on to the memories of those that come after us, and not till then that we are conscious of an earnest desire to brighten the links of the chain that binds us to those who have gone before, and to keep it fast and strong.

Catharine Maria Sedgwick was born December 28, 1789, in Stockbridge, Massachusetts. Her father, a state senator and Massachusetts Supreme Court justice, was a great influence on her. Her mother suffered from melancholia, which twice developed into periods of insanity. It fell to Catharine and a black servant named Mumbet to take care of the household, the six other children, and Mrs. Sedgwick. As a result, her formal schooling was spasmodic. She briefly attended Mrs. Bell's Academy in Albany and Miss Paine's Finishing School in Boston, where she "learned to parse glibly" but ran up a large bill at local stores "in mad squanderings for raisins, sweets, and Malaga wine." She received at least six marriage proposals but refused them all.

In 1821 Catharine's brother Theodore asked her to write an anti-Calvinist tract. She enjoyed the assignment and the tract grew into a novel, *A New England Tale*, published in 1822. The book was a major success and instantly established her as the most popular American female novelist of the day. She published four more novels between 1824 and 1835. Twenty-two years elapsed before publication of her sixth and final novel, *Married or Single?*, the intent of which was to "lessen the stigma placed on the term old maid."

For most of her adult life, Catharine spent summers in Stockbridge in the Berkshires and winters in New York City. In addition to her career as an author, she played an active role in the prison reform movement. From 1848 until her death, she was director of the Women's Prison Association in New York. She died in 1867 at the age of seventy-seven and was buried in the Sedgwick family plot in Stockbridge.

Catharine's writing is from "Recollections of Childhood," included in Life and Letters of Catharine Maria Sedgwick, *edited by Mary E. Dewey and published by Harper in 1871.*

Floride Clemson Lee

1863
Sep. 7th Niagara Falls
Clifton House, Canada
My Darling Mother,

   Here we are at last at the great falls. We arrived safe, & sound, after dark last evening, so we did not see the falls until (I am ashamed to say it) ten o'clock this morning. The rest of the party seemed to be disappointed, not so with me, my highest expectations were more than realized. I must say I was silly enough to cry when they first caught my sight. As you have been here, I suppose you know that from this side, & the porches of this house, you have a "full & particular" view of Goat Island, & both the bodies of water. I never imagined any thing so grand. . . .

*A*t the falls

Floride Clemson Lee was born December 29, 1842, on her grandfather's plantation, Fort Hill, in South Carolina. Her mother was Senator John C. Calhoun's favorite daughter. In 1844 Calhoun influenced President Zachary Taylor to appoint his son-in-law as chargé d'affaires to Belgium.

   The Clemson family moved to Brussels with one slave and a nurse to take care of Floride and her brother. They enjoyed six years abroad until President Taylor's death in 1850 brought a new administration to Washington, and Mr. Clemson was recalled. Upon his return he purchased 100 acres in Maryland and became a gentleman farmer. He conducted scientific experiments on his farm and developed a reputation as an agricultural chemist.

   Floride was sent to Miss Barton's School in Philadelphia in 1856. She made a pact with her mother that they would exchange letters at least once a week. Floride thrived at school, but her mother missed her and worried constantly about her health, so she returned after two years.

   In 1860 the Clemsons moved to Washington, D.C., when Mr. Clemson was appointed superintendent of agricultural affairs. Floride became good friends with President James Buchanan's niece, who served as official hostess for her bachelor uncle. Through her friendship Floride was invited to numerous official functions and met many important people.

   With Lincoln's inauguration, Mr. Clemson resigned his position in the Department of the Interior, and the family returned to South Carolina for the duration of the Civil War.

Floride's writing is from a September 7, 1863, letter sent to her mother from Niagara Falls. It is included in A Rebel Came Home: The Diary and Letters of Floride Clemson, 1863-1866, *edited by Charles M. McGee, Jr., and Ernest M. Lancer, Jr., and published by the University of South Carolina Press, 1989.*

Floride married Gideon Lee, a wealthy man eighteen years her senior, in July 1869. They settled in Carmel, New York, where their only child, a daughter, was born in 1870. One year later, Floride became ill and died at the age of twenty-nine.

DECEMBER 30

Rachel Foster Avery

Doctor's orders

circa 1912

Well here I am mad as a hopper at the Doctor and Lucy and everybody else. The Dr. positively refused to let me go tomorrow, simply said I should not, after I said I would. I must say for the Doctor, she does not often get angry but she did this time and her anger made me forget mine, for I was angry because I felt Dr. and Lucy had planned to keep me at home, and I did not like feeling compelled to back my word. It has been a kind of big headed pride on my part that I keep my engagements at whatever cost to myself and to be forced not to do so against my will was a little too much. Yet deep down inside of me I felt the doctor had the right of it. If I call on her when I need her she has a right to dictate terms or refuse to respond to my request for assistance and when she said, "did you not go last Sunday when I told you not to and did I not come to you and get you just in time to keep you from becoming delirious and have I not done all I could for you all the week to get you well and don't you suppose I know better than you do what you are fit to do." I felt as if I were about five years old and was being spanked.

Rachel Foster Avery was born December 30, 1858, in Pittsburgh. Her parents, both Quakers, were anti-slavery and pro-suffrage. The first suffrage meetings in Pittsburgh were held in their home.

Rachel and her sisters were educated at private schools in Philadelphia, after which Rachel travelled extensively abroad, embraced socialism, and studied political economy at the University of Zurich. In 1879 she attended the National American Woman Suffrage Association convention, where she began her lifelong friendship with Susan B. Anthony (February 15).

Rachel's writing is from a letter to her friend Mary Dennett (April 4), Mary Dennett Collection, Schlesinger Library, Radcliffe College, Cambridge, Massachusetts.

Rachel organized suffrage conventions in New England and the Midwest. Susan B. Anthony referred to her as "my dear, first adopted niece." She gradually delegated more and more of the organizational work to Rachel, so that she could be free to travel and lecture.

In November 1888 Rachel married Cyrus Miller Avery, the son of an active suffragist from Chicago. Miss Anthony disapproved of the marriage fearing Rachel would abandon the cause of suffrage in favor of her husband and three daughters. Her fears were unfounded, however, as Rachel never slackened her efforts.

Miss Anthony retired as head of the National American Woman Suffrage Association in 1901, and Rachel resigned as corresponding secretary the following year, although she stayed active within the movement. Miss Anthony commented on Rachel's invaluable assistance, "I should never have been able to carry on the work of the society as its president for so many years but for her able cooperation. . . . She has done the drudgery of this association for more than twenty years."

Rachel died of pneumonia in 1919 at the age of sixty, having lived long enough to see the suffrage amendment passed by Congress.

Mary Anne Sadlier

1903

Never shall I forget the demoniacal expression of his once handsome features as he waved his arm and called on the others to burn down the "Mass-house" and clear the city of the rascally Irish. The sight has never since left my eyes; sleeping and waking it is ever before me, and the thought of that hell-inspired ruffian being *my son* is like a fiery dart sticking for ever and ever in my heart. . . .

Her ruffian son

Mary Anne Madden Sadlier was born December 31, 1820, in Cootehill, County Cavan, Ireland. After her mother's death, she was reared by her father. She showed promise as a writer at an early age and contributed poems to *La Belle Assemblée* when she was only eighteen.

After Mary's father died in 1844 she emigrated to New York City. Two years later she married James Sadlier, the owner of a Catholic publishing house. For the next fourteen years they resided in Montreal, Canada, where he operated a

Mary's writing is from her novel, Confessions of an Apostate, *published by Arno Press in 1903.*

branch of the company. They raised three daughters, three sons, and a foster son.

Mary began writing seriously during her years in Montreal. She published several novels, a collection of short stories, and numerous articles in Catholic periodicals such as the *Boston Pilot* and the *New York Tablet*. She was a leader in conservative Catholic poetry and prose. When the Sadliers returned to New York in 1860, she became active in New York's Catholic charities. Many of her novels were about Irish-Catholic immigrants in the United States and revealed much about mid-century Irish life. Her book *Willie Burke: A Tale of the Irish Orphan in America* sold 7,000 copies in its first month of publication. In all, she produced sixty books during her lifetime.

In 1888 Mary returned to Montreal to be close to her married children. She received the Laetare Medal from Notre Dame University in 1895 for her work on behalf of Catholicism. She died in 1903 at the age of eighty-two.

Picture credits

Mary Kenney O'Sullivan	JANUARY 8	Schlesinger Library, Radcliffe College
Harriet Maxwell Converse	JANUARY 11	New York Historical Society
Theresa Helburn	JANUARY 12	Harvard Theatre Collection
Ellis R. Shipp, M.D.	JANUARY 20	Schlesinger Library, Radcliffe College
Maud Wood Park	JANUARY 25	Sophia Smith Collection, Smith College
Elisabet Ney	JANUARY 26	Schlesinger Library, Radcliffe College
Cordelia Howard	FEBRUARY 1	Harvard Theatre Collection
Elizabeth Blackwell	FEBRUARY 3	Schlesinger Library, Radcliffe College
Harriet Robinson	FEBRUARY 8	Schlesinger Library, Radcliffe College
Susan B. Anthony	FEBRUARY 15	Schlesinger Library, Radcliffe College
Katherine Pettit	FEBRUARY 23	The Doris Ulman Foundation, Berea College
Sarah Morgan Dawson	FEBRUARY 28	Schlesinger Library, Radcliffe College
Mary Patrick	MARCH 10	Library of Congress
Wanda Gág	MARCH 11	Library of Congress
Clara Morris	MARCH 17	Sophia Smith Collection, Smith College
Fanny Davenport	APRIL 10	Harvard Theatre Collection
Margaret Houston	APRIL 11	The Center for American History, the University of Texas at Austin
Mary Booth	APRIL 19	Duyckinck Family Papers, New York Public Library
Ellen Glasgow	APRIL 22	Schlesinger Library, Radcliffe College
Cecilia Beaux	MAY 1	Schlesinger Library, Radcliffe College
Elizabeth Cochrane Seaman (Nellie Bly)	MAY 5	Library of Congress
Mari Sandoz	MAY 11	University of Nebraska
Margaret Sloan	MAY 15	"Shattered Dream" University of South Carolina Press
Antoinette Blackwell	MAY 20	Schlesinger Library, Radcliffe College
Kate Barnard	MAY 23	Library of Congress
Jeannette Rankin	JUNE 11	Library of Congress
Malvina Hoffman	JUNE 15	Schlesinger Library, Radcliffe College
Chrystal Herne	JUNE 17	Harvard Theatre Collection
Rebecca Davis	JUNE 24	Schlesinger Library, Radcliffe College
Helen Keller	JUNE 27	Schlesinger Library, Radcliffe College
Susan Glaspell	JULY 1	Library of Congress
Millie-Christine McKoy	JULY 11	Regional Museum of Spartanburg County
Florence Tuttle	JULY 23	Sophia Smith Collection, Smith College
Ella Boole	JULY 26	Library of Congress
Mary Beard	AUGUST 5	Schlesinger Library, Radcliffe College
Florence Bailey	AUGUST 8	Smith College Archives
Elizabeth Smith	AUGUST 12	Library of Congress
Phoebe Ann Moses (Annie Oakley)	AUGUST 13	Buffalo Bill Historical Center, Cody, WY
Ethel Dreier	AUGUST 21	Sophia Smith Collection, Smith College
Maud Powell	AUGUST 22	Library of Congress
Sophia Kerr	AUGUST 23	Schlesinger Library, Radcliffe College
Madeleine Doty	AUGUST 24	Sophia Smith Collection, Smith College
Nora Gordon	AUGUST 25	Spelman College Archives
Jane Addams	SEPTEMBER 6	Library of Congress
Karen Horney	SEPTEMBER 16	Schlesinger Library, Radcliffe College
Grace Espy Patton	OCTOBER 5	Colorado State University
Della Fox	OCTOBER 13	Harvard Theatre Collection

Belva Lockwood	OCTOBER 24	Sophia Smith Collection, Smith College
Fanny Brice	OCTOBER 29	Harvard Theatre Collection
Eleanor Patterson	NOVEMBER 7	Library of Congress
Grace Abbott	NOVEMBER 17	Library of Congress
Mary Hallock Foote	NOVEMBER 19	Stanford University Library
Rose Pesotta	NOVEMBER 20	Library of Congress
Mabel Daniels	NOVEMBER 27	Schlesinger Library, Radcliffe College
Harriet Chalmers Bliss Ford	NOVEMBER 28	Sophia Smith Collection, Smith College
Adella Prentiss Hughes	NOVEMBER 29	Schlesinger Library, Radcliffe College
Florence Clemson	DECEMBER 29	Special Collections, University Libraries, Clemson University

Reference collections

Grateful acknowledgment is made to the following museums, libraries, historical societies and individuals for courtesy in granting access to their collections:

University of North Florida	Jacksonville, FL
The Library of Congress	Washington, D.C.
The Historical Society of York County	York, PA
Wellesley College, Wellesley College Archives	Wellesley, MA
Harvard University, Harvard Theatre Collection	Cambridge, MA
Harvard University, Harvard University Collection	Cambridge, MA
Harvard University, Houghton Library	Cambridge, MA
Harvard University, Widener Library	Cambridge, MA
Radcliffe College, Schlesinger Library	Cambridge, MA
Harvard Medical School, Harvard Medical School Library	Cambridge, MA
Cornell University, Labor Management Documentation Center	Ithaca, NY
Boston Public Library, Rare Books	Boston, MA
Smith College, Sophia Smith Collection	Northampton, MA
Smith College, Smith College Archives	Northampton, MA
Cabrini College, Cabriniana Room	Radnor, PA
Archives of American Art	Washington, D.C.
Hampton University, Hampton University Archives	Hampton, VA
University of Texas at Austin, Baker Texas History Center	Austin, TX
Herbert Hoover Presidential Library	West Branch, IA
University of Vermont, Bailey Howe Library	Burlington, VT
Berea College, Southern Appalachian Archives	Berea, KY
American Philosophical Society	Philadelphia, PA
Antioch College, Antiochiana College Archives	Yellow Springs, OH
The Center for the Study of the Consumer Movement	Mount Vernon, NY
Consumer Union Foundation Archives, University of North Dakota in Grand Forks	Grand Forks ND
Orin G. Libby Manuscript Collection, Harvard University, Gray Herbarium	Cambridge, MA
South Carolina Historical Society	Charleston, SC
University of California at Berkeley, Department of Botany	Berkeley, CA
Boston Atheneum	Boston, MA
Barrie Barstow Greenbie	Amherst, MA
Delia Heming Cantor	Scarsdale, NY
G. Lloyd Martin	Brick, NJ
Barbara Groves	Wenham, MA
Mrs. Anne Sims Morison	Cambridge, MA
Richard Boyle O'Reilly Hocking	Madison, NH
Chester Historical Society	West Chester, PA
Duke University, William R. Perkins Library	Durham, SC
Hamilton College Library	Hamilton, NY
Sharon Public Library	Sharon, MA
State Historical Society of Wisconsin Archives	Madison, WI
Wayne County Historical Society	Honesdale, PA
A'Lelia Bundles	Alexandria, VA

Index

Elizabeth Rogers Mason Cabot	MAY 25
Saint Frances Xavier Cabrini	JULY 15
Mabel Buland Campbell	OCTOBER 21
Persia Crawford Campbell	MARCH 15
Harriet Starr Cannon	MAY 7
Evelyn Maurine Carrington	AUGUST 30
Ada Jack Carver	APRIL 7
Alice Cary	APRIL 26
Phoebe Cary	SEPTEMBER 4
Willa Cather	DECEMBER 7
Sarah Flournoy Moore Chapin	MARCH 14
Louise Smith Clappe	JULY 28
Mary Devereaux Clarke	MAY 13
Kate McPhelim Cleary	AUGUST 20
Fannia Mary Cohn	APRIL 5
Ann Raney Coleman	NOVEMBER 5
Miriam Davis Colt	DECEMBER 18
Katharine Coman	NOVEMBER 23
Hannah Chaplin Conant	SEPTEMBER 5
Claribel Cone	NOVEMBER 14
Harriet Maxwell Converse	JANUARY 11
Anna Maria Green Cook	SEPTEMBER 22
Anna J. Cooper	AUGUST 10
Prudence Crandall	SEPTEMBER 3
Caresse Crosby	APRIL 20
Rachel Crothers	DECEMBER 12
Elizabeth Bacon Custer	APRIL 8
Mabel Wheeler Daniels	NOVEMBER 27
Flora Adams Darling	JULY 25
Fanny Davenport	APRIL 10
Paulina Wright Davis	AUGUST 7
Rebecca Harding Davis	JUNE 24
Sarah Morgan Dawson	FEBRUARY 28
Rebecca Pennell Dean	MARCH 12
Mary Ware Dennett	APRIL 4
Angela Diller	AUGUST 1
Catharine Marvin Dimmick	JANUARY 27
Mary Abigail Dodge	MARCH 31
Tamsen Donner	NOVEMBER 1
Sarah Anne Dorsey	FEBRUARY 16
Madeleine Zabriskie Doty	AUGUST 24
Neltje De Graff Doubleday	OCTOBER 23
Anna Palmer Draper	SEPTEMBER 11
Ruth Draper	DECEMBER 2
Ethel Eyre Valentine Dreier	AUGUST 21
Ella Elgar Bird Dumont	JULY 3
Amelia Mary Earhart	JULY 24
Annis Ford Eastman	APRIL 24
Crystal Eastman	JUNE 25
Elaine Goodale Eastman	OCTOBER 9
Linda Anne Eastman	JULY 17
Myra Fairbanks Eells	MAY 26
Ellen Russell Emerson	JANUARY 16
Mary Fife Emerson	MAY 12
Angna Enters	APRIL 18
Janet Ayer Fairbank	JUNE 7
Mary Cutler Fairchild	JUNE 21
Beatrix Jones Farrand	JUNE 19
Jessie Redmon Fauset	APRIL 27
Amy Fay	MAY 21
Marian Anthon Fish	JUNE 8

Dorothy Canfield Fisher	FEBRUARY 17
Elizabeth Chester Fisk	FEBRUARY 18
Janet Flanner	MARCH 13
Sarah Lee Brown Fleming	JANUARY 10
Eliza Lee Cabot Follen	AUGUST 15
Mary Hallock Foote	NOVEMBER 19
Harriet Chalmers Ford	NOVEMBER 28
Sarah Jane Foster	OCTOBER 12
Della Fox	OCTOBER 13
Margaret Alsip Frink	APRIL 25
Wanda Hazel Gág	MARCH 11
Irene McCoy Gaines	OCTOBER 25
Zona Gale	AUGUST 26
Mary Sewall Gardner	FEBRUARY 5
Alice Gerstenberg	AUGUST 2
Lillian Moller Gilbreth	MAY 24
Elizabeth Meriwether Gilmer	NOVEMBER 18
Lillian Gish	OCTOBER 14
Ellen Glasgow	APRIL 22
Susan Keating Glaspell	JULY 1
Caroline Gordon	OCTOBER 6
Nora Antonia Gordon	AUGUST 25
Rebecca Gratz	MARCH 4
Marjorie Barstow Greenbie	AUGUST 4
Rosetta Sherwood Hall	SEPTEMBER 19
Sharlot Mabridth Hall	OCTOBER 27
Margherita Arlina Hamm	APRIL 29
Phebe Coffin Hanaford	MAY 6
Frances Watkins Harper	SEPTEMBER 24
Elizabeth Johnson Harris	DECEMBER 16
Mary Belle Harris	AUGUST 19
Minnie Hauk	NOVEMBER 16
Elizabeth Ross Haynes	JULY 30
Lillian Weston Hazen	OCTOBER 31
Theresa Helburn	JANUARY 12
Abby Maria Hemenway	OCTOBER 7
Alice Henry	MARCH 21
Chrystal Katharine Herne	JUNE 17
Caroline Maria Hewins	OCTOBER 10
Margaret Dwight Hitchcock	MAY 16
Agnes Boyle O'Reilly Hocking	MAY 19
Malvina Cornell Hoffman	JUNE 15
Louise Beatty Homer	APRIL 30
Hulda Minthorn Hoover	MAY 4
Lugenia Burns Hope	FEBRUARY 19
Hedda Hopper	MAY 2
Karen Danielsen Horney	SEPTEMBER 16
Margaret Lea Houston	APRIL 11
Cordelia Howard	FEBRUARY 1
Julia Ward Howe	MAY 27
Adella Prentiss Hughes	NOVEMBER 29
Harriot Kezia Hunt	NOVEMBER 9
Emily Huntington	JANUARY 3
Fannie Hurst	OCTOBER 18
Ida Henrietta Hyde	SEPTEMBER 8
Inez Haynes Irwin	MARCH 2
Lucy Crump Jefferson	NOVEMBER 3
Adelaide Johnson	SEPTEMBER 26
Georgia Douglas Johnson	SEPTEMBER 10
Halle Johnson	OCTOBER 17
Elizabeth Garver Jordan	MAY 9

Sara Murray Jordan	OCTOBER 20
Sarah Hall Boardman Judson	NOVEMBER 4
Helen Keller	JUNE 27
Florence Kelley	SEPTEMBER 12
Clara Louise Kellogg	JULY 9
Electa Kellogg	NOVEMBER 12
Kate Kennedy	MAY 31
Jennie Kimball	JUNE 23
Rebekah Kohut	SEPTEMBER 9
Lucile Wolf Heming Koshland	JUNE 6
Selma Kronold	AUGUST 18
Rose Wilder Lane	DECEMBER 5
Marion Florence Lansing	JUNE 10
Nella Larsen	APRIL 13
Dorothy Paulis Lathrop	APRIL 16
Agnes Christina Laut	FEBRUARY 11
Florence Lawrence	JANUARY 2
Elizabeth Blair Lee	JUNE 20
Floride Clemson Lee	DECEMBER 29
Mary Elizabeth Lee	MARCH 23
Frances Leigh	MAY 28
Clara Temple Leonard	DECEMBER 19
Edmonia Lewis	JULY 4
Belva Bennett Lockwood	OCTOBER 24
Harriet Stone Lothrop	JUNE 22
Martha Perry Lowe	NOVEMBER 21
Amy Lowell	FEBRUARY 9
Annie Lowry	NOVEMBER 13
Marian Nevins MacDowell	NOVEMBER 22
Jean Kenyon Mackenzie	JANUARY 6
Clara Dargan Maclean	OCTOBER 11
Anne Sullivan Macy	APRIL 14
Helen Adelia Manville	AUGUST 3
Helen Marot	JUNE 9
Georgia Madden Martin	MAY 3
Lillien Jane Martin	JULY 7
Lydia Lucretia Mossman Martin	JUNE 28
Anne Henrietta Martin	SEPTEMBER 30
Emma Marwedel	FEBRUARY 27
Abigail Williams May	APRIL 21
Katherine Mayo	JANUARY 24
Rosalie McClendon	AUGUST 27
Josephine Clifford McCrackin	NOVEMBER 25
Catharine Waugh McCulloch	JUNE 4
Cornelia Peake McDonald	JUNE 14
Susan McGroarty	FEBRUARY 13
Millie-Christine McKoy	JULY 11
Leila Mechlin	MAY 29
Lucy Sprague Mitchell	JULY 2
Aubertine Woodward Moore	SEPTEMBER 27
Ella Sheppard Moore	FEBRUARY 4
Anne Morgan	FEBRUARY 24
Mary Kimball Morgan	DECEMBER 8
Clara Morris	MARCH 17
Phoebe Ann Moses	AUGUST 13
Emma Schoenmacher Mott	JANUARY 7
Franc Johnson Newcomb	MARCH 30
Frances Newman	DECEMBER 13
Effie Lee Newsome	JANUARY 19
Elisabet Ney	JANUARY 26
Margaret Morse Nice	DECEMBER 6

516

Minerva Parker Nichols	MAY 14
Mabel Normand	NOVEMBER 10
Mary Blanche Norton	JANUARY 23
Leonel Ross O'Bryan	NOVEMBER 11
Mary Kenney O'Sullivan	JANUARY 8
Frances Sargent Locke Osgood	JUNE 18
Bertha Honoré Palmer	MAY 22
Maud Wood Park	JANUARY 25
Mary Mills Patrick	MARCH 10
Eleanor Medill Patterson	NOVEMBER 7
Grace Espy Patton	OCTOBER 5
Anna Claypoole Peale	MARCH 6
Elia Wilkinson Peattie	JANUARY 15
Annie Smith Peck	OCTOBER 19
Elizabeth Pennell	FEBRUARY 21
Lucy Fitch Perkins	JULY 12
Lilla Cabot Perry	JANUARY 13
Rose Pesotta	NOVEMBER 20
Katherine Pettit	FEBRUARY 23
Mary Wright Plummer	MARCH 8
Louise Pound	JUNE 30
Maud Powell	AUGUST 22
Elizabeth Payson Prentiss	OCTOBER 26
Ann Preston	DECEMBER 1
Nancy Gardner Prince	SEPTEMBER 15
Ann Browder Pruett	JANUARY 18
Jeannette Pickering Rankin	JUNE 11
Ellen Spaulding Reed	AUGUST 14
Mary Reed	DECEMBER 4
Ellen Henrietta Swallow Richards	DECEMBER 3
Fannie Moore Richards	OCTOBER 1
Marilla Marks Ricker	MARCH 18
Norma Collins Roberts	MARCH 16
Anna Mary Robertson	SEPTEMBER 7
Harriet Hanson Robinson	FEBRUARY 8
Edith Kermit Roosevelt	AUGUST 6
Anne Ryan	JULY 20
Pauline Morton Sabin	APRIL 23
Mary Anne Sadlier	DECEMBER 31
Lucy Maynard Salmon	JULY 27
Deborah Sampson	DECEMBER 17
Jessie Sampter	MARCH 22
Mari Sandoz	MAY 11
Margaret Sanger	SEPTEMBER 14
Margaret Munson Sangster	FEBRUARY 22
Augusta Christine Fells Savage	FEBRUARY 29
Francis Sawyer	JUNE 13
Hannah Kent Schoff	JUNE 3
Evelyn Dunn Scott	JANUARY 17
Vida Dutton Scudder	DECEMBER 15
Caroline Seabury	JUNE 1
Elizabeth Cochrane Seaman	MAY 5
Anne Douglas Sedgwick	MARCH 28
Catharine Maria Sedgwick	DECEMBER 28
Grace Gallatin Seton	JANUARY 28
Lydia Sexton	APRIL 12
Jessie Field Shambaugh	JUNE 26
May French Sheldon	MAY 10
Kate Shelley	SEPTEMBER 25
Milicent Washburn Shinn	APRIL 15
Ellis Reynolds Shipp	JANUARY 20

Olivia Shipp	MAY 17
Ruth McCormick Simms	MARCH 27
Leila Davidson Simpson	AUGUST 16
Margaret Sloan	MAY 15
Annie Trumbull Slosson	MAY 18
Elizabeth Oakes Smith	AUGUST 12
Margaret Bayard Smith	FEBRUARY 20
Eliza Hart Spalding	AUGUST 11
Anne Spencer	FEBRUARY 6
Cornelia Phillips Spencer	MARCH 20
Eliza Allen Starr	AUGUST 29
Ellen Gates Starr	MARCH 19
Emma Stebbins	SEPTEMBER 1
Lillian M. N. Stevens	MARCH 1
Carrie Adell Strahorn	JANUARY 1
Gene Stratton-Porter	AUGUST 17
Anna Louise Strong	NOVEMBER 24
Clara A. Swain	JULY 18
Mary Morris Talbert	SEPTEMBER 17
Eva March Tappan	DECEMBER 26
Mary Hawes Terhune	DECEMBER 21
Mary Church Terrell	SEPTEMBER 23
Clara Thompson	OCTOBER 3
Eloise Bibb Thompson	JUNE 29
Jeannette Meyers Thurber	JANUARY 29
Frances Christine Fisher Tiernan	JULY 5
Eunice Tietjens	JULY 29
Katherine Westcott Tingley	JULY 6
Florence Guertin Tuttle	JULY 23
Sophie Kerr Underwood	AUGUST 23
Maggie Newton Van Cott	MARCH 25
Bertha Van Hoosen	MARCH 26
Miriam Van Waters	OCTOBER 4
Mary Ann Farlow Vincent	SEPTEMBER 18
Sarah Breedlove Walker	DECEMBER 23
Elizabeth Stuart Phelps Ward	AUGUST 31
Josephine Washington	JULY 31
Margaret Murray Washington	MARCH 9
Sukey Vickery Watson	JUNE 12
Marguerite Milton Wells	FEBRUARY 10
Ida Bell Wells-Barnett	JULY 16
Mary Allen West	JULY 13
Candace Thurber Wheeler	MARCH 24
Alma Bridwell White	JUNE 16
Anna White	JANUARY 21
Eartha Mary Magdalene White	NOVEMBER 8
Ellen Gould Harmon White	NOVEMBER 26
Anne Whitney	SEPTEMBER 2
Kate Douglas Wiggin	SEPTEMBER 28
Laura Ingalls Wilder	FEBRUARY 7
Louise Beebe Wilder	JANUARY 30
Fannie Barrier Williams	FEBRUARY 12
Eliza Azelia Williams	DECEMBER 11
Jennie Fowler Willing	JANUARY 22
Isabel Mack Willson	SEPTEMBER 20
Harriet Lathrop Winslow	APRIL 9
Rose Guggenheim Winslow	DECEMBER 27
Helen Thompson Wooley	NOVEMBER 6
Constance Fenimore Woolson	MARCH 5
Katharine Prescott Wormeley	JANUARY 14
Elizabeth Wright	APRIL 3

Lois Stiles Edgerly

Lois Stiles Edgerly lives with her husband William, in Cambridge, Massachusetts, and Ocean Park, Maine.

Women's Words, Women's Stories is her second collection of nineteenth-century American women's writings. She is the author of *Give Her This Day: A Daybook of Women's Words* (Tilbury House, Publishers, 1990).